Microeconomics

A Contemporary Introduction

9e

William A. McEachern
University of Connecticut

SOUTH-WESTERN
CENGAGE Learning™

Australia • Brazil • Japan • Korea • Mexico • Singapore • Spain • United Kingdom • United States

SOUTH-WESTERN
CENGAGE Learning™

Microeconomics: A Contemporary Introduction, 9e

William A. McEachern

Vice President of Editorial, Business: Jack W. Calhoun

Publisher: Joe Sabatino

Acquisitions Editor: Steven Scoble

Sr. Developmental Editor: Susanna C. Smart

Editorial Assistant: Allyn Bissmeyer

Marketing Manager: John Carey

Associate Marketing Manager: Betty Jung

Content Project Manager: Corey Geissler

Sr. Frontlist Buyer, Manufacturing: Kevin Kluck

Marketing Communications Manager: Sarah Greber

Production Service: S4Carlisle Publishing Services

Art Director: Michelle Kunkler

Internal Designer: Albonetti Design

Cover Designer: Albonetti Design

Cover Image: © Jonathan Evans/ Getty Images, Inc.

Rights Acquisitions Specialists: John Hill & Deanna Ettinger

For product information and technology assistance, contact us at
Cengage Learning Customer & Sales Support, 1-800-354-9706

For permission to use material from this text or product,
submit all requests online at **www.cengage.com/permissions**
Further permissions questions can be emailed to
permissionrequest@cengage.com

Library of Congress Control Number: 2010930339

ISBN-13: 978-0-538-45371-4
ISBN-10: 0-538-45371-0

South-Western Cengage Learning
5191 Natorp Boulevard
Mason, OH 45040
USA

Cengage Learning products are represented in Canada by Nelson Education, Ltd.

For your course and learning solutions, visit **www.cengage.com**

Purchase any of our products at your local college store or at our preferred online store **www.CengageBrain.com**

Printed in the United States of America
1 2 3 4 5 6 7   14 13 12 11 10

About the Author

William A. McEachern started teaching large sections of economic principles when he joined the University of Connecticut in 1973. In 1980, he began offing teaching workshops around the country, and, in 1990, he created *The Teaching Economist*, a newsletter that focuses on making teaching more effective and more fun.

His research in public finance, public policy, and industrial organization has appeared in a variety of journals, including *Economic Inquiry, National Tax Journal, Journal of Industrial Economics, Quarterly Review of Economics and Finance, Southern Economic Journal, Econ Journal Watch, Kyklos,* and *Public Choice.* His books and monographs include *Managerial Control and Performance* (D.C. Heath), *School of Finance Reform* (CREUES), and *Tax-Exempt Property and Tax Capitalization in Metropolitan Areas* (CREUES). He has also contributed chapters to edited volumes such as *Rethinking Economic Principles* (Irwin), *Impact Evaluations of Vertical Restraint Cases* (Federal Trade Commission), and *Public Choice Economics* (University of Michigan Press).

Professor McEachern has advised federal, state, and local governments on policy matters and directed a bipartisan commission examining Connecticut's finances. He has been quoted in or written for publications such as the *Times* of London, *New York Times, Wall Street Journal, Christian Science Monitor, USA Today, Challenge Magazine, Connection,* CBS MarketWatch.com, and *Reader's Digest.* He has also appeared on Now with Bill Moyers, Voice of America, and National Public Radio.

In 1984, Professor McEachern won the University of Connecticut Alumni Association's Faculty Award for Distinguished Public Service and in 2000 won the Association's Faculty Excellence in Teaching Award. He is the only person in the university's history to receive both. He was born in Portsmouth, N.H., earned an undergraduate degree with honors from College of the Holy Cross, served three years as an Army Officer, and earned an M.A. and Ph.D. from the University of Virginia.

To Pat

Brief Contents

Part 6   International Economics

Contents

Preface

Economics has a short history but a long past. As a distinct discipline, economics has been studied for only a few hundred years, yet civilizations have confronted the economic problem of scarce resources and unlimited wants for millennia. Economics, the discipline, may be centuries old, but it's new every day, with fresh evidence that refines and extends economic theory. What could be newer than the financial crisis, the recession, the policy responses, and how all this affected individual choices in the household and the firm? In this edition of *Microeconomics: A Contemporary Introduction*, I draw on more than three decades of teaching and research experience to convey the vitality, timeliness, and relevance of economics.

Lead by Example

Remember the last time you were in unfamiliar parts and had to ask for directions? Along with the directions came the standard comment, "You can't miss it!" So how come you missed it? Because the "landmark," so obvious to locals, was invisible to you, a stranger. Writing a principles textbook is much like giving directions. Familiarity is a must, but that very familiarity can cloud the author's ability to see the material through the fresh eyes of a new student. One could revert to a tell-all approach, but that will bury students in information. An alternative is to opt for the minimalist approach, writing abstractly about good *x* and good *y*, units of labor and units of capital, or the proverbial widget. But that shorthand turns economics into a foreign language.

Good directions rely on landmarks familiar to us all—a stoplight, a fork in the road, a white picket fence. Likewise, a good textbook builds bridges from the familiar to the new. That's what I try to do—*lead by example*. By beginning with examples that draw on common experience, I try to create graphic images that need little explanation, thereby eliciting from the reader that light of recognition, that "Aha!" I believe that the shortest distance between an economic principle and student comprehension is a lively example. Examples should convey the point quickly and directly. Having to explain an example is like having to explain a joke—the point gets lost. Throughout the book, I try to provide just enough intuition and institutional detail to get the point across. My emphasis is on economic ideas, not economic jargon.

Students show up the first day of class with at least 17 years of experience with economic choices, economic institutions, and economic events. Each grew up in a household—the most important economic institution in a market economy. As consumers, students are familiar with fast-food outlets, cineplexes, car dealerships, online retailers, and scores of stores at the mall. Most students have supplied labor to the job market—more than half had jobs in high school. Students also interact with government—they know about sales taxes, driver's licenses, speed limits, and public schools. And students have a growing familiarity with the rest of the world. Thus, students have abundant experience with economics. This rich lode of personal experience offers a perfect starting point. Rather than try to create for students a new world of economics—a new way of thinking, my approach is to build on student experience—on what Alfred Marshall called "the ordinary business of life."

This book starts with what students bring to the party. For example, to explain resource substitution, rather than rely on abstract units of labor and capital, I begin with washing a car, where the mix can vary from a drive-through car wash (much capital and little labor) to a Saturday morning charity car wash (much labor and little capital). Down-to-earth examples turn the abstract into the concrete to help students remember and learn. Because instructors can cover only a portion of a textbook in the classroom, textbook material should be self-contained and self-explanatory. This gives instructors the flexibility to emphasize in class topics of special interest.

What's New with the Ninth Edition

This edition builds on previous success with additional examples, more questions along the way, and frequent summaries as a chapter unfolds. By making the material both more natural and more personal, I try to engage students in a collaborative discussion. Chapters have been streamlined for a clearer, more intuitive presentation, with fresh examples, new or revised case studies, and additional exhibits to crystalize key points.

In terms of overarching themes, this revision places more emphasis on the institutional underpinnings of a market economy—the "rules of the game" that shape markets and promote economic development. This includes more examples, new case studies, and a new chapter on economic development and transitional economies. My emphasis on the institutional tissue that supports a market economy also underscores the role of manners, customs, and conventions in market exchange. To the extent possible, I draw on examples and lessons learned during the financial crisis, the recession, and policy responses.

It goes without saying that all data have been revised to reflect the most recent figures available. Time sensitive examples and discussions have also been updated. Here are other relevant revisions by chapter.

Introductory Chapters: 1–4

As with earlier editions, topics common to both macro- and microeconomics are covered in the first four chapters. Limiting introductory material to four chapters saves precious class time, particularly at those institutions where students can take macro and micro courses in either order (and so must cover introductory chapters twice). New or revised features in the introductory chapters include:

Ch. 1: *The Art and Science of Economic Analysis* This chapter provides more detail on the implications of rational self-interest, and adds an additional paragraph about macroeconomics. By elaborating a bit more about macroeconomics here, I can discuss how the recession affected particular micro decisions in other introductory chapters and in the micro chapters.

Ch. 2: *Economic Tools and Economic Systems* The case study on the opportunity cost of college notes that 40 percent of college students hold jobs during the academic year, and the case study discussing the best and worst countries in which to do business, the pool of countries grows to 183.

Ch. 3: *Economic Decision Makers* I offer more detailed examples of home production. The case study on user-generated products includes more social networks such as Twitter. I discuss how the recession influenced household production. The case study on the information revolution and household production now references the impact of the recession on telecommuting.

Ch.4: *Demand, Supply, and Markets* I add a current example about how a plunge in copper prices affected quantity supplied. To explain how prices reflect scarcity, I discuss why the rental price of a truck from San Francisco to Austin is so much higher than the rental price of one going from Austin to San Francisco.

Microeconomic Chapters: 5–18

My approach to microeconomics underscores the role of time and information in production and consumption. I also allow macro issues to affect the micro side. For example, a new case study in Chapter 12, the labor chapter, looks at how the General Motors and Chrysler bailouts affected union workers. And a new case study in Chapter 18, the income distribution chapter, looks at how the recession affected high-income households. The presentation also reflects the growing interest in the economic institutions that underpin impersonal market activity. More generally, I try to convey the idea that most microeconomic principles operate like gravity: Market forces exert pressure, whether or not individual economic actors understand them. At every opportunity, I try to turn the abstract into the concrete. New or revised features in the microeconomic chapters include:

Ch. 5: *Elasticity of Demand and Supply* To show the unintended consequences of public policy, I discuss a finding that smokers compensate for higher cigarette taxes by smoking each cigarette more intensively—that is, by sucking more nicotine from each cigarette.

Ch. 6: *Consumer Choice and Demand* The growing appeal of local produce has tripled the number of farmers' markets in the United States since 1995, showing how tastes change. In the case study on government subsidized health care I discuss how Medicare fraud has replaced illegal drugs as the top crime in Florida.

Ch. 7: *Production and Cost in the Firm* Diseconomies of scale are presented by discussing the world's largest cruise liner, which can accommodate 6,300 but is too large to visit some of the world's most popular destinations. In addition, the financial crisis of 2008 is presented, discussing how it resulted in part because some financial institutions had grown so large and complex that top executives couldn't accurately assess the risks of the financial products they were buying and selling.

Ch. 8: *Perfect Competition* I discuss a study of 732 firms in the United States, France, Germany, and the United Kingdom that finds that firms in competitive industries are more efficient than other firms. And I spell out the problems that arise with the competitive model when there are barriers to exit.

Ch. 9: *Monopoly* I discuss the impact of the recession on the jewelry business—another example of how the macro economy spills into the micro economy. I also mention that China has a world monopoly on the supply of pandas, and to enforce that monopoly—that is, to restrict supply—China requires that any offspring from the pandas rented to zoos around the world become China's property.

Ch. 10: *Monopolistic Competition and Oligopoly* In the section on cartels, I cite research showing that cheating increases as the number of firms in the cartel grows. In the discussion of price wars, I describe the dollar-menu duel of cheeseburgers between the McDonald's McDouble and the Burger King Dollar Double.

Ch. 11: *Resource Markets* The case study on the lumber industry as an example of derived demand now reflects the bottom falling out of the housing market—more macro leaking into micro. Lumber prices dropped 70 percent. To help explain the shape of a resource supply curve, I note how a higher price for oil enables producers to drill deeper, explore more remote areas, and squeeze oil from tar sands that contain less of it.

Ch. 12: *Labor Markets and Labor Unions* In the "Winner Take All" case study, I add more reasons why U.S. executive pay has increased so much. I expand the discussion of geographic wage differences, and provide a new case study about the federal bailout of GM and Chrysler and how it affected the United Auto Workers.

Ch. 13: *Capital, Interest, Entrepreneurship, and Corporate Finance* I simplify the presentation of investment. A topic that gets more attention in this edition is entrepreneurship, reflected in the chapter title. I have added a major section discussing the sources of entrepreneurship along with examples of specific entrepreneurs and what they created.

Ch. 14: *Transaction Costs, Imperfect Information, and Behavioral Economics* In the previous edition, this chapter was titled "Transaction Costs, Imperfect Information, and Market Behavior." The substitution of "Behavioral Economics" for "Market Behavior" in the title reflects the coverage of behavioral economics in this edition. I have added a 1,350-word section entitled "Behavioral Economics" that offers an overview of the subject and includes a case study that looks at why some economists are paying more attention to issues of self-control.

Ch. 15: *Economic Regulation and Antitrust Policy* I note how critics charged that the Securities and Exchange Commission failed to uncover the massive fraud by Bernie Madoff, despite receiving many complaints about him, because the agency may have been captured by the industry it was supposed to be regulating.

Ch. 16: *Public Goods and Public Choice* The case study on farm subsidies reflects the latest legislation. In the discussing the underground economy, I list names used in other countries to describe it, including the shady economy, informal economy, second economy, etc. The case study on campaign finance reform reflects the 2010 Supreme Court decision.

Ch. 17: *Externalities and the Environment* I add oil spills as a third source of water pollution and distinguish between spills on land and spills offshore. Then I present the case study about BP's spill in the Gulf of Mexico. The case study does more than explain events; it raises some fundamental questions about the definition of negative externalities.

Ch. 18: *Income Distribution and Poverty* I point out that one reason for the increase in earnings inequality is that more jobs in the U.S. labor market pay workers for their productivity—using bonus pay, commissions, or piece-rate contracts. I cite research showing that one of the many problems with housing discrimination is that people stuck in neighborhoods where few have jobs cannot take advantage of the better job networking available in neighborhoods where more people are working. I add a new case study discussing how the recession affected high-income households.

International Chapters: 19–21

This edition reflects the growing impact of the world economy on U.S. economic welfare. International issues are introduced early and discussed often. For example, the rest of the world is introduced in Chapter 1 and profiled in Chapter 3. Comparative advantage and the production possibilities frontier are discussed from a global perspective in Chapter 2. International coverage is woven throughout the text. By comparing the U.S. experience with that of other countries around the world, students gain a better perspec-tive about such topics as unionization trends, antitrust laws, pollution, conservation, environmental laws, tax rates, and the distribution of income. International references are scattered throughout the book, including a number of relevant case studies.

Again, every effort is made to give students a feel for the numbers. For example, to convey the importance of U.S. consumers in the world economy, I note that Americans represent less than 5 percent of the world's population, but they buy more than half the Rolls Royces and diamonds sold worldwide. New or revised features in the international chapters include:

Ch. 19 *International Trade* I discuss how the recession reduced the trade deficit as U.S. consumers cut back on all their purchases, including what they spent on foreign products. I now describe the terms of trade in a way that matches the slope of the production possibilities frontier in each country. I discuss how the national defense argument for trade restrictions has been extended to justify recent efforts to block China from buying American oil or steel companies.

Ch. 20: *International Finance* I describe how the recession shrank the U.S. trade deficit relative to GDP from 5.9 percent in 2007 to 3.5 percent in 2009, and identify some of those few countries with which the U.S. has a trade surplus. A case study notes how China seeks every trade advantage, especially for the 125 state-owned enterprises run directly by the central government. Between 2007 and 2010, China's holding of U.S. Treasury securities more than doubled from $400 billion to $900 billion.

Ch. 21: *Economic Development* I offer a brief summary of transitional economies and focus the chapter more on "Economic Development." A case study considers a new method of estimating economic growth in countries where data are poor or nonexistent by measuring differences over time in the intensity of night lights on the ground using a satellite camera high above the Earth. In the section entitled "Entrepreneurship," I highlight the role of McDonald's and other franchises that train a cadre of managers from poor countries and offer customers there an idea of what's possible in the way of service, cleanliness, and quality. To the section about how exporting subsidized food to developing countries has hurt poor farmers in those countries, I add a discussion of how sending used clothing from richer countries has hurt the local textile industry in recipient countries.

Student-Friendly Features

In some principles textbooks, chapters are broken up by boxed material, qualifying footnotes, and other distractions that disrupt the flow of the material. Students aren't sure when or if they should read such segregated elements. But this book has a natural flow. Each chapter opens with a few off-beat questions and then follows with a logical narrative. Case studies appear in the natural sequence of the chapter, not as separate boxes. Students can thus read each chapter from the opening questions to the conclusion and summary. I also adhere to a "just-in-time" philosophy, introducing material just as it's needed to build an argument. Footnotes are used sparingly and then only to cite sources, not to qualify or extend material in the text.

This edition is more visual than its predecessors, with more exhibits to reinforce key findings. Exhibit titles convey the central points, and more exhibits now have summary captions. Captions have been edited for clarity and brevity. The point is to make the exhibits more self-contained. Students learn more if concepts are presented both in words and in exhibits. Additional summary paragraphs have been added throughout each chapter; these summaries begin with the bold-faced identifier **"To Review"**. Economic jargon has been reduced. Although the number of terms defined in the margin has increased modestly, definitions have been pared to make them clearer and less like entries from a dictionary. In short, economic principles are now more transparent (a textbook should not be like some giant Easter egg hunt, where it's up to the student to figure out what the author is trying to say). Overall, the ninth edition is a cleaner presentation, a straighter shot into the student's brain.

Color is used systematically within graphs, charts, and tables to ensure that students can easily see what's going on. Throughout the book, demand curves are blue and supply curves are red. Color shading distinguishes key areas of many graphs, and color identifies outcomes in others. For example, economic profit and welfare gains are always shaded blue and economic loss and welfare losses are always shaded pink. In short, color is more than mere eye candy—it is coordinated consistently and with forethought to help students learn (a dyslexic student once told me she found the book's color guide quite helpful). Students benefit from these visual cues.

NET BOOKMARKS   Each chapter includes a Net Bookmark. These margin notes identify interesting Web sites that illustrate real-world examples, giving students a chance to develop their research skills. They can be accessed through the McEachern Student Web site at www.cengage.com/economics/mceachern.

THE MCEACHERN TEXT   *Web site (www.cengage.com/economics/mceachern)* The Web site designed to be used with this textbook provides chapter-by-chapter online study aids that include a glossary and Internet features, among others. Some of the highlights include:

KEY TERMS GLOSSARY   A convenient, online glossary enables students to use the point-and-click flashcard functionality of the glossary to test themselves on key terminology.

IN-TEXT WEB FEATURES   To streamline navigation, the site links directly to Web sites discussed in the Internet-enhanced in-text features for each chapter—Net Bookmarks and e-Activities. These applications provide students with opportunities to interact with the material by performing real-world analyses.

CourseMate: Engaging, Affordable

Interested in a simple way to *complement* your text and course content with study and practice materials?

Cengage Learning's Economics CourseMate brings course concepts to life with interactive learning, study, and exam preparation tools that support the printed textbook. Watch student comprehension soar as your class works with the printed textbook and the textbook-specific website. Economics CourseMate goes beyond the book to deliver what you need!

Microeconomics: A Contemporary Introduction CourseMate includes:

- Interactive eBook
- Quizzes
- Flashcards
- Videos
- Graphing Tutorials
- News, Debates, and Data
- Engagement Tracker

Engagement Tracker

How do you assess your students' engagement in your course? How do you know your students have read the material or viewed the resources you've assigned? How can you tell if your students are struggling with a concept? With CourseMate, you can use the included Engagement Tracker to assess student preparation and engagement. Use the tracking tools to see progress for the class as a whole or for individual students. Identify students at risk early in the course. Uncover which concepts are most difficult for your class. Monitor time on task. Keep your students engaged.

Interactive Teaching and Learning Tools

CourseMate includes interactive teaching and learning tools: quizzes, flashcards, videos and more. These assets enable students to review for tests, prepare for class, and address the needs of students' varied learning styles. *Economics, 10e* CourseMate also includes Economic Applications (news, policy debates, and data) and Graphing Workshop.

Interactive eBook

In addition to interactive teaching and learning tools, CourseMate includes an interactive eBook. Students can take notes, highlight, search and interact with embedded media specific to their book. Use it as a supplement to the printed text, or as a substitute—the choice is up to your students with CourseMate.

Find out more at: www.cengage.com.

The Support Package

The teaching and learning support package that accompanies *Economics: A Contemporary Introduction* provides instructors and students with focused, accurate, and innovative supplements to the textbook.

STUDY GUIDES   Written by John Lunn of Hope College, study guides are available for the full textbook, as well as for the micro and macro "split" versions. Every chapter of each study guide corresponds to a chapter in the text and offers (1) an introduction; (2) a chapter outline, with definitions of all terms; (3) a discussion of the chapter's main points; (4) a *lagniappe*, or bonus, which supplements material in the chapter and includes a "Question to Think About"; (5) a list of key terms; (6) a variety of true-false, multiple-choice, and discussion questions; and (7) answers to all the questions.

INSTRUCTOR'S MANUAL   The *Instructor's Manual*, revised by Robert Sandman, Wilmington College, is keyed to the text. For each textbook chapter, it includes (1) a detailed lecture outline and brief overview, (2) a summary of main points, (3) pedagogical tips that expand on points raised in the chapter and indicate use of PowerPoint slides, (4) suggested answers to all end-of-chapter questions and problems, and (5) optional Experiential Exercises.

TEACHING ASSISTANCE MANUAL   Revised by me, the *Teaching Assistance Manual* provides additional support beyond the *Instructor's Manual*. It is especially useful to new instructors, graduate assistants, and teachers interested in generating more class discussion. This manual offers (1) overviews and outlines of each chapter, (2) chapter objectives and quiz material, (3) material for class discussion, (4) topics warranting special attention, (5) supplementary examples, and (6) "What if?" discussion questions. Appendices provide guidance on (1) presenting material; (2) generating and sustaining class discussion; (3) preparing, administering, and grading quizzes; and (4) coping with the special problems confronting foreign graduate assistants.

TEST BANKS   Thoroughly revised for currency and accuracy by Kenneth Slaysman, York College of Pennsylvania, the microeconomics and macroeconomics test banks contain over 6,600 questions in multiple-choice and true-false formats. All multiple-choice questions are rated by degree of difficulty, and are labeled with AACSB compliance tags.

EXAMVIEW—COMPUTERIZED TESTING SOFTWARE   ExamView is an easy-to-use test-creation software package available in versions compatible with Microsoft Windows and Apple Macintosh. It contains all the questions in the printed test banks. Instructors can add or edit questions, instructions, and answers; select questions by previewing them on the screen; and then choose them by number or at random. Instructors can also create and administer quizzes online, either over the Internet, through a local area network (LAN), or through a wide area network (WAN).

MICROSOFT POWERPOINT LECTURE SLIDES   Lecture slides revised by Andreea Chiritescu of Eastern Illinois University, contain tables and graphs from the textbook, and are intended to enhance lectures and help integrate technology into the classroom.

MICROSOFT POWERPOINT FIGURE SLIDES   These PowerPoint slides contain key figures from the text. Instructors who prefer to prepare their own lecture slides can use these figures as an alternative to the text's PowerPoint lecture slides.

THE TEACHING ECONOMIST   Since 1990, I have edited *The Teaching Economist*, a newsletter aimed at making teaching more interesting and more fun. The newsletter discusses imaginative ways to present topics—for example, how to "sensationalize" economic concepts, useful resources on the Internet, economic applications from science fiction, recent research in teaching and learning, and more generally, ways to teach just for the fun of it. A regular feature of *The Teaching Economist*, "The Grapevine," offers teaching ideas suggested by colleagues from across the country. The latest issue—and back issues—of *The Teaching Economist* are available online at cengage.com/economics/mceachern/theteachingeconomist/index.html.

APLIA   Started in 2000 by economist and instructor, Paul Romer, more students are currently using an Aplia Integrated Textbook Solution for principles of economics than are using all other web-based learning programs combined. Because the assignments in Aplia are automatically graded, you can assign homework more frequently to ensure your students are putting forth a full effort and getting the most out of your class. Assignments are closely tied to the text and each McEachern Aplia course has a digital edition of the textbook embedded right in the Aplia program. This digital text is now in the Aplia Text format, which gives students the same interactive experience they get on Web sites they use in their personal lives.

NEWS VIDEOS   Video segments from news sources bring the real world to your classroom to illustrate how economics is an important part of daily life and how the text material applies to current events. Contact your Cengage Learning sales consultant for access.

WEBTUTOR TOOLBOX   WebTutor Toolbox offers basic online study tools including learning objectives, flashcards, and practice quizzes.

CUSTOM SOLUTIONS: FLEX-TEXT   Create a text as unique as your course: quickly, simply, and affordably. As part of our *Flex-Text* program you can add your personal touch to *Economics: A Contemporary Introduction* with a course-specific cover and up to 32 pages of your own content, at no additional cost. Or, consider adding one of our bonus options in economics (economic issues pertaining to education, health care, social security, unemployment, inflation, and international trade) or our quick guide to time value of money (on time value of money concepts). Contact your sales consultant to learn more about this and other custom options to fit your course.

Acknowledgments

Many people contributed to this book's development. I gratefully acknowledge the insights, comments, and criticisms of those who have reviewed the book for this and previous editions or provided feedback on particular points. Their remarks changed my thinking on many points and improved the book.

Steve Abid,
Grand Rapids Community College

Basil Al-Hashimi,
Mesa Community College - Red Mountain

Polly Reynolds Allen,
University of Connecticut

Mary Allender,
University of Portland

Jeffrey Alstete,
Iona College

Hassan Y. Aly,
Ohio State University

Ted Amato,
University of North Carolina, Charlotte

Donna Anderson,
University of Wisconsin, La Crosse

Richard Anderson,
Texas A&M University

Kyriacos Aristotelous,
Otterbein College

James Aylesworth,
Lakeland Community College

Mohsen Bahmani Mohsen Bahmani-Oskooee,
University of Wisconsin, Milwaukee

Dale Bails,
Christian Brothers College

Benjamin Balak,
Rollins College

A. Paul Ballantyne,
University of Colorado at Colorado Springs

Andy Barnett,
Auburn University

Bharati Basu,
Central Michigan University

Klaus Becker,
Texas Tech University

Charles Bennett,
Gannon University

Trisha L. Bezmen,
Old Dominion University

Jay Bhattacharya,
Okaloosa Walton Community College

Gerald W. Bialka,
University of North Florida

William Bogart,
Case Western Reserve University

Andrew M. Bonacic,
Adirondack College

Kenneth Boyer,
Michigan State University

David Brasfield,
Murray State University

Jurgen Brauer,
Augusta College

Taggert Brooks,
University of Wisconsin, La Crosse

Gardner Brown, Jr.,
University of Washington

Eric Brunner,
Morehead State University

Francine Butler,
Grand View College

Judy Butler,
Baylor University

Charles Callahan III,
SUNY College at Brockport

Giorgio Canarella,
California State University, Los Angeles

Shirley Cassing,
University of Pittsburgh

Shi-fan Chu,
University of Nevada–Reno

Ronald Cipcic,
Kalamazoo Valley Community College

Larry Clarke,
Brookhaven College

Rebecca Cline,
Middle Georgia College

Stephen Cobb,
Xavier University

Doug Conway,
Mesa Community College

Mary E. Cookingham,
Michigan State University

James P. Cover,
University of Alabama

James Cox,
DeKalb College

Jerry Crawford,
Arkansas State University

Thomas Creahan,
Morehead State University

Carl Davidson,
Michigan State University

Elynor Davis,
Georgia Southern University

Susan Davis,
SUNY College at Buffalo

A. Edward Day,
University of Central Florida

David Dean,
University of Richmond

Janet Deans,
Chestnut Hill College

Dennis Debrecht,
Carroll College

David Denslow,
University of Florida

Kruti R. Dholakia,
Grayson County College

Gary Dymski,
University of California–Riverside

John Edgren,
Eastern Michigan University

Ron D. Elkins,
Central Washington University

Donald Elliott, Jr.,
Southern Illinois University

G. Rod Erfani,
Transylvania University

Gisela Meyer Escoe,
University of Cincinnati

Mark Evans,
*California State University,
Bakersfield*

Jamie Falcon,
*University of Maryland Baltimore
County*

Gregory Falls,
Central Michigan University

Eleanor Fapohunda,
SUNY College at Farmingdale

Mohsen Fardmanesh,
Temple University

Paul Farnham,
Georgia State University

Rudy Fichtenbaum,
Wright State University

T. Windsor Fields,
James Madison University

Rodney Fort,
Washington State University

Richard Fowles,
University of Utah

Roger Frantz,
San Diego State University

Julie Gallaway,
Southwest Montana State University

Gary Galles,
Pepperdine University

Edward Gamber,
Lafayette College

Adam Gifford,
California State University, Northridge

J. P. Gilbert,
MiraCosta College

Robert Gillette,
University of Kentucky

Art Goldsmith,
Washington and Lee University

Rae Jean Goodman,
U.S. Naval Academy

Robert Gordon,
San Diego State University

Fred Graham,
American University

Philip Graves,
University of Colorado, Boulder

Gary Greene,
Manatee Community College

Harpal S. Grewal,
Claflin College

Carolyn Grin,
Grand Rapids Community College

Daniel Gropper,
Auburn University

Simon Hakim,
Temple University

Robert Halvorsen,
University of Washington

Nathan Eric Hampton,
St. Cloud State University

Mehdi Haririan,
Bloomsburg University

William Hart,
Miami University

Baban Hasnat,
SUNY College at Brockport

Travis Lee Hayes,
*Chattanooga State Technical
Community College*

Julia Heath,
University of Memphis

James Heisler,
Hope College

James Henderson,
Baylor University

Michael Heslop,
*Northern Virginia Community
College*

James R. Hill,
Central Michigan University

Jane Smith Himarios,
University of Texas, Arlington

Calvin Hoerneman,
Delta College

Tracy Hofer,
*University of Wisconsin, Stevens
Point*

George E. Hoffer,
Virginia Commonwealth University

Dennis Hoffman,
Arizona State University

Bruce Horning,
Fordham University

Calvin Hoy,
County College of Morris

Jennifer Imazeki,
San Diego State University

Beth Ingram,
University of Iowa

Paul Isley,
Grand Valley State University

Joyce Jacobsen,
Wesleyan University

Nancy Jianakoplos,
Colorado State University

Claude Michael Jonnard,
Fairleigh Dickinson University

Nake Kamrany,
University of Southern California

Bryce Kanago,
Miami University

John Kane,
SUNY College at Oswego

David Kennett,
Vassar College

William Kern,
Western Michigan University

Robert Kleinhenz,
*California State University,
Fullerton*

Faik Koray,
Louisiana State University

Joseph Kotaska,
Monroe Community College

Barry Kotlove,
Edmonds Community College

Marie Kratochvil,
Nassau Community College

Joseph Lammert,
Raymond Walters College

Christopher Lee,
*Saint Ambrose University,
Davenport*

Jim Lee,
Fort Hays State University

Dennis Leyden,
*University of North Carolina,
Greensboro*

Carl Liedholm,
Michigan State University

Hyoung-Seok Lim,
Ohio State University

C. Richard Long,
Georgia State University

Ken Long,
New River Community College

Michael Magura,
University of Toledo

Thomas Maloy,
Muskegon Community College

Gabriel Manrique,
Winona State University

Barbara Marcus,
Davenport College

Robert Margo,
Vanderbilt University

Nelson Mark,
Ohio State University

Richard Martin,
Agnes Scott College

Peter Mavrokordatos,
Tarrant County College

Wolfgang Mayer,
University of Cincinnati

Bruce McCrea,
Lansing Community College

John McDowell,
Arizona State University

KimMarie McGoldrick,
University of Richmond

David McKee,
Kent State University

James McLain,
University of New Orleans

Mark McNeil,
Irvine Valley College

Michael A. McPherson,
University of North Texas

Scott Eric Merryman,
University of Oregon

Michael Metzger,
University of Central Oklahoma

Art Meyer,
Lincoln Land Community College

Carrie Meyer,
George Mason University

Charles Meyrick,
Housatonic Community College

Martin Milkman,
Murray State University

Green R. Miller,
Morehead State University

Bruce D. Mills,
Troy State University, Montgomery

Milton Mitchell,
University of Wisconsin, Oshkosh

Shannon Mitchell,
Virginia Commonwealth University

Barry Morris,
University of North Alabama

Tina Mosleh,
Ohlone College

Kathryn Nantz,
Fairfield University

Paul Natke,
Central Michigan University

Rick Nelson,
Lansing Community College

Heather Newsome,
Baylor University

Farrokh Nourzad,
Marquette University

Maureen O'Brien,
University of Minnesota, Duluth

Norman P. Obst,
Michigan State University

Joan Q. Osborne,
Palo Alto College

Jeffrey Phillips,
Thomas College

Jeffrey D. Prager,
East Central College

Fernando Quijano,
Dickinson State University

Jaishankar Raman,
Valparaiso University

Reza Ramazani,
St. Michael's University

Carol Rankin,
Xavier University

Mitch Redlo,
Monroe Community College

Kevin Rogers,
Mississippi State University

Scanlon Romer,
Delta College

Duane Rosa,
West Texas A&M University

Robert Rossana,
Wayne State University

Mark Rush,
University of Florida

Richard Saba,
Auburn University

Simran Sahi,
University of Minnesota, Twin Cities

Richard Salvucci,
Trinity University

Rexford Santerre,
University of Connecticut

George D. Santopietro,
Radford University

Sue Lynn Sasser,
University of Central Oklahoma

Ward Sayre,
Kenyon College

Ted Scheinman,
Mt. Hood Community College

Peter Schwartz,
University of North Carolina, Charlotte

Carol A. Scotese,
Virginia Commonwealth University

Shahrokh Shahrokhi,
San Diego State University

Roger Sherman,
University of Houston

Michael Shields,
Central Michigan University

Alden Shiers,
California Polytechnic State University

Virginia Shingleton,
Valparaiso University

Frederica Shockley,
California State University, Chico

William Shughart II,
University of Mississippi

Paul Sicilian,
Grand Valley State University

Charles Sicotte,
Rock Valley College

Calvin Siebert,
University of Iowa

Gerald P. W. Simons,
Grand Valley State University

Brian W. Sloboda,
University of Phoenix

Phillip Smith,
DeKalb College

V. Kerry Smith,
Duke University

David Spencer,
Brigham Young University

Jane Speyrer,
University of New Orleans

Joanne Spitz,
University of Massachusetts

Mark Stegeman,
Virginia Polytechnic Institute

Houston Stokes,
University of Illinois, Chicago

Robert Stonebreaker,
Indiana University of Pennsylvania

Michael Stroup,
Stephen Austin State University

William Swift,
Pace University

James Swofford,
University of South Alabama

Linghui Tang,
Drexel University

Donna Thompson,
Brookdale Community College

John Tribble,
Russell Sage College

Lee J. Van Scyoc,
University of Wisconsin, Oshkosh

Percy Vera,
Sinclair Community College

Han X. Vo,
Winthrop University

Jin Wang,
University of Wisconsin, Stevens Point

Gregory Wassall,
Northeastern University

William Weber,
Eastern Illinois University

David Weinberg,
Xavier University

Bernard Weinrich,
St. Louis Community College

Donald Wells,
University of Arizona

Robert Whaples,
Wake Forest University

Mark Wheeler,
Western Michigan University

Michael White,
St. Cloud State University

Richard Winkelman,
Arizona State University

Stephan Woodbury,
Michigan State University

Kenneth Woodward,
Saddleback College

Patricia Wyatt,
Bossier Parish Community College

Peter Wyman,
Spokane Falls Community College

Mesghena Yasin,
Morehead State University

Edward Young,
University of Wisconsin, Eau Claire

Michael J. Youngblood,
Rock Valley College

William Zeis,
Bucks Community College

I also thank the many contributions and comments from the group of instructors who participated in the Online Survey of my book, or responded to our phone surveys:

Richard U. Agesa,
Marshall University

John Beck,
Gonzaga University

Randall Bennett,
Gonzaga University

Andrew M. Bonacic,
Adirondack College

Joseph Daniels,
Marquette University

Maria Davis,
Indian River State College

Mary Sue DePuy,
Arizona Western College

Erwin F. Erhardt, ,
III ,University of Cincinnati

George Hoffer,
Virginia Commonwealth University

Judy Hurtt,
East Central Community College

E.M. Jankovic,
Fairfield University

Sunita Kumari,
St. Petersburg College

J. Franklin Lee,
Pitt Community College

Harry Miley,
South Carolina State University

Kaustav Misra,
Mississippi State University

Phillip Mixon,
Troy University

John Rapczak,
Community College of Rhode Island

Richard Rouch,
Volunteer State Community College

Jeff Wiltzius,
Indian River State College

Sourushe Zandvakili,
University of Cincinnati

To practice what I preach, I relied on the division of labor based on comparative advantage to help put together an attractive teaching package. John Lunn of Hope College authored the study guides. Robert Sandman of Wilmington College revised the instructors manual, developed Internet activities, and helped update a number of exhibits. Kenneth Slaysman of York College of Pennsylvania reworked the test banks. And Andreea Chiritescu of Eastern Illinois University revised the PowerPoint lecture slides. I thank them all for their help and for their imagination.

The talented professionals at South-Western Cengage provided invaluable editorial, administrative, and sales support. I owe a special debt to Susan Smart, senior developmental editor, who nurtured the manuscript through reviews, revisions, editing, and production. She also helped with Internet activities, photography selection, and coordinated the work of others who contributed to the publishing package. For the fresh look of the book, I owe a debt to Michelle Kunkler, art director, Lisa Albonetti, designer, and John Hill, photography manager. I am also grateful to the content project manager, Corey Geissler, and S4-Carlisle Publishing Services, who helped create the printed pages. Sharon Morgan has been valuable as the media editor. I would also like to thank Sarah Greber, senior marketing communications manager, who has been most helpful, especially with the publication of my newsletter, *The Teaching Economist*.

I am most grateful to Jack Calhoun, vice president and editorial director; Steve Scoble, senior acquisitions editor and problem solver; and John Carey, the senior marketing manager, whose knowledge of the book dates back to the beginning. As good as the book may be, all our efforts would be wasted unless students get to read it. To that end, I greatly appreciate the dedicated service and sales force of South-Western Cengage, who have contributed in a substantial way to the book's success.

Finally, I owe an abiding debt to my wife, Pat, who provided abundant encouragement and support along the way and read the entire manuscript.

William A. McEachern

The Art and Science of Economic Analysis

Siri Stafford/Getty Images

- Why are comic-strip and TV characters like Foxtrot, the Simpsons, and the Family Guy missing a finger on each hand?

- Why do the kids on South Park have hands that look like mittens? And where is Dilbert's mouth?

- Why does Japan have nearly 10 times more vending machines per capita than does Europe?

- In what way are people who pound on vending machines relying on theory?

- Why is a good theory like a California Closet?

- What's the big idea with economics?

- Finally, how can it be said that in economics "what goes around comes around"?

These and other questions are answered in this chapter, which introduces the art and science of economic analysis.

You have been reading and hearing about economic issues for years—unemployment, inflation, poverty, recessions, federal deficits, college tuition, airfares, stock prices, computer prices, gas prices. When explanations of such issues go into any depth, your eyes may glaze over and you may tune out, the same way you do when a weather forecaster tries to provide an in-depth analysis of high-pressure fronts colliding with moisture carried in from the coast.

What many people fail to realize is that economics is livelier than the dry accounts offered by the news media. Economics is about making choices, and you make economic choices every day—choices about whether to get a part-time job or focus on your studies, live in a dorm or off campus, take a course in accounting or one in history, get married or stay single, pack a lunch or buy a sandwich. You already know much more about economics than you realize. You bring to the subject a rich personal experience, an experience that will be tapped throughout the book to reinforce your understanding of the basic ideas.

Topics discussed in this chapter include:

- The economic problem
- Marginal analysis
- Rational self-interest
- Scientific method
- Normative versus positive analysis
- Pitfalls of economic thinking

The Economic Problem: Scarce Resources, Unlimited Wants

Would you like a new car, a nicer home, better meals, more free time, a more interesting social life, more spending money, more leisure, more sleep? Who wouldn't? But even if you can satisfy some of these desires, others keep popping up. *The problem is that, although your wants, or desires, are virtually unlimited, the resources available to satisfy these wants are scarce.* A resource is *scarce* when it is not freely available—that is, when its price exceeds zero. Because resources are scarce, you must choose from among your many wants, and whenever you choose, you must forgo satisfying some other wants. The problem of scarce resources but unlimited wants exists to a greater or lesser extent for each of the 6.9 billion people on earth. Everybody—cab driver, farmer, brain surgeon, dictator, shepherd, student, politician—faces the problem. For example, a cab driver uses time and other scarce resources, such as the taxi, knowledge of the city, driving skills, and gasoline, to earn income. That income, in turn, buys housing, groceries, clothing, trips to Disney World, and thousands of other goods and services that help satisfy some of the driver's unlimited wants. **Economics** examines how people use their scarce resources to satisfy their unlimited wants. Let's pick apart the definition, beginning with resources, then goods and services, and finally focus on the heart of the matter—economic choice, which arises from scarcity.

Resources

Resources are the inputs, or factors of production, used to produce the goods and services that people want. *Goods and services are scarce because resources are scarce.* Resources sort into four broad categories: labor, capital, natural resources, and entrepreneurial ability. **Labor** is human effort, both physical and mental. Labor includes the effort of the cab driver and the brain surgeon. Labor itself comes from a more fundamental resource: *time.* Without time we can accomplish nothing. We allocate our time to alternative uses: We can *sell* our time as labor, or we can *spend* our time doing other things, like sleeping, eating, studying, playing sports, going online, attending class, watching TV, or just relaxing with friends.

   Capital includes all human creations used to produce goods and services. Economists often distinguish between physical capital and human capital. *Physical capital* consists

economics
The study of how people use their scarce resources to satisfy their unlimited wants

resources
The inputs, or factors of production, used to produce the goods and services that people want; resources consist of labor, capital, natural resources, and entrepreneurial ability

labor
The physical and mental effort used to produce goods and services

capital
The buildings, equipment, and human skills used to produce goods and services

of factories, tools, machines, computers, buildings, airports, highways, and other human creations used to produce goods and services. Physical capital includes the cab driver's taxi, the surgeon's scalpel, and the building where your economics class meets (or, if you are taking this course online, your computer and online connectors). *Human capital* consists of the knowledge and skill people acquire to increase their productivity, such as the cab driver's knowledge of city streets, the surgeon's knowledge of human anatomy, and your knowledge of economics.

Natural resources include all *gifts of nature*, such as bodies of water, trees, oil reserves, minerals, even animals. Natural resources can be divided into renewable resources and exhaustible resources. A *renewable resource* can be drawn on indefinitely if used conservatively. Thus, timber is a renewable resource if felled trees are replaced to regrow a steady supply. The air and rivers are renewable resources if they are allowed sufficient time to cleanse themselves of any pollutants. More generally, biological resources like fish, game, livestock, forests, rivers, groundwater, grasslands, and soil are renewable if managed properly. An *exhaustible resource*—such as oil or coal—does not renew itself and so is available in a limited amount. Once burned, each barrel of oil or ton of coal is gone forever. The world's oil and coal deposits are exhaustible.

A special kind of human skill called **entrepreneurial ability** is the talent required to dream up a new product or find a better way to produce an existing one. This special skill comes from an entrepreneur. An **entrepreneur** is a profit-seeking decision maker who starts with an idea, organizes an enterprise to bring that idea to life, and then assumes the risk of operation. An entrepreneur pays resource owners for the opportunity to employ their resources in the firm. Every firm in the world today, such as Ford, Microsoft, Google, and Dell, began as an idea in the mind of an entrepreneur.

Resource owners are paid **wages** for their labor, **interest** for the use of their capital, and **rent** for the use of their natural resources. Entrepreneurial ability is rewarded by **profit**, which equals the *revenue* from items sold minus the *cost* of the resources employed to make those items. The word *profit* comes from the Latin *proficere*, which means "to benefit." The entrepreneur benefits from what's left over after paying other resource suppliers. Sometimes the entrepreneur suffers a loss. Resource earnings are usually based on the *time* these resources are employed. Resource payments therefore have a time dimension, as in a wage of $10 *per hour*, interest of 6 percent *per year*, rent of $600 *per month*, or profit of $10,000 *per year*.

Goods and Services

Resources are combined in a variety of ways to produce goods and services. A farmer, a tractor, 50 acres of land, seeds, and fertilizer combine to grow the good: corn. One hundred musicians, musical instruments, chairs, a conductor, a musical score, and a music hall combine to produce the service: Beethoven's *Fifth Symphony*. Corn is a **good** because it is something you can see, feel, and touch; it requires scarce resources to produce; and it satisfies human wants. The book you are now holding, the chair you are sitting in, the clothes you are wearing, and your next meal are all goods. The performance of the *Fifth Symphony* is a **service** because it is intangible, yet it uses scarce resources to satisfy human wants. Lectures, movies, concerts, phone service, broadband connections, yoga lessons, dry cleaning, and haircuts are all services.

Because goods and services are produced using scarce resources, they are themselves scarce. *A good or service is scarce if the amount people desire exceeds the amount available at a zero price.* Because we cannot have all the goods and services we would like, we must continually choose among them. We must choose among more pleasant living quarters, better meals, nicer clothes, more reliable transportation, faster computers, and so on. Making choices in a world of **scarcity** means we must pass up some goods and

natural resources
All gifts of nature used to produce goods and services; includes renewable and exhaustible resources

entrepreneurial ability
The imagination required to develop a new product or process, the skill needed to organize production, and the willingness to take the risk of profit or loss

entrepreneur
A profit-seeking decision maker who starts with an idea, organizes an enterprise to bring that idea to life, and assumes the risk of the operation

wages
Payment to resource owners for their labor

interest
Payment to resource owners for the use of their capital

rent
Payment to resource owners for the use of their natural resources

profit
Reward for entrepreneurial ability; sales revenue minus resource cost

good
A tangible product used to satisfy human wants

service
An activity, or intangible product, used to satisfy human wants

scarcity
Occurs when the amount people desire exceeds the amount available at a zero price

services. But not everything is scarce. In fact some things we would prefer to have less of. For example, we would prefer to have less garbage, less spam email, and less pollution. Things we want none of even at a zero price are called *bads*, the opposite of goods.

A few goods and services seem *free* because the amount available at a zero price exceeds the amount people want. For example, air and seawater often seem free because we can breathe all the air we want and have all the seawater we can haul away. Yet, despite the old saying "The best things in life are free," most goods and services are scarce, not free, and even those that appear to be free come with strings attached. For example, *clean* air and *clean* seawater have become scarce. *Goods and services that are truly free are not the subject matter of economics. Without scarcity, there would be no economic problem and no need for prices.*

Sometimes we mistakenly think of certain goods as free because they involve no apparent cost to us. Napkins seem to be free at Starbucks. Nobody stops you from taking a fistful. Supplying napkins, however, costs the company millions each year and prices reflect that cost. Some restaurants make special efforts to keep napkin use down—such as packing them tightly into the dispenser or making you ask for them.

You may have heard the expression "There is no such thing as a free lunch." There is no free lunch because all goods and services involve a cost to someone. The lunch may seem free to you, but it draws scarce resources away from the production of other goods and services, and whoever provides a free lunch often expects something in return. A Russian proverb makes a similar point but with a bit more bite: "The only place you find free cheese is in a mousetrap." Albert Einstein once observed, "Sometimes one pays the most for things one gets for nothing."

Economic Decision Makers

There are four types of decision makers in the economy: households, firms, governments, and the rest of the world. Their interaction determines how an economy's resources are allocated. *Households* play the starring role. As consumers, households demand the goods and services produced. As resource owners, households supply labor, capital, natural resources, and entrepreneurial ability to firms, governments, and the rest of the world. *Firms, governments,* and *the rest of the world* demand the resources that households supply and then use these resources to supply the goods and services that households demand. The rest of the world includes foreign households, foreign firms, and foreign governments that supply resources and products to U.S. markets and demand resources and products from U.S. markets.

Markets are the means by which buyers and sellers carry out exchange. By bringing together the two sides of exchange, markets determine price, quantity, and quality. Markets are often physical places, such as supermarkets, department stores, shopping malls, or yard sales. But markets also include other mechanisms by which buyers and sellers communicate, such as classified ads, radio and television ads, telephones, bulletin boards, online sites, and face-to-face bargaining. These market mechanisms provide information about the quantity, quality, and price of products offered for sale. Goods and services are bought and sold in **product markets**. Resources are bought and sold in **resource markets**. The most important resource market is the labor, or job, market. Think about your own experience looking for a job, and you'll already have some idea of that market.

A Simple Circular-Flow Model

Now that you have learned a bit about economic decision makers, consider how they interact. Such a picture is conveyed by the **circular-flow model**, which describes the flow of resources, products, income, and revenue among economic decision makers.

market
A set of arrangements by which buyers and sellers carry out exchange at mutually agreeable terms

product market
A market in which a good or service is bought and sold

resource market
A market in which a resource is bought and sold

circular-flow model
A diagram that traces the flow of resources, products, income, and revenue among economic decision makers

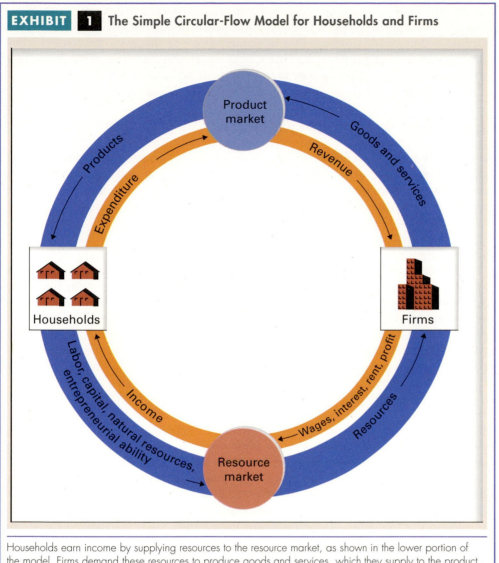

EXHIBIT   1   The Simple Circular-Flow Model for Households and Firms

Households earn income by supplying resources to the resource market, as shown in the lower portion of the model. Firms demand these resources to produce goods and services, which they supply to the product market, as shown in the upper portion of the model. Households spend their income to demand these goods and services. This spending flows through the product market as revenue to firms.

The simple circular-flow model focuses on the primary interaction in a market economy—that between households and firms. Exhibit 1 shows households on the left and firms on the right; please take a look.

Households supply labor, capital, natural resources, and entrepreneurial ability to firms through resource markets, shown in the lower portion of the exhibit. In return, households demand goods and services from firms through product markets, shown on the upper portion of the exhibit. Viewed from the business end, firms demand labor, capital, natural resources, and entrepreneurial ability from households through resource markets, and firms supply goods and services to households through product markets.

The flows of resources and products are supported by the flows of income and expenditure—that is, by the flow of money. So let's add money. The demand and supply of resources come together in resource markets to determine what firms pay for resources. These resource prices—wages, interest, rent, and profit—flow as *income* to households. The demand and supply of products come together in product markets to determine what households pay for goods and services. These product prices of goods and services flow as *revenue* to firms. Resources and products flow in one direction—in this case, counterclockwise—and the corresponding payments flow in the other direction—clockwise. What goes around comes around. Take a little time now to trace the logic of the circular flows.

The Art of Economic Analysis

An economy results as millions of individuals attempt to satisfy their unlimited wants. Because their choices lie at the heart of the economic problem—coping with scarce resources but unlimited wants—these choices deserve a closer look. Learning about the forces that shape economic choice is the first step toward mastering the art of economic analysis.

Rational Self-Interest

A key economic assumption is that individuals, in making choices, rationally select what they perceive to be in their best interests. By *rational,* economists mean simply that people try to make the best choices they can, given the available time and information. People may not know with certainty which alternative will turn out to be the best. They simply select the alternatives they *expect* will yield the most satisfaction and happiness. In general, **rational self-interest** means that each individual tries to maximize the expected benefit achieved with a given cost or to minimize the expected cost of achieving a given benefit.

Rational self-interest should not be viewed as blind materialism, pure selfishness, or greed. We all know people who are tuned to radio station WIIFM (What's In It For Me?). For most of us, however, self-interest often includes the welfare of our family, our friends, and perhaps the poor of the world. Even so, our concern for others is influenced by the personal cost of that concern. We may readily volunteer to drive a friend to the airport on Saturday afternoon but are less likely to offer a ride if the plane leaves at 6:00 A.M. When we donate clothes to an organization such as Goodwill Industries, they are more likely to be old and worn than brand new. People tend to give more to charities when their contributions are tax deductible and when contributions garner social approval in the community (as when contributor names are made public or when big donors get buildings named after them). TV stations are more likely to donate airtime for public-service announcements during the dead of night than during prime time (in fact, 80 percent of such announcements air between 11:00 P.M. and 7:00 A.M.[1]). In Asia some people burn money to soothe the passage of a departed loved one. But they burn fake money, not real money. The notion of self-interest does not rule out concern for others; it simply means that concern for others is influenced by the same economic forces that affect other economic choices. *The lower the personal cost of helping others, the more help we offer.* We don't like to think that our behavior reflects our self-interest, but it usually does. As Jane Austen wrote in *Pride and Prejudice,* "I have been a selfish being all my life, in practice, though not in principle."

Choice Requires Time and Information

Rational choice takes time and requires information, but time and information are scarce and therefore valuable. If you have any doubts about the time and information needed to make choices, talk to someone who recently purchased a home, a car, or a personal

rational self-interest
Each individual tries to maximize the expected benefit achieved with a given cost or to minimize the expected cost of achieving a given benefit

net bookmark
To make good use of the Internet, you need Adobe Acrobat Reader. You can download it from http://get.adobe.com/reader/. An economic question is: Why does Adobe give its Reader away free?

1.   Sally Goll Beatty, "Media and Agencies Brawl Over Do-Good Advertising," *Wall Street Journal,* 29 September 1997.

computer. Talk to a corporate official trying to decide whether to introduce a new product, sell online, build a new factory, or buy another firm. Or think back to your own experience in choosing a college. You probably talked to friends, relatives, teachers, and guidance counselors. You likely used school catalogs, college guides, and Web sites. You may have visited some campuses to meet the admissions staff and anyone else willing to talk. The decision took time and money, and it probably involved aggravation and anxiety.

Because information is costly to acquire, we are often willing to pay others to gather and digest it for us. College guidebooks, stock analysts, travel agents, real estate brokers, career counselors, restaurant critics, movie reviewers, specialized Web sites, and *Consumer Reports* magazine attest to our willingness to pay for information that improves our choices. As we'll see next, *rational decision makers continue to acquire information as long as the additional benefit expected from that information exceeds the additional cost of gathering it.*

Economic Analysis Is Marginal Analysis

Economic choice usually involves some adjustment to the existing situation, or status quo. Amazon.com must decide whether to add an additional line of products. The school superintendent must decide whether to hire another teacher. Your favorite jeans are on sale, and you must decide whether to buy another pair. You are wondering whether to carry an extra course next term. You just finished lunch and are deciding whether to order dessert.

Economic choice is based on a comparison of the *expected marginal benefit* and the *expected marginal cost* of the action under consideration. **Marginal** means incremental, additional, or extra. Marginal refers to a change in an economic variable, a change in the status quo. *A rational decision maker changes the status quo if the expected marginal benefit from the change exceeds the expected marginal cost.* For example, Amazon .com compares the marginal benefit expected from adding a new line of products (the additional sales revenue) with the marginal cost (the additional cost of the resources required). Likewise, you compare the marginal benefit you expect from eating dessert (the additional pleasure or satisfaction) with its marginal cost (the additional money, time, and calories).

marginal
Incremental, additional, or extra; used to describe a change in an economic variable

Typically, the change under consideration is small, but a marginal choice can involve a major economic adjustment, as in the decision to quit school and find a job. For a firm, a marginal choice might mean building a plant in Mexico or even filing for bankruptcy. By focusing on the effect of a marginal adjustment to the status quo, the economist is able to cut the analysis of economic choice down to a manageable size. Rather than confront a bewildering economic reality head-on, the economist begins with a marginal choice to see how this choice affects a particular market and shapes the economic system as a whole. Incidentally, to the noneconomist, *marginal* usually means relatively inferior, as in "a movie of marginal quality." Forget that meaning for this course and instead think of *marginal* as meaning incremental, additional, or extra.

Microeconomics and Macroeconomics

Although you have made thousands of economic choices, you probably seldom think about your own economic behavior. For example, why are you reading this book right now rather than doing something else? **Microeconomics** is the study of your economic behavior and the economic behavior of others who make choices about such matters as how much to study and how much to party, how much to borrow and how much to save, what to buy and what to sell. Microeconomics examines individual economic choices and how markets coordinate the choices of various decision makers. Microeconomics explains how price and quantity are determined in individual markets—the market for breakfast cereal, sports equipment, or used cars, for instance.

microeconomics
The study of the economic behavior in particular markets, such as that for computers or unskilled labor

macroeconomics

The study of the economic behavior of entire economies, as measured, for example, by total production and employment

economic fluctuations

The rise and fall of economic activity relative to the long-term growth trend of the economy; also called business cycles

You have probably given little thought to what influences your own economic choices. You have likely given even less thought to how your choices link up with those made by millions of others in the U.S. economy to determine economy-wide measures such as total production, employment, and economic growth. **Macroeconomics** studies the performance of the economy as a whole. Whereas microeconomics studies the individual pieces of the economic puzzle, as reflected in particular markets, macroeconomics puts all the pieces together to focus on the big picture.

The national economy usually grows over time, but along the way it sometimes stumbles, experiencing *recessions* in economic activity, as reflected by a decline in production, employment, and other aggregate measures. **Economic fluctuations** are the rise and fall of economic activity relative to the long-term growth trend of the economy. These fluctuations, or *business cycles,* vary in length and intensity, but they usually involve the entire nation and often other nations too. For example, the U.S. economy now produces more than four times as much as it did in 1960, despite experiencing eight recessions since then, including the painful recession of 2007–2009.

To Review: The art of economic analysis focuses on how people use their scarce resources in an attempt to satisfy their unlimited wants. Rational self-interest guides individual choice. Choice requires time and information, and involves a comparison of the expected marginal benefit and the expected marginal cost of alternative actions. Microeconomics looks at the individual pieces of the economic puzzle; macroeconomics fits the pieces together to form the big picture.

The Science of Economic Analysis

economic theory, or economic model

A simplification of reality used to make predictions about cause and effect in the real world

Economists use scientific analysis to develop theories, or models, that help explain economic behavior. An **economic theory**, or **economic model**, is a simplification of economic reality that *is used to make predictions about the real world*. A theory, or model, such as the circular-flow model, captures the important elements of the problem under study but need not spell out every detail and interrelation. In fact, adding more details may make a theory more unwieldy and, therefore, less useful. For example, a wristwatch is a model that tells time, but a watch festooned with extra features is harder to read at a glance and is therefore less useful as a time-telling model. The world is so complex that we must simplify it to make sense of things. Store mannequins simplify the human form (some even lack arms and heads). Comic strips and cartoons simplify characters—leaving out fingers or a mouth, for instance. You might think of economic theory as a stripped-down, or streamlined, version of economic reality.

A good theory helps us understand a messy and confusing world. Lacking a theory of how things work, our thinking can become cluttered with facts, one piled on another, as in a messy closet. You could think of a good theory as a closet organizer for the mind. A good theory offers a helpful guide to sorting, saving, and understanding information.

The Role of Theory

Most people don't understand the role of theory. Perhaps you have heard, "Oh, that's fine in theory, but in practice it's another matter." The implication is that the theory in question provides little aid in practical matters. People who say this fail to realize that they are merely substituting their own theory for a theory they either do not believe or do not understand. They are really saying, "I have my own theory that works better."

All of us employ theories, however poorly defined or understood. Someone who pounds on the Pepsi machine that just ate a quarter has a crude theory about how that machine works. One version of that theory might be "The quarter drops through a series of *whatchamacallits,* but sometimes it gets stuck. *If* I pound on the machine, *then* I can free up the quarter and send it on its way." Evidently, this theory is widespread enough that people continue to pound on machines that fail to perform (a real problem for the vending machine industry and one reason newer machines are fronted with glass). Yet, if you were to ask these mad pounders to explain their "theory" about how the machine works, they would look at you as if you were crazy.

The Scientific Method

To study economic problems, economists employ a process of theoretical investigation called the *scientific method,* which consists of four steps, as outlined in Exhibit 2.

Step One: Identify the Question and Define Relevant Variables

The scientific method begins with curiosity: Someone wants to answer a question. Thus, the first step is to identify the economic question and define the variables relevant to a solution. For example, the question might be "What is the relationship between the price of Pepsi and

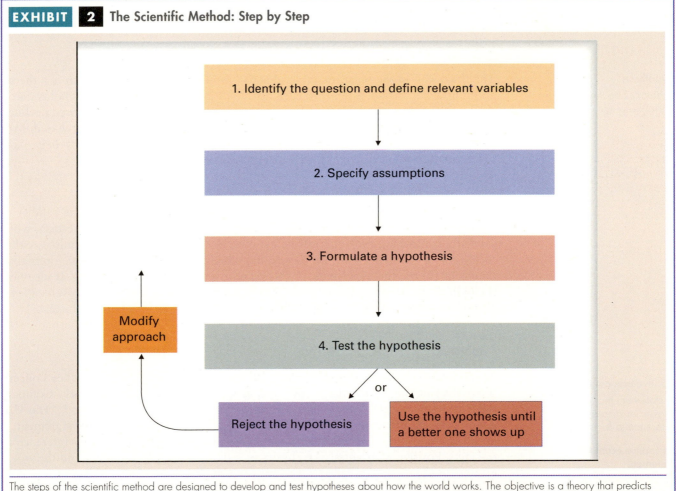

EXHIBIT   2   The Scientific Method: Step by Step

1. Identify the question and define relevant variables

2. Specify assumptions

3. Formulate a hypothesis

4. Test the hypothesis

or

Reject the hypothesis

Use the hypothesis until a better one shows up

Modify approach

The steps of the scientific method are designed to develop and test hypotheses about how the world works. The objective is a theory that predicts outcomes more accurately than the best alternative theory. A hypothesis is rejected if it does not predict as accurately as the best alternative. A rejected hypothesis can be modified or reworked in light of the test results.

the quantity of Pepsi purchased?" In this case, the relevant variables are price and quantity. A **variable** is a measure that can take on different values at different times. The variables of concern become the elements of the theory, so they must be selected with care.

Step Two: Specify Assumptions

The second step is to specify the assumptions under which the theory is to apply. One major category of assumptions is the **other-things-constant assumption**—in Latin, the *ceteris paribus* assumption. The idea is to identify the variables of interest and then focus exclusively on the relationships among them, assuming that nothing else important changes—that other things remain constant. Again, suppose we are interested in how the price of Pepsi influences the amount purchased. To isolate the relation between these two variables, we assume that there are no changes in other relevant variables such as consumer income, the average temperature, or the price of Coke.

We also make assumptions about how people behave; these are called **behavioral assumptions**. The primary behavioral assumption is rational self-interest. Earlier we assumed that each decision maker pursues self-interest rationally and makes choices accordingly. Rationality implies that each consumer buys the products expected to maximize his or her level of satisfaction. Rationality also implies that each firm supplies the products expected to maximize the firm's profit. These kinds of assumptions are called behavioral assumptions because they specify how we expect economic decision makers to behave—what makes them tick, so to speak.

Step Three: Formulate a Hypothesis

The third step in the scientific method is to formulate a **hypothesis**, which is a theory about how key variables relate to each other. For example, one hypothesis holds that if the price of Pepsi goes up, other things constant, then the quantity purchased declines. The hypothesis becomes a prediction of what happens to the quantity purchased if the price increases. *The purpose of this hypothesis, like that of any theory, is to help make predictions about cause and effect in the real world.*

Step Four: Test the Hypothesis

In the fourth step, by comparing its predictions with evidence, we test the validity of a hypothesis. To test a hypothesis, we must focus on the variables in question, while carefully controlling for other effects assumed not to change. The test leads us either to (1) reject the hypothesis, or theory, if it predicts worse than the best alternative theory or (2) use the hypothesis, or theory, until a better one comes along. If we reject the hypothesis, we can go back and modify our approach in light of the results. Please spend a moment now reviewing the steps of the scientific method in Exhibit 2.

Normative Versus Positive

Economists usually try to explain how the economy works. Sometimes they concern themselves not with how the economy *does* work but how it *should* work. Compare these two statements: "The U.S. unemployment rate is 9.7 percent." and "The U.S. unemployment rate should be lower." The first, called a **positive economic statement**, is an assertion about economic reality that can be supported or rejected by reference to the facts. Positive economics, like physics or biology, attempts to understand the world around us. The second, called a **normative economic statement**, reflects an opinion. And an opinion is merely that—it cannot be shown to be true or false by reference to the facts. Positive statements concern what *is*; normative statements concern what, in someone's opinion, *should be*. Positive statements need not necessarily be true, but

variable
A measure, such as price or quantity, that can take on different values at different times

other-things-constant assumption
The assumption, when focusing on the relation among key economic variables, that other variables remain unchanged; in Latin, *ceteris paribus*

behavioral assumption
An assumption that describes the expected behavior of economic decision makers, what motivates them

hypothesis
A theory about how key variables relate

positive economic statement
A statement that can be proved or disproved by reference to facts

normative economic statement
A statement that reflects an opinion, which cannot be proved or disproved by reference to the facts

they must be subject to verification or refutation by reference to the facts. Theories are expressed as positive statements such as "If the price of Pepsi increases, then the quantity demanded decreases."

Most of the disagreement among economists involves normative debates—such as the appropriate role of government—rather than statements of positive analysis. To be sure, many theoretical issues remain unresolved, but economists generally agree on most fundamental theoretical principles—that is, about positive economic analysis. For example, in a survey of 464 U.S. economists, only 6.5 percent disagreed with the statement "A ceiling on rents reduces the quantity and quality of housing available." This is a positive statement because it can be shown to be consistent or inconsistent with the evidence. In contrast, there was much less agreement on normative statements such as "The distribution of income in the United States should be more equal." Half the economists surveyed "generally agreed," a quarter "generally disagreed," and a quarter "agreed with provisos."[2]

Normative statements, or value judgments, have a place in a policy debate such as the proper role of government, provided that statements of opinion are distinguished from statements of fact. In such policy debates, you are entitled to your own opinion, but you are not entitled to your own facts.

Economists Tell Stories

Despite economists' reliance on the scientific method for developing and evaluating theories, economic analysis is as much art as science. Formulating a question, isolating the key variables, specifying the assumptions, proposing a theory to answer the question, and devising a way to test the predictions all involve more than simply an understanding of economics and the scientific method. Carrying out these steps requires good intuition and the imagination of a storyteller. Economists explain their theories by telling stories about how they think the economy works. To tell a compelling story, an economist relies on case studies, anecdotes, parables, the personal experience of the listener, and supporting data. Throughout this book, you'll hear stories that bring you closer to the ideas under consideration. The stories, such as the one about the Pepsi machine, breathe life into economic theory and help you personalize abstract ideas. As another example, here is a case study on the popularity of vending machines in Japan.

WORLD OF BUSINESS

CASE STUDY

e activity
Do you want to see more pictures of unusual vending machines in Japan? Go to http://www.toxel.com/tech and scroll down to find the search box. Enter "14 Cool Vending Machines from Japan." In the search results, click on the link for Read Full Post.

A Yen for Vending Machines   Japan faces a steady drop in the number of working-age people. Here are three reasons why: (1) Japan's birthrate has dropped to a record low, (2) Japan allows little immigration, and (3) Japan's population is aging. As a result, unemployment has usually been lower in Japan than in other countries. For example, Japan's unemployment rate in 2010 was only about half that of the United States and Europe. Because labor is relatively scarce in Japan, it is relatively costly. To sell products, Japanese retailers rely more on physical capital, particularly vending machines, which obviously eliminate the need for sales clerks.

Japan has more vending machines per capita than any other country on the planet—twice as many as the United States and nearly 10 times as many as Europe. And vending machines in Japan sell a wider range of products than elsewhere, including beer, sake, whiskey, rice, fresh eggs, beef, vegetables, pizza, entire meals, fried foods, fresh flowers, clothes, toilet paper, fishing supplies including bait, video

2. Richard M. Alston et al., "Is There a Consensus Among Economists in the 1990s?" *American Economic Review*, 82 (May 1992): 203–209, Table 1.

© AndySmyStock/Alamy

games, software, ebooks, toys, DVDs, mobile phone recharging, and even X-rated comic books. Japan's vending machines are also more sophisticated. Newer models come with video monitors and touch-pad screens. Wireless chips alert vendors when supplies run low. Some cigarette and liquor machines have artificial vision that reportedly are better at estimating age than are nightclub bouncers. Sanyo makes a giant machine that sells up to 200 different items at three different temperatures. Some cold-drink dispensers automatically raise prices in hot weather. Thousands of machines allow cell phone users to pay by pressing a few buttons on their phones.

As noted earlier, it is common practice in the United States to shake down vending machines that malfunction. Such abuse increases the probability the machines will fail again, leading to a cycle of abuse. Vending machines in Japan are less abused, in part because they are more sophisticated and more reliable and in part because the Japanese generally have greater respect for private property and, consequently, a lower crime rate (e.g., Japan's theft rate is about half the U.S. rate).

Forty percent of all soft-drink sales in Japan are through vending machines, compared to only 12 percent of U.S. sales. Japanese sales per machine are double the U.S. rate. Research shows that most Japanese consumers prefer an anonymous machine to a salesperson. Despite the abundance of vending machines in Japan, more growth is forecast, spurred on by a shrinking labor pool, technological innovations, and wide acceptance of machines there.

Sources: "Machines That Can See," *The Economist*, 5 March 2009; Hiroko Tabuchi, "Beef Bowl Economics," *New York Times*, 30 January 2010; and Trends in Japan at http://web-japan.org/trends/lifestyle/lif060720.html. For a photo gallery of vending machines in Japan go to http://www.photomann.com/japan/machines/.

This case study makes two points. First, producers combine resources in a way that conserves, or economizes on, the resource that is more costly—in this case, labor. Second, the customs and conventions of the marketplace can differ across countries, and this variance can result in different types of economic arrangements, such as the more extensive use of vending machines in Japan.

Predicting Average Behavior

The goal of an economic theory is to predict the impact of an economic event on economic choices and, in turn, the effect of these choices on particular markets or on the economy as a whole. Does this mean that economists try to predict the behavior of particular consumers or producers? Not necessarily, because a specific individual may behave in an unpredictable way. But the unpredictable actions of numerous individuals tend to cancel one another out, so the *average behavior* of groups can be predicted more accurately. For example, if the federal government cuts personal income taxes, certain households may decide to save the entire tax cut. On average, however, household spending increases. Likewise, if Burger King cuts the price of Whoppers, the manager can better predict how much sales will increase than how a specific customer coming through the door will respond. *The random actions of individuals tend to offset one another, so the average behavior of a large group can be predicted more accurately than the behavior of a particular individual.* Consequently, economists tend to focus on the average, or typical, behavior of people in groups—for example, as average taxpayers or average Whopper consumers—rather than on the behavior of a specific individual.

Some Pitfalls of Faulty Economic Analysis

Economic analysis, like other forms of scientific inquiry, is subject to common mistakes in reasoning that can lead to faulty conclusions. Here are three sources of confusion.

The Fallacy That Association Is Causation

In the last two decades, the number of physicians specializing in cancer treatment increased sharply. At the same time, the incidence of some cancers increased. Can we conclude that physicians cause cancer? No. To assume that event A caused event B simply because the two are associated in time is to commit the **association-is-causation fallacy**, a common error. The fact that one event precedes another or that the two events occur simultaneously does not necessarily mean that one causes the other. Remember: Association is not necessarily causation.

The Fallacy of Composition

Perhaps you have been to a rock concert where everyone stands to get a better view. At some concerts, most people even stand on their chairs. But even standing on chairs does not improve the view if others do the same, unless you are quite tall. Likewise, arriving early to buy game tickets does not work if many have the same idea. These are examples of the **fallacy of composition**, which is an erroneous belief that what is true for the individual, or the part, is also true for the group, or the whole.

The Mistake of Ignoring the Secondary Effects

In many cities, public officials have imposed rent controls on apartments. The primary effect of this policy, the effect policy makers focus on, is to keep rents from rising. Over time, however, fewer new apartments get built because renting them becomes less profitable. Moreover, existing rental units deteriorate because owners have plenty of customers anyway. Thus, the quantity and quality of housing may decline as a result of what appears to be a reasonable measure to keep rents from rising. The mistake was to ignore the **secondary effects**, or the unintended consequences, of the policy. Economic actions have secondary effects that often turn out to be more important than the primary effects. Secondary effects may develop more slowly and may not be immediately obvious, but good economic analysis tries to anticipate them and take them into account.

If Economists Are So Smart, Why Aren't They Rich?

Why aren't economists rich? Well, some are, earning over $25,000 per appearance on the lecture circuit. Others top $2 million a year as consultants and expert witnesses.[3] Economists have been appointed to federal cabinet posts, such as secretaries of commerce, defense, labor, state, and treasury, and to head the U.S. Federal Reserve System. Economics is the only social science and the only business discipline for which the prestigious Nobel Prize is awarded, and pronouncements by economists are reported in the media daily. *The Economist,* a widely respected news weekly from London, has argued that economic ideas have influenced policy "to a degree that would make other social scientists drool."[4]

The economics profession thrives because its models usually do a better job of making economic sense out of a confusing world than do alternative approaches. But not all economists are wealthy, nor is personal wealth the goal of the discipline. In a similar vein, not all doctors are healthy (some even smoke), not all carpenters live in perfectly built homes, not all marriage counselors are happily married, and not all

association-is-causation fallacy
The incorrect idea that if two variables are associated in time, one must necessarily cause the other

fallacy of composition
The incorrect belief that what is true for the individual, or part, must necessarily be true for the group, or the whole

secondary effects
Unintended consequences of economic actions that may develop slowly over time as people react to events

3.   As reported by George Anders, "An Economist's Courtroom Bonanza," *Wall Street Journal*, 19 March 2007.
4.   "The Puzzling Failure of Economics," *Economist*, 23 August 1997, p. 11.

child psychologists have well-adjusted children. Still, those who study economics do reap financial rewards, as discussed in this closing case study, which looks at the link between a college major and annual earnings.

THE INFORMATION ECONOMY

College Major and Annual Earnings   Earlier in the chapter, you learned that economic choice involves comparing the expected marginal benefit and the expected marginal cost. Surveys show that students go to college because they believe a college diploma is the ticket to better jobs and higher pay. Put another way, for nearly two-thirds of U.S. high school graduates, the expected marginal benefit of college apparently exceeds the expected marginal cost. The cost of college will be discussed in the next chapter; the focus here is on the benefits of college, particularly expected earnings.

Among college graduates, all kinds of factors affect earnings, such as general ability, effort, occupation, college attended, college major, and highest degree earned. PayScale.com collected real time information on annual pay from its 10 million users. The site focused on the 20 popular college majors where most graduates go into the private sector (this excluded public sector majors such as education and social work, where pay is relatively low). To isolate the effects of a college major on earnings, only workers with a bachelor's as their highest degree were included in the results. Exhibit 3 shows the median earnings in 2008 by major for two groups of college graduates: (1) those with zero to five years of job experience and (2) those with 10 to 20 years of job experience. Majors are listed from the top down by the median annual pay of those with between zero and five years experience, indentified by the light green bars. The top pay of $60,500 went to those majoring in computer engineering; indeed, the top five slots went to engineering and computer graduates. Economics ranked sixth out of twenty majors with a median pay of $48,100, or 20 percent below the top pay. Criminal justice majors held the bottom spot of $34,200, which was 44 percent below the top pay.

The dark green bars show the median pay by major for those with 10 to 20 years of job experience. Those majoring in computer engineering still lead the field with $104,000, an increase of 72 percent over the pay of newer graduates with that degree. Economics majors with 10 to 20 years of job experience saw a 100 percent pay increase to $96,200. While economics majors with zero to five years experience were paid 20 percent less than the top paying major, among those with at least a decade of job experience, the median pay for economics majors moved up to within 7 percent of the top pay. In fact, economics majors saw their median pay grow more both in dollar terms and in percentage terms than did any other major. This suggests that those who study economics acquire skills that appreciate with experience.

The bump in median pay based on experience for the 19 other majors averaged 67 percent. Criminal justice remained the lowest paying major among those with 10 to 20 years of experience. Note that the majors ranked toward the top of the list tend to be more quantitative and analytical. The selection of a relatively more challenging major such as economics may send a favorable signal to future employers.

Remember, the survey was limited to those whose highest degree was the baccalaureate, so it excluded the many economics majors who went on to pursue graduate studies in law, business administration, economics, public administration, journalism, and other fields (a different study found that lawyers with undergraduate degrees in economics earned more on average than lawyers with other majors).

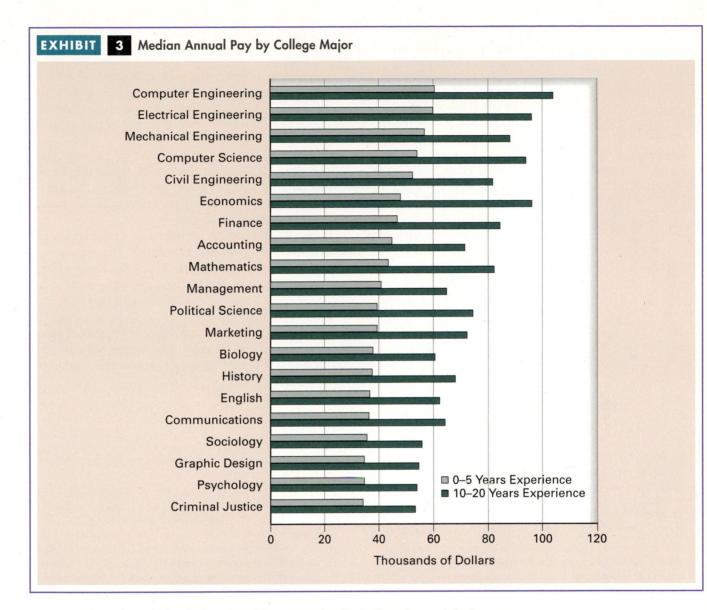

EXHIBIT 3 Median Annual Pay by College Major

A number of world leaders majored in economics, including three of the last seven U.S. presidents, Chile's president and billionaire, Sabastian Pinera (who earned a Ph.D. in economics from Harvard), Turkey's first female prime minister, Tansu Ciller (who earned a Ph.D. in economics from the University of Connecticut), U.S. Supreme Court justices Steven Breyer and Anthony Kennedy, and former justice Sandra Day O'Connor. Other notable economics majors include billionaire Donald Trump, former eBay president (and billionaire) Meg Whitman, Microsoft chief executive officer (and billionaire) Steve Ballmer, CNN founder (and billionaire) Ted Turner, Intel president Paul Otellini, NFL Patriot's coach Bill Belichick, Governor Arnold Schwarzenegger, and Scott Adams, creator of Dilbert, the mouthless wonder.

Sources: Kurt Badenhausen, "Most Lucrative College Major," *Forbes.com*, 18 June 2008 at http://www.forbes .com/2008/06/18/college-majors-lucrative-lead-cx_kb_0618majors.html. "The World's Billionaires," *Forbes*, 11 March 2010; and R. Kim Craft and Joe Baker, "Do Economists Make Better Lawyers?, "*Journal of Economic Education*," 34 (Summer 2003): 263–281. For a survey of employment opportunities, go to the U.S. Labor Department's *Occupational Outlook Handbook* at http://www.bls.gov/oco/.

Conclusion

This textbook describes how economic factors affect individual choices and how all these choices come together to shape the economic system. Economics is not the whole story, and economic factors are not always the most important. But economic considerations have important and predictable effects on individual choices, and these choices affect the way we live.

Sure, economics is a challenging discipline, but it is also an exciting and rewarding one. The good news is that you already know a lot about economics. To use this knowledge, however, you must cultivate the art and science of economic analysis. You must be able to simplify the world to formulate questions, isolate the relevant variables, and then tell a persuasive story about how these variables relate.

An economic relation can be expressed in words, represented as a table of quantities, described by a mathematical equation, or illustrated as a graph. The appendix to this chapter introduces graphs. You may find this unnecessary. If you are already familiar with relations among variables, slopes, tangents, and the like, you can probably just browse. But if you have little recent experience with graphs, you might benefit from a more careful reading with pencil and paper in hand.

The next chapter introduces key tools of economic analysis. Subsequent chapters use these tools to explore economic problems and to explain economic behavior that may otherwise seem puzzling. You must walk before you can run, however, and in the next chapter, you take your first wobbly steps.

Summary

1. Economics is the study of how people choose to use their scarce resources to produce, exchange, and consume goods and services in an attempt to satisfy unlimited wants. The economic problem arises from the conflict between scarce resources and unlimited wants. If wants were limited or if resources were not scarce, there would be no need to study economics.

2. Economic resources are combined in a variety of ways to produce goods and services. Major categories of resources include labor, capital, natural resources, and entrepreneurial ability. Because economic resources are scarce, only a limited number of goods and services can be produced with them. Therefore, goods and services are also scarce so choices must be made.

3. Microeconomics focuses on choices made in households, firms, and governments and how these choices affect particular markets, such as the market for used cars. Choice is guided by rational self-interest. Choice typically requires time and information, both of which are scarce and valuable.

4. Whereas microeconomics examines the individual pieces of the puzzle, macroeconomics steps back to consider the big picture—the performance of the economy as a whole as reflected by such measures as total production, employment, the price level, and economic growth.

5. Economists use theories, or models, to help understand the effects of an economic change, such as a change in price or income, on individual choices and how these choices affect particular markets and the economy as a whole. Economists employ the scientific method to study an economic problem by (a) formulating the question and identifying relevant variables, (b) specifying the assumptions under which the theory operates, (c) developing a theory, or hypothesis, about how the variables relate, and (d) testing that theory by comparing its predictions with the evidence. A theory might not work perfectly, but it is useful as long as it predicts better than competing theories do.

6. Positive economics aims to discover how the economy works. Normative economics is concerned more with how, in someone's opinion, the economy should work. Those who are not careful can fall victim to the fallacy that association is causation, to the fallacy of composition, and to the mistake of ignoring secondary effects.

Key Concepts

Economics 2	Capital 2	Entrepreneur 3
Resources 2	Natural resources 3	Wages 3
Labor 2	Entrepreneurial ability 3	Interest 3

Rent   3

Profit   3

Good   3

Service   3

Scarcity   3

Market   4

Product market   4

Resource market   4

Circular-flow model   4

Rational self-interest   6

Marginal   7

Microeconomics   7

Macroeconomics   8

Economic fluctuations   8

Economic theory, or economic model   8

Variable   10

Other-things-constant assumption   10

Behavioral assumption   10

Hypothesis   10

Positive economic statement   10

Normative economic statement   10

Association-is-causation fallacy   13

Fallacy of composition   13

Secondary effects   13

Questions for Review

1. **DEFINITION OF ECONOMICS**   What determines whether or not a resource is scarce? Why is the concept of scarcity important to the definition of economics?

2. **RESOURCES**   To which category of resources does each of the following belong?

   a. A taxi
   b. Computer software
   c. One hour of legal counsel
   d. A parking lot
   e. A forest
   f. The Mississippi River
   g. An individual introducing a new way to market products on the Internet

3. **GOODS AND SERVICES**   Explain why each of the following would *not* be considered "free" for the economy as a whole:

   a. Food vouchers
   b. U.S. aid to developing countries
   c. Corporate charitable contributions
   d. Noncable television programs
   e. Public high school education

4. **ECONOMIC DECISION MAKERS**   Which group of economic decision makers plays the leading role in the economic system? Which groups play supporting roles? In what sense are they supporting actors?

5. **MICRO VERSUS MACRO**   Determine whether each of the following is primarily a microeconomic or a macroeconomic issue:

   a. What price to charge for an automobile
   b. Measuring the impact of tax policies on total consumer spending in the economy
   c. A household's decisions about what to buy
   d. A worker's decision regarding how much to work each week
   e. Designing a government policy to increase total employment

6. **MICRO VERSUS MACRO**   Some economists believe that to really understand macroeconomics, you must first understand microeconomics. How does microeconomics relate to macroeconomics?

7. **NORMATIVE VERSUS POSITIVE ANALYSIS**   Determine whether each of the following statements is normative or positive:

   a. The U.S. unemployment rate was below 10.0 percent in 2010.
   b. The inflation rate in the United States is too high.
   c. The U.S. government should increase the minimum wage.
   d. U.S. trade restrictions cost consumers $40 billion annually.

8. **ROLE OF THEORY**   What good is economic theory if it can't predict the behavior of a specific individual?

Problems and Exercises

9. **RATIONAL SELF-INTEREST**   Discuss the impact of rational self-interest on each of the following decisions:

   a. Whether to attend college full time or enter the workforce full time
   b. Whether to buy a new textbook or a used one
   c. Whether to attend a local college or an out-of-town college

10. **RATIONAL SELF-INTEREST**   If behavior is governed by rational self-interest, why do people make charitable contributions of time and money?

11. **MARGINAL ANALYSIS**   The owner of a small pizzeria is deciding whether to increase the radius of delivery area by one mile. What considerations must be taken into account if such a decision is to increase profitability?

12. **TIME AND INFORMATION**   It is often costly to obtain the information necessary to make good decisions. Yet your own interests can be best served by rationally weighing all options available to you. This requires informed decision making. Does this mean that making uninformed decisions is irrational? How do you determine how much information is the right amount?

13. **Case Study: A Yen for Vending Machines**   Do vending machines conserve on any resources other than labor? Does your answer offer any additional insight into the widespread use of vending machines in Japan?

14. **Case Study: A Yen for Vending Machines**   Suppose you had the choice of purchasing identically priced lunches from a vending machine or at a cafeteria. Which would you choose? Why?

15. PITFALLS OF ECONOMIC ANALYSIS   Review the discussion of pitfalls in economic thinking in this chapter. Then identify the fallacy, or mistake in thinking, in each of the following statements:

    a. Raising taxes always increases government revenues.
    b. Whenever there is a recession, imports decrease. Therefore, to stop a recession, we should increase imports.
    c. Raising the tariff on imported steel helps the U.S. steel industry. Therefore, the entire economy is helped.
    d. Gold sells for about $1,000 per ounce. Therefore, the U.S. government could sell all the gold in Fort Knox at $1,000 per ounce and reduce the national debt.

16. ASSOCIATION VERSUS CAUSATION   Suppose I observe that communities with lots of doctors tend to have relatively high rates of illness. I conclude that doctors cause illness. What's wrong with this reasoning?

17. **Case Study: College Major and Career Earnings**   Because some college majors pay nearly twice as much as others, why would students pursuing their rational self-interest choose a lower paying major?

Global Economic Watch Exercises

Login to www.cengagebrain.com and access the Global Economic Watch to do these exercises.

18. GLOBAL ECONOMIC WATCH   Go to the Global Economic Crisis Resource Center. Select Global Issues in Context. In the Basic Search box at the top of the page, enter the phrase "selfish." On the Results page, scroll down to the Magazines section. Choose the red link to View All. Scroll down to click on the link for the December 8, 2008, article "Going Green for Selfish Reasons." Are the companies described acting out of rational self-interest?

19. GLOBAL ECONOMIC WATCH   Go to the Global Economic Crisis Resource Center. Select Global Issues in Context. In the Basic Search box at the top of the page, enter either the term "microeconomic" or the term "macroeconomic." Choose one of the resources and write a summary in your own words. Especially emphasize how the resource is an example of microeconomics or macroeconomics.

Appendix
Understanding Graphs

Take out a pencil and a blank piece of paper. Go ahead. Put a point in the middle of the paper. This is your point of departure, called the **origin**. With your pencil at the origin, draw a straight line off to the right. This line is called the **horizontal axis**. The value of the variable *x* measured along the horizontal axis increases as you move to the right of the origin. Now mark off this line from 0 to 20, in increments of 5 units each. Returning to the origin, draw another line, this one straight north. This line is called the **vertical axis**. The value of the variable *y* measured along the vertical axis increases as you move north of the origin. Mark off this line from 0 to 20, in increments of 5 units each.

Within the space framed by the two axes, you can plot possible combinations of the variables measured along each axis. Each point identifies a value measured along the horizontal, or *x*, axis *and* a value measured along the vertical, or *y*, axis. For example, place point *a* in your graph to reflect the combination where *x* equals 5 units and *y* equals 15 units. Likewise, place point *b* in your graph to reflect 10 units of *x* and 5 units of *y*. Now compare your results with points shown in Exhibit 4.

A **graph** is a picture showing how variables relate, and a picture can be worth a thousand words. Take a look at Exhibit 5, which shows the U.S. annual unemployment rate since 1900. The year is measured along the horizontal axis and the unemployment rate is measured as a percentage along the vertical axis. Exhibit 5 is a *time-series graph*, which shows the value of a variable, in this case the percent of the labor force unemployed, over time. If you had to describe the information presented in Exhibit 5 in words, the explanation could take many words. The picture shows not only how one year compares to the next but also how one decade compares to another and how the unemployment rate trends over time. The sharply higher unemployment rate during the Great Depression of the 1930s is unmistakable. *Graphs convey information in a compact and efficient way.*

This appendix shows how graphs express a variety of possible relations among variables. Most graphs of interest in this book reflect the relationship between

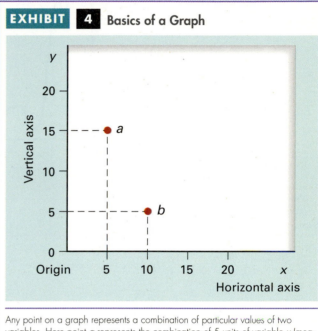

EXHIBIT 4 Basics of a Graph

Any point on a graph represents a combination of particular values of two variables. Here point *a* represents the combination of 5 units of variable *x* (measured on the horizontal axis) and 15 units of variable *y* (measured on the vertical axis). Point *b* represents 10 units of *x* and 5 units of *y*.

two economic variables, such as the unemployment rate and the year, the price of a product and the quantity demanded, or the price of production and the quantity supplied. Because we focus on just two variables at a time, we usually assume that other relevant variables remain constant.

One variable often depends on another. The time it takes you to drive home depends on your average speed. Your weight depends on how much you eat. The amount of Pepsi you buy depends on the price. A *functional relation* exists between two variables when the value of one variable *depends* on the value of another variable. The value of the **dependent variable** depends on the value of the **independent variable**. The task of the economist is to isolate economic relations and determine the direction of causality, if any. Recall that one of the pitfalls of economic

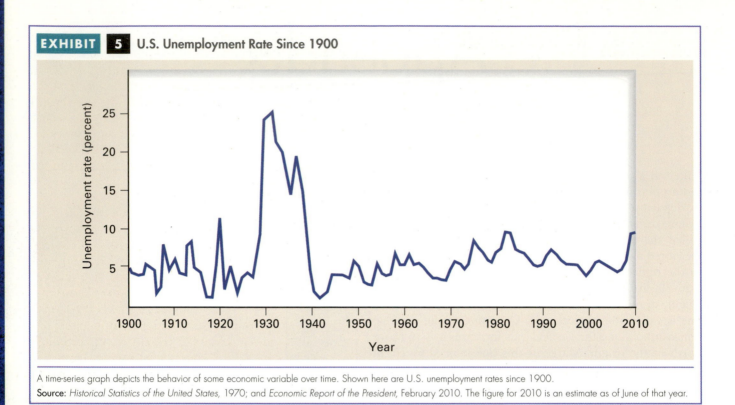

EXHIBIT 5 U.S. Unemployment Rate Since 1900

A time-series graph depicts the behavior of some economic variable over time. Shown here are U.S. unemployment rates since 1900.

Source: *Historical Statistics of the United States,* 1970; and *Economic Report of the President,* February 2010. The figure for 2010 is an estimate as of June of that year.

---

thinking is the erroneous belief that association is causation. We cannot conclude that, simply because two events relate in time, one causes the other. There may be no relation between the two events.

Drawing Graphs

Let's begin with a simple relation. Suppose you are planning to drive across country and want to figure out how far you will travel each day. You plan to average 50 miles per hour. Possible combinations of driving time and distance traveled per day appear in Exhibit 6. One column lists the hours driven per day, and the next column lists the number of miles traveled per day, assuming an average speed of 50 miles per hour. The distance traveled, the *dependent* variable, depends on the number of hours driven, the *independent* variable. Combinations of hours driven and distance traveled are shown as *a, b, c, d,* and *e*. Each combination is represented by a point in Exhibit 7. For example, point *a* shows that if you drive for 1 hour, you travel 50 miles. Point *b* indicates that if you drive for 2 hours, you travel 100 miles. By connecting the points, or possible combinations, we create a

EXHIBIT 6 Schedule Relating Distance Traveled to Hours Driven

	Hours Driven per Day	Distance Traveled per Day (miles)
a	1	50
b	2	100
c	3	150
d	4	200
e	5	250

The distance traveled per day depends on the number of hours driven per day, assuming an average speed of 50 miles per hour. This table shows combinations of hours driven and distance traveled. These combinations are shown as points in Exhibit 7.

line running upward and to the right. This makes sense, because the longer you drive, the farther you travel. Assumed constant along this line is your average speed of 50 miles per hour.

Types of relations between variables include the following:

1. As one variable increases, the other increases—as in Exhibit 7; this is called a **positive,** or **direct, relation** between the variables.

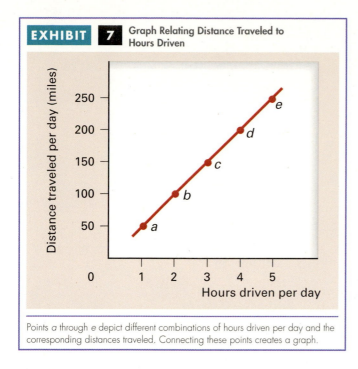

EXHIBIT 7 Graph Relating Distance Traveled to Hours Driven

Points *a* through *e* depict different combinations of hours driven per day and the corresponding distances traveled. Connecting these points creates a graph.

2. As one variable increases, the other decreases; this is called a **negative**, or **inverse**, **relation**.
3. As one variable increases, the other remains unchanged; the two variables are said to be *independent*, or *unrelated*.

One of the advantages of graphs is that they easily convey the relation between variables. We do not need to examine the particular combinations of numbers; we need only focus on the shape of the curve.

The Slopes of Straight Lines

A more precise way to describe the shape of a curve is to measure its slope. The **slope of a line** indicates how much the vertical variable changes for a given increase in the horizontal variable. Specifically, the slope between any two points along any straight line is the vertical change between these two points divided by the horizontal increase, or

$$\text{Slope} = \frac{\text{Change in the vertical distance}}{\text{Increase in the horizontal distance}}$$

Each of the four panels in Exhibit 8 indicates a vertical change, given a 10-unit increase in the horizontal variable. In panel (a), the vertical distance increases by 5 units when the horizontal distance increases by 10 units.

The slope of the line is therefore 5/10, or 0.5. Notice that the slope in this case is a positive number because the relation between the two variables is positive, or direct. This slope indicates that for every 1-unit increase in the horizontal variable, the vertical variable increases by 0.5 units. The slope, incidentally, does not imply causality; the increase in the horizontal variable does not necessarily *cause* the increase in the vertical variable. The slope simply measures the relation between an increase in the horizontal variable and the associated change in the vertical variable.

In panel (b) of Exhibit 8, the vertical distance declines by 7 units when the horizontal distance increases by 10 units, so the slope equals −7/10, or −0.7. The slope in this case is a negative number because the two variables have a negative, or inverse, relation. In panel (c), the vertical variable remains unchanged as the horizontal variable increases by 10, so the slope equals 0/10, or 0. These two variables are not related. Finally, in panel (d), the vertical variable can take on any value, although the horizontal variable remains unchanged. Again, the two variables are not related. In this case, any change in the vertical measure, for example a 10-unit change, is divided by 0, because the horizontal value does not change. Any change divided by 0 is mathematically undefined, but as the line tilts toward vertical, its slope gets incredibly large. For practical purposes, we will assume that the slope of this line is not undefined but infinitely large.

The Slope, Units of Measurement, and Marginal Analysis

The mathematical value of the slope depends on the units measured on the graph. For example, suppose copper tubing costs $1 a foot. Graphs depicting the relation between total cost and quantity purchased are shown in Exhibit 9. In panel (a), the total cost increases by $1 for each 1-foot increase in the amount of tubing purchased. Thus, the slope equals 1/1, or 1. If the cost per foot remains the same but units are measured not in *feet* but in *yards,* the relation between total cost and quantity purchased is as depicted in panel (b). Now total cost increases by $3 for each 1-*yard* increase in output, so the slope equals 3/1, or 3. Because different units are used to measure the copper tubing, the two panels reflect different slopes, even though the cost is $1 per foot in each panel. Keep in mind that *the slope depends in part on the units of measurement.*

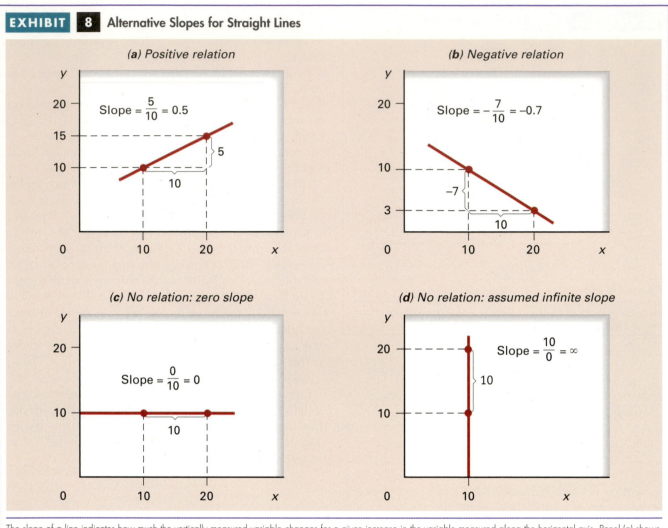

EXHIBIT 8 Alternative Slopes for Straight Lines

(a) Positive relation

$$\text{Slope} = \frac{5}{10} = 0.5$$

(b) Negative relation

$$\text{Slope} = -\frac{7}{10} = -0.7$$

(c) No relation: zero slope

$$\text{Slope} = \frac{0}{10} = 0$$

(d) No relation: assumed infinite slope

$$\text{Slope} = \frac{10}{0} = \infty$$

The slope of a line indicates how much the vertically measured variable changes for a given increase in the variable measured along the horizontal axis. Panel (a) shows a positive relation between two variables; the slope is 0.5, a positive number. Panel (b) depicts a negative, or inverse, relation. When the x variable increases, the y variable decreases; the slope is −0.7, a negative number. Panels (c) and (d) represent situations in which two variables are unrelated. In panel (c), the y variable always takes on the same value; the slope is 0. In panel (d), the x variable always takes on the same value; the slope is mathematically undefined but we simplify by assuming the slope is infinite.

Economic analysis usually involves *marginal analysis*, such as the marginal cost of one more unit of output. The slope is a convenient device for measuring marginal effects because it reflects the change in total cost, measured along the vertical axis, for each 1-unit change in output, measured along the horizontal axis. For example, in panel (a) of Exhibit 9, the marginal cost of another *foot* of copper tubing is $1, which also equals the slope of the line. In panel (b), the marginal cost of another *yard* of tubing is $3, which again is the slope of that line. Because of its applicability to marginal analysis, the slope has special relevance in economics.

The Slopes of Curved Lines

The slope of a straight line is the same everywhere along the line, but the slope of a curved line differs along the curve, as shown in Exhibit 10. To find the slope of a curved line at a particular point, draw a straight line that just touches the curve at that point but does not cut or cross the curve. Such a line is called a tangent to the curve at that point. The slope of the **tangent** gives the slope of the curve at that point. Look at line *A*, which is tangent to the curve at point *a*. As the horizontal value increases from 0 to 10, the vertical value drops along *A* from

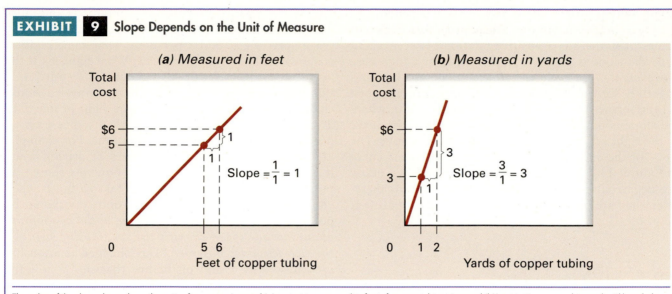

EXHIBIT 9 Slope Depends on the Unit of Measure

(a) Measured in feet

Total cost

$6
5

Slope $= \frac{1}{1} = 1$

1
1

0   5 6

Feet of copper tubing

(b) Measured in yards

Total cost

$6

3

Slope $= \frac{3}{1} = 3$

3
1

0   1 2

Yards of copper tubing

The value of the slope depends on the units of measure. In panel (a), output is measured in feet of copper tubing; in panel (b), output is measured in yards. Although the cost is $1 per foot in each panel, the slope is different in the two panels because copper tubing is measured using different units.

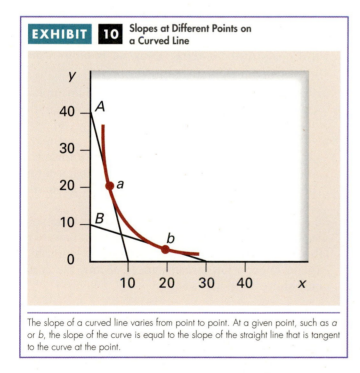

EXHIBIT 10 Slopes at Different Points on a Curved Line

y

40   A
30
20   a
10   B
0   b
     10 20 30 40   x

The slope of a curved line varies from point to point. At a given point, such as a or b, the slope of the curve is equal to the slope of the straight line that is tangent to the curve at the point.

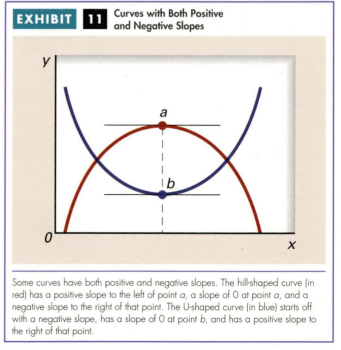

EXHIBIT 11 Curves with Both Positive and Negative Slopes

y

a

b

0   x

Some curves have both positive and negative slopes. The hill-shaped curve (in red) has a positive slope to the left of point a, a slope of 0 at point a, and a negative slope to the right of that point. The U-shaped curve (in blue) starts off with a negative slope, has a slope of 0 at point b, and has a positive slope to the right of that point.

40 to 0. Thus, the vertical change divided by the horizontal change equals −40/10, or −4, which is the slope of the curve at point a. This slope is negative because the vertical value decreases as the horizontal value increases. Line B, a line tangent to the curve at point b, has the slope −10/30, or −0.33. As you can see, the curve depicted in Exhibit 10 gets flatter as the horizontal variable increases, so the value of its slope approaches zero.

Other curves, of course, will reflect different slopes as well as different changes in the slope along the curve. Downward-sloping curves have negative slopes, and upward-sloping curves, positive slopes. Sometimes curves, such as those in Exhibit 11, are more complex, having both positive and negative ranges, depending on the horizontal value. In the hill-shaped curve, for small values of *x*, there is a positive relation between *x* and *y*, so the slope is positive. As the value of *x* increases, however, the slope declines and eventually becomes negative. We can divide the curve into two segments: (1) the segment between the origin and point *a*, where the slope is positive; and (2) the segment of the curve to the right of point *a*, where the slope is negative. The slope of the curve at point *a* is 0. The U-shaped curve in Exhibit 11 represents the opposite relation: *x* and *y* are negatively related until point *b* is reached; thereafter, they are positively related. The slope equals 0 at point *b*.

Line Shifts

Let's go back to the example of your cross-country trip, where we were trying to determine how many miles you would travel per day. Recall that we measured hours driven per day on the horizontal axis and miles traveled per day on the vertical axis, assuming an average speed of 50 miles per hour. That same relation is shown as line *T* in Exhibit 12. What happens if the average speed is 40 miles per hour? The entire relation between hours driven and distance traveled would change, as shown by the shift to the right of line *T* to *T'*. With a slower average speed, any distance traveled per day now requires more driving time. For example, 200 miles traveled requires 4 hours of driving when the average speed is 50 miles per hour (as shown by point *d* on curve *T*), but 200 miles takes 5 hours when your speed averages 40 miles per hour (as shown by point *f* on curve *T'*). Thus, *a change in the assumption about average speed changes the relationship between the two variables observed*. This changed relationship is expressed by a shift of the line that shows how the two variables relate.

That ends our once-over of graphs. Return to this appendix when you need a review.

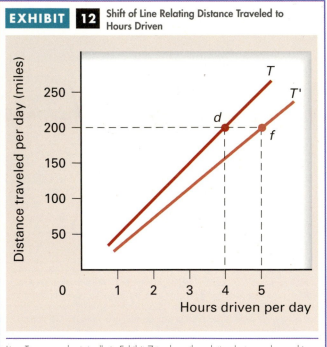

EXHIBIT 12 Shift of Line Relating Distance Traveled to Hours Driven

Line *T* appeared originally in Exhibit 7 to show the relation between hours driven and distance traveled per day, assuming an average speed of 50 miles per hour. If the average speed is only 40 miles per hour, the entire relation shifts to the right to *T'*, indicating that any given distance traveled requires more driving time. For example, 200 miles traveled takes 4 hours of driving at 50 miles per hour but 5 hours at 40 miles per hour. This figure shows how a change in assumptions, in this case, the average speed assumed, can shift the entire relationship between two variables.

Appendix Questions

1. **UNDERSTANDING GRAPHS** Look at Exhibit 5 and answer the following questions:

   a. In what year (approximately) was the unemployment rate the highest? In what year was it the lowest?

   b. In what decade, on average, was the unemployment rate highest? In what decade was it lowest?

   c. Between 1950 and 1980, did the unemployment rate generally increase, decrease, or remain about the same?

2. **DRAWING GRAPHS** Sketch a graph to illustrate your idea of each of the following relationships. Be sure to label each axis appropriately. For each relationship, explain under what circumstances, if any, the curve could shift:

   a. The relationship between a person's age and height

   b. Average monthly temperature in your home town over the course of a year

   c. A person's income and the number of hamburgers consumed per month

   d. The amount of fertilizer added to an acre and the amount of corn grown on that land in one growing season

   e. An automobile's horsepower and its gasoline mileage (in miles per gallon)

3. SLOPE Suppose you are given the following data on wage rates and number of hours worked:

Point	Hourly Wage	Hours Worked per Week
a	$0	0
b	5	0
c	10	30
d	15	35
e	20	45
f	25	50

a. Construct and label a set of axes and plot these six points. Label each point a, b, c, and so on. Which variable do you think should be measured on the vertical axis, and which variable should be measured on the horizontal axis?

b. Connect the points. Describe the resulting curve. Does it make sense to you?

c. Compute the slope of the curve between points a and b. Between points b and c. Between points c and d. Between points d and e. Between points e and f. What happens to the slope as you move from point a to point f?

Economic Tools and Economic Systems

2

© 2010 Digital Vision/Jupiterimages Corporation

○ Why are you reading this book right now rather than doing something else?

○ What is college costing you?

○ Why will you eventually major in one subject rather than continue to take courses in different ones?

○ Why is fast food so fast?

○ Why is there no sense crying over spilt milk?

These and other questions are addressed in this chapter, which introduces some tools of economic analysis—some tools of the trade.

Chapter 1 introduced the idea that scarcity forces us to make choices, but the chapter said little about how to make economic choices. This chapter develops a framework for evaluating economic alternatives. First, we consider the cost involved in selecting one alternative over others. Next, we develop tools to explore the choices available to individuals and to the economy as a whole. Finally, we examine the questions that different economies must answer—questions about what goods and services to produce, how to produce them, and for whom to produce them.

Topics discussed include:

- Opportunity cost
- Comparative advantage
- Specialization
- Division of labor
- Production possibilities frontier
- Economic systems
- Three economic questions
- Capitalism and command system

Choice and Opportunity Cost

Think about a choice you just made: the decision to begin reading this chapter right now rather than use your time to study for another course, play sports, watch TV, go online, get some sleep, hang with friends, or do something else. Suppose it's late and your best alternative to reading right now is getting some sleep. The cost of reading is passing up the opportunity of sleep. Because of scarcity, whenever you make a choice, you must pass up another opportunity; you must incur an *opportunity cost*.

Opportunity Cost

opportunity cost
The value of the best alternative forgone when an item or activity is chosen

What do we mean when we talk about the cost of something? Isn't it what we must give up—must forgo—to get that thing? The **opportunity cost** of the chosen item or activity is *the value of the best alternative that is forgone.* You can think of opportunity cost as the *opportunity lost*. Sometimes opportunity cost can be measured in terms of money, although, as we shall see, money is usually only part of opportunity cost.

How many times have you heard people say they did something because they "had nothing better to do"? They actually mean they had nothing else going on. Yet, according to the idea of opportunity cost, people *always* do what they do because they have nothing better to do. The choice selected seems, at the time, preferable to any other possible alternative. You are reading this chapter right now because you have nothing better to do. In fact, you are attending college for the same reason: College appears more attractive than your best alternative, as discussed in the following case study.

BRINGING THEORY TO LIFE

The Opportunity Cost of College   What is your opportunity cost of attending college full time this year? What was the best alternative you gave up? If you held a full-time job, you would have some idea of the income you gave up to attend college. Suppose you expected to earn $20,000 a year, after taxes, from a full-time job. As a full-time college student, you plan to work part time during the academic year and full time during the summer, earning a total of $10,000 after taxes (about 40 percent of college students hold jobs during the academic year). Thus, by attending college this year, you gave up after-tax earnings of $10,000 (= $20,000 − $10,000).

What about the direct cost of college itself? Suppose you are paying $6,000 this year for in-state tuition, fees, and books at a public college (paying out-of-state rates would tack on $6,000 to that, and attending a private college would add about $15,000). *The opportunity cost of paying for tuition, fees, and books is what you and your family could otherwise have purchased with that money.*

How about room and board? Expenses for room and board are not necessarily an opportunity cost because, even if you were not attending college, you would still need to live somewhere and eat something, though these could differ from your college costs. Likewise, whether or not you attended college, you would still buy goods such as CDs, clothes, and toiletries, and services such as laundry, haircuts, and mobile service. Your spending for such products is not an opportunity cost of attending college but the personal cost that arises regardless of what you do. So for simplicity, assume that room, board, and personal expenses are the same whether or not you attend college. The forgone earnings of $10,000 plus the $6,000 for tuition, fees, and books yield an opportunity cost of $16,000 this year for a student paying in-state rates at a public college. Opportunity cost jumps to about $22,000 for students paying out-of-state rates and to about $31,000 for those at private colleges. Scholarships, but not loans, would reduce your opportunity cost (why not loans?).

This analysis assumes that other things remain constant. But if, in your view, attending college is more of a pain than you expected your best alternative to be, then the opportunity cost of college is even higher. In other words, if you are one of those people who find college difficult, often boring, and in most ways more unpleasant than a full-time job, then the money cost understates your opportunity cost, because your best alternative offers a more enjoyable quality of life. If, on the other hand, you believe the wild and crazy life of a college student is more enjoyable than a full-time job would be, then the dollar figures overstate your opportunity cost, because your best alternative involves a less satisfying quality of life.

Apparently, you view college as a good investment in your future, even though it's costly and perhaps even painful. College graduates on average earn about twice as much per year as high school graduates, a difference that exceeds $1 million over a lifetime. These pay-gains from college prompt some college students to pile up debts to finance their education. Among those earning a bachelor's degrees at public four-year institutions in 2008, 38 percent graduated without education debt, but 6 percent were more than $40,000 in debt. One medical school graduate accumulated an education debt of $550,000 (counting unpaid interest and default charges).

Still, college is not for everyone. Some find the opportunity cost too high. For example, Bill Gates and Paul Allen dropped out of college to cofound Microsoft (both are now among the richest people on earth). Tiger Woods, once an economics major at Stanford, dropped out after two years to earn a fortune in professional golf. And Paula Creamer, who skipped college to play golf, won her first $1 million sooner than any LPGA player in tour history. High school basketball players who believed they were ready for the pros, such as Kobe Bryant and LeBron James, also skipped college (now players can't enter the pros until reaching 19 years of age and out of high school at least a year), as do most tennis pros. Many actors even dropped out of high school to follow their dreams, including Jim Carrey, Russell Crowe, Tom Cruise, Johnny Depp, Robert DeNiro, Cameron Diaz, Colin Farrell, Nicole Kidman, Jude Law, Lindsay Lohan, Demi Moore, Keanu Reeves, Kiefer Sutherland, Hilary Swank, Charlize Theron, and Kate Winslet.

Sources: Elyse Ashburn, "Why Do Students Drop Out? Because They Must Work at Jobs Too," *Chronicle of Higher Education,* 9 December 2009; Mary Pilon, "The $550,000 Student Loan Burden," *Wall Street Journal,* 13 February 2010; "The World's Billionaires," *Forbes,* 11 March 2010; and "College Board Connect to College Success" at http://www.collegeboard.com/.

Opportunity Cost Is Subjective

Like beauty, opportunity cost is in the eye of the beholder. It is subjective. Only the individual making the choice can identify the most attractive alternative. But the chooser seldom knows the actual value of what was passed up, because that alternative is "the road not taken." If you give up an evening of pizza and conversation with friends to work on a research paper, you will never know exactly what you gave up. You know only what you *expected*. Evidently, you expected the benefit of working on that paper to exceed the benefit of the best alternative. (Incidentally, focusing on the best alternative forgone makes all other alternatives irrelevant.)

Calculating Opportunity Cost Requires Time and Information

Economists assume that people rationally choose the most valued alternative. This does not mean you exhaustively assess the value of all possibilities. You assess alternatives as long as the expected marginal benefit of gathering more information about your options exceeds the expected marginal cost (even if you are not aware of making such conscious calculations). In other words, you do the best you can for yourself.

Because learning about alternatives is costly and time consuming, some choices are based on limited or even wrong information. Indeed, some choices may turn out badly (you went for a picnic but it rained; the movie you rented stunk; your new shoes pinch; your new exercise equipment gets no exercise; the stock you bought tanked). Regret about lost opportunities is captured in the common expression "coulda, woulda, shoulda." At the time you made the selection, however, you thought you were making the best use of all your scarce resources, including the time required to gather and evaluate information about your choices.

Time: The Ultimate Constraint

The Sultan of Brunei is among the richest people on earth, worth billions based on huge oil revenues that flow into his tiny country. He and his royal family (which has ruled since 1405) live in a palace with 1,788 rooms, 257 bathrooms, and a throne room the size of a football field. The family owns hundreds of cars, including dozens of Rolls-Royces; he can drive any of these or pilot one of his seven planes, including the 747 with gold-plated furniture. Supported by such wealth, the Sultan would appear to have overcome the economic problem of scarcity. Though he can buy just about whatever he wants, he lacks the time to enjoy his stuff. If he pursues one activity, he cannot at the same time do something else. Each activity involves an opportunity cost. Consequently, the Sultan must choose from among the competing uses of his scarcest resource, time. Although your alternatives are less exotic, you too face a time constraint, especially as the college term winds down.

Opportunity Cost Varies With Circumstance

Opportunity cost depends on your alternatives. This is why you are more likely to study on a Tuesday night than on a Saturday night. The opportunity cost of studying is lower on a Tuesday night, because your alternatives are less attractive than on a Saturday night, when more is going on. Suppose you go to a movie on Saturday night. Your opportunity cost is the value of your best alternative forgone, which might be attending a college game. For some of you, studying on Saturday night may rank well down the list of possibilities—perhaps ahead of reorganizing your closet but behind doing your laundry.

Opportunity cost is subjective, but in some cases, money paid for goods and services is a reasonable approximation. For example, the opportunity cost of the new DVD player you bought is the benefit from spending that $100 on the best forgone alternative. The money measure may leave out some important elements, however, particularly the value of the time involved. For example, watching the latest hit movie costs you not only the $10 admission price but also the time needed to get there, watch the movie, and return home.

Even religious practices are subject to opportunity cost. For example, about half the U.S. population attends religious services at least once a month. In some states, so-called blue laws prohibit retail activity on Sunday. Some states have repealed these laws in recent years, thus raising the opportunity cost of church attendance. Researchers have found that when a state repeals its blue laws, religious attendance declines as do church donations. These results do not seem to be linked to any decline in religiosity before the repeal.[1]

Sunk Cost and Choice

Suppose you have just finished grocery shopping and are wheeling your cart toward the checkout counters. How do you decide which line to join? Easy. You pick the one with the shortest expected wait. Suppose that barely moves for 10 minutes, when you notice that a cashier has opened a new line and invites you to check out. Do you switch to the open cashier, or do you think, "Since I've already spent 10 minutes in this line, I'm staying put"? The 10 minutes you waited represents a **sunk cost**, which is a cost that already been incurred and cannot be recovered, regardless of what you do next. You should ignore sunk costs in making economic choices. Hence, you should switch. *Economic decision makers should consider only those costs that are affected by the choice. Sunk costs have already been incurred and are not affected by the choice, so they are irrelevant.* Likewise, you should walk out on a bad movie, even if you spent $10 to get in. Your $10 is gone, and sitting through that stinker only makes you worse off. The irrelevance of sunk costs is underscored by proverbs such as "Don't throw good money after bad," "Let bygones be bygones," "That's water over the dam," and "There's no sense crying over spilt milk." The milk has already spilled, so whatever you do now cannot change that. Or, as Tony Soprano would say, "Fuhgeddaboudit!"

Now that you have some idea about opportunity cost, let's see how it helps solve the economic problem.

sunk cost
A cost that has already been incurred, cannot be recovered, and thus is irrelevant for present and future economic decisions

Comparative Advantage, Specialization, and Exchange

Suppose you live in a dormitory. You and your roommate have such tight schedules that you each can spare only about an hour a week for mundane tasks like ironing shirts and typing papers (granted, in reality you may not iron shirts or type papers, but this example will help you understand some important principles). Each of you must turn in a typed three-page paper every week, and you each prefer ironed shirts when you have the time. Let's say it takes you a half hour to type a handwritten paper. Your roommate

1. See Jonathan Gruber and Daniel Hungerman, "The Church vs. the Mall: What Happens When Religion Faces Increased Secular Competition?" *Quarterly Journal of Economics,* 123 (May 2008): 831–862.

is from the hunt-and-peck school and takes about an hour. But your roommate is a talented ironer and can iron a shirt in 5 minutes flat (or should that be, iron it flat in 5 minutes?). You take twice as long, or 10 minutes, to iron a shirt.

During the hour set aside each week for typing and ironing, typing takes priority. If you each do your own typing and ironing, you type your paper in a half hour and iron three shirts in the remaining half hour. Your roommate spends the entire hour typing the paper, leaving no time for ironing. Thus, if you each do your own tasks, the combined output is two typed papers and three ironed shirts.

The Law of Comparative Advantage

Before long, you each realize that total output would increase if you did all the typing and your roommate did all the ironing. In the hour available for these tasks, you type both papers and your roommate irons 12 shirts. As a result of specialization, total output increases by 9 shirts! You strike a deal to exchange your typing for your roommate's ironing, so you each end up with a typed paper and 6 ironed shirts. Thus, *each of you is better off as a result of specialization and exchange*. By specializing in the task that you each do better, you rely on the **law of comparative advantage**, which states that the individual with the lower opportunity cost of producing a particular output should specialize in that output. You face a lower opportunity cost of typing than does your roommate, because in the time it takes to type a paper, you could iron 3 shirts whereas your roommate could iron 12 shirts. And if you face a lower opportunity cost of typing, your roommate must face a lower opportunity cost of ironing (try working that out).

law of comparative advantage
The individual, firm, region, or country with the lowest opportunity cost of producing a particular good should specialize in that good

Absolute Advantage Versus Comparative Advantage

The gains from specialization and exchange so far are obvious. A more interesting case is if you are faster at both tasks. Suppose the example changes only in one respect: Your roommate takes 12 minutes to iron a shirt compared with your 10 minutes. You now have an *absolute advantage* in both tasks, meaning each task takes you less time than it does your roommate. More generally, having an **absolute advantage** means making something using fewer resources than other producers require.

Does your absolute advantage in both activities mean specialization is no longer a good idea? Recall that the law of comparative advantage states that the individual with *the lower opportunity cost* of producing a particular good should specialize in that good. You still take 30 minutes to type a paper and 10 minutes to iron a shirt, so your opportunity cost of typing the paper remains at three ironed shirts. Your roommate takes an hour to type a paper and 12 minutes to iron a shirt, so your roommate could iron five shirts in the time it takes to type a paper. Your opportunity cost of typing a paper is ironing three shirts; for your roommate, it's ironing five shirts. *Because your opportunity cost of typing is lower than your roommate's, you still have a comparative advantage in typing.* Consequently, your roommate must have a comparative advantage in ironing (again, try working this out to your satisfaction). Therefore, you should do all the typing and your roommate, all the ironing. Although you have an absolute advantage in both tasks, your **comparative advantage** calls for specializing in the task for which you have the lower opportunity cost—in this case, typing.

If neither of you specialized, you could type one paper and iron three shirts. Your roommate could still type just the one paper. Your combined output would be two papers and three shirts. If you each specialized according to comparative advantage, in an hour you could type both papers and your roommate could iron five shirts. Thus,

absolute advantage
The ability to make something using fewer resources than other producers use

comparative advantage
The ability to make something at a lower opportunity cost than other producers face

specialization increases total output by two ironed shirts. Even though you are better at both tasks than your roommate, you are comparatively better at typing. Put another way, your roommate, although worse at both tasks, is not quite as bad at ironing as at typing.

Don't think that this is just common sense. Common sense would lead you to do your own ironing and typing, because you are better at both. *Absolute advantage focuses on who uses the fewest resources, but comparative advantage focuses on what else those resources could produce—that is, on the opportunity cost of those resources.* Comparative advantage is the better guide to who should do what.

The law of comparative advantage applies not only to individuals but also to firms, regions of a country, and entire nations. Individuals, firms, regions, or countries with the lowest opportunity cost of producing a particular good should specialize in producing that good. Because of such factors as climate, workforce skills, natural resources, and capital stock, certain parts of the country and certain parts of the world have a comparative advantage in producing particular goods. From Washington State apples to Florida oranges, from software in India to hardware in Taiwan—*resources are allocated most efficiently across the country and around the world when production and trade conform to the law of comparative advantage.*

Specialization and Exchange

In the previous example, you and your roommate specialized and then exchanged output. No money was involved. In other words, you engaged in **barter**, where products are traded directly for other products. Barter works best in simple economies with little specialization and few traded goods. But for economies with greater specialization, *money* facilitates exchange. Money—coins, bills, checks, and debit cards—is a *medium of exchange* because it is the one thing that everyone accepts in return for goods and services.

Because of specialization and comparative advantage, most people consume little of what they produce and produce little of what they consume. Each individual specializes, then exchanges that product for money, which in turn is exchanged for other products. Did you make anything you are wearing? Probably not. Think about the degree of specialization that went into your cotton shirt. A farmer in a warm climate grew the cotton and sold it to someone who spun it into thread, who sold it to someone who wove it into fabric, who sold it to someone who sewed the shirt, who sold it to a wholesaler, who sold it to a retailer, who sold it to you. Many specialists in the chain of production created that shirt.

Evidence of specialization is all around us. Shops at the mall specialize in products ranging from luggage to lingerie. Restaurants range from subs to sushi. Or let your fingers do the walking through the help-wanted ads or *Yellow Pages,* where you will find thousands of specializations. Without moving a muscle, you can observe the division of labor within a single industry by watching the credits roll at the end of a movie. The credits list scores of specialists—from gaffer (lighting electrician) to assistant location scout. As an extreme example, more than 3,000 specialists helped create the movie *Avatar*.[2] Even a typical TV drama, such as *Grey's Anatomy* or *CSI: Miami*, requires hundreds of specialists.

Some specialties may seem odd. For example, professional mourners in Taiwan are sometimes hired by grieving families to scream, wail, and otherwise demonstrate the deep grief befitting a proper funeral. The sharp degree of specialization is perhaps most obvious online, where the pool of potential customers is so vast that individual sites

barter
The direct exchange of one product for another without using money

---

2. As reported in Hendrik Hertzberg, "And the Oscar Goes To," *The New Yorker*, 15 & 22 February 2010, p. 46.

become finely focused. For example, you can find sites specializing in musical bowls, tongue studs, toe rings, brass knuckles, mouth harps, ferret toys, and cat bandannas—just to name a few of the hundreds of thousands of specialty sites. You won't find such precise specialization at the mall. Adam Smith said the degree of specialization is limited by the extent of the market. Online sellers draw on the broadest customer base in the world to find a market niche.

Division of Labor and Gains From Specialization

division of labor
Breaking down the production of a good into separate tasks

Picture a visit to McDonald's: "Let's see, I'll have a Big Mac, an order of fries, and a chocolate shake." Less than a minute later your order is ready. It would take you much longer to make a homemade version of this meal. Why is the McDonald's meal faster, cheaper, and—for some people—tastier than one you could make yourself? Why is fast food so fast? McDonald's takes advantage of the gains resulting from the **division of labor**. Each worker, rather than preparing an entire meal, specializes in separate tasks. This division of labor allows the group to produce much more.

How is this increase in productivity possible? First, the manager can assign tasks according to *individual preferences and abilities*—that is, according to the law of comparative advantage. The worker with the friendly smile and pleasant personality can handle the customers up front; the one with the strong back but few social graces can handle the heavy lifting out back. Second, a worker who performs the same task again and again gets better at it (experience is a good teacher). The worker filling orders at the drive-through, for example, learns to deal with special problems that arise. As another example, consider the experience gained by someone screening bags at airport security. Experience helps the screener distinguish the harmful from the harmless. Third, specialization means no time is lost moving from one task to another. Finally, and perhaps most importantly, the **specialization of labor** allows for the introduction of more sophisticated production techniques—techniques that would not make sense on a smaller scale. For example, McDonald's large shake machine would be impractical in the home. *Specialized machines make each worker more productive.*

specialization of labor
Focusing work effort on a particular product or a single task

To summarize: The specialization of labor (a) takes advantage of individual preferences and natural abilities, (b) allows workers to develop more experience at a particular task, (c) reduces the need to shift between different tasks, and (d) permits the introduction of labor-saving machinery. Specialization and the division of labor occur not only among individuals but also among firms, regions, and indeed entire countries. The cotton shirt mentioned earlier might involve growing cotton in one country, turning it into cloth in another, making the shirt in a third, and selling it in a fourth.

We should also acknowledge the downside of specialization. Doing the same thing all day can become tedious. Consider, for example, the assembly line worker whose sole task is to tighten a particular bolt. Such a monotonous job could drive that worker bonkers or lead to repetitive motion injury. Thus, the gains from dividing production into individual tasks must be weighed against any problems caused by assigning workers to repetitive, tedious, and potentially harmful jobs. Fortunately, many routine tasks, particularly on assembly lines, can be turned over to robots.

The Economy's Production Possibilities

The focus to this point has been on how individuals choose to use their scarce resources to satisfy their unlimited wants or, more specifically, how they specialize based on comparative advantage. This emphasis on the individual has been appropriate because the economy is shaped by the choices of individual decision makers, whether they are consumers, producers, or public officials. Just as resources are scarce for the individual, they are also scarce for the economy as a whole (no fallacy of composition here). An economy has millions of different resources that can be combined in all kinds of ways to produce millions of different goods and services. This section steps back from the immense complexity of the real economy to develop another simple model, which explores the economy's production options.

Efficiency and the Production Possibilities Frontier, or PPF

Let's develop a model to get some idea of how much an economy can produce with the resources available. What are the economy's production capabilities? Here are the model's assumptions:

1. To simplify matters, output is limited to just two broad classes of products: consumer goods and capital goods.
2. The focus is on production during a given period—in this case, a year.
3. The economy's resources are fixed in both quantity and quality during that period.
4. Society's knowledge about how these resources combine to produce output—that is, the available *technology*—does not change during the year.
5. Also assumed fixed during the period are the "rules of the game" that facilitate production and exchange. These include such things as the legal system, property rights, tax laws, patent laws, and the manners, customs, and conventions of the market.

The point of these simplifying assumptions is to freeze in time the economy's resources, technology, and rules of the game so we can focus on the economy's production options. Otherwise, the production possibilities of the economy would be a moving target.

Given the resources, technology, and rules of the game available in the economy, the **production possibilities frontier**, or **PPF**, identifies possible combinations of the two types of goods that can be produced when all available resources are employed efficiently. *Resources are employed efficiently when there is no change that could increase the production of one good without decreasing the production of the other good.* **Efficiency** involves getting the most from available resources.

The economy's PPF for consumer goods and capital goods is shown by the curve *AF* in Exhibit 1. Point *A* identifies the amount produced per year if all the economy's resources are used efficiently to produce consumer goods. Point *F* identifies the amount produced per year if all the economy's resources are used efficiently to produce capital goods. Points along the curve between *A* and *F* identify possible combinations of the two goods that can be produced when all the economy's resources are used efficiently.

Inefficient and Unattainable Production

Points inside the PPF, such as *I* in Exhibit 1, identify combinations that do not employ resources efficiently. Note that *C* yields more consumer goods and no fewer capital goods than *I*. And *E* yields more capital goods and no fewer consumer goods than *I*. Indeed, any point along the PPF between *C* and *E*, such as *D*, yields both more consumer goods and more capital goods than *I*. Hence, combination *I* is *inefficient*. By using resources more efficiently, the economy can produce more of at least one good without reducing the production of the other good. Points outside the PPF, such as *U* in Exhibit 1, identify *unattainable* combinations, given the availability of resources, technology, and rules of the game. Thus, *the PPF not only shows efficient combinations of production but also serves as the boundary between inefficient combinations inside the frontier and unattainable combinations outside the frontier.*

Production possibilities frontier (PPF)

A curve showing alternative combinations of goods that can be produced when available resources are used efficiently; a boundary line between inefficient and unattainable combinations

efficiency

The condition that exists when there is no way resources can be reallocated to increase the production of one good without decreasing the production of another; getting the most from available resources

EXHIBIT **1** The Economy's Production Possibilities Frontier

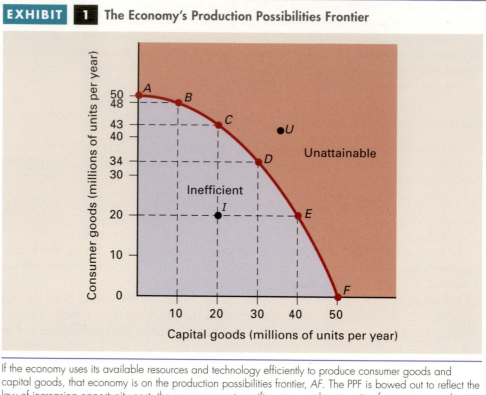

If the economy uses its available resources and technology efficiently to produce consumer goods and capital goods, that economy is on the production possibilities frontier, *AF*. The PPF is bowed out to reflect the law of increasing opportunity cost; the economy must sacrifice more and more units of consumer goods to produce an additional increment of capital goods. Note that more consumer goods must be given up in moving from *E* to *F* than in moving from *A* to *B*, although in each case the gain in capital goods is 10 million units. Points inside the PPF, such as *I*, represent inefficient use of resources. Points outside the PPF, such as *U*, represent unattainable combinations.

The Shape of the Production Possibilities Frontier

Any movement along the PPF involves producing less of one good to produce more of the other. Movements down along the curve indicate that the opportunity cost of more capital goods is fewer consumer goods. For example, moving from point *A* to point *B* *increases* capital production from none to 10 million units but *reduces* consumer units from 50 million to 48 million. Increasing capital goods to 10 million reduces consumer goods only a little. Capital production initially employs resources (such as heavy machinery used to build factories) that add few consumer units but are quite productive in making capital.

As shown by the dashed lines in Exhibit 1, each additional 10 million units of capital produced reduce consumer goods by successively larger amounts. The resources used to produce more capital are increasingly better suited to producing consumer goods. *The opportunity cost of making more capital goods increases, because resources in the economy are not all perfectly adaptable to the production of both types of goods.* The shape of the production possibilities frontier reflects the **law of increasing opportunity cost.** If the economy uses all resources efficiently, the law of increasing opportunity cost states that each additional increment of one good requires the economy to sacrifice successively larger and larger increments of the other good.

The PPF derives its bowed-out shape from the law of increasing opportunity cost. For example, whereas the first 10 million units of capital have an opportunity cost of only

law of increasing opportunity cost

To produce more of one good, a successively larger amount of the other good must be sacrificed

2 million consumer units, the final 10 million units of capital—that is, the increase from *E* to *F*—have an opportunity cost of 20 million consumer units. Notice that the slope of the PPF shows the opportunity cost of an increment of capital. As the economy moves down the curve, the curve becomes steeper, reflecting the higher opportunity cost of capital goods in terms of forgone consumer goods. The law of increasing opportunity cost also applies when shifting from capital goods to consumer goods. Incidentally, if resources were perfectly adaptable to the production of both consumer goods and capital goods, the PPF would be a straight line, reflecting a constant opportunity cost along the PPF.

What Can Shift the Production Possibilities Frontier?

Any production possibilities frontier assumes the economy's resources, technology, and rules of the game are fixed during the period under consideration. Over time, however, the PPF may shift if resources, technology, or the rules of the game change. **Economic growth** is an expansion in the economy's production possibilities as reflected by an outward shift of the PPF.

economic growth
An increase in the economy's ability to produce goods and services; reflected by an outward shift of the economy's production possibilities frontier

Changes in Resource Availability

If people decide to work longer hours, the PPF shifts outward, as shown in panel (a) of Exhibit 2. An increase in the size or health of the labor force, an increase in the skills of the labor force, or an increase in the availability of other resources, such as new oil discoveries, also shifts the PPF outward. In contrast, a decrease of resources shifts the PPF inward, as depicted in panel (b). For example, in 1990 Iraq invaded Kuwait, setting oil fields ablaze and destroying much of Kuwait's physical capital. In West Africa, the encroaching sands of the Sahara destroy thousands of square miles of farmland each year. And in northwest China, a rising tide of wind-blown sand has claimed grasslands, lakes, and forests, and swallowed entire villages, forcing tens of thousands of people to flee.

The new PPFs in panels (a) and (b) appear to be parallel to the original ones, indicating that the resources that changed could produce both capital goods and consumer goods. For example, an increase in electrical power can enhance the production of both, as shown in panel (a). If a resource such as farmland benefits just consumer goods, then increased availability or productivity of that resource shifts the PPF more along the consumer goods axis, as shown in panel (c). Panel (d) shows the effect of an increase in a resource such as construction equipment that is suited only to capital goods.

Increases in the Capital Stock

An economy's PPF depends in part on the stock of human and physical capital. The more capital an economy produces one period, the more output can be produced the next period. Thus, producing more capital goods this period (for example, more machines in the case of physical capital or more education in the case of human capital) shifts the economy's PPF outward the next period.

Technological Change

A technological discovery that employs resources more efficiently could shift the economy's PPF outward. Some discoveries enhance the production of both consumer goods and capital goods, as shown in panel (a) of Exhibit 2. For example, the Internet has increased each firm's ability to find available resources. A technological discovery that benefits consumer goods only, such as more disease-resistant crops, is reflected by a rotation outward of the PPF along the consumer goods axis, as shown in panel (c).

EXHIBIT **2** Shifts of the Economy's Production Possibilities Frontier

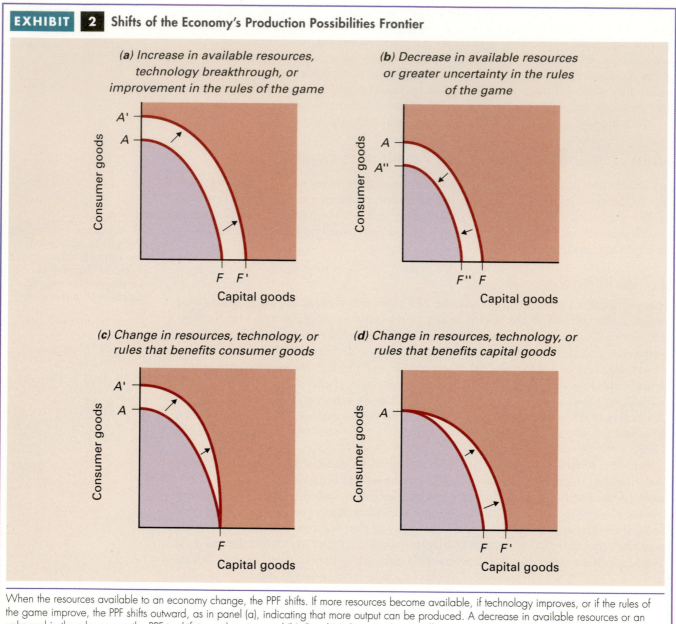

(a) *Increase in available resources, technology breakthrough, or improvement in the rules of the game*

(b) *Decrease in available resources or greater uncertainty in the rules of the game*

(c) *Change in resources, technology, or rules that benefits consumer goods*

(d) *Change in resources, technology, or rules that benefits capital goods*

When the resources available to an economy change, the PPF shifts. If more resources become available, if technology improves, or if the rules of the game improve, the PPF shifts outward, as in panel (a), indicating that more output can be produced. A decrease in available resources or an upheaval in the rules causes the PPF to shift inward, as in panel (b). Panel (c) shows a change affecting consumer goods production. More consumer goods can now be produced at any given level of capital goods. Panel (d) shows a change affecting capital goods production.

Note that point *F* remains unchanged because the breakthrough does not affect the production of capital goods. Panel (d) shows a technological advance in the production of capital goods, such as better software for designing heavy machinery.

Improvements in the Rules of the Game

The **rules of the game** are the formal and informal institutions that support the economy—the laws, customs, manners, conventions, and other institutional under-pinnings that encourage people to pursue productive activity. A more stable political environment and more reliable property rights increase the incentive to work and to invest, and thus help the economy grow. For example, people have more incentive to work if taxes claim less of their paychecks. People have more incentive to invest if they are confident that their investment will not be appropriated by government, stolen by thieves, destroyed by civil unrest, or blown up by terrorists. Improvements in the rules of the game shift the economy's PPF outward. On the other hand, greater uncertainty about the rules of the game reduces the economy's productive capacity as reflected by an inward shift of the PPF. The following case study underscores the importance of the rules of the game.

PUBLIC POLICY

CASE STUDY

e activity
You can see how difficult it is to do business in 183 countries by examining the rankings in the annual report on Doing Business. Find this and previous reports on other topics at the World Bank Group's Web site at http://www.doingbusiness.org.

Rules of the Game and Economic Development Rules of the game can affect the PPF by either nurturing or discouraging economic development. Businesses supply jobs, tax revenue, and consumer products, but owning and operating a business is risky even in the best of times. How hard is it for an entrepreneur to start a business, import products for sale, comply with tax laws, and settle business disputes? The World Bank, a nonprofit international organization, has developed a composite measure that rolls answers to all these questions into a single measure and ranks 183 countries from best to worst based on their ease of doing business. Exhibit 3 lists the best 10 and the worst 10 countries in terms of the ease of doing business. The countries with the friendliest business climate all have a high standard of living and a sophisticated economy. The United States ranks fourth best, behind Singapore, New Zealand, and Hong Kong. The 10 most difficult countries all have a low standard of living, a poor economy, and nine are in Africa.

Consider, for example, the burden facing a business that wants to sell an imported product. No business in the African country of Burundi makes bicycles, so a shop selling bicycles there must import them. Bicycles are shipped to Burundi via a port in Tanzania. In all, it takes the shop owner at least 10 documents and at least 71 days to get the bicycles from the port in Tanzania to the bicycle shop. Contrast this with 3 documents, and 5 days needed to import products in Denmark. Burundi is one of the poorest countries on earth, based on per capita income. Denmark is among the richest, with a per capita income about 120 times that of Burundi.

How does the burden imposed by business taxes differ across countries? In Burundi, businesses are subject to a tax rate totalling 279 percent of profit. So all business profits and much more are eaten up by taxes, in the process destroying the primary reason to even open a business. Meanwhile, a business in Hong Kong pays a tax rate amounting to only 24 percent of profit.

Of course, some level of business regulation and taxation is necessary to ensure public health and safety and to nurture market competition. Few would argue, however, that the world's most prosperous economies have allowed businesses to go wild. But why would a country impose taxes and regulations so severe as to kill business development, thereby choking off the jobs, taxes, and consumer products that go with it? One possible explanation is that many countries with the worst business climate were once under colonial rule and have not yet developed the ability to operate

ALESSANDRO DELLA BELLA/KEYSTONE//landov

EXHIBIT 3	Best 10 and Worst 10 Among 183 Countries Based on Ease of Doing Business

Best 10	Worst 10
1. Singapore	174. Niger
2. New Zealand	175. Eritrea
3. Hong Kong, China	176. Burundi
4. United States	177. Venezuela
5. United Kingdom	178. Chad
6. Denmark	179. Republic of Congo
7. Ireland	180. São Tomé and Principe
8. Canada	181. Guinea-Bissau
9. Australia	182. Democratic Republic of Congo
10. Norway	183. Central African Republic

Source: *Doing Business in 2010: Reforming Through Difficult Times*, (World Bank Publications, 2010) at http://www.doingbusiness.org/documents/fullreport/2010/DB10-full-report.pdf.

government efficiently. Another possibility is that governments in poor countries usually offer the most attractive jobs around. Politicians create government jobs for friends, relatives, and supporters. Overseeing bureaucratic regulations gives all these people something to do, and high tax rates are needed to pay the salaries of all these political cronies.

Perhaps the darkest explanation for the bad business climate in some countries is that business regulations and tax laws provide government bureaucrats with more opportunities for graft and corruption. For example, the more government documents needed to execute a business transaction, the more opportunities to seek bribes. In other words, obstacles are put in the way of business so that government bureaucrats can demand bribes to circumvent those obstacles. Even Irish rocker Bono, a long-time supporter of aid to Africa, has called for "advances in fighting the evils of corruption in Africa." Regardless of the explanation, poor countries are poor in part because they have not yet developed the rules of the game that nurture a prosperous economy.

Source: *Doing Business in 2010: Reforming Through Difficult Times*, (World Bank Publications, 2010) also available at http://www.doingbusiness.org/documents/fullreport/2010/DB10-full-report.pdf; and Bono, "A Time for Miracles," *Time*, 2 April 2007.

What We Learn From the PPF

The PPF demonstrates several ideas introduced so far. The first is *efficiency:* The PPF describes efficient combinations of output, given the economy's resources, technology, and rules of the game. The second idea is *scarcity:* Given the resources, technology, and rules of the game, the economy can produce only so much output per period. The PPF slopes downward, because more of one good means less of the other good, thus demonstrating *opportunity cost.* The PPF's bowed-out shape reflects the *law of increasing opportunity cost*, which arises because some resources are not perfectly adaptable to the production of each type of good. And a shift outward in the PPF reflects *economic growth*.

Finally, because society must somehow select a specific combination of output—a single point—along the PPF, the PPF also underscores the need for *choice*. Selecting a particular combination determines not only consumer goods available this period, but also the capital stock available next period. One thing the PPF does not tell us is which combination to choose. The PPF tells us only about the costs, not the benefits, of the two goods. To make a selection, we need to know about both costs *and* benefits. How society goes about choosing a particular combination depends on the nature of the economic system, as you will see next.

Economic Systems

Each point along the economy's production possibilities frontier is an efficient combination of outputs. Whether the economy produces efficiently and how the economy selects the most preferred combination depends on the decision-making rules employed. But regardless of how decisions are made, each economy must answer three fundamental questions.

Three Questions Every Economic System Must Answer

What goods and services are to be produced? How are they to be produced? And for whom are they to be produced? An **economic system** is the set of mechanisms and institutions that resolve the *what, how,* and *for whom* questions. Some criteria used to distinguish among economic systems are (1) who owns the resources, (2) what decision-making process is used to allocate resources and products, and (3) what types of incentives guide economic decision makers.

economic system
The set of mechanisms and institutions that resolve the what, how, and for whom questions

What Goods and Services Are to Be Produced?

Most of us take for granted the incredible number of choices that go into deciding what gets produced—everything from which new kitchen appliances are introduced, which roads get built, to which of the 10,000 movie scripts purchased by U.S. studios each year get to be among the 500 movies made.[3] Although different economies resolve these and millions of other questions using different decision-making rules and mechanisms, all economies must somehow make such choices.

How Are Goods and Services to Be Produced?

The economic system must determine how output gets produced. Which resources should be used, and how should they be combined to make stuff? How much labor should be used and at what skill levels? What kinds of machines should be used? What new technology should be incorporated into the latest video games? Should the office complex be built in the city or closer to the interstate highway? Millions of individual decisions determine which resources are employed and how these resources are combined.

For Whom Are Goods and Services to Be Produced?

Who will actually consume the goods and services produced? The economic system must determine how to allocate the fruits of production among the population. Should everyone receive equal shares? Should the weak and the sick get more? Should those

3. As reported in Ian Parker, "The Real McKee," *New Yorker*, 20 October 2003.

willing to wait in line get more? Should goods be allocated according to height? Weight? Religion? Age? Gender? Race? Looks? Strength? Political connections? The value of resources supplied? The question "For whom are goods and services to be produced?" is often referred to as the *distribution question.*

Although the three economic questions were discussed separately, they are closely related. The answer to one depends on the answers to the others. For example, an economy that distributes goods and services uniformly to all will, no doubt, answer the what-will-be-produced question differently than an economy that somehow allows more personal choice. As we have seen, laws about resource ownership and the role of government determine the "rules of the game"—the set of conditions that shape individual incentives and constraints. Along a spectrum ranging from the freest to the most regimented types of economic systems, *pure capitalism* would be at one end and the *pure command system* at the other.

Pure Capitalism

pure capitalism

An economic system characterized by the private ownership of resources and the use of prices to coordinate economic activity in unregulated markets

private property rights

An owner's right to use, rent, or sell resources or property

net 📖 bookmark

The Center for International Comparisons at the University of Pennsylvania at http://pwt .econ.upenn.edu/ is a good source of information on the performance of economies around the world.

Under **pure capitalism**, the rules of the game include the private ownership of resources and the market distribution of products. Owners have *property rights* to the use of their resources and are therefore free to supply those resources to the highest bidder. **Private property rights** allow individual owners to use resources or to charge others for their use. Any income derived from supplying labor, capital, natural resources, or entrepreneurial ability goes to the individual resources owners. Producers are free to make and sell whatever they think will be profitable. Consumers are free to buy whatever goods they can afford. All this voluntary buying and selling is coordinated by unrestricted markets, where buyers and sellers make their intentions known. Market prices guide resources to their most productive use and channel goods and services to the consumers who value them the most.

Under pure capitalism, markets answer the what, how, and for whom questions. That's why capitalism is also referred to as a *market system.* Markets transmit information about relative scarcity, provide individual incentives, and distribute income among resource suppliers. No individual or small group coordinates these activities. Rather, it is the voluntary choices of many buyers and sellers responding only to their individual incentives and constraints that direct resources and products to those who value them the most.

According to Adam Smith (1723–1790), market forces allocate resources as if by an "invisible hand"—an unseen force that harnesses the pursuit of self-interest to direct resources where they earn the greatest reward. According to Smith, *although each individual pursues his or her self-interest, the "invisible hand" of market forces promotes the general welfare.* Capitalism is sometimes called *laissez-faire;* translated from the French, this phrase means "to let do," or to let people do as they choose without government intervention. Thus, under capitalism, voluntary choices based on rational self-interest are made in unrestricted markets to answer the questions what, how, and for whom.

As we will see in later chapters, pure capitalism has its flaws. The most notable market failures are:

1. No central authority protects property rights, enforces contracts, and otherwise ensures that the rules of the game are followed.
2. People with no resources to sell could starve.
3. Some producers may try to monopolize markets by eliminating the competition.

4. The production or consumption of some goods involves side effects that can harm or benefit people not involved in the market transaction.
5. Private firms have no incentive to produce so-called *public goods,* such as national defense, because private firms cannot prevent nonpayers from enjoying the benefits of public goods.

Because of these limitations, countries have modified pure capitalism to allow some role for government. Even Adam Smith believed government should play a role. The United States is among the most market-oriented economies in the world today.

Pure Command System

In a **pure command system**, resources are directed and production is coordinated not by market forces but by the "command," or central plan, of government. In theory at least, instead of private property, there is public, or *communal*, ownership of property. That's why central planning is sometimes called *communism*. Government planners, as representatives of all the people, answer the three questions through *central plans* spelling out how much steel, how many cars, and how much housing to produce. They also decide how to produce these goods and who gets them.

In theory, the pure command system incorporates individual choices into collective choices, which, in turn, are reflected in the central plans. In fact, command economies often have names that focus on collective choice, such as the People's Republic of China and the Democratic People's Republic of Korea (North Korea). In practice, the pure command system also has flaws, most notably:

1. Running an economy is so complicated that some resources are used inefficiently.
2. Because nobody in particular owns resources, each person has less incentive to employ them in their highest-valued use, so some resources are wasted.
3. Central plans may reflect more the preferences of central planners than those of society.
4. Because government is responsible for all production, the variety of products tends to be more limited than in a capitalist economy.
5. Each individual has less personal freedom in making economic choices.

Because of these limitations, countries have modified the pure command system to allow a role for markets. North Korea is perhaps the most centrally planned economy in the world today.

Mixed and Transitional Economies

No country on earth exemplifies either type of economic system in its pure form. Economic systems have grown more alike over time, with the role of government increasing in capitalist economies and the role of markets increasing in command economies. The United States represents a **mixed system**, with government directly accounting for a little more than one-third of all economic activity. What's more, U.S. governments at all levels regulate the private sector in a variety of ways. For example, local zoning boards determine lot sizes, home sizes, and the types of industries allowed. Federal bodies regulate workplace safety, environmental quality, competitive fairness, food and drug quality, and many other activities.

Although both ends of the spectrum have moved toward the center, capitalism has gained the most converts in recent decades. Perhaps the benefits of markets are no better illustrated than where a country, as a result of war or political upheaval, became

pure command system
An economic system characterized by the public ownership of resources and centralized planning

mixed system
An economic system characterized by the private ownership of some resources and the public ownership of other resources; some markets are regulated by government

divided by ideology into a capitalist economy and a command economy, such as with Taiwan and China or South Korea and North Korea. In each case, the economies began with similar human and physical resources, but once they went their separate ways, economic growth diverged sharply, with the capitalist economies outperforming the command economies. For example, Taiwan's production per capita in 2010 was four times that of China's, and South Korea's production per capita was 15 times that of North Korea's.

Consider the experience of the pilgrims in 1620 while establishing Plymouth Colony. They first tried communal ownership of the land. That turned out badly. Crops were neglected and food shortages developed. After three years of near starvation, the system was changed so that each family was assigned a plot of land and granted the fruits of that plot. Yields increased sharply. The pilgrims learned that people take better care of what they own individually; common ownership often leads to common neglect.

Recognizing the incentive power of property rights and markets, some of the most die-hard central planners are now allowing a role for markets. For example, about one-fifth of the world's population lives in China, which grows more market oriented each day, even going so far as to give private property constitutional protection on a par with state property. In a poll of Chinese citizens, 74 percent agreed that "the free enterprise system is the best system on which to base the future of the world." Among Americans polled, 71 percent agreed with that statement.[4] Two decades ago, the former Soviet Union dissolved into 15 independent republics; most converted state-owned enterprises into private firms. From Moscow to Beijing, from Hungary to Mongolia, the transition to mixed economies now underway in former command economies will shape the world for decades to come.

Economies Based on Custom or Religion

Finally, some economic systems are molded largely by custom or religion. For example, caste systems in India and elsewhere restrict occupational choices. Charging interest is banned under Islamic law. Family relations also play significant roles in organizing and coordinating economic activity. Even in the United States, some occupations are still dominated by women, others by men, largely because of tradition. Your own pattern of consumption and choice of occupation may be influenced by some of these considerations.

Conclusion

Although economies can answer the three economic questions in a variety of ways, this book focuses primarily on the mixed market system, such as exists in the United States. This type of economy blends *private choice,* guided by the price system in competitive markets, with *public choice,* guided by democracy in political markets. The study of mixed market systems grows more relevant as former command economies try to develop markets. The next chapter focuses on the economic actors in a mixed economy and explains why and how government gets into the act.

4.   As reported in "Capitalism, Comrade," *Wall Street Journal,* 18 January 2006.

Summary

1. Resources are scarce, but human wants are unlimited. Because you cannot satisfy all your wants, you must choose, and whenever you choose, you must forgo some option. Choice involves an opportunity cost. The opportunity cost of the selected option is the value of the best alternative forgone.

2. The law of comparative advantage says that the individual, firm, region, or country with the lowest opportunity cost of producing a particular good should specialize in that good. Specialization according to the law of comparative advantage promotes the most efficient use of resources.

3. The specialization of labor increases efficiency by (a) taking advantage of individual preferences and natural abilities, (b) allowing each worker to develop expertise and experience at a particular task, (c) reducing the need to shift between different tasks, and (d) allowing for the introduction of more specialized machines and large-scale production techniques.

4. The production possibilities frontier, or PPF, shows the productive capabilities of an economy when all resources are used efficiently. The frontier's bowed-out shape reflects the law of increasing opportunity cost, which arises because some resources are not perfectly adaptable to the production of different goods. Over time, the PPF can shift in or out as a result of changes in the availability of resources, in technology, or in the rules of the game. The PPF demonstrates several economic concepts, including efficiency, scarcity, opportunity cost, the law of increasing opportunity cost, economic growth, and the need for choice.

5. All economic systems, regardless of their decision-making processes, must answer three basic questions: What is to be produced? How is it to be produced? And for whom is it to be produced? Economies answer the questions differently, depending on who owns the resources and how economic activity is coordinated. Economies can be directed by market forces, by the central plans of government officials, or, in most cases, by a mix of the two.

Key Concepts

Opportunity cost   28

Sunk cost   31

Law of comparative advantage   32

Absolute advantage   32

Comparative advantage   32

Barter   33

Division of labor   34

Specialization of labor   34

Production possibilities frontier (PPF)   35

Efficiency   35

Law of increasing opportunity cost   36

Economic growth   37

Economic system   41

Pure capitalism   42

Private property rights   42

Pure command system   43

Mixed system   43

Questions for Review

1. **OPPORTUNITY COST**   Discuss the ways in which the following conditions might affect the opportunity cost of going to a movie tonight:

   a. You have a final exam tomorrow.
   b. School will be out for one month starting tomorrow.
   c. The same movie will be on TV next week.
   d. The Super Bowl is on TV.

2. **OPPORTUNITY COST**   Determine whether each of the following statements is true, false, or uncertain. Explain your answers:

   a. The opportunity cost of an activity is the total value of all the alternatives passed up.
   b. Opportunity cost is an objective measure of cost.
   c. When making choices, people carefully gather all available information about the costs and benefits of alternative choices.
   d. A decision maker seldom knows the actual value of a forgone alternative and therefore must make decisions based on expected values.

3. **COMPARATIVE ADVANTAGE**   "You should never buy precooked frozen foods because the price you pay includes the labor costs of preparing food." Is this conclusion always valid, or can it be invalidated by the law of comparative advantage?

4. **SPECIALIZATION AND EXCHANGE**   Explain how the specialization of labor can lead to increased productivity.

5. **PRODUCTION POSSIBILITIES**   Under what conditions is it possible to increase production of one good without decreasing production of another good?

6. **PRODUCTION POSSIBILITIES**   Under what conditions would an economy be operating inside its PPF? On its PPF? Outside its PPF?

7. **SHIFTING PRODUCTION POSSIBILITIES**   In response to an influx of undocumented workers, Congress made it a federal offense to hire them. How do you think this measure affected the U.S. production possibilities frontier? Do you think all industries were affected equally?

8. PRODUCTION POSSIBILITIES "If society decides to use its resources efficiently (that is, to produce *on* its production possibilities frontier), then future generations will be worse off because they will not be able to use these resources." If this assertion is true, full employment of resources may not be a good thing. Comment on the validity of this assertion.

9. ECONOMIC QUESTIONS What basic economic questions must be answered in a barter economy? In a primitive economy? In a capitalist economy? In a command economy?

10. ECONOMIC SYSTEMS What are the major differences between a pure capitalist system and a pure command system? Is the United States closer to a pure capitalist system or to a pure command system?

Problems and Exercises

11. Case Study: The Opportunity Cost of College During the Vietnam War, colleges and universities were overflowing with students. Was this bumper crop of students caused by a greater expected return on a college education or by a change in the opportunity cost of attending college? Explain.

12. SUNK COST AND CHOICE Suppose you go to a restaurant and buy an expensive meal. Halfway through, despite feeling quite full, you decide to clean your plate. After all, you think, you paid for the meal, so you are going to eat all of it. What's wrong with this thinking?

13. OPPORTUNITY COST You can either spend spring break working at home for $80 per day for five days or go to Florida for the week. If you stay home, your expenses will total about $100. If you go to Florida, the airfare, hotel, food, and miscellaneous expenses will total about $700. What's your opportunity cost of going to Florida?

14. ABSOLUTE AND COMPARATIVE ADVANTAGE You have the following information concerning the production of wheat and cloth in the United States and the United Kingdom:

Labor Hours Required to Produce One Unit

	United Kingdom	United States
Wheat	2	1
Cloth	6	5

a. What is the opportunity cost of producing a unit of wheat in the United Kingdom? In the United States?
b. Which country has an absolute advantage in producing wheat? In producing cloth?
c. Which country has a comparative advantage in producing wheat? In producing cloth?
d. Which country should specialize in producing wheat? In producing cloth?

15. SPECIALIZATION Provide some examples of specialized markets or retail outlets. What makes the Web so conducive to specialization?

16. SHAPE OF THE PPF Suppose a production possibilities frontier includes the following combinations:

Cars	Washing Machines
0	1,000
100	600
200	0

a. Graph the PPF, assuming that it has no curved segments.
b. What is the cost of producing an additional car when 50 cars are being produced?

c. What is the cost of producing an additional car when 150 cars are being produced?
d. What is the cost of producing an additional washing machine when 50 cars are being produced? When 150 cars are being produced?
e. What do your answers tell you about opportunity costs?

17. PRODUCTION POSSIBILITIES Suppose an economy uses two resources (labor and capital) to produce two goods (wheat and cloth). Capital is relatively more useful in producing cloth, and labor is relatively more useful in producing wheat. If the supply of capital falls by 10 percent and the supply of labor increases by 10 percent, how will the PPF for wheat and cloth change?

18. PRODUCTION POSSIBILITIES There's no reason why a production possibilities frontier could not be used to represent the situation facing an individual. Imagine your own PPF. Right now—today—you have certain resources—your time, your skills, perhaps some capital. And you can produce various outputs. Suppose you can produce combinations of two outputs, call them studying and partying.

a. Draw your PPF for studying and partying. Be sure to label the axes of the diagram appropriately. Label the points where the PPF intersects the axes, as well as several other points along the frontier.
b. Explain what it would mean for you to move upward and to the left along your personal PPF. What kinds of adjustments would you have to make in your life to make such a movement along the frontier?
c. Under what circumstances would your personal PPF shift outward? Do you think the shift would be a "parallel" one? Why, or why not?

19. SHIFTING PRODUCTION POSSIBILITIES Determine whether each of the following would cause the economy's PPF to shift inward, outward, or not at all:

a. An increase in average length of annual vacations
b. An increase in immigration
c. A decrease in the average retirement age
d. The migration of skilled workers to other countries

20. Case Study: Rules of the Game and Economic Development Why is the standard of living higher in countries where doing business is easier? Why do governments collect any taxes or impose any regulations at all?

21. ECONOMIC SYSTEMS The United States is best described as having a mixed economy. What are some elements of command in the U.S. economy? What are some elements of tradition?

Global Economic Watch Exercises

Login to www.cengagebrain.com and access the Global Economic Watch to do these exercises.

22. GLOBAL ECONOMIC WATCH Go to the Global Economic Crisis Resource Center. Select Global Issues in Context. In the Basic Search box at the top of the page, enter the phrase "Build Ontario's economy." On the Results page, scroll down to the Global Viewpoints section. Click on the link for the December 8, 2009, article "Build Ontario's economy on battle-tested financial sector." Use your understanding of opportunity cost to explain the idea that the Canadian province of Ontario has a comparative advantage in the financial sector.

23. GLOBAL ECONOMIC WATCH   Go to the Global Economic Crisis Resource Center. Select Global Issues in Context. In the Basic Search box at the top of the page, enter the term "capitalism." Find one resource that supports capitalism and one that criticizes. Write a summary of the viewpoints in your own words.

Economic Decision Makers

©iStockphoto.com/Ramona d'Viola

- If we live in the age of specialization, then why haven't specialists taken over all production?

- For example, why do most of us still do our own laundry and perform dozens of other tasks for ourselves?

- In what sense has some production moved from the household to the firm and then back to the household?

- If the "invisible hand" of competitive markets is so efficient, why does government get into the act?

Answers to these and other questions are addressed in this chapter, which discusses the four economic decision makers: households, firms, governments, and the rest of the world.

To develop a better feel for how the economy works, you must get more acquainted with the key players. You already know more about them than you may realize. You grew up in a household. You have dealt with firms all your life, from Sony to Subway. You know much about governments, from taxes to public schools. And you have a growing awareness of the rest of the world, from online sites, to imports, to foreign travel. This chapter draws on your abundant personal experience with economic decision makers to consider their makeup and goals.

Topics discussed include:

- Evolution of the household
- Evolution of the firm
- Types of firms
- Market failures and government remedies
- Taxing and public spending
- International trade and finance

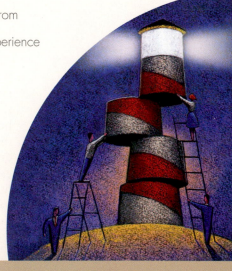

The Household

Households play the starring role in a market economy. Their demand for goods and services determines what gets produced. And their supply of labor, capital, natural resources, and entrepreneurial ability produces that output. As demanders of goods and services and suppliers of resources, households make all kinds of choices, such as what to buy, how much to save, where to live, and where to work. Although a household usually consists of several individuals, we will view each household as acting like a single decision maker.

The Evolution of the Household

In earlier times, when the economy was primarily agricultural, a farm household was largely self-sufficient. Each family member often specialized in a specific farm task—cooking meals, making clothes, tending livestock, planting crops, and so on. These early households produced what they consumed and consumed what they produced. With the introduction of new seed varieties, better fertilizers, and labor-saving machinery, farm productivity increased sharply. Fewer farmers were needed to grow enough food to feed a nation. At the same time, the growth of urban factories increased the demand for factory labor. As a result, many workers moved from farms to cities, where they became more specialized but less self-sufficient.

Households evolved in other ways. For example, in 1950, only about 15 percent of married women with young children were in the labor force. Since then, higher levels of education among women and a growing demand for their labor increased women's earnings, thus raising their opportunity cost of working in the home. This higher opportunity cost contributed to their growing labor force participation. Today about 70 percent of women with children under 18 are in the labor force.

The rise of two-earner households has affected the family as an economic unit. Households produce less for themselves and demand more from the market. For example, child-care services and fast-food restaurants have displaced some household production (Americans now consume about one-third of their calories away from home). The rise in two-earner families has reduced specialization within the household—a central feature of the farm family. Nonetheless, some production still occurs in the home, as we'll explore later.

Households Maximize Utility

There are more than 115 million U.S. households. All those who live together under one roof are considered part of the same household. What exactly do households attempt to accomplish in making decisions? Economists assume that people try to maximize their level of satisfaction, sense of well-being, happiness, and overall welfare. In short, households attempt to maximize **utility**. Households, like other economic decision makers, are viewed as rational, meaning that they try to act in their best interests and do not deliberately try to make themselves less happy. Utility maximization depends on each household's subjective goals, not on some objective standard. For example, some households maintain neat homes with well-groomed lawns; others pay little attention to their homes and use their lawns as junkyards.

utility
The satisfaction received from consumption; sense of well-being

Households as Resource Suppliers

Households use their limited resources—labor, capital, natural resources, and entre-preneurial ability—in an attempt to satisfy their unlimited wants. They can use these resources to produce goods and services in their homes. For example, they can cook, wash, sew, dust, iron, sweep, vacuum, mop, mow, paint, and fix a leaky faucet. They can also sell these resources in the resource market and use the income to buy goods and services in the product market. The most valuable resource sold by most house-holds is labor.

Panel (a) of Exhibit 1 shows the sources of personal income received by U.S. households in 2009, when personal income totaled $12.0 trillion. As you can see, 60 percent of personal income came from wages and salaries. A distant second was transfer payments (to be discussed next), at 16 percent of personal income, followed by personal interest at 10 percent, and proprietors' income at 8 percent. *Proprietors* are people who work for themselves rather than for employers; farmers, plumbers, and doctors are often self-employed. Proprietors' income should also be considered a form of labor income. *Over two-thirds of personal income in the United States comes from labor earnings rather than from the ownership of other resources such as capital or natural resources.*

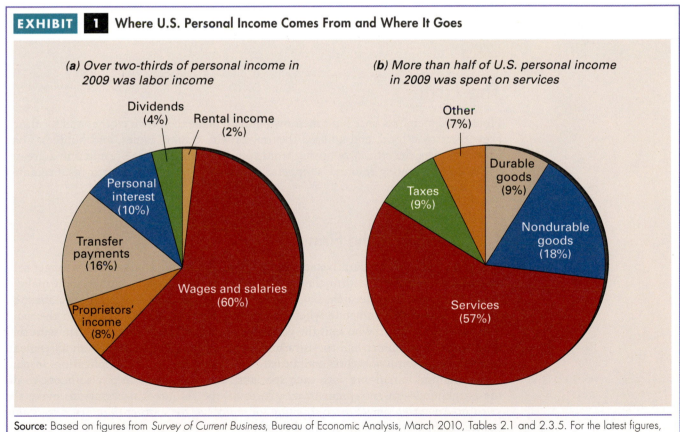

EXHIBIT 1   Where U.S. Personal Income Comes From and Where It Goes

(a) *Over two-thirds of personal income in 2009 was labor income*

Dividends (4%)
Rental income (2%)
Personal interest (10%)
Transfer payments (16%)
Proprietors' income (8%)
Wages and salaries (60%)

(b) *More than half of U.S. personal income in 2009 was spent on services*

Other (7%)
Durable goods (9%)
Taxes (9%)
Nondurable goods (18%)
Services (57%)

Source: Based on figures from *Survey of Current Business*, Bureau of Economic Analysis, March 2010, Tables 2.1 and 2.3.5. For the latest figures, go to http://www.bea.gov/scb/index.htm.

Because of a limited education, disability, discrimination, poor health, the time demands of caring for small children, or just bad luck, some households have few resources that are valued in the market. Society has made the political decision that individuals in such circumstances should receive short-term public assistance. Consequently, the government gives some households **transfer payments**, which are outright grants. *Cash transfers* are monetary payments, such as welfare benefits, Social Security, unemployment compensation, and disability benefits. *In-kind transfers* provide for specific goods and services, such as food, health care, and housing.

Households as Demanders of Goods and Services

What happens to personal income once it comes into the household? Most goes to personal consumption, which sorts into three broad spending categories: (1) *durable goods*—that is, goods expected to last three or more years—such as an automobile or a refrigerator; (2) *nondurable goods,* such as food, clothing, and gasoline; and (3) *services,* such as haircuts, air travel, and medical care. As you can see from panel (b) of Exhibit 1, spending on durable goods in 2009 claimed 9 percent of U.S. personal income; nondurables, 18 percent; and services, 57 percent. Taxes claimed 9 percent, and all other categories, including savings, claimed just 7 percent. So more than half of all personal income went for services—the fastest growing sector, because many services, such as child care, are shifting from do-it-yourself home production to market purchases.

The Firm

Household members once built their own homes, made their own clothes and furniture, grew their own food, and amused themselves with books, games, and hobbies. Over time, however, the efficiency arising from comparative advantage resulted in a greater specialization among resource suppliers. This section takes a look at firms, beginning with their evolution.

The Evolution of the Firm

Specialization and comparative advantage explain why households are no longer self-sufficient. But why is a firm the natural result? For example, rather than make a woolen sweater from scratch, couldn't a consumer take advantage of specialization by negotiating with someone who produced the wool, another who spun the wool into yarn, and a third who knit the yarn into a sweater? Here's the problem with that model: If the consumer had to visit each of these specialists and reach an agreement, the resulting *transaction costs* could easily erase the gains from specialization. Instead of visiting and bargaining with each specialist, the consumer can pay someone to do the bargaining—an entrepreneur, who hires all the resources necessary to make the sweater. *An entrepreneur, by contracting for many sweaters rather than just one, is able to reduce the transaction costs per sweater.*

For about 200 years, profit-seeking entrepreneurs relied on "putting out" raw material, like wool and cotton, to rural households that turned it into finished products, like woolen goods made from yarn. The system developed in the British Isles, where workers' cottages served as tiny factories, especially during winter months, when farming chores were few (so the opportunity cost was low). This approach, which came to be known as the *cottage industry system,* still exists in some parts of the world. You might think of this system as partway between household self-sufficiency and the modern firm.

As the British economy expanded in the 18th century, entrepreneurs began organizing the stages of production under one roof. Technological developments, such as waterpower and later steam power, increased the productivity of each worker and helped shift employment from rural areas to urban factories. *Work, therefore, became organized in large, centrally powered factories that (1) promoted a more efficient division of labor, (2) allowed for the direct supervision of production, (3) reduced transportation costs, and (4) facilitated the use of machines far bigger than anything used in the home.* The development of large-scale factory production, known as the **Industrial Revolution**, began in Great Britain around 1750 and spread to the rest of Europe, North America, and Australia.

Production, then, evolved from self-sufficient rural households to the cottage industry system, where specialized production occurred in the household, to production in a firm. Today, entrepreneurs combine resources in firms such as factories, mills, offices, stores, and restaurants. **Firms** are economic units formed by profit-seeking entrepreneurs who combine labor, capital, and natural resources to produce goods and services. Just as we assume that households try to maximize utility, we assume that firms try to *maximize profit*. Profit, the entrepreneur's reward, equals sales revenue minus the cost of production, including the opportunity cost of the entrepreneur's time.

Industrial Revolution
Development of large-scale factory production that began in Great Britain around 1750 and spread to the rest of Europe, North America, and Australia

firms
Economic units formed by profit-seeking entrepreneurs who employ resources to produce goods and services for sale

Types of Firms

There are more than 30 million for-profit businesses in the United States. Two-thirds are small retail businesses, small service operations, part-time home-based businesses, and small farms. Each year more than a million new businesses start up and many fail. Firms are organized in one of three ways: as a sole proprietorship, as a partnership, or as a corporation.

Sole Proprietorships

The simplest form of business organization is the **sole proprietorship**, a single-owner firm. Examples include self-employed plumbers, farmers, and dentists. Most sole proprietorships consist of just the self-employed proprietor—there are no hired employees. To organize a sole proprietorship, the owner simply opens for business by, for example, taking out a classified ad announcing availability for plumbing services or whatever. The owner is in complete control. But he or she faces unlimited liability and could lose everything, including a home and other personal assets, to settle business debts or other claims against the business. Also, because the sole proprietor has no partners or other investors, raising enough money to get the business up and running and keep it going can be a challenge. One final disadvantage is that a sole proprietorship usually goes out of business when the proprietor dies or leaves the business. Still, a sole proprietorship is the most common type of business, accounting most recently for 71 percent of all U.S. businesses. Nonetheless, because this type of firm is typically small, proprietorships generate just a tiny portion of all U.S. business sales—only 4 percent. But keep in mind that many of the largest businesses in the world today began as an idea of a sole proprietor.

sole proprietorship
A firm with a single owner who has the right to all profits but who also bears unlimited liability for the firm's losses and debts

Partnerships

partnership

A firm with multiple owners who share the profits and bear unlimited liability for the firm's losses and debts

A more complicated form of business is the **partnership**, which involves two or more individuals who agree to combine their funds and efforts in return for a share of any profit or loss. Law, accounting, and medical partnerships typify this business form. Partners have strength in numbers and often find it easier than sole proprietors to raise enough funds to get the business going. But partners may not always agree. Also, each partner usually faces unlimited liability for any debts or claims against the partnership, so one partner could lose everything because of another's mistake. Finally, the death or departure of one partner can disrupt the firm's continuity and require a complete reorganization. The partnership is the least common form of U.S. business, making up only 10 percent of all firms and 13 percent of all business sales.

Corporations

corporation

A legal entity owned by stockholders whose liability is limited to the value of their stock ownership

By far the most influential form of business is the corporation. A **corporation** is a legal entity established through articles of incorporation. Shares of stock confer corporate ownership, thereby entitling stockholders to a claim on any profit. A major advantage of the corporate form is that many investors—hundreds, thousands, even millions—can pool their funds, so incorporating represents the easiest way to amass large sums to finance the business. Also, stockholders' liability for any loss is limited to the value of their stock, meaning stockholders enjoy *limited liability*. A final advantage of this form of organization is that the corporation has a life apart from its owners. The corporation survives even if ownership changes hands, and it can be taxed, sued, and even charged with a crime as if it were a person.

The corporate form has some disadvantages as well. A stockholder's ability to influence corporate policy is limited to voting for a board of directors, which oversees the operation of the firm. Each share of stock usually carries with it one vote. The typical stockholder of a large corporation owns only a tiny fraction of the shares and thus has little say. Whereas the income from sole proprietorships and partnerships is taxed only once, corporate income gets whacked twice—first as corporate profits and second as stockholder income, either as corporate dividends or as realized capital gains. A *realized capital gain* is any increase in the market price of a share that occurs between the time the share is purchased and the time it is sold.

A hybrid type of corporation has evolved to take advantage of the limited liability feature of the corporate structure while reducing the impact of double taxation. The *S corporation* provides owners with limited liability, but profits are taxed only once—as income on each shareholder's personal income tax return. To qualify as an S corporation, a firm must have no more than 100 stockholders and no foreign stockholders.

Corporations make up only 19 percent of all U.S. businesses, but because they tend to be much larger than the other two business forms, corporations account for 83 percent of all business sales. Exhibit 2 shows, by business type, the percentage of U.S. firms and the percentage of U.S. sales. *The sole proprietorship is the most important in sheer numbers, but the corporation is the most important in total sales.*

Cooperatives

cooperative

An organization consisting of people who pool their resources to buy and sell more efficiently than they could individually

A **cooperative**, or "co-op" for short, is a group of people who cooperate by pooling their resources to buy and sell more efficiently than they could independently. Cooperatives try to minimize costs and operate with limited liability of members. The government

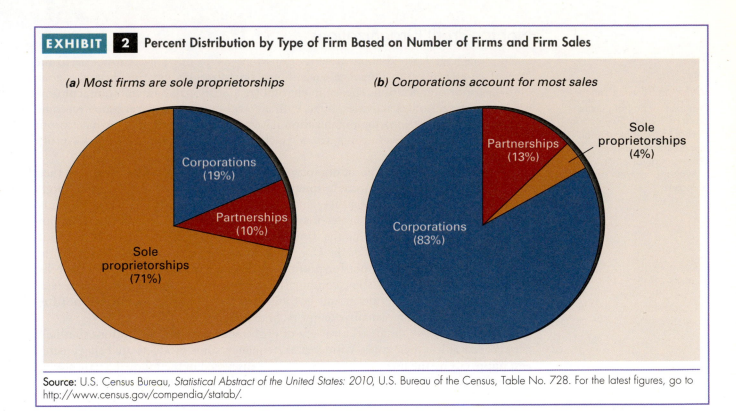

EXHIBIT **2** **Percent Distribution by Type of Firm Based on Number of Firms and Firm Sales**

(a) Most firms are sole proprietorships

- Corporations (19%)
- Partnerships (10%)
- Sole proprietorships (71%)

(b) Corporations account for most sales

- Partnerships (13%)
- Sole proprietorships (4%)
- Corporations (83%)

Source: U.S. Census Bureau, *Statistical Abstract of the United States: 2010*, U.S. Bureau of the Census, Table No. 728. For the latest figures, go to http://www.census.gov/compendia/statab/.

grants most cooperatives tax-exempt status. There are two types: consumer cooperatives and producer cooperatives.

Consumer Cooperatives

A *consumer cooperative* is a retail business owned and operated by some or all of its customers in order to reduce costs. Some cooperatives require members to pay an annual fee and others require them to work a certain number of hours each year. Members sometimes pay lower prices than other customers or may share in any revenues that exceed costs. In the United States, consumer cooperatives operate credit unions, electric-power facilities, health plans, apartment buildings, and grocery stores, among other businesses. Many college bookstores are cooperatives. For example, the UConn Co-op is owned by about 30,000 students, faculty, and staff. These members receive discounts on their purchases.

Producer Cooperatives

In a *producer cooperative,* producers join forces to buy supplies and equipment and to market their output. Each producer's objective is to reduce costs and increase profits. Federal legislation allows farmers to cooperate without violating antitrust laws. Firms in other industries could not do this legally. Farmers pool their funds to purchase machinery and supplies, provide storage and processing facilities, and transport products to market. Sunkist, for example, is a farm cooperative owned and operated by about 6,500 citrus growers in California and Arizona.

Not-for-Profit Organizations

So far, you have learned about organizations that try to maximize profits or, in the case of cooperatives, to minimize costs. Some organizations have neither as a goal. **Not-for-profit organizations** engage in charitable, educational, humanitarian, cultural, professional, and other activities, often with a social purpose. Any revenue exceeding cost is plowed back into the organization. Government agencies do not have profit as a goal either, but governments are not included in this definition of not-for-profit organizations.

Like businesses, not-for-profit organizations evolved to help people accomplish their goals. Examples include nonprofit hospitals, private schools and colleges, religious organizations, the Red Cross, Greenpeace, charitable foundations, soup kitchens, orchestras, museums, labor unions, and professional organizations. There are about 1.5 million not-for-profit organizations in the United States. They employ about 12 million workers, or about 8 percent of the U.S. work force with not-for-profit hospitals the largest employers. But even not-for-profit organizations must somehow pay the bills. Revenue typically includes some combination of voluntary contributions and service charges, such as college tuition and hospital charges. In the United States, not-for-profit organizations are usually exempt from taxes.

Thus far we have discussed a variety of profit and nonprofit institutions that help people accomplish their goals. With greater frequency, some products are being created and improved by the users of those products, as discussed in the following case study.

CASE STUDY

e activity

You can find more information and links about user-generated products—or user-generated content (UGC)—if you go to Wikipedia. Discover UGC characteristics and development, types, adoption by mass media, and criticisms at http://en.wikipedia.org/wiki/User-generated_content.

THE INFORMATION ECONOMY

User-Generated Products   In a market economy, new products and processes are usually developed by profit-seeking entrepreneurs, but sometimes sheer curiosity and the challenge of solving difficult problems lead to new and better ways of doing things. For example, loose communities of computer programmers have been collaborating for decades. By the early 1990s, they formed a grass roots movement known as "open source," which was fueled by the Internet. In 1991, Linus Torvalds, a student at the University of Helsinki in Finland, wrote the core program for what would become known as the Linux operating system. He posted his program online and invited anyone to tinker with the coding. Word spread, and computer aficionados around the world began spending their free time making Linux better.

Other software has developed in the open-source arena. For example, from the University of Illinois came web server software named Apache, and Swedish researchers developed database software called MySQL. The *Free Software Directory* lists more than 5,000 free software packages. The term *free* refers not only to the dollar cost of the software, which is zero, but to what you can do with the software—you can examine it, modify it, and redistribute it to anyone. Free user-generated software now includes the most widely used web server (Apache) and the second most popular desktop operating system (Linux), web browser (Firefox), and office suite (OpenOffice).

Other user-generated products include some familiar names—Wikipedia, MySpace, Facebook, YouTube, and Twitter. Wikipedia is a free online encyclopedia written and edited by volunteers. The idea is that collaboration over time will improve

AP Photo/Cameron Bloch

content much the way that open-source software has evolved. Wikipedia claims to be one of the most visited online sites. Founder Jimmy Wales says he spent a half million dollars getting Wikipedia going, but now the project relies on volunteers and donations.

MySpace and Facebook are social networking sites that allow users to post personal profiles, blogs, photos, music, videos, and more. The main attraction of these sites is material provided by users. The companies simply provide the software and hardware backbone to support the network. MySpace, founded in July 2003, was sold in July 2005 for about $330 million. Facebook was started by a college sophomore in 2004; the company had 500 million users by 2010 and an estimated market value of $10 billion.

YouTube is an online site that allows users to post their own videos and view those posted by others. Searching is easy. For example, "comparative advantage" turned up more than 150 videos, including "Econ Concepts in 60 Seconds." When sold to Google in 2006, YouTube had only 67 employees and no profit. Still, because visitors were viewing more than 100 million videos a day, all those eyeballs offered tremendous advertising potential. Google paid $1.7 billion for a company with no profit.

Finally, Twitter is a social networking and microblogging service that allows users to send and receive "tweets," which are messages limited to 140 characters. Delivery can be online via the Twitter Web site, by cell phones, or by using other applications. The company had about 100 million users in 2010, but projects one billion users by 2013.

User-generated products are not new. Radio call-in shows have been making money off callers for decades. But the Internet has increased opportunities for users to create new products and to improve existing products. Most of the users are just having fun. The more users involved, the more attractive that product is to each user. That's why networking and video sites try to dominate their markets.

Sources: Jaron Lanier, *You Are Not a Gadget*, (Knopf, 2010); "A World of Connections," *The Economist*, 5 February 2010; and Jessica Vascellaro, "Facebook CEO in No Rush to 'Friend' Wall Street," *Wall Street Journal*, 3 March 2010. The *Free Software Directory* is found at http://directory.fsf.org/.

Why Does Household Production Still Exist?

If firms are so efficient at reducing transaction and production costs, why don't they make everything? Why do households still perform some tasks, such as cooking and cleaning? *If a household's opportunity cost of performing a task is below the market price, then the household usually performs that task.* People with a lower opportunity cost of time do more for themselves. For example, janitors are more likely to mow their lawns than are physicians. Let's look at some reasons for household production.

No Skills or Special Resources Are Required

Some activities require so few skills or special resources that householders find it cheaper to do the jobs themselves. Sweeping the kitchen floor requires only a broom and some time so it's usually performed by household members. Sanding a wooden floor, however, involves special machinery and expertise, so this service is usually left to professionals. Similarly, although you wouldn't hire someone to brush your teeth, dental work is not for amateurs. *Households usually perform domestic chores that demand neither expertise nor special machinery.*

Household Production Avoids Taxes

Suppose you are deciding whether to pay someone $3,000 to paint your house or do it yourself. If the income tax rate is one-third, you must earn $4,500 before taxes to have the $3,000 after taxes to pay for the job. And the painter who charges you $3,000 nets only $2,000 after paying $1,000 in taxes. Thus, you must earn $4,500 so that the painter can take home $2,000. If you paint the house yourself, no taxes are involved. The tax-free nature of do-it-yourself activity favors household production over market transactions.

Household Production Reduces Transaction Costs

Getting estimates, hiring a contractor, negotiating terms, and monitoring job performance all take time and require information. Doing the job yourself reduces these transaction costs. Household production also allows for more personal control over the final product than is usually available through the market. For example, some people prefer home cooking, because they can prepare home-cooked meals to individual tastes.

Household production often grows during hard times. The economic recession of 2007–2009 prompted some families to shift from market purchases to household production to save money. For example, sales of hair clippers used for home haircuts increased 10 percent in 2008 and 11 percent in 2009.[1]

Technological Advances Increase Household Productivity

Information Revolution

Technological change spawned by the microchip and the Internet that enhanced the acquisition, analysis, and transmission of information

Technological breakthroughs are not confined to market production. Vacuum cleaners, washers and dryers, dishwashers, microwave ovens, and other modern appliances reduce the time and often the skill required to perform household tasks. Also, new technologies such as Blu-ray players, DVRs, HDTVs, broadband downloads, and computer games enhance home entertainment. Indeed, microchip-based technologies have shifted some production from the firm back to the household, as discussed in the following case study.

CASE STUDY

e activity

Economists have begun to study the economic implications of the virtual office and other virtual phenomena. Try visiting Google (http://www.google.com) and Yahoo (http://www.yahoo.com). Search for the words *virtual* and *economics,* and see what you find.

THE INFORMATION ECONOMY

The Electronic Cottage   The Industrial Revolution shifted production from rural cottages to urban factories. But the **Information Revolution** spawned by the microchip and the Internet has decentralized the acquisition, analysis, and transmission of information. These days, someone who claims to work at a home office is not necessarily referring to corporate headquarters but to a spare bedroom. According to a recent survey, the number of telecommuters, or "remote workers," has more than doubled in the last decade. Pushing the trend are worsening traffic, higher gas prices, wider access to broadband, growing self-employment resulting from layoffs during the recession of 2007–2009, and even the threat of terrorism. The average commute is 23 miles, and eliminating that can save about $1,000 a year in gas and can avoid putting more than 6,000 pounds of carbon dioxide into the atmosphere. What's more, it often makes sense to try a new business at home before moving to a separate, more costly, location. Most small businesses are home-based, at least at the start.

---

1. Mary Pilon, "Per Capita Savings: Home Barbering Grows in Recession," *Wall Street Journal,* 31 August 2009.

From home, people can write a document with coworkers scattered throughout the world, then discuss the project online in real time or have a videoconference on Skype (McDonald's saves millions in travel costs by videoconferencing). Software allows thousands of employees to share electronic files. A 2010 survey found the majority of those who use computers for most of their work believe they could work at home. When Accenture moved headquarters from Boston to a suburb, the company replaced 120 tons of paper records with an online database accessible anytime from anywhere in the world.

To support those who work at home, an entire industry has sprung up, with magazines, newsletters, Web sites, and national conferences. In fact, an office need not even be in a specific place. Some people now work in virtual offices, which have no permanent locations. With iPhones, BlackBerries, or other links, remote workers, can conduct business on the road—literally, "deals on wheels."

Chip technology is decentralizing production, shifting work from a central office either back to the household or to no place in particular. More generally, the Internet has reduced transaction costs, whether it's a market report authored jointly by researchers from around the world or a new computer system assembled from parts ordered over the Internet. Easier communication has even increased contact among distant research scholars. For example, economists living in distant cities are four times more likely to collaborate now than they were two decades ago.

Sources: Betty Beard, "Survey: Most Could Work from Home," *Arizona Republic*, 6 March 2010; Colleen DeBaise, "For More Workers, Home is Where the Office Is," *Wall Street Journal*, 3 January 2010; and Daniel Hamermesh and Sharon Oster, "Tools or Toys? The Impact of High Technology on Scholarly Productivity," *Economic Inquiry*, 40 (October 2002): 539–555. For information about how to run a business from home, go to http://www.ows.doleta.gov/unemploy/self.asp.

The Government

You might think that production by households and firms could satisfy all consumer wants. Why must yet another economic decision maker get into the act? After all, governments play some role in every nation on earth.

The Role of Government

Sometimes the unrestrained operation of markets yields undesirable results. Too many of some goods and too few of other goods get produced. This section discusses the sources of **market failure** and how society's overall welfare may be improved through government intervention in the market.

market failure

A condition that arises when the unregulated operation of markets yields socially undesirable results

Establishing and Enforcing the Rules of the Game

Market efficiency depends on people like you using your resources to maximize your utility. But what if you were repeatedly robbed of your paycheck on your way home from work? Or what if, after you worked two weeks in a new job, your boss called you a sucker and said you wouldn't get paid? Why bother working? The market system would break down if you could not safeguard your private property or if you could not enforce contracts. Governments safeguard private property through police protection and enforce contracts through a judicial system. More generally, governments try to make sure that market participants abide by the rules of the game. These rules are established through government laws and regulations and also through the customs and conventions of the marketplace.

Promoting Competition

Although the "invisible hand" of competition usually promotes an efficient allocation of resources, some firms try to avoid competition through *collusion*, which is an agreement among firms to divide the market and fix the price. Or an individual firm may try to eliminate the competition by using unfair business practices. For example, to drive out local competitors, a large firm may temporarily sell at a price below cost. Government antitrust laws try to promote competition by prohibiting collusion and other anticompetitive practices.

Regulating Natural Monopolies

monopoly

A sole supplier of a product with no close substitutes

Competition usually keeps the product price below the price charged by a **monopoly**, a sole supplier to the market. In rare instances, however, a monopoly can produce and sell the product for less than could competing firms. For example, electricity is delivered more efficiently by a single firm that wires the community than by competing firms each stringing its own wires. When it is cheaper for one firm to serve the market than for two or more firms to do so, that one firm is called a **natural monopoly**. Since a natural monopoly faces no competition, it maximizes profit by charging a higher price than would be optimal from society's point of view. A lower price and greater output would improve social welfare. Therefore, the government usually regulates a natural monopoly, forcing it to lower its price and increase output.

natural monopoly

One firm that can supply the entire market at a lower per-unit cost than could two or more firms

Providing Public Goods

So far this book has been talking about private goods, which have two important features. First, private goods are *rival* in consumption, meaning that the amount consumed by one person is unavailable for others to consume. For example, when you and some friends share a pizza, each slice they eat is one less available for you. Second, the supplier of a private good can easily exclude those who fail to pay. Only paying customers get pizza. Thus, private goods are said to be *exclusive*. So **private goods**, such as pizza, are both rival in consumption and exclusive. In contrast, **public goods** are *nonrival* in consumption. For example, your family's benefit from a safer neighborhood does not reduce your neighbor's benefit. What's more, once produced, public goods are available to all. Suppliers cannot easily prevent consumption by those who fail to pay. For example, reducing terrorism is *nonexclusive*. It benefits all in the community, regardless of who pays to reduce terrorism and who doesn't. Because public goods are *nonrival* and *nonexclusive*, private firms cannot sell them profitably. The government, however, has the authority to enforce tax collections for public goods. Thus, the government provides public goods and funds them with taxes.

private good

A good, such as pizza, that is both rival in consumption and exclusive

public good

A good that, once produced, is available for all to consume, regardless of who pays and who doesn't; such a good is nonrival and nonexclusive, such as a safer community

Dealing With Externalities

externality

A cost or a benefit that affects neither the buyer nor seller, but instead affects people not involved in the market transaction

Market prices reflect the private costs and private benefits of producers and consumers. But sometimes production or consumption imposes costs or benefits on third parties—on those who are neither suppliers nor demanders in a market transaction. For example, a paper mill fouls the air breathed by nearby residents, but the price of paper usually fails to reflect such costs. Because these pollution costs are outside, or external to, the market, they are called *externalities*. An **externality** is a cost or a benefit that falls on a third party. A negative externality imposes an external cost, such as factory pollution, auto emissions, or traffic congestion. A positive externality confers an external benefit, such as getting a good education, getting inoculated against a disease (thus reducing the possibility of infecting others), or driving carefully. Because market prices usually do not reflect externalities, governments often use taxes, subsidies, and regulations to discourage negative externalities and encourage positive externalities. For example, a polluting factory may face taxes and regulations aimed at curbing that pollution. And because more educated people can read road signs and have options that pay better than crime, governments try to encourage education with free public schools, subsidized higher education, and by keeping people in school until their 16th birthdays.

A More Equal Distribution of Income

As mentioned earlier, some people, because of poor education, mental or physical disabilities, bad luck, or perhaps the need to care for small children, are unable to support themselves and their families. Because resource markets do not guarantee even a minimum level of income, transfer payments reflect society's willingness to provide a basic standard of living to all households. Most Americans agree that government should redistribute income to the poor (note the normative nature of this statement). Opinions differ about who should receive benefits, how much they should get, what form benefits should take, and how long benefits should last.

Full Employment, Price Stability, and Economic Growth

Perhaps the most important responsibility of government is fostering a healthy economy, which benefits just about everyone. The government—through its ability to tax, to spend, and to control the money supply—attempts to promote full employment, price stability, and economic growth. Pursuing these objectives by taxing and spending is called **fiscal policy**. Pursuing them by regulating the money supply is called **monetary policy**. Macroeconomics examines both policies.

Government's Structure and Objectives

The United States has a *federal system* of government, meaning that responsibilities are shared across levels of government. State governments grant some powers to local governments and surrender some powers to the national, or federal, government. As the system has evolved, the federal government has primary responsibility for national security, economic stability, and market competition. State governments fund public higher education, prisons, and—with aid from the federal government—highways and welfare. Local governments provide primary and secondary education with aid from the state, plus police and fire protection. Here are some distinguishing features of government.

Difficulty in Defining Government Objectives

We assume that households try to maximize utility and firms try to maximize profit, but what about governments—or, more specifically, what about government decision makers? What do they try to maximize? One problem is that our federal system consists of not one but many governments—more than 89,500 separate jurisdictions in all, including 1 nation, 50 states, 3,033 counties, 35,991 cities and towns, 13,051 school districts, and 37,381 special districts. What's more, because the federal government relies on offsetting, or countervailing, powers across the executive, legislative, and judicial branches, government does not act as a single, consistent decision maker. Even within the federal executive branch, there are so many agencies and bureaus that at

net ✦ bookmark

The annual *Economic Report of the President* is an invaluable source of information on current economic policy. It also contains many useful data tables. You can find it online at http://www.gpoaccess.gov/eop/.

fiscal policy
The use of government purchases, transfer payments, taxes, and borrowing to influence economy-wide variables such as inflation, employment, and economic growth

monetary policy
Regulation of the money supply to influence economy-wide variables such as inflation, employment, and economic growth

times they seem to work at cross-purposes. For example, at the same time as the U.S. Surgeon General required health warnings on cigarette packages, the U.S. Department of Agriculture pursued policies to benefit tobacco growers. Given this thicket of jurisdictions, branches, and bureaus, one useful theory of government behavior is that elected officials try to maximize the number of votes they get in the next election. So let's assume that elected officials are vote maximizers. In this theory, vote maximization guides the decisions of elected officials who, in turn, oversee government employees.

Voluntary Exchange Versus Coercion

Market exchange relies on the voluntary behavior of buyers and sellers. Don't like tofu? No problem—don't buy any. But in political markets, the situation is different. Any voting rule except unanimous consent must involve some government coercion. Public choices are enforced by the police power of the state. Those who don't pay their taxes could go to jail, even though they may object to some programs those taxes support, such as capital punishment or the war in Afghanistan.

No Market Prices

Another distinguishing feature of governments is that public output is usually offered at either a zero price or at some price below the cost of providing it. If you now pay in-state tuition at a public college or university, your tuition probably covers only about half the state's cost of providing your education. Because the revenue side of the government budget is usually separate from the expenditure side, there is no necessary link between the cost of a program and the benefit. In the private sector, the expected marginal benefit of a product is at least as great as marginal cost; otherwise, nobody would buy it.

The Size and Growth of Government

One way to track the impact of government over time is by measuring government outlays relative to the U.S. *gross domestic product,* or *GDP,* which is the total value of all final goods and services produced in the United States. In 1929, the year the Great Depression began, all government outlays, mostly by state and local governments, totaled about 10 percent of GDP. At the time, the federal government played a minor role. In fact, during the nation's first 150 years, federal outlays, except during war years, never exceeded 3 percent relative to GDP.

The Great Depression, World War II, a change in macroeconomic thinking, and extraordinary measures following the financial crisis of 2008 boosted the share of government outlays to 41 percent of GDP in 2010 with about two-thirds of that by the federal government. In comparison, government outlays relative to GDP were 41 percent in Japan, 44 percent in Canada, 48 percent in Germany, 51 percent in Italy, 53 percent in the United Kingdom, and 55 percent in France. Government outlays by the 28 largest industrial economies averaged 45 percent of GDP in 2010.[2] Thus, government outlays in the United States relative to GDP are below that of most other advanced economies.

Let's look briefly at the composition of federal outlays. Since 1960, defense spending has declined from over half of federal outlays to about one-fifth by 2011, as shown in Exhibit 3. Redistribution—Social Security, Medicare, and welfare programs—has been the mirror image of defense spending, jumping from only about one-fifth of federal outlays in 1960 to nearly half by 2011.

2. The Organization of Economic Cooperation and Development, *OECD Economic Outlook,* 87 (May 2010), Annex Table 25.

EXHIBIT **3** **Redistribution Has Grown and Defense Has Declined as Share of Federal Outlays Since 1960**

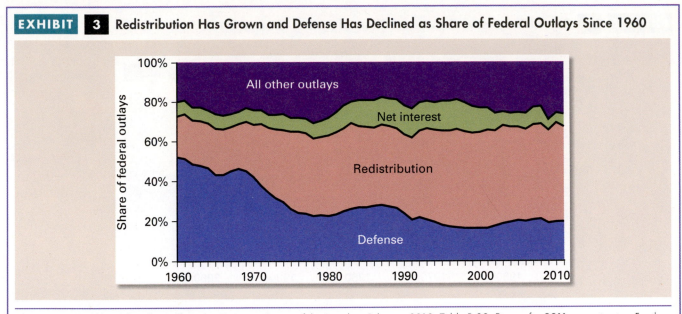

Source: Computed based on figures from the *Economic Report of the President*, February 2010, Table B-80. Figures for 2011 are estimates. For the latest figures, go to http://gpoaccess.gov/eop/.

Sources of Government Revenue

Taxes provide the bulk of revenue at all levels of government. The federal government relies primarily on the individual income tax, state governments rely on income and sales taxes, and local governments rely on the property tax. Other revenue sources include user charges, such as highway tolls, and borrowing. For additional revenue, some states also act as monopolies in certain markets, such as for lottery tickets and for liquor.

Exhibit 4 focuses on the composition of federal revenue since 1960. The share made up by the individual income tax has remained relatively steady, ranging from a low of 42 percent in the mid-1960s to a high of 50 percent in 2001, before settling down to 44 percent in 2011. The share from payroll taxes more than doubled from 15 percent in 1960 to 36 percent in 2011. *Payroll taxes* are deducted from paychecks to support Social Security and Medicare, which fund retirement income and medical care for the elderly. Corporate taxes and revenue from other sources, such as excise (sales) taxes and user charges, have declined as a share of federal revenue since 1960.

Tax Principles and Tax Incidence

The structure of a tax is often justified on the basis of one of two general principles. First, a tax could relate to the individual's ability to pay, so those with a greater ability pay more taxes. Income or property taxes often rely on this **ability-to-pay tax principle**. Alternatively, the **benefits-received tax principle** relates taxes to the benefits taxpayers receive from the government activity funded by the tax. For example, the tax on gasoline funds highway construction and maintenance, thereby linking tax payment to road use, since those who drive more, pay more gas taxes.

Tax incidence indicates who actually bears the burden of the tax. One way to evaluate tax incidence is by measuring the tax as a percentage of income. Under

ability-to-pay tax principle
Those with a greater ability to pay, such as those earning higher incomes or those owning more property, should pay more taxes

benefits-received tax principle
Those who get more benefits from the government program should pay more taxes

tax incidence
The distribution of tax burden among taxpayers; who ultimately pays the tax

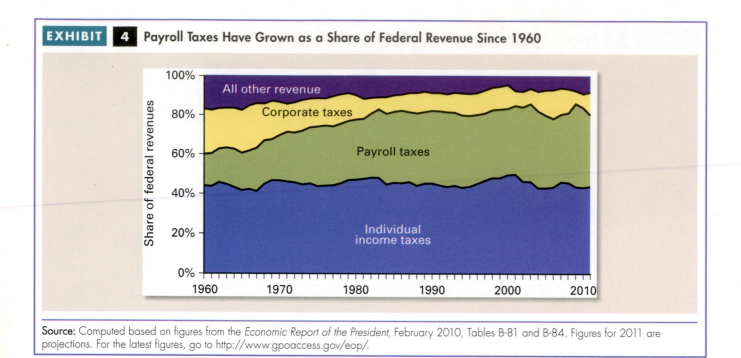

EXHIBIT 4 Payroll Taxes Have Grown as a Share of Federal Revenue Since 1960

Source: Computed based on figures from the *Economic Report of the President*, February 2010, Tables B-81 and B-84. Figures for 2011 are projections. For the latest figures, go to http://www.gpoaccess.gov/eop/.

proportional taxation

The tax as a percentage of income remains constant as income increases; also called a flat tax

progressive taxation

The tax as a percentage of income increases as income increases

marginal tax rate

The percentage of each additional dollar of income that goes to the tax

regressive taxation

The tax as a percentage of income decreases as income increases

proportional taxation, taxpayers at all income levels pay the same percentage of their income in taxes. A proportional income tax is also called a flat tax, since the tax as a percentage of income remains constant, or flat, as income increases. Note that under proportional taxation, although taxes remain constant as a percentage of income, the dollar amount of taxes increases proportionately as income increases.

Under **progressive taxation,** the percentage of income paid in taxes increases as income increases. The **marginal tax rate** indicates the percentage of each additional dollar of income that goes to taxes. Because high marginal rates reduce the after-tax return from working or investing, high marginal rates can reduce people's incentives to work and invest. The six marginal rates applied to the U.S. personal income tax ranged from 10 to 35 percent in 2010, down from a range of 15 to 39.6 percent in 2000. The top rate was scheduled to return to 39.6 percent in 2011.

The top marginal tax bracket each year during the history of the personal income tax is shown by Exhibit 5. Although the top marginal rate is now lower than it was during most other years, high-income households still pay most of the federal income tax collected. Nearly half of all U.S. households pay no federal income tax. According to the U.S. Internal Revenue Service, the top 1 percent of tax filers, based on income, paid 40.4 percent of all income taxes collected in 2007. Their average tax rate was 22.5 percent. And the top 10 percent of tax filers paid 71.2 percent of all income taxes collected. Their average tax rate was 18.9 percent. In contrast, the bottom 50 percent of tax filers paid only 2.9 percent of all income taxes collected. Their tax rate averaged only 3.0 percent. Whether we look at marginal tax rates or average tax rates, the U.S. income tax is progressive. High-income filers pay the overwhelming share of income taxes.

Finally, under **regressive taxation,** the percentage of income paid in taxes decreases as income increases, so the marginal tax rate declines as income increases. Most U.S. *payroll taxes* are regressive, because they impose a flat rate up to a certain level of income, above which the marginal rate drops to zero. For example, Social Security taxes were levied on

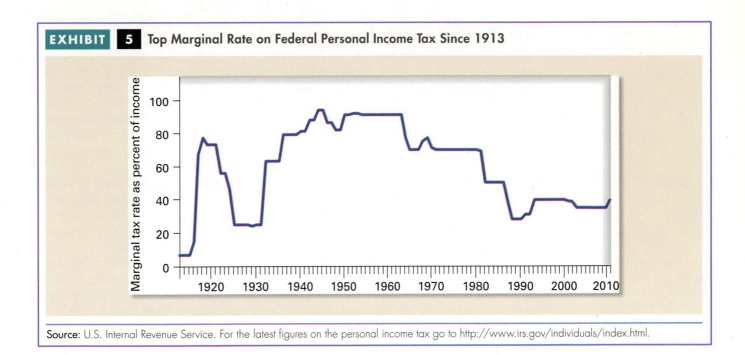

EXHIBIT 5 Top Marginal Rate on Federal Personal Income Tax Since 1913

Source: U.S. Internal Revenue Service. For the latest figures on the personal income tax go to http://www.irs.gov/individuals/index.html.

the first $106,800 of workers' pay in 2010. Half the 12.4 percent tax is paid by employers and half by employees (the self-employed pay the entire 12.4 percent).

Taxes often do more than fund public programs. Some taxes discourage certain activity. For example, a pollution tax can help clean the air. A tax on gasoline can encourage people to work at home, car pool, or use public transportation. Some taxes have unintended consequences. For example, in Egypt a property tax is not imposed until a building is complete. To avoid such taxes, builders never finish the job; multi-story dwellings are usually missing the top floor. As another example of how taxes can distort the allocation of resources, property taxes in Amsterdam and Vietnam were originally based on the width of the building. As a result, buildings in those places are extremely narrow.

This discussion of revenue sources brings to a close, for now, our examination of the role of government in the U.S. economy. Government has a pervasive influence on the economy, and its role is discussed throughout the book.

The Rest of the World

So far, the focus has been on institutions within the United States—that is, on *domestic* households, firms, and governments. This focus is appropriate because our primary objective is to understand the workings of the U.S. economy, by far the largest in the world. But the rest of the world affects what U.S. households consume and what U.S. firms produce. For example, Japan and China supply all kinds of manufactured goods to America, thereby affecting U.S. prices, wages, and profits. Likewise, political events in the Persian Gulf can affect what Americans pay for oil. Foreign decision makers, therefore, influence the U.S. economy—what we produce and what we consume. The *rest of the world* consists of the households, firms, and governments in the other 200 or so sovereign nations throughout the world.

International Trade

In the previous chapter, you learned about comparative advantage and the gains from specialization. These gains explain why householders stopped doing everything for themselves and began to specialize. International trade arises for the same reasons. *International trade occurs because the opportunity cost of producing specific goods differs across countries.* Americans import raw materials like crude oil, bauxite (aluminum ore), and coffee beans and finished goods like cameras, DVD players, and cut diamonds. U.S. producers export sophisticated products like computer software, aircraft, and movies, as well as agricultural products like wheat, corn, and cotton.

Trade between the United States and the rest of the world has increased in recent decades. In 1970, U.S. exports of goods and services amounted to only 6 percent of the gross domestic product. That has increased to about 10 percent today. The top 10 destinations for U.S. exports in order of importance are Canada, Mexico, China, Japan, United Kingdom, Germany, Netherlands, South Korea, France, and Brazil.

merchandise trade balance
The value during a given period of a country's exported goods minus the value of its imported goods

balance of payments
A record of all economic transactions during a given period between residents of one country and residents of the rest of the world

The **merchandise trade balance** equals the value of exported goods minus the value of imported goods. Goods in this case are distinguished from services, which show up in another trade account. For the last quarter century, the United States has imported more goods than it has exported, resulting in a merchandise trade deficit. Just as a household must pay for its spending, so too must a nation. The merchandise trade deficit must be offset by a surplus in one or more of the other *balance-of-payments* accounts. A nation's **balance of payments** is the record of all economic transactions between its residents and residents of the rest of the world.

Exchange Rates

foreign exchange
Foreign money needed to carry out international transactions

The lack of a common currency complicates trade between countries. How many U.S. dollars buy a Porsche? An American buyer cares only about the dollar cost; the German carmaker cares only about the *euros* received (the common currency of 16 European countries). To facilitate trade funded by different currencies, a market for foreign exchange has developed. **Foreign exchange** is foreign currency needed to carry out international transactions. The supply and demand for foreign exchange comes together in *foreign exchange markets* to determine the exchange rate. The *exchange rate* measures the price of one currency in terms of another. For example, the exchange rate between the euro and the dollar might indicate that one euro exchanges for $1.20. At that exchange rate, a Porsche selling for €100,000 costs $120,000. The exchange rate affects the prices of imports and exports and thus helps shape the flow of foreign trade.

Trade Restrictions

tariff
A tax on imports

quota
A legal limit on the quantity of a particular product that can be imported or exported

Despite clear gains from international specialization and exchange, nearly all nations restrict trade to some extent. These restrictions can take the form of (1) **tariffs**, which are taxes on imports; (2) **quotas**, which are limits on the quantity of a particular good that can be imported or exported; and (3) other trade restrictions. If specialization according to comparative advantage is so beneficial, why do most countries restrict trade? Restrictions benefit certain domestic producers that lobby their governments for these benefits. For example, U.S. growers of sugarcane have benefited from legislation restricting imports, thereby raising U.S. sugar prices. These higher prices hurt domestic consumers, but consumers are usually unaware of this harm. Trade restrictions interfere with the free flow of products across borders and tend to hurt the overall economy.

Conclusion

This chapter examined the four economic decision makers: households, firms, governments, and the rest of the world. Domestic households are by far the most important, for they supply resources and demand goods and services.

If you were to stop reading right now, you would already know more economics than most people. But to understand market economies, you must learn how markets work. The next chapter introduces demand and supply.

Summary

1. Most household income arises from the sale of labor, and most household income is spent on personal consumption, primarily services.

2. Household members once built their own homes, made their own clothes and furniture, grew their own food, and supplied their own entertainment. Over time, however, the efficiency arising from comparative advantage resulted in a greater specialization among resource suppliers.

3. Firms bring together specialized resources and in the process reduce the transaction costs of bargaining with all these resource providers. U.S. firms can be organized in three different ways: as sole proprietorships, partnerships, or corporations. Because corporations are typically large, they account for the bulk of sales.

4. When private markets yield undesirable results, government may intervene to address these market failures. Government programs are designed to (a) protect private property and enforce contracts; (b) promote competition; (c) regulate natural monopolies; (d) provide public goods; (e) discourage negative externalities and encourage positive externalities; (f) promote a more even distribution of income; and (g) promote full employment, price stability, and economic growth.

5. In the United States, the federal government has primary responsibility for providing national defense, ensuring market competition, and promoting stability of the economy. State governments provide public higher education, prisons, and—with aid from the federal government—highways and welfare. And local governments provide police and fire protection, and, with help from the state, local schools.

6. The federal government relies primarily on the personal income tax, states rely on income and sales taxes, and localities rely on the property tax. A tax is often justified based on (a) the individual's ability to pay or (b) the benefits the taxpayer receives from the activities financed by the tax.

7. The rest of the world is also populated by households, firms, and governments. International trade creates gains that arise from comparative advantage. The balance of payments summarizes transactions between the residents of one country and the residents of the rest of the world. Although consumers gain from comparative advantage, nearly all countries impose trade restrictions to protect specific domestic industries.

Key Concepts

Utility 50
Transfer payments 52
Industrial Revolution 53
Firms 53
Sole proprietorship 53
Partnership 54
Corporation 54
Cooperative 54
Not-for-profit organizations 56
Information Revolution 58

Market failure 59
Monopoly 60
Natural monopoly 60
Private good 60
Public good 60
Externality 60
Fiscal policy 61
Monetary policy 61
Ability-to-pay tax principle 63
Benefits-received tax principle 63

Tax incidence 63
Proportional taxation 64
Progressive taxation 64
Marginal tax rate 64
Regressive taxation 64
Merchandise trade balance 66
Balance of payments 66
Foreign exchange 66
Tariff 66
Quota 66

Questions for Review

1. **HOUSEHOLDS AS DEMANDERS OF GOODS AND SERVICES** Classify each of the following as a durable good, a nondurable good, or a service:

   a. A gallon of milk
   b. A lawn mower
   c. A DVD player
   d. A manicure
   e. A pair of shoes
   f. An eye exam
   g. A personal computer
   h. A neighborhood teenager mowing a lawn

2. **Case Study: The Electronic Cottage** How has the development of personal computer hardware and software reversed some of the trends brought on by the Industrial Revolution?

3. **EVOLUTION OF THE FIRM** Explain how production after the Industrial Revolution differed from production under the cottage industry system.

4. **HOUSEHOLD PRODUCTION** What factors does a householder consider when deciding whether to produce a good or service at home or buy it in the marketplace?

5. **CORPORATIONS** How did the institution of the firm get a boost from the advent of the Industrial Revolution? What type of business organization existed before this?

6. **SOLE PROPRIETORSHIPS** What are the disadvantages of the sole proprietorship form of business?

7. **COOPERATIVES** How do cooperatives differ from typical businesses?

8. **Case Study: User-Generated Products** Why are users willing to help create certain products even though few, if any, users are paid for their efforts?

9. **GOVERNMENT** Often it is said that government is necessary when private markets fail to work effectively and fairly. Based on your reading of the text, discuss how private markets might break down.

10. **EXTERNALITIES** Suppose there is an external cost, or negative externality, associated with production of a certain good. What's wrong with letting the market determine how much of this good will be produced?

11. **GOVERNMENT REVENUE** What are the sources of government revenue in the United States? Which types of taxes are most important at each level of government? Which two taxes provide the most revenue to the federal government?

12. **OBJECTIVES OF THE ECONOMIC DECISION MAKERS** In economic analysis, what are the assumed objectives of households, firms, and the government?

13. **INTERNATIONAL TRADE** Why does international trade occur? What does it mean to run a deficit in the merchandise trade balance?

14. **INTERNATIONAL TRADE** Distinguish between a tariff and a quota. Who benefits from and who is harmed by such restrictions on imports?

Problems and Exercises

15. **EVOLUTION OF THE HOUSEHOLD** Determine whether each of the following would increase or decrease the opportunity costs for mothers who choose not to work outside the home. Explain your answers.

    a. Higher levels of education for women
    b. Higher unemployment rates for women
    c. Higher average pay levels for women
    d. Lower demand for labor in industries that traditionally employ large numbers of women

16. **HOUSEHOLD PRODUCTION** Many households supplement their food budget by cultivating small vegetable gardens. Explain how each of the following might influence this kind of household production:

    a. Both husband and wife are professionals who earn high salaries.
    b. The household is located in a city rather than in a rural area.
    c. The household is located in a region where there is a high sales tax on food.
    d. The household is located in a region that has a high property tax rate.

17. **GOVERNMENT** Complete each of the following sentences:

    a. When the private operation of a market leads to overproduction or underproduction of some good, this is known as a(n) _____.
    b. Goods that are nonrival and nonexclusive are known as _____.
    c. _____ are cash or in-kind benefits given to individuals as outright grants from the government.
    d. A(n) _____ confers an external benefit on third parties that are not directly involved in a market transaction.
    e. _____ refers to the government's pursuit of full employment and price stability through variations in taxes and government spending.

18. TAX RATES Suppose taxes are related to income level as follows:

Income	Taxes
$1,000	$200
$2,000	$350
$3,000	$450

a. What percentage of income is paid in taxes at each level?
b. Is the tax rate progressive, proportional, or regressive?
c. What is the marginal tax rate on the first $1,000 of income? The second $1,000? The third $1,000?

Global Economic Watch Exercises

Login to www.cengagebrain.com and access the Global Economic Watch to do these exercises.

19. GLOBAL ECONOMIC WATCH Go to the Global Economic Crisis Resource Center. Select Global Issues in Context. In the Basic Search box at the top of the page, enter the phrase "Not-So-Free Ride." On the Results page, scroll down to the Magazines section. Click on the link for the April 20, 2008, article "Not-So-Free Ride." Can you list negative externalities of driving in addition to the ones described in the article?

20. GLOBAL ECONOMIC WATCH Go to the Global Economic Crisis Resource Center. Global Issues in Context. In the Basic Search box at the top of the page, enter the terms "tax rate" and/or "tax rates." Find resources that are no more than three years old that describe tax rates in two foreign countries. Write an analysis of these tax rates in your own words.

Demand, Supply, and Markets

4

© Jason Moore/Alamy

○ Why do roses cost more on Valentine's Day than during the rest of the year?

○ Why do TV ads cost more during the Super Bowl ($3.0 million for 30 seconds in 2010) than during *Nick at Nite* reruns?

○ Why do Miami hotels charge more in February than in August?

○ Why do surgeons earn more than butchers?

○ Why do basketball pros earn more than hockey pros?

○ Why do economics majors earn more than most other majors?

Answers to these and most economic questions boil down to the workings of demand and supply—the subject of this chapter.

This chapter introduces demand and supply and shows how they interact in competitive markets. *Demand and supply are the most fundamental and the most powerful of all economic tools*—important enough to warrant a chapter. Indeed, some believe that if you program a computer to answer "demand and supply" to every economic question, you could put many economists out of work. An understanding of the two ideas will take you far in mastering the art and science of economic analysis. This chapter uses more graphs, so you may need to review the Chapter 1 appendix as a refresher.

Topics discussed include:

- Demand and quantity demanded
- Movement along a demand curve
- Shift of a demand curve
- Supply and quantity supplied
- Movement along a supply curve
- Shift of a supply curve
- Markets and equilibrium
- Disequilibrium

Demand

How many six packs of Pepsi will people buy each month at a price of $4? What if the price is $3? What if it's $5? The answers reveal the relationship between the price of a six pack and the quantity of Pepsi demanded. Such a relationship is called the *demand* for Pepsi. **Demand** indicates the quantity consumers are both *willing and able* to buy at each possible price during a given time period, other things constant. Because demand pertains to a specific period—a day, a week, a month—think of demand as the *amounts purchased per period* at each possible price. Also, notice the emphasis on *willing and able*. You may be *able* to buy a new Harley-Davidson Sportster Forty-Eight for $10,500 because you can afford one, but you may not be *willing* to buy one if motorcycles don't interest you.

demand

A relation between the price of a good and the quantity that consumers are willing and able to buy per period, other things constant

The Law of Demand

In 1962, Sam Walton opened his first store in Rogers, Arkansas, with a sign that read: "Wal-Mart Discount City. We sell for less." Wal-Mart now sells more than any other retailer in the world because prices there are among the lowest around. As a consumer, you understand why people buy more at a lower price. Sell for less, and the world will beat a path to your door. Wal-Mart, for example, sells on average over 20,000 pairs of shoes *an hour*. This relation between the price and the quantity demanded is an economic law. The **law of demand** says that quantity demanded varies inversely with price, other things constant. Thus, the higher the price, the smaller the quantity demanded; the lower the price, the greater the quantity demanded.

law of demand

The quantity of a good that consumers are willing and able to buy per period relates inversely, or negatively, to the price, other things constant

Demand, Wants, and Needs

Consumer demand and consumer wants are not the same. As we have seen, wants are unlimited. You may want a new Mercedes-Benz SL600 Roadster convertible, but the $139,100 price tag is likely beyond your budget (that is, the quantity you demand at that price is zero). Nor is demand the same as need. You may need a new muffler for your car, but a price of $300 is just too high for you right now. If, however, the price drops enough—say, to $200—then you become both willing and able to buy one.

The Substitution Effect of a Price Change

What explains the law of demand? Why, for example, is more demanded at a lower price? The explanation begins with unlimited wants confronting scarce resources. Many goods and services could satisfy particular wants. For example, you can satisfy your hunger with pizza, tacos, burgers, chicken, or hundreds of other foods. Similarly, you can satisfy your desire for warmth in the winter with warm clothing, a home-heating system, a trip to Hawaii, or in many other ways. Clearly, some alternatives have more appeal than others (a trip to Hawaii is more fun than warm clothing). In a world without scarcity, everything would be free, so you would always choose the most attractive alternative. Scarcity, however, is a reality, and the degree of scarcity of one good relative to another helps determine each good's relative price.

substitution effect of a price change

When the price of a good falls, that good becomes cheaper compared to other goods so consumers tend to substitute that good for other goods

Notice that the definition of *demand* includes the other-things-constant assumption. Among the "other things" assumed to remain constant are the prices of other goods. For example, if the price of pizza declines while other prices remain constant, pizza becomes relatively cheaper. Consumers are more *willing* to purchase pizza when its relative price falls; they substitute pizza for other goods. This principle is called the **substitution effect of a price change**. On the other hand, an increase in the price of pizza, other things constant, increases the opportunity cost of pizza—that is, the amount of other goods you must give up to buy pizza. This higher opportunity cost causes consumers to substitute other goods for the now higher-priced pizza, thus reducing their quantity of pizza demanded. Remember that *it is the change in the relative price—the price of one good relative to the prices of other goods—that causes the substitution effect.* If all prices changed by the same percentage, there would be no change in relative prices and no substitution effect.

The Income Effect of a Price Change

A fall in the price of a good increases the quantity demanded for a second reason. Suppose you earn $30 a week from a part-time job, so $30 is your money income. **Money income** is simply the number of dollars received per period, in this case, $30 per week. Suppose you spend all that on pizza, buying three a week at $10 each. What if the price drops to $6? At the lower price, you can now afford five pizzas a week. Your money income remains at $30 per week, but the decrease in the price has increased your **real income**—that is, your income measured in terms of what it can buy. The price reduction, other things constant, increases the purchasing power of your income, thereby increasing your ability to buy pizza. The quantity of pizza you demand will likely increase because of this **income effect of a price change**. You may not increase your quantity demanded to five pizzas, but you could. If you decide to purchase four pizzas a week when the price drops to $6, you would still have $6 remaining to buy other stuff. Thus, the income effect of a lower price increases your real income and thereby increases your ability to purchase all goods, making you better off. The income effect is reflected in Wal-Mart's slogan, which trumpets low prices: "Save money. Live better." Because of the income effect, consumers typically increase their quantity demanded when the price declines.

Conversely, an increase in the price of a good, other things constant, reduces real income, thereby reducing your *ability* to purchase all goods. Because of the income effect, consumers typically reduce their quantity demanded when the price increases. Again, note that money income, not real income, is assumed to remain constant along a demand curve. A change in price changes your real income, so real income varies along a demand curve. The lower the price, the greater your real income.

The Demand Schedule and Demand Curve

Demand can be expressed as a *demand schedule* or as a *demand curve.* Panel (a) of Exhibit 1 shows a hypothetical demand schedule for pizza. In describing demand, we must specify the units measured and the period considered. In our example, the unit is a 12-inch regular pizza and the period is a week. The schedule lists possible prices, along with the quantity demanded at each price. At a price of $15, for example, consumers demand 8 million pizzas per week. As you can see, the lower the price, other things constant, the greater the quantity demanded. Consumers substitute pizza for other foods. And as the price falls, real income increases, causing consumers to increase the quantity of pizza they demand. If the price drops as low as $3, consumers demand 32 million per week.

The demand schedule in panel (a) appears as a **demand curve** in panel (b), with price measured on the vertical axis and the quantity demanded per week on the horizontal axis. Each price-quantity combination listed in the demand schedule in the left panel becomes a point in the right panel. Point *a,* for example, indicates that if the price is $15, consumers demand 8 million pizzas per week. Connecting points forms the demand curve for pizza, labeled *D.* (By the way, some demand curves are straight lines, some are curved lines, and some are even jagged lines, but they all are called demand *curves.*)

money income
The number of dollars a person receives per period, such as $400 per week

real income
Income measured in terms of the goods and services it can buy; real income changes when the price changes

income effect of a price change
A fall in the price of a good increases consumers' real income, making consumers more able to purchase goods; for a normal good, the quantity demanded increases

demand curve
A curve showing the relation between the price of a good and the quantity consumers are willing and able to buy per period, other things constant

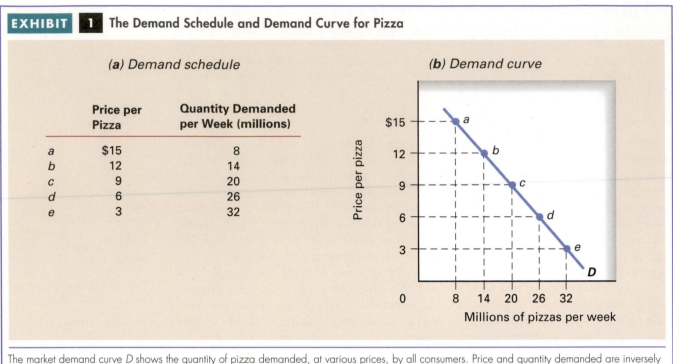

EXHIBIT 1   The Demand Schedule and Demand Curve for Pizza

(a) Demand schedule

	Price per Pizza	Quantity Demanded per Week (millions)
a	$15	8
b	12	14
c	9	20
d	6	26
e	3	32

(b) Demand curve

The market demand curve D shows the quantity of pizza demanded, at various prices, by all consumers. Price and quantity demanded are inversely related.

A demand curve slopes downward, reflecting the *law of demand*: Price and quantity demanded are inversely related, other things constant. Besides money income, also assumed constant along the demand curve are the prices of other goods. Thus, along the demand curve for pizza, the price of pizza changes *relative to the prices of other goods*. The demand curve shows the effect of a change in the *relative price* of pizza—that is, relative to other prices, which do not change.

Take care to distinguish between *demand* and *quantity demanded*. The *demand* for pizza is not a specific amount, but rather the *entire relationship* between price and quantity demanded—represented by the demand schedule or the demand curve. An individual point on the demand curve indicates the **quantity demanded** at a particular price. For example, at a price of $12, the quantity demanded is 14 million pizzas per week. If the price drops from $12 to, say, $9, this is shown in Exhibit 1 by *a movement along the demand curve*—in this case from point *b* to point *c*. Any movement along a demand curve reflects a *change in quantity demanded,* not a change in demand.

The law of demand applies to the millions of products sold in grocery stores, department stores, clothing stores, shoe stores, drugstores, music stores, bookstores, hardware stores, other retailers, travel agencies, and restaurants, as well as through mail-order catalogs, the *Yellow Pages,* classified ads, online sites, stock markets, real estate markets, job markets, flea markets, and all other markets. The law of demand applies even to choices that seem more personal than economic, such as whether or not to own a pet. For example, after New York City passed an anti-dog-litter law, law-abiding owners had to follow their dogs around the city with scoopers, plastic bags—whatever would do the job. Because the law in effect raised the personal cost of owning a dog, the

quantity demanded

The amount of a good consumers are willing and able to buy per period at a particular price, as reflected by a point on a demand curve

quantity of dogs demanded decreased. Some dogs were abandoned, increasing strays in the city. The number of dogs left at animal shelters doubled. The law of demand predicts this inverse relation between cost, or price, and quantity demanded.

It is useful to distinguish between **individual demand**, which is the demand of an individual consumer, and **market demand**, which is the sum of the individual demands of all consumers in the market. In most markets, there are many consumers, sometimes millions. Unless otherwise noted, when we talk about demand, we are referring to market demand, as shown in Exhibit 1.

Shifts of the Demand Curve

A demand curve isolates the relation between the price of a good and quantity demanded when other factors that could affect demand remain unchanged. What are those other factors, and how do changes in them affect demand? Variables that can affect market demand are (1) the money income of consumers, (2) prices of other goods, (3) consumer expectations, (4) the number or composition of consumers in the market, and (5) consumer tastes. How do changes in each affect demand?

Changes in Consumer Income

Exhibit 2 shows the market demand curve D for pizza. This demand curve assumes a given level of money income. Suppose consumer income increases. Some consumers are then willing and able to buy more pizza at each price, so market demand increases. The demand curve shifts to the right from D to D'. For example, at a price of $12,

individual demand
The relation between the price of a good and the quantity purchased by an individual consumer per period, other things constant

market demand
The relation between the price of a good and the quantity purchased by all consumers in the market during a given period, other things constant; sum of the individual demands in the market

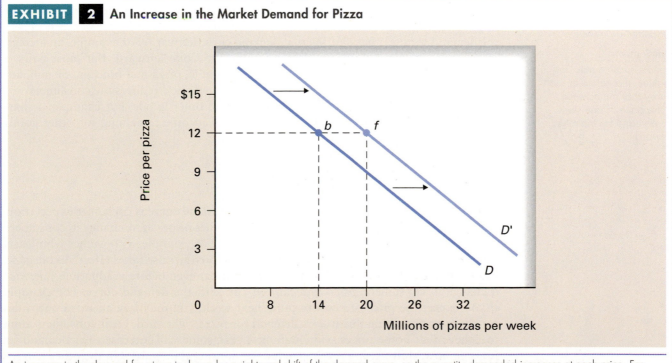

EXHIBIT 2 An Increase in the Market Demand for Pizza

An increase in the demand for pizza is shown by a rightward shift of the demand curve, so the quantity demanded increases at each price. For example, the quantity of pizza demanded at a price of $12 increases from 14 million (point b) to 20 million (point f).

the amount of pizza demanded increases from 14 million to 20 million per week, as indicated by the movement from point *b* on demand curve *D* to point *f* on demand curve *D′*. In short, *an increase in demand—that is, a rightward shift of the demand curve—means that consumers are willing and able to buy more pizza at each price.*

Goods are classified into two broad categories, depending on how consumers respond to changes in money income. The demand for a **normal good** increases as money income increases. Because pizza is a normal good, its demand curve shifts rightward when money income increases. Most goods are normal. In contrast, demand for an **inferior good** actually decreases as money income increases, so the demand curve shifts leftward. Examples of inferior goods include bologna sandwiches, used furniture, and used clothes. As money income increases, consumers tend to switch from these inferior goods to normal goods (such as roast beef sandwiches, new furniture, and new clothes).

Changes in the Prices of Other Goods

Again, the prices of other goods are assumed to remain constant along a given demand curve. Now let's bring these other prices into play. Consumers have various ways of trying to satisfy any particular want. Consumers choose among substitutes based on relative prices. For example, pizza and tacos are substitutes, though not perfect ones. An increase in the price of tacos, other things constant, reduces the quantity of tacos demanded along a given taco demand curve. An increase in the price of tacos also increases the demand for pizza, shifting the demand curve for pizza to the right. Two goods are considered **substitutes** if an increase in the price of one shifts the demand for the other rightward and, conversely, if a decrease in the price of one shifts demand for the other leftward.

Goods used in combination are called **complements**. Examples include Coke and pizza, milk and cookies, computer software and hardware, and airline tickets and rental cars. Two goods are considered **complements** if an increase in the price of one decreases the demand for the other, shifting that demand curve leftward. For example, an increase in the price of pizza shifts the demand curve for Coke leftward. But most pairs of goods selected at random are *unrelated*—for example, pizza and housing, or milk and gasoline. Still, an increase in the price of an unrelated good reduces the consumers' real income and can reduce the demand for pizza and other goods. For example, a sharp increase in housing prices reduces the amount of income remaining for other goods, such as pizza.

Changes in Consumer Expectations

Another factor assumed constant along a given demand curve is consumer expectations about factors that influence demand, such as incomes or prices. A change in consumers' *income expectations* can shift the demand curve. For example, a consumer who learns about a pay raise might increase demand well before the raise takes effect. A college senior who lands that first real job may buy a new car even before graduation. Likewise, a change in consumers' *price expectations* can shift the demand curve. For example, if you expect the price of pizza to jump next week, you may buy an extra one today for the freezer, shifting this week's demand for pizza rightward. Or if consumers come to believe that home prices will climb next year, some will increase their demand for housing now, shifting this year's demand for housing rightward. On the other hand, if housing prices are expected to fall next year, some consumers will postpone purchases, thereby shifting this year's housing demand leftward.

normal good
A good, such as new clothes, for which demand increases, or shifts rightward, as consumer income rises

inferior good
A good, such as used clothes, for which demand decreases, or shifts leftward, as consumer income rises

substitutes
Goods, such as Coke and Pepsi, that relate in such a way that an increase in the price of one shifts the demand for the other rightward

complements
Goods, such as milk and cookies, that relate in such a way that an increase in the price of one shifts the demand for the other leftward

Changes in the Number or Composition of Consumers

As mentioned earlier, the market demand curve is the sum of the individual demand curves of all consumers in the market. If the number of consumers changes, the demand curve will shift. For example, if the population grows, the demand curve for pizza will shift rightward. Even if total population remains unchanged, demand could shift with a change in the composition of the population. For example, an increase over time in the teenage population could shift pizza demand rightward. A baby boom would shift rightward the demand for car seats and baby food. A growing Latino population would affect the demand for Latino foods.

Changes in Consumer Tastes

Do you like anchovies on your pizza? How about sauerkraut on your hot dogs? Are you into tattoos and body piercings? Is music to your ears more likely to be rock, country, hip-hop, reggae, R&B, jazz, funk, Latin, gospel, new age, or classical? Choices in food, body art, music, clothing, books, movies, TV—indeed, all consumer choices—are influenced by consumer tastes. **Tastes** are nothing more than your likes and dislikes as a consumer. What determines tastes? Your desires for food when hungry and drink when thirsty are largely biological. So too is your desire for comfort, rest, shelter, friendship, love, status, personal safety, and a pleasant environment. Your family background affects some of your tastes—your taste in food, for example, has been shaped by years of home cooking. Other influences include the surrounding culture, peer pressure, and religious convictions. So economists can say a little about the origin of tastes, but they claim no special expertise in understanding how tastes develop and change over time. Economists recognize, however, that tastes have an important impact on demand. For example, although pizza is popular, some people just don't like it and those who are lactose intolerant can't stomach the cheese topping. Thus, most people like pizza but some don't.

In our analysis of consumer demand, *we will assume that tastes are given and are relatively stable*. Tastes are assumed to remain constant along a given demand curve. A change in the tastes for a particular good would shift that good's demand curve. For example, a discovery that the tomato sauce and cheese combination on pizza promotes overall health could change consumer tastes, shifting the demand curve for pizza to the right. But because a change in tastes is so difficult to isolate from other economic changes, we should be reluctant to attribute a shift of the demand curve to a change in tastes. We try to rule out other possible reasons for a shift of the demand curve before accepting a change in tastes as the explanation.

That wraps up our look at changes in demand. Before we turn to supply, you should remember the distinction between a **movement along a given demand curve** and a **shift of a demand curve**. A change in *price,* other things constant, causes a *movement along a demand curve,* changing the quantity demanded. A change in one of the determinants of demand other than price causes a *shift of a demand curve,* changing demand.

Supply

Just as demand is a relation between price and quantity demanded, supply is a relation between price and quantity supplied. **Supply** indicates how much producers are *willing* and *able* to offer for sale per period at each possible price, other things constant. The **law of supply** states that the quantity supplied is usually directly related to its price,

---

tastes
Consumer preferences; likes and dislikes in consumption; assumed to remain constant along a given demand curve

movement along a demand curve
Change in quantity demanded resulting from a change in the price of the good, other things constant

shift of a demand curve
Movement of a demand curve right or left resulting from a change in one of the determinants of demand other than the price of the good

supply
A relation between the price of a good and the quantity that producers are willing and able to sell per period, other things constant

law of supply
The amount of a good that producers are willing and able to sell per period is usually directly related to its price, other things constant

other things constant. Thus, the lower the price, the smaller the quantity supplied; the higher the price, the greater the quantity supplied.

The Supply Schedule and Supply Curve

supply curve
A curve showing the relation between price of a good and the quantity producers are willing and able to sell per period other things constant

Exhibit 3 presents the market *supply schedule* and market **supply curve** *S* for pizza. Both show the quantities supplied per week at various possible prices by the thousands of pizza makers in the economy. As you can see, price and quantity supplied are directly, or positively, related. Producers offer more at a higher price than at a lower price, so the supply curve slopes upward.

There are two reasons why producers offer more for sale when the price rises. First, as the price increases, other things constant, a producer becomes more *willing* to supply the good. Prices act as signals to existing and potential suppliers about the rewards for producing various goods. A higher pizza price attracts resources from lower-valued uses. *A higher price makes producers more willing to increase quantity supplied.*

Higher prices also increase the producer's *ability* to supply the good. The law of increasing opportunity cost, as noted in Chapter 2, states that the opportunity cost of producing more of a particular good rises as output increases—that is, the *marginal cost* of production increases as output increases. Because producers face a higher marginal cost for additional output, they need to get a higher price for that output to be *able* to increase the quantity supplied. *A higher price makes producers more able to increase quantity supplied.* As a case in point, a higher price for gasoline increases oil companies' ability to extract oil from tar sands, to drill deeper, and to explore in less accessible areas, such as the remote jungles of the Amazon, the stormy waters of the North Sea, and the frozen tundra above the Arctic Circle. For example, at a market

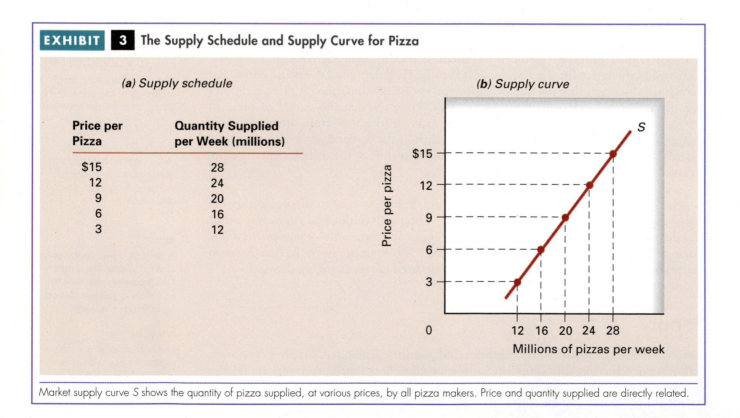

EXHIBIT   3   The Supply Schedule and Supply Curve for Pizza

(a) Supply schedule

Price per Pizza	Quantity Supplied per Week (millions)
$15	28
12	24
9	20
6	16
3	12

(b) Supply curve

Market supply curve *S* shows the quantity of pizza supplied, at various prices, by all pizza makers. Price and quantity supplied are directly related.

price of $50 per barrel, extracting oil from tar sands is unprofitable, but at price of $55 per barrel, producers are able to supply millions of barrels per month from tar sands.

Thus, a higher price makes producers more *willing* and more *able* to increase quantity supplied. Producers are more *willing* because production becomes more attractive than other uses of the resources involved. Producers are more *able* because they can afford to cover the higher marginal cost that typically results from increasing output.

On the other hand, a lower price makes production less attractive, so suppliers are less willing and less able to offer the good. For example, a mining company "reacted quickly to steep copper price declines in 2008 by curbing production at its North American sites and implementing layoffs at its mines and corporate headquarters."[1]

As with demand, we distinguish between *supply* and *quantity supplied*. *Supply* is the entire relationship between prices and quantities supplied, as reflected by the supply schedule or supply curve. **Quantity supplied** refers to a particular amount offered for sale at a particular price, as reflected by a point on a given supply curve. We also distinguish between **individual supply**, the supply of an individual producer, and **market supply**, the sum of individual supplies of all producers in the market. Unless otherwise noted, the term *supply* refers to market supply.

Shifts of the Supply Curve

The supply curve isolates the relation between the price of a good and the quantity supplied, other things constant. Assumed constant along a supply curve are the determinants of supply other than the price of the good, including (1) the state of technology, (2) the prices of resources, (3) the prices of other goods, (4) producer expectations, and (5) the number of producers in the market. Let's see how a change in each affects the supply curve.

Changes in Technology

Recall from Chapter 2 that the state of technology represents the economy's knowledge about how to combine resources efficiently. Along a given supply curve, technology is assumed to remain unchanged. If a better technology is discovered, production costs will fall; so suppliers will be more willing and able to supply the good at each price. For example, new techniques helped Marathon Oil cut drilling time for a new well from 56 days in 2006 to only 24 days in 2009.[2] Consequently, supply will increase, as reflected by a rightward shift of the supply curve. For example, suppose a new, high-tech oven that costs the same as existing ovens bakes pizza in half the time. Such a breakthrough would shift the market supply curve rightward, as from *S* to *S'* in Exhibit 4, where more is supplied at each possible price. For example, at a price of $12, the amount supplied increases from 24 million to 28 million pizzas, as shown in Exhibit 4 by the movement from point *g* to point *h*. In short, *an increase in supply—that is, a rightward shift of the supply curve—means that producers are willing and able to sell more pizza at each price.*

quantity supplied
The amount offered for sale per period at a particular price, as reflected by a point on a given supply curve

individual supply
The relation between the price of a good and the quantity an individual producer is willing and able to sell per period, other things constant

market supply
The relation between the price of a good and the quantity all producers are willing and able to sell per period, other things constant

---

1.   Andrew Johnson, "Freeport Outsourcing Will Cut 60 Valley Jobs," *Arizona Republic*, 23 February 2010.
2.   Ben Casselman, "Oil Industry Boom—in North Dakota," *Wall Street Journal*, 26 February 2010.

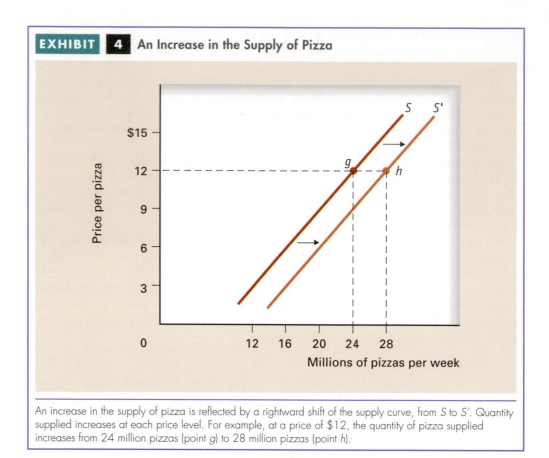

EXHIBIT 4 An Increase in the Supply of Pizza

An increase in the supply of pizza is reflected by a rightward shift of the supply curve, from S to S'. Quantity supplied increases at each price level. For example, at a price of $12, the quantity of pizza supplied increases from 24 million pizzas (point g) to 28 million pizzas (point h).

Changes in the Prices of Resources

The prices of resources employed to make the good affect the cost of production and therefore the supply of the good. For example, suppose the price of mozzarella cheese falls. This reduces the cost of making pizza, so producers are more willing and better able to supply it. The supply curve for pizza shifts rightward, as shown in Exhibit 4. On the other hand, an increase in the price of a resource reduces supply, meaning a shift of the supply curve leftward. For example, a higher price of mozzarella increases the cost of making pizza. Higher production costs decrease supply, as reflected by a leftward shift of the supply curve.

Changes in the Prices of Other Goods

Nearly all resources have alternative uses. The labor, building, machinery, ingredients, and knowledge needed to run a pizza business could produce other goods instead. A drop in the price of one of these other goods, with the price of pizza unchanged, makes pizza production more attractive. For example, if the price of Italian bread declines, some bread makers become pizza makers so the supply of pizza increases, shifting the supply curve of pizza rightward as in Exhibit 4. On the other hand, if the price of Italian bread increases, supplying pizza becomes relatively less attractive compared to supplying Italian bread. As resources shift from pizza to bread, the supply of pizza decreases, or shifts to the left.

Changes in Producer Expectations

Changes in producer expectations can shift the supply curve. For example, a pizza maker expecting higher pizza prices in the future may expand his or her pizzeria now, thereby shifting the supply of pizza rightward. When a good can be easily stored (crude oil, for example, can be left in the ground), expecting higher prices in the future might prompt some producers to *reduce* their current supply while awaiting the higher price. Thus, an expectation of higher prices in the future could either increase or decrease current supply, depending on the good. More generally, any change affecting future profitability, such as a change in business taxes, could shift the supply curve now.

Changes in the Number of Producers

Because market supply sums the amounts supplied at each price by all producers, market supply depends on the number of producers in the market. If that number increases, supply will increase, shifting supply to the right. If the number of producers decreases, supply will decrease, shifting supply to the left. As an example of increased supply, the number of gourmet coffee bars has more than quadrupled in the United States since 1990 (think Starbucks), shifting the supply curve of gourmet coffee to the right.

Finally, note again the distinction between a **movement along a supply curve** and a **shift of a supply curve**. A change in *price*, other things constant, causes *a movement along a supply curve*, changing the quantity supplied. A change in one of the determinants of supply other than price causes a *shift of a supply curve*, changing supply.

You are now ready to bring demand and supply together.

movement along a supply curve
Change in quantity supplied resulting from a change in the price of the good, other things constant

shift of a supply curve
Movement of a supply curve left or right resulting from a change in one of the determinants of supply other than the price of the good

Demand and Supply Create a Market

Demanders and suppliers have different views of price. Demanders pay the price and suppliers receive it. Thus, a higher price is bad news for consumers but good news for producers. As the price rises, consumers reduce their quantity demanded along the demand curve and producers increase their quantity supplied along the supply curve. How is this conflict between producers and consumers resolved?

Markets

Markets sort out differences between demanders and suppliers. A *market,* as you know from Chapter 1, includes all the arrangements used to buy and sell a particular good or service. Markets reduce **transaction costs**—the costs of time and information required for exchange. For example, suppose you are looking for a summer job. One approach might be to go from employer to employer looking for openings. But this could have you running around for days or weeks. A more efficient strategy would be to pick up a copy of the local newspaper or go online and look for openings. Classified ads and Web sites, which are elements of the job market, reduce the transaction costs of bringing workers and employers together.

The coordination that occurs through markets takes place not because of some central plan but because of Adam Smith's "invisible hand." For example, the auto dealers in your community tend to locate together, usually on the outskirts of town, where land is cheaper. The dealers congregate not because they all took an economics course or because they like one another's company but because grouped together they become a more attractive destination for car buyers. A dealer who makes the mistake of locating

transaction costs
The costs of time and information required to carry out market exchange

away from the others misses out on a lot of business. Similarly, stores locate together so that more shoppers will be drawn by the call of the mall. From Orlando theme parks to Broadway theaters to Las Vegas casinos, suppliers congregate to attract demanders. Some groupings can be quite specialized. For example, shops in Hong Kong that sell dress mannequins cluster along Austin Road. And diamond merchants in New York City congregate within a few blocks.

Market Equilibrium

To see how a market works, let's bring together market demand and market supply. Exhibit 5 shows the market for pizza, using schedules in panel (a) and curves in panel (b). Suppose the price initially is $12. At that price, producers supply 24 million

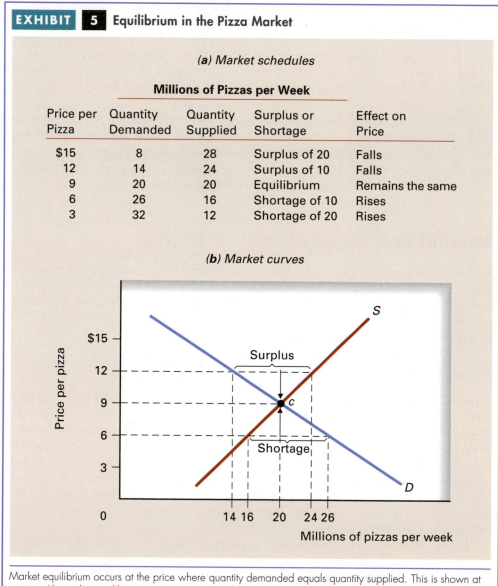

EXHIBIT   5   Equilibrium in the Pizza Market

(a) Market schedules

Millions of Pizzas per Week

Price per Pizza	Quantity Demanded	Quantity Supplied	Surplus or Shortage	Effect on Price
$15	8	28	Surplus of 20	Falls
12	14	24	Surplus of 10	Falls
9	20	20	Equilibrium	Remains the same
6	26	16	Shortage of 10	Rises
3	32	12	Shortage of 20	Rises

(b) Market curves

Market equilibrium occurs at the price where quantity demanded equals quantity supplied. This is shown at point c. Above the equilibrium price, quantity supplied exceeds quantity demanded. This creates a surplus, which puts downward pressure on the price. Below the equilibrium price, quantity demanded exceeds quantity supplied. The resulting shortage puts upward pressure on the price.

pizzas per week, but consumers demand only 14 million, resulting in an *excess quantity supplied,* or a **surplus,** of 10 million pizzas per week. Suppliers don't like getting stuck with unsold pizzas. Their desire to eliminate the surplus puts downward pressure on the price, as shown by the arrow pointing down in the graph. As the price falls, producers reduce their quantity supplied and consumers increase their quantity demanded. The price continues to fall as long as quantity supplied exceeds quantity demanded.

Alternatively, suppose the price initially is $6. You can see from Exhibit 5 that at that price consumers demand 26 million pizzas but producers supply only 16 million, resulting in an *excess quantity demanded,* or a **shortage,** of 10 million pizzas per week. Producers quickly notice they have sold out and those customers still demanding pizzas are grumbling. Profit-maximizing producers and frustrated consumers create market pressure for a higher price, as shown by the arrow pointing up in the graph. As the price rises, producers increase their quantity supplied and consumers reduce their quantity demanded. The price continues to rise as long as quantity demanded exceeds quantity supplied.

Thus, *a surplus creates downward pressure on the price, and a shortage creates upward pressure.* As long as quantity demanded differs from quantity supplied, this difference forces a price change. Note that a shortage or a surplus depends on the price. There is no such thing as a general shortage or a general surplus, only a shortage or a surplus at a particular price.

A market reaches equilibrium when the quantity demanded equals quantity supplied. In **equilibrium,** the independent plans of buyers and sellers exactly match, so market forces exert no pressure for change. In Exhibit 5, the demand and supply curves intersect at the *equilibrium point,* identified as point *c.* The *equilibrium price* is $9 per pizza, and the *equilibrium quantity* is 20 million per week. At that price and quantity, the market *clears.* Because there is no shortage or surplus, there is no pressure for the price to change. The demand and supply curves form an "x" at the intersection. The equilibrium point is found where "x" marks the spot.

A market finds equilibrium through the independent actions of thousands, or even millions, of buyers and sellers. In one sense, the market is personal because each consumer and each producer makes a personal decision about how much to buy or sell at a given price. In another sense, the market is impersonal because it requires no conscious communication or coordination among consumers or producers. The price does all the talking. *Impersonal market forces synchronize the personal and independent decisions of many individual buyers and sellers to achieve equilibrium price and quantity.* Prices reflect relative scarcity. For example, to rent a 26-foot truck one-way from San Francisco to Austin, U-Haul recently charged $3,236. Its one-way charge for that same truck from Austin to San Francisco was just $399. Why the difference? Far more people wanted to move from San Francisco to Austin than vice versa, so U-Haul had to pay its own employees to drive the empty trucks back from Texas. Rental rates reflected that extra cost.

surplus
At a given price, the amount by which quantity supplied exceeds quantity demanded; a surplus usually forces the price down

shortage
At a given price, the amount by which quantity demanded exceeds quantity supplied; a shortage usually forces the price up

equilibrium
The condition that exists in a market when the plans of buyers match those of sellers, so quantity demanded equals quantity supplied and the market clears

Changes in Equilibrium Price and Quantity

Equilibrium occurs when the intentions of demanders and suppliers exactly match. Once a market reaches equilibrium, that price and quantity prevail until something happens to demand or supply. A change in any determinant of demand or supply usually changes equilibrium price and quantity in a predictable way, as you'll see.

net bookmark
The Inomics search engine at http://www.inomics.com/cgi/show is devoted solely to economics. Use it to investigate topics related to demand and supply and to other economic models.

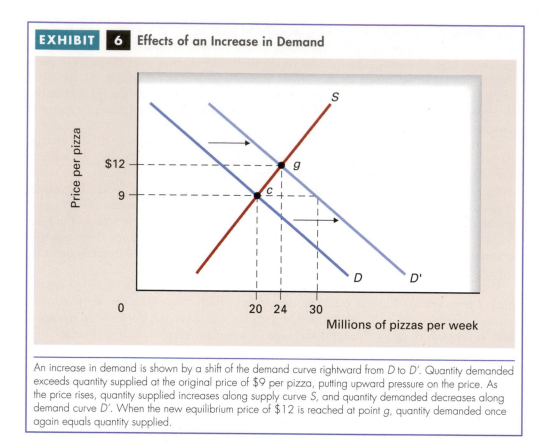

EXHIBIT **6** **Effects of an Increase in Demand**

An increase in demand is shown by a shift of the demand curve rightward from D to D'. Quantity demanded exceeds quantity supplied at the original price of $9 per pizza, putting upward pressure on the price. As the price rises, quantity supplied increases along supply curve S, and quantity demanded decreases along demand curve D'. When the new equilibrium price of $12 is reached at point g, quantity demanded once again equals quantity supplied.

Shifts of the Demand Curve

In Exhibit 6, demand curve D and supply curve S intersect at point c to yield the initial equilibrium price of $9 and the initial equilibrium quantity of 20 million 12-inch regular pizzas per week. Now suppose that one of the determinants of demand changes in a way that increases demand, shifting the demand curve to the right from D to D'. Any of the following could shift the demand for pizza rightward: (1) an increase in the money income of consumers (because pizza is a normal good); (2) an increase in the price of a substitute, such as tacos, or a decrease in the price of a complement, such as Coke; (3) a change in consumer expectations that causes people to demand more pizzas now; (4) a growth in the number of pizza consumers; or (5) a change in consumer tastes—based, for example, on a discovery that the tomato sauce on pizza has antioxidant properties that improve overall health.

After the demand curve shifts rightward to D' in Exhibit 6, the amount demanded at the initial price of $9 is 30 million pizzas, which exceeds the amount supplied of 20 million by 10 million pizzas. This shortage puts upward pressure on the price. As the price increases, the quantity demanded decreases along the new demand curve D', and the quantity supplied increases along the existing supply curve S until the two quantities are equal once again at equilibrium point g. The new equilibrium price is $12, and the new equilibrium quantity is 24 million pizzas per week. Thus, given an upward-sloping supply curve, an increase in demand increases both equilibrium price and quantity. A decrease in demand would lower both equilibrium price and quantity.

These results can be summarized as follows: *Given an upward-sloping supply curve, a rightward shift of the demand curve increases both equilibrium price and quantity and a leftward shift decreases both equilibrium price and quantity.*

Shifts of the Supply Curve

Let's now consider shifts of the supply curve. In Exhibit 7, as before, we begin with demand curve D and supply curve S intersecting at point c to yield an equilibrium price of $9 and an equilibrium quantity of 20 million pizzas per week. Suppose one of the determinants of supply changes, increasing supply from S to S'. Changes that could shift the supply curve rightward include (1) a technological breakthrough in pizza ovens; (2) a reduction in the price of a resource such as mozzarella cheese; (3) a decline in the price of another good such as Italian bread; (4) a change in expectations that encourages pizza makers to expand production now; or (5) an increase in the number of pizzerias.

After the supply curve shifts rightward in Exhibit 7, the amount supplied at the initial price of $9 increases from 20 million to 30 million, so producers now supply 10 million more pizzas than consumers demand. This surplus forces the price down. As the price falls, the quantity supplied declines along the new supply curve and the quantity demanded increases along the existing demand curve until a new equilibrium point d is established. The new equilibrium price is $6, and the new equilibrium quantity is 26 million pizzas per week. In short, an increase in supply reduces the price and increases the quantity. On the other hand, a decrease in supply increases the price but decreases the quantity. Thus, *given a downward-sloping demand curve, a rightward shift of the supply curve decreases price but increases quantity, and a leftward shift increases price but decreases quantity.*

EXHIBIT 7 Effects of an Increase in Supply

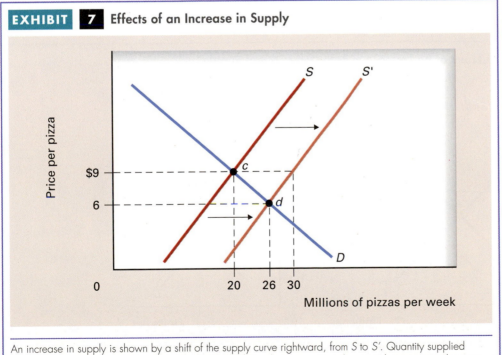

An increase in supply is shown by a shift of the supply curve rightward, from S to S'. Quantity supplied exceeds quantity demanded at the original price of $9 per pizza, putting downward pressure on the price. As the price falls, quantity supplied decreases along supply curve S', and quantity demanded increases along demand curve D. When the new equilibrium price of $6 is reached at point d, quantity demanded once again equals quantity supplied.

Simultaneous Shifts of Demand and Supply Curves

As long as only one curve shifts, we can say for sure how equilibrium price and quantity will change. If both curves shift, however, the outcome is less obvious. For example, suppose both demand and supply increase, or shift rightward, as in Exhibit 8. Note that in panel (a), demand shifts more than supply, and in panel (b), supply shifts more than demand. In both panels, equilibrium quantity increases. The change in equilibrium price, however, depends on which curve shifts more. If demand shifts more, as in panel (a), equilibrium price increases. For example, between 1995 and 2005, the demand for housing increased more than the supply, so both price and quantity increased. But if supply shifts more, as in panel (b), equilibrium price decreases. For example, in the last decade, the supply of personal computers has increased more than the demand, so price has decreased and quantity increased.

Conversely, if both demand and supply decrease, or shift leftward, equilibrium quantity decreases. But, again, we cannot say what will happen to equilibrium price unless we examine relative shifts. (You can use Exhibit 8 to consider decreases in demand and supply by viewing D' and S' as the initial curves.) If demand shifts more, the price will fall. If supply shifts more, the price will rise.

If demand and supply shift in opposite directions, we can say what will happen to equilibrium price. Equilibrium price will increase if demand increases and supply decreases. Equilibrium price will decrease if demand decreases and supply increases. Without reference to particular shifts, however, we cannot say what will happen to equilibrium quantity.

These results are no doubt confusing, but Exhibit 9 summarizes the four possible combinations of changes. Using Exhibit 9 as a reference, please take the time right now to work through some changes in demand and supply to develop a feel for the results. Then, in the following case study, evaluate changes in the market for professional basketball.

EXHIBIT 8 Indeterminate Effect of an Increase in Both Demand and Supply

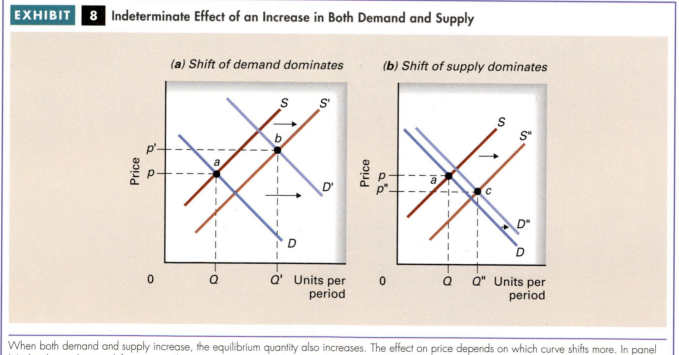

When both demand and supply increase, the equilibrium quantity also increases. The effect on price depends on which curve shifts more. In panel (a), the demand curve shifts more, so the price rises. In panel (b), the supply curve shifts more, so the price falls.

EXHIBIT 9 **Effects of Shifts of Both Demand and Supply**

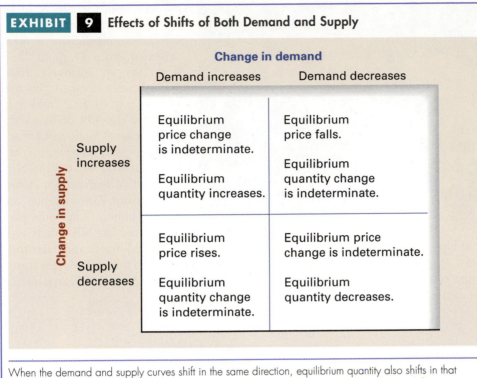

When the demand and supply curves shift in the same direction, equilibrium quantity also shifts in that direction. The effect on equilibrium price depends on which curve shifts more. If the curves shift in opposite directions, equilibrium price will move in the same direction as demand. The effect on equilibrium quantity depends on which curve shifts more.

WORLD OF BUSINESS

The Market for Professional Basketball   Toward the end of the 1970s, the NBA seemed on the brink of collapse. Attendance had sunk to little more than half the capacity. Some teams were nearly bankrupt. Championship games didn't even merit prime-time television coverage. But in the 1980s, three superstars turned things around. Michael Jordan, Larry Bird, and Magic Johnson added millions of fans and breathed new life into the sagging league. Successive generations of stars, including Dwayne Wade, Kevin Durant, and LeBron James, continue to fuel interest.

Since 1980 the league has expanded from 22 to 30 teams and attendance has more than doubled. More importantly, league revenue from broadcast rights jumped nearly *50-fold* from $19 million per year in the 1978–1982 contract to $930 million per year in the current contract, which runs to 2016. Popularity also increased around the world as international players, such as Dirk Nowitzki of Germany and Yao Ming of China, joined the league (basketball is now the most widely played team sport in China). NBA rosters now include more than 80 international players. The NBA formed marketing alliances with global companies such as Coca-Cola and McDonald's, and league playoffs are now televised in more than 200 countries in 45 languages to a potential market of 3 billion people.

What's the key resource in the production of NBA games? Talented players. Exhibit 10 shows the market for NBA players, with demand and supply in 1980 as D_{1980} and S_{1980}. The intersection of these two curves generated an average pay in 1980 of $170,000, or $0.17 million, for the 300 or so players then in the league. Since 1980, the talent pool expanded somewhat, so the supply curve in 2010 was more like S_{2010} (almost

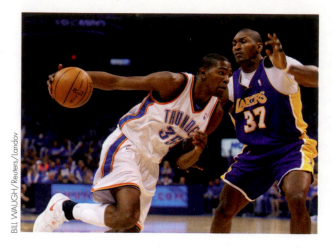

by definition, the supply of the top few hundred players in the world is limited). But demand exploded from D_{1980} to D_{2010}. With supply relatively fixed, the greater demand boosted average pay to $6.0 million by 2010 for the 450 or so players in the league. Such pay attracts younger and younger players. Stars who entered the NBA right out of high school include Kobe Bryant, Kevin Garnett, and LeBron James. (After nine players entered the NBA draft right out of high school in 2005, the league, to stem the flow, required draft candidates to be at least 19 years old and out of high school at least one year. So talented players started turning pro after their first year of college; in 2008, for example, 12 college freshman were drafted including five of the top seven picks.)

EXHIBIT 10   NBA Pay Leaps

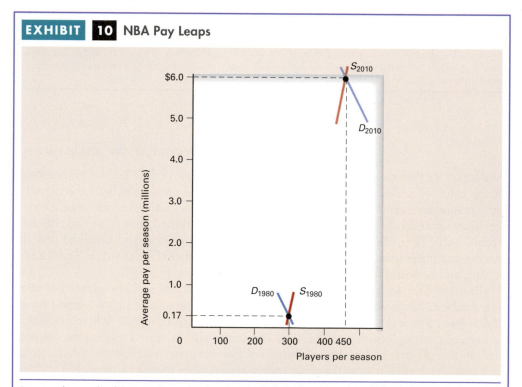

Because the supply of the world's top few hundred basketball players is relatively fixed by definition, the big jump in the demand for such talent caused average league pay to explode. Average pay increased from $170,000 in 1980 to $6,000,000 in 2010. Because the number of teams in the NBA increased, the number of players in the league grew from about 300 to about 450.

Sources: Howard Beck, "Falk Says NBA and Players Headed for Trouble," *New York Times,* 13 February 2010; Jonathan Abrams, "NBA's Shrinking Salary Cap Could Shake Up 2010 Free Agency," *New York Times,* 8 July 2010; and U.S. Census Bureau, *Statistical Abstract of the United States: 2010* at http://www.census.gov/compendia/statab/.

But rare talent alone does not command high pay. Top rodeo riders, top bowlers, and top women basketball players also possess rare talent, but the demand for their talent is not sufficient to support pay anywhere near NBA levels. NBA players earn on average nearly 100 times more than WNBA players. For example, Diana Taurasi, a great University of Connecticut player, earned only $40,800 her first WNBA season. Some sports aren't even popular enough to support professional leagues.

NBA players are now the highest-paid team athletes in the world—earning at least double that of professionals in baseball, football, and hockey. Both demand *and* supply determine average pay. But the NBA is not without its problems. In 2010 NBA players received 57 percent of all team revenue. Some team owners say they have been losing money, so they want to cut the share of revenue going to players. To cut costs, some teams, such as the Detroit Pistons, have traded their highest paid players.

Disequilibrium

A surplus exerts downward pressure on the price, and a shortage exerts upward pressure. Markets, however, don't always reach equilibrium quickly. During the time required to adjust, the market is said to be in disequilibrium. **Disequilibrium** is usually temporary as the market gropes for equilibrium. But sometimes, often as a result of government intervention, disequilibrium can last a while, perhaps decades, as we will see next.

Price Floors

Sometimes public officials set prices above their equilibrium levels. For example, the federal government regulates some agriculture prices in an attempt to ensure farmers a higher and more stable income than they would otherwise earn. To achieve higher prices, the government sets a **price floor**, or a *minimum* selling price that is above the equilibrium price. Panel (a) of Exhibit 11 shows the effect of a $2.50 per gallon price floor for milk. At that price, farmers supply 24 million gallons per week, but consumers demand only 14 million gallons, yielding a surplus of 10 million gallons. This surplus milk will pile up on store shelves, eventually souring. To take it off the market, the government usually agrees to buy the surplus milk. The federal government, in fact, has spent billions buying and storing surplus agricultural products. Note, to have an impact, a price floor must be set *above* the equilibrium price. A price floor set at or below the equilibrium price wouldn't matter (how come?). Price floors distort markets and reduce economic welfare.

Price Ceilings

Sometimes public officials try to keep a price below the equilibrium level by setting a **price ceiling**, or a *maximum* selling price. Concern about the rising cost of rental housing in some cities prompted city officials to impose rent ceilings. Panel (b) of Exhibit 11 depicts the demand and supply of rental housing. The vertical axis shows monthly rent, and the horizontal axis shows the quantity of rental units. The equilibrium, or market-clearing, rent is $1,000 per month, and the equilibrium quantity is 50,000 housing units. Suppose city officials set a maximum rent of $600 per month. At that ceiling price, 60,000 rental units are demanded, but only 40,000 supplied, resulting in a housing shortage of 20,000 units. Because of the price ceiling, the rental price no longer rations housing to those who value it the most. Other devices emerge to ration housing,

disequilibrium
The condition that exists in a market when the plans of buyers do not match those of sellers; a temporary mismatch between quantity supplied and quantity demanded as the market seeks equilibrium

price floor
A minimum legal price below which a product cannot be sold; to have an impact, a price floor must be set above the equilibrium price

price ceiling
A maximum legal price above which a product cannot be sold; to have an impact, a price ceiling must be set below the equilibrium price

EXHIBIT 11   Price Floors and Price Ceilings

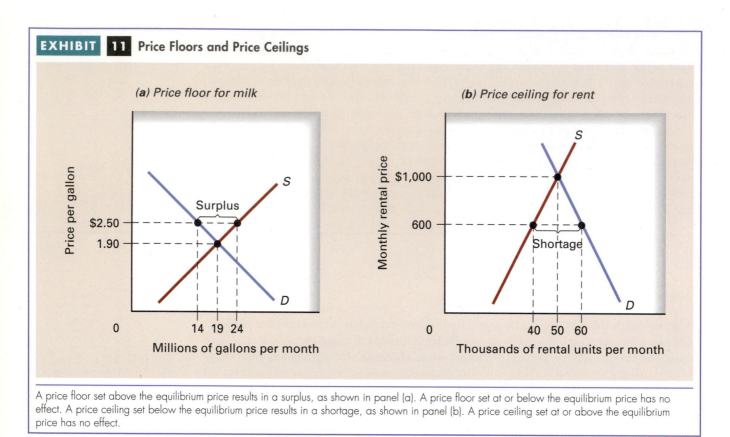

A price floor set above the equilibrium price results in a surplus, as shown in panel (a). A price floor set at or below the equilibrium price has no effect. A price ceiling set below the equilibrium price results in a shortage, as shown in panel (b). A price ceiling set at or above the equilibrium price has no effect.

such as long waiting lists, personal connections, and the willingness to make under-the-table payments, such as "key fees," "finder's fees," high security deposits, and the like. To have an impact, a price ceiling must be set *below* the equilibrium price. A price ceiling set at or above the equilibrium level wouldn't matter. Price floors and ceilings distort markets and reduce economic welfare. Let's take a closer look at rent ceilings in New York City in the following case study.

CASE STUDY

e activity

The New York State Division of Housing and Community Renewal features a number of fact sheets on rent control, stabilization, rent adjustments, special rights programs, and much more, at their Web site. Visit the site to see what kinds of problems exist with services, utilities, and other issues, at http://www.dhcr.state.ny.us/Rent/FactSheets/.

BRINGING THEORY TO LIFE

Rent Ceilings in New York City   New York City rent controls began after World War II, when greater demand for rental housing threatened to push rents higher. To keep rents from rising to their equilibrium level, city officials imposed rent ceilings. Since the quantity demanded at the ceiling rent exceeded the quantity supplied, a housing shortage resulted, as was sketched out in panel (b) of Exhibit 11. Thus, the perverse response to a tight housing market was a policy that reduced the supply of housing over time. The city-wide vacancy rate was recently just 3 percent.

Prior to rent controls, builders in New York City completed about 30,000 housing units a year and 90,000 units in the peak year. After rent controls, new construction dropped sharply. To stimulate supply, the city periodically promised rent-ceiling exemptions for new construction. But three times the city broke that promise after the housing was built. So builders remain understandably wary. During the peak year of the last decade only about 10,000 new housing units were built.

The excess demand for housing in the rent-controlled sector spilled into the free-market sector, increasing demand there. This greater demand raised rents in the free-market sector, making a rent-controlled apartment that much more attractive.

New York City rent regulations now cover about 70 percent of the 2.1 million rental apartments in the city.

Tenants in rent-controlled apartments are entitled to stay until they die, and with a little planning, they can pass the apartment to their heirs. Rent control forces tenants into housing choices they would not otherwise make. After the kids have grown and one spouse has died, the last parent standing usually remains in an apartment too big for one person but too much of a bargain to give up. An heir will often stay for the same reason. Some people keep rent-controlled apartments as weekend retreats for decades after they have moved from New York. All this wastes valuable resources and worsens the city's housing shortage.

Since there is excess quantity demanded for rent-controlled apartments, landlords have less incentive to maintain apartments in good shape. A survey found that about 30 percent of rent-controlled housing in the United States was deteriorating versus only 8 percent of free-market housing. Similar results have been found for England and France. Sometimes the rent is so low that owners simply abandon their property. During one decade, owners abandoned a third of a million units in New York City. So rent controls reduce both the quality and the quantity of housing available.

You would think that rent control benefits the poor most, but it hasn't worked out that way. Henry Pollakowski, an MIT housing economist, concludes that tenants in low- and moderate-income areas get little or no benefit from rent control. But some rich people living in a rent-controlled apartment in the nicest part of town get a substantial windfall. Someone renting in upscale sections of Manhattan might pay only $1,000 a month for a three-bedroom apartment that would rent for $12,000 a month on the open market. According to a recent study, more than 87,000 New York City households with incomes exceeding $100,000 a year benefited from rent control by paying below-market rents.

Once a tenant leaves a rent-controlled apartment, landlords can raise the rent on the next tenant and under some circumstances can escape rent controls entirely. With so much at stake, landlords under rent control have a strong incentive to oust a tenant. Some landlords have been known to pay $5,000 bounties to doormen who report tenants violating their lease (for example, the apartment is not the tenant's primary residence or the tenant is illegally subletting). Landlords also hire private detectives to identify lease violators. And landlords use professional "facilitators" to negotiate with tenants about moving out. Many tenants end up getting paid hundreds of thousands of dollars for agreeing to move. Some have been paid more than $1 million. Facilitators can often find tenants a better apartment in the free-market sector along with enough cash to cover the higher rent for, say, 10 years. Since the rental market is in disequilibrium, other markets, such as the market for buying out tenants, kick in.

Sources: Edward Glaeser and Erzo Luttmer, "The Misallocation of Housing Under Rent Control," *American Economic Review*, 93 (September 1993): 1027–1046; Henry Pollakowski, "Who Really Benefits from New York City's Rent Regulation System?" Civic Report 34 (March 2003) at http://manhattan-institute.org/pdf/cr_34.pdf. Janny Scott, "Illegal Sublets Put Private Eyes on the Cast," *New York Times*, 27 January 2007; and Eileen Norcross, "Rent Control Is the Real New York Scandal," *Wall Street Journal*, September 13, 2008. The New York City Rent Guideline Board's Web site is at http://www.housingnyc.com/html/resources/dhcr/dhcr1.html.

Government intervention is not the only source of market disequilibrium. Sometimes, when new products are introduced or when demand suddenly changes, it takes a while to reach equilibrium. For example, popular toys, best-selling books, and chart-busting CDs sometimes sell out. On the other hand, some new products attract few customers and pile up unsold on store shelves, awaiting a "clearance sale."

Conclusion

Demand and supply are the building blocks of a market economy. Although a market usually involves the interaction of many buyers and sellers, few markets are consciously designed. Just as the law of gravity works whether or not we understand Newton's principles, market forces operate whether or not participants understand demand and supply. These forces arise naturally, much the way car dealers cluster on the outskirts of town to attract more customers.

Markets have their critics. Some observers may be troubled, for example, that an NBA star like Kevin Garnett earns a salary that could pay for 500 new schoolteachers, or that corporate executives, such as the head of Goldman Sachs, a financial firm, earns enough to pay for 1,000 new schoolteachers, or that U.S. consumers spend over $40 billion on their pets. On your next trip to the supermarket, notice how much shelf space goes to pet products—often an entire aisle. PetSmart, a chain store, sells over 12,000 different pet items. Veterinarians offer cancer treatment, cataract removal, root canals, even acupuncture. Kidney dialysis for a pet can cost over $75,000 per year.

In a market economy, consumers are kings and queens. Consumer sovereignty rules, deciding what gets produced. Those who don't like the market outcome usually look to government for a solution through price ceilings and price floors, regulations, income redistribution, and public finance more generally.

Summary

1. Demand is a relationship between the price of a product and the quantity consumers are willing and able to buy per period, other things constant. According to the law of demand, quantity demanded varies negatively, or inversely, with the price, so the demand curve slopes downward.

2. A demand curve slopes downward for two reasons. A price decrease makes consumers (a) more *willing* to substitute this good for other goods and (b) more *able* to buy the good because the lower price increases real income.

3. Assumed to remain constant along a demand curve are (a) money income, (b) prices of other goods, (c) consumer expectations, (d) the number or composition of consumers in the market, and (e) consumer tastes. A change in any of these could shift, or change, the demand curve.

4. Supply is a relationship between the price of a good and the quantity producers are willing and able to sell per period, other things constant. According to the law of supply, price and quantity supplied are usually positively, or directly, related, so the supply curve typically slopes upward.

5. The supply curve slopes upward because higher prices make producers (a) more *willing* to supply this good rather than supply other goods that use the same resources and (b) more *able* to cover the higher marginal cost associated with greater output rates.

6. Assumed to remain constant along a supply curve are (a) the state of technology; (b) the prices of resources used to produce the good; (c) the prices of other goods that could be produced with these resources; (d) supplier expectations; and (e) the number of producers in this market. A change in any of these could shift, or change, the supply curve.

7. Demand and supply come together in the market for the good. A market provides information about the price, quantity, and quality of the good. In doing so, a market reduces the transaction costs of exchange—the costs of time and information required for buyers and sellers to make a deal. The interaction of demand and supply guides resources and products to their highest-valued use.

8. Impersonal market forces reconcile the personal and independent plans of buyers and sellers. Market equilibrium, once established, will continue unless there is a change in a determinant that shapes demand or supply. Disequilibrium is usually temporary while markets seek equilibrium, but sometimes

disequilibrium lasts a while, such as when government regulates the price.

9. A price floor is the minimum legal price below which a particular good or service cannot be sold. The federal government imposes price floors on some agricultural products to help farmers achieve a higher and more stable income than would be possible with freer markets. If the floor price is set above the market clearing price, quantity supplied exceeds quantity demanded. Policy makers must figure out some way to prevent this surplus from pushing the price down.

10. A price ceiling is a maximum legal price above which a particular good or service cannot be sold. Governments sometimes impose price ceilings to reduce the price of some consumer goods such as rental housing. If the ceiling price is below the market clearing price, quantity demanded exceeds the quantity supplied, creating a shortage. Because the price system is not allowed to clear the market, other mechanisms arise to ration the product among demanders.

Key Concepts

Demand   72
Law of demand   72
Substitution effect of a price change   72
Money income   73
Real income   73
Income effect of a price change   73
Demand curve   73
Quantity demanded   74
Individual demand   75
Market demand   75
Normal good   76

Inferior good   76
Substitutes   76
Complements   76
Tastes   77
Movement along a demand curve   77
Shift of a demand curve   77
Supply   77
Law of supply   77
Supply curve   78
Quantity supplied   79
Individual supply   79

Market supply   79
Movement along a supply curve   81
Shift of a supply curve   81
Transaction costs   81
Surplus   83
Shortage   83
Equilibrium   83
Disequilibrium   89
Price floor   89
Price ceiling   89

Questions for Review

1. LAW OF DEMAND   What is the law of demand? Give two examples of how you have observed the law of demand at work in the "real world." How is the law of demand related to the demand curve?

2. CHANGES IN DEMAND   What variables influence the demand for a normal good? Explain why a reduction in the price of a normal good does not increase the demand for that good.

3. SUBSTITUTION AND INCOME EFFECTS   Distinguish between the substitution effect and income effect of a price change. If a good's price increases, does each effect have a positive or a negative impact on the quantity demanded?

4. DEMAND   Explain the effect of an increase in consumer income on the demand for a good.

5. INCOME EFFECTS   When moving along the demand curve, income must be assumed constant. Yet one factor that can cause a change in the quantity demanded is the "income effect." Reconcile these seemingly contradictory facts.

6. DEMAND   If chocolate is found to have positive health benefits, would this lead to a shift of the demand curve or a movement along the demand curve?

7. SUPPLY   What is the law of supply? Give an example of how you have observed the law of supply at work. What is the relationship between the law of supply and the supply curve?

8. CHANGES IN SUPPLY   What kinds of changes in underlying conditions can cause the supply curve to shift? Give some examples and explain the direction in which the curve shifts.

9. SUPPLY   If a severe frost destroys some of Florida's citrus crop, would this lead to a shift of the supply curve or a movement along the supply curve?

10. MARKETS   How do markets coordinate the independent decisions of buyers and sellers?

11. Case Study: The Market for Professional Basketball   In what sense can we speak of a market for professional basketball? Who are the demanders and who are the suppliers? What are some examples of how changes in supply or demand conditions have affected this market?

Problems and Exercises

12. **Shifting Demand**   Using demand and supply curves, show the effect of each of the following on the market for cigarettes:

    a. A cure for lung cancer is found.
    b. The price of cigars increases.
    c. Wages increase substantially in states that grow tobacco.
    d. A fertilizer that increases the yield per acre of tobacco is discovered.
    e. There is a sharp increase in the price of matches, lighters, and lighter fluid.
    f. More states pass laws restricting smoking in restaurants and public places.

13. **Substitutes and Complements**   For each of the following pair of goods, determine whether the goods are substitutes, complements, or unrelated:

    a. Peanut butter and jelly
    b. Private and public transportation
    c. Coke and Pepsi
    d. Alarm clocks and automobiles
    e. Golf clubs and golf balls

14. **Equilibrium**   "If a price is not an equilibrium price, there is a tendency for it to move to its equilibrium level. Regardless of whether the price is too high or too low to begin with, the adjustment process will increase the quantity of the good purchased." Explain, using a demand and supply diagram.

15. **Equilibrium**   Assume the market for corn is depicted as in the table that appears below.

    a. Complete the table below.
    b. What market pressure occurs when quantity demanded exceeds quantity supplied? Explain.
    c. What market pressure occurs when quantity supplied exceeds quantity demanded? Explain.
    d. What is the equilibrium price?
    e. What could change the equilibrium price?
    f. At each price in the first column of the table, how much is sold?

16. **Market Equilibrium**   Determine whether each of the following statements is true, false, or uncertain. Then briefly explain each answer.

    a. In equilibrium, all sellers can find buyers.
    b. In equilibrium, there is no pressure on the market to produce or consume more than is being sold.

    c. At prices above equilibrium, the quantity exchanged exceeds the quantity demanded.
    d. At prices below equilibrium, the quantity exchanged is equal to the quantity supplied.

17. **Demand and Supply**   How do you think each of the following affected the world price of oil? (Use demand and supply analysis.)

    a. Tax credits were offered for expenditures on home insulation.
    b. The Alaskan oil pipeline was completed.
    c. The ceiling on the price of oil was removed.
    d. Oil was discovered in the North Sea.
    e. Sport utility vehicles and minivans became popular.
    f. The use of nuclear power declined.

18. **Demand and Supply**   What happens to the equilibrium price and quantity of ice cream in response to each of the following? Explain your answers.

    a. The price of dairy cow fodder increases.
    b. The price of beef decreases.
    c. Concerns arise about the fat content of ice cream. Simultaneously, the price of sugar (used to produce ice cream) increases.

19. **Equilibrium**   Consider the following graph in which demand and supply are initially D and S, respectively. What are the equilibrium price and quantity? If demand increases to D', what are the new equilibrium price and quantity? What happens if the government does not allow the price to change when demand increases?

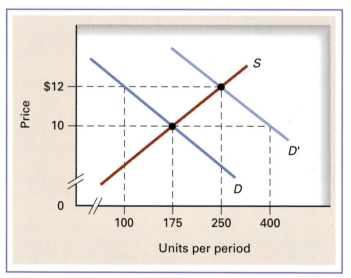

Price per Bushel ($)	Quantity Demanded (millions of bushels)	Quantity Supplied (millions of bushels)	Surplus/ Shortage	Will Price Rise or Fall?
1.80	320	200	_____	_____
2.00	300	230	_____	_____
2.20	270	270	_____	_____
2.40	230	300	_____	_____
2.60	200	330	_____	_____
2.80	180	350	_____	_____

20. CHANGES IN EQUILIBRIUM   What are the effects on the equilibrium price and quantity of steel if the wages of steelworkers rise and, simultaneously, the price of aluminum rises?

21. PRICE FLOOR   There is considerable interest in whether the minimum wage rate contributes to teenage unemployment. Draw a demand and supply diagram for the unskilled labor market, and discuss the effects of a minimum wage. Who is helped and who is hurt by the minimum wage?

22. Case Study: Rent Ceilings in New York City   Suppose the demand and supply curves for rental housing units have the typical shapes and that the rental housing market is in equilibrium. Then, government establishes a rent ceiling below the equilibrium level.

a. What happens to the quantity of housing available?
b. What happens to the quality of housing and why?
c. Who benefits from rent control?
d. Who loses from rent control?
e. How do landlords of rent-controlled apartments try to get tenants to leave?

Global Economic Watch Exercises

Login to www.cengagebrain.com and access the Global Economic Watch to do these exercises.

23. GLOBAL ECONOMIC WATCH   Go to the Global Economic Crisis Resource Center. Select Global Issues in Context. In the Basic Search box at the top of the page, enter the phrase "Law of Supply, Demand." On the Results page, go to the Global Viewpoints section. Click on the link for the November 21, 1984, article "Law of Supply, Demand Applies to Everyone." Did the article describe a surplus of supply or a shortage of supply?

24. GLOBAL ECONOMIC WATCH   Go to the Global Economic Crisis Resource Center. Select Global Issues in Context. Go to the menu at the top of the page and click on the tab for Browse Issues and Topics. Choose Business and Economy. Click on the link for Oil Prices. Find an article from the past 12 months. Compare and contrast the information about oil prices in the article from Problem 23 and in the current article. Use *demand, supply,* and *equilibrium* in your analysis.

Elasticity of Demand and Supply

5

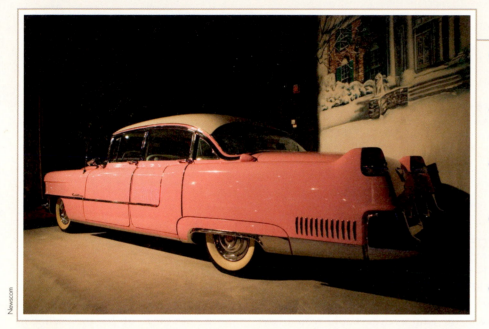

- What does the demand curve look like when price is no object?
- What does the supply curve look like for Cadillacs once owned by Elvis Presley?
- Why do higher cigarette taxes cut smoking by teenagers more than by other age groups?
- Why are consumers more sensitive to the price of Post Raisin Bran than to the price of cereal more generally?
- Why does an abundant harvest often spell trouble for farmers?

Answers to these and other questions are explored in this chapter, which takes a closer look at demand and supply.

As you learned in Chapter 1, macroeconomics concentrates on aggregate markets—on the big picture. But the big picture is a mosaic pieced together from individual decisions made by households, firms, governments, and the rest of the world. To understand how a market economy works, you must take a closer look at these individual choices, especially at the role of prices. In a market economy, prices tell producers and consumers about the relative scarcity of products and resources.

A downward-sloping demand curve and an upward-sloping supply curve form a powerful analytical tool. To use this tool wisely, you need to learn more about these curves. The more you know, the better you can predict the effects of a change in the price on quantity. Decision makers are willing to pay dearly for such knowledge. For example, Taco Bell would like to know what happens to sales if taco prices change. Governments would like to know how a hike in cigarette taxes affects teenage smoking. Colleges would like to know how tuition increases affect enrollments. And subway officials would like to know how fare changes affect ridership. To answer such questions, you must learn how responsive consumers and producers are to price changes. This chapter introduces the idea of *elasticity*, a measure of *responsiveness*.

Topics discussed include:

- Price elasticity of demand
- Determinants of price elasticity
- Price elasticity and total revenue

- Price elasticity of supply
- Income elasticity of demand
- Cross-price elasticity of demand

Price Elasticity of Demand

Just before a recent Thanksgiving, Delta Airlines cut fares for some seats on more than 10,000 domestic flights. Was that a good idea? A firm's success or failure often depends on how much it knows about the demand for its product. For Delta's total revenue to increase, the gain in tickets sold would have to more than make up for the decline in ticket prices. Likewise, the operators of Taco Bell would like to know what happens to sales if the price drops from, say, $1.10 to $0.90 per taco. The law of demand tells us that a lower price increases quantity demanded, but by how much? How sensitive is quantity demanded to a change in price? After all, if quantity demanded increases enough, a price cut could be a profitable move for Taco Bell.

Calculating Price Elasticity of Demand

Let's get more specific about how sensitive changes in quantity demanded are to changes in price. Take a look at the demand curve in Exhibit 1. At the initial price of $1.10 per taco, consumers demand 95,000 a day. If the price drops to $0.90, quantity demanded increases to 105,000. Is such a response a little or a lot? The *price elasticity of demand* measures, in a standardized way, how responsive consumers are to a change in price. *Elasticity* is another word for *responsiveness*. In simplest terms, the **price elasticity of demand** measures the percentage change in quantity demanded divided by the percentage change in price, or:

price elasticity of demand
Measures how responsive quantity demanded is to a price change; the percentage change in quantity demanded divided by the percentage change in price

$$\text{Price elasticity of demand} = \frac{\text{Percentage change in quantity demanded}}{\text{Percentage change in price}}$$

So what's the price elasticity of demand when the price of tacos falls from $1.10 to $0.90—that is, what's the price elasticity of demand between points *a* and *b* in Exhibit 1? For price elasticity to be a clear and reliable measure, we should get the same result between points *a* and *b* as we get between points *b* and *a*. To ensure that consistency,

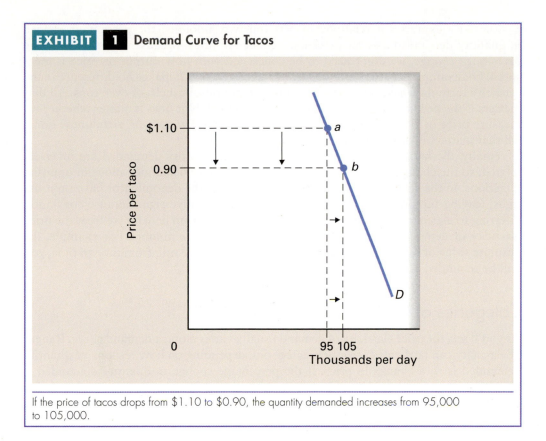

EXHIBIT 1 Demand Curve for Tacos

If the price of tacos drops from $1.10 to $0.90, the quantity demanded increases from 95,000 to 105,000.

we must take the average of the initial price and the new price and use that as the base for computing the percentage change in price. For example, in Exhibit 1, the base used to calculate the percentage change in price is the average of $1.10 and $0.90, which is $1.00. The percentage change in price is therefore the change in price, −$0.20, divided by $1.00, which works out to be −20 percent.

The same holds for changes in quantity demanded. In Exhibit 1, the base used for computing the percentage change in quantity demanded is the average of 95,000 and 105,000, which is 100,000. So the percentage increase in quantity demanded is the change in quantity demanded, 10,000, divided by 100,000, which works out to be 10 percent. So the resulting price elasticity of demand between points *a* and *b* (and between points *b* and *a*) is the percentage increase in quantity demanded, 10 percent, divided by the percentage decrease in price, −20 percent, which is −0.5 (=10%/−20%).

Let's generalize the **price elasticity formula**. If the price changes from p to p', other things constant, the quantity demanded changes from q to q'. The change in price can be represented as Δp and the change in quantity as Δq. The formula for calculating the price elasticity of demand E_D between the two points is the percentage change in quantity demanded divided by the percentage change in price, or:

$$E_D = \frac{\Delta q}{(q+q')/2} \div \frac{\Delta p}{(p+p')/2}$$

Again, because the average quantity and average price are used as the bases for computing percentage change, the same elasticity results whether going from the higher price to the lower price or the other way around.

price elasticity formula
Percentage change in quantity demanded divided by the percentage change in price; the average quantity and the average price are used as bases for computing percentage changes in quantity and in price

Elasticity expresses a relationship between two amounts: the percentage change in quantity demanded and the percentage change in price. Because the focus is on the *percentage change*, we don't need to be concerned with how output or price is measured. For example, suppose the good in question is apples. It makes no difference in the elasticity formula whether we measure apples in pounds, bushels, or even tons. All that matters is the percentage change in quantity demanded. Nor does it matter whether we measure price in U.S. dollars, Mexican pesos, Zambian kwacha, or Vietnamese dong. All that matters is the percentage change in price.

Finally, the law of demand states that price and quantity demanded are inversely related, so the change in price and the change in quantity demanded move in opposite directions. In the elasticity formula, the numerator and the denominator have opposite signs, leaving the price elasticity of demand with a negative sign. Because constantly referring to elasticity as a negative number gets old fast, from here on we treat the price elasticity of demand as an absolute value, or as a positive number. For example, the absolute value of the elasticity measured in Exhibit 1 is 0.5. Still, from time to time, you will be reminded that we are discussing absolute values.

Categories of Price Elasticity of Demand

As you'll see, the price elasticity of demand usually varies along a demand curve. Ranges of elasticity can be divided into three categories, depending on how responsive quantity demanded is to a change in price. If the percentage change in quantity demanded is less than the percentage change in price, the resulting elasticity has an absolute value between 0 and 1.0. That portion of the demand curve is said to be **inelastic**, meaning that quantity demanded is relatively unresponsive to a change in price. For example, the elasticity derived in Exhibit 1 between points *a* and *b* was 0.5, so that portion of the demand curve is inelastic. If the percentage change in quantity demanded just equals the percentage change in price, the resulting elasticity has an absolute value of 1.0, and that portion of a demand curve is **unit elastic**. Finally, if the percentage change in quantity demanded exceeds the percentage change in price, the resulting elasticity has an absolute value exceeding 1.0, and that portion of a demand curve is said to be **elastic**. In summary, *the price elasticity of demand is inelastic if its absolute value is between 0 and 1.0, unit elastic if equal to 1.0, and elastic if greater than 1.0.*

Elasticity and Total Revenue

Knowledge of price elasticity of demand is especially valuable to producers, because it indicates the effect of a price change on total revenue. **Total revenue** (TR) is the price (p) multiplied by the quantity demanded (q) at that price, or $TR = p \times q$. What happens to total revenue when price decreases? Well, according to the law of demand, a lower price increases quantity demanded, which tends to increase total revenue. But, a lower price means producers get less for each unit sold, which tends to decrease total revenue. The overall impact of a lower price on total revenue therefore depends on the net result of these opposite effects. *If the positive effect of a greater quantity demanded more than offsets the negative effect of a lower price, then total revenue rises.* More specifically, if demand is elastic, the percentage increase in quantity demanded exceeds the percentage decrease in price, so total revenue increases. If demand is unit elastic, the percentage increase in quantity demanded just equals the percentage decrease in price, so total revenue remains unchanged. Finally, if demand is inelastic, the positive impact of an increase in quantity demanded on total revenue is more than offset by the negative impact of a decrease in price, so total revenue falls.

inelastic demand

A change in price has relatively little effect on quantity demanded; the percentage change in quantity demanded is less than the percentage change in price; the resulting price elasticity has an absolute value less than 1.0

unit-elastic demand

The percentage change in quantity demanded equals the percentage change in price; the resulting price elasticity has an absolute value of 1.0

elastic demand

A change in price has a relatively large effect on quantity demanded; the percentage change in quantity demanded exceeds the percentage change in price; the resulting price elasticity has an absolute value exceeding 1.0

total revenue

Price multiplied by the quantity demanded at that price

Price Elasticity and the Linear Demand Curve

A look at elasticity along a particular type of demand curve, the linear demand curve, ties together the ideas discussed so far. A **linear demand curve** is simply a straight-line demand curve, as in panel (a) of Exhibit 2. Panel (b) shows the total revenue generated by each price-quantity combination along the demand curve in panel (a). Recall that total revenue equals price times quantity. Please take a moment to see how the demand curve and total revenue curve relate.

Because the demand curve is linear, its slope is constant, so a given decrease in price always causes the same unit increase in quantity demanded. For example, along the demand curve in Exhibit 2, a $10 drop in price always increases quantity demanded by

linear demand curve
A straight-line demand curve; such a demand curve has a constant slope but usually has a varying price elasticity

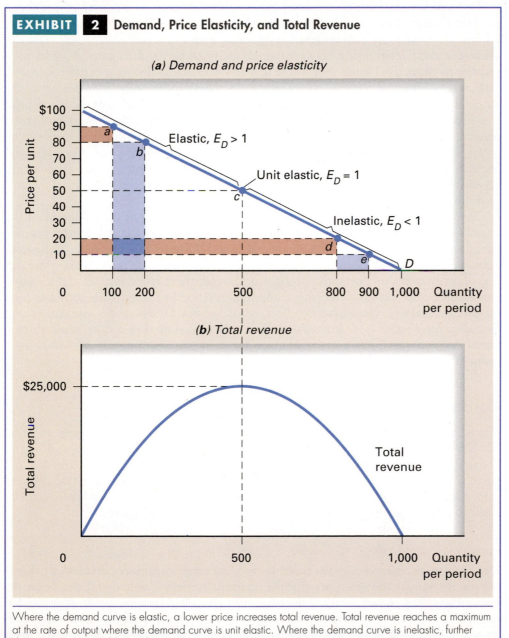

EXHIBIT 2 Demand, Price Elasticity, and Total Revenue

(a) Demand and price elasticity

(b) Total revenue

Where the demand curve is elastic, a lower price increases total revenue. Total revenue reaches a maximum at the rate of output where the demand curve is unit elastic. Where the demand curve is inelastic, further decreases in price reduce total revenue.

100 units. But the price elasticity of demand is larger on the higher-price end of the demand curve than on the lower-price end. Here's why. Consider a movement from point *a* to point *b* on the upper end of the demand curve in Exhibit 2. The $10 price drop is a percentage change of 10/85, or 12 percent. The 100-unit increase in quantity demanded is a percentage change of 100/150, or 67 percent. Therefore, the price elasticity of demand between points *a* and *b* is 67%/12%, which equals 5.6. Between points *d* and *e* on the lower end, however, the $10 price decrease is a percentage change of 10/15, or 67 percent, and the 100-unit quantity increase is a percentage change of 100/850, or only 12 percent. The price elasticity of demand is 12%/67%, or 0.2. In other words, *if the demand curve is linear, consumers are more responsive to a given price change when the initial price is high than when it's low.*

Demand becomes less elastic as we move down the curve. At a point halfway down the linear demand curve in Exhibit 2, the elasticity is 1.0. *This halfway point divides a linear demand curve into an elastic upper half and an inelastic lower half.* You can observe a clear relationship between the elasticity of demand in panel (a) and total revenue in panel (b). Notice that where demand is elastic, a decrease in price increases total revenue because the gain in revenue from selling more units (represented by the large blue rectangle) exceeds the loss in revenue from selling all units at the lower price (the small pink rectangle). But where demand is inelastic, a price decrease reduces total revenue because the gain in revenue from selling more units (the small blue rectangle) is less than the loss in revenue from selling all units at the lower price (the large pink rectangle). And where demand is unit elastic, the gain and loss of revenue exactly cancel each other out, so total revenue at that point remains constant (thus, total revenue peaks in the lower panel).

To review, total revenue increases as the price declines until the midpoint of the linear demand curve is reached, where total revenue peaks. In Exhibit 2, total revenue peaks at $25,000 where quantity demanded equals 500 units. To the right of the midpoint of the demand curve, total revenue declines as the price falls. More generally, regardless of whether demand is straight or curved, there is a consistent relationship between the price elasticity of demand and total revenue: *A price decline increases total revenue if demand is elastic, has no effect on total revenue if demand is unit elastic, and decreases total revenue if demand is inelastic.* Finally, note that a downward-sloping linear demand curve has a constant slope but a varying elasticity, so *the slope of a demand curve is not the same as the price elasticity of demand.*

Constant-Elasticity Demand Curves

Again, price elasticity measures the responsiveness of consumers to a change in price. The shape of the demand curve for a firm's product is key in the pricing and output decision. This responsiveness varies along a linear demand curve unless the demand curve is horizontal or vertical, as in panels (a) and (b) of Exhibit 3. These two demand curves, along with the special demand curve in panel (c), are all called *constant-elasticity demand curves* because the elasticity does not change along the curves.

Perfectly Elastic Demand Curve

The horizontal demand curve in panel (a) indicates that consumers demand all that is offered for sale at the given price *p* (the quantity actually demanded depends on the amount supplied at that price). If the price rises above *p*, however, quantity demanded drops to zero. This is a **perfectly elastic demand curve**, and its elasticity value is infinity, a number too large to be defined. You may think this an odd sort of demand curve: Consumers, as a result of a small increase in price, go from demanding as much as is

net bookmark

The $5 footlong sandwich at Subway was a fast-food hit. Was elasticity a key to its success? Go to http://www .businessweek.com and search for "The Accidental Hero." Read about the franchise owner who introduced the $5 footlong and what happened to Subway sales after the price cut.

perfectly elastic demand curve

A horizontal line reflecting a situation in which any price increase would reduce quantity demanded to zero; the elasticity has an absolute value of infinity

---

EXHIBIT 3 Constant-Elasticity Demand Curves

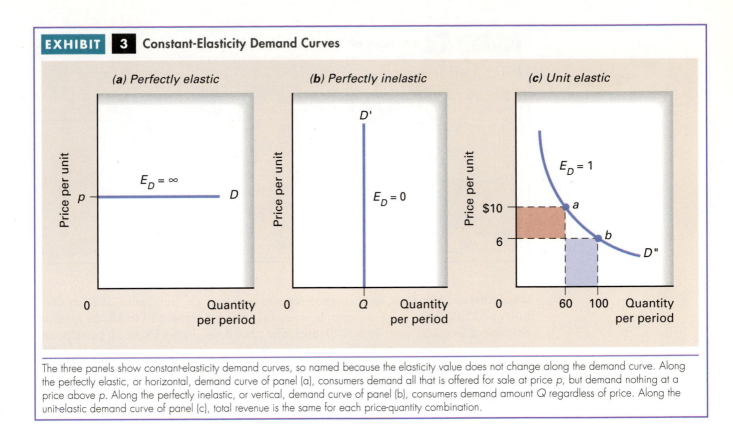

The three panels show constant-elasticity demand curves, so named because the elasticity value does not change along the demand curve. Along the perfectly elastic, or horizontal, demand curve of panel (a), consumers demand all that is offered for sale at price *p*, but demand nothing at a price above *p*. Along the perfectly inelastic, or vertical, demand curve of panel (b), consumers demand amount *Q* regardless of price. Along the unit-elastic demand curve of panel (c), total revenue is the same for each price-quantity combination.

---

supplied to demanding none of the good. Consumers are so sensitive to price changes that they tolerate no price increase. As you will see in a later chapter, this behavior reflects the demand for the output of any individual producer when many producers supply identical products at the market price of *p*.

Perfectly Inelastic Demand Curve

Along the vertical demand curve in panel (b) of Exhibit 3, quantity demanded does not vary when the price changes. This demand curve expresses consumer sentiment when "price is no object." For example, if you are extremely rich and need insulin to survive, price would be no object. No matter how high the price, you would continue to demand whatever it takes. And if the price of insulin should drop, you would not increase your quantity demanded. Another example of perfectly inelastic demand comes from Shakespeare's play *Richard III*. After his horse is slain in battle, the king, at the mercy of the enemy, cries out, "A horse! A horse! My kingdom for a horse!" The king is willing to pay a high price indeed—his kingdom—for a horse. On a less lofty level, Ben Franklin expressed a similar sentiment when he observed, "Necessity never made a good bargain." Because the percentage change in quantity demanded is zero for any given percentage change in price, the numerical value of the price elasticity is zero. A vertical demand curve is called a **perfectly inelastic demand curve**.

Unit-Elastic Demand Curve

Panel (c) in Exhibit 3 presents a demand curve that is unit elastic everywhere. Along a **unit-elastic demand curve**, any percentage change in price causes the exact opposite percentage change in quantity demanded. Because changes in price and in quantity

perfectly inelastic demand curve

A vertical line reflecting a situation in which any price change has no effect on the quantity demanded; the elasticity value is zero

unit-elastic demand curve

Everywhere along the demand curve, the percentage change in price causes an equal but offsetting percentage change in quantity demanded, so total revenue remains the same; the elasticity has an absolute value of 1.0

EXHIBIT   4   Summary of Price Elasticity of Demand

Effects of a 10 Percent Increase in Price

Absolute Value of Price Elasticity	Type of Demand	What Happens to Quantity Demanded	What Happens to Total Revenue
$E_D = 0$	Perfectly inelastic	No change	Increases by 10 percent
$0 < E_D < 1$	Inelastic	Drops by less than 10 percent	Increases by less than 10 percent
$E_D = 1$	Unit elastic	Drops by 10 percent	No change
$1 < E_D < \infty$	Elastic	Drops by more than 10 percent	Decreases
$E_D = \infty$	Perfectly elastic	Drops to 0	Drops to 0

demanded are offsetting, total revenue remains constant for every price-quantity combination along the curve. For example, when the price falls from $10 to $6, the quantity demanded increases from 60 to 100 units. The price drops by $4/$8, or 50 percent, and the quantity increases by 40/80, or 50 percent. The pink shaded rectangle shows the loss in total revenue from cutting the price; the blue shaded rectangle shows the gain in total revenue from selling more at the lower price. Because the demand curve is unit elastic, the revenue gained from selling more just offsets the revenue lost from lowering the price, so total revenue remains unchanged at $600.

Each demand curve in Exhibit 3 is called a **constant-elasticity demand curve** because the elasticity is the same all along the curve. In contrast, the downward-sloping linear demand curve examined earlier had a different elasticity value at each point along the curve. Exhibit 4 lists the absolute values for the five categories of price elasticity we have discussed, summarizing the effects of a 10 percent price increase on quantity demanded and on total revenue. Give this exhibit some thought now, and see if you can draw a demand curve for each category of elasticity.

constant-elasticity demand curve

The type of demand that exists when price elasticity is the same everywhere along the curve; the elasticity value is unchanged

Determinants of the Price Elasticity of Demand

So far we have explored the technical properties of demand elasticity and discussed why it varies along a downward-sloping demand curve. But we have yet to consider why elasticity is different for different goods. Several factors influence the price elasticity of demand.

Availability of Substitutes

As we saw in Chapter 4, your particular wants can be satisfied in a variety of ways. A rise in the price of pizza makes other food relatively cheaper. If close substitutes are available, an increase in the price of pizza prompts some consumers to buy substitutes. But if nothing else satisfies like pizza, the quantity of pizza demanded does not decline as much. *The greater the availability of substitutes and the more similar these substitutes are to the good in question, the greater that good's price elasticity of demand.*

The number and similarity of substitutes depend on how the good is defined. *The more narrow the definition, the more substitutes and, thus, the more elastic the demand*. For example, the demand for Post Raisin Bran is more elastic than the demand for raisin bran more generally because there are more substitutes for Post Raisin Bran, including Kellogg's Raisin Bran and Total Raisin Bran, than for raisin bran more generally. The demand for raisin bran, however, is more elastic than the demand for breakfast cereals more generally because the consumer has many substitutes for raisin bran, such as cereals made from corn, rice, wheat, or oats, and processed with or without honey, nuts, fruit, or chocolate. To give you some idea of the range of elasticities, the price elasticity of demand for Post Raisin Bran has been estimated to be −2.5 versus −0.9 for all breakfast cereals.[1]

Pro team owners worry that live TV broadcasts cut game attendance, especially now that more households enjoy large-screen HDTVs plus DVRs with playback and slow-motion capabilities. A study of attendance at Scottish Premier League soccer matches found that TV broadcasts cut pay-at-the-gate attendance by 30 percent.[2] This is why home teams black out TV coverage if a game is not sold out before a certain date.

Certain goods—some prescription drugs, for instance—have no close substitutes. The demand for such goods tends to be less elastic than for goods with close substitutes, such as Bayer aspirin. Much advertising is aimed at establishing in the consumer's mind the uniqueness of a particular product—an effort to convince consumers "to accept no substitutes." Why might a firm want to make the demand for its product less elastic?

Share of the Consumer's Budget Spent on the Good

Recall that a higher price reduces quantity demanded in part because a higher price reduces the real spending power of consumer income. Because spending on some goods claims a large share of the consumer's budget, a change in the price of such a good has a substantial impact on the consumer's *ability* to buy it. An increase in the price of housing, for example, reduces the ability to buy housing. The income effect of a higher price reduces the quantity demanded. In contrast, the income effect of an increase in the price of, say, paper towels is trivial because paper towels represent such a tiny share of any budget. *The more important the item is as a share of the consumer's budget, other things constant, the greater is the income effect of a change in price, so the more elastic is the demand for the item.* Hence, the quantity of housing demanded is more responsive to a given percentage change in price than is the quantity of paper towels demanded.

Length of Adjustment Period

Consumers can substitute lower-priced goods for higher-priced goods, but finding substitutes usually takes time. Suppose your college announces a sharp increase in room and board fees, effective next term. Some students will move off campus before that term begins; others may wait until the next academic year. Over time, the college may get fewer applicants and more incoming students will choose off-campus housing. The longer the adjustment period, the greater the consumers' ability to substitute away from relatively higher-priced products toward lower-priced substitutes. Thus, *the longer the period of adjustment, the more responsive the change in quantity demanded is to a given change in price.* Here's another example: Between 1973 and 1974, OPEC (Organization of the Petroleum Exporting Countries) raised gasoline prices 45 percent, but the quantity

1. See Jerry A. Hausman, "The Price Elasticity of Demand for Breakfast Cereal," in *The Economics of New Goods*, T. F. Bresnahan and J. J. Gordon, eds. (Chicago: University of Chicago Press, 1997).
2. Grant Allan and Graeme Roy, "Does Television Crowd Out Spectators?," *Journal of Sports Economics*, 5 (December 2008): 592–605.

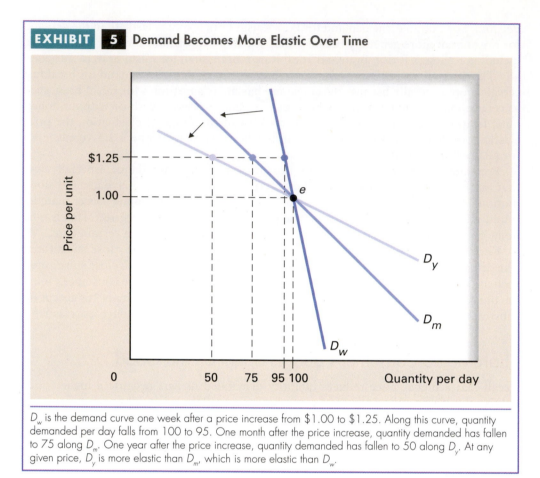

EXHIBIT 5   Demand Becomes More Elastic Over Time

D_w is the demand curve one week after a price increase from $1.00 to $1.25. Along this curve, quantity demanded per day falls from 100 to 95. One month after the price increase, quantity demanded has fallen to 75 along D_m. One year after the price increase, quantity demanded has fallen to 50 along D_y. At any given price, D_y is more elastic than D_m, which is more elastic than D_w.

demanded initially decreased just 8 percent. As more time passed, however, people bought smaller cars and relied more on public transportation. They also bought more energy-efficient appliances and insulated their homes better. Thus, the percentage change in quantity demanded was greater the longer consumers adjusted to the price hike.

Exhibit 5 shows how demand becomes more elastic over time. Given an initial price of $1.00 at point e, let D_w be the demand curve one week after a price change; D_m, one month after; and D_y, one year after. Suppose the price increases to $1.25. The more time consumers have to respond to the price increase, the greater the reduction in quantity demanded. The demand curve D_w shows that one week after the price increase, the quantity demanded has not declined much—in this case, from 100 to 95 per day. The demand curve D_m indicates a reduction to 75 per day after one month, and demand curve D_y shows a reduction to 50 per day after one year. Notice that among these demand curves and over the range starting from point e, the flatter the demand curve, the more price elastic the demand. Here, elasticity seems linked to the slope because we begin from a common point—the price-quantity combination at point e.

Elasticity Estimates

Let's look at some estimates of the price elasticity of demand for particular goods and services. Remember, finding alternatives when the price increases takes time. Thus, when estimating price elasticity, economists often distinguish between a period during which

EXHIBIT **6** **Selected Price Elasticities of Demand (Absolute Values)**

Product	Short Run	Long Run
Cigarettes (among adults)	—	0.4
Electricity (residential)	0.1	1.9
Air travel	0.1	2.4
Medical care and hospitalization	0.3	0.9
Gasoline	0.4	1.5
Milk	0.4	—
Fish (cod)	0.5	—
Wine	0.7	1.2
Movies	0.9	3.7
Natural gas (residential)	1.4	2.1
Automobiles	1.9	2.2
Chevrolets	—	4.0

Sources: F. Chaloupka, "Rational Addictive Behavior and Cigarette Smoking," *Journal of Political Economy*, (August 1991); Hsaing-tai Cheng and Oral Capps, Jr., "Demand for Fish," *American Journal of Agricultural Economics*, (August 1998); J. Johnson et al., "Short-Run and Long-Run Elasticities for Canadian Consumption of Alcoholic Beverages," *Review of Economics and Statistics*, (February 1992); Douglas Young et al., "Alcohol Consumption, Measurement Error, and Beverage Prices," *Journal of Studies on Alcohol*, (March 2003); J. Griffin, *Energy Conservation in the OECD*, 1980–2000 (Balinger, 1979); and H. Houthakker and L. Taylor, *Consumer Demand in the United States: Analysis and Projections*, 2nd ed. (Harvard University Press, 1970).

consumers have little time to adjust—let's call it the *short run*—and a period during which consumers can more fully adjust to a price change—let's call it the *long run*. Exhibit 6 provides short-run and long-run price elasticity estimates for selected products.

The price elasticity of demand is greater in the long run because consumers have more time to adjust. For example, if the price of electricity rose today, consumers in the short run might cut back a bit in their use of electrical appliances, and those in homes with electric heat might lower the thermostat in winter. Over time, however, consumers would switch to more energy-efficient appliances, insulate their homes better, and perhaps switch from electric heat. So the demand for electricity is more elastic in the long run than in the short run, as shown in Exhibit 6. In fact, in every instance where estimates for both the short run and the long run are available, demand is more elastic in the long run than the short run. Notice also that the demand for Chevrolets is more elastic than the demand for automobiles more generally. Chevrolets have many more substitutes than do automobiles in general. There are no close substitutes for cigarettes, even in the long run, so the demand for cigarettes among adults is price inelastic. Elasticity measures are of more than just academic interest, as discussed in the following case study.

BEHAVIORAL ECONOMICS

CASE STUDY

Deterring Young Smokers As the U.S. Surgeon General warns on each pack of cigarettes, smoking can be hazardous to your health. Researchers estimate that cigarettes kill 440,000 Americans a year—10 times more than traffic accidents. Smoking is the overwhelming cause of lung cancer, the top cancer killer among women. Smoking is also the leading cause of heart disease, emphysema, and stroke.

According to the U.S. Centers for Disease Control and Prevention, each pack of cigarettes sold in the United States costs society more than $7 in higher health care costs

e activity

The CDC stated that anti-smoking efforts targeting high school teens have been successful-including TV ads, *...continued*

e activity continued
school campaigns, and higher cost per pack. Read more at http://www.cdc.gov/tobacco/youth/index.htm. Find information about smoking cessation at http://www.lungusa.org/stop-smoking/.

and lost worker productivity. These costs exceed $150 billion a year, which works out to be about $3,400 per smoker per year.

Thus, smoking imposes major health and economic costs. Policy makers try to reduce these costs by discouraging smoking, especially among young people. About 80 percent of adult smokers began before the age of 18. Each day, about 3,500 U.S. teens under 18 try smoking for the first time, and about a third of those become regular smokers.

One way to reduce youth smoking is to prohibit cigarette sales to minors. A second way is to raise the price through higher cigarette taxes (the price now tops $9 per pack in New York City). The amount by which a given price hike reduces teen smoking depends on the price elasticity of demand. This elasticity is higher for teens than for adults. Why are teenagers more sensitive to price changes than adults? First, recall that one factor affecting elasticity is the importance of the item in the consumer's budget. Because teen income is relatively low, the share of income spent on cigarettes usually exceeds the share spent by adult smokers. Second, peer pressure shapes a young person's decision to smoke more than an adult's decision to continue smoking (if anything, adults face negative peer pressure for smoking). Teens often begin smoking by mooching cigarettes from peers. Thus, the effect of a higher price gets magnified among young smokers because that higher price also reduces smoking by peers. With fewer peers smoking, teens face less pressure and less opportunity to smoke. And, third, young people not yet addicted to nicotine are more sensitive to price increases than are adult smokers, who are more

AP Photo/Bob Child

likely to be already hooked. The experience from other countries supports the effectiveness of higher cigarette taxes in reducing teen smoking. For example, a large tax increase on cigarettes in Canada cut youth smoking by two-thirds.

Another way to reduce smoking is to change consumer tastes through health warnings. In Canada, these warnings include photos showing how smoking can affect the brain, teeth, and gums, and a wilted cigarette depicts male impotence. In Australia, labels show gangrenous limbs, underweight babies, cancerous mouths, and blind eyes. Belgium adds corpses to the gallery of horrors. In California, a combination of higher cigarette taxes and an ambitious awareness program contributed to a 5 percent decline in lung cancer among women, even as the disease rose 13 percent in the rest of the country. (As of 2010, state taxes varied from a low of 7 cents per pack in South Carolina to a high of $3.46 in Rhode Island.)

But higher cigarette taxes can have unintended consequences. Researchers have found that smokers compensate for tax hikes by smoking each cigarette more intensively—that is, by sucking more smoke and nicotine from each cigarette. This poses an added health risk.

More generally, the message about the dangers of smoking, which seem to work, along with the higher cost of cigarettes has had an impact over time. Only about 20 percent of American adults now smoke, down from more than half in the 1960s.

Sources: Rosemary Avery et al., "Private Profits and Public Health: Does Advertising of Smoking Cessation Products Encourage Smokers to Quit?," *Journal of Political Economy*, 115 (June 2007): 447-481. Petter Lundborg and Henrik Andersson, "Gender, Risk Perceptions, and Smoking Behavior," *Journal of Health Economics*, 27 (September 2008): 1299–1311; Jerome Adda and Francesca Cornaglia, "Taxes, Cigarette Consumption, and Smoking Intensity," *American Economic Review*, 96 (September 2006): 1013–1028; and Deliana Kostova et al., "Prices and Cigarette Demand: Evidence from Youth Tobacco Use in Developing Countries," NBER Working Paper 15781, (February 2010).

Price Elasticity of Supply

Prices signal both sides of the market about the relative scarcity of products. Higher prices discourage consumption but encourage production. Lower prices encourage consumption but discourage production. The price elasticity of demand measures how responsive consumers are to a price change. Likewise, the **price elasticity of supply** measures how responsive producers are to a price change. Supply elasticity is calculated in the same way as demand elasticity. In simplest terms, the price elasticity of supply equals the percentage change in quantity supplied divided by the percentage change in price. Because a higher price usually increases quantity supplied, the percentage change in price and the percentage change in quantity supplied move in the same direction, so the price elasticity of supply is usually a positive number.

Exhibit 7 depicts a typical upward-sloping supply curve. As you can see, if the price increases from p to p', the quantity supplied increases from q to q'. Price and quantity supplied move in the same direction. Let's look at the elasticity formula for the supply curve. The price elasticity of supply is:

$$E_S = \frac{\Delta q}{(q + q')/2} \div \frac{\Delta p}{(p + p')/2}$$

where Δq is the change in quantity supplied and Δp is the change in price. This is the same formula used to compute the price elasticity of demand except that q here is quantity supplied, not quantity demanded. The terminology for supply elasticity is the same as for demand elasticity: If supply elasticity is less than 1.0, supply is **inelastic**; if it equals 1.0, supply is **unit elastic**; and if it exceeds 1.0, supply is **elastic**.

price elasticity of supply
A measure of the responsiveness of quantity supplied to a price change; the percentage change in quantity supplied divided by the percentage change in price

inelastic supply
A change in price has relatively little effect on quantity supplied; the percentage change in quantity supplied is less than the percentage change in price; the price elasticity of supply is less than 1.0

unit-elastic supply
The percentage change in quantity supplied equals the percentage change in price; the price elasticity of supply equals 1.0

elastic supply
A change in price has a relatively large effect on quantity supplied; the percentage change in quantity supplied exceeds the percentage change in price; the price elasticity of supply exceeds 1.0

EXHIBIT 7 Price Elasticity of Supply

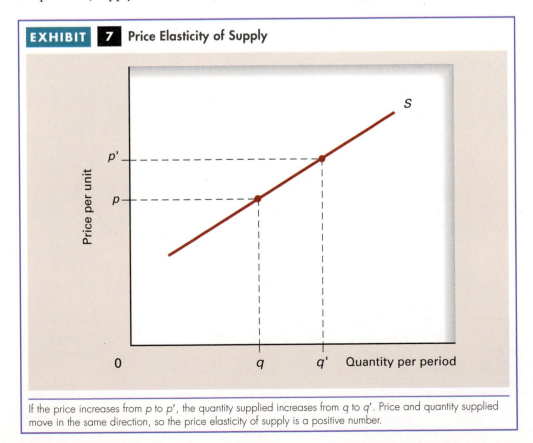

If the price increases from p to p', the quantity supplied increases from q to q'. Price and quantity supplied move in the same direction, so the price elasticity of supply is a positive number.

Constant Elasticity Supply Curves

Again, price elasticity of supply measures the responsiveness of producers to a change in price. This responsiveness varies along a linear supply curve unless the curve is horizontal or vertical, as in panels (a) and (b) of Exhibit 8, or passes through the origin, as in panel (c). These three supply curves are called *constant-elasticity supply curves* because the elasticity does not change along the curves.

Perfectly Elastic Supply Curve

At one extreme is the horizontal supply curve, such as supply curve S in panel (a) of Exhibit 8. In this case, producers supply none of the good at a price below p but supply any amount at price p (the quantity actually supplied at price p depends on the amount demanded at that price). Because a tiny increase from a price just below p to a price of p results in an unlimited quantity supplied, this is called a **perfectly elastic supply curve**, which has a numerical value of infinity. As individual consumers, we typically face perfectly elastic supply curves. When we go to the supermarket, we usually can buy as much as we want at the prevailing price but none at a lower price. Obviously all consumers together cannot buy an unlimited amount at the prevailing price (recall the fallacy of composition from Chapter 1).

Perfectly Inelastic Supply Curve

The least responsive relationship is where there is no change in the quantity supplied regardless of the price, as shown by the vertical supply curve S' in panel (b) of Exhibit 8. Because the percentage change in quantity supplied is zero, regardless of the change in price, the price elasticity of supply is zero. This is a **perfectly inelastic supply curve**.

perfectly elastic supply curve
A horizontal line reflecting a situation in which any price decrease drops the quantity supplied to zero; the elasticity value is infinity

Perfectly inelastic supply curve
A vertical line reflecting a situation in which a price change has no effect on the quantity supplied; the elasticity value is zero

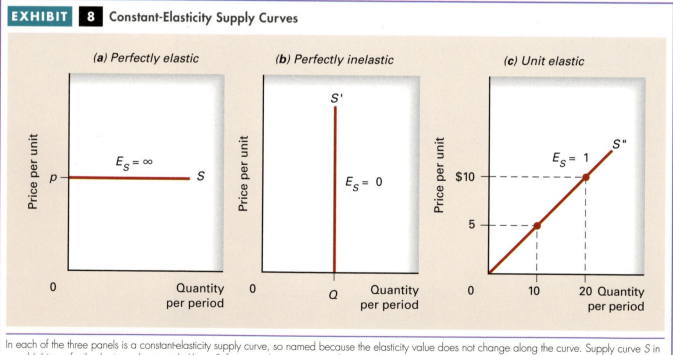

EXHIBIT   8   Constant-Elasticity Supply Curves

(a) Perfectly elastic   *(b) Perfectly inelastic*   *(c) Unit elastic*

In each of the three panels is a constant-elasticity supply curve, so named because the elasticity value does not change along the curve. Supply curve S in panel (a) is perfectly elastic, or horizontal. Along S, firms supply any amount of output demanded at price p, but supply none at prices below p. Supply curve S' is perfectly inelastic, or vertical. S' shows that the quantity supplied is independent of the price. In panel (c), S'', a straight line from the origin, is a unit-elastic supply curve. Any percentage change in price results in the same percentage change in quantity supplied.

Any good in fixed supply, such as Picasso paintings, 1995 Dom Perignon champagne, or Cadillacs once owned by Elvis Presley, has a perfectly inelastic supply curve.

Unit-Elastic Supply Curve

Any supply curve that is a straight line from the origin—such as S'' in panel (c) of Exhibit 8—is a **unit-elastic supply curve**. This means a percentage change in price always generates an identical percentage change in quantity supplied. For example, along S'' a doubling of the price results in a doubling of the quantity supplied. Note that unit elasticity is based not on the slope of the line but on the fact that the linear supply curve is a ray from the origin.

unit-elastic supply curve
A percentage change in price causes an identical percentage change in quantity supplied; depicted by a supply curve that is a straight line from the origin; the elasticity value equals 1.0

Determinants of Supply Elasticity

The elasticity of supply indicates how responsive producers are to a change in price. Their response depends on how easy it is to alter quantity supplied when the price changes. If the cost of supplying additional units rises sharply as output expands, then a higher price causes little increase in quantity supplied, so supply tends to be inelastic. But if the marginal cost rises slowly as output expands, the lure of a higher price prompts a large increase in quantity supplied. In this case, supply is more elastic.

One determinant of supply elasticity is the length of the adjustment period under consideration. Just as demand becomes more elastic over time as consumers adjust to price changes, supply also becomes more elastic over time as producers adjust to price changes. The longer the adjustment period under consideration, the more able producers are to adapt to a price change. Exhibit 9 presents different supply curves for each of

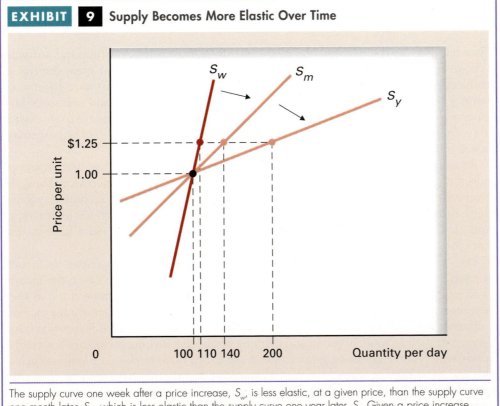

EXHIBIT   9   Supply Becomes More Elastic Over Time

The supply curve one week after a price increase, S_w, is less elastic, at a given price, than the supply curve one month later, S_m, which is less elastic than the supply curve one year later, S_y. Given a price increase from \$1.00 to \$1.25, quantity supplied per day increases to 110 units after one week, to 140 units after one month, and to 200 units after one year.

three periods. S_w is the supply curve when the period of adjustment is a week. As you can see, a higher price generates little response in quantity supplied because firms have little time to adjust. This supply curve is inelastic between \$1.00 and \$1.25.

S_m is the supply curve when the adjustment period under consideration is a month. Firms have more time to vary output. Thus, supply is more elastic when the adjustment period is a month than when it's a week. Supply is yet more elastic when the adjustment period is a year, as is shown by S_y. As the adjustment period lengthens, the supply response increases. For example, if the price of oil increases, oil producers in the short run can try to pump more from existing wells, but in the long run, a higher price stimulates more exploration. Research confirms the positive link between the price elasticity of supply and the length of the adjustment period. *The elasticity of supply is typically greater the longer the period of adjustment.*

The ability to increase quantity supplied in response to a higher price differs across industries. For example, oil was discovered on Alaska's north slope in 1967; but oil did not begin to flow south until a decade later. More generally, the response time is slower for suppliers of oil, electricity, and timber (where expansion may take years, if not decades) than for suppliers of window-washing services, lawn maintenance, and hot-dog vending (where expansion may take only days).

Other Elasticity Measures

Price elasticities of demand and supply are frequently used in economic analysis, but two other elasticity measures also provide valuable information.

Income Elasticity of Demand

What happens to the demand for new cars, fresh vegetables, or computer software if consumer income increases by, say, 10 percent? The answer is of great interest to producers because it helps them predict the effect of changing consumer income on quantity sold and on total revenue. The **income elasticity of demand** measures how responsive demand is to a change in consumer income. Specifically, *the income elasticity of demand measures the percentage change in demand divided by the percentage change in income that caused it.*

As noted in Chapter 4, the demand for some products, such as used furniture and used clothing, actually declines, or shifts leftward, as income increases. Thus, the income elasticity of demand for such goods is negative. Goods with income elasticities less than zero are called *inferior goods.* But the demand for most goods increases, or shifts rightward, as income increases. These are called *normal goods* and have income elasticities greater than zero.

Let's take a closer look at normal goods. Suppose demand increases as income increases but by a smaller percentage than income increases. In such cases, the income elasticity is greater than 0 but less than 1. For example, people buy more food as their incomes rise, but the percentage increase in demand is less than the percentage increase in income. Normal goods with income elasticities less than 1 are called *income inelastic.* *Necessities* such as food, housing, and clothing often have income elasticities less than 1. Goods with income elasticity greater than 1 are called *income elastic.* *Luxuries* such as high-end cars, vintage wines, and meals at upscale restaurants have income elasticities greater than 1. By the way, the terms *inferior goods, necessities,* and *luxuries* are not value judgments about the merits of particular goods; these terms are simply convenient ways of classifying economic behavior.

income elasticity of demand

The percentage change in demand divided by the percentage change in consumer income; the value is positive for normal goods and negative for inferior goods

EXHIBIT 10 Selected Income Elasticities of Demand

Product	Income Elasticity	Product	Income Elasticity
Wine	5.03	Physicians' services	0.75
Private education	2.46	Coca-Cola	0.68
Automobiles	2.45	Beef	0.62
Owner-occupied housing	1.49	Food	0.51
Furniture	1.48	Coffee	0.51
Dental service	1.42	Cigarettes	0.50
Restaurant meals	1.40	Gasoline and oil	0.48
Spirits ("hard" liquor)	1.21	Rental housing	0.43
Shoes	1.10	Pork	0.18
Chicken	1.06	Beer	−0.09
Clothing	0.92	Flour	−0.36

Sources: Ivan Bloor, "Food for Thought," *Economic Review*, (September 1999); F. Gasmi et al., "Econometric Analysis of Collusive Behavior in a Soft-Drink Market," *Journal of Economics and Management Strategy*, (Summer 1992); X. M. Gao et al., "A Microeconomic Model Analysis of U.S. Consumer Demand for Alcoholic Beverages," *Applied Economics*, (January 1995); H. Houthakker and L. Taylor, *Consumer Demand in the United States: Analyses and Projections*, 2nd ed. (Harvard University Press, 1970); C. Huang et al., "The Demand for Coffee in the United States, 1963–77," *Quarterly Review of Economics and Business*, (Summer 1980); and G. Brester and M. Wohlgenant, "Estimating Interrelated Demands for Meats Using New Measures for Ground and Table Cut Beef," *American Journal of Agricultural Economics*, (November 1991).

Exhibit 10 presents income elasticity estimates for some goods and services. The figures indicate, for example, that as income increases, consumers spend proportionately more on wine, restaurant meals, and owner-occupied housing. Spending on food and rental housing also increases as income increases, but less than proportionately. Spending on beer declines as income increases. So as income rises, the demand for restaurant meals increases more in percentage terms than does the demand for food, and the demand for owner-occupied housing increases more in percentage terms than does the demand for rental housing. The demand for wine increases sharply, while the demand for beer declines. Flour also has negative income elasticity. According to these estimates, beer and flour are inferior goods.

As we have seen, the demand for food is income inelastic. The demand for food also tends to be price inelastic. This combination of income and price inelasticity creates special problems for farmers, as discussed in the following case study.

BRINGING THEORY TO LIFE

The Market for Food and the "Farm Problem" Despite decades of federal support and billions of tax dollars spent on various farm-assistance programs, the number of American farmers continues its long slide, dropping from 10 million in 1948 to under 3 million today. The demise of the family farm can be traced to the price and income elasticities of demand for farm products and to technological breakthroughs that increased supply.

Many of the forces that determine farm production are beyond a farmer's control. Temperature, rainfall, pests, and other natural forces affect crop size and quality. For example, favorable weather boosted crop production 16 percent in one recent year. Such increases create special problems for farmers because the demand for most farm

CASE STUDY

e activity

What are the forces shaping U.S. agriculture today? The Economic Research Service of the U.S. Department of Agriculture provides some answers with its briefing book *...continued*

Fuse/Jupiter Images

crops, such as milk, eggs, corn, potatoes, oats, sugar, and beef, is price inelastic.

The effect of inelastic demand on farm revenue is illustrated in Exhibit 11. Suppose that in a normal year, farmers supply 10 billion bushels of grain at a market price of $5 a bushel. Annual farm revenue, which is price times quantity, totals $50 billion in our example. What if favorable weather boosts grain production to 11 billion bushels, an increase of 10 percent? Because demand is price inelastic, the average price in our example must fall by more than 10 percent to, say, $4 per bushel to sell the extra billion bushels. Thus, the 10 percent increase in farm production gets sold only if the price drops from $5 to $4, or by 20 percent.

Total revenue declines from $50 billion to $44 billion. So, despite a 10 percent rise in production, total revenue drops. *Because demand is price inelastic, total revenue falls when the price falls.* Of course, for farmers, the upside of inelastic demand is that a lower-than-normal crop results in higher total revenue. For example, one recent drought sent corn prices up 50 percent, increasing farm revenue in the process. So weather-generated changes in farm production create year-to-year swings in farm revenue.

Fluctuations in farm revenue are compounded in the long run by the *income inelasticity* of demand for grain and, more generally, for food. As household incomes grow over time, spending on food may increase because consumers substitute prepared foods and restaurant meals for home cooking. But this move up the food chain has little effect on the total demand for farm products. Thus, as the economy grows over

e activity continued

at http://www.ers.usda.gov/ Emphases/Competitive/. Find out what the latest edition says about the current state of the American farm family. How have farm size and the number of family farms been changing? How does farm family income compare to average household income? What percent of farm income is a result of government farm support policies?

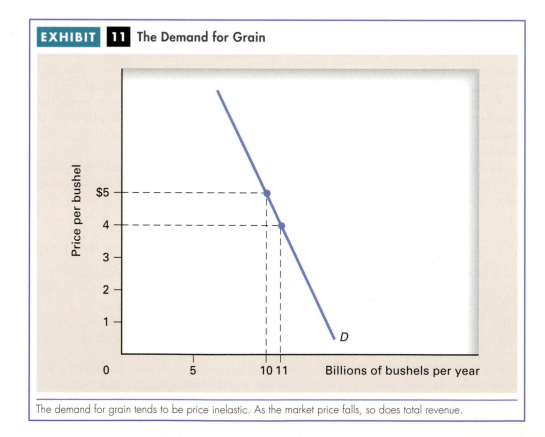

EXHIBIT   11   The Demand for Grain

The demand for grain tends to be price inelastic. As the market price falls, so does total revenue.

EXHIBIT 12 The Effect of Increases in Demand and Supply on Farm Revenue

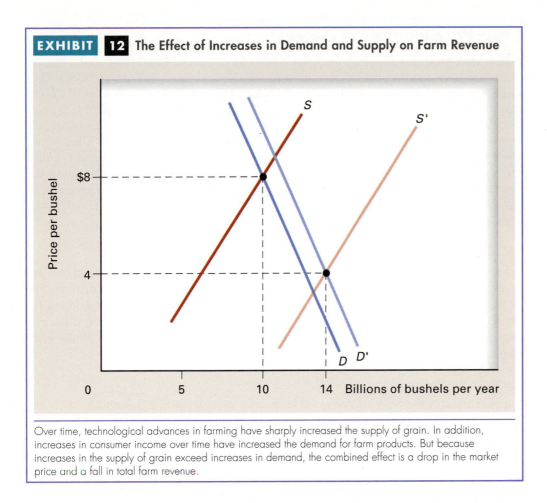

Over time, technological advances in farming have sharply increased the supply of grain. In addition, increases in consumer income over time have increased the demand for farm products. But because increases in the supply of grain exceed increases in demand, the combined effect is a drop in the market price and a fall in total farm revenue.

time and incomes rise, the demand for farm products tends to increase but by less than the increase in income. This modest increase in demand from *D* to *D'* is reflected in Exhibit 12.

Because of technological improvements in production, however, the supply of farm products has increased sharply. Developments such as more sophisticated machines, better fertilizer, and healthier seeds have increased farm output per hour of labor 11-fold since 1950. For example, farmers can now seed at night using a 32-row planter and global positioning satellites. With new strains of pest-resistant plants, farmers have cut insecticide applications from seven per season to one or none.

Exhibit 12 shows a big increase in the supply of grain from *S* to *S'*. Because the supply increase exceeds the demand increase, the price declines. And because the demand for grain is price inelastic, the percentage drop in price exceeds the percentage increase in output. The combined effect in our example is lower total revenue. In the real world, the effect over time is not quite so bleak, but farmers have been getting a declining share of consumer spending for decades. Between 1960 and 2009, for example, total consumer spending on all goods and services (adjusted for inflation) in the United States increased more than 400 percent, but total farm revenue increased only 40 percent.

Sources: Scott Kilman and Lauren Etter, "Recession Finally Hits Down on the Farm," *Wall Street Journal*, 28 August 2009; Bruce L. Gardner, "Changing Economic Perspective on the Farm Problem," *Journal of Economic Literature*, 30 (March 1992): 62–105; and *Economic Report of the President*, February 2010, Tables B-99 at http://www.gpoaccess.gov/eop/2010/2010_erp .pdf; For current economic research at the U.S. Department of Agriculture, go to http://www.ers.usda.gov/.

Cross-Price Elasticity of Demand

A firm that produces an entire line of products has a special interest in how a change in the price of one item affects the demand for another. For example, the Coca-Cola Company needs to know how changing the price of Cherry Coke affects sales of Classic Coke. The company also needs to know the relationship between the price of Coke and the demand for Pepsi and vice versa. Likewise, Apple needs to know how changing the price of one iPhone model affects the demand for the other iPhone models. The responsiveness of the demand for one good to changes in the price of another good is called the **cross-price elasticity of demand**. This is defined as the percentage change in the demand of one good divided by the percentage change in the price of another good. Its numerical value can be positive, negative, or zero, depending on whether the two goods in question are substitutes, complements, or unrelated, respectively.

cross-price elasticity of demand

The percentage change in the demand of one good divided by the percentage change in the price of another good; it's positive for substitutes, negative for complements, and zero for unrelated goods

Substitutes

If an increase in the price of one good leads to an increase in the demand for another good, their cross-price elasticity is positive and the two goods are *substitutes*. For example, an increase in the price of Coke, other things constant, shifts the demand for Pepsi rightward, so the two are substitutes. The cross-price elasticity between Coke and Pepsi has been estimated at about 0.7, indicating that a 10 percent increase in the price of one increases the demand for the other by 7 percent.[3]

Complements

If an increase in the price of one good leads to a decrease in the demand for another, their cross-price elasticity is negative and the goods are *complements*. For example, an increase in the price of gasoline, other things constant, shifts the demand for tires leftward because people drive less and replace their tires less frequently. Gasoline and tires have a negative cross-price elasticity and are complements.

To Review: The cross-price elasticity of demand is positive for substitutes and negative for complements. Most pairs of goods selected at random are unrelated, so their cross-price elasticity is zero, such as socks and sushi.

Conclusion

Because this chapter has been more quantitative than earlier ones, the mechanics may have overshadowed the intuitive appeal and neat simplicity of elasticity. *Elasticity measures the willingness and ability of buyers and sellers to alter their behavior in response to changes in their economic circumstances.* Firms try to estimate the price elasticity of demand for their products. Governments also have an ongoing interest in various elasticities. For example, state governments want to know the effect of an increase in the sales tax on total tax receipts, and local governments want to know how an increase in income affects the demand for real estate and thus the revenue generated by a given property tax rate. International groups are interested in elasticities; for example, OPEC is concerned about the price elasticity of demand for oil—in the short run and in the long run. Because a corporation often produces an entire line of products, it also has a special interest in cross-price elasticities. Some corporate economists estimate elasticities for a living. The appendix to this chapter shows how price elasticities of demand and supply shed light on who ultimately pays a tax.

3. F. Gasmi, J. J. Laffont, and Q. Vuong, "Econometric Analysis of Collusive Behavior in a Soft-Drink Market," *Journal of Economics and Management Strategy*, 1 (June 1992): 277–311.

Summary

1. The price elasticities of demand and supply show how responsive buyers and sellers are to changes in the price of a good. More elastic means more responsive.

2. When the percentage change in quantity demanded exceeds the percentage change in price, demand is price elastic. If demand is price elastic, a price increase reduces total revenue and a price decrease increases total revenue. When the percentage change in quantity demanded is less than the percentage change in price, demand is price inelastic. If demand is price inelastic, a higher price increases total revenue and a lower price reduces total revenue. When the percentage change in quantity demanded equals the percentage change in price, demand is unit elastic; a price change does not affect total revenue.

3. Along a straight-lined, downward-sloping demand curve, the elasticity of demand declines steadily as the price falls. A constant-elasticity demand curve, on the other hand, has the same elasticity everywhere.

4. Demand is more elastic (a) the greater the availability of substitutes; (b) the more narrowly the good is defined; (c) the larger the share of the consumer's budget spent on the good; and (d) the longer the time period consumers have to adjust to a change in price.

5. The price elasticity of supply measures the responsiveness of quantity supplied to price changes. This depends on how much the marginal cost of production changes as output changes. If marginal cost rises sharply as output expands, quantity supplied is less responsive to price increases and is thus less elastic. Also, the longer the time period producers have to adjust to price changes, the more elastic the supply.

6. Income elasticity of demand measures the responsiveness of demand to changes in consumer income. Income elasticity is positive for normal goods and negative for inferior goods.

7. The cross-price elasticity of demand measures the impact of a change in the price of one good on the demand for another good. Two goods are defined as substitutes, complements, or unrelated, depending on whether their cross-price elasticity of demand is positive, negative, or zero, respectively.

Key Concepts

Price elasticity of demand   98
Price elasticity formula   99
Inelastic demand   100
Unit-elastic demand   100
Elastic demand   100
Total revenue   100
Linear demand curve   101

Perfectly elastic demand curve   102
Perfectly inelastic demand curve   103
Unit-elastic demand curve   103
Constant-elasticity demand curve   104
Price elasticity of supply   109
Inelastic supply   109
Unit-elastic supply   109

Elastic supply   109
Perfectly elastic supply curve   110
Perfectly inelastic supply curve   110
Unit-elastic supply curve   111
Income elasticity of demand   112
Cross-price elasticity of demand   116

Questions for Review

1. CATEGORIES OF PRICE ELASTICITY OF DEMAND   For each of the following absolute values of price elasticity of demand, indicate whether demand is elastic, inelastic, perfectly elastic, perfectly inelastic, or unit elastic. In addition, determine what would happen to total revenue if a firm raised its price in each elasticity range identified.
    a. $E_D = 2.5$
    b. $E_D = 1.0$
    c. $E_D = \infty$
    d. $E_D = 0.8$

2. ELASTICITY AND TOTAL REVENUE   Explain the relationship between the price elasticity of demand and total revenue.

3. PRICE ELASTICITY AND THE LINEAR DEMAND CURVE   How is it possible for many price elasticities to be associated with a single demand curve?

4. DETERMINANTS OF PRICE ELASTICITY   Why is the price elasticity of demand for Coca-Cola greater than the price elasticity of demand for soft drinks generally?

5. DETERMINANTS OF PRICE ELASTICITY   Would the price elasticity of demand for electricity be more elastic over a shorter or a longer period of time?

6. DETERMINANTS OF PRICE ELASTICITY   What factors help determine the price elasticity of demand? What factors help determine the price elasticity of supply?

7. CROSS-PRICE ELASTICITY   Using demand and supply curves, predict the impact on the price and quantity demanded of Good 1 of an increase in the price of Good 2 if the two goods are substitutes. What if the two goods are complements?

8. OTHER ELASTICITY MEASURES   Complete each of the following sentences:

    a. The income elasticity of demand measures, for a given price, the _____ in quantity demanded divided by the _____ income from which it resulted.

    b. If a decrease in the price of one good causes a decrease in demand for another good, the two goods are _____.

    c. If the value of the cross-price elasticity of demand between two goods is approximately zero, they are considered _____.

Problems and Exercises

9. CALCULATING PRICE ELASTICITY OF DEMAND   Suppose that 50 units of a good are demanded at a price of $1 per unit. A reduction in price to $0.20 results in an increase in quantity demanded to 70 units. Show that these data yield a price elasticity of 0.25. By what percentage would a 10 percent rise in the price reduce the quantity demanded, assuming price elasticity remains constant along the demand curve?

10. PRICE ELASTICITY AND TOTAL REVENUE   Fill in the blanks for each price-quantity combination listed in the following table. What relationship have you depicted?

P	Q	Price Elasticity	Total Revenue
$9	1	_____	_____
$8	2	_____	_____
$7	3	_____	_____
$6	4	_____	_____
$5	5	_____	_____
$4	6	_____	_____
$3	7	_____	_____
$2	8	_____	_____

11. Case Study: Deterring Young Smokers   Why is the price elasticity of demand for cigarettes among teenagers greater than it is among those 20 and over?

12. INCOME ELASTICITY OF DEMAND   Calculate the income elasticity of demand for each of the following goods:

	Quantity Demanded When Income Is $10,000	Quantity Demanded When Income Is $20,000
Good 1	10	25
Good 2	4	5
Good 3	3	2

13. PRICE ELASTICITY OF SUPPLY   Calculate the price elasticity of supply for each of the following combinations of price and quantity supplied. In each case, determine whether supply is elastic, inelastic, perfectly elastic, perfectly inelastic, or unit elastic.

    a. Price falls from $2.25 to $1.75; quantity supplied falls from 600 units to 400 units.
    b. Price falls from $2.25 to $1.75; quantity supplied falls from 600 units to 500 units.
    c. Price falls from $2.25 to $1.75; quantity supplied remains at 600 units.
    d. Price increases from $1.75 to $2.25; quantity supplied increases from 466.67 units to 600 units.

Use the following diagram to answer the next two questions.

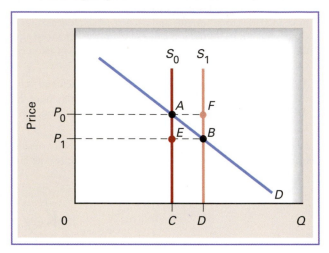

14. Case Study: The Market for Food and the "Farm Problem"   Interpret this diagram as showing the market demand and supply curves for agricultural products. Suppose that demand is inelastic over the relevant range of prices and supply increased from S_0 to S_1. What areas in the figure would you use to illustrate the net change in farmers' total revenue as a result of the increase in supply?

15. Case Study: The Market for Food and the "Farm Problem"   Again suppose that this diagram represents the market for agricultural products and that supply has increased from S_0 to S_1. To aid farmers, the federal government decides to stabilize the price at P_0 by buying up surplus farm products. Show on the diagram how much this would cost the government. By how much would farm income change compared to what it would have been without government intervention?

16. CROSS-PRICE ELASTICITY   Rank the following in order of increasing (from negative to positive) cross-price elasticity of demand with coffee. Explain your reasoning.

    Bleach

    Tea

    Cream

    Cola

Appendix
Price Elasticity and Tax Incidence

A contributing factor to the Revolutionary War was a British tax on tea imported by the American Colonies. The tea tax led to the Boston Tea Party, during which colonists dumped tea leaves into Boston Harbor. There was confusion about who would ultimately pay such a tax: Would it be paid by suppliers, demanders, or both? As you will see, tax incidence—that is, who pays a tax—depends on the price elasticities of demand and supply.

Demand Elasticity and Tax Incidence

Panel (a) of Exhibit 13 depicts the market for tea leaves, with demand D and supply S. Before the tax is imposed, the intersection of demand and supply yields a market price of $1.00 per ounce and a market quantity of

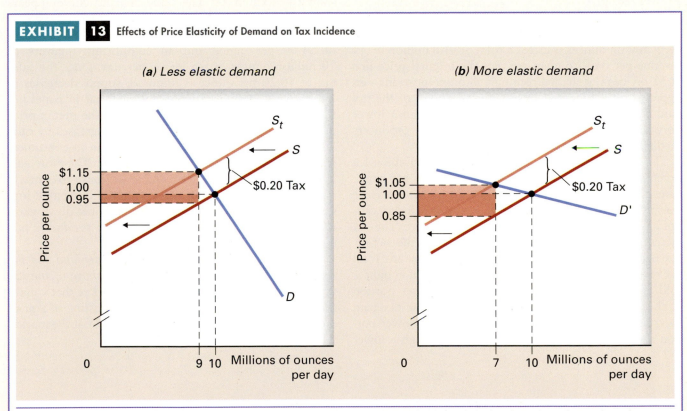

EXHIBIT 13 Effects of Price Elasticity of Demand on Tax Incidence

(a) Less elastic demand

(b) More elastic demand

The imposition of a $0.20-per-ounce tax on tea shifts the supply curve leftward from S to S_t. In panel (a), which has a less elastic demand curve, the market price rises from $1.00 to $1.15 per ounce and the market quantity falls from 10 million to 9 million ounces. In panel (b), which has a more elastic demand curve, the same tax leads to an increase in price from $1.00 to $1.05; market quantity falls from 10 million to 7 million ounces. The more elastic the demand curve, the more the tax is paid by producers in the form of a lower net-of-tax receipt.

10 million ounces per day. Now suppose a tax of $0.20 is imposed on each ounce sold. Recall that the supply curve represents the amount that producers are willing and able to supply at each price. Because the government now collects $0.20 in tax for each ounce sold, that amount must be added to the original supply curve to get a supply curve that includes the tax. Thus, the shift of the supply curve from S to S_t reflects the decrease in supply resulting from the tax. *The effect of a tax on tea is to decrease the supply by the amount of the tax.* The demand curve remains the same because nothing happened to demand; only the quantity demanded changes.

The result of the tax in panel (a) is to raise the equilibrium price from $1.00 to $1.15 and to decrease the equilibrium quantity from 10 million to 9 million ounces. As a result of the tax, consumers pay $1.15, or $0.15 more per ounce, and producers receive $0.95 after the tax, or $0.05 less per ounce. Thus, consumers pay $0.15 of the $0.20 tax as a higher price, and producers pay $0.05 as a lower receipt.

The shaded rectangle of panel (a) shows the total tax collected, which equals the tax per ounce of $0.20 times the 9 million ounces sold, for a total of $1.8 million in tax revenue per day. You can see that the original price line at $1 divides the shaded rectangle into two portions—an upper portion (light pink) showing the share of the tax paid by consumers through a higher price and a lower portion (dark pink) showing the tax paid by producers through a lower net-of-tax receipt.

The same situation is depicted in panel (b) of Exhibit 13, except that demand is more elastic than in the left panel. Consumers in panel (b) cut their quantity demanded more sharply in response to a price change, so producers cannot as easily pass the tax along at a higher price. The tax increases the price by $0.05, to $1.05, and the net-of-tax receipt to suppliers declines by $0.15 to $0.85. Total tax revenue equals $0.20 per ounce times 7 million ounces sold, or $1.4 million per day. Again, the upper portion of the shaded rectangle shows the share of the tax paid by consumers through a higher price, and the lower portion shows the share paid by producers through a lower

net-of-tax receipt. The tax is the difference between the amount consumers pay and the amount producers receive.

More generally, as long as the supply curve slopes upward, the more price elastic the demand, the more tax producers pay as a lower net-of-tax receipt and the less consumers bear as a higher price. Also notice that the amount sold decreases more in panel (b) than in panel (a): Other things constant, the total tax revenue declines more when demand is more elastic. Because tax revenue falls as the price elasticity of demand increases, governments around the world tend to tax products with inelastic demand, such as cigarettes, liquor, gasoline, gambling, salt, coffee, and, yes, tea.

Supply Elasticity and Tax Incidence

The effect of the elasticity of supply on tax incidence is shown in Exhibit 14. The same demand curve appears in both panels, but the supply curve is more elastic in panel (a). Again we begin with an equilibrium price of $1.00 per ounce and an equilibrium quantity of 10 million ounces of tea leaves per day. Once the sales tax of $0.20 per ounce is imposed, supply decreases in both panels to reflect the tax. Notice that in panel (a), the price rises to $1.15, or $0.15 above the pretax price of $1.00, while in panel (b), the price increases by only $0.05. Thus, more of the tax is passed on to consumers in panel (a), where supply is more elastic. The more easily suppliers can cut production in response to a newly imposed tax, the more of the tax consumers pay. More generally, as long as the demand curve slopes downward, *the more elastic the supply, the less tax producers pay and the more consumers pay.*

We conclude that *the less elastic the demand and the more elastic the supply, the greater the share of the tax paid by consumers.* The side of the market that's more nimble (that is, more price elastic) in adjusting to a price increase is more able to stick the other side of the market with more of the tax.

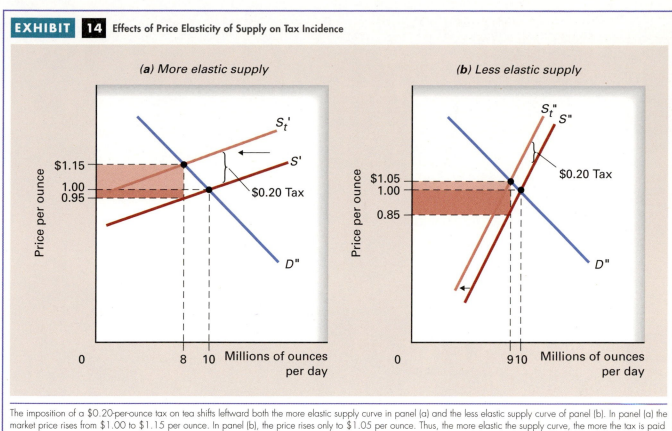

EXHIBIT **14** Effects of Price Elasticity of Supply on Tax Incidence

(a) More elastic supply

(b) Less elastic supply

The imposition of a $0.20-per-ounce tax on tea shifts leftward both the more elastic supply curve in panel (a) and the less elastic supply curve of panel (b). In panel (a) the market price rises from $1.00 to $1.15 per ounce. In panel (b), the price rises only to $1.05 per ounce. Thus, the more elastic the supply curve, the more the tax is paid by consumers as a higher price.

Appendix Questions

1. The claim is often made that a tax on a specific good is simply passed on to consumers. Under what conditions of demand and supply elasticities does this occur? Under what conditions is little of the tax passed on to consumers?

2. Suppose a tax is imposed on a good with a perfectly elastic supply curve.

   a. Who pays the tax?
   b. Using demand and supply curves, show how much tax is collected.
   c. How would this tax revenue change if the supply curve becomes less elastic?

3. During the 1980s, the U.S. Congress imposed a high sales tax on yachts, figuring that the rich could afford to pay for this luxury. But so many jobs were lost in the boat-building industry that the measure was finally repealed. What did Congress get wrong in imposing this luxury tax?

Consumer Choice and Demand

6

Fuse/Jupiter Images

○ Why are newspapers sold in vending machines that allow you to take more than one?

○ How much do you eat when you can eat all you want?

○ Why don't restaurants allow doggie bags with their all-you-can-eat specials?

○ What cures cabin fever and spring fever?

○ Why is water cheaper than diamonds even though water is essential to life while diamonds are simply bling?

To answer these and other questions, we take a closer look at consumer demand, a key building block in economics.

You have already learned two reasons why demand curves slope downward. The first is the *substitution effect* of a price change. When the price of a good falls, consumers substitute that now-cheaper good for other goods. The second is the *income effect* of a price change. When the price of a good falls, real incomes increase, boosting consumers' ability to buy more.

Demand is so important that it needs more attention. This chapter develops the law of demand based on the utility, or satisfaction, of consumption. As usual, the assumption is that you and other consumers try to maximize utility, or satisfaction. The point of this chapter is not to teach you how to maximize utility—that comes naturally. But learning the theory behind your behavior will help you understand the implications of that behavior, making predictions more accurate.

Topics discussed include:

- Total and marginal utility
- Law of diminishing marginal utility
- Measuring utility
- Utility-maximizing condition
- Consumer surplus
- Role of time in demand
- Time price of goods

Utility Analysis

Suppose you and a friend are dining out. After dinner, your friend asks how you liked your meal. You wouldn't say, "I liked mine twice as much as you liked yours." Nor would you say, "It deserves a rating of 86 on the Consumer Satisfaction Index." The utility, or satisfaction, you derive from that meal cannot be compared with another person's experience, nor can your utility be measured based on some uniform standard. But you might say something such as, "I liked it better than my last meal here" or "I liked it better than campus food." More generally, you can say whether one of your experiences is more satisfying than another. Even if you say nothing about your likes and dislikes, we can draw conclusions about your preferences by observing your behavior. For example, we can conclude that you prefer apples to oranges if, when the two are priced the same, you buy apples every time.

Tastes and Preferences

As introduced in Chapter 3, *utility* is the sense of pleasure, or satisfaction, that comes from consumption. Utility is subjective. The utility you derive from a particular good, service, or activity depends on your *tastes and preferences*—your likes and dislikes in consumption. Some things are extremely appealing to you and others are not. You may not understand, for example, why someone would pay good money for sharks' fin soup, calves' brains, polka music, or martial arts movies. Why are most baby carriages sold in the United States navy blue, whereas they are yellow in Italy and chartreuse in Germany? And why do Australians favor chicken-flavored potato chips and chicken-flavored salt?

As noted in Chapter 4, your desires for food and drink are largely biological, as is your desire for comfort, rest, shelter, friendship, love, status, personal safety, and a pleasant environment. Your family background shapes some of your tastes, such as food preferences. Other influences include your culture, peer pressure, and religious convictions. So economists can say something about the origin of tastes, but they claim no particular expertise. *Economists assume simply that tastes are given and are relatively stable—that is, different people may have different tastes, but an individual's tastes are not constantly in flux.* To be sure, tastes for some products do change over time. Here are four examples: (1) over the last two decades, hiking boots and work boots replaced running shoes as everyday footwear among many college students, (2) Americans began consuming leaner cuts of beef after a report linked the fat in red meat to a greater risk of cancer, (3) because of the decline in the popularity of baseball cards, the number of shops that sell and trade these cards fell from about

10,000 in the early 1990s to less than 1,600 by 2010; and (4) the increased appeal of locally grown produce has tripled the number of farmers markets in the United States since 1995.

Although some tastes do change over time, economists believe they are stable enough to allow us to examine relationships such as that between price and quantity demanded. If tastes were not relatively stable, then we could not reasonably make the other-things-constant assumption required for demand analysis. We could not even draw a demand curve.

The Law of Diminishing Marginal Utility

Suppose it's a hot summer day and you are extremely thirsty after running four miles. You pour yourself an 8-ounce glass of ice water. That first glass is wonderful, and it puts a serious dent in your thirst. The next glass is not quite as wonderful, but it is still pretty good. The third one is just fair; and the fourth glass you barely finish.

What can we say about the *utility*, or satisfaction, you get from water? Let's first distinguish between *total utility* and *marginal utility*. **Total utility** is the total satisfaction you derive from consumption. In this example, total utility is the total satisfaction you get from four glasses of water. **Marginal utility** is the change in total utility resulting from a one-unit change in consumption. For example, the marginal utility of a third glass of water is the change in total utility resulting from drinking that third glass.

Your experience with water reflects an economic law—the **law of diminishing marginal utility**. This law states that the more of a good you consume per period, other things constant, the smaller the increase in your total utility from additional consumption—that is, the smaller the marginal utility of each additional unit consumed. The marginal utility you derive from each additional glass of water declines as you drink more. You enjoy the first glass a lot, but each additional glass provides less and less marginal utility. If forced to drink a fifth glass, you wouldn't like it; your marginal utility would be negative—you would experience *disutility*.

Diminishing marginal utility is a feature of all consumption. A second foot-long sub sandwich at one meal, for most people, would provide little or no marginal utility. You might still enjoy a second movie on Friday night, but a third would probably be too much to take. In fact, almost anything repeated enough could become torture, such as being forced to watch the same movie or listen to the same song over and over and over. Yes, variety is the spice of life.

A long, cold winter spent cooped up inside can cause "cabin fever." Each additional cold day brings more disutility. But the fever breaks with the arrival of the first warm day of spring, which is something special. That first warm, glorious day causes such delirious joy that this jump in marginal utility has its own fevered name—"spring fever." Spring fever is eventually "cured" by many warm days like the first. By the time August rolls around, you attach much less marginal utility to yet another warm day.

For some goods, the drop in marginal utility with additional consumption is greater. A second copy of the same daily newspaper would likely provide you no marginal utility (in fact, the design of newspaper vending machines relies on the fact that people will take no more than one).[1] Likewise, a second viewing of the same movie at one sitting usually yields no additional utility. More generally, expressions such as "Been there, done that" and "Same old, same old" convey the idea that, for many activities, things

total utility
The total satisfaction you derive from consumption; this could refer to either your total utility of consuming a particular good or your total utility from all consumption

marginal utility
The change in your total utility from a one-unit change in your consumption of a good

law of diminishing marginal utility
The more of a good a person consumes per period, the smaller the increase in total utility from consuming one more unit, other things constant

---

1. This example appears in Marshall Jevons, *The Fatal Equilibrium* (Cambridge, Mass.: MIT Press, 1985).

start to get old fast. Restaurants depend on the law of diminishing marginal utility when they hold all-you-can-eat specials—and no doggie bags allowed, because the deal is all you can eat now, not now and over the next few days.

Measuring Utility

So far, the description of utility has used such words as *wonderful, good,* and *fair.* The analysis can't be pushed very far with such subjective language. To predict consumer behavior, we need to develop a consistent way of viewing utility.

Units of Utility

Let's go back to the water example. Although there really is no objective way of measuring utility, if pressed, you could be more specific about how much you enjoyed each glass of water. For example, you might say the second glass was half as good as the first, the third was half as good as the second, the fourth was half as good as the third, and you passed up a fifth glass because you expected no positive utility. To get a handle on this, let's assign arbitrary numbers to the utility you get from water, so the pattern reflects your expressed level of satisfaction. Let's say the first glass provides you with 40 units of utility, the second with 20, the third with 10, and the fourth with 5. A fifth glass, if you were forced to drink it, would cause negative utility, or disutility—in this case, say, −2 units. *Developing numerical values for utility allows us to be more specific about the utility of consumption.* If it would help, you could think of these units more playfully as thrills, kicks, or jollies—as in, getting your kicks from consumption.

By attaching a numerical measure to utility, we can compare the total utility a particular consumer gets from different goods as well as the marginal utility that a consumer gets from additional consumption. Thus, we can employ units of utility to evaluate a consumer's preferences. Note, however, that we cannot compare utility levels across consumers. *Each person has a uniquely subjective utility scale.*

The first column of Exhibit 1 lists possible quantities of water you might consume after running four miles on a hot day. The second column presents the total utility derived from that consumption, and the third column shows the marginal utility of each additional glass of water. Recall that marginal utility is the change in total utility from consuming an additional unit of the good. You can see from the second column that total utility increases with each of the first four glasses but by smaller and smaller amounts. The third column shows that the first glass of water yields 40 units of utility, the second glass yields an additional 20 units, and so on. Marginal utility declines

EXHIBIT   1   Utility Derived From Drinking Water After Running Four Miles

Amount Consumed (8-ounce glasses)	Total Utility	Marginal Utility
0	0	—
1	40	40
2	60	20
3	70	10
4	75	5
5	73	−2

after the first glass of water, becoming negative with the fifth glass. *At any level of consumption, marginal utilities sum to yield the total utility of that amount.* Total utility is graphed in panel (a) of Exhibit 2. Again, because of diminishing marginal utility, each additional glass of water adds less to total utility, so total utility increases for the first four glasses but at a decreasing rate. Panel (b) shows the law of diminishing marginal utility.

Utility Maximization in a World Without Scarcity

Economists assume that your purpose for drinking water, as with all consumption, is to *maximize your total utility.* So how much water do you consume? If the price of water is zero, you drink water as long as doing so increases total utility. Each of the first four glasses of water adds to your total utility. *If a good is free, you increase consumption as long as marginal utility is positive.* Let's broaden the analysis to a world of two goods—pizza and movie rentals. We continue to translate the satisfaction you receive from consumption into units of utility. Based on your tastes and preferences, suppose

EXHIBIT 2 Total Utility and Marginal Utility You Derive From Drinking Water After Running Four Miles

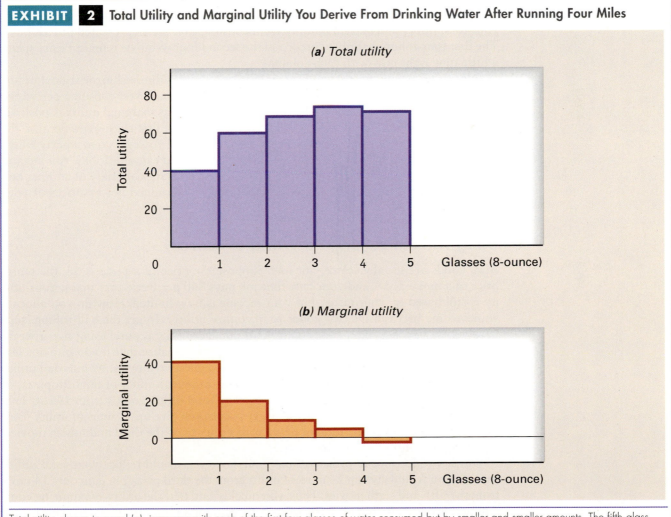

Total utility, shown in panel (a), increases with each of the first four glasses of water consumed but by smaller and smaller amounts. The fifth glass causes total utility to fall, implying that marginal utility is negative, as shown in panel (b).

EXHIBIT	3	Total and Marginal Utilities From Pizza and Movies						

Pizza				Movie Rentals			
(1)	(2)	(3)	(4)	(5)	(6)	(7)	(8)
Consumed per Week	Total Utility	Marginal Utility	Marginal Utility per Dollar if $p = \$8$	Viewed per Week	Total Utility	Marginal Utility	Marginal Utility per Dollar if $p = \$4$
0	0	—	—	0	0	—	—
1	56	56	7	1	40	40	10
2	88	32	4	2	68	28	7
3	**112**	**24**	**3**	3	88	20	5
4	130	18	2¼	**4**	**100**	**12**	**3**
5	142	12	1½	5	108	8	2
6	150	8	1	6	114	6	1½

your total utility and marginal utility from consumption are as presented in Exhibit 3. The first four columns apply to pizza and the second four to movie rentals. Please spend a little time right now with each column.

Notice from columns (3) and (7) that each good shows diminishing marginal utility. Given this set of preferences, how much of each good would you consume per week? At a zero price, you would increase consumption as long as marginal utility is positive. Thus, you would consume at least the first six pizzas and first six movies because the sixth unit of each good yields positive marginal utility. Did you ever go to a party where the food and drinks were free to you? How much did you eat and drink? You ate and drank until you didn't want any more—that is, until the marginal utility of another bite and another sip fell to zero. Your consumption was determined not by prices or your income but simply by your tastes.

Utility Maximization in a World of Scarcity

Alas, goods are usually scarce, not free. Suppose the price of a pizza is $8, the rental price of a movie is $4, and your part-time job pays $40 per week after taxes. Your utility is still based on your tastes, but your income is now limited. How do you allocate your income between the two goods to maximize utility? To get the ball rolling, suppose you start off spending your entire $40 budget on pizza, purchasing five a week, which yields a total of 142 units of utility. You quickly realize that if you buy one less pizza, you free up enough income in your budget to rent two movies. Would total utility increase? Sure. You give up 12 units of utility, the marginal utility of the fifth pizza, to get 68 units of utility from the first two movies. Total utility zooms from 142 to 198. Then you notice that if you cut back to three pizzas, you give up 18 units of utility from the fourth pizza but gain a total of 32 units of utility from the third and fourth movies. This is another utility-increasing move.

Further reductions in pizza consumption, however, would reduce your total utility because you would give up 24 units of utility from the third pizza but gain only 14 units from the fifth and sixth movies. Thus, you quickly find that the utility-maximizing combination is three pizzas and four movies per week, for a total utility of 212. This means spending $24 on pizza and $16 on movies. *You are in equilibrium when consuming this combination because any affordable change would reduce your utility.*

Utility-Maximizing Conditions

Once a consumer is in equilibrium, there is no way to increase utility by reallocating the budget. Any change decreases utility. But, wait, there's more: In equilibrium, the last dollar spent on each good yields the same marginal utility. Let's see how this works. Column (4) shows the marginal utility of pizza divided by a price of $8. Column (8) shows the marginal utility of movies divided by a price of $4. The equilibrium combination of three pizzas and four movies exhausts the $40 budget and adds 3 units of utility for the last dollar spent on each good. **Consumer equilibrium** is achieved when the budget is exhausted and the last dollar spent on each good yields the same marginal utility. In equilibrium, the marginal utility of a pizza divided by its price equals the marginal utility of a movie divided by its price. In short, the consumer gets the same bang from the last buck spent on each good. This equality can be expressed as:

$$\frac{MU_p}{p_p} = \frac{MU_m}{p_m}$$

where MU_p is the marginal utility of pizza, p_p is the price of pizza, MU_m is the marginal utility of movies, and p_m is the rental price. The consumer reallocates spending until the last dollar spent on each product yields the same marginal utility. Although this example considers only two goods, the logic of utility maximization applies to any number of goods.

In equilibrium, higher-priced goods must yield more marginal utility than lower-priced goods—enough additional utility to compensate for their higher price. Because a pizza costs twice as much as a movies rental, the marginal utility of the final pizza purchased must, in equilibrium, be twice that of the final movie rented. Indeed, the marginal utility of the third pizza, 24, is twice that of the fourth movie, 12. Economists do not claim that you consciously equate the ratios of marginal utility to price, but they do claim that you act as if you made such calculations. Thus, you decide how much of each good to purchase by considering your tastes, market prices, and your income. Consumers maximize utility by equalizing the marginal utility from the last dollar spent on each good. This approach resolved what had been an economic puzzle, as discussed in the following case study.

consumer equilibrium
The condition in which an individual consumer's budget is exhausted and the last dollar spent on each good yields the same marginal utility; therefore, utility is maximized

BRINGING THEORY TO LIFE

Water, Water, Everywhere   Centuries ago, economists puzzled over the price of diamonds relative to the price of water. Diamonds are mere bling—-certainly not a necessity of life in any sense. Water is essential to life and has hundreds of valuable uses. Yet diamonds are expensive, while water is cheap. For example, the $10,000 spent on a high-quality one-carat diamond could buy about 10,000 bottles of water or about 2.8 million gallons of municipally supplied water (which sells for about 35 cents per 100 gallons in New York City). However measured, diamonds are extremely expensive relative to water. For the price of a one-carat diamond, you could buy enough water to last two lifetimes.

How can something as useful as water cost so much less than something of such limited use as diamonds? In 1776, Adam Smith discussed what has come to be called the *diamonds-water paradox*. Because water is essential to life, the total utility derived from water greatly exceeds the total utility derived from diamonds. Yet the market value of a good is based not on its total utility but on what consumers are willing and able to pay for an additional unit—that is, on its *marginal utility*. Because water is so abundant in nature, we consume it to the point where the marginal utility of the last gallon purchased is relatively low. Because diamonds are relatively scarce compared

CASE STUDY

e activity
Almost any question you might have about water supply and use in the United States can be answered by visiting the U.S. Geological Survey's Water Q&A Web page at http://ga.water. usgs.gov/edu/mqanda.html. Various terms are linked to pages with additional information. Another great source is the Environmental Protection Agency at http:// www.epa.gov/ebtpages/water. html. This site includes links to many water issues such as the economic effects of pollution.

to water, the marginal utility of the last diamond purchased is relatively high. Thus, water is cheap and diamonds expensive. As Ben Franklin said "We will only know the worth of water when the well is dry."

Speaking of water, sales of bottled water are growing faster than any other beverage category—creating a $15 billion U.S. industry, an average of 25 gallons per person in 2010. Bottled water ranks behind only soft drinks in sales, outselling coffee, milk, and beer. The United States offers the world's largest market for bottled water—importing water from places such as Italy, France, Sweden, Wales, even Fiji. "Water bars" in cities such as Newport, Rhode Island, and San Francisco feature bottled water as the main attraction. A 9-ounce bottle of Evian water costs $1.49. That amounts to $21.19 per gallon, or nearly 10 times more than gasoline. You think that's pricey? Bling H_2O is available in bottles decorated with Swarovski crystals and sells for more than $50 a bottle—that's about 100 times more than gasoline.

Why would consumers pay a premium for bottled water when water from the tap costs virtually nothing? After all, some bottled water comes from municipal taps (for example, New York City water is also bottled and sold under the brand name Tap'dNY). First, many people do not view the two as good substitutes. Some people have concerns about the safety of tap water, and they consider bottled water a healthy alternative (about half those surveyed in a Gallup Poll said they won't drink water straight from the tap). Second, even those who drink tap water find bottled water a convenient option away from home. And third, some bottled water is now lightly flavored or fortified with vitamins. People who buy bottled water apparently feel the additional benefit offsets the additional cost.

Fast-food restaurants now offer bottled water as a healthy alternative to soft drinks. Soft-drink sales have been declining for more than a decade as bottled water sales have climbed. But if you can't fight 'em, join 'em: Pepsi's Aquafina is the top-selling bottled water in America, and Coke's Dasani ranks second.

Sources: Dana Cimilluca et al., "Coke Near Deal for Bottler," *Wall Street Journal*, 25 February 2010; Jack Healy, "Five-cent Deposits Set for Bottled Water," *New York Times*, 24 October 2009; and Charles Duhigg, "That Tap Water Is Legal But May Be Unhealthy," *New York Times*, 16 December 2009. The Definitive Bottled Water site is http://www.bottledwaterweb.com/, and the New York City drinking water department is at http://www.nyc.gov/html/dep/html/drinking_water/index.shtml.

Marginal Utility and the Law of Demand

How does utility analysis relate to your demand for pizza? The discussion so far yields a single point on your demand curve for pizza: At a price of $8, you demand three pizzas per week. This is based on income of $40 per week, a price of $4 per movie rental, and your tastes reflected by the utility tables in Exhibit 3. Knowing that three pizzas are demanded when the price is $8 offers no clue about the shape of your demand curve for pizza. To generate another point, let's see what happens to quantity demanded if the price of pizza changes, while keeping other things constant (such as tastes, income, and the price of movie rentals). Suppose the price of a pizza drops from $8 to $6.

Exhibit 4 is the same as Exhibit 3, except the price per pizza is $6. Your original choice was three pizzas and four movie rentals. At that combination and with the price of pizza now $6, the marginal utility per dollar spent on the third pizza is 4, while the marginal utility per dollar spent on the fourth movie remains at 3. The marginal utilities of the last dollar spent on each good are no longer equal. What's more, the original

> **EXHIBIT 4**   Total and Marginal Utilities From Pizza and Movies After the Price of Pizza Decreases From $8 to $6

	Pizza				Movie Rentals			
(1)	(2)	(3)	(4)		(5)	(6)	(7)	(8)
Consumed per Week	Total Utility	Marginal Utility	Marginal Utility per Dollar if $p = \$6$		Viewed per Week	Total Utility	Marginal Utility	Marginal Utility per Dollar if $p = \$4$
0	0	—	—		0	0	—	—
1	56	56	9⅓		1	40	40	10
2	88	32	5⅓		2	68	28	7
3	112	24	4		3	88	20	5
4	**130**	**18**	**3**		**4**	**100**	**12**	**3**
5	142	12	2		5	108	8	2
6	150	8	1⅓		6	114	6	1½

combination of three pizzas and four movies now leaves $6 unspent. So you could still buy your original combination but have $6 left to spend (this, incidentally, shows the income effect of the lower price). You can increase utility by adjusting your consumption. Take a moment now to see if you can figure out what the new equilibrium should be.

In light of your utility schedules in Exhibit 4, you would increase your consumption to four pizzas per week. This strategy exhausts your budget and equates the marginal utilities of the last dollar expended on each good. Your movie rentals remain unchanged. The marginal utility of the fourth pizza, 18, divided by the price of $6 yields 3 units of utility per dollar of expenditure, the same as you get from the fourth movie. You are in equilibrium once again. Total utility increases by the 18 units you derive from the fourth pizza. Thus, you are clearly better off as a result of the price decrease.

We now have a second point on your demand curve for pizza—if the price is $6, you demand four pizzas. The two points are presented as *a* and *b* in Exhibit 5. We could continue to change the price of pizza and thereby generate additional points on the demand curve, but you can get some idea of the demand curve's downward slope from these two points. The shape of the demand curve for pizza matches our expectations based on the law of demand: Price and quantity demanded are inversely related. (Try estimating your price elasticity of demand between points *a* and *b*. Hint: What does your total spending on pizza tell you?)

We have gone to some lengths to see how you (or any consumer) maximize utility. Given prices and your income, your tastes and preferences naturally guide you to the best bundle. You are not even conscious of your behavior. The urge to maximize utility is like the force of gravity—both work whether or not you understand them. Even animal behavior seems consistent with the law of demand. Wolves, for example, exhibit no territorial concerns when game is plentiful. But when game becomes scarce, wolves carefully mark their territory and defend it against intruders. Thus, wolves appear to value game more when it is scarce.

Now that you have some idea of utility, let's consider an application of utility analysis.

Consumer Surplus

In our earlier example, total utility increased when the price of pizza fell from $8 to $6. In this section, we take a closer look at how consumers benefit from a lower price. Suppose your demand for foot-long sub sandwiches is as shown in Exhibit 6. Recall

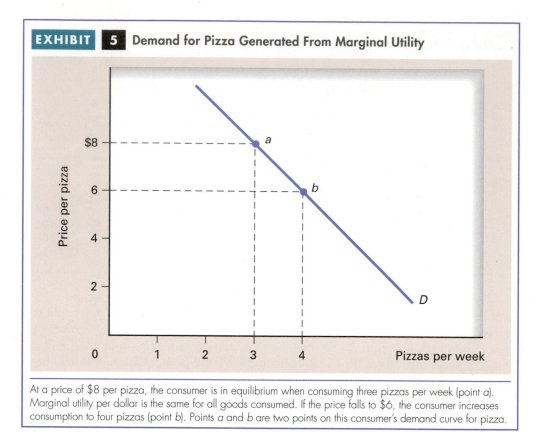

EXHIBIT 5   Demand for Pizza Generated From Marginal Utility

Price per pizza (y-axis)

$8 ----- a

6 ----- b

4

2

D

0   1   2   3   4   Pizzas per week

At a price of $8 per pizza, the consumer is in equilibrium when consuming three pizzas per week (point *a*). Marginal utility per dollar is the same for all goods consumed. If the price falls to $6, the consumer increases consumption to four pizzas (point *b*). Points *a* and *b* are two points on this consumer's demand curve for pizza.

that in constructing an individual's demand curve, we hold tastes, income, and the prices of other goods constant. Only the price of the good in question varies. At a price of $8 or above, you find that the marginal utility of other goods that you could buy for $8 is higher than the marginal utility of a sub sandwich. Consequently, you buy no subs. At a price of $7, you are willing and able to buy one per month, so the marginal utility of that first sub exceeds the marginal utility you expected from spending that $7 on your best alternative—say, a movie ticket. A price of $6 prompts you to buy two subs a month. The second is worth at least $6 to you. At a price of $5, you buy three subs, and at $4, you buy four. *The value of the sub purchased must at least equal the price; otherwise, you wouldn't buy it.* Along the demand curve, therefore, the price reflects your **marginal valuation** of the good, or the dollar value to you of the marginal utility derived from consuming each additional unit.

Notice that if the price is $4, you can purchase four subs for $4 each, even though you would have been willing to pay more for each of the first three subs. The first sandwich provides marginal utility that you valued at $7; the second you valued at $6; and the third you valued at $5. In fact, if you had to, rather than go without subs, you would have been willing to pay $7 for the first, $6 for the second, and $5 for the third. The dollar value of the total utility of the first four sandwiches is $7 + $6 + $5 + $4 = $22 per month. But when the price is $4, you get all four for a total of $16. Thus, a price of $4 confers a **consumer surplus**, or a consumer bonus, equal to the difference between the maximum amount you would have been willing to pay ($22) rather than go without subs altogether and what you actually pay ($16). When the price is $4, your consumer surplus is $22 − $16 = $6, as approximated by the six darker shaded blocks in Exhibit 6. Consumer surplus equals the value of the total utility you receive from

Marginal valuation

The dollar value of the marginal utility derived from consuming each additional unit of a good

consumer surplus

The difference between the most a consumer would pay for a given quantity of a good and what the consumer actually pays

EXHIBIT **6** **Consumer Surplus From Sub Sandwiches**

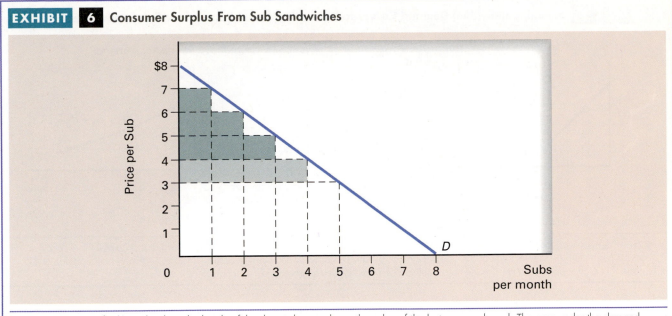

At a given quantity of sub sandwiches, the height of the demand curve shows the value of the last one purchased. The area under the demand curve for a specific quantity shows the total value a consumer attaches to that quantity. At a price of $4, the consumer purchases four subs. The first one is valued at $7, the second at $6, the third at $5, and the fourth at $4. The consumer values four at $22. Because the consumer pays $4 per sub, all four can be purchased for $16. The difference between what the consumer would have been willing to pay ($22) and what the consumer actually pays ($16) is called consumer surplus. When the price is $4, the consumer surplus is $6, as represented by the dark shaded area under the demand curve above $4. When the price of subs falls to $3, consumer surplus increases by $4, as reflected by the lighter shaded area.

consuming the sandwiches minus your total spending on them. *Consumer surplus is reflected by the area under the demand curve but above the price.*

If the price falls to $3, you buy five subs a month. Apparently, you feel that the marginal utility from the fifth one is worth at least $3. The lower price means that you get all five for $3 each, even though each except the fifth one is worth more to you than $3. Your consumer surplus when the price is $3 is the value of the total utility from the first five, which is $7 + $6 + $5 + $4 + $3 = $25, minus your cost, which is $3 × 5 = $15. Thus, your consumer surplus is $25 − $15 = $10, as indicated by both the dark and the light shaded blocks in Exhibit 6. So if the price declines to $3, your consumer surplus increases by $4, as reflected by the four lighter-shaded blocks in Exhibit 6. You can see how consumers benefit from lower prices.

Incidentally, in some cases your consumer surplus is huge, such as from a bottle of water if you are dying of thirst, a winter coat if you are at risk of freezing, or a pair of glasses if you can't see without them.

Market Demand and Consumer Surplus

Let's talk now about the market demand for a good, assuming the market consists of you and two other consumers. *The market demand curve is simply the horizontal sum of the individual demand curves for all consumers in the market.* Exhibit 7 shows how the demand curves for three consumers in the market for sub sandwiches sum horizontally to yield the market demand. At a price of $4, for example, you demand four subs per month, Brittany demands two, and Chris demands none. The market demand at a price of $4 is therefore six sandwiches. At a price of $2, you demand six per month, Brittany four, and Chris two, for a market demand of 12. *The market demand*

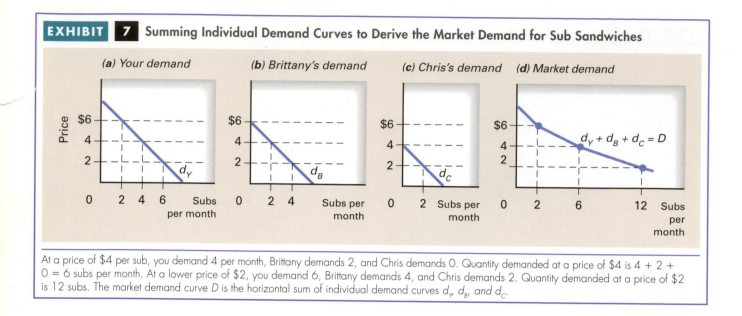

EXHIBIT 7   Summing Individual Demand Curves to Derive the Market Demand for Sub Sandwiches

At a price of $4 per sub, you demand 4 per month, Brittany demands 2, and Chris demands 0. Quantity demanded at a price of $4 is 4 + 2 + 0 = 6 subs per month. At a lower price of $2, you demand 6, Brittany demands 4, and Chris demands 2. Quantity demanded at a price of $2 is 12 subs. The market demand curve D is the horizontal sum of individual demand curves d_Y, d_B, and d_C.

curve shows the total quantity demanded per period by all consumers at various prices. Consumer surplus can be used to examine market demand as well as individual demand. *At a given price, consumer surplus for the market is the difference between the most consumers would pay for that quantity and the amount they do pay.*

Instead of just three consumers in the market, suppose there are many. Exhibit 8 presents market demand for a good with millions of consumers. If the price is $2 per unit, each person adjusts his or her quantity demanded until the marginal valuation of the final unit purchased equals $2. But each consumer also gets to buy all other units

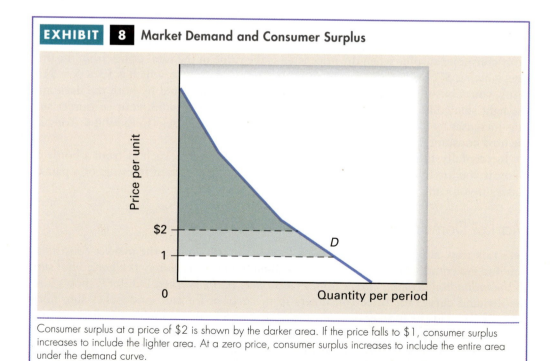

EXHIBIT 8   Market Demand and Consumer Surplus

Consumer surplus at a price of $2 is shown by the darker area. If the price falls to $1, consumer surplus increases to include the lighter area. At a zero price, consumer surplus increases to include the entire area under the demand curve.

for $2 each. In Exhibit 8, the dark shading, bounded above by the demand curve and below by the price line at $2, depicts the consumer surplus. The light shading shows the gain in consumer surplus if the price drops to $1. Notice that if this good were given away, the consumer surplus would not be that much greater than when the price is $1.

Consumer surplus is the net benefit consumers get from market exchange. It can be used to measure economic welfare and to compare the effects of different market structures, different tax structures, and different public programs, such as for medical care, as discussed in the following case study.

PUBLIC POLICY

The Marginal Value of Free Medical Care Certain Americans, such as the elderly and those on welfare, receive government-subsidized medical care. State and federal taxpayers spend more than $750 billion a year providing medical care to 94 million Medicare and Medicaid recipients, or more than $8,000 per beneficiary. Medicaid is the largest and fastest growing spending category in most state budgets. Beneficiaries pay only a tiny share of Medicaid costs; most services are free.

The problem with giving something away is that a beneficiary consumes it to the point where the marginal value reaches zero, although the marginal cost to taxpayers can be sizable. This is not to say that people derive no benefit from these programs. Although beneficiaries may attach little or no value to the final unit consumed, they likely derive a substantial consumer surplus from all the other units they consume. For example, suppose that Exhibit 8 represents the demand for health care by Medicaid beneficiaries. If the price they face is zero, each beneficiary consumes health care to the point where the demand curve intersects the horizontal axis—that is, where his or her marginal valuation is zero. Although they attach little or no value to their final unit of Medicaid-funded health care, their consumer surplus is the entire area under the demand curve.

One way to reduce the cost to taxpayers without significantly harming beneficiaries is to charge a token amount—say, $1 per doctor visit. Beneficiaries would eliminate visits they value less than $1. This practice would yield significant savings to taxpayers but would still leave beneficiaries with abundant health care and a substantial consumer surplus (measured in Exhibit 8 as the area under the demand curve but above the $1 price). As a case in point, one Medicaid experiment in California required some beneficiaries to pay $1 per visit for their first two office visits per month (after two visits, the price of additional visits reverted to zero). A control group continued to receive free medical care. The $1 charge reduced office visits by 8 percent compared to the control group. Medical care, like other goods and services, is also sensitive to its time cost (a topic discussed in the next section). For example, a 10 percent increase in the average travel time to a free outpatient clinic reduced visits by 10 percent. Similarly, when the relocation of a free health clinic at one college increased students' average walking time by 10 minutes, visits dropped 40 percent.

Another problem with giving something away is that beneficiaries are less vigilant about getting honest value, and this may increase the possibility of waste, fraud, and abuse. According to President Obama, "improper payments" for Medicaid and Medicare cost taxpayers nearly $100 billion in 2009. Medicaid fraud has replaced illegal drugs as the top crime in Florida. Crooks were charging the government for medical supplies

CASE STUDY

e activity
This case study points out that patients have little incentive to monitor physician behavior when they do not pay the bill. In an attempt to control costs, Medicare reduces the reimbursement rate for services provided by physicians. How do you suppose physicians respond? Auditors with the Centers for Medicare and Medicaid Services (CMS) examined physician behavior and found that they increase the volume and intensity of work in response to declining prices to maintain revenue. CMS's easy-to-read report on physician response, which includes several real examples, can be found at http://www.cms.gov/ActuarialStudies/. Under Actuarial Studies, click on Physician Response.

Ackerman Gruber Images

that were not delivered or not needed (some supposed beneficiaries were dead). People won't tolerate padded bills and fake claims if they have to pay their own bills.

Finally, program beneficiaries have less incentive to pursue healthy behaviors themselves in their diet, their exercise, and the like. This doesn't necessarily mean certain groups don't deserve heavily subsidized medical care. The point is that when something is free, people consume it until their marginal value is zero, they pay less attention to getting honest value, and they take less personal responsibility for their own health.

Some Medicare beneficiaries visit one or more medical specialists most days of the week. Does all this medical attention improve their health care? Not according to a long-running Dartmouth Medical School study. Researchers there found no apparent medical benefit and even some harm from such overuse. As one doctor lamented, "The system is broken. I'm not being a mean ogre, but when you give something away for free, there is nothing to keep utilization down."[2] Even a modest money cost or time cost would reduce utilization, yet would still leave beneficiaries with quality health care and a substantial consumer surplus. Research suggests that up to 30 percent of all medical care is unnecessary.

Federal legislation in 2010 expanded the coverage of Medicaid and extended insurance coverage to many without it. Research by Michael Anderson and others suggests that one result will be a "substantial increase in care provided to currently uninsured individuals." No question, better health care can improve the quality of life, but overusing a service because the price is zero also wastes scarce resources.

Sources: Michael Anderson, Carlos Dobkin, and Tal Gross, "The Effects of Health Insurance Coverage on the Use of Medical Services," NBER Working Paper 15823 (March 2010); David Card, Carlos Dobkin, and Nicole Maestras, "The Impact of Nearly Universal Insurance Coverage on Health Care Utilization," *American Economic Review*, 98 (December 2008): 2242–2258; Elliot Fisher et al., "The Implications of Regional Variation in Medicare Spending," *Annals of Internal Medicine*, 18 February 2003; Gina Kolata, "Law May Do Little to Help Curb Unnecessary Care," *New York Times*, 29 March 2010; and Steven Rhoads, "Marginalism," in *The Fortune Encyclopedia of Economics*, edited by D. R. Henderson (New York: Warner, 1993): 31–33. A transcript of President Obama's remarks about 'improper payments' is at http://www.whitehouse.gov/the-press-office/remarks-president-health-insurance-reform-st-charles-mo. For more on Medicare and Medicaid, go to http://www.cms.hhs.gov/.

The Role of Time in Demand

Because consumption does not occur instantly, time plays a role in demand analysis. Consumption takes time and, as Ben Franklin said, time is money—time has a positive value for most people. Consequently, consumption has a *money price* and a *time price*. Goods are demanded because of the benefits they offer. It is not the microwave oven, personal computer, airline trip, or headache medicine that you value but the services they provide. Other things constant, you would gladly pay more to get the same benefit in less time, as with faster ovens, computers, airline trips, and headache relief. Likewise, you are willing to pay more for seedless grapes, seedless oranges, and seedless watermelon.

Your willingness to pay a premium for time-saving goods and services depends on the opportunity cost of your time. Differences in the value of time among consumers help explain differences in the consumption patterns observed in the economy. For example, a retired couple has more leisure time than a working couple and may clip discount coupons and search the newspapers for bargains, sometimes even going from store to store for particular grocery items on sale that week. The working couple tends to ignore the coupons and sales, eats out more often, and shops more at convenience stores, where they pay more for the "convenience." The retired couple is more inclined to drive to a vacation destination, whereas the working couple flies.

2.   As reported by Gina Kolata, "Patients in Florida Lining Up for All That Medicare Covers," *New York Times*, 13 September 2003.

Just inside the gates at Disneyland, Disney World, and Universal Studios are boards listing the waiting times of each attraction and ride. At that point, the dollar cost of admission has already been paid, so the marginal dollar cost of each ride and attraction is zero. The waiting times offer a menu of the marginal *time costs* of each ride or attraction. Incidentally, people willing to pay up to $55 an hour at Disney World and $60 an hour at Disneyland (plus the price of admission), until recently, could take VIP tours that bypass the lines. And at Universal Studios, you can still pay extra for a pass to the front of the line. How much would you pay to avoid the lines?

Differences in the opportunity cost of time among consumers shape consumption patterns and add another dimension to our analysis of demand.

Conclusion

This chapter has analyzed consumer choice by focusing on utility, or satisfaction. We assumed that utility could be measured in some systematic way for a particular consumer, even though utility measures could not be compared across consumers. The goal has been to explore utility maximization and predict how consumers react to a change in price. We judge a theory not by the realism of its assumptions but by the accuracy of its predictions. Based on this criterion, the theory of consumer choice presented in this chapter has proven to be quite useful.

Again, to maximize utility, you or any other consumer don't need to understand the material presented in this chapter. Economists assume that the urge to maximize utility is natural and instinctive. In this chapter, we simply tried to analyze that process. A more general approach to consumer choice, one that does not require a specific measure of utility, is developed in the appendix to this chapter.

Summary

1. Utility is the sense of pleasure or satisfaction that comes from consumption; it is the want-satisfying power of goods, services, and activities. The utility you get from consuming a particular good depends on your tastes. The law of diminishing marginal utility says that the more of a particular good you consume per period, other things constant, the smaller the gain in total utility from each additional unit consumed. The total utility derived from a good is the sum of the marginal utilities from each additional unit of the good. At some point, additional consumption could reduce total utility.

2. Utility is subjective. Each consumer makes a personal assessment of the want-satisfying power of consumption. By translating an individual's subjective measure of satisfaction into units of utility, we can predict the quantity demanded at a given price as well as the effect of a change in price on quantity demanded.

3. The consumer's objective is to maximize utility within the limits imposed by income and prices. In a world without scarcity, utility is maximized by consuming each good until its marginal utility reaches zero. In the real world—a world shaped by scarcity as reflected by prices—utility is maximized when the budget is exhausted and the marginal utility of the final unit consumed divided by that good's price is identical for each different good.

4. Utility analysis can be used to construct an individual consumer's demand curve. By observing the effects of a change in price on consumption, we can generate points that trace a demand curve.

5. Consumers typically receive a surplus, or a bonus, from consumption. Consumer surplus is the difference between the maximum amount consumers would pay for a given quantity of the good rather than go without it and the amount they actually pay. Consumer surplus increases as the price declines.

6. Consumption involves a money price and a time price. People are willing to pay a higher money price for products that save time.

Key Concepts

Total utility 125	Law of diminishing marginal utility 125	Marginal valuation 132
Marginal utility 125	Consumer equilibrium 129	Consumer surplus 132

Questions for Review

1. **LAW OF DIMINISHING MARGINAL UTILITY** Some restaurants offer "all you can eat" meals. How is this practice related to diminishing marginal utility? What restrictions must the restaurant impose on the customer to make a profit?

2. **LAW OF DIMINISHING MARGINAL UTILITY** Complete each of the following sentences:

   a. Your tastes determine the _____ you derive from consuming a particular good.

   b. _____ utility is the change in _____ utility resulting from a _____ change in the consumption of a good.

   c. As long as marginal utility is positive, total utility is _____.

   d. The law of diminishing marginal utility states that as an individual consumes more of a good during a given time period, other things constant, total utility _____.

3. **MARGINAL UTILITY** Is it possible for marginal utility to be negative while total utility is positive? If yes, under what circumstances is it possible?

4. **UTILITY-MAXIMIZING CONDITIONS** For a particular consumer, the marginal utility of cookies equals the marginal utility of candy. If the price of a cookie is less than the price of candy, is the consumer in equilibrium? Why or why not? If not, what should the consumer do to attain equilibrium?

5. **UTILITY-MAXIMIZING CONDITIONS** Suppose that marginal utility of Good $X = 100$, the price of X is $10 per unit, and the price of Y is $5 per unit. Assuming that the consumer is in equilibrium and is consuming both X and Y, what must the marginal utility of Y be?

6. **UTILITY-MAXIMIZING CONDITIONS** Suppose that the price of X is twice the price of Y. You are a utility maximizer who allocates your budget between the two goods. What must be true about the equilibrium relationship between the marginal utility levels of the last unit consumed of each good? What must be true about the equilibrium relationship between the marginal utility levels of the last dollar spent on each good?

7. **Case Study: Water, Water Everywhere** What is the diamonds-water paradox, and how is it explained? Use the same reasoning to explain why bottled water costs so much more than tap water.

8. **CONSUMER SURPLUS** The height of the demand curve at a given quantity reflects the marginal valuation of the last unit of that good consumed. For a normal good, an increase in income shifts the demand curve to the right and therefore increases its height at any quantity. Does this mean that consumers get greater marginal utility from each unit of this good than they did before? Explain.

9. **CONSUMER SURPLUS** Suppose supply of a good is perfectly elastic at a price of $5. The market demand curve for this good is linear, with zero quantity demanded at a price of $25. Given that the slope of this linear demand curve is -0.25, draw a supply and demand graph to illustrate the consumer surplus that occurs when the market is in equilibrium.

10. **Case Study: The Marginal Value of Free Medical Care** Medicare recipients pay a monthly premium for coverage, must meet an annual deductible, and have a co-payment for doctors' office visits. President George W. Bush introduced some coverage of prescription medications (prior to that, there was none). What impact would an increase in the monthly premium have on their consumer surplus? What would be the impact of a reduction in co-payments? What is the impact on consumer surplus of offering some coverage for prescription medication?

11. **ROLE OF TIME IN DEMAND** In many amusement parks, you pay an admission fee to the park but you do not need to pay for individual rides. How do people choose which rides to go on?

Problems and Exercises

12. **UTILITY MAXIMIZATION** The following tables illustrate Eileen's utilities from watching first-run movies in a theater and from renting movies from a video store. Suppose that she has a monthly movie budget of $36, each movie ticket costs $6, and each video rental costs $3.

Movies in a Theater

Q	TU	MU	MU/P
0	0	___	___
1	200	___	___
2	290	___	___
3	370	___	___
4	440	___	___
5	500	___	___
6	550	___	___
7	590	___	___

Movies from a Video Store

Q	TU	MU	MU/P
0	0	___	___
1	250	___	___
2	295	___	___
3	335	___	___
4	370	___	___
5	400	___	___
6	425	___	___

   a. Complete the tables.

   b. Do these tables show that Eileen's preferences obey the law of diminishing marginal utility? Explain your answer.

   c. How much of each good does Eileen consume in equilibrium?

   d. Suppose the prices of both types of movies drop to $1 while Eileen's movie budget shrinks to $10. How much of each good does she consume in equilibrium?

13. UTILITY MAXIMIZATION   Suppose that a consumer has a choice between two goods, X and Y. If the price of X is $2 and the price of Y is $3, how much of X and Y does the consumer purchase, given an income of $17? Use the following information about marginal utility:

Units	MU_x	MU_y
1	10	5
2	8	4
3	2	3
4	2	2
5	1	2

14. THE LAW OF DEMAND AND MARGINAL UTILITY   Daniel allocates his budget of $24 per week among three goods. Use the following table of marginal utilities for good A, good B, and good C to answer the questions below:

Q_A	MU_A	Q_B	MU_B	Q_C	MU_C
1	50	1	75	1	25
2	40	2	60	2	20
3	30	3	40	3	15
4	20	4	30	4	10
5	15	5	20	5	7.5

a. If the price of A is $2, the price of B is $3, and the price of C is $1, how much of each does Daniel purchase in equilibrium?

b. If the price of A rises to $4 while other prices and Daniel's budget remain unchanged, how much of each does he purchase in equilibrium?

c. Using the information from parts (a) and (b), draw the demand curve for good A. Be sure to indicate the price and quantity demanded for each point on the curve.

15. CONSUMER SURPLUS   Suppose the linear demand curve for shirts slopes downward and that consumers buy 500 shirts per year when the price is $30 and 1,000 shirts per year when the price is $25.

a. Compared to the prices of $30 and $25, what can you say about the marginal valuation that consumers place on the 300th shirt, the 700th shirt, and the 1,200th shirt they might buy each year?

b. With diminishing marginal utility, are consumers deriving any consumer surplus if the price is $25 per shirt? Explain.

c. Use a market demand curve to illustrate the change in consumer surplus if the price drops from $30 to $25.

Global Economic Watch Exercises

Login to www.cengagebrain.com and access the Global Economic Watch to do these exercises.

16. GLOBAL ECONOMIC WATCH   Go to the Global Economic Crisis Resource Center. Select Global Issues in Context. In the Basic Search box at the top of the page, enter the phrase "applied economics." On the Results page, go to the Magazines section. Click on the link for the December 31, 2003, book review "How Economics Works." Think about the first paragraph of the book review. Do you expect to experience diminishing marginal utility in your economics course?

17. GLOBAL ECONOMIC WATCH and Case Study: The Marginal Value of Free Medical Care   Go to the Global Economic Crisis

Resource Center. Select Global Issues in Context. Go to the menu at the top of the page and click on the tab for Browse Issues and Topics. Choose Health and Medicine. Click on the link for Access to Health Care. At the bottom of the Overview section, select View Full Overview. Read about access to health care in three categories of countries: developing nations, the United States, and industrialized nations with national health insurance systems. Describe the consumer surplus of the average citizen in each category of country.

Appendix
Indifference Curves and Utility Maximization

The approach used in the body of the chapter required a numerical measure of utility to determine optimal consumption. Economists have developed a more general approach to consumer behavior, one that does not rely on a numerical measure of utility. All this approach requires is that consumers be able to indicate their preferences for various combinations of goods. For example, the consumer should be able to say whether combination *A* is preferred to combination *B*, combination *B* is preferred to combination *A*, or each combination is equally preferred. This approach discussed in this appendix is more general and more flexible than the one developed in the body of the chapter. But it's also a little more complicated.

Consumer Preferences

An **indifference curve** shows all combinations of goods that provide the consumer with the same satisfaction, or the same utility. Thus, the consumer finds all combinations on a curve equally preferred. Because each bundle of goods yields the same level of utility, the consumer is *indifferent* about which combination is actually consumed. We can best understand the use of indifference curves through the following example.

In reality, consumers choose among thousands of goods and services, but to keep the analysis manageable, suppose only two are available: pizzas and movie rentals. In Exhibit 9, the horizontal axis measures the number of pizzas you buy per week, and the vertical axis measures the number of movies you rent per week. Point *a*, for example, consists of one pizza and eight movie rentals. Suppose you are given a choice of combination *a* or some combination with more pizza. The question is: Holding your total utility constant, how many movie rentals would you be willing to give up to get a second pizza? As you can see, in moving from point *a* to point *b*, you are willing to give up four movies to get a second pizza. Total utility is the same at points *a* and *b*. The marginal utility of that additional pizza is just sufficient to compensate you for the utility lost from decreasing your movie rentals by four. Thus, at point *b*, you are eating two pizzas and watching four movies a week.

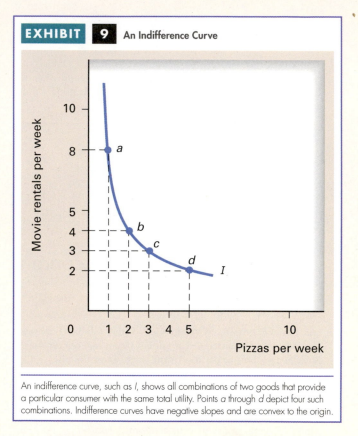

EXHIBIT 9 An Indifference Curve

An indifference curve, such as *I*, shows all combinations of two goods that provide a particular consumer with the same total utility. Points *a* through *d* depict four such combinations. Indifference curves have negative slopes and are convex to the origin.

In moving from point *b* to point *c*, again total utility is constant; you are now willing to give up only one movie for another pizza. At point *c*, your consumption bundle consists of three pizzas and three movies. Once at point *c*, you are willing to give up another movie only if you get two more pizzas in return. Combination *d*, therefore, consists of five pizzas and two movies.

Points *a*, *b*, *c*, and *d* connect to form indifference curve *I*, which represents possible combinations of pizza and movie rentals that would provide you the same total utility. Because points on the curve offer the same total utility, you are indifferent about which combination you choose—hence the name *indifference curve*. One sign of indifference is a willingness to allow someone else to choose for you. Expressions of indifference often include the phrases "Whatever" and "I could take it or leave it."

Note that we don't know, nor do we need to know, the value you attach to the utility reflected by the indifference curve—that is, no particular number is attached to the utility along *I*. *Combinations of goods along an indifference curve reflect some constant, though unspecified, level of utility.* So, unlike the approach adopted in the body of the chapter, indifference curves need not be measured in units of utility.

For you to remain indifferent among consumption alternatives, the increase in utility from eating more pizzas must just offset the decrease in utility from watching fewer movies. Thus, along an indifference curve, the quantity of pizza and the quantity of movies are inversely related. Because of this inverse relationship, *indifference curves slope downward to the right.*

Indifference curves are also *convex to the origin,* which means they are bowed inward toward the origin. The indifference curve gets flatter as you move down it. Here's why. Your willingness to substitute pizza for movies depends on how much of each you already consume. At combination *a,* for example, you watch eight movies and eat only one pizza a week. Because there are many movies relative to pizza, you are willing to give up four to get another pizza. Once you reach point *b,* your pizza consumption has doubled, so you are not quite so willing to give up movies to get a third pizza. In fact, you forgo just one movie to get another pizza. This moves you from point *b* to point *c.*

The **marginal rate of substitution**, or **MRS**, between pizza and movies indicates the number of movies that you are willing to give up to get one more pizza, neither gaining nor losing utility in the process. Because the MRS measures your willingness to trade movies for pizza, it depends on the amount of each good you are currently consuming. Mathematically, the MRS is equal to the absolute value of the slope of the indifference curve. Recall that the slope of any line is the vertical change between two points on the line divided by the corresponding horizontal change. For example, in moving from combination *a* to combination *b* in Exhibit 9, you are willing to give up four movies to get another pizza; the slope between these two points equals −4, so the MRS is 4. In the move from *b* to *c,* the slope is −1, so the MRS is 1. And from *c* to *d,* the slope is −½, so the MRS is ½.

The **law of diminishing marginal rate of substitution** says that as your consumption of pizza increases, the number of movies that you are willing to give up to get another pizza declines. This law applies to most pairs of goods. Because your marginal rate of substitution of movies for pizza declines as your pizza consumption increases, the indifference curve has a diminishing slope, meaning that it is convex when viewed from the origin.

As you move down the indifference curve, your pizza consumption increases, so the marginal utility of additional pizza decreases. Conversely, the number of movies you rent decreases, so their marginal utility increases. Thus, in moving down the indifference curve, you require more pizza to offset the loss of each movie.

We have focused on a single indifference curve, which indicates some constant though unspecified level of utility. We can use the same approach to generate a series of indifference curves, called an **indifference map**. An indifference map is a graphical representation of a consumer's tastes. Each curve reflects a different level of utility. Part of such a map is shown in Exhibit 10, where indifference curves for a particular consumer, in this case you, are labeled I_1, I_2, I_3, and I_4. Each consumer has a unique indifference map based on his or her preferences.

Because both goods yield marginal utility, you, the consumer, prefer more of each, rather than less. Curves farther from the origin represent greater consumption levels and, therefore, higher levels of utility. The utility level along I_2 is higher than that along I_1. I_3 reflects a higher level of utility than I_2, and so on. We can show this best by drawing a line from the origin and following it to higher indifference curves. Such a line has been included in Exhibit 10. By following that line to higher and higher

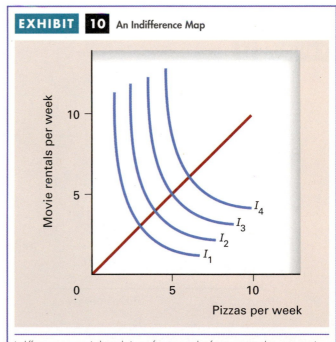

EXHIBIT 10 An Indifference Map

Indifference curves I_1 through I_4 are four examples from a particular consumer's indifference map. Indifference curves farther from the origin depict higher levels of utility. A line intersects each higher indifference curve, reflecting more of both goods.

indifference curves, you can see that the combination on each successive indifference curve reflects more of *both* goods. Because you value both goods, the greater amounts of each reflected on higher indifference curves represent higher levels of utility.

Indifference curves in a consumer's indifference map don't intersect. Exhibit 11 shows why. If indifference curves did cross, as at point *i*, then every point on indifference curve *I* and every point on curve *I′* would have to reflect the same level of utility as at point *i*. But because point *k* in Exhibit 11 is a combination with more pizza and more movies than point *j*, point *k* must represent a higher level of utility. This contradiction means that indifference curves cannot intersect.

Let's summarize the properties of indifference curves:

1. A particular indifference curve reflects a constant level of utility, so *the consumer is indifferent among all consumption combinations along a given curve*. Combinations are equally attractive.
2. If total utility is to remain constant, an increase in the consumption of one good must be offset by a decrease in the consumption of the other good, so *each indifference curve slopes downward to the right*.
3. Because of the law of diminishing marginal rate of substitution, *indifference curves bow in toward the origin*.

4. Higher indifference curves represent higher levels of utility.
5. Indifference curves do not intersect.

An indifference map is a graphical representation of a consumer's tastes for the two goods. Given a consumer's indifference map, how much of each good is consumed? To determine that, we must consider the relative prices of the goods and the consumer's income. In the next section, we focus on the consumer's budget.

The Budget Line

The **budget line** depicts all possible combinations of movies and pizzas, given their prices and your budget. Suppose, as in the body of this chapter, movies rent for $4, pizza sells for $8, and your budget is $40 per week. If you spend the entire $40 on movies, you can afford 10 per week. Alternatively, if you spend the entire $40 on pizzas, you can afford 5 per week. In Exhibit 12, your budget line meets the vertical axis at 10 movie rentals and meets the horizontal axis at 5 pizzas. We connect

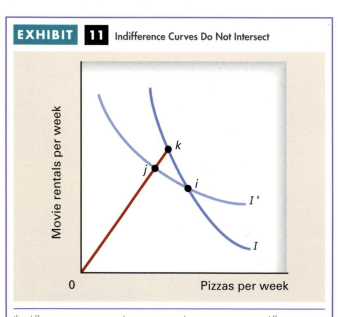

EXHIBIT 11 Indifference Curves Do Not Intersect

If indifference curves crossed, as at point *i*, then every point on indifference curve *I* and every point on indifference curve *I′* would have to reflect the same level of utility as at point *i*. But point *k* is a combination with more pizza and more movies than point *j*, so *k* must reflect a higher level of utility. This contradiction indicates that indifference curves cannot intersect.

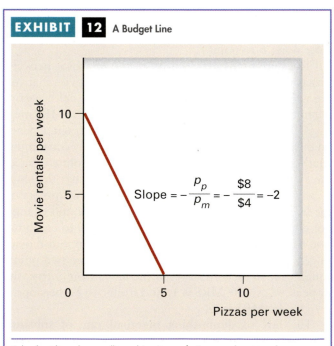

EXHIBIT 12 A Budget Line

$$\text{Slope} = -\frac{p_p}{p_m} = -\frac{\$8}{\$4} = -2$$

A budget line shows all combinations of pizza and movies that can be purchased at fixed prices with a given amount of income. If all income is spent on movies, 10 can be rented. If all income is spent on pizzas, 5 can be purchased. Points between the vertical intercept and the horizontal intercept show combinations of pizzas and movies. The slope of this budget line is −2, illustrating that the price of 1 pizza is 2 movies.

the intercepts to form the budget line. You can purchase any combination on your budget line, or your budget constraint. You might think of the budget line as your *consumption possibilities frontier*.

Let's find the slope of the budget line. At the point where the budget line meets the vertical axis, the maximum number of movies you can rent equals your income (I) divided by the movie rental price (p_m), or I/p_m. At the point where the budget line meets the horizontal axis, the maximum quantity of pizzas that you can purchase equals your income divided by the price of a pizza (p_p), or I/p_p. The slope of the budget line between the vertical intercept in Exhibit 12 and the horizontal intercept equals the vertical change, or $-I/p_m$, divided by the horizontal change, or I/p_p:

$$\text{Slope of budget line} = \frac{I/p_m}{I/p_p} - \frac{p_p}{p_m}$$

Note that the income term cancels out, so the slope of a budget line depends only on relative prices. In our example the slope is $-\$8/\$4$, which equals -2. The slope of the budget line indicates the cost of another pizza in terms of forgone movies. You must give up two movies for each additional pizza.

The indifference curve indicates what you are *willing* to buy. The budget line shows what you are *able* to buy. We must therefore bring together the indifference curve and the budget line to find out what quantities of each good you are both *willing* and *able* to buy.

Consumer Equilibrium at the Tangency

As always, the consumer's objective is to maximize utility. We know that indifference curves farther from the origin represent higher levels of utility. You, as a utility-maximizing consumer, select a combination along the budget line in Exhibit 13 that lies on the highest attainable indifference curve. Given prices and income, you maximize utility at the combination depicted by point *e* in Exhibit 13, where indifference curve I_2 just touches, or *is tangent to,* your budget line. At point *e,* you buy 3 pizzas at $8 each and rent 4 movies at $4 each, exhausting your budget of $40 per week. Other attainable combinations along the budget line reflect lower levels of utility. For example, point *a* is on the budget line, making it a combination you are *able* to purchase, but *a* is on a lower indifference curve, I_1. "Better" indifference

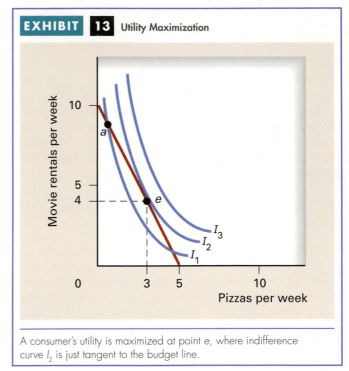

EXHIBIT **13** Utility Maximization

A consumer's utility is maximized at point *e*, where indifference curve I_2 is just tangent to the budget line.

curves, such as I_3, lie completely above the budget line and thus are unattainable.

Because you maximize utility at point *e*, that combination is an equilibrium outcome. Note that the indifference curve is tangent to the budget line at the equilibrium point. At the point of tangency, the slope of the indifference curve equals the slope of the budget line. Recall that the absolute value of the slope of the indifference curve is your marginal rate of substitution, and the absolute value of the slope of the budget line equals the price ratio. In equilibrium, therefore, your marginal rate of substitution between movies and pizza, MRS, must equal the ratio of the price of pizza to the price of movie rentals:

$$MRS = \frac{p_p}{p_m}$$

The marginal rate of substitution of pizza for movie rentals can also be found from the marginal utilities of pizza and movies presented in the chapter. Exhibit 3 indicated that, at the consumer equilibrium, the marginal utility you derived from the third pizza was 24 and the marginal utility you derived by the fourth movie was 12. Because the marginal utility of pizza (MU_p) is 24 and the marginal utility of movies (MU_m) is 12, in moving to that equilibrium, you were willing to give up two movies to get one more pizza. Thus, the marginal rate of substitution of pizza for movies equals the ratio of pizza's marginal utility (MU_p) to movie's marginal utility (MU_m), or

$$MRS = \frac{MU_p}{MU_m}$$

In fact, the absolute value of the slope of the indifference curve equals MU_p/MU_m. Since the absolute value of the slope of the budget line equals p_p/p_m, the equilibrium condition for the indifference curve approach can be written as

$$\frac{MU_p}{p_p} = \frac{MU_m}{p_m}$$

This equation is the same equilibrium condition for utility maximization developed in the chapter using marginal utility analysis. The equality says that in equilibrium—that is, when the consumer maximizes utility—the last dollar spent on each good yields the same marginal utility. If this equality did not hold, the consumer could increase utility by adjusting consumption until the equality occurs.

Effects of a Change in Price

What happens to quantity demanded when the price changes? The answer can be found by deriving the demand curve. We begin at point *e,* our initial equilibrium, in panel (a) of Exhibit 14. At point *e,* you eat 3 pizzas and watch 4 movies per week. Suppose that the price of pizzas falls from $8 to $6, other things constant. The price drop means that if the entire budget were spent on pizza, you could buy 6.67 (=$40/$6). Your money income remains at $40 per week, but your real income has increased because of the lower pizza price. Because the rental price of movies has not changed, however, 10 remains the maximum number you can rent. Thus, the budget line's vertical intercept remains fixed at 10 movies, but the lower end of the budget line rotates to the right from 5 pizzas to 6.67 pizzas.

After the price of pizza changes, the new equilibrium occurs at *e″*, where pizza purchases increase from 3 to 4 and, as it happens, movie rentals remains at 4. Thus, price and the quantity of pizza demanded are inversely related. The demand curve in panel (b) of Exhibit 14 shows how price and quantity demanded are related. Specifically, if the price of pizza falls from $8 per unit to $6 per unit, other things constant, your quantity demanded increases from 3 to 4. Because you are on a higher indifference curve at *e″*, you are clearly better off after the price reduction (your consumer surplus has increased).

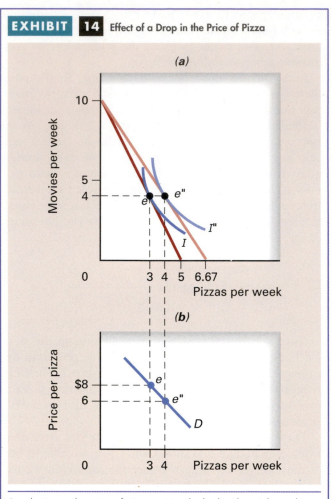

EXHIBIT 14 Effect of a Drop in the Price of Pizza

A reduction in the price of pizza rotates the budget line rightward in panel (a). The consumer is back in equilibrium at point *e″* along the new budget line. Panel (b) shows that a drop in the price of pizza from $8 to $6 increases quantity demanded from 3 to 4 pizzas. Price and quantity demanded are inversely related.

Income and Substitution Effects

The law of demand was initially explained in terms of an income effect and a substitution effect of a price change. You now have the tools to examine these two effects more precisely. Suppose the price of a pizza falls from $8 to $4, other things constant. You can now purchase a maximum of 10 pizzas with a budget of $40 per week. As shown in Exhibit 15, the budget-line intercept rotates out from 5 to 10 pizzas. After the price change, the quantity of pizzas demanded increases from 3 to 5. The increase in utility shows how you benefit from the price decrease.

The increase in the quantity of pizzas demanded can be broken down into the substitution effect and the income effect of a price change. When the price of pizza falls, the

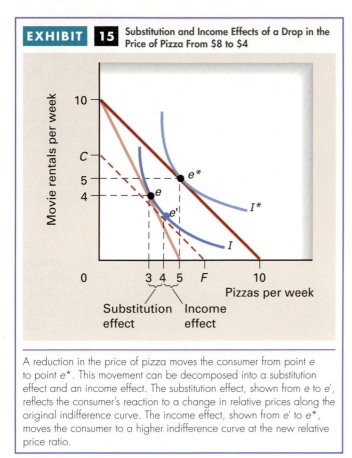

EXHIBIT 15 Substitution and Income Effects of a Drop in the Price of Pizza From $8 to $4

A reduction in the price of pizza moves the consumer from point *e* to point *e**. This movement can be decomposed into a substitution effect and an income effect. The substitution effect, shown from *e* to *e'*, reflects the consumer's reaction to a change in relative prices along the original indifference curve. The income effect, shown from *e'* to *e**, moves the consumer to a higher indifference curve at the new relative price ratio.

change in relative prices shows up through the change in the slope of the budget line. To derive the substitution effect, let's initially assume that you must maintain the same level of utility after the price change as before. In other words, let's suppose your utility level has not yet changed, but the relative prices you face have changed. We want to learn how you would adjust to the price change. A new budget line reflecting just the change in relative prices, not a change in utility, is shown by the dashed line, *CF*, in Exhibit 15. Given the new relative prices, you would increase the quantity of pizza demanded to the point on indifference curve *I* where the indifference curve is just tangent to the dashed budget line. That tangency keeps utility at the initial level but reflects the new relative prices. Thus, we adjust your budget line to correspond to the new relative prices, but we adjust your income level so that your utility remains unchanged.

You move down along indifference curve *I* to point *e'*, buying more pizza but renting fewer movies. These changes in quantity demanded reflect the *substitution effect* of lower pizza prices. The substitution effect always increases the quantity demanded of the good whose price has dropped. Because consumption bundle *e'* represents

the same level of utility as consumption bundle *e*, you are neither better off nor worse off at point *e'*.

But at point *e'*, you have not spent your full budget. The drop in the price of pizza has increased the quantity of pizza you can buy, as shown by the expanded budget line that runs from 10 movie rentals to 10 pizzas. Your *real income* has increased because of the lower price of pizza. As a result, you are able to attain point *e** on indifference curve *I**. At this point, you buy 5 pizzas and rent 5 movies. Because prices remain constant during the move from *e'* to *e**, the change in consumption is due solely to a change in real income. Thus, the change in the quantity demanded from 4 to 5 pizzas reflects the *income effect* of the lower pizza price.

We can now distinguish between the substitution effect and the income effect of a drop in the price of pizza. The substitution effect is shown by the move from point *e* to point *e'* in response to a change in the relative price of pizza, with your utility held constant along *I*. The income effect is shown by the move from *e'* to *e** in response to an increase in your real income, with relative prices held constant.

The overall effect of a change in the price of pizza is the sum of the substitution effect and the income effect. In our example, the substitution effect accounts for a one-unit increase in the quantity of pizza demanded, as does the income effect. Thus, when the price falls from $8 to $4, the income and substitution effects combine to increase the quantity of pizza demanded by two units. The income effect is not always positive. For inferior goods, the income effect is negative; so as the price falls, the income effect can cause the consumption of one of the goods to fall, offsetting part or even all the substitution effect. Incidentally, notice that as a result of the increase in your real income, movie rentals increase as well—from 4 to 5 rentals per week in our example, though it is not always the case that the income effect is positive.

Conclusion

Indifference curve analysis does not require us to attach numerical values to particular levels of utility, as marginal utility theory does. The results of indifference curve analysis support the conclusions drawn from our simpler models: price and quantity demanded are inversely related. Indifference curves provide a logical way of viewing consumer choice, but consumers need not be aware of this approach to make rational choices. The purpose of the analysis in this chapter is to predict consumer behavior—not to advise consumers how to maximize utility. They already know that instinctively.

Appendix Questions

1. CONSUMER PREFERENCES   The absolute value of the slope of the indifference curve equals the marginal rate of substitution. If two goods were *perfect* substitutes, what would the indifference curves look like? Explain.

2. EFFECTS OF A CHANGE IN PRICE   Chris has an income of $90 per month to allocate between Goods A and B. Initially the price of A is $3 and the price of B is $4.

   a. Draw Chris's budget line, indicating its slope if units of A are measured on the horizontal axis and units of B are on the vertical axis.

   b. Add an indifference curve to your graph and label the point of consumer equilibrium. Indicate Chris's consumption level of A and B. Explain why this is a consumer equilibrium. What can you say about Chris's total utility at this equilibrium?

   c. Now suppose the price of A rises to $4. Draw the new budget line, a new point of equilibrium, and the consumption level of Goods A and B. What is Chris's marginal rate of substitution at the new equilibrium point?

   d. Draw the demand curve for Good A, labeling the different price-quantity combinations determined in parts (b) and (c).

Production and Cost in the Firm

7

- Why do too many cooks spoil the broth?
- Why do movie theaters have so many screens?
- Why don't they add even more?
- If you go into business for yourself, how much must you earn just to break even?
- Why might your average fall even though your grades improved from the previous term?

Answers to these and other questions are discovered in this chapter, which introduces production and cost in the firm.

The previous chapter explored the consumer behavior shaping the demand curve. You were asked to think like a consumer, or demander. This chapter examines the producer behavior shaping the supply curve. You must now think like a producer, or supplier. You may feel more natural as a consumer (after all, you *are* one), but you already know a lot more about producers than you may realize. You have been around them all your life—Wal-Mart, Starbucks, Google, Exxon, Amazon.com, Home Depot, McDonald's, Twitter, Facebook, Pizza Hut, Ford, the Gap, grocery stores, drugstores, convenience stores, bookstores, and hundreds more. So you already have some idea how businesses operate. They all have the same goal—they try to maximize profit, which is revenue minus cost. This chapter introduces the cost side of the profit equation.

Topics discussed include:

- Explicit and implicit costs
- Economic and normal profit
- Increasing and diminishing returns
- Short-run costs
- Long-run costs
- Economies and diseconomies of scale

Cost and Profit

With demand, we assume that consumers try to maximize utility, a goal that motivates their behavior. With supply, we assume that producers try to maximize *profit,* and this goal motivates their behavior. *Firms try to earn a profit by transforming resources into salable products.* Over time, firms that survive and grow are those that are more profitable. Unprofitable firms eventually fail. Each year, millions of new firms enter the marketplace and many leave. The firm's decision makers must choose what goods and services to produce and what resources to employ. They must make plans while confronting uncertainty about consumer demand, resource availability, and the intentions of other firms in the market. *The lure of profit is so strong, however, that eager entrepreneurs are always ready to pursue their dreams.*

Explicit and Implicit Costs

To hire a resource, a firm must pay at least the resource's *opportunity cost*—that is, at least what the resource could earn in its best alternative use. For most resources, a cash payment approximates the opportunity cost. For example, the $3 per pound that Domino's Pizza pays for cheese must at least equal the cheese producer's opportunity cost of supplying it. Firms do not make direct cash payments for resources they own. For example, a firm pays no rent to operate in a company-owned building. Similarly, small-business owners usually don't pay themselves an hourly wage. Yet these resources are not free. *Whether hired in resource markets or owned by the firm, all resources have an opportunity cost.* Company-owned buildings can be rented or sold; small-business owners can find other work.

    A firm's **explicit costs** are its actual cash payments for resources: wages, rent, interest, insurance, taxes, and the like. In addition to these direct cash outlays, or explicit costs, the firm also incurs **implicit costs,** which are the opportunity costs of using resources owned by the firm or provided by the firm's owners. Examples include the use of a company-owned building, use of company funds, or the time of the firm's owners. Like explicit costs, implicit costs are opportunity costs. But unlike explicit costs, implicit costs require no cash payment and no entry in the firm's *accounting statement,* which records its revenues, explicit costs, and accounting profit.

Alternative Measures of Profit

An example may help clarify the distinction between explicit and implicit costs. Wanda Wheeler earns $50,000 a year as an aeronautical engineer with the Skyhigh Aircraft Corporation. On her way home from work one day, she gets an idea for a rounder, more friction-resistant airplane wheel. She decides to quit her job and start a business, which she calls Wheeler Dealer. To buy the necessary machines

explicit cost
Opportunity cost of resources employed by a firm that takes the form of cash payments

implicit cost
A firm's opportunity cost of using its own resources or those provided by its owners without a corresponding cash payment

and equipment, she withdraws $20,000 from a savings account earning interest of $1,000 a year. She hires an assistant and starts producing the wheel using the spare bay in her condominium's parking garage, which she had been renting to a neighbor for $100 a month.

Sales are slow at first—people keep telling her she is just trying to reinvent the wheel—but her wheel eventually gets rolling. When Wanda reviews the firm's performance after the first year, she is pleased. As you can see in the top portion of Exhibit 1, company revenue in 2010 totaled $105,000. After paying her assistant and for materials and equipment, the firm shows an accounting profit of $64,000. **Accounting profit** equals total revenue minus explicit costs. Accountants use this profit to determine a firm's taxable income.

But accounting profit ignores the opportunity cost of Wanda's own resources used in the firm. First is the opportunity cost of her time. Remember, she quit a $50,000-a-year job to work full time on her business, thereby forgoing that salary. Second is the $1,000 in annual interest she passes up by funding the operation with her own savings. And third, by using the spare bay in the garage for the business, she forgoes $1,200 per year in rental income. The forgone salary, interest, and rental income are implicit costs because she no longer earns income from the best alternative uses of these resources.

Economic profit equals total revenue minus all costs, both implicit and explicit; *economic profit takes into account the opportunity cost of all resources used in production.* In Exhibit 1, accounting profit of $64,000 less implicit costs of $52,200 yields an economic profit of $11,800. Economic profit is what Wanda Wheeler earns as an entrepreneur—an amount over and above what her resources could earn in their best alternative use. What would happen to the accounting statement if Wanda decided to pay herself a salary of $50,000 per year? Explicit costs would increase by $50,000, and implicit costs would decrease by $50,000. Thus, accounting profit would decrease by $50,000, but economic profit would not change because it already reflects both implicit and explicit costs.

There is one other profit measure to consider. The accounting profit just sufficient to ensure that *all* resources used by the firm earn their opportunity cost is called a **normal profit.** Wheeler Dealer earns a normal profit when accounting profit equals implicit costs—the sum of the salary Wanda gave up at her regular job ($50,000), the interest she gave up by using her own savings ($1,000), and the rent she gave up on her garage ($1,200). Thus, if the accounting profit is $52,200 per year—the opportunity cost of resources Wanda supplies to the firm—the company earns a normal profit. *Any*

accounting profit
A firm's total revenue minus its explicit costs

economic profit
A firm's total revenue minus its explicit and implicit costs

normal profit
The accounting profit earned when all resources earn their opportunity cost

---

EXHIBIT 1   Wheeler Dealer Accounts, 2010

Total revenue		$105,000
Less explicit costs:		
Assistant's salary	−$21,000	
Material and equipment	−$20,000	
Equals accounting profit		$64,000
Less implicit costs:		
Wanda's forgone salary	−$50,000	
Forgone interest on savings	−$1,000	
Forgone garage rental	−$1,200	
Equals economic profit		$11,800

accounting profit in excess of a normal profit is economic profit. If accounting profit is large enough, it can be divided into normal profit and economic profit. The $64,000 in accounting profit earned by Wanda's firm consists of (1) a normal profit of $52,200, which covers her implicit costs—the opportunity cost of resources she supplies the firm, and (2) an economic profit of $11,800, which is over and above what these resources, including Wanda's time, could earn in their best alternative use.

As long as economic profit is positive, Wanda is better off running her own firm than working for Skyhigh Aircraft. If total revenue had been only $50,000, an accounting profit of only $9,000 would cover less than one-fifth of her salary, to say nothing of her forgone rent and interest. Because Wanda would not have covered her implicit costs, she would not be earning even a normal profit and would be better off back in her old job.

To understand profit maximization, you must develop a feel for both revenue and cost. In this chapter, you begin learning about the cost of production, starting with the relationship between inputs and outputs.

Production in the Short Run

We shift now from a discussion of profit, which is why firms exist, to a discussion of how firms operate. Suppose a new McDonald's just opened in your neighborhood and business is booming far beyond expectations. The manager responds to the unexpected demand by quickly hiring more workers. But cars are still backed up into the street waiting for a parking space. The solution is to add a drive-through window, but such an expansion takes time.

Fixed and Variable Resources

variable resource

Any resource that can be varied in the short run to increase or decrease production

fixed resource

Any resource that cannot be varied in the short run

short run

A period during which at least one of a firm's resources is fixed

long run

A period during which all resources under the firm's control are variable

Some resources, such as labor, are called **variable resources** because they can be varied quickly to change the output rate. But adjustments in other resources take more time. Resources that cannot be altered easily—the size of the building, for example—are called **fixed resources**. When considering the time required to change the quantity of resources employed, economists distinguish between the short run and the long run. In the **short run**, at least one resource is fixed. In the **long run**, no resource is fixed.

Output can be changed in the short run by adjusting variable resources, but the size, or *scale,* of the firm is fixed in the short run. In the long run, all resources can be varied. The length of the long run differs from industry to industry because the nature of production differs. For example, the size of a McDonald's outlet can be increased more quickly than can the size of an auto plant. Thus, the long run for that McDonald's is shorter than the long run for an automaker.

The Law of Diminishing Marginal Returns

Let's focus on the short-run link between resource use and the rate of output by considering a hypothetical moving company called Smoother Mover. Suppose the company's fixed resources, such as a warehouse, are already in place and that labor is the only variable resource. Exhibit 2 relates the amount of labor employed to the amount of output produced. Labor is measured in worker-days, which is one worker for one day, and output is measured in tons of furniture moved per day. The first column shows the amount of labor employed, which ranges from 0 to 8 worker-days. The second column

EXHIBIT	2	The Short-Run Relationship Between Units of Labor and Tons of Furniture Moved

Units of the Variable Resource (worker-days)	Total Product (tons moved per day)	Marginal Product (tons moved per day)
0	0	–
1	2	2
2	5	3
3	9	4
4	12	3
5	14	2
6	15	1
7	15	0
8	14	−1

Marginal product increases as the firm hires each of the first three workers, reflecting increasing marginal returns. Then marginal product declines, reflecting diminishing marginal returns. Adding more workers may, at some point, actually reduce total product (as occurs here with an eighth worker) because workers start getting in each other's way.

shows the tons of furniture moved per day, or the **total product,** at each level of employment. The relationship between the amount of resources employed and total product is called the firm's **production function.** The third column shows the **marginal product** of each worker—that is, the change in total product resulting from an additional unit of labor, assuming other resources remain unchanged. Spend a little time now getting acquainted with the three columns.

Increasing Marginal Returns

Without labor, nothing gets moved, so total product is 0. If one worker is hired, that worker must do all the driving, packing, crating, and moving. Some of the larger items, such as couches and major appliances, cannot easily be moved by a single worker. Still, in our example one worker moves 2 tons of furniture per day. When a second worker is hired, some division of labor occurs, and two together can move the big stuff more easily, so production more than doubles to 5 tons per day. The marginal product of the second worker is 3 tons per day. Adding a third worker allows for a finer division of labor. For example, one can pack fragile items while the other two do the heavy lifting. Total product is 9 tons per day, 4 tons more than with two workers. Because the marginal product increases, the firm experiences **increasing marginal returns** from labor as each of the first three workers is hired.

Diminishing Marginal Returns

A fourth worker's marginal product is less than that of a third worker. Hiring still more workers increases total product by successively smaller amounts, so the marginal product declines after three workers. With that fourth worker, the **law of diminishing marginal returns** takes hold. This law states that as more of a variable resource is combined with a given amount of another resource, marginal product eventually declines. *The law of diminishing marginal returns is the most important feature of production in the short run.* As more and more labor is hired, marginal product could even turn negative, so total product would decline. For example, when Smoother Mover hires an eighth worker, workers start getting in each other's way, and they take up valuable space in the moving van. As a result, an eighth worker actually subtracts from total

total product
A firm's total output

production function
The relationship between the amount of resources employed and a firm's total product

marginal product
The change in total product that occurs when the use of a particular resource increases by one unit, all other resources constant

increasing marginal returns
The marginal product of a variable resource increases as each additional unit of that resource is employed

law of diminishing marginal returns
As more of a variable resource is added to a given amount of another resource, marginal product eventually declines and could become negative

net 📖 bookmark

Unit labor cost is the term used to describe the cost of labor per unit of output. Because labor costs generally represent the largest share of costs, this value is closely watched by businesspeople and government analysts. Look at the most recent data on unit labor costs at http://stats.bls.gov/news. release/prod2.toc.htm from the Bureau of Labor Statistics. What is the current trend? What forces may be pushing unit labor costs downward? What does this mean for the profitability of firms?

fixed cost

Any production cost that is independent of the firm's rate of output

variable cost

Any production cost that changes as the rate of output changes

output, yielding a negative marginal product. Likewise, a McDonald's outlet can hire only so many workers before congestion and confusion in the work area cut total product ("too many cooks spoil the broth").

The Total and Marginal Product Curves

Exhibit 3 illustrates the relationship between total product and marginal product, using data from Exhibit 2. Note that because of increasing marginal returns, marginal product in panel (b) increases with each of the first three workers. With marginal product increasing, total product in panel (a) increases at an increasing rate (although this is hard to see in Exhibit 3). But once decreasing marginal returns set in, which begins with the fourth worker, marginal product declines. Total product continues to increase but at a decreasing rate. As long as marginal product is positive, total product increases. Where marginal product turns negative, total product starts to fall. Exhibit 3 summarizes all this by sorting production into three ranges: increasing marginal returns, diminishing but positive marginal returns, and negative marginal returns. These ranges for marginal product correspond with total product that increases at an increasing rate, increases at a decreasing rate, and declines.

Costs in the Short Run

Now that we have examined the relationship between the amount of resources used and the rate of output, let's consider how the cost of production varies as output varies. There are two kinds of costs in the short run: fixed and variable. Fixed cost pays for fixed resources and variable cost pays for variable resources. A firm must pay a **fixed cost** even if no output is produced. For example, in the steel industry, giant ovens must remain hot even when the plant isn't making steel. Otherwise, bricks inside would disintegrate. And a huge vacuum that sucks out pollutants must run continuously because turning its motors off and on can damage them.[1] Similarly, even if Smoother Mover hires no labor and moves no furniture, it incurs property taxes, insurance, vehicle registration, plus any opportunity cost for warehouse and equipment. By definition, fixed cost is just that: fixed—it does not vary with output in the short run. Suppose the *fixed cost* for Smoother Mover is $200 per day.

Variable cost, as the name implies, is the cost of variable resources—in this case, labor. When no labor is employed, output is zero, as is variable cost. As workers are hired, output increases, as does variable cost. Variable cost depends on the amount of labor employed and on the wage. If the wage is $100 per day, *variable cost* equals the number of workers hired times $100.

Total Cost and Marginal Cost in the Short Run

Exhibit 4 offers cost data for Smoother Mover. The table lists the cost of production associated with alternative rates of output. Column (1) shows possible rates of output in the short run, measured in tons of furniture moved per day.

Total Cost

Column (2) shows the fixed cost (*FC*) at each rate of output. Note that fixed cost, by definition, remains constant at $200 per day regardless of output. Column (3) shows the labor needed to produce each rate of output based on the productivity figures reported in the previous two exhibits. For example, moving 2 tons a day requires one

---

1.   Robert Guy Matthews, "Fixed Costs Chafe Steel Mills," *Wall Street Journal*, 10 June 2009.

EXHIBIT   3   The Total and Marginal Product of Labor

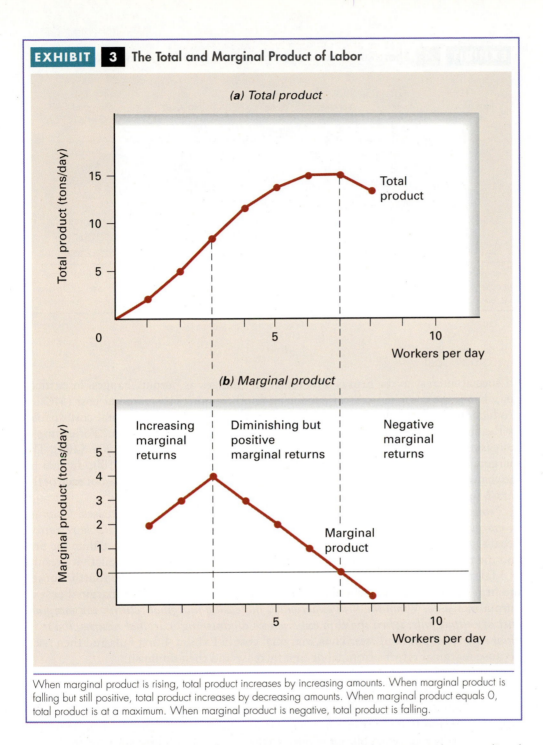

When marginal product is rising, total product increases by increasing amounts. When marginal product is falling but still positive, total product increases by decreasing amounts. When marginal product equals 0, total product is at a maximum. When marginal product is negative, total product is falling.

worker, 5 tons requires two workers, and so on. Only the first six workers are listed because additional workers would add nothing to output and so would not be hired. Column (4) lists variable cost (VC) per day, which equals $100 times the number of workers employed. For example, the variable cost of moving 9 tons of furniture per day is $300 because this output rate requires three workers. Column (5) lists the **total cost** (TC), the sum of fixed cost and variable cost: $TC = FC + VC$. As you can see, when output is zero, variable cost is zero, so total cost consists entirely of the fixed cost of $200. Incidentally, because total cost is the opportunity cost of all resources used by the firm, total cost includes a normal profit but not an economic profit. Think about that.

total cost
The sum of fixed cost and variable cost, or $TC = FC + VC$

EXHIBIT 4   Short-Run Total and Marginal Cost Data for Smoother Mover

(1) Tons Moved per Day (q)	(2) Fixed Cost (FC)	(3) Workers per Day	(4) Variable Cost (VC)	(5) Total Cost $(TC = FC + VC)$	(6) Marginal Cost $MC = \Delta TC/\Delta q$
0	$200	0	$0	$200	—
2	200	1	100	300	$50.00
5	200	2	200	400	33.33
9	200	3	300	500	25.00
12	200	4	400	600	33.33
14	200	5	500	700	50.00
15	200	6	600	800	100.00

Because of increasing marginal returns from the first three workers, marginal cost declines at first, as shown in column (6). Because of diminishing marginal returns beginning with the fourth worker, marginal cost starts increasing.

Marginal Cost

marginal cost

The change in total cost resulting from a one-unit change in output; the change in total cost divided by the change in output, or $MC = \Delta TC/\Delta q$

Of special interest to the firm is how total cost changes as output changes. In particular, what is the marginal cost of producing another unit? The **marginal cost** (*MC*) of production listed in column (6) of Exhibit 4 is simply the change in total cost divided by the change in output, or $MC = \Delta TC/\Delta q$, where Δ means "change in." For example, increasing output from 0 to 2 tons increases total cost by $100 (=$300−$200). The marginal cost of each of the first 2 tons is the change in total cost, $100, divided by the change in output, 2 tons, or $100/2, which equals $50. The marginal cost of each of the next 3 tons is $100/3, or $33.33.

Notice in column (6) that marginal cost first decreases, then increases. *Changes in marginal cost reflect changes in the marginal productivity of the variable resource.* Because of increasing marginal returns, the second worker produces more than the first and the third worker produces more than the second. This greater productivity results in a falling marginal cost for the first 9 tons moved. Beginning with the fourth worker, the firm experiences diminishing marginal returns from labor, so the marginal cost of output increases. *When the firm experiences increasing marginal returns, the marginal cost of output falls; when the firm experiences diminishing marginal returns, the marginal cost of output increases.* Thus, marginal cost in Exhibit 4 first falls and then rises, because marginal returns from labor first increase and then diminish.

Total and Marginal Cost Curves

Exhibit 5 shows cost curves for the data in Exhibit 4. Because fixed cost does not vary with output, the fixed cost curve is a horizontal line at the $200 level in panel (a). Variable cost is zero when output is zero, so the *variable cost curve* starts from the origin. The *total cost curve* sums the fixed cost curve and the variable cost curve. Because a constant fixed cost is added to variable cost, the total cost curve is simply the variable cost curve shifted vertically by the fixed cost.

In panel (b) of Exhibit 5, marginal cost declines until the ninth unit of output and then increases, reflecting labor's increasing and then diminishing marginal returns. There is a relationship between the two panels because the change in total cost resulting from a one-unit change in production equals the marginal cost. With each successive unit of output, total cost increases by the marginal cost of that unit. Thus, *the slope of the total*

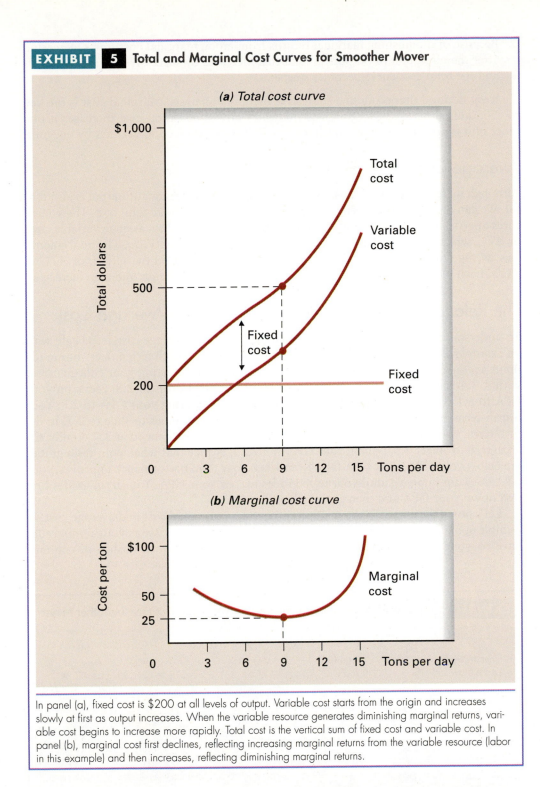

EXHIBIT 5 Total and Marginal Cost Curves for Smoother Mover

(a) Total cost curve

(b) Marginal cost curve

In panel (a), fixed cost is $200 at all levels of output. Variable cost starts from the origin and increases slowly at first as output increases. When the variable resource generates diminishing marginal returns, variable cost begins to increase more rapidly. Total cost is the vertical sum of fixed cost and variable cost. In panel (b), marginal cost first declines, reflecting increasing marginal returns from the variable resource (labor in this example) and then increases, reflecting diminishing marginal returns.

cost curve at each rate of output equals the marginal cost at that rate of output. The total cost curve can be divided into two sections, based on what happens to marginal cost:

1. Because of increasing marginal returns from labor, marginal cost at first declines, so total cost initially increases by successively smaller amounts and the total cost curve becomes less steep.

2. Because of diminishing marginal returns from labor, marginal cost starts increasing after the ninth unit of output, so total cost increases by successively larger amounts and the total cost curve becomes steeper.

Keep in mind that economic analysis is marginal analysis. Marginal cost is the key to economic decisions. Marginal cost indicates how much total cost increases if one more unit is produced or how much total cost drops if production declines by one unit.

Average Cost in the Short Run

average variable cost
Variable cost divided by output, or $AVC = VC/q$

average total cost
Total cost divided by output, or $ATC = TC/q$; the sum of average fixed cost and average variable cost, or $ATC = AFC + AVC$

Although marginal cost is of most interest, the average cost per unit of output is also useful. We can distinguish between average variable cost and average total cost. These measures appear in columns (5) and (6) of Exhibit 6. Column (5) lists **average variable cost,** or AVC, which equals variable cost divided by output, or $AVC = VC/q$. The final column lists **average total cost,** or ATC, which equals total cost divided by output, or $ATC = TC/q$. Each measure of average cost first declines as output expands and then increases.

The Relationship Between Marginal Cost and Average Cost

To understand the relationship between marginal cost and average cost, let's begin with an example of college grades. Think about how your grades each term affect your grade point average (GPA). Suppose you do well your first term, starting your college career with a 3.4 (out of 4.0). Your grades for the second term drop to 2.8, reducing your GPA to 3.1. You slip again in the third term to a 2.2, lowering your GPA to 2.8. Your fourth-term grades improve a bit to 2.4, but your GPA continues to slide to 2.7. In the fifth term, your grades improve to 2.7, leaving your GPA unchanged at 2.7. And in the sixth term, you get 3.3, pulling your GPA up to 2.8. Notice that when your term grades are below your GPA, your GPA falls. Even when your term performance improves, your GPA does not improve until your term grades *exceed* your GPA. Your term grades first pull down your GPA and then eventually pull it up.

Let's now take a look at the relationship between marginal cost and average cost. In Exhibit 6, marginal cost has the same relationship to average cost as your term grades have to your GPA. You can observe this marginal-average relationship in columns

EXHIBIT 6   Short-Run Total, Marginal, and Average Cost Data for Smoother Mover

(1) Tons Moved per Day (q)	(2) Variable Cost (VC)	(3) Total Cost (TC = FC + VC)	(4) Marginal Cost (MC = ΔTC/Δq)	(5) Average Variable Cost (AVC = VC/q)	(6) Average Total Cost (ATC = TC/q)
0	$0	$200	0	—	∞
2	100	300	$50.00	$50.00	$150.00
5	200	400	33.33	40.00	80.00
9	300	500	25.00	33.33	55.55
12	400	600	33.33	33.33	50.00
14	500	700	50.00	35.71	50.00
15	600	800	100.00	40.00	53.33

Marginal cost first falls then increases because of increasing then diminishing marginal returns from labor. As long as marginal cost is below average cost, average cost declines. Once marginal cost exceeds average cost, average cost increases. Columns (4), (5), and (6) show the relation between marginal and average costs.

(4) and (5). Because of increasing marginal returns from the first three workers, marginal cost falls for the first 9 tons of furniture moved. Because marginal cost is below average cost, marginal cost pulls down average cost. Marginal cost equals average variable cost when output is 12 tons, and marginal cost exceeds average variable cost when output exceeds 12 tons, so marginal cost pulls up average variable cost.

Exhibit 7 shows the same marginal cost curve first presented in Exhibit 5, along with average cost curves based on data in Exhibit 6. At low rates of output, marginal cost declines as output expands because of increasing marginal returns from labor. As long as marginal cost is below average cost, marginal cost pulls down average cost as output expands. At higher rates of output, marginal cost increases because of diminishing marginal returns from labor. Once marginal cost exceeds average cost, marginal cost pulls up average cost. The fact that marginal cost first pulls average cost down and then pulls it up explains why the average cost curves have U shapes. The shapes of the average variable cost curve and the average total cost curve are determined by the shape of the marginal cost curve, so each is shaped by increasing, then diminishing, marginal returns.

Notice also that the rising marginal cost curve intersects both the average variable cost curve and the average total cost curve where these average curves reach their minimum. This occurs because the marginal pulls down the average where the marginal is below the average and pulls up the average where the marginal is above the average. One more thing: The distance between the average variable cost curve and the average total cost curve is *average fixed cost,* which gets smaller as the rate of output increases. (Why does average fixed cost get smaller?)

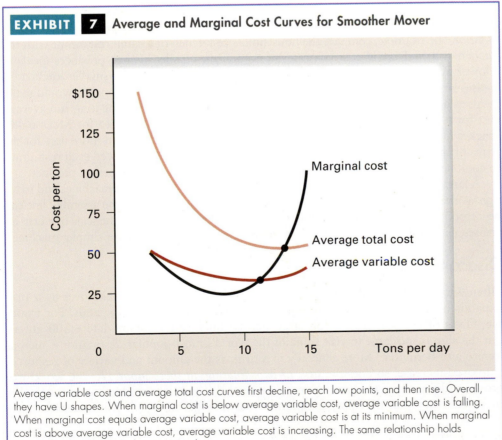

EXHIBIT 7 Average and Marginal Cost Curves for Smoother Mover

Average variable cost and average total cost curves first decline, reach low points, and then rise. Overall, they have U shapes. When marginal cost is below average variable cost, average variable cost is falling. When marginal cost equals average variable cost, average variable cost is at its minimum. When marginal cost is above average variable cost, average variable cost is increasing. The same relationship holds between marginal cost and average total cost.

The law of diminishing marginal returns determines the shapes of short-run cost curves. When the marginal product of labor increases, the marginal cost of output falls. Once diminishing marginal returns take hold, the marginal cost of output rises. Thus, marginal cost first falls and then rises. And the marginal cost curve dictates the shapes of the average cost curves. When marginal cost is less than average cost, average cost declines. When marginal cost is above average cost, average cost increases. Got it? If not, please reread this paragraph.

Costs in the Long Run

So far, the analysis has focused on how costs vary as the rate of output expands in the short run for a firm of a given size. In the long run, all inputs that are under the firm's control can be varied, so there is no fixed cost. The long run is not just a succession of short runs. The long run is best thought of as a *planning horizon.* In the long run, the choice of input combinations is flexible. But once the size of the plant has been selected and the concrete has been poured, the firm has fixed costs and is operating in the short run. Firms plan for the long run, but they produce in the short run. We turn now to long-run costs.

Economies of Scale

economies of scale
Forces that reduce a firm's average cost as the scale of operation increases in the long run

Like short-run average cost curves, a firm's long-run average cost curve is U-shaped. Recall that the shape of the short-run average total cost curve is determined primarily by increasing and diminishing marginal returns from the variable resource. A different principle shapes the long-run cost curve. If a firm experiences **economies of scale**, long-run average cost falls as output expands. Consider some sources of economies of scale. *A larger size often allows for larger, more specialized machines and greater specialization of labor.* For example, compare the household-size kitchen of a small restaurant with the kitchen at a McDonald's. At low rates of output, the smaller kitchen produces meals at a lower average cost than does McDonald's. But if production in the smaller kitchen increases beyond, say, 100 meals per day, a kitchen on the scale of McDonald's would make meals at a lower average cost. Thus, because of economies of scale, the long-run average cost for a restaurant may fall as size increases. As an example, the idea for McDonald's snack wrap started when a franchisee suggested that the company find more uses for the strips of chicken served with dipping sauce. Selling more chicken allowed each restaurant to cook new batches more frequently, which meant customers got a fresher product.[2]

A larger scale of operation allows a firm to use larger, more efficient machines and to assign workers to more specialized tasks. Production techniques such as the assembly line can be introduced only if the rate of output is sufficiently large. Typically, as the scale of a firm increases, capital substitutes for labor and complex machines substitute for simpler machines.

Diseconomies of Scale

diseconomies of scale
Forces that may eventually increase a firm's average cost as the scale of operation increases in the long run

Often another force, called **diseconomies of scale**, may eventually take over as a firm expands its plant size, increasing long-run average cost as output expands. For example, Oasis of the Sea, the world's largest cruise liner, can accommodate 6,300 guests, but the ship is too large to visit some of the world's most popular destinations, such as Venice and Bermuda.[3] More generally in a firm, as the amount and variety of resources employed increase, so does the *task of coordinating all these inputs.* As the workforce grows, additional layers of management are needed to monitor production. In the thicket of bureaucracy that develops, communications may get mangled. Top executives have

2.   As reported by Janet Adamy, "For McDonald's It's a Wrap," *Wall Street Journal,* 30 January 2007.
3.   Sarah Nassauer, "What It Takes to Keep a City Afloat," *Wall Street Journal,* 3 March 2010.

more difficulty keeping in touch with the factory floor because information is distorted as it moves up and down the chain of command. Indeed, in large organizations, rumors may become a primary source of information, reducing efficiency and increasing average cost.

The crisis of 2008 resulted in part because some financial institutions had grown so large and complex that top executives couldn't accurately assess the risks of the financial products they were buying and selling. One could argue that such firms were experiencing diseconomies of scale. For example, "Former Citigroup CEO Charles Prince apologized for his firm's role in the financial crisis, suggesting bank executives were wholly unaware of the risks posed by collateralized debt securities on the firm's books."[4]

Note that *diseconomies of scale result from a larger firm size, whereas diminishing marginal returns result from using more variable resources in a firm of a given size.*

The Long-Run Average Cost Curve

Because of the special nature of technology in the industry, suppose a firm must choose from among three possible plant sizes: small, medium, and large. Exhibit 8 presents this simple case. The average total cost curves for the three sizes are *SS'*, *MM'*, and *LL'*. Which size should the firm build to minimize average cost? The appropriate size, *or scale,* for the firm depends on how much output the firm wants to produce. For example, if *q* is the desired output, average cost is lowest with a small plant size. If the desired output is *q'*, the medium plant size offers the lowest average cost. With the medium plant, the firm experiences economies of scale. With the large plant, the firm experiences diseconomies of scale.

EXHIBIT 8 Short-Run Average Total Cost Curves Form the Long-Run Average Cost Curve, or Planning Curve

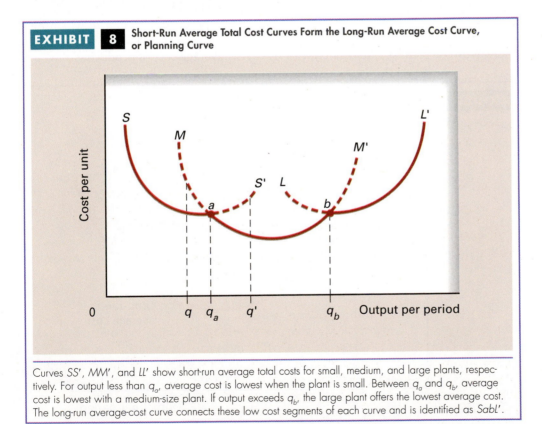

Curves *SS'*, *MM'*, and *LL'* show short-run average total costs for small, medium, and large plants, respectively. For output less than q_a, average cost is lowest when the plant is small. Between q_a and q_b, average cost is lowest with a medium-size plant. If output exceeds q_b, the large plant offers the lowest average cost. The long-run average-cost curve connects these low cost segments of each curve and is identified as *SabL'*.

---

4. As reported by Michael Crittenden, "Citi's Prince: I'm Sorry," *Wall Street Journal,* 8 April 2010. For more evidence see David Wessel, *In Fed We Trust,* (Crown Business, 2009); Michael Lewis, *The Big Short,* (Norton, 2010); and Roger Lowenstein, *The End of Wall Street,* (Penguin Press, 2010).

More generally in Exhibit 8, for output less than q_a, average cost is lowest when the plant is small. For output between q_a and q_b, average cost is lowest for the medium plant. And for output that exceeds q_b average cost is lowest when the plant is large. The **long-run average cost curve**, or *LRAC* curve, sometimes called the firm's *planning curve*, connects portions of the three short-run average cost curves that are lowest for each output rate. In Exhibit 8, that curve consists of the line segments connecting S, a, b, and L'. So even though the firm experiences diseconomies of scale with the largest plant size, the large firm is the one to build if the firm needs to produce more than q_b.

Now suppose there are many possible plant sizes. Exhibit 9 presents a sample of short-run cost curves shown in pink. The long-run average cost curve, shown in red, is formed by connecting the points on the various short-run average cost curves that represent the lowest per-unit cost for each rate of output. Each of the short-run average cost curves is tangent to the long-run average cost curve, or *planning curve*. If we could display enough short-run cost curves, we would have a different plant size for each rate of output. *These points of tangency represent the least-cost way of producing each particular rate of output, given resource prices and the technology.* For example, the short-run average total cost curve ATC_1 is tangent to the long-run average cost curve at point a, where \$11 is the lowest average cost of producing output q. Note, however, that other output rates along ATC_1 have a lower average cost. For example, the average cost of producing q' is only \$10, as identified at point b. Point b depicts the lowest average cost along ATC_1. So, while the point of tangency reflects the least-cost way of producing a particular rate of output, that tangency point does not reflect the minimum average cost for this particular plant size.

If the firm decides to produce q', which size plant should it choose to minimize the average cost of production? Output rate q' could be produced at point b, which represents the minimum average cost along ATC_1. But average cost is lower with a larger plant. With the plant size associated with ATC_2, the average cost of producing q' would

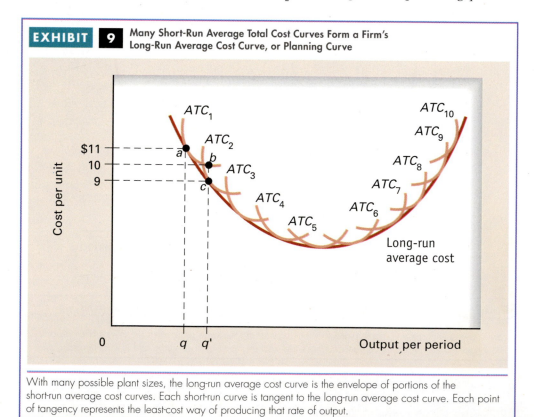

EXHIBIT 9 Many Short-Run Average Total Cost Curves Form a Firm's Long-Run Average Cost Curve, or Planning Curve

With many possible plant sizes, the long-run average cost curve is the envelope of portions of the short-run average cost curves. Each short-run curve is tangent to the long-run average cost curve. Each point of tangency represents the least-cost way of producing that rate of output.

be minimized at $9 per unit at point *c. Each point of tangency between a short-run average cost curve and the long-run average cost curve represents the least-cost way of producing that particular rate of output.*

In the long run, a firm can vary the inputs under its control. Some resources, however, are not under the firm's control, and the inability to vary them may contribute to diseconomies of scale. Let's consider economies and diseconomies of scale at movie theaters in the following case study.

BRINGING THEORY TO LIFE

Scale Economies and Diseconomies at the Movies   Movie theaters experience both economies and diseconomies of scale. A theater with one screen needs someone to sell tickets, usually another to sell popcorn (concession stand sales account for well over half the profit at most theaters), and yet another to run the movie projector. If a second movie screen is added, the same staff can perform these tasks for both screens. Thus, by selling tickets to both movies, the ticket seller becomes more productive. Furthermore, construction costs per screen are reduced because only one lobby and one set of rest rooms are required. The theater may get a better deal from movie distributors, can run bigger, more noticeable newspaper ads, and can spread the cost over more films. This is why we see theater owners adding more and more screens; they are taking advantage of economies of scale. Since 1990, the number of movie screens in the United States has grown faster than the number of theaters, so the average number of screens per theater has increased. There are now an average of 13 screens per movie theater. Europe has experienced similar growth.

But why stop at, say, 10 or even 20 screens per theater? Why not 30 or 40 screens, particularly in thickly populated areas with sufficient demand? One problem with expanding the number of screens is that traffic congestion around the theater grows with the number of screens at that location. Public roads are a resource the theater cannot control. Also, the supply of popular films may not be large enough to fill so many screens (though some theaters have diversified beyond movies by broadcasting live baseball games, operas, rock concerts and other events). Finally, time itself is a resource that the firm cannot easily control. Only certain hours are popular with moviegoers. Scheduling becomes more difficult because the manager must space out starting and ending times to avoid the crush that occurs when too many customers come and go at the same time. No more "prime time" can be created. (To spread out the customers, theaters offer discounts for morning or early afternoon showings.) Thus, theater owners lack control over such inputs as the public roads, the supply of films, and the amount of "prime time" in the day. These factors contribute to diseconomies of scale.

Sources: Jeffrey McCracken and Lauren Schuker, "Movie Theaters Secure Financing for Digital Upgrade," *Wall Street Journal*, 25 February 2010; Brooks Barnes, "At Cineplexes, Sport, Opera, Maybe a Movie," *New York Times*, 23 March 2008; Sandy Cohen, "Movie Fans Prefer the Theater Experience," *Forbes*, 7 March 2007; and *Statistical Abstract of the United States: 2010*, U.S. Census Bureau, http://www.census.gov/compendia/statab/.

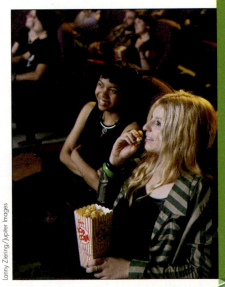

Lanny Ziering/Jupiter Images

It is possible for average cost to neither increase nor decrease with changes in firm size. If neither economies of scale nor diseconomies of scale are apparent over some range of output, a firm experiences **constant long-run average cost**. Perhaps economies and diseconomies of scale exist simultaneously in the firm but have offsetting effects. Exhibit 10 presents a firm's long-run average cost curve, or *LRAC* curve, which is divided into output

constant long-run average cost

A cost that occurs when, over some range of output, long-run average cost neither increases nor decreases with changes in firm size

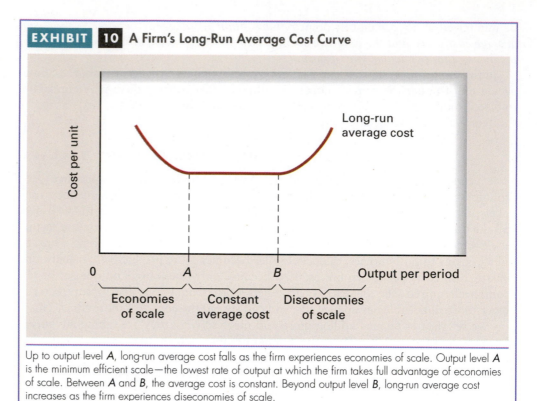

EXHIBIT **10** **A Firm's Long-Run Average Cost Curve**

Up to output level *A*, long-run average cost falls as the firm experiences economies of scale. Output level *A* is the minimum efficient scale—the lowest rate of output at which the firm takes full advantage of economies of scale. Between *A* and *B*, the average cost is constant. Beyond output level *B*, long-run average cost increases as the firm experiences diseconomies of scale.

segments reflecting economies of scale, constant long-run average costs, and diseconomies of scale. Output must reach quantity *A* for the firm to achieve the **minimum efficient scale**, which is the lowest rate of output at which long-run average cost is at a minimum.

Economies and Diseconomies of Scale at the Firm Level

Our discussion so far has referred to a particular plant—a movie theater or a restaurant, for example. But a firm could also be a collection of plants, such as the hundreds of movie theaters in a chain or the thousands of McDonald's restaurants. More generally, we can distinguish between economies and diseconomies of scale at the *plant level*—that is, at a particular location—and at the *firm level,* where the firm is a collection of plants. The following case study explores issues of multiplant scale economies and diseconomies.

WORLD OF BUSINESS

Scale Economies and Diseconomies at McDonald's   McDonald's experiences economies of scale at the plant, or restaurant, level because of its specialization of labor and machines, but it also benefits from economies of scale at the firm level. Experience gained from decades of selling hamburgers can be shared with new managers through centralized training programs. Costly research and efficient production techniques can also be shared across thousands of locations. For example, McDonald's took three years to decide on the exact temperature of the holding cabinets for its hamburger patties. What's more, the cost of advertising and promoting McDonald's through sponsorship of world events such as the Olympics can be spread across 32,000 restaurants in more than 120 countries.

   Some diseconomies may also arise in such large-scale operations. The fact that the menu must be reasonably uniform across thousands of locations means that if customers

---

minimum efficient scale

The lowest rate of output at which a firm takes full advantage of economies of scale

---

CASE STUDY

e activity

Surf the world of McDonald's at http://www.aboutmcdonalds.com/country/map.html. Because tastes vary, you can see that the McDonald's menu also varies. If you can read a foreign language, try to find a McDonald's page for a country where it is spoken.

in some parts of the country or the world do not like a product, it may not get on the menu, even though it might be popular elsewhere. Another problem with a uniform menu is that the ingredients must be available around the world and cannot be subject to droughts or sharp swings in price. For example, McDonald's considered adding a shrimp salad to the menu but decided not to when advised the move could deplete the nation's shrimp supply.

McDonald's has moved aggressively into overseas markets (about 10 percent of the beef sold in Japan goes into McDonald's hamburgers). Planning across so many markets has grown increasingly complex. For example, McDonald's is kosher in Israel, closes five times a day for Muslim prayer in Saudi Arabia, and serves mutton burgers in India, where cows are worshiped, not eaten. Running a worldwide operation also exposes the company to regional risks, such as environmental protests in Brazil, mad-cow disease in Europe, and terrorist bombings of outlets in France, Indonesia, Russia, and Turkey.

Change usually comes slowly in some large corporations, but the profit motive has forced McDonald's to reinvent itself. McDonald's has reorganized its U.S. operation into regions, allowing managers in each region more leeway in pricing and promotion. McDonald's has also become more flexible by putting mini-restaurants in airports, gas stations, and Wal-Marts. The company has been opening new stores and closing unprofitable ones. And McDonald's has reduced the time required to develop new products. For example, whereas Chicken McNuggets were seven years in the making, Chicken Wraps took less than a year to develop. This greater flexibility across countries and regions, the increased willingness to close unprofitable restaurants, and the reduction in product development time all reflect McDonald's effort to cope with diseconomies of scale.

Sources: Daniel Gross, "Who Won the Recession? McDonald's," *Slate*, 11 August 2009, at http://www.slate.com/id/2224862/. Janet Adamy, "For McDonald's It's a Wrap," *Wall Street Journal*, 30 January 2007; Tess Stynes, "McDonald's Posts Robust Sales," *Wall Street Journal*, 8 March 2010; James L. Watson, ed., *Golden Arches East: McDonald's in East Asia* (Stanford University Press, 1998); and McDonald's Web site at http://www.mcdonalds.com/.

Other large firms do what they can to reduce diseconomies of scale at the firm level. For example, IBM undertook a massive restructuring program to decentralize into six smaller decision-making groups. Some big corporations have even spun off parts of their operation to form new corporations. For example, Hewlett-Packard split off Agilent Technologies, AT&T created Lucent Technologies, and Time Warner spun off AOL.

Conclusion

By considering the relationship between production and cost, we have developed the foundation for a theory of firm behavior. Despite what may appear to be a tangle of short-run and long-run cost curves, *only two relationships between resources and output underlie all the curves. In the short run, it's increasing and diminishing returns from the variable resource. In the long run, it's economies and diseconomies of scale.* If you understand the sources of these two phenomena, you grasp the central points of the chapter. Our examination of production and cost in the short run and long run lays the groundwork for a firm's supply curve, to be covered in the next chapter. But before that, the appendix develops a more sophisticated approach to production and cost.

Summary

1. Explicit costs are opportunity costs of resources employed by a firm that take the form of cash payments. Implicit costs are the opportunity costs of using resources owned by the firm. A firm earns a normal profit when total revenue covers all implicit and explicit costs. Economic profit equals total revenue minus both explicit and implicit costs.

2. Resources that can be varied quickly to increase or decrease output are called variable resources. In the short run, at least one resource is fixed. In the long run, all resources are variable.

3. A firm may initially experience increased marginal returns as it takes advantage of increased specialization of the variable resource. But the law of diminishing marginal returns indicates that the firm eventually reaches a point where adding more units of the variable resource yields an ever-smaller marginal product.

4. The law of diminishing marginal returns from the variable resource is the most important feature of production in the short run and explains why marginal cost and average cost eventually increase as output expands.

5. In the long run, all inputs under the firm's control are variable, so there is no fixed cost. The firm's long-run average cost curve, also called its planning curve, is an envelope formed by a series of short-run average total cost curves. The long run is best thought of as a planning horizon.

6. A firm's long-run average cost curve, like its short-run average cost curves, is U-shaped. As output expands, average cost at first declines because of economies of scale—a larger plant size allows for bigger and more specialized machinery and a more extensive division of labor. Eventually, average cost stops falling. Average cost may be constant over some range. If output expands still further, the plant may experience diseconomies of scale as the cost of coordinating resources grows. Economies and diseconomies of scale can occur at the plant level and at the firm level.

7. In the long run, a firm selects the most efficient size for the desired rate of output. Once that size is chosen, some resources become fixed, so the firm is back operating in the short run. Thus, the firm plans for the long run but produces in the short run.

Key Concepts

Explicit cost   148

Implicit cost   148

Accounting profit   149

Economic profit   149

Normal profit   149

Variable resource   150

Fixed resource   150

Short run   150

Long run   150

Total product   151

Production function   151

Marginal product   151

Increasing marginal returns   151

Law of diminishing marginal returns   151

Fixed cost   152

Variable cost   152

Total cost   153

Marginal cost   154

Average variable cost   156

Average total cost   156

Economies of scale   158

Diseconomies of scale   158

Long-run average cost curve   160

Constant long-run average cost   161

Minimum efficient scale   162

Questions for Review

1. EXPLICIT AND IMPLICIT COSTS   Amos McCoy is currently raising corn on his 100-acre farm and earning an accounting profit of $100 per acre. However, if he raised soybeans, he could earn $200 per acre. Is he currently earning an economic profit? Why or why not?

2. EXPLICIT AND IMPLICIT COSTS   Determine whether each of the following is an explicit cost or an implicit cost:

   a. Payments for labor purchased in the labor market
   b. A firm's use of a warehouse that it owns and could rent to another firm
   c. Rent paid for the use of a warehouse not owned by the firm
   d. The wages that owners could earn if they did not work for themselves

3. ALTERNATIVE MEASURES OF PROFIT   Calculate the accounting profit or loss as well as the economic profit or loss in each of the following situations:

   a. A firm with total revenues of $150 million, explicit costs of $90 million, and implicit costs of $40 million
   b. A firm with total revenues of $125 million, explicit costs of $100 million, and implicit costs of $30 million
   c. A firm with total revenues of $100 million, explicit costs of $90 million, and implicit costs of $20 million
   d. A firm with total revenues of $250,000, explicit costs of $275,000, and implicit costs of $50,000

4. ALTERNATIVE MEASURES OF PROFIT   Why is it reasonable to think of normal profit as a type of cost to the firm?

5. **SHORT RUN VERSUS LONG RUN**   What distinguishes a firm's short-run period from its long-run period?

6. **LAW OF DIMINISHING MARGINAL RETURNS**   As a farmer, you must decide how many times during the year to plant a new crop. Also, you must decide how far apart to space the plants. Will diminishing returns be a factor in your decision making? If so, how will it affect your decisions?

7. **MARGINAL COST**   What is the difference between fixed cost and variable cost? Does each type of cost affect short-run marginal cost? If yes, explain how each affects marginal cost. If no, explain why each does or does not affect marginal cost.

8. **MARGINAL COST**   Explain why the marginal cost of production *must* increase if the marginal product of the variable resource is decreasing.

9. **COSTS IN THE SHORT RUN**   What effect would each of the following have on a firm's short-run marginal cost curve and its fixed cost curve?

   a. An increase in the wage rate
   b. A decrease in property taxes
   c. A rise in the purchase price of new capital
   d. A rise in energy prices

10. **COSTS IN THE SHORT RUN**   Identify each of the curves in the following graph:

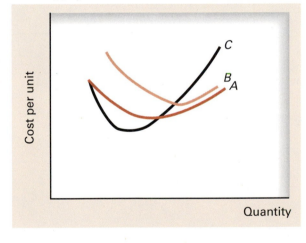

11. **MARGINAL COST AND AVERAGE COST**   Explain why the marginal cost curve must intersect the average total cost curve and the average variable cost curve at their minimum points. Why do the average total cost and average variable cost curves get closer to one another as output increases?

12. **MARGINAL COST AND AVERAGE COST**   In Exhibit 7 in this chapter, the output level where average total cost is at a minimum is greater than the output level where average variable cost is at a minimum. Why?

13. **LONG-RUN AVERAGE COST CURVE**   What types of changes could shift the long-run average cost curve? How would these changes also affect the short-run average total cost curve?

14. **LONG-RUN AVERAGE COST CURVE**   Explain the shape of the long-run average cost curve. What does "minimum efficient scale" mean?

15. **Case Study: At the Movies**   The case study notes that the concession stand accounts for well over half the profits at most theaters. Given this, what are the benefits of the staggered movie times allowed by multiple screens? What is the benefit to a multiscreen theater of locating at a shopping mall?

16. **Case Study: Scale Economies and Diseconomies at McDonald's**   How does having a menu that is uniform around the country provide McDonald's with economies of scale? How is menu planning made more complex by expanding into other countries?

Problems and Exercises

17. **PRODUCTION IN THE SHORT RUN**   Complete the following table. At what point does diminishing marginal returns set in?

Units of the Variable Resource	Total Product	Marginal Product
0	0	—
1	10	—
2	22	—
3	—	9
4	—	4
5	34	—

18. **TOTAL COST AND MARGINAL COST**   Complete the following table, assuming that each unit of labor costs $75 per day.

Quantity of Labor per Day	Output per Day	Fixed Cost	Variable Cost	Total Cost	Marginal Cost
0	—	$300	$__	$__	$__
1	5	—	75	—	15
2	11	—	150	450	12.5
3	15	—	—	525	—
4	18	—	300	600	25
5	20	—	—	—	37.5

a. Graph the fixed cost, variable cost, and total cost curves for these data.
b. What is the marginal product of the third unit of labor?
c. What is average total cost when output is 18 units per day?

19. TOTAL COST AND MARGINAL COST   Complete the following table, where L is units of labor, Q is units of output, and MP is the marginal product of labor.

L	Q	MP	VC	TC	MC·	ATC
0	0	—	$ 0	$ 12	—	—
1	6	—	$ 3	$15	—	—
2	15	—	$ 6	—	—	—
3	21	—	$ 9	—	—	—
4	24	—	$ 12	—	—	—
5	26	—	$ 15	—	—	—

a. At what level of labor input do the marginal returns from labor begin to diminish?
b. What is the average variable cost when $Q = 24$?
c. What is this firm's fixed cost?
d. What is the wage rate per day?

20. RELATIONSHIP BETWEEN MARGINAL COST AND AVERAGE COST   Assume that labor and capital are the only inputs used by a firm. Capital is fixed at 5 units, which cost $100 each. Workers can be hired for $200 each. Complete the following table to show average variable cost (AVC), average total cost (ATC), and marginal cost (MC).

Quantity of Labor	Total Output	AVC	ATC	MC
0	0	—	—	—
1	100	—	—	—
2	250	—	—	—
3	350	—	—	—
4	400	—	—	—
5	425	—	—	—

21. LONG-RUN COSTS   Suppose the firm has only three possible scales of production as shown below:

a. Which scale of production is most efficient when $Q = 65$?
b. Which scale of production is most efficient when $Q = 75$?
c. Trace out the long-run average cost curve on the diagram.

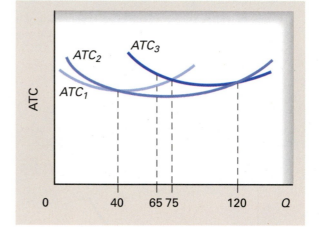

Appendix

A Closer Look at Production and Cost

This appendix develops a model for determining how a profit-maximizing firm combines resources to produce a particular rate of output. The quantity of output that can be produced with a given amount of resources depends on the existing *state of technology,* which is the prevailing knowledge of how resources can be combined. Let's begin by considering the technological possibilities available to the firm.

The Production Function and Efficiency

The ways in which resources can be combined to produce output are summarized by a firm's production function. The *production function* identifies the most that can be produced per time period using various combinations of resources, for a given state of technology. The production function can be presented as an equation, a graph, or a table.

The production function summarized in Exhibit 11 reflects, for a hypothetical firm, the output resulting from various combinations of resources. This firm uses only two resources: capital and labor. The amount of capital used is listed down the left side of the table and the amount of labor across the top. For example, if 1 unit of capital is combined with 7 units of labor, the firm can produce 290 units of output per month. The firm produces the maximum possible output given the combination of resources used; that same output could not be produced with fewer resources. Thus, we say that production is **technologically efficient.**

We can examine the effects of adding labor to capital by starting with any level of capital and reading across the table. For example, when the firm uses 1 unit of capital and 1 unit of labor, it produces 40 units of output per month. If the amount of labor increases by 1 unit and the amount of capital remains constant, output increases to 90 units, so the marginal product of labor is 50 units. If the amount of labor employed increases from 2 to 3 units, other things constant, output goes to 150 units, yielding a marginal product of 60 units. By reading across the table, you find that the marginal product of labor first rises,

EXHIBIT 11	A Firm's Production Function Using Labor and Capital: Production per Month						

Units of Capital Employed per Month	Units of Labor Employed per Month						
	1	2	3	4	5	6	7
1	40	90	150	200	240	270	290
2	90	140	200	250	290	315	335
3	150	195	260	310	345	370	390
4	200	250	310	350	385	415	440
5	240	290	345	385	420	450	475
6	270	320	375	415	450	475	495
7	290	330	390	435	470	495	510

showing increasing marginal returns from labor, and then declines, showing diminishing marginal returns. Similarly, by holding the amount of labor constant and following down the column, you find that the marginal product of capital also reflects first increasing marginal returns and then diminishing marginal returns.

Isoquants

Notice from the tabular presentation of the production function in Exhibit 11 that different combinations of resources yield the same rate of output. For example, several combinations of labor and capital yield 290 units of output per month (try to find the four combinations). Some of the information provided in Exhibit 11 can be presented more clearly in graphical form. In Exhibit 12, labor is measured along the horizontal axis and capital along the vertical axis. Combinations that yield 290 units of output are presented in Exhibit 12 as points *a, b, c,* and *d.* These points can be connected to form an *isoquant,* Q_1, a curve that shows the possible combinations of the two inputs that produce 290 units of output per month. Likewise, Q_2 shows combinations of inputs that yield 415 units of output, and Q_3, 475 units of output. (The isoquant colors match the corresponding entries in the production function table in Exhibit 11.)

An **isoquant**, such as Q_1 in Exhibit 12, is a curve that shows all the technologically efficient combinations of two resources, such as labor and capital, that produce a certain rate of output. *Iso* is from the Greek word meaning "equal," and *quant* is short for "quantity"; so *isoquant* means "equal quantity." Along a particular isoquant, such as Q_1, the output remains constant—in this case, 290 units per month—but the quantities of inputs vary. To produce a particular rate of output, the firm can use resource combinations ranging from much capital and little labor to little capital and much labor. For example, a paving contractor can put in a new driveway with 10 workers using shovels, wheelbarrows, and hand rollers. The same job can also be done with only two workers, a road grader, and a paving machine. A charity car wash is labor intensive, involving many workers per car, plus buckets, sponges, and hose. In contrast, a professional car wash is fully automated, requiring only one worker to turn on the machine and collect the money. An isoquant depicts alternative combinations of resources that produce the same output. Although we have included only three isoquants in Exhibit 12, there is a different isoquant for every amount listed in Exhibit 11. Indeed, there is a different isoquant for every amount the firm could possibly produce. Let's consider some properties of isoquants:

1. Isoquants farther from the origin represent greater output rates.

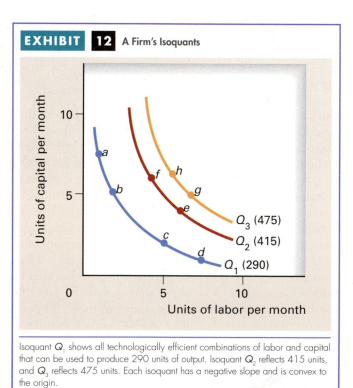

EXHIBIT 12 A Firm's Isoquants

Isoquant Q_1 shows all technologically efficient combinations of labor and capital that can be used to produce 290 units of output. Isoquant Q_2 reflects 415 units, and Q_3 reflects 475 units. Each isoquant has a negative slope and is convex to the origin.

2. Isoquants have negative slopes because along a given isoquant, the quantity of labor employed inversely relates to the quantity of capital employed.

3. Isoquants do not intersect because each isoquant refers to a specific rate of output. An intersection would indicate that the same combination of resources could, with equal efficiency, produce two different rates of output.

4. *Isoquants are usually convex to the origin*, which means that any isoquant becomes flatter as you move down along the curve.

The slope of an isoquant measures the ability of additional units of one resource—in this case, labor—to substitute in production for another resource—in this case, capital. As noted already, the isoquant has a negative slope. The absolute value of the slope of an isoquant is the **marginal rate of technical substitution**, or **MRTS**, between two resources. The MRTS is the rate at which labor substitutes for capital without affecting output. When much capital and little labor are used, the marginal productivity of capital is relatively small and the marginal productivity of labor is relatively great. One unit of labor substitutes for a relatively large amount of capital. For example, in moving from point *a* to *b* along isoquant Q_1 in Exhibit 12, one unit of labor substitutes for two units of capital, so the MRTS between points *a* and *b* equals 2. But as more labor and less capital are employed, the marginal product of labor declines and the marginal product of capital increases, so it takes more labor to make up for a one-unit reduction in capital. For example, in moving from point *c* to point *d*, two units of labor substitute for one unit of capital; thus, the MRTS between points *c* and *d* equals ½.

The extent to which one input substitutes for another, as measured by the marginal rate of technical substitution, is linked to the marginal productivity of each input. For example, between points *a* and *b*, one unit of labor replaces two units of capital, yet output remains constant. So labor's marginal product, MP_L—that is, the additional output resulting from an additional unit of labor—must be twice as large as capital's marginal product, MP_C. In fact, *anywhere along the isoquant, the marginal rate of technical substitution of labor for capital equals the marginal product of labor divided by the marginal product of capital, which also equals the absolute value of the slope of the isoquant*, or:

$$|\text{Slope of isoquant}| = MRTS = MP_L/MP_C$$

where the vertical lines on either side of "Slope of isoquant" indicate the absolute value. For example, the slope between points *a* and *b* equals −2 and has an absolute value of 2, which equals both the marginal rate of substitution of labor for capital and the ratio of marginal productivities. Between points *b* and *c*, three units of labor substitute for three units of capital, while output remains constant at 290. Thus, the slope between *b* and *c* is −3/3, for an absolute value of 1. Note that the absolute value of the isoquant's slope declines as we move down the curve because larger increases in labor are required to offset each one-unit decline in capital. Put another way, as less capital is employed, its marginal product increases, and as more labor is employed, its marginal product decreases.

If labor and capital were perfect substitutes in production, the rate at which labor substituted for capital would remain fixed along the isoquant, so the isoquant would be a downward-sloping straight line. Because most resources are *not* perfect substitutes, however, the rate at which one substitutes for another changes along an isoquant. As we move down along an isoquant, more labor is required to offset each one-unit decline in capital, so the isoquant becomes flatter and is convex to the origin.

Isocost Lines

Isoquants graphically illustrate a firm's production function for all quantities of output the firm could possibly produce. We turn now to the question of what combination of resources to employ to minimize the cost of producing a given rate of output. The answer, as we'll see, depends on the cost of resources.

Suppose a unit of labor costs the firm $1,500 per month, and a unit of capital costs $2,500 per month. The total cost (*TC*) of production per month is

$$TC = (w \times L) + (r \times C)$$
$$= \$1,500L + \$2,500C$$

where *w* is the monthly wage rate, *L* is the quantity of labor employed, *r* is the monthly cost of capital, and *C* is the quantity of capital employed. An **isocost line** identifies all combinations of capital and labor the firm can hire for a given total cost. Again, *iso* is Greek for "equal," so an isocost line is a line representing resource combinations of equal cost. In Exhibit 13, for example, the line *TC* = $15,000 identifies all combinations of labor and capital that cost the firm $15,000 per month. The entire $15,000 could pay for either 6 units of capital or 10 units of labor per month. Or the firm could employ any other combination of the two resources along the isocost line.

Recall that the slope of any line is the vertical change between two points on the line divided by the corresponding horizontal change. At the point where the isocost line meets the vertical axis, the quantity of capital that can be purchased equals the total cost divided by the monthly

cost of a unit of capital, or *TC/r*. At the point where the isocost line meets the horizontal axis, the quantity of labor that can be hired equals the firm's total cost divided by the monthly wage, or *TC/w*. The slope of any isocost line in Exhibit 13 can be calculated by considering a movement from the vertical intercept to the horizontal intercept. That is, we divide the vertical change (−*TC/r*) by the horizontal change (*TC/w*), as follows:

$$\text{Slope of isocost line} = -\frac{TC/r}{TC/w} = \frac{-w}{r}$$

The slope of the isocost line is the negative of the price of labor divided by the price of capital, or −*w/r*, which indicates the relative prices of the inputs. In our example, the absolute value of the slope of the isocost line equals *w/r*, or

$$\begin{aligned}|\text{Slope of isocost line}| &= w/r \\ &= \$1,500/\$2,500 \\ &= 0.6\end{aligned}$$

The monthly wage is 0.6, or six-tenths, of the monthly cost of a unit of capital, so hiring one more unit of labor, without changing total cost, implies that the firm must employ 0.6 fewer units of capital.

A firm is not confined to a particular isocost line. This is why Exhibit 13 includes three of them, each corresponding to a different total budget. In fact, there is a different isocost line for every possible budget. *These isocost*

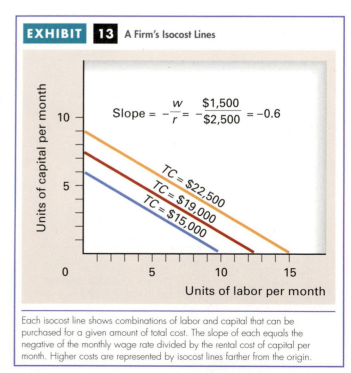

EXHIBIT 13   A Firm's Isocost Lines

Slope = $-\dfrac{w}{r} = -\dfrac{\$1,500}{\$2,500} = -0.6$

TC = $22,500
TC = $19,000
TC = $15,000

Units of capital per month (vertical axis)
Units of labor per month (horizontal axis)

Each isocost line shows combinations of labor and capital that can be purchased for a given amount of total cost. The slope of each equals the negative of the monthly wage rate divided by the rental cost of capital per month. Higher costs are represented by isocost lines farther from the origin.

lines are parallel because each reflects the same relative resource prices. Resource prices in our example are assumed to be constant regardless of the amount of each resource the firm employs.

The Choice of Input Combinations

Exhibit 14 brings together the isoquants and the isocost line. Suppose the firm has decided to produce 415 units of output and wants to minimize the cost of doing so. The firm could select point *f*, where 6 units of capital combine with 4 units of labor to produce 415 units. This combination, however, would cost $21,000 at prevailing prices. Because the profit-maximizing firm wants to produce its chosen output at the minimum cost, it tries to find the isocost line closest to the origin that still touches the isoquant. The isoquant for 415 units of output is tangent to the isocost line at point *e*. This resource combination costs $19,000. From the point of tangency, any movement in either direction along an isoquant increases the cost. So *the tangency between the isocost line and the isoquant shows the minimum cost required to produce a given output.*

Look at what's going on at the point of tangency. At point *e* in Exhibit 14, the isoquant and the isocost line have the same slope. As mentioned already, the absolute value of the slope of an isoquant equals the *marginal rate of technical substitution* between labor and capital, and the

absolute value of the slope of the isocost line equals the *ratio of the input prices.* So when a firm produces output in the least costly way, the marginal rate of technical substitution must equal the ratio of the resource prices, or:

$$\text{MRTS} = w/r = \$1{,}500/\$2{,}500 = 0.6$$

This equality shows that the firm adjusts resource use so that the rate at which one input substitutes for another in production—that is, the marginal rate of technical substitution—equals the rate at which one resource exchanges for another in resource markets, which is w/r. If this equality does not hold, the firm could adjust its input mix to produce the same output for less.

The Expansion Path

Imagine a set of isoquants representing each possible rate of output. Given the relative cost of resources, we could then draw isocost lines to determine the optimal combination of resources for producing each rate of output. The points of tangency in Exhibit 15 show the least-cost input combinations for producing several output rates. For example, output rate Q_2 can be produced most cheaply using *C* units of capital and *L* units of labor. The line formed by connecting these tangency points is the firm's **expansion path**. The expansion path need not be a straight line, although it generally slopes upward, indicating that the firm expands the use of both resources in the long run as output increases. Note that we have assumed that the prices of inputs remain constant as the firm varies output along the expansion path, so the isocost lines at the points of tangency are parallel—that is, they have the same slope.

The expansion path indicates the lowest long-run total cost for each rate of output. For example, the firm can produce output rate Q_2 for TC_2, output rate Q_3 for TC_3, and so on. Similarly, the firm's long-run average cost curve indicates, at each rate of output, the total cost divided by the rate of output. The firm's expansion path and the firm's long-run average cost curve represent alternative ways of portraying costs in the long run, given resource prices and technology.

We can use Exhibit 15 to distinguish between short-run and long-run adjustments in output. Let's begin with the firm producing Q_2 at point *b*, which requires *C* units of capital and *L* units of labor. Now suppose that in the short run, the firm wants to increase output to Q_3. If capital is fixed in the short run, the only way to produce Q_3 is by increasing the quantity of labor employed to *L´*, which requires moving to point *h* in Exhibit 15. Point *h* is not

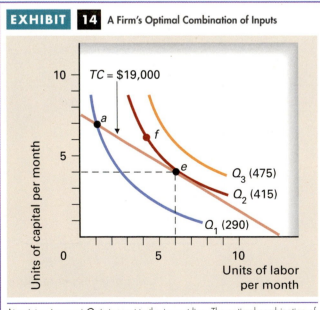

EXHIBIT 14   A Firm's Optimal Combination of Inputs

TC = $19,000

Units of capital per month (vertical axis, values 5, 10)

Units of labor per month (horizontal axis, values 5, 10)

Q_3 (475)
Q_2 (415)
Q_1 (290)

At point *e*, isoquant Q_2 is tangent to the isocost line. The optimal combination of inputs is 6 units of labor and 4 units of capital. The most that can be produced for $19,000 is 415 units. Another way of looking at this is that point *e* identifies the least costly way of producing 415 units.

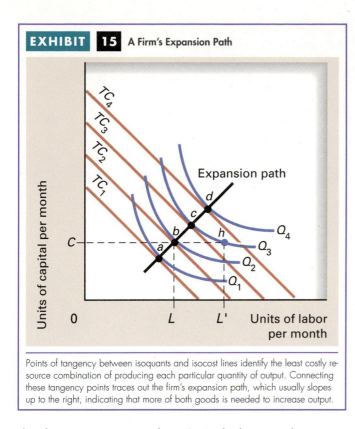

EXHIBIT **15** A Firm's Expansion Path

Units of capital per month (vertical axis)

TC$_4$
TC$_3$
TC$_2$
TC$_1$

Expansion path

d
c
b
C ---- a
h
Q_4
Q_3
Q_2
Q_1

0 L L' Units of labor per month

Points of tangency between isoquants and isocost lines identify the least costly resource combination of producing each particular quantity of output. Connecting these tangency points traces out the firm's expansion path, which usually slopes up to the right, indicating that more of both goods is needed to increase output.

increase would also be reflected by an upward shift of the average total cost curve.

Summary

A firm's *production function* specifies the relationship between resource use and output, given prevailing technology. An *isoquant* is a curve that illustrates the possible combinations of resources that produce a particular rate of output. An *isocost* line presents the combinations of resources the firm can employ, given resource prices and the firm's total budget. For a given rate of output—that is, for a given isoquant—the firm minimizes total cost by choosing the lowest isocost line that just touches, or is tangent to, the isoquant. The least-cost combination of resources depends on the productivity of resources and their relative cost. Economists believe that although firm owners may not understand the material in this appendix, they must act as if they do to maximize profit.

Appendix Questions

1. CHOICE OF INPUT COMBINATIONS   Suppose that a firm's cost per unit of labor is $100 per day and its cost per unit of capital is $400 per day.

   a. Draw the isocost line for a total cost per day of $2,000. Label the axes.
   b. If the firm is producing efficiently, what is the marginal rate of technical substitution between labor and capital?
   c. Demonstrate your answer to part (b) using isocost lines and isoquant curves.

2. THE EXPANSION PATH   How are the expansion path and the long-run average cost curve related?

the cheapest way to produce Q_3 in the long run because it is not a tangency point. In the long run, all resources are variable, and if the firm wishes to produce Q_3, it should minimize total cost by adjusting from point h to point c.

One final point: If the relative prices of resources change, the least-cost resource combination also changes, so the firm's expansion path changes. For example, if the price of labor increases, capital becomes cheaper relative to labor. Efficient production therefore calls for less labor and more capital. With the cost of labor higher, the firm's total cost for each rate of output rises. Such a cost

Perfect Competition

8

○ What do wheat and Google have in common?

○ Why might a firm continue to operate even when it's losing money?

○ Why do many firms fail to earn an economic profit?

○ How can it be said that the more competitive the industry, the less individual firms compete with each other?

○ What's the difference between making stuff right and making the right stuff?

○ And what's so perfect about perfect competition?

Answers to these and other questions are provided in this chapter, which examines the first of four market structures—perfect competition

The previous chapter developed cost curves for an individual firm in the short run and in the long run. In light of these costs, how much should a firm produce and what price should it charge? To discover the firm's profit-maximizing output and price, we revisit an old friend— demand. Demand and supply, together, guide the firm to maximize any profit or minimize any loss. In the next few chapters, we examine how firms respond to their economic environments in deciding what to supply, in what quantities, and at what price. We continue to assume that firms try to maximize profit.

Topics discussed include:

- Market structure
- Price takers
- Marginal revenue
- Golden rule of profit maximization
- Loss minimization
- Short-run supply curve
- Long-run supply curve
- Competition and efficiency
- Producer surplus
- Gains from exchange

An Introduction to Perfect Competition

Market structure describes the important features of a market, such as the number of suppliers (are there many or few?), the product's degree of uniformity (do firms in the market supply identical products, or are there differences across firms?), the ease of entry into and exit from the market (can firms come and go easily or are entry and exit blocked?), and the forms of competition among firms (do firms compete based on price alone or do they also compete through advertising and product differences?). The various features will become clearer as we examine each of the four market structures in the next few chapters. *A firm's decisions about how much to produce or what price to charge depend on the structure of the market.*

Before we get started, a few words about terminology. An *industry* consists of all firms that supply output to a particular *market*, such as the auto market, the shoe market, or the wheat market. The terms *industry* and *market* are used interchangeably throughout this chapter.

Perfectly Competitive Market Structure

We begin with **perfect competition**, in some ways the most basic of market structures. A *perfectly competitive* market is characterized by (1) many buyers and sellers—so many that each buys or sells only a tiny fraction of the total amount in the market; (2) firms sell a **commodity**, which is a standardized product, such as a bushel of wheat, an ounce of gold, or a share of Google stock; such a product does not differ across suppliers; (3) buyers and sellers are fully informed about the price and availability of all resources and products; and (4) firms and resources are freely mobile—that is, over time they can easily enter or leave the industry without facing obstacles like patents, licenses, and high capital costs.

If these conditions exist in a market, an individual buyer or seller has no control over the price. Price is determined by market demand and supply. Once the market establishes the price, any firm is free to supply whatever quantity maximizes profit. *A perfectly competitive firm is so small relative to the market that the firm's supply decision does not affect the market price.* Examples of perfectly competitive markets include those for most agricultural products, such as wheat, corn, and livestock; markets for basic metals, such as gold, silver, and copper; markets for widely traded stock, such as Google, Bank of America, and General Electric; and markets for foreign exchange, such as yen, euros, and pesos. Again, there are so many buyers and sellers that the actions of any one cannot influence the market price. For example, about 65,000 farmers in the United States raise hogs, and tens of millions of U.S. households buy pork products. The model of perfect competition allows us to make a number of predictions that hold up pretty well when compared to the real world. Perfect competition is also an important benchmark for evaluating the efficiency of other types of markets. Let's look at demand under perfect competition.

Demand Under Perfect Competition

Suppose the market in question is the world market for wheat and the firm in question is a wheat farm in Kansas. In the world market for wheat, there are hundreds of thousands of farms, so any one supplies only a tiny fraction of market output. For example, the thousands of wheat farmers in Kansas together produce less than 3 percent of the world's supply of wheat. In Exhibit 1, the market price of wheat of $5 per bushel is determined in panel (a) by the intersection of the market demand curve *D* and the market

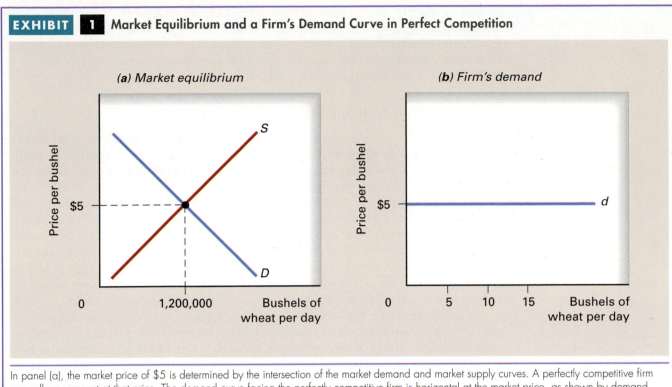

EXHIBIT 1 Market Equilibrium and a Firm's Demand Curve in Perfect Competition

(a) Market equilibrium

(b) Firm's demand

In panel (a), the market price of $5 is determined by the intersection of the market demand and market supply curves. A perfectly competitive firm can sell any amount at that price. The demand curve facing the perfectly competitive firm is horizontal at the market price, as shown by demand curve *d* in panel (b).

supply curve *S*. Once the market determines the price, any farmer can sell all he or she wants to at that market price.

Each farm is so small relative to the market that each has no impact on the market price. Because all farmers produce an identical product—bushels of wheat, in this case—anyone who charges more than the market price sells no wheat. For example, a farmer charging $5.05 per bushel would find no buyers. Of course, any farmer is free to charge less than the market price, but why do that when all wheat can be sold at the market price? Farmers aren't stupid (if they are, they don't last long). *The demand curve facing an individual farmer is, therefore, a horizontal line drawn at the market price.* In our example, the demand curve facing an individual farmer, identified as *d* in panel (b), is drawn at the market price of $5 per bushel. Thus, each farmer faces a horizontal, or a *perfectly elastic,* demand curve for wheat. A perfectly competitive firm is called a **price taker** because that firm must "take," or accept, the market price—as in "take it or leave it."

It has been said, "In perfect competition there is no competition." Ironically, two neighboring wheat farmers in perfect competition are not really rivals. They both can sell all they want at the market price. The amount one sells has no effect on the market price or on the amount the other can sell.

price taker
A firm that faces a given market price and whose quantity supplied has no effect on that price; a perfectly competitive firm that decides to produce must accept, or "take," the market price

Short-Run Profit Maximization

Each firm tries to maximize economic profit. Firms that ignore this strategy don't survive for long. Economic profit equals total revenue minus total cost, including both explicit and implicit costs. Implicit cost, remember, is the opportunity cost of resources owned by the firm and includes a normal profit. Economic profit is any profit above normal profit. How do firms maximize profit? You have already learned that a perfectly competitive firm has no control over price. What that firm does control is its rate of output—its quantity supplied. The question each wheat farmer asks is this: *How much should I produce to earn the most profit?*

Total Revenue Minus Total Cost

The firm maximizes economic profit by finding the quantity at which total revenue exceeds total cost by the greatest amount. The firm's total revenue is simply its output times the price. Column (1) in Exhibit 2 shows the farmer's output possibilities measured in bushels of wheat per day. Column (2) shows the market price of $5 per bushel, a price that does not vary with the farmer's output. Column (3) shows the farmer's total revenue, which is output times price, or column (1) times column (2). And column (4) shows the farmer's total cost of supplying each quantity shown. Total cost already includes a normal profit, so total cost includes all opportunity costs. Although the table does not distinguish between fixed and variable costs, fixed cost must equal $15 per day because total cost is $15 when output is zero. The presence of fixed cost tells us that at least one resource is fixed, so the farm must be operating in the short run.

At each output rate, total revenue in column (3) minus total cost in column (4) yields the farmer's economic profit or economic loss in column (7). As you can see, total revenue exceeds total cost at rates of output between 7 and 14 bushels, so the farm earns an *economic profit* at those output rates. Economic profit is maximized at $12 per day when the farm produces 12 bushels of wheat per day (the $12 and 12 bushels combination here is just a coincidence).

These results are graphed in panel (a) of Exhibit 3, which shows the total revenue and total cost curves. As output increases by 1 bushel, total revenue increases

---

EXHIBIT 2 Maximizing Short-Run Profit for a Perfectly Competitive Firm

(1) Bushels of Wheat per Day (q)	(2) Marginal Revenue (Price) (p)	(3) Total Revenue ($TR = q \times p$)	(4) Total Cost (TC)	(5) Marginal Cost ($MC = \Delta TC/\Delta q$)	(6) Average Total Cost ($ATC = TC/q$)	(7) Economic Profit or Loss = $TR - TC$
0	—	$ 0	$15.00	—	—	$-15.00
1	$ 5	5	19.75	$ 4.75	$19.75	−14.75
2	5	10	23.50	3.75	11.75	−13.50
3	5	15	26.50	3.00	8.83	−11.50
4	5	20	29.00	2.50	7.25	−9.00
5	5	25	31.00	2.00	6.20	−6.00
6	5	30	32.50	1.50	5.42	−2.50
7	5	35	33.75	1.25	4.82	1.25
8	5	40	35.25	1.50	4.41	4.75
9	5	45	37.25	2.00	4.14	7.75
10	5	50	40.00	2.75	4.00	10.00
11	5	55	43.25	3.25	3.93	11.75
12	5	60	48.00	4.75	4.00	12.00
13	5	65	54.50	6.50	4.19	10.50
14	5	70	64.00	9.50	4.57	6.00
15	5	75	77.50	13.50	5.17	−2.50
16	5	80	96.00	18.50	6.00	−16.00

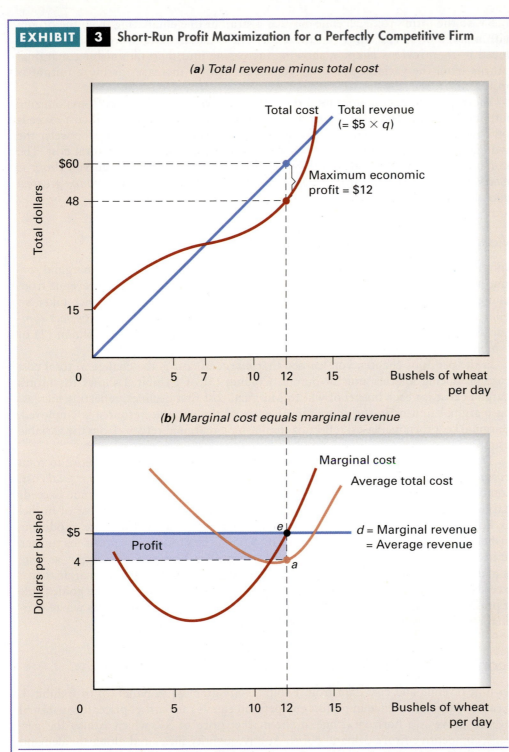

EXHIBIT 3 Short-Run Profit Maximization for a Perfectly Competitive Firm

(a) Total revenue minus total cost

Total cost

Total revenue (= $5 × q)

$60

Maximum economic profit = $12

48

15

0   5   7   10 12   15   Bushels of wheat per day

Total dollars

(b) Marginal cost equals marginal revenue

Marginal cost

Average total cost

$5   e   d = Marginal revenue = Average revenue

Profit

4   a

0   5   10 12   15   Bushels of wheat per day

Dollars per bushel

In panel (a), the total revenue curve for a perfectly competitive firm is a straight line with a slope of 5, the market price. Total cost increases with output, first at a decreasing rate and then at an increasing rate. Economic profit is maximized where total revenue exceeds total cost by the greatest amount, which occurs at 12 bushels of wheat per day. In panel (b), marginal revenue is a horizontal line at the market price of $5. Economic profit is maximized at 12 bushels of wheat per day, where marginal revenue equals marginal cost (point e). That profit equals 12 bushels multiplied by the amount by which the market price of $5 exceeds the average total cost of $4. Economic profit is identified by the shaded rectangle.

by \$5, so the farm's total revenue curve is a straight line emanating from the origin, with a slope of 5. The short-run total cost curve has the backward S shape introduced in the previous chapter, showing increasing and then diminishing marginal returns from the variable resource. Total cost always increases as more output is produced.

Subtracting total cost from total revenue is one way to find the profit-maximizing output. For output less than 7 bushels and greater than 14 bushels, total cost exceeds total revenue. The economic loss is measured by the vertical distance between the two curves. Between 7 and 14 bushels per day, total revenue exceeds total cost. The economic profit, again, is measured by the distance between the two curves. *Profit is maximized at the rate of output where total revenue exceeds total cost by the greatest amount.* Profit is greatest when 12 bushels are produced per day.

Marginal Revenue Equals Marginal Cost

marginal revenue (MR)

The firm's change in total revenue from selling an additional unit; a perfectly competitive firm's marginal revenue is also the market price

Another way to find the profit-maximizing rate of output is to focus on marginal revenue and marginal cost. **Marginal revenue**, or **MR**, is the change in total revenue from selling another unit of output. In perfect competition, each firm is a price taker, so selling one more unit increases total revenue by the market price. Thus, *in perfect competition, marginal revenue is the market price*—in this example, \$5. Column (2) of Exhibit 2 presents the farm's marginal revenue for each bushel of wheat.

In the previous chapter, you learned that *marginal cost* is the change in total cost from producing another unit of output. Column (5) of Exhibit 2 shows the farm's marginal cost for each bushel of wheat. Marginal cost first declines, reflecting increasing marginal returns in the short run as more of the variable resource is employed. Marginal cost then increases, reflecting diminishing marginal returns from the variable resource.

The firm increases production as long as each additional unit adds more to total revenue than to total cost—that is, as long as marginal revenue exceeds marginal cost. Comparing columns (2) and (5) in Exhibit 2, we see that marginal revenue exceeds marginal cost for each of the first 12 bushels of wheat. The marginal cost of bushel 13, however, is \$6.50, compared with its marginal revenue of \$5. Therefore, producing bushel 13 would reduce economic profit by \$1.50. The farmer, as a profit maximizer, limits output to 12 bushels per day. More generally, a firm expands output as long as marginal revenue exceeds marginal cost and stops expanding before marginal cost exceeds marginal revenue. A shorthand expression for this approach is the **golden rule of profit maximization**, which says that a profit-maximizing firm produces where marginal revenue equals marginal cost.

golden rule of profit maximization

To maximize profit or minimize loss, a firm should produce the quantity at which marginal revenue equals marginal cost; this rule holds for all market structures

Economic Profit in the Short Run

average revenue

Total revenue divided by quantity, or $AR = TR/q$; in all market structures, average revenue equals the market price

Per-unit revenue and cost data from Exhibit 2 are graphed in panel (b) of Exhibit 3. Because marginal revenue in perfect competition equals the market price, the marginal revenue curve is a horizontal line at the market price of \$5, which is also the perfectly competitive firm's demand curve. At any quantity measured along the demand curve, marginal revenue is the price. Because the perfectly competitive firm can sell any amount for the same price per unit, marginal revenue is also **average revenue**, or **AR**. Average revenue equals total revenue divided by quantity, or $AR = TR/q$. Regardless of the output rate, therefore, the following equality holds along a perfectly competitive firm's demand curve:

$$\text{Market price} = \text{Marginal revenue} = \text{Average revenue}$$

The marginal cost curve intersects the marginal revenue curve at point *e,* where output is about 12 bushels per day. At lower rates of output, marginal revenue exceeds marginal cost, so the farm could increase profit by expanding output. At higher rates of output, marginal cost exceeds marginal revenue, so the farm could increase profit by reducing output. Profit itself appears as the shaded rectangle. The height of that rectangle, *ae,* equals the price (or average revenue) of $5 minus the average total cost of $4. Price minus average total cost yields an average profit of $1 per bushel. Profit per day, $12, equals the average profit per bushel, $1 (denoted by *ae*), times the 12 bushels produced.

Note that with the total cost and total revenue curves, we measure economic profit by the vertical *distance* between the two curves, as shown in panel (a). But with the per-unit curves of panel (b), we measure economic profit by an *area*—that is, by multiplying the average profit of $1 per bushel times the 12 bushels sold.

Minimizing Short-Run Losses

A firm in perfect competition has no control over the market price. Sometimes that price may be so low that a firm loses money no matter how much it produces. Such a firm can either continue to produce at a loss or temporarily shut down. But even if the firm shuts down, it cannot, *in the short run,* go out of business or produce something else. The short run is by definition a period too short to allow existing firms to leave the industry. In a sense, firms are stuck in their industry in the short run.

Fixed Cost and Minimizing Losses

When facing a loss, should a firm temporarily shut down? Intuition suggests the firm should. But keep in mind that the firm faces two types of costs in the short run: fixed cost, such as property taxes and fire insurance, which must be paid even if the firm produces nothing, and variable cost, such as labor, which depends on the amount produced. A firm that shuts down in the short run must still pay its fixed cost. But, by producing, a firm's revenue may cover variable cost and a portion of fixed cost. *A firm produces rather than shuts down if total revenue exceeds the variable cost of production.* After all, if total revenue exceeds variable cost, that excess covers at least a portion of fixed cost.

Let's look at the same cost data presented in Exhibit 2, but now suppose the market price of wheat is only $3 a bushel, not $5. This new situation is presented in Exhibit 4. Because of the lower price, total cost in column (4) exceeds total revenue in column (3) at all output rates. Each quantity thus yields a loss, as indicated by column (8). If the firm produces nothing, it loses the fixed cost of $15 per day. But, by producing anywhere from 6 to 12 bushels, the firm can cut that loss. From column (8), you can see that the loss is minimized at $10 per day where 10 bushels are produced. Compared to shutting down, producing 10 bushels adds $5 more to total revenue than to total cost. That $5 pays some of the firm's fixed cost.

Panel (a) of Exhibit 5 presents the firm's total cost and total revenue curves for data in Exhibit 4. The total cost curve remains as in Exhibit 3. Because the price is $3, the total revenue curve now has a slope of 3, so it's flatter than at a price of $5. The total revenue curve now lies below the total cost curve for all output rates. The vertical distance between the two curves measures the loss at each output rate. If the farmer produces nothing, the loss is the fixed cost of $15 per day. The vertical distance between the two curves is minimized at 10 bushels, where the loss is $10 per day.

EXHIBIT 4   Minimizing Short-Run Losses for a Perfectly Competitive Firm

(1) Bushels of Wheat per Day (q)	(2) Marginal Revenue (Price) (p)	(3) Total Revenue (TR = q × p)	(4) Total Cost (TC)	(5) Marginal Cost (MC = ΔTC/Δq)	(6) Average Total Cost (ATC = TC/q)	(7) Average Variable Cost (AVC = VC/q)	(8) Economic Profit or Loss = TR − TC
0	—	$ 0	$15.00	—	—	—	$−15.00
1	$3	3	19.75	$ 4.75	$19.75	$4.75	−16.75
2	3	6	23.50	3.75	11.75	4.25	−17.50
3	3	9	26.50	3.00	8.83	3.83	−17.50
4	3	12	29.00	2.50	7.25	3.50	−17.00
5	3	15	31.00	2.00	6.20	3.20	−16.00
6	3	18	32.50	1.50	5.42	2.92	−14.50
7	3	21	33.75	1.25	4.82	2.68	−12.75
8	3	24	35.25	1.50	4.41	2.53	−11.25
9	3	27	37.25	2.00	4.14	2.47	−10.25
10	3	30	40.00	2.75	4.00	2.50	−10.00
11	3	33	43.25	3.25	3.93	2.57	−10.25
12	3	36	48.00	4.75	4.00	2.75	−12.00
13	3	39	54.50	6.50	4.19	3.04	−15.50
14	3	42	64.00	9.50	4.57	3.50	−22.00
15	3	45	77.50	13.50	5.17	4.17	−32.50
16	3	48	96.00	18.50	6.00	5.06	−48.00

Marginal Revenue Equals Marginal Cost

We get the same result using marginal analysis. The per-unit data from Exhibit 4 are graphed in panel (b) of Exhibit 5. First we find the rate of output where marginal revenue equals marginal cost. Marginal revenue equals marginal cost at an output of 10 bushels per day. At that output, the market price of $3 exceeds the average variable cost of $2.50. Because price exceeds average variable cost, total revenue covers variable cost plus a portion of fixed cost. Specifically, $2.50 of the price pays the average variable cost, and the remaining $0.50 helps pay some of average fixed cost (average fixed cost equals average total cost of $4.00 minus average variable cost of $2.50). This still leaves a loss of $1 per bushel, which when multiplied by 10 bushels yields an economic loss of $10 per day, identified in panel (b) by the pink-shaded rectangle. *The bottom line is that the firm produces rather than shuts down if there is some rate of output where the price at least covers average variable cost.* (Why is the farmer in the short run better off operating at a loss rather than shutting down?)

Shutting Down in the Short Run

If total revenue exceeds variable costs, the farmer produces in the short run. You may have read or heard of firms reporting a loss; most continue to operate. In fact, many new firms lose money during the first few years of operations. Still, they hang on because they hope to be profitable eventually (for example, the TV network UPN lost more than $1 billion during its first 11 years before merging with the WB network to form the CW network). But *if average variable cost exceeds the price at all rates of output, the firm shuts down.* After all, why produce if doing so only increases the loss? For example, a wheat price of $2 would fall below the average variable cost at all rates

EXHIBIT 5 Short-Run Loss Minimization for a Perfectly Competitive Firm

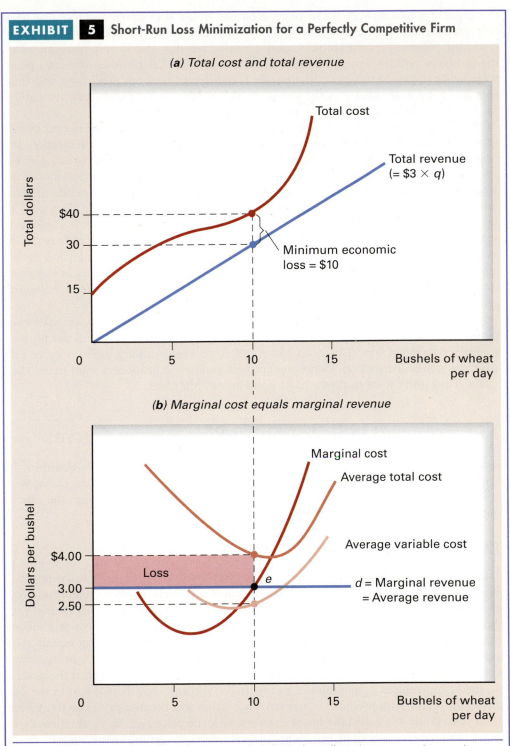

(a) Total cost and total revenue

(b) Marginal cost equals marginal revenue

Because total cost always exceeds total revenue in panel (a), the firm suffers a loss no matter how much is produced. The loss is minimized where output is 10 bushels per day. Panel (b) shows that marginal revenue equals marginal cost at point *e*. The loss is equal to output of 10 multiplied by the difference between average total cost ($4) and price ($3). Because price exceeds average variable cost ($2.50), the firm is better off continuing to produce in the short run, since revenue covers some fixed cost.

of output. Faced with such a low price, a farmer would shut down and lose just fixed cost, rather than produce and lose both fixed cost plus some variable cost.

From column (7) of Exhibit 4, you can also see that the lowest price at which the farmer would just cover average variable cost is $2.47 per bushel, when output is 9 bushels per day. At this price, the farmer is indifferent between producing and shutting down, because either way the loss is the $15 per day in fixed cost. Any price above $2.47 allows the farmer, by producing, to also cover some fixed cost.

Shutting down is not the same as going out of business. In the short run, even a firm that shuts down keeps productive capacity intact—paying rent, insurance, and property taxes, keeping water pipes from freezing in the winter, and so on. For example, Dairy Queen shuts down for the winter in cooler climates, a business serving a college community may close during term breaks, an auto plant responds to slack sales by temporarily halting production, and Yahoo recently shut down for a week to save money. A firm that shuts down does not escape fixed cost. When demand picks up again, production resumes. If the market outlook remains grim, the firm may decide to leave the market, but that's a long-run decision. The short run is defined as a period during which some costs are fixed, so a firm cannot escape those costs in the short run, no matter what it does. *Fixed cost is sunk cost in the short run, whether the firm produces or shuts down.*

Likewise, a concert promoter may cancel an event because of poor ticket sales even though the hall has already been rented. And a movie producer may pull the plug on a nearly completed film that looks like a turkey to avoid sinking millions more into advertising and distribution. Concert promoters and movie producers want to cut their losses. They don't want to throw more good money after bad.

The Firm and Industry Short-Run Supply Curves

If average variable cost exceeds price at all output rates, the firm shuts down in the short run. But if price exceeds average variable cost, the firm produces the quantity at which marginal revenue equals marginal cost. As we'll see, a firm changes the rate of output if the market price changes.

The Short-Run Firm Supply Curve

The relationship between price and quantity is summarized in Exhibit 6. Points 1, 2, 3, 4, and 5 identify where the marginal cost curve intersects alternative marginal revenue, or demand, curves. At a price as low as p_1, the firm shuts down rather than produce at point 1 because that price is below average variable cost. So the loss-minimizing output rate at price p_1 is zero, as identified by q_1. At price p_2, the price just equals average variable cost, so the firm is indifferent between producing q_2 and shutting down; either way the firm loses fixed cost. Point 2 is called the *shutdown point*. If the price is p_3, the firm produces q_3 to minimize its loss (see if you can identify that loss in the diagram). At p_4, the firm produces q_4 to earn a normal profit, because price equals average total cost. Point 4 is called the *break-even point*. If the price rises to p_5, the firm earns short-run economic profit by producing q_5 (see if you can identify that economic profit in the diagram).

At prices below p_2, the firm shuts down in the short run. The quantity supplied when the price is p_2 or higher is determined by the intersection of the firm's marginal cost curve and its demand, or marginal revenue, curve. As long as the price covers average variable cost, the firm supplies the quantity at which the upward-sloping marginal cost curve intersects the marginal revenue, or demand, curve. Thus, that portion of the

EXHIBIT **6** **Summary of a Perfectly Competitive Firm's Short-Run Output Decisions**

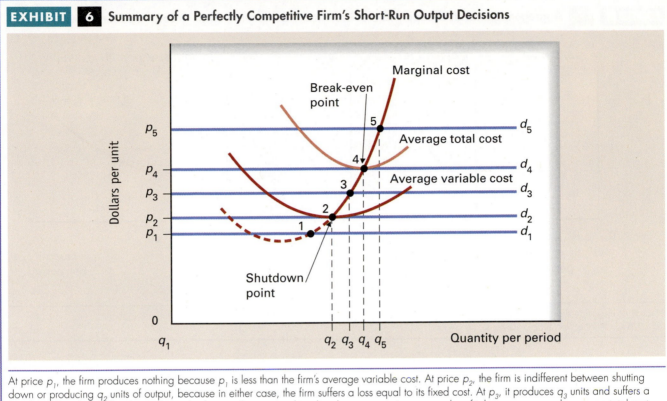

At price p_1, the firm produces nothing because p_1 is less than the firm's average variable cost. At price p_2, the firm is indifferent between shutting down or producing q_2 units of output, because in either case, the firm suffers a loss equal to its fixed cost. At p_3, it produces q_3 units and suffers a loss that is less than its fixed cost. At p_4, the firm produces q_4 and just breaks even, earning a normal profit, because p_4 equals average total cost. Finally, at p_5, the firm produces q_5 and earns an economic profit. The firm's short-run supply curve is that portion of its marginal cost curve at or rising above the minimum point of average variable cost (point 2).

firm's marginal cost curve that intersects and rises above the lowest point on its average variable cost curve becomes the **short-run firm supply curve**. In Exhibit 6, the short-run supply curve is the upward-sloping portion of the marginal cost curve, beginning at point 2, the shutdown point. The solid portion of the short-run supply curve indicates the quantity the firm offers for sale at each price.

The Short-Run Industry Supply Curve

Exhibit 7 presents examples of how supply curves for three firms with identical marginal cost curves can be summed *horizontally* to form the short-run industry supply curve (in perfect competition, there are many more firms). The **short-run industry supply curve** is the horizontal sum of all firms' short-run supply curves. At a price below p, no output is supplied. At price p, each of the three firms supplies 10 units, so the market supplies 30 units. At p', which is above p, each firm supplies 20 units, so the market supplies 60 units.

Firm Supply and Market Equilibrium

Exhibit 8 shows the relationship between the short-run profit-maximizing output of the individual firm and market equilibrium price and quantity. Suppose there are 100,000 identical wheat farmers in this industry. Their individual supply curves (represented by

short-run firm supply curve
A curve that shows how much a firm supplies at each price in the short run; in perfect competition, that portion of a firm's marginal cost curve that intersects and rises above the low point on its average variable cost curve

short-run industry supply curve
A curve that indicates the quantity supplied by the industry at each price in the short run; in perfect competition, the horizontal sum of each firm's short-run supply curve

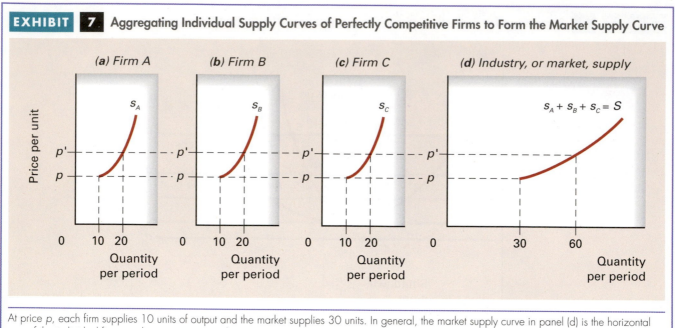

EXHIBIT 7   Aggregating Individual Supply Curves of Perfectly Competitive Firms to Form the Market Supply Curve

At price p, each firm supplies 10 units of output and the market supplies 30 units. In general, the market supply curve in panel (d) is the horizontal sum of the individual firm supply curves s_A, s_B, and s_C.

the portions of the marginal cost curve at or rising above the average variable cost) are summed horizontally to yield the market, or industry, supply curve. The market supply curve appears in panel (b), where it intersects the market demand curve to determine the market price of $5 per bushel. At that price, each farmer supplies 12 bushels per day,

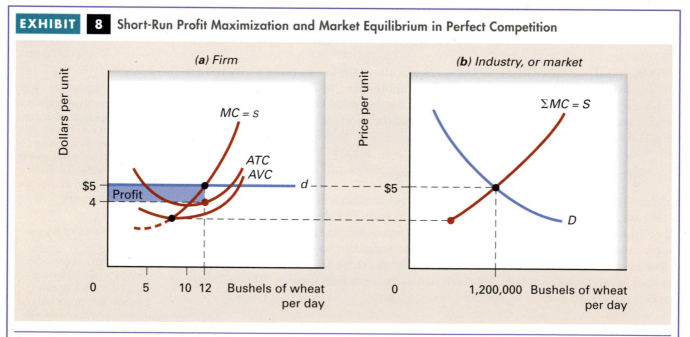

EXHIBIT 8   Short-Run Profit Maximization and Market Equilibrium in Perfect Competition

The market supply curve S in panel (b) is the horizontal sum of the supply curves of all 100,000 firms in this perfectly competitive industry. The intersection of S with the market demand curve D determines the market price of $5. That price, in turn, determines the height of the perfectly elastic demand curve facing the individual firm in panel (a). That firm produces 12 bushels per day (where marginal cost equals marginal revenue of $5) and earns economic profit in the short run of $1 per bushel, or $12 in total per day.

as shown in panel (a), which sums to 1,200,000 bushels for the market, as shown in panel (b). Each farmer in the short run earns an economic profit of $12 per day, represented by the shaded rectangle in panel (a).

To Review: A perfectly competitive firm supplies the short-run quantity that maximizes profit or minimizes loss. When confronting a loss, a firm either produces an output that minimizes that loss or shuts down temporarily. Given the conditions for perfect competition, the market converges toward the equilibrium price and quantity. But how is that equilibrium actually reached? In the real world, markets operate based on customs and conventions, which vary across markets. For example, the rules acceptable on the New York Stock Exchange are not the same as those followed in the market for fresh fish. The following case study discusses one mechanism for reaching equilibrium—auctions.

WORLD OF BUSINESS

Auction Markets   Flower markets are global. About three-quarters of flowers purchased in the United States are imported. More than half the world's cut flowers move through the auction system in the Netherlands. Five days a week, in a huge building 10 miles outside Amsterdam, some 2,500 buyers gather to participate in FloraHolland Aalsmeer, the largest auction of its kind in the world. Every day over 20 million flowers and plants from thousands of growers around the globe are auctioned off in the world's largest roofed building, spread across the equivalent of 100 football fields. Flowers are grouped and auctioned off by type—long-stemmed roses, tulips, and so on. Hundreds of buyers sit in theater settings with their fingers on buttons. Nearly as many buyers bid online from remote locations. Once the flowers are presented, a clock-like instrument starts ticking off descending prices until a buyer pushes a button. The winning bidder gets to choose how many and which items to take. The clock starts again until another buyer stops it, and so on, until all flowers are sold. Auctions occur rapidly—on average a transaction takes place every 4 seconds.

This is an example of a *Dutch auction,* which starts at a high price and works down. Dutch auctions are more common when selling multiple lots of similar, though not identical, items, such as flowers in Amsterdam, tobacco in Canada, and fish in seaports around the world. Because there is some difference among the products for sale in a given market—for example, some flower lots are in better condition than others—this is not quite perfect competition because perfectly competitive markets sell identical products.

More common than the Dutch auction is the *English open outcry auction,* where bidding starts at a low price and moves up until only one buyer remains. Products sold this way include stocks, bonds, wine, art (think Sotheby's and Christie's), antiques, and livestock. On markets such as the Chicago Board of Trade, prices for commodities such as wheat, gold, and coffee beans are continuously determined in the trading pits using variations of an open outcry auction.

The birth of the Internet has breathed new life into auctions. Web sites such as eBay, uBid, and hundreds more hold online auctions for old maps, used computers, wine, airline tickets, antiques, military memorabilia, comic books, paperweights— you name it. The largest online site, eBay, offers over

© Sion Touhig/Sygma./Corbis

2,000 categories in a forum that mimics a live auction. Internet auctions allow specialized sellers to reach a world of customers. A listing on eBay, for example, could reach millions of people in more than 100 countries.

Computers are taking over markets in other ways. In New York, Chicago, Philadelphia, London, and Frankfurt, hand-waving traders in what seem like mosh pits are being replaced by electronic trading. The Nasdaq was the world's first virtual stock market. There is no Nasdaq trading floor as there is with the New York Stock Exchange. On the French futures exchange, after electronic trading was added as an option to the open-outcry system, electronic trading dominated within a matter of months. *Computers reduce the transaction costs of market exchange.*

Sources: Constance Cacey, "Petal Pushers," *New York Times*, 25 February 2007; Eric Felton, "The Flower, the Leaf and the Lobby: A Valentine's Tale," *Wall Street Journal*, 15 February 2010; and Lynette Evans, "Following the Flowers," *San Francisco Chronicle*, 3 March 2007. The FloraHolland Web site (in English) is at http://www.floraholland.com/en/Pages/default.aspx.

net 📖 bookmark

Quick links to numerous online auctions, such as eBay, can be found at the most popular search engines (see Google at http://www.google.com). What are the most frequently listed types of goods available through online auctions? Are these the types of goods you would expect to find offered in perfectly competitive market? Can you distinguish which goods are fads? Some of the search engines bring you directly to auctions for particular goods, but are they running the auction? Who is "powering" the auction processes? Does the auctioning business appear to be perfectly competitive?

Perfect Competition in the Long Run

In the short run, the quantity of variable resources can change, but other resources, which mostly determine firm size, are fixed. In the long run, however, a firm has time to enter and leave and to adjust its size—that is, to adjust its *scale* of operations. In the long run, there is no distinction between fixed and variable cost because all resources under the firm's control are variable.

Short-run economic profit encourages new firms to enter the market in the long run and may prompt existing firms to get bigger. Economic profit attracts resources from industries where firms are losing money or earning only a normal profit. This expansion in the number and size of firms shifts the industry supply curve rightward in the long run, driving down the price. New firms continue to enter a profitable industry and existing firms continue to expand as long as economic profit is greater than zero. Entry and expansion stop only when the resulting increase in supply drives down the price enough to erase economic profit. In the case of wheat farming, economic profit attracts new wheat farmers and may encourage existing wheat farmers to expand. *Short-run economic profit attracts new entrants in the long run and may cause existing firms to expand. Market supply thereby increases, driving down the market price until economic profit disappears.*

On the other hand, a short-run loss forces some firms to leave the industry in the long run or to reduce their scale of operation. In the long run, departures and reductions in scale shift the market supply curve to the left, thereby increasing the market price until remaining firms just break even—that is, earn a normal profit.

Zero Economic Profit in the Long Run

In the long run, firms in perfect competition earn just a normal profit, which means zero economic profit. Exhibit 9 shows a firm and the market in long-run equilibrium. Market supply adjusts as firms enter or leave or change their size. *This long-run adjustment continues until the market supply curve intersects the market demand curve at a price that corresponds to the lowest point on each firm's long-run average cost curve, or LRAC curve.* Because the long run is a period during which all resources under a firm's control are variable, a *firm in the long run is forced by competition to adjust its*

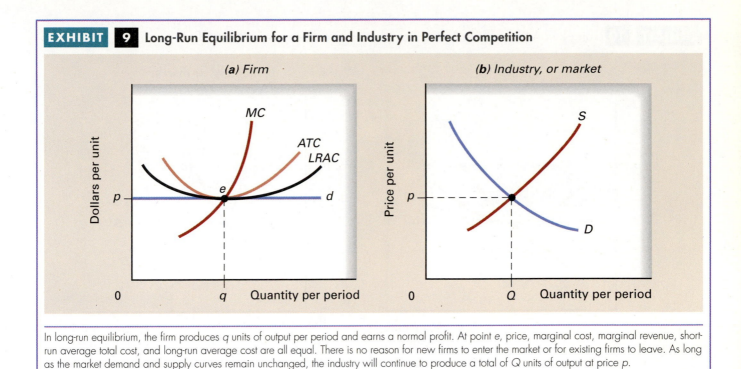

EXHIBIT 9 Long-Run Equilibrium for a Firm and Industry in Perfect Competition

(a) Firm

(b) Industry, or market

MC

ATC
LRAC

p ---- e   d

Dollars per unit

0   q Quantity per period

S

p ------------

Price per unit

D

0   Q Quantity per period

In long-run equilibrium, the firm produces q units of output per period and earns a normal profit. At point e, price, marginal cost, marginal revenue, short-run average total cost, and long-run average cost are all equal. There is no reason for new firms to enter the market or for existing firms to leave. As long as the market demand and supply curves remain unchanged, the industry will continue to produce a total of Q units of output at price p.

scale until average cost is minimized. A firm that fails to minimize average cost will not survive in the long run. At point e in panel (a) of Exhibit 9, the firm is in equilibrium, producing q units per period and earning just a normal profit. At point e, price, marginal cost, short-run average total cost, and long-run average cost are all equal. No firm in the market has any reason to change its output, and no outside firm has any incentive to enter this industry, because firms in this market are earning normal, but not economic, profit. In other words, all resources employed in this industry earn their opportunity costs.

The Long-Run Adjustment to a Change in Demand

To explore the long-run adjustment process, let's consider how a firm and an industry respond to an increase in market demand. Suppose that the costs facing each firm do not depend on the number of firms in the industry (an assumption explained soon).

Effects of an Increase in Demand

Exhibit 10 shows a perfectly competitive firm and industry in long-run equilibrium, with the market supply curve intersecting the market demand curve at point a in panel (b). The market-clearing price is p, and the market quantity is Q_a. The firm, shown in panel (a), supplies q units at that market price, earning a normal profit. This representative firm produces where price, or marginal revenue, equals marginal cost, short-run average total cost, and long-run average cost. (Remember, a normal profit is included in the firm's average cost curves.)

Now suppose market demand increases, as reflected by a rightward shift of the market demand curve, from D to D' in panel (b), causing the market price to increase in the short run to p'. Each firm responds to the higher price by expanding output

EXHIBIT 10   Long-Run Adjustment in Perfect Competition to an Increase in Demand

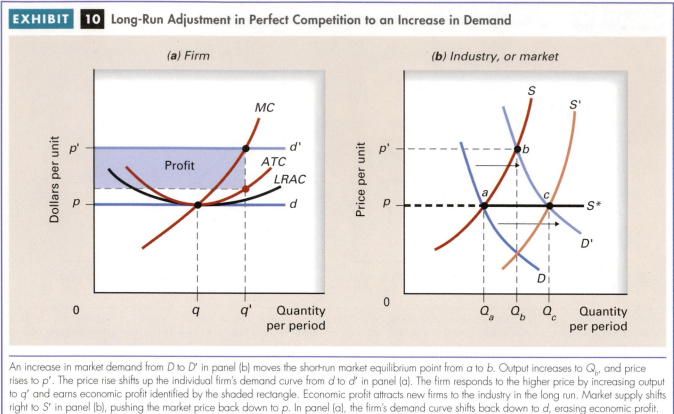

(a) Firm

(b) Industry, or market

An increase in market demand from *D* to *D'* in panel (b) moves the short-run market equilibrium point from *a* to *b*. Output increases to Q_b, and price rises to *p'*. The price rise shifts up the individual firm's demand curve from *d* to *d'* in panel (a). The firm responds to the higher price by increasing output to *q'* and earns economic profit identified by the shaded rectangle. Economic profit attracts new firms to the industry in the long run. Market supply shifts right to *S'* in panel (b), pushing the market price back down to *p*. In panel (a), the firm's demand curve shifts back down to *d*, erasing economic profit. The short-run adjustment is from point *a* to point *b* in panel (b), but the long-run adjustment is from point *a* to point *c*.

along its short-run supply, or marginal cost, curve until its quantity supplied increases to *q'*, shown in panel (a) of Exhibit 10. At that output, the firm's marginal cost curve intersects the new marginal revenue curve, which is also the firm's new demand curve, *d'*. Note that in the short run, each firm now earns an economic profit, shown by the shaded rectangle. Because all firms increase their quantity supplied, industry quantity supplied increases to Q_b in panel (b).

Economic profit attracts new firms in the long run. Their entry shifts the market supply curve to the right, which forces the price down. Firms continue to enter as long as they can earn economic profit. The market supply curve eventually shifts out to *S'*, where it intersects *D'* at point *c*, returning the price to its initial equilibrium level, *p*. The firm's demand curve drops from *d'* back down to *d*. As a result, each firm reduces output from *q'* back to *q*, and once again, each earns just a normal profit. Notice that although industry output increases from Q_a to Q_c, each firm's output returns to *q*. In this example, the additional output comes entirely from new firms drawn to the industry rather than from more output by existing firms (existing firms don't expand in this example because an increase in scale would increase average cost).

New firms are attracted to the industry by short-run economic profits resulting from the increase in demand. But this new entry shifts out market supply, forcing the market price down until economic profit disappears. In panel (b) of Exhibit 10, the short-run adjustment to increased demand is from point *a* to point *b;* the long-run adjustment moves to point *c*.

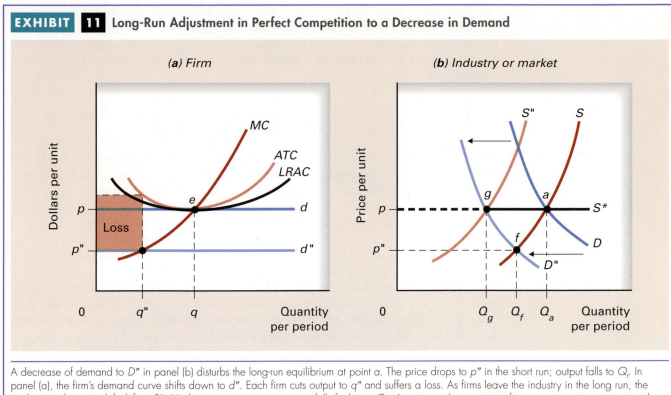

EXHIBIT 11   Long-Run Adjustment in Perfect Competition to a Decrease in Demand

A decrease of demand to D'' in panel (b) disturbs the long-run equilibrium at point a. The price drops to p'' in the short run; output falls to Q_f. In panel (a), the firm's demand curve shifts down to d''. Each firm cuts output to q'' and suffers a loss. As firms leave the industry in the long run, the market supply curve shifts left to S''. Market price rises to p as output falls further to Q_g. At price p, the remaining firms once again earn a normal profit. Thus, the short-run adjustment is from point a to point f in panel (b); the long-run adjustment is from point a to point g.

Effects of a Decrease in Demand

Next, let's trace the effects of a decrease of demand on the long-run market adjustment. The initial long-run equilibrium in Exhibit 11 is the same as in Exhibit 10. Market demand and supply curves intersect at point a in panel (b), yielding an equilibrium price p and an equilibrium quantity Q_a. As shown in panel (a), each firm earns a normal profit in the long run by producing output rate q, where price, or marginal revenue, equals marginal cost, short-run average total cost, and long-run average cost.

Now suppose that market demand declines, as reflected in panel (b) by a leftward shift of the market demand curve, from D back to D''. In the short run, this forces the market price down to p''. With the market price lower, the demand curve facing each individual firm drops from d to d''. Each firm responds in the short run by reducing quantity supplied to q'' where the firm's marginal cost equals its now-lower marginal revenue, or price. Market output falls to Q_f. Because the lower market price is below average total cost, each firm operates at a loss. This loss is shown by the shaded rectangle in Exhibit 11. Note, the price must still be above the average variable cost, because the firm's short-run supply curve, MC, is defined as that portion of the firm's marginal cost curve at or above its average variable cost curve.

A short-run loss forces some firms out of business in the long run. As firms exit, market supply decreases, or shifts leftward, so the price increases along market demand curve D''. Firms continue to leave until the market supply curve decreases to S'', where it intersects D'' at point g. Market output has fallen to Q_g, and price has returned to p. With the price back up to p, remaining firms once again earn a normal profit. When the dust settles, each remaining firm produces q, the initial equilibrium quantity. But, because some firms have left the industry, market output has fallen from Q_a to Q_g. Again, note that the adjustment involves the departure of firms from the industry rather than a reduction in the scale of firms, as a reduction in scale would increase each firm's long-run average cost.

The Long-Run Industry Supply Curve

Thus far, we have looked at a perfectly competitive firm's and industry's response to changes in demand, distinguishing between a short-run adjustment and a long-run adjustment. In the short run, a firm alters quantity supplied by moving up or down its marginal cost curves (that portion at or above average variable cost) until marginal cost equals marginal revenue, or price. If the price is too low to cover minimum average variable cost, a firm shuts down in the short run. Short-run economic profit (or loss) prompts some firms in the long run to enter (or leave) the industry or to adjust firm size until remaining firms earn just a normal profit.

In Exhibits 10 and 11, we began with an initial long-run equilibrium point; then, in response to a shift of the demand curve, we found a new long-run equilibrium point. In each case, the price changed in the short run but not in the long run. Market output increased in Exhibit 10 and decreased in Exhibit 11. Connecting these long-run equilibrium points yields the *long-run industry supply curve,* labeled S^* in Exhibits 10 and 11. The **long-run industry supply curve** shows the relationship between price and quantity supplied once firms fully adjust to any short-term economic profit or loss resulting from a change in demand.

Constant-Cost Industries

The industry we have examined thus far is called **constant-cost industry** because each firm's long-run average cost curve does not shift up or down as industry output changes. In a **constant-cost industry**, each firm's per-unit costs are independent of the number of firms in the industry. *The long-run supply curve for a constant-cost industry is horizontal,* as is depicted by S^* in Exhibits 10 and 11. A constant-cost industry uses such a small portion of the resources available that increasing industry output does not bid up resource prices. For example, output in the pencil industry can expand without bidding up the prices of wood, graphite, and rubber, because the pencil industry uses such a tiny share of the market supply of these resources.

Increasing-Cost Industries

The firms in some industries encounter higher average costs as industry output expands in the long run. Firms in these **increasing-cost industries** find that expanding output bids up the prices of some resources or otherwise increases per-unit production costs, and these higher costs shift up each firm's cost curves. For example, a market expansion of oil production could bid up the prices of drilling rigs and the wages of petroleum engineers and geologists, raising per-unit production costs for each oil producer. Likewise, more housing construction could bid up what developers must pay for land, carpenters, lumber, and other building materials.

To illustrate the equilibrium adjustment process for an increasing-cost industry, we begin again in long-run equilibrium in Exhibit 12, with the firm shown in panel (a) and the industry in panel (b). Market demand curve D in panel (b) intersects short-run market supply curve S at equilibrium point a to yield market price p_a and market

long-run industry supply curve A curve that shows the relationship between price and quantity supplied by the industry once firms adjust in the long run to any change in market demand

constant-cost industry An industry that can expand or contract without affecting the long-run per-unit cost of production; the long-run industry supply curve is horizontal

increasing-cost industry An industry that faces higher per-unit production costs as industry output expands in the long run; the long-run industry supply curve slopes upward

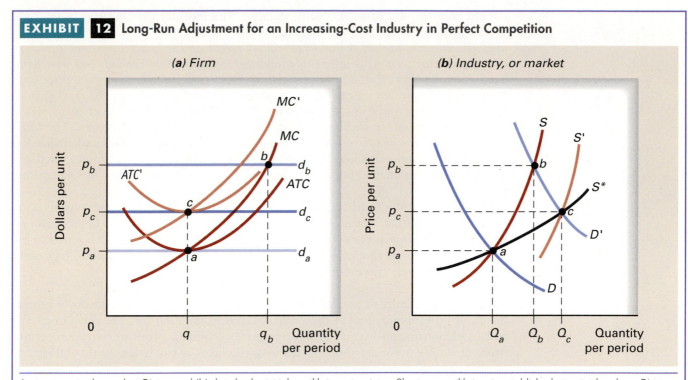

EXHIBIT 12 Long-Run Adjustment for an Increasing-Cost Industry in Perfect Competition

(a) Firm

(b) Industry, or market

An increase in demand to D' in panel (b) disturbs the initial equilibrium at point a. Short-run equilibrium is established at point b, where D' intersects the short-run market supply curve S. At the higher price p_b, the firm's demand curve shifts up to d_b, and its output increases to q_b in panel (a). At point b, the firm is now earning economic profit, which attracts new firms. As new firms enter, input prices get bid up, so each firm's marginal and average cost curves rise. New firms increase the short-run market supply curve from S to S'. The intersection of the new market supply curve, S', with D' determines the market price, p_c. At p_c, individual firms are earning a normal profit. Point c shows the long-run equilibrium combination of price and quantity. By connecting long-run equilibrium points a and c in panel (b), we obtain the upward-sloping long-run market supply curve S^* for this increasing-cost industry.

quantity Q_a. When the price is p_a, the demand (and marginal revenue) curve facing each firm is d_a as shown in panel (a). The firm supplies quantity q, where the price, or marginal revenue, equals marginal cost. At that output, average total cost equals the price, so the firm earns no economic profit in this long-run equilibrium.

Suppose an increase in the demand for this product shifts the market demand curve in panel (b) to the right from D to D'. The new demand curve intersects the short-run market supply curve S at point b, yielding the market price p_b and market quantity Q_b. With this price increase, each firm's demand curve shifts from d_a up to d_b. The firm's new short-run equilibrium occurs at point b in panel (a), where the marginal cost curve intersects the new demand curve, which is also the marginal revenue curve. Each firm produces output q_b. In the short run, each firm earns an economic profit equal to q_b times the difference between price p_b and the average total cost at that rate of output. So far, the sequence of events is the same as for a constant-cost industry.

Economic profit attracts new firms. Because this is an increasing-cost industry, new entrants drive up the cost of production, raising each firm's marginal and average cost curves. In panel (a) of Exhibit 12, MC and ATC shift up to MC' and ATC'. (We assume for simplicity that new average cost curves are vertical shifts of the initial ones, so the minimum efficient plant size remains the same.)

The entry of new firms also shifts the short-run industry supply curve to the right in panel (b), thus reducing the market price along D'. *New firms enter the industry until the combination of a higher production cost and a lower price squeezes economic profit to zero.* This long-run equilibrium occurs when the entry of new firms has shifted the short-run industry supply curve out to S', which lowers the price until it equals the minimum on each firm's new average total cost curve. The market price does not fall back to the initial equilibrium level because each firm's average total cost curve has increased, or shifted up, with the expansion of industry output. The intersection of the new short-run market supply curve, S', and the new market demand curve, D', determines the new long-run market equilibrium point, c. Points a and c in panel (b) are both on the *upward-sloping* long-run supply curve $S*$ for this increasing-cost industry.

In constant-cost industries, each firm's costs depend simply on the scale of its plant and its rate of output. For increasing-cost industries, each firm's costs depend also on the number of firms in the market. By bidding up the price of resources, long-run expansion in an increasing-cost industry increases each firm's marginal and average costs. The long-run supply curve slopes upward, like $S*$ in Exhibit 12.

To Review: Firms in perfect competition can earn an economic profit, a normal profit, or an economic loss in the short run. But in the long run, the entry or exit of firms and adjustments in each firm's size squeeze economic profit to zero. Competitive firms earn only a normal profit in the long run. This is true whether the industry in question experiences constant costs or increasing costs in the long run. Notice that, regardless of the nature of costs in the industry, the market supply curve is more elastic in the long run than in the short run. In the long run, firms can adjust all their resources, so they are better able to respond to changes in price. One final point: Firms in an industry could theoretically experience a lower average cost as industry output expands in the long run, resulting in a downward-sloping long-run industry supply curve. But such an outcome is considered so rare that we do not examine it.

As mentioned at the outset, perfect competition provides a useful benchmark for evaluating the efficiency of markets. Let's examine the qualities of perfect competition that make it so useful.

Perfect Competition and Efficiency

How does perfect competition stack up as an efficient user of resources? Two concepts of efficiency are used to judge market performance. The first, called *productive efficiency,* refers to producing output at the least possible cost. The second, called *allocative efficiency,* refers to producing the output that consumers value the most. *Perfect competition guarantees both productive efficiency and allocative efficiency in the long run.*

Productive Efficiency: Making Stuff Right

productive efficiency
The condition that exists when production uses the least-cost combination of inputs; minimum average cost in the long run

Productive efficiency occurs when the firm produces at the minimum point on its long-run average cost curve, so the market price equals the minimum average cost. The entry and exit of firms and any adjustment in the scale of each firm ensure that each firm produces at the minimum of its long-run average cost curve. Firms that do not reach minimum long-run average cost must, to avoid continued losses, either adjust their scale or leave the industry. Thus, *perfect competition produces output at minimum average cost in the long run.*

Allocative Efficiency: Making the Right Stuff

Just because *production* occurs at the least possible cost does not mean that the *allocation* of resources is the most efficient one possible. The products may not be the ones consumers want. This situation is akin to that of the airline pilot who informs passengers that there's good news and bad news: "The good news is that we're making record time. The bad news is that we're lost!" Likewise, firms may be producing goods efficiently but producing the wrong goods—that is, making stuff right but making the wrong stuff.

Allocative efficiency occurs when firms produce the output that consumers value most. How do we know that perfect competition guarantees allocative efficiency? The answer lies with the market demand and supply curves. Recall that the demand curve reflects the marginal value that consumers attach to each unit of the good, so the market price is the amount people are willing and able to pay for the final unit they consume. We also know that, in both the short run and the long run, the equilibrium price in perfect competition equals the marginal cost of supplying the last unit sold. Marginal cost measures the opportunity cost of resources employed to produce that last unit sold. Thus, the demand and supply curves intersect at the combination of price and quantity at which *the marginal value, or the marginal benefit, that consumers attach to the final unit purchased, just equals the opportunity cost of the resources employed to produce that unit.*

As long as marginal benefit equals marginal cost, the last unit produced is valued by consumers as much as, or more than, any other good those resources could have produced. There is no way to reallocate resources to increase the total value of all output in the economy. Thus, there is no way to reallocate resources to increase the total utility or total benefit consumers reap from production. *When the marginal benefit that consumers derive from a good equals the marginal cost of producing that good, that market is said to be allocatively efficient.*

Marginal benefit = Marginal cost

Firms not only are making stuff right, they are making the right stuff.

> **allocative efficiency**
> The condition that exists when firms produce the output most preferred by consumers; marginal benefit equals marginal cost

What's so Perfect About Perfect Competition?

If the marginal cost of supplying a good just equals the marginal benefit to consumers, does this mean that market exchange confers no net benefits to participants? No. Market exchange usually benefits both consumers and producers. Recall that consumers enjoy a surplus from market exchange because the most they would be willing and able to pay for each unit of the good usually exceeds what they actually do pay. Exhibit 13 depicts a market in short-run equilibrium. The *consumer surplus* in this exhibit is represented by blue shading, which is the area below the demand curve but above the market-clearing price of $10.

Producers in the short run also usually derive a net benefit, or a surplus, from market exchange, because what they receive for their output exceeds the least they would accept to supply that quantity in the short run. Recall that the short-run market supply curve is the sum of each firm's marginal cost curve at or above its minimum average variable cost. Point *m* in Exhibit 13 is the minimum point on the market supply curve; it indicates that at a price of $5, quantity supplied is 100,000 units. At prices below $5, quantity supplied would be zero because firms could not cover average variable cost. A price of $5 just covers average variable cost.

If the market price rises to $6, quantity supplied increases until marginal cost equals $6. Market output increases from 100,000 to 120,000 units. Total revenue in

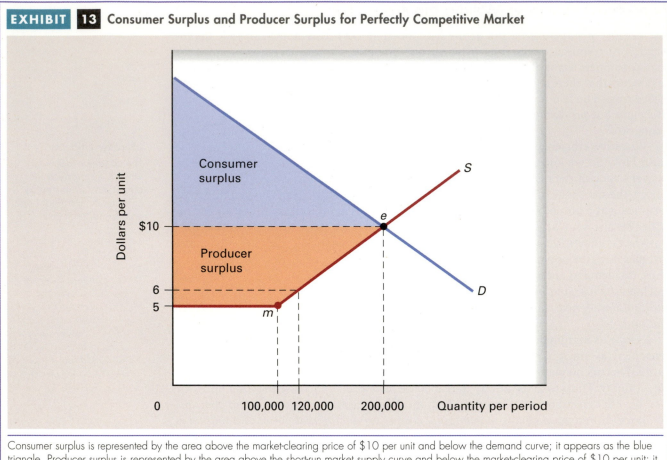

EXHIBIT 13 Consumer Surplus and Producer Surplus for Perfectly Competitive Market

Consumer surplus is represented by the area above the market-clearing price of $10 per unit and below the demand curve; it appears as the blue triangle. Producer surplus is represented by the area above the short-run market supply curve and below the market-clearing price of $10 per unit; it appears as the gold area. At a price of $5 per unit, there would be no producer surplus. At a price of $6 per unit, producer surplus would be the gold shaded area between $5 and $6. A price of $5 just covers each firm's average variable cost. .

this market increases from $500,000 to $720,000. Part of the higher revenue covers the higher marginal cost of production. But the rest provides a bonus to producers. After all, suppliers would have offered the first 100,000 units for only $5 each. If the price is $6, firms get to supply these 100,000 units for $6 each. Producer surplus at a price of $6 is the gold-shaded area between the prices of $5 and $6.

producer surplus

A bonus for producers in the short run; the amount by which total revenue from production exceeds variable cost

In the short run, **producer surplus** equals the total revenue producers are paid minus their variable cost of production. In Exhibit 13, the market-clearing price is $10 per unit, and producer surplus is depicted by the gold-shaded area between a price of $5 and the market price of $10. The most the firm can lose in the short run is to shut down. Any price that exceeds average variable cost, which is $5 in this example, reduces that short-run loss, and generates a producer surplus. A high enough price could yield economic profit.

social welfare

The overall well-being of people in the economy; maximized when the marginal cost of production equals the marginal benefit to consumers

The combination of consumer surplus and producer surplus shows the gains from voluntary exchange. Productive and allocative efficiency in the short run occurs at equilibrium point *e*, which also is the combination of price and quantity that maximizes the sum of consumer surplus and producer surplus, thus maximizing social welfare. **Social welfare** is the overall well-being of people in the economy. Even though marginal cost equals marginal benefit for the final unit produced and consumed, both producers and consumers usually derive a surplus, or a bonus, from market exchange.

The gains from market exchange have been examined in an experimental setting, as discussed in the following case study.

INFORMATION ECONOMY

Experimental Economics   Economists have limited opportunities to carry out the kind of controlled experiments available in the physical and biological sciences. But about four decades ago, Professor Vernon Smith began some experiments to see how quickly and efficiently a group of test subjects could achieve market equilibrium. His original experiment involved 22 students, 11 designated as "buyers" and 11 as "sellers." Each buyer was given a card indicating the value of purchasing one unit of a hypothetical commodity; these values ranged from $3.25 down to $0.75, forming a downward-sloping demand curve. Each seller was given a card indicating the cost of supplying one unit of that commodity; these costs ranged from $0.75 up to $3.25, forming an upward-sloping supply curve. Each buyer and seller knew only what was on his or her own card.

To provide incentives, participants were told they would get a cash bonus at the end of the experiment based on the difference between the price they negotiated in the market and their value (for buyers) or their cost (for sellers). For example, if a buyer assigned a $3.25 value was able to purchase the good for $1.50, that buyer would receive a cash bonus of $1.75 for that transaction. The point is that both buyers and sellers had a cash incentive to play the game for keeps. As a way of trading, Smith employed a system in which any buyer or seller could announce a bid or an offer to the entire group—a system called a *double-continuous auction*—based on rules similar to those governing stock markets and commodity exchanges. A transaction occurred whenever any buyer accepted an offer to sell or when any seller accepted an offer to buy. *Smith found that the price quickly moved to the market-clearing level,* which in his experiment was $2.00.

Economists have since carried out thousands of experiments to test the properties of markets. These show that under most circumstances, markets are extremely efficient in moving goods from producers with the lowest costs to consumers who place the highest value on the goods. This movement maximizes the sum of consumer and producer surplus and thus maximizes social welfare. One surprising finding is how few participants it takes to establish a market price. Market experiments sometimes use only four buyers and four sellers, each capable of trading several units. Some experiments use only two sellers, yet the competitive model performs well under double-continuous auction rules. Professor Smith won the Nobel Prize for his work in experimental economics.

Incidentally, most U.S. retail markets, such as supermarkets and department stores, use *posted-offer pricing*—that is, the price is marked, not negotiated. Experiments show that posted pricing does not adjust to changing market conditions as quickly as does a double-continuous auction. Despite their slow response time, posted prices may be the choice for large, relatively stable markets, because posted prices involve low transaction costs—that is, buyer and seller don't have to haggle over each transaction (imagine negotiating the price with a Wal-Mart clerk for each item you wanted to buy). In contrast, double-continuous-auction pricing

involves high transaction costs and, in the case of some stock and commodity markets, requires thousands of people in full-time negotiations to maintain prices at their equilibrium levels (although, as discussed in the previous case study, the Internet is reducing these transaction costs).

Experiments provide empirical support for economic theory and yield insights about how market rules affect market outcomes. Experiments also help create markets that did not exist before, such as the market for pollution rights or for broadcast spectrum rights—markets to be discussed in later chapters. Experiments also offer a safe and inexpensive way for people in emerging market and transitional economies to learn how markets work. The rapid development of online auctions has opened up a world of data for experimentalists.

Experimental economics is a hot topic for research and industry. For example, the number of papers published in the field jumped from fewer than 20 a year in the 1970s to more than ten times that today. The field also has its own research journals, including *Experimental Economics*. Most top U.S. business schools employ experimental economists. Some top corporations, such as Google, Hewlett-Packard, and IBM, as well as many universities created experimental-economics labs.

Sources: Vernon Smith, "Experimental Methods in Economics," *The New Palgrave Dictionary of Economics*, Vol. 2, edited by J. Eatwell et al. (Stockton, 1987), pp. 241–249; Vernon Smith, "Behavioral Economics and the Foundations of Economics," *Journal of Socio-Economics* (Issue 2, 2005), pp. 135–150; and Francesco Guala, *The Methodology of Experimental Economics* (Cambridge University Press, 2005). The academic journal *Experimental Economics* can be found at http://www.springer.com/economics/economic+theory/journal/10683.

Conclusion

Let's review the assumptions of a perfectly competitive market and see how each relates to ideas developed in this chapter. *First,* there are many buyers and many sellers. This assumption ensures that no individual buyer or seller can influence the price (although recent experiments show that competition occurs even with few buyers and sellers). *Second,* firms produce a commodity, or a uniform product. If consumers could distinguish between the products of different suppliers, they might prefer one firm's product even at a higher price, so different producers could sell at different prices. In that case, not every firm would be a price taker—that is, each firm's demand curve would no longer be horizontal. *Third,* market participants have full information about all prices and all production processes. Otherwise, some producers could charge more than the market price, and some uninformed consumers would pay that higher price. Also, through ignorance, some firms might select outdated technology or fail to recognize opportunities for short-run economic profits. *Fourth,* all resources are mobile in the long run, with nothing preventing firms in the long run from entering profitable markets or leaving losing markets. If firms couldn't enter profitable markets, then some firms already in that market could earn economic profit in the long run. If firms couldn't exit losing markets, then market supply couldn't decline enough in the long run to erase the economic losses of remaining firms.

Perfect competition is not the most common market structure observed in the real world. The markets for agricultural products, metals such as gold and silver, widely traded stocks, and foreign exchange come close to being perfect. But even if not a single example could be found, the model would still be useful for analyzing market behavior. As you will see in the next two chapters, perfect competition provides a valuable benchmark for evaluating the efficiency of other market structures.

Summary

1. Market structure describes important features of the economic environment in which firms operate. These features include the number of buyers and sellers in the market, the ease or difficulty of entering and leaving the market, differences in the product across firms, and the forms of competition among firms.

2. A perfectly competitive market is characterized by (a) a large number of buyers and sellers, each too small to influence the market price; (b) firms in the market supply a commodity, which is a product undifferentiated across producers; (c) buyers and sellers possess full information about the availability and prices of all resources, goods, and technologies; and (d) firms and resources are freely mobile in the long run.

3. The market price in perfect competition is determined by the intersection of the market demand and market supply curves. Each firm then faces a demand curve that is a horizontal line at the market price. The firm's demand curve also indicates the average revenue and marginal revenue received at each rate of output. Firms in perfect competition are said to be price takers because no firm can influence the market price. Each firm can vary only the amount it supplies at that price.

4. For a firm to produce in the short run, rather than shut down, the market price must at least cover the firm's average variable cost. If price is below average variable cost, the firm shuts down. That portion of the marginal cost curve at or rising above the average variable cost curve becomes the perfectly competitive firm's short-run supply curve. The horizontal sum of each firm's supply curve forms the market supply curve. As long as price covers average variable cost, each perfectly competitive firm maximizes profit or minimizes loss by producing where marginal revenue equals marginal cost.

5. Because firms are not free to enter or leave the market in the short run, economic profit or loss is possible. In the long run, however, firms enter or leave the market and otherwise adjust their scale of operation until any economic profit or loss is eliminated.

6. Competition drives each firm in the long run to produce at the lowest point on its long-run average cost curve. At this rate of output, marginal revenue equals marginal cost and each also equals the price and average cost. Firms that fail to produce at this least-cost combination do not survive in the long run.

7. In the short run, a firm's change in quantity supplied is shown by moving up or down its marginal cost, or supply, curve. In the long run, firms enter or leave the market and existing firms may change their scale of operation until firms still in the industry earn just a normal profit. As the industry expands or contracts in the long run, the long-run industry supply curve has a shape that reflects either constant costs or increasing costs.

8. Perfectly competitive markets exhibit both productive efficiency (because output is produced using the most efficient combination of resources available) and allocative efficiency (because the goods produced are those most valued by consumers). In equilibrium, a perfectly competitive market allocates goods so that the marginal cost of the final unit produced equals the marginal value that consumers attach to that final unit. In the long run, market pressure minimizes the average cost of production. Voluntary exchange in competitive markets maximizes the sum of consumer surplus and producer surplus, thus maximizing social welfare.

Key Concepts

Market structure   174

Perfect competition   174

Commodity   174

Price taker   175

Marginal revenue (MR)   178

Golden rule of profit maximization   178

Average revenue   178

Short-run firm supply curve   183

Short-run industry supply curve   183

Long-run industry supply curve   190

Constant-cost industry   190

Increasing-cost industry   190

Productive efficiency   192

Allocative efficiency   193

Producer surplus   194

Social welfare   194

Questions for Review

1. MARKET STRUCTURE Define *market structure*. What factors are considered in determining the market structure of a particular industry?

2. DEMAND UNDER PERFECT COMPETITION What type of demand curve does a perfectly competitive firm face? Why?

3. TOTAL REVENUE Look back at Exhibit 3, panel (a) in this chapter. Explain why the total revenue curve is a straight line from the origin, whereas the slope of the total cost curve changes.

4. PROFIT IN THE SHORT RUN Look back at Exhibit 3, panel (b), in this chapter. Why doesn't the firm choose the output that

maximizes average profit (i.e., the output where average cost is the lowest)?

5. **The Short-Run Firm Supply Curve**   An individual competitive firm's short-run supply curve is the portion of its marginal cost curve that equals or rises above the average variable cost. Explain why.

6. **Case Study: Auction Markets**   Which of the characteristics of the perfectly competitive market structure are found in FloraHolland Aalsmeer?

7. **Long-Run Industry Supply**   Why does the long-run industry supply curve for an increasing-cost industry slope upward? What increases costs in an increasing-cost industry?

8. **Perfect Competition and Efficiency**   Define productive efficiency and allocative efficiency. What conditions must be met to achieve them?

9. **Case Study: Experimental Economics**   In Professor Vernon Smith's experiment, which "buyers" ended up with a surplus at the market-clearing price of $2? Which "sellers" had a surplus? Which "buyers" or "sellers" did not engage in transactions?

Problems and Exercises

10. **Short-Run Profit Maximization**   A perfectly competitive firm has the following fixed and variable costs in the short run. The market price for the firm's product is $150.

Output	FC	VC	TC	TR	Profit/Loss
0	$100	$0	___	___	___
1	$100	$100	___	___	___
2	$100	$180	___	___	___
3	$100	$300	___	___	___
4	$100	$440	___	___	___
5	$100	$600	___	___	___
6	$100	$780	___	___	___

a. Complete the table.
b. At what output rate does the firm maximize profit or minimize loss?
c. What is the firm's marginal revenue at each positive rate of output? Its average revenue?
d. What can you say about the relationship between marginal revenue and marginal cost for output rates below the profit-maximizing (or loss-minimizing) rate? For output rates above the profit-maximizing (or loss-minimizing) rate?

11. **The Short-Run Firm Supply Curve**   Use the following data to answer the questions below:

Q	VC	MC	AVC
1	$10	___	___
2	$16	___	___
3	$20	___	___
4	$25	___	___
5	$31	___	___
6	$38	___	___
7	$46	___	___
8	$55	___	___
9	$65	___	___

a. Calculate the marginal cost and average variable cost for each level of production.
b. How much would the firm produce if it could sell its product for $5? For $7? For $10?

c. Explain your answers.
d. Assuming that its fixed cost is $3, calculate the firm's profit at each of the production levels determined in part (b).

12. **The Short-Run Firm Supply Curve**   Each of the following situations could exist for a perfectly competitive firm in the short run. In each case, indicate whether the firm should produce in the short run or shut down in the short run, or whether additional information is needed to determine what it should do in the short run.

a. Total cost exceeds total revenue at all output levels.
b. Total variable cost exceeds total revenue at all output levels.
c. Total revenue exceeds total fixed cost at all output levels.
d. Marginal revenue exceeds marginal cost at the current output level.
e. Price exceeds average total cost at all output levels.
f. Average variable cost exceeds price at all output levels.
g. Average total cost exceeds price at all output levels.

13. **Perfect Competition in the Long Run**   Draw the short- and long-run cost curves for a competitive firm in long-run equilibrium. Indicate the long-run equilibrium price and quantity.

a. Discuss the firm's short-run response to a reduction in the price of a variable resource.
b. Assuming that this is a constant-cost industry, describe the process by which the industry returns to long-run equilibrium following a change in market demand.

14. **The Long-Run Industry Supply Curve**   A normal good is being produced in a constant-cost, perfectly competitive industry. Initially, each firm is in long-run equilibrium.

a. Graphically illustrate and explain the short-run adjustments for the market and the firm to a decrease in consumer incomes. Be sure to discuss any changes in output levels, prices, profits, and the number of firms.
b. Next, show on your graph and explain the long-run adjustment to the income change. Be sure to discuss any changes in output levels, prices, profits, and the number of firms.

15. **The Long-Run Industry Supply Curve**   The following graph shows possible long-run market supply curves for a perfectly competitive industry. Determine which supply curve

indicates a constant-cost industry and which an increasing-cost industry.

a. Explain the difference between a constant-cost industry and an increasing-cost industry.
b. Distinguish between the long-run impact of an increase in market demand in a constant-cost industry and the impact in an increasing-cost industry.

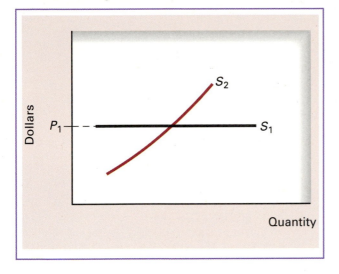

16. WHAT'S SO PERFECT ABOUT PERFECT COMPETITION   Use the following data to answer the questions.

Quantity	Marginal Cost	Marginal Benefit
0	—	—
1	$ 2	$10
2	$ 3	$ 9
3	$ 4	$ 8
4	$ 5	$ 7
5	$ 6	$ 6
6	$ 8	$ 5
7	$10	$ 4
8	$12	$ 3

a. For the product shown, assume that the minimum point of each firm's average variable cost curve is at $2. Construct a demand and supply diagram for the product and indicate the equilibrium price and quantity.
b. On the graph, label the area of consumer surplus as *f*. Label the area of producer surplus as *g*.
c. If the equilibrium price were $2, what would be the amount of producer surplus?

Global Economic Watch Exercises

Login to www.cengagebrain.com and access the Global Economic Watch to do these exercises.

17. GLOBAL ECONOMIC WATCH   Go to the Global Economic Crisis Resource Center. Select Global Issues in Context. In the Basic Search box at the top of the page, enter the phrase "Green Shoots." On the Results page, go to the Magazines section. Click on the link for the March 13, 2010, article "Green Shoots; Agribusiness in India." As you read the article, concentrate on the fourth paragraph, which describes the traditional market structure for Indian agriculture. How well does the description fit the four characteristics of perfect competition?

18. GLOBAL ECONOMIC WATCH   Go to the Global Economic Crisis Resource Center. Select Global Issues in Context. In the Basic Search box at the top of the page, enter the term "perfect competition." Find three or four resources that discuss the economic definition of *perfect competition*. Writing in your own words, analyze whether the authors support or dispute the idea that perfect competition is realistic and applicable.

Monopoly

9

AP Photo/Rick Rycroft

- How can a firm monopolize a market?
- Why aren't most markets monopolized?
- Why don't most monopolies last?
- Why don't monopolies charge the highest possible price?
- How has China monopolized the world market for pandas?
- Why is the head of Starbucks worried about his coffee becoming a commodity?
- Do student and senior discounts come from corporate generosity?
- Why are there so many different airfares for the same flight?

These and other questions are answered in this chapter, which looks at our second market structure—monopoly.

Monopoly is from the Greek, meaning "one seller." In some parts of the United States, monopolists sell electricity, cable TV service, and local phone service. Monopolists also sell postage stamps, hot dogs at sports arenas, some patented products, some prescription drugs, and other goods and services with no close substitutes. You have probably heard about the evils of monopoly. You may have even played the board game *Monopoly* on a rainy day. Now we sort out fact from fiction.

Like perfect competition, pure monopoly is not as common as other market structures. But by understanding monopoly, you grow more familiar with market structures that lie between the extremes of perfect competition and pure monopoly. This chapter examines the sources of monopoly power, how a monopolist maximizes profit, differences between monopoly and perfect competition, and why a monopolist sometimes charges different prices for the same product.

Topics include:

- Barriers to entry
- Price elasticity and marginal revenue
- Profit maximization and loss minimization

- Monopoly and resource allocation
- Welfare cost of monopoly
- Price discrimination
- The monopolist's dream

net 📖 bookmark

For more information about patents—their purpose, what can be patented, how to apply, what rights are included—go to the U.S. Patent and Trademark Office's Web page on General Information Concerning Patents at http://www.uspto.gov/web/offices/pac/doc/general/. How does the Patent Office treat the information provided about a new invention? Why do you suppose that some firms prefer not to seek patent protection for new inventions? What types of intellectual property, other than new machines and processes, can be protected by patents?

barrier to entry

Any impediment that prevents new firms from entering an industry and competing on an equal basis with existing firms

patent

A legal barrier to entry that grants the holder the exclusive right to sell a product for 20 years from the date the patent application is filed

innovation

The process of turning an invention into a marketable product

Barriers to Entry

As noted in Chapter 3, a *monopoly* is the sole supplier of a product with no close substitutes. Why do some markets come to be dominated by a single supplier? A monopolized market is characterized by **barriers to entry**, which are restrictions on the entry of new firms into an industry. Because of barriers, new firms cannot profitably enter that market. Let's examine three types of entry barriers: legal restrictions, economies of scale, and control of an essential resource.

Legal Restrictions

One way to prevent new firms from entering a market is to make entry illegal. Patents, licenses, and other legal restrictions imposed by the government provide some producers with legal protection against competition.

Patents and Invention Incentives

In the United States, a **patent** awards an inventor the exclusive right to produce a good or service for 20 years from the date the patent is filed with the patent office. Originally enacted in 1790, patent laws encourage inventors to invest the time and money required to discover and develop new products and processes. If others could simply copy successful products, inventors would be less interested in incurring the up-front costs of invention. Abraham Lincoln said that "the patent system added the fuel of interest to the fire of genius." The 20-year clock starts ticking as soon as the application is filed, thus providing a stimulus to turn inventions into marketable products, a process called **innovation**.

Licenses and Other Entry Restrictions

Governments often confer monopoly status by awarding an individual firm the exclusive right to supply a particular good or service. Federal licenses give certain firms the right to broadcast radio and TV signals. State licenses authorize suppliers of medical care, haircuts, and legal advice. A license may not grant a monopoly, but it does block entry and often gives firms the power to charge prices above the competitive level. Thus, a license can serve as an effective barrier against new competitors. Governments also grant monopoly rights to sell hot dogs at civic auditoriums, collect garbage, provide bus and taxi service, and supply other services ranging from electricity to cable

TV. Sometimes the government itself may claim that right by outlawing competitors. For example, many state governments sell liquor and lottery tickets, and the U.S. Postal Service has the exclusive right to deliver first-class mail to your mailbox.

Economies of Scale

A monopoly sometimes occurs naturally when a firm experiences *economies of scale,* as reflected by the downward-sloping, long-run average cost curve shown in Exhibit 1. In such instances, a single firm can supply market demand at a lower average cost per unit than could two or more firms, each producing less. Put another way, market demand is not great enough to allow more than one firm to achieve sufficient economies of scale. Thus, a single firm emerges from the competitive process as the only low-cost supplier in the market. For example, even though electricity *production* has become more competitive, electricity *transmission* still exhibits economies of scale. Once wires are strung throughout a community, the cost of linking an additional household to the power grid is relatively small. Consequently, the average cost of delivering electricity declines as more and more households are wired into an existing system.

A monopoly that emerges from the nature of costs is called a *natural monopoly,* to distinguish it from the artificial monopolies created by government patents, licenses, and other legal barriers to entry. A new entrant cannot sell enough to experience the economies of scale achieved by an established natural monopolist. Therefore,

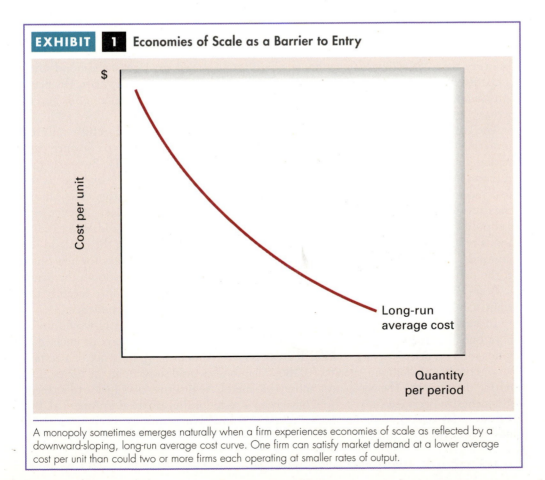

EXHIBIT   1   Economies of Scale as a Barrier to Entry

Long-run average cost

Cost per unit

Quantity per period

A monopoly sometimes emerges naturally when a firm experiences economies of scale as reflected by a downward-sloping, long-run average cost curve. One firm can satisfy market demand at a lower average cost per unit than could two or more firms each operating at smaller rates of output.

market entry is naturally blocked. A later chapter gets into the regulation of natural monopolies.

Control of Essential Resources

Sometimes the source of monopoly power is a firm's control over some resource critical to production. Here are some examples. Alcoa was the sole U.S. maker of aluminum from the late 19th century until World War II. Its monopoly power initially stemmed from production patents that expired in 1909, but for the next three decades, it controlled the supply of bauxite, the key raw material in making aluminum. Professional sports leagues try to block the formation of competing leagues by signing the best athletes to long-term contracts and by seeking the exclusive of sports stadiums and arenas. China is a monopoly supplier of pandas to the world's zoos. The National Zoo in Washington, D.C., for example, rents its pair of pandas from China for $1 million a year. Other zoos have similar arrangements. To limit the supply, China stipulates that any offspring becomes China's property.[1] For example, in 2010 a male offspring of the Washington pair was shipped back to China. Finally, for decades, the world's diamond trade was controlled primarily by De Beers Consolidated Mines, which mined diamonds and also bought most of the world's supply of rough diamonds, as discussed in the following case study.

CASE STUDY

e activity

At http://www
.adiamondisforever.com, you
can learn a lot about buying
diamonds but nothing about
the sponsoring firm—De Beers.
For information about the
company, check http://www
.debeersgroup.com. What
are the current prospects
for De Beers' grip on the
diamond market? De Beers
is not standing idly by while
Canadian diamonds come
into the market. The company
has set up operations in
Canada. What have they
accomplished there thus
far? Find out at the De Beers
Canada Web site at http://
www.debeerscanada.com.

WORLD OF BUSINESS

Is a Diamond Forever?   In 1866, a child walking along the Orange River in South Africa picked up an odd-looking pebble that turned out to be a 21-carat diamond. That discovery on a farm owned by Johannes De Beers sparked the largest diamond mine in history. When the Great Depression caused a slump in diamond prices, De Beers Consolidated Mines undertook efforts to control the world supply of diamonds and to increase consumer demand for them.

The company was able to increase consumer demand through a carefully tailored marketing program. De Beers spends about $200 million a year trying to convince people that diamonds are scarce, valuable, and perfect reflections of love. De Beers' slogan, "A diamond is forever," was recently acclaimed by the magazine *Advertising Age* as the most recognized and effective marketing slogan of the twentieth century. The phrase sends several messages, including (1) a diamond is so durable that it lasts forever, and so should love; (2) diamonds should remain in the family and not be sold; and (3) diamonds retain their value over time. This slogan is aimed at increasing the demand for diamonds and keeping secondhand diamonds, which are good substitutes for new ones, off the market, where they could otherwise increase supply and drive down the price. De Beers came up with the idea of a diamond engagement ring and more recently the "right-hand ring," a diamond worn by a woman as a sign of her independence.

To limit the supply of rough diamonds reaching the market, De Beers would invite about one hundred wholesalers to London, where each was offered a box of uncut diamonds for a set price—no negotiating. If De Beers needed to prop up the price of a certain size and quality of diamond, then few of those diamonds would show up in the boxes, thus limiting their supply. The company's actions violated U.S. antitrust laws (prior to a recent settlement, De Beers executives could have been arrested if they traveled to America). But there were no laws prohibiting U.S. wholesalers from buying from De Beers (as long as those transactions occurred outside U.S. borders).

---

1.   D'Vera Cohn, "Zoos Find Pandas Don't Make the Cash to Cover the Keep," *Washington Post,* 7 August 2005.

A monopoly that relies on the control of a key resource loses market power once that control slips away. In the mid-1990s, De Beers began losing control of some rough diamond supplies. Russian miners were selling half their diamonds to independent dealers. Australia's Argyle mine, now the world's largest, stopped selling to De Beers in 1996. And Yellowknife, a huge Canadian mine, began operations in 1998, but De Beers was guaranteed only about one-third of its output. As a result of all this erosion, De Beers' share of the world's uncut diamond supply slipped from nearly 90 percent in the mid-1980s to about 40 percent in 2010. Worse still for De Beers, newly developed synthetic diamonds are starting to appear on the jewelry market (they already account for 90 percent of industrial diamonds). To counter that threat, De Beers supplies precision equipment to help jewelers spot synthetics.

In a reversal of policy, De Beers has abandoned efforts to control the world diamond supply. In 2006, the company paid $300 million to settle a number of lawsuits charging anticompetitive practices in the United States and Europe. The company also agreed to comply with antitrust laws in the future. De Beers now hopes to become the "supplier of choice" by marketing the De Beers brand of diamonds at its own jewelry stores. De Beers had more than three dozen such stores worldwide as of 2010, including shops in New York and Beverly Hills. (Americans account for only 5 percent of the world's population but for nearly half the world's retail diamond purchases.) In an effort to differentiate its diamonds, De Beers has started etching its "Forevermark" on some stones, a microscopic engraving of authenticity. Some other diamond suppliers are starting to etch their own marks.

Another problem De Beers and other diamond suppliers face was dramatized by the Hollywood movie *Blood Diamond*, starring Leonardo DiCaprio. The terms *blood diamonds* and *conflict diamonds* refer to diamonds sold to fund civil wars that have killed or displaced millions of people in Africa, the source of much of the world's rough diamonds. Some customers are now asking for "conflict-free" diamonds. For its part, De Beers guarantees that its diamonds are "conflict free." Global economic turmoil in 2008 and 2009 also hurt diamond sales. Industrywide, revenue from diamond jewelry sales fell 16 percent in 2009 to $65 billion.

De Beers is an example of the legal and practical difficulties of maintaining a profitable monopoly. Once the company's control over uncut diamonds slipped away, so did its monopoly power. After losing that power, the company had less incentive to pursue its anticompetitive practices.

Sources: Vanessa O'Connell, "Diamond Industry Makeover Sends Fifth Avenue to Africa," *Wall Street Journal*, 26 October 2009; Tina Gooch, "Conflict Diamonds or Illicit Diamonds?" *Natural Resource Journal*, 48 (Winter 2008): 189–214; Robb Stewart, "Will Diamonds Sparkle Again for De Beers?" *Wall Street Journal*, 11 February 2010; and the De Beers home page at http://www.adiamondisforever.com/.

Monopoly profits often spring from supplying something that other producers can't match. For example, Starbucks over the years has built up a unique "experience" for the customer, including baristas who know customer orders by heart and a comfortable atmosphere that encourages patrons to relax and linger. That uniqueness has given Starbucks the market power to grow and to charge a premium price that has rocketed the company's stock price more than 25-fold since 1992. But a recent memo from the company chairman to employees warned that the pressure to grow could "commoditize" Starbucks, making it more vulnerable to competition from other coffee shops and even from fast-food chains. Once a product loses its uniqueness—in this case, by going from a special experience to just another cup of coffee—the supplier loses market power and profitability.[2]

Local monopolies are more common than national or international monopolies. In rural areas, monopolies may include the only grocery store, movie theater, restaurant, or gas station for miles around. These are natural monopolies for products sold in local markets. But long-lasting monopolies are rare because economic profit attracts competitors. Also, over time, technological change tends to break down barriers to entry. For example, the development of wireless transmission of long-distance calls created competitors to AT&T. Wireless transmission is also erasing the monopoly held by local cable TV providers and even local phone service. Likewise, text messaging, email, the Internet, and firms such as FedEx and UPS now compete with the U.S. Postal Service's monopoly, as described in a later case study.

Revenue for the Monopolist

Because a monopoly, by definition, supplies the entire market, the demand for a monopolist's output is also the market demand. The demand curve therefore slopes downward, reflecting the law of demand—price and quantity demanded are inversely related. Let's look at demand, average revenue, and marginal revenue for a monopolist.

Demand, Average Revenue, and Marginal Revenue

Suppose De Beers controls the diamond market. Exhibit 2 shows the demand curve for high-quality 1-carat diamonds. De Beers, for example, can sell three diamonds a day at $7,000 each. That price-quantity combination yields total revenue of $21,000 (=$7,000 × 3). Total revenue divided by quantity is the *average revenue per diamond,* which also is $7,000. Thus, the monopolist's price equals the average revenue per unit. To sell a fourth diamond, De Beers must lower the price to $6,750. Total revenue from selling four diamonds is $27,000 (=$6,750 × 4), and average revenue is $6,750. All along the demand curve, price equals average revenue. Therefore, *the demand curve is also the monopolist's average revenue curve,* just as the perfectly competitive firm's demand curve is that firm's average revenue curve.

What's the marginal revenue from selling a fourth diamond? When De Beers drops the price from $7,000 to $6,750, total revenue increases from $21,000 to $27,000. Thus, *marginal revenue*—the change in total revenue from selling one more diamond— is $6,000, which is less than the price, or average revenue, of $6,750. *For a monopolist, marginal revenue is less than the price, or average revenue.* Recall that for a perfectly competitive firm, marginal revenue equals the price, or average revenue, because that firm can sell all it supplies at the market price.

The Gains and Loss From Selling One More Unit

A closer look at Exhibit 2 reveals why a monopolist's marginal revenue is less than the price. By selling another diamond, De Beers gains the revenue from that sale. For example, De Beers gets $6,750 from the fourth diamond, as shown by the blue-shaded vertical rectangle marked "Gain." But to sell that fourth unit, De Beers must sell all four diamonds

---

2.   The company memo is discussed in Janet Adamy, "Starbucks Chairman Says Trouble May Be Brewing," *Wall Street Journal,* 24 February 2007.

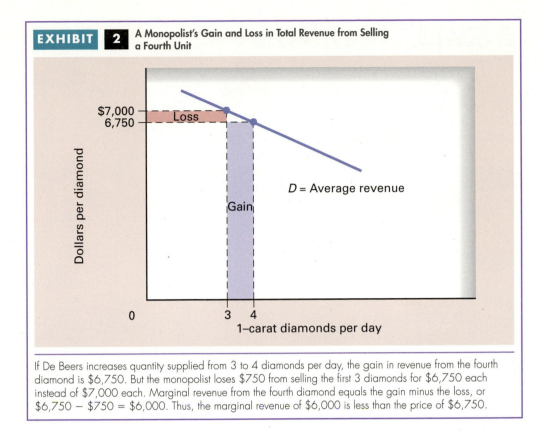

EXHIBIT   2   A Monopolist's Gain and Loss in Total Revenue from Selling a Fourth Unit

If De Beers increases quantity supplied from 3 to 4 diamonds per day, the gain in revenue from the fourth diamond is $6,750. But the monopolist loses $750 from selling the first 3 diamonds for $6,750 each instead of $7,000 each. Marginal revenue from the fourth diamond equals the gain minus the loss, or $6,750 − $750 = $6,000. Thus, the marginal revenue of $6,000 is less than the price of $6,750.

for $6,750 each. Thus, to sell a fourth diamond, De Beers must sacrifice $250 on each of the first three diamonds, which could have been sold for $7,000 each. This loss in revenue from the first three units totals $750 (=$250 × 3) and is identified in Exhibit 2 by the pink-shaded horizontal rectangle marked "Loss." The net change in total revenue from selling the fourth diamond—that is, the marginal revenue from the fourth diamond— equals the *gain* minus the *loss,* which equals $6,750 minus $750, or $6,000. So marginal revenue equals the gain minus the loss, or the price minus the revenue forgone by selling all units for a lower price. Because a monopolist's marginal revenue equals the price minus the loss, you can see why the marginal revenue is less than the price.

Incidentally, this analysis assumes that all units are sold at the market price; for example, the four diamonds are sold for $6,750 each. Although this is usually true, later in the chapter you learn how some monopolists try to increase profit by charging different customers different prices.

Revenue Schedules

Let's flesh out more fully the revenue schedules behind the demand curve of Exhibit 2. Column (1) of Exhibit 3 lists the quantity of diamonds demanded per day, and column (2) lists the corresponding price, or average revenue. Together, the two columns are the demand schedule for 1-carat diamonds. The price in column (2) times the quantity in column (1) yields the monopolist's *total revenue* schedule in column (3). So $TR = p \times Q$. As De Beers sells more, total revenue increases until quantity reaches 15 diamonds.

Marginal revenue, the change in total revenue from selling one more diamond, appears in column (4). In shorthand, $MR = \Delta TR/\Delta Q$, or the change in total revenue divided by

EXHIBIT **3** Revenue for De Beers, a Monopolist

(1) 1-Carat Diamonds per Day (Q)	(2) Price (average revenue) (p)	(3) Total Revenue (TR = p × Q)	(4) Marginal Revenue (MR = ΔTR/ΔQ)
0	$7,750	0	—
1	7,500	$ 7,500	$7,500
2	7,250	14,500	7,000
3	7,000	21,000	6,500
4	6,750	27,000	6,000
5	6,500	32,500	5,500
6	6,250	37,500	5,000
7	6,000	42,000	4,500
8	5,750	46,000	4,000
9	5,500	49,500	3,500
10	5,250	52,500	3,000
11	5,000	55,000	2,500
12	4,750	57,000	2,000
13	4,500	58,500	1,500
14	4,250	59,500	1,000
15	4,000	60,000	500
16	3,750	60,000	0
17	3,500	59,500	-500

To sell more, the monopolist must lower the price on all units sold. Because the revenue lost from selling all units at a lower price must be subtracted from the revenue gained from selling another unit, marginal revenue is less than the price. At some point, marginal revenue turns negative, as shown here when the price is reduced to $3,500.

the change in quantity. Note in Exhibit 3 that after the first unit, marginal revenue is less than price. As the price declines, the gap between price and marginal revenue widens. As the price declines, the *loss* from selling all diamonds for less increases (because quantity increases) and the *gain* from selling another diamond decreases (because the price falls).

Revenue Curves

The schedules in Exhibit 3 are graphed in Exhibit 4, which shows the demand and marginal revenue curves in panel (a) and the total revenue curve in panel (b). Recall that total revenue equals price times quantity. Note that *the marginal revenue curve is below the demand curve and that total revenue reaches a maximum where marginal revenue is zero.* Please take a minute now to study these relationships—they are important.

Again, along the demand curve, price equals average revenue, so the demand curve is also the monopolist's average revenue curve. In Chapter 5 you learned that the price elasticity for a straight-line demand curve declines as you move down the curve. When demand is elastic—that is, when the percentage increase in quantity demanded more than offsets the percentage decrease in price—a decrease in price increases total revenue. Therefore, *where demand is elastic, marginal revenue is positive, and total revenue increases as the price falls.* On the other hand, where demand is inelastic—that is, where the percentage increase in quantity demanded is less than the percentage decrease in price—a decrease in price reduces total revenue. In other words, the loss in revenue from selling all diamonds for the lower price overwhelms the gain in revenue from

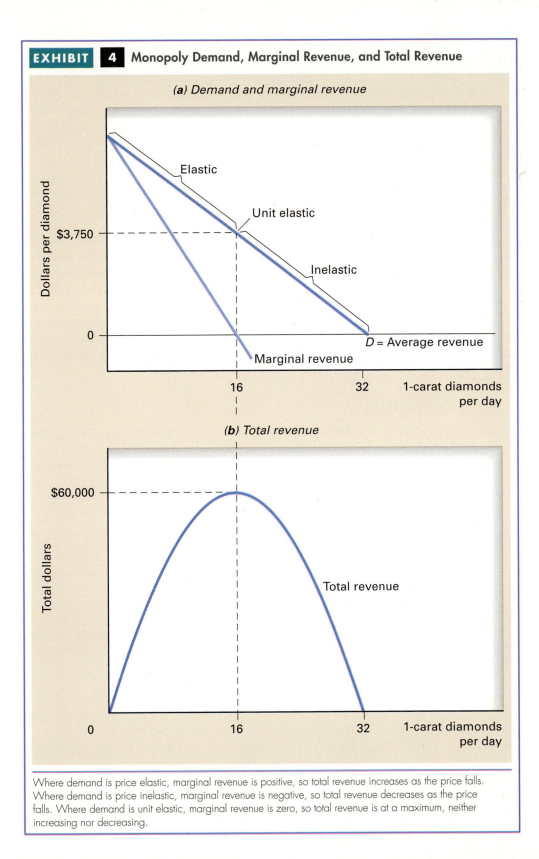

EXHIBIT **4** **Monopoly Demand, Marginal Revenue, and Total Revenue**

(a) Demand and marginal revenue

Where demand is price elastic, marginal revenue is positive, so total revenue increases as the price falls. Where demand is price inelastic, marginal revenue is negative, so total revenue decreases as the price falls. Where demand is unit elastic, marginal revenue is zero, so total revenue is at a maximum, neither increasing nor decreasing.

selling more diamonds. Therefore, *where demand is inelastic, marginal revenue is negative, and total revenue decreases as the price falls.*

From Exhibit 4, you can see that marginal revenue turns negative if the price drops below $3,750, indicating inelastic demand below that price. *A profit-maximizing monopolist would never expand output to the inelastic range of demand because doing so would reduce total revenue.* It would make no sense to sell more if total revenue drops in the process. Also note that demand is unit elastic at the price of $3,750. At that price, marginal revenue is zero and total revenue reaches a maximum.

The Firm's Costs and Profit Maximization

In perfect competition, each firm's choice is confined to *quantity* because the market has already determined the price. The perfect competitor is a *price taker. The monopolist, however, can choose either the price or the quantity, but choosing one determines the other—they come in pairs.* For example, if De Beers decides to sell 10 diamonds a day, consumers would demand that many only at a price of $5,250 per diamond. Alternatively, if De Beers decides to sell diamonds for $6,000 each, consumers would demand 7 a day. Because the monopolist can choose any price-quantity combination on the demand curve, we say the monopolist is a *price maker.* More generally, any firm that has some control over what price to charge is a **price maker**.

price maker

A firm with some power to set the price because the demand curve for its output slopes downward; a firm with market power

Profit Maximization

Exhibit 5 repeats revenue schedules from Exhibits 3 and 4 and also includes a short-run cost schedule similar to those already introduced in the two previous chapters. Please take a little time now to become familiar with this table. Then ask yourself this

EXHIBIT 5   Short-Run Costs and Revenue for a Monopolist

(1) Diamonds per Day (Q)	(2) Price (p)	(3) Total Revenue (TR = p × Q)	(4) Marginal Revenue (MR = ΔTR/ΔQ)	(5) Total Cost (TC)	(6) Marginal Cost (MC = ΔTC/ΔQ)	(7) Average Total Cost (ATC = TC/Q)	(8) Total Profit or Loss (= TR − TC)
0	$7,750	0	—	$ 15,000	—	—	$−15,000
1	7,500	$ 7,500	$7,500	19,750	$ 4,750	$19,750	−12,250
2	7,250	14,500	7,000	23,500	3,750	11,750	−9,000
3	7,000	21,000	6,500	26,500	3,000	8,833	−5,500
4	6,750	27,000	6,000	29,000	2,500	7,250	−2,000
5	6,500	32,500	5,500	31,000	2,000	6,200	1,500
6	6,250	37,500	5,000	32,500	1,500	5,417	5,000
7	6,000	42,000	4,500	33,750	1,250	4,821	8,250
8	5,750	46,000	4,000	35,250	1,500	4,406	10,750
9	5,500	49,500	3,500	37,250	2,000	4,139	12,250
10	5,250	52,500	3,000	40,000	2,750	4,000	12,500
11	5,000	55,000	2,500	43,250	3,250	3,932	11,750
12	4,750	57,000	2,000	48,000	4,750	4,000	9,000
13	4,500	58,500	1,500	54,500	6,500	4,192	4,000
14	4,250	59,500	1,000	64,000	9,500	4,571	−4,500
15	4,000	60,000	500	77,500	13,500	5,167	−17,500
16	3,750	60,000	0	96,000	18,500	6,000	−36,000
17	3,500	59,500	−500	121,000	25,000	7,118	−61,500

question: Which price-quantity combination should De Beers select to maximize profit? As was the case with perfect competition, the monopolist can approach profit maximization in two ways—the total approach and the marginal approach.

Total Revenue Minus Total Cost

The profit-maximizing monopolist employs the same decision rule as the competitive firm. *The monopolist supplies the quantity at which total revenue exceeds total cost by the greatest amount.* Economic profit appears in column (8) of Exhibit 5. As you can see, maximum profit is $12,500 per day, which occurs at 10 diamonds per day. At that quantity, total revenue is $52,500 and total cost is $40,000.

Marginal Revenue Equals Marginal Cost

De Beers, as a profit-maximizing monopolist, increases output if it adds more to total revenue than to total cost. So De Beers expands output as long as marginal revenue, shown in column (4) of Exhibit 5, exceeds marginal cost, shown in column (6). But De Beers stops short of producing where marginal cost exceeds marginal revenue. Again, profit is maximized at $12,500 when 10 diamonds per day are sold. For the 10th diamond, marginal revenue is $3,000 and marginal cost is $2,750. As you can see, if output exceeds 10 diamonds per day, marginal cost exceeds marginal revenue. An 11th diamond's marginal cost of $3,250 exceeds its marginal revenue of $2,500. For simplicity, we say that *the profit-maximizing output occurs where marginal revenue equals marginal cost,* which, you will recall, is the golden rule of profit maximization.

Graphical Solution

The revenue and cost schedules in Exhibit 5 are graphed in Exhibit 6, with per-unit cost and revenue curves in panel (a) and total cost and revenue curves in panel (b). The intersection of the two marginal curves at point *e* in panel (a) indicates that profit is maximized when 10 diamonds are sold. At that quantity, we move up to the demand curve to find the profit-maximizing price of $5,250. Average total cost of $4,000 is identified by point *b*. The average profit per diamond equals the price of $5,250 minus the average total cost of $4,000. Economic profit is the average profit per unit of $1,250 multiplied by the 10 diamonds sold, for a total profit of $12,500 per day, as identified by the blue-shaded rectangle. *So the profit-maximizing rate of output is found where the marginal cost curve intersects the marginal revenue curve.*

In panel (b), the firm's profit or loss is measured by the vertical distance between the total revenue and total cost curves. De Beers expands output if the increase in total revenue from selling another diamond exceeds the increase in total cost. *The profit-maximizing firm produces where total revenue exceeds total cost by the greatest amount.* Again, profit is maximized where De Beers sells 10 diamonds per day. Total profit in panel (b) is measured by the *vertical distance* between the two total curves; in panel (a), total profit is measured by the shaded *area* formed by multiplying average profit per unit by the number of units sold.

One common myth about monopolies is that they charge the highest price possible. But the monopolist is interested in maximizing profit, not price. What the monopolist can charge is limited by consumer demand. De Beers, for example, could charge $7,500, but selling only one diamond would result in a big loss. Indeed, De Beers could charge $7,750 or more but would sell no diamonds. So charging the highest possible price is not consistent with maximizing profit. A monopolist may be able to set the price, but the quantity demanded at that price is determined by consumers. *Even the most powerful monopolist must obey the law of demand.*

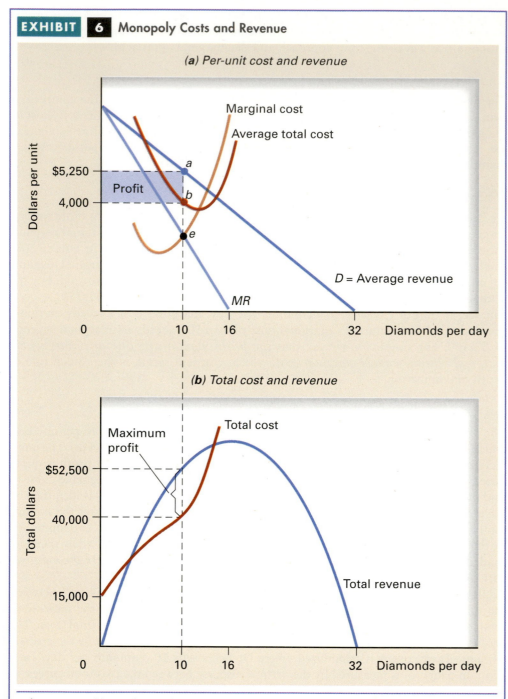

EXHIBIT 6 Monopoly Costs and Revenue

(a) Per-unit cost and revenue

(b) Total cost and revenue

Profit is maximized by producing where marginal cost equals marginal revenue, which is point *e* in panel (a). A profit-maximizing monopolist supplies 10 diamonds per day and charges $5,250 per diamond. Total profit, shown by the blue rectangle in panel (a), is $12,500, the profit per unit multiplied by the number of units sold. In panel (b), profit is maximized by producing where total revenue exceeds total cost by the greatest amount, which occurs at an output rate of 10 diamonds per day. Maximum profit is total revenue ($52,500) minus total cost ($40,000), or $12,500. In panel (a) profit is measured by an area and in panel (b) by a vertical distance. That's because panel (a) measures cost, revenue, and profit per unit of output while panel (b) measures them as totals.

Short-Run Losses and the Shutdown Decision

A monopolist is not assured an economic profit. Although a monopolist is the sole supplier of a good with no close substitutes, the demand for that good may not generate economic profit in either the short run or the long run. After all, many new products are protected from direct competition by patents, yet most of the 200,000, or so, U.S. patents issued each year never turn into profitable products. And even a monopolist that is initially profitable may eventually suffer losses because of rising costs, falling demand, or market entry of similar products. For example, Coleco, the original mass producer of Cabbage Patch dolls, went bankrupt after that craze died down. And Cuisinart, the company that introduced the food processor, soon faced many imitators and filed for bankruptcy (though the name lives on). In the short run, the loss-minimizing monopolist, like the loss-minimizing perfect competitor, must decide whether to produce or to shut down. *If the price covers average variable cost, the monopolist produces, at least in the short run. If not, the monopolist shuts down, at least in the short run.*

Exhibit 7 brings average variable cost back into the picture. Recall from Chapter 7 that average variable cost and average fixed cost sum to average total cost. Loss minimization occurs in Exhibit 7 at point *e*, where the marginal revenue curve intersects the marginal cost curve. At the equilibrium rate of output, *Q*, price *p* is found on the demand curve at point *b*. That price exceeds average variable cost, at point *c*, but is below average total cost, at point *a*. Because price covers average variable cost and a portion of average fixed cost, this monopolist loses less by producing *Q* than by

EXHIBIT **7** The Monopolist Minimizes Losses in the Short Run

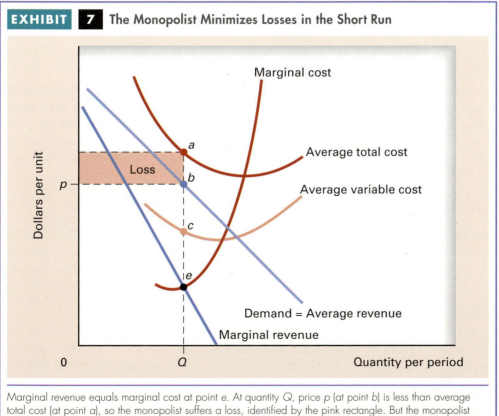

Marginal revenue equals marginal cost at point *e*. At quantity *Q*, price *p* (at point *b*) is less than average total cost (at point *a*), so the monopolist suffers a loss, identified by the pink rectangle. But the monopolist continues to produce rather than shut down in the short run because price exceeds average variable cost (at point *c*).

shutting down. The loss, identified by the shaded rectangle, is the average loss per unit, *ab*, times the quantity sold, *Q*. The firm shuts down in the short run if the average variable cost curve is above the demand curve, or average revenue curve, at all output rates.

Recall that a perfectly competitive firm's supply curve is that portion of the marginal cost curve at or above the average variable cost curve. The intersection of a monopolist's marginal revenue and marginal cost curves identifies the profit-maximizing (or loss-minimizing) quantity, but the price is found up on the demand curve. Because the equilibrium quantity can be found along a monopolist's marginal cost curve, but the equilibrium price appears on the demand curve, no single curve traces points showing unique combinations of both the price and quantity supplied. Because no curve reflects combinations of price and quantity supplied, *there is no monopolist supply curve.*

Long-Run Profit Maximization

For perfectly competitive firms, the distinction between the short run and the long run is important because entry and exit of firms can occur in the long run, erasing any economic profit or loss. For the monopolist, the distinction between the short run and long run is less relevant. *If a monopoly is insulated from competition by high barriers that block new entry, economic profit can persist into the long run.* Yet short-run profit is no guarantee of long-run profit. For example, suppose the monopoly relies on a patent. Patents last only so long and even while a product is under patent, the monopolist often must defend it in court (patent litigation has nearly doubled in the last decade). On the other hand, a monopolist may be able to erase a loss (most firms lose money initially) or increase profit in the long run by adjusting the scale of the firm or by advertising to increase demand. A monopolist unable to erase a loss will, in the long run, leave the market.

Monopoly and the Allocation of Resources

If monopolists are no greedier than perfect competitors (because both maximize profit), if monopolists do not charge the highest possible price (because the highest price would reduce quantity demanded to zero), and if monopolists are not guaranteed a profit (because demand for the product may be weak), then what's the problem with monopoly? To get a handle on the problem, let's compare monopoly with the benchmark established in the previous chapter—perfect competition.

Price and Output Under Perfect Competition

Let's begin with the long-run equilibrium price and output in a perfectly competitive market. Suppose the long-run market supply curve in perfect competition is horizontal, as shown by S_c in Exhibit 8. Because this is a constant-cost industry, the horizontal long-run supply curve also shows marginal cost and average total cost at each quantity. Equilibrium in perfect competition occurs at point *c*, where the market demand and market supply curves intersect to yield price p_c and quantity Q_c. Remember, the demand curve reflects the marginal benefit of each unit purchased. In competitive equilibrium, the marginal benefit of the final unit sold equals the marginal cost to society of producing that final unit. As noted in the previous chapter, when the marginal benefit that consumers derive from a good equals the marginal cost of producing that good, that market is said to be efficient and to maximize social welfare. There is no way of reallocating resources to increase the total value of output or to increase social welfare. Because consumers are able to purchase Q_c units at price p_c, they enjoy a net benefit from consumption, or a consumer surplus, measured by the entire shaded triangle, acp_c.

EXHIBIT   8   Perfect Competition and Monopoly Compared

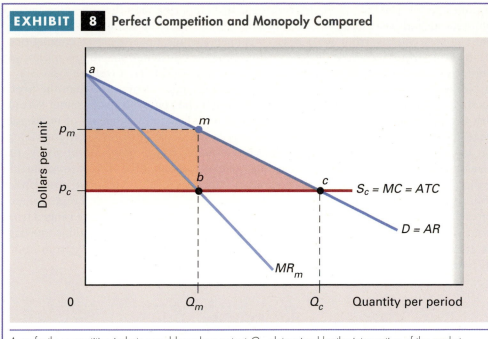

A perfectly competitive industry would produce output Q_c, determined by the intersection of the market demand curve D and the market supply curve S_c. The price would be p_c. A monopoly that could produce output at the same minimum average cost as a perfectly competitive industry would produce output Q_m, determined at point b, where marginal cost intersects marginal revenue. The monopolist would charge price p_m. Thus, given the same costs, output is lower and price is higher under monopoly than under perfect competition.

Price and Output Under Monopoly

With only one firm in the industry, the industry demand curve D in Exhibit 8 becomes the monopolist's demand curve, so the price the monopolist charges determines the market quantity. Because the monopolist's demand curve slopes downward, the marginal revenue curve also slopes downward and is beneath the demand curve, as is indicated by MR_m in Exhibit 8. Suppose the monopolist can produce at the same constant cost in the long run as can firms in the perfectly competitive industry. The monopolist maximizes profit by equating marginal revenue with marginal cost, which occurs at point b, yielding equilibrium price p_m and market output Q_m. Again, the price shows the consumers' marginal benefit for unit Q_m. This marginal benefit, identified at point m, exceeds the monopolist's marginal cost, identified at point b. Because marginal benefit exceeds marginal cost, society would be better off if output expanded beyond Q_m. *The monopolist restricts quantity below what would maximize social welfare.* Even though the monopolist restricts output, consumers still derive some benefit, just not as much as with perfect competition. Consumer surplus is shown by the smaller triangle, amp_m.

Allocative and Distributive Effects

Consider the allocative and distributive effects of monopoly versus perfect competition. In Exhibit 8, consumer surplus under perfect competition is the large triangle, acp_c. Under monopoly, consumer surplus shrinks to the smaller triangle amp_m, which in this example is only one-fourth as large (how do we know that?). The monopolist earns economic profit equal to the shaded rectangle. By comparing the situation under perfect competition with that under monopoly, you can see that the monopolist's economic profit comes entirely from what was consumer surplus under perfect competition. Because the profit rectangle reflects a transfer from consumer surplus to monopoly profit, this amount is not lost to society and so is not considered a welfare loss.

Notice, however, that consumer surplus has been reduced by more than the profit rectangle. Consumers also lose the triangle *mcb,* which is part of the consumer surplus with perfect competition. The *mcb* triangle is called the **deadweight loss of monopoly** because it is a loss to consumers but a gain to nobody. This loss results from *the allocative inefficiency arising from the higher price and reduced output of a monopoly.* Again, society would be better off if output exceeded the monopolist's profit-maximizing quantity, because the marginal benefit of more output exceeds its marginal cost. Under monopoly, the price, or marginal benefit, always exceeds marginal cost. Empirical estimates of the annual deadweight loss of monopoly in the United States have ranged from about 1 percent to about 5 percent of national income. Applied to national income data for 2010, these estimates imply a deadweight loss of monopoly ranging from about $475 to $2,400 per capita—not a trivial amount.

deadweight loss of monopoly

Net loss to society when a firm with market power restricts output and increases the price

Problems Estimating the Deadweight Loss of Monopoly

The actual cost of monopoly could differ from the deadweight loss described so far. These costs could be lower or higher. Here's the reasoning.

Why the Deadweight Loss of Monopoly Might Be Lower

If economies of scale are substantial enough, a monopolist might be able to produce output at a lower cost per unit than could competitive firms. Therefore, the price, or at least the cost of production, could be lower under monopoly than under competition. The deadweight loss shown in Exhibit 8 may also overstate the true cost of monopoly because monopolists might, in response to public scrutiny and political pressure, keep prices below the profit-maximizing level. Although monopolists would like to earn as much profit as possible, they realize that if the public outcry over high prices and high profit grows loud enough, some sort of government intervention could reduce or even erase that profit. For example, the prices and profit of drug companies, which individually are monopoly suppliers of patented medicines, come under scrutiny from time to time by elected officials who propose regulating drug prices or taxing "windfall profits." Drug firms might try to avoid such treatment by keeping prices below the level that would maximize profit. Finally, a monopolist might keep the price below the profit-maximizing level to avoid attracting competitors to the market. For example, some observers claim that Alcoa, when it was the only U.S. producer of aluminum, kept prices low enough to discourage new entry by potential rivals.

Why the Deadweight Loss Might Be Higher

Another line of reasoning suggests that the deadweight loss of monopoly might be greater than shown in our simple diagram. *If resources must be devoted to securing and maintaining a monopoly position, monopolies may impose a greater welfare loss than simple models suggest.* For example, radio and TV broadcasting rights confer on the recipient the use of a particular band of the scarce broadcast spectrum. In the past, these rights have been given away by government agencies to the applicants deemed most deserving. Because these rights are so valuable, numerous applicants have spent millions on lawyers' fees, lobbying expenses, and other costs to make themselves appear the most deserving. The efforts devoted to securing and maintaining a monopoly position are largely a social waste because they use up scarce resources but add not one unit to output. Activities undertaken by individuals or firms to influence public policy to directly or indirectly redistribute income to themselves are referred to as **rent seeking**.

The monopolist, insulated from the rigors of competition in the marketplace, might also grow fat and lazy—and become inefficient. Because some monopolies could still earn an economic profit even if the firm is inefficient, corporate executives might waste resources by creating a more comfortable life for themselves. Long lunches, afternoon golf, plush offices, corporate jets, and excessive employee benefits might make company life more pleasant, but they increase production costs and raise prices.

Monopolists have also been criticized for being slow to adopt the latest production techniques, being reluctant to develop new products, and generally lacking innovation. Because monopolists are largely insulated from the rigors of competition, they might take it easy. It's been said "The best of all monopoly profits is a quiet life."

The following case study discusses the performance of one of the nation's oldest monopolies, the U.S. Postal Service.

rent seeking
Activities undertaken by individuals or firms to influence public policy in a way that increases their incomes

PUBLIC POLICY

CASE STUDY

The Mail Monopoly The U.S. Post Office was granted a monopoly in 1775 and has operated under federal protection ever since. In 1971, Congress converted the Post Office Department into a semi-independent agency called the U.S. Postal Service, or USPS, which had total revenue of about $70 billion in 2009. Because of the national recession, revenue in 2009 was down 9 percent from 2008 and about the same as in 2006. More than 650,000 employees at 37,000 post offices deliver an average of 177 billion pieces of mail a year to 144 million home and business addresses. This amounts to about 40 percent of the world's total mail delivery. USPS pays no taxes and is exempt from local zoning laws. It has a legal monopoly in delivering regular, first-class letters and has the exclusive right to use the space inside your mailbox. Other delivery services such as FedEx or UPS cannot deliver to mail boxes or post office boxes.

The USPS monopoly has suffered in recent years because of rising costs and growing competition from new technologies. The price of a first-class stamp climbed from 6 cents in 1970 to 44 cents by 2010—a growth rate twice that of inflation. Long-distance phone service, one possible substitute for first-class mail, is much cheaper today than in 1970. New technologies such as email, ecards, online bill-payment, text messaging, and social-networking sites also displace USPS delivery services (email messages now greatly outnumber first-class letters). Because its monopoly applies only to regular first-class mail, USPS has lost chunks of other business to private firms offering lower rates and better service. The United Parcel Service (UPS), for example, is more mechanized and more containerized than the USPS and thus has lower costs and less breakage. The USPS has tried to emulate UPS but with only limited success. After Hurricane Katrina, it took seven months to reopen the USPS processing and distribution center in New Orleans. Rivals UPS, FedEx, and DHL all restored service within three weeks.

When the Postal Service raised third-class ("junk" mail) rates, businesses substituted other forms of advertising, including cable TV, telemarketing, and the Internet. UPS and

e activity
How has the U.S. Postal Service dealt with competition and change? A chapter in its online history, at http://www.usps.com, describes the reforms made in the 1990s to compete with for-profit firms and email. What role do forces of competition play in rate setting? Online cost calculators are provided by both USPS at http://postcalc.usps.gov/ and UPS (United Parcel Service) at http://www.ups.com. Try finding the cost of sending a 2-lb. package to Fairbanks, Alaska (or to Miami, Florida, if you're in Alaska!). Which is cheaper—USPS or UPS? Why?

other rivals now account for most ground-shipped packages. Even USPS's first-class monopoly is being threatened, because FedEx and others have captured 90 percent of the overnight mail business. Thus, USPS is losing business because of competition from overnight mail and from new technologies.

USPS has been fighting back, trying to leverage its monopoly power while increasing efficiency. On the electronic front, USPS tried to offer online postage purchases, online bill-paying service, and online document transmission service. But these new products were scrapped as failures. Changing technology and competition have been eroding USPS's government-granted monopoly. USPS lost about $4 billion in 2009 and said that without drastic changes, losses would total $238 billion over the next decade. Even a legal monopoly can lose money. Proposed changes include postage increases and dropping Saturday delivery.

Sources: Corey Dade, "Post Office Renews Campaign to End Saturday Mail Service," *Wall Street Journal*, 3 March 2010; Liz Robbins, "Postal Service Revives Cutback Plans," *New York Times*, 2 March 2010; "The Trap: The Curse of Long-term Unemployment Will Bedevil the Economy," *The Economist*, 14 January 2010; and the USPS home page at http://www .usps.com.

Not all economists believe that monopolies manage their resources with any less vigilance than perfect competitors do. Some argue that because monopolists are protected from rivals, they are in a good position to capture the fruits of any innovation and therefore are more innovative than competitive firms are. Others believe that if a monopolist strays from the path of profit maximization, its share price will drop enough to attract someone who will buy a controlling interest and shape up the company. This market for corporate control is said to keep monopolists on their toes.

Price Discrimination

In the model developed so far, to sell more output, a monopolist must lower the price. In reality, a monopolist can sometimes increase profit by charging higher prices to those who value the product more. This practice of charging different prices to different groups of consumers is called **price discrimination**. For example, children, students, and senior citizens often pay lower admission prices to ball games, movies, amusement parks, and other events. You may believe that firms do this out of some sense of fairness to certain groups, but the primary goal is to boost profits. Let's see how and why.

price discrimination

Increasing profit by charging different groups of consumers different prices for the same product

Conditions for Price Discrimination

To practice price discrimination, a firm's product must meet certain conditions. First, the demand curve for the firm's product must slope downward, indicating that the firm is a price maker—the producer has some market power, some ability to set the price. Second, there must be at least two groups of consumers for the product, each with a different price elasticity of demand. Third, the firm must be able, at little cost, to charge each group a different price for essentially the same product. Finally, the firm must be able to prevent those who pay the lower price from reselling the product to those facing the higher price.

A Model of Price Discrimination

Exhibit 9 shows the effects of price discrimination. Consumers are sorted into two groups with different demand elasticities. For simplicity, let's assume that the firm produces at a constant long-run average and marginal cost of $1.00. *At a given price,* the price elasticity of demand in panel (b) is greater than that in panel (a). Think of panel (b) as reflecting the demand of college students, senior citizens, or some other group more sensitive to the price. *This firm maximizes profit by finding the price in each market that equates marginal revenue with marginal cost.* For example, consumers with a lower price elasticity pay $3.00, and those with a higher price elasticity pay $1.50. Profit maximization means charging a lower price to the group with the more elastic demand. Despite the price difference, the firm gets the same marginal revenue of $1.00 from the last unit sold to each group. Note that charging both groups $3.00 would erase any profit from that right-hand group of consumers, who would be priced out of the market. Charging both groups $1.50 would lead to negative marginal revenue from the left-hand group, which would reduce profit. No single price could generate the profit achieved through price discrimination.

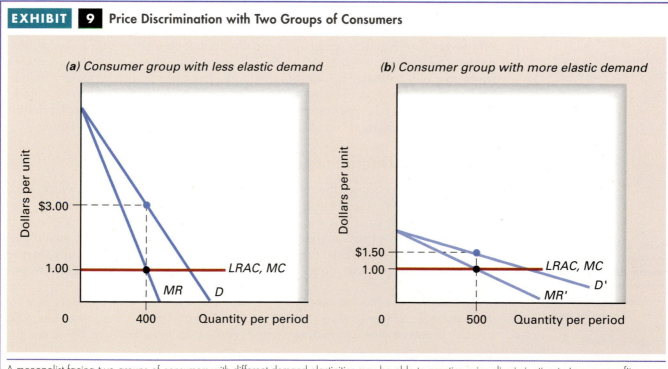

EXHIBIT 9 **Price Discrimination with Two Groups of Consumers**

A monopolist facing two groups of consumers with different demand elasticities may be able to practice price discrimination to increase profit or reduce any loss. With marginal cost the same in both markets, the firm charges a higher price to the group in panel (a), which has less elastic demand than the group in panel (b).

Examples of Price Discrimination

Let's look at some examples of price discrimination. Because businesspeople face unpredictable yet urgent demands for travel, and because their employers pay such expenses, businesspeople tend to be less sensitive to price than are householders. In other words, businesspeople have a less elastic demand for travel than do householders, so airlines try to maximize profits by charging businesses more than households. Business-class tickets cost much more than coach-class tickets. Business seats offer more room than coach seats, and the food is a little better, but the difference in ticket prices far exceeds differences in the airline's cost of providing each service. Even within a class of tickets, airlines charge different rates based on how far in advance tickets are purchased. Householders usually plan their trips well in advance and often spend the weekend. But business travel is more unpredictable, more urgent, and seldom involves a weekend stay. The airlines sort out the two groups by limiting discount fares to travelers who buy tickets well in advance. More generally, airlines use computer models to price discriminate depending on the circumstances. Still, an airline's ability to charge a higher price for a particular seat is limited by competition from other airlines.

Here are other examples of price discrimination: IBM wanted to charge business users of its laser printer more than home users. To distinguish between the two groups, IBM decided to slow down the home printer to 5 pages a minute (versus 10 for the business model). To do this, they added an extra chip that inserted pauses between pages.[3] Thus, IBM could sell the home model for less than the business model without cutting into sales of its business model. Intel offered two versions of the same computer chip; the cheaper version was the expensive version with some extra work done to reduce its speed. And Adobe stripped some features from its Photoshop CD to offer a cheaper version, Photoshop Elements.

Major amusement parks, such as Disney World and Universal Studios, distinguish between local residents and out-of-towners when it comes to the price of admission. Out-of-towners typically spend substantial amounts on airlines and lodging just to be there, so they are less sensitive to the admission price than are local residents. The problem is how to charge a lower price to locals. The parks do this by making discount coupons available at local businesses, such as dry cleaners, which vacationers are less likely to visit. The Las Vegas monorail sorts out the locals from the visitors by charging $1 for those presenting a Nevada driver's license and $5 for those without one.

Perfect Price Discrimination: The Monopolist's Dream

The demand curve shows the marginal value of each unit consumed, which is also the maximum amount consumers would pay for each unit. If the monopolist could charge a different price for each unit sold—a price reflected by the height of the demand curve—the firm's marginal revenue from selling one more unit would equal the price of that unit. Thus, the demand curve would become the firm's marginal revenue curve. A **perfectly discriminating monopolist** would charge a different price for each unit sold.

In Exhibit 10, again for simplicity, the monopolist is assumed to produce at a constant average and marginal cost in the long run. A perfectly discriminating monopolist, like any producer, would maximize profit by producing the quantity at which marginal

perfectly discriminating monopolist

A monopolist who charges a different price for each unit sold; also called the monopolist's dream

---

3. Carl Shapiro and Hal Varian, *Information Rules: A Strategic Guide to the Network Economy* (Boston: Harvard Business School Press, 1999), p. 59.

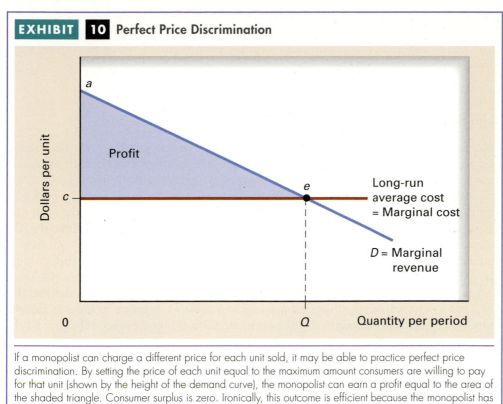

EXHIBIT **10** **Perfect Price Discrimination**

a

Dollars per unit

Profit

c ——————————————————— *e* ——————————— Long-run average cost = Marginal cost

D = Marginal revenue

0   *Q*   Quantity per period

If a monopolist can charge a different price for each unit sold, it may be able to practice perfect price discrimination. By setting the price of each unit equal to the maximum amount consumers are willing to pay for that unit (shown by the height of the demand curve), the monopolist can earn a profit equal to the area of the shaded triangle. Consumer surplus is zero. Ironically, this outcome is efficient because the monopolist has no incentive to restrict output, so there is no deadweight loss.

revenue equals marginal cost. Because the demand curve is now the marginal revenue curve, the profit-maximizing quantity occurs where the demand, or marginal revenue, curve intersects the marginal cost curve, identified at point *e* in Exhibit 10. Price discrimination is a way of increasing profit. The area of the shaded triangle *aec* shows the perfectly discriminating monopolist's economic profit.

By charging a different price for each unit sold, the perfectly discriminating monopolist is able to convert every dollar of consumer surplus into economic profit. Although this practice seems unfair to consumers, perfect price discrimination gets high marks based on allocative efficiency. Because such a monopolist does not have to lower the price to all customers to sell more, there is no reason to restrict output. In fact, because this is a constant-cost industry, Q is the same quantity produced in perfect competition (though in perfect competition, the triangle *aec* would be consumer surplus, not economic profit). As in the perfectly competitive outcome, the marginal benefit of the final unit produced and consumed just equals its marginal cost. And although perfect price discrimination yields no consumer surplus, the total benefit consumers derive from consuming this good just equals their total cost. Note also that because the monopolist does not restrict output, *there is no deadweight loss.* Thus, perfect price discrimination enhances social welfare when compared with monopoly output in the absence of price discrimination. But the monopolist reaps all net gains from production, while consumers just break even on the deal because their total benefit equals their total cost.

The pricing of cell phone service reflects a firm's effort to capture more consumer surplus as profit. Pricing alternatives include (1) a per-minute price with no basic fee,

(2) a flat rate for the month plus a price per minute, and (3) a flat rate for unlimited calls. These alternatives allow the company to charge those who use fewer minutes more per minute than those who call more. Such suppliers are trying to convert some consumer surplus into profit.

Conclusion

Pure monopoly, like perfect competition, is not that common. Perhaps the best examples are firms producing patented items that provide unique benefits, such as certain prescription drugs, but patents eventually expire so generic substitutes become available. Some firms may enjoy monopoly power in the short run, but the lure of economic profit encourages rivals to hurdle seemingly high entry barriers in the long run. Changing technology also works against monopoly in the long run. For example, the railroad monopoly was erased by the interstate highway system. AT&T's monopoly on long-distance phone service crumbled as wireless technology replaced copper wire. The U.S. Postal Service's monopoly on first-class mail is being eroded by fax machines, texting, Twittering, email, e-payments, and private firms offering overnight delivery. De Beers has lost its grip on the diamond market. And cable TV is losing its local monopoly to technological breakthroughs in fiber-optics technology, wireless broadband, and the Internet.

Although perfect competition and pure monopoly are rare, our examination of them yields a framework to help understand market structures that lie between the two extremes. Many firms have some degree of monopoly power—that is, they face downward-sloping demand curves. The next chapter discusses the two market structures that lie in the gray region between perfect competition and monopoly.

Summary

1. A monopolist sells a product with no close substitutes. Short-run economic profit earned by a monopolist can persist in the long run only if the entry of new firms is blocked. Three barriers to entry are (a) legal restrictions, such as patents and operating licenses; (b) economies of scale over a broad range of output; and (c) control over a key resource.

2. Because a monopolist is the sole supplier of a product with no close substitutes, a monopolist's demand curve is also the market demand curve. Because a monopolist that does not price discriminate can sell more only by lowering the price for all units sold, marginal revenue is less than the price. Where demand is price elastic, marginal revenue is positive and total revenue increases as the price falls. Where demand is price inelastic, marginal revenue is negative and total revenue decreases as the price falls. A monopolist never voluntarily produces where demand is inelastic because raising the price and reducing output would increase total revenue.

3. If the monopolist can at least cover variable cost, profit is maximized or loss is minimized in the short run by finding the output rate that equates marginal revenue with marginal cost. At the profit-maximizing quantity, the price is found on the demand curve.

4. In the short run, a monopolist, like a perfect competitor, can earn economic profit but will shut down unless price at least covers average variable cost. In the long run, a monopolist, unlike a perfect competitor, can continue to earn economic profit as long as entry of potential competitors is blocked.

5. If costs are similar, a monopolist charges a higher price and supplies less output than does a perfectly competitive industry. Monopoly usually results in a deadweight loss when compared with perfect competition because the loss of consumer surplus exceeds the gains in monopoly profit.

6. To increase profit through price discrimination, the monopolist must have at least two identifiable groups of customers, each with a different price elasticity of demand at a given price, and must be able to prevent customers charged the lower price from reselling to those facing the higher price.

7. A perfect price discriminator charges a different price for each unit sold, thereby converting all consumer surplus into economic profit. Perfect price discrimination seems unfair because the monopolist reaps maximum profit and consumers get no consumer surplus. Yet perfect price discrimination is as efficient as perfect competition because the monopolist has no incentive to restrict output, so there is no deadweight loss.

Key Concepts

Questions for Review

1. **BARRIERS TO ENTRY** Complete each of the following sentences:

    a. A U.S. _____ awards inventors the exclusive right to production for 20 years.

    b. Patents and licenses are examples of government-imposed _____ that prevent entry into an industry.

    c. When economies of scale make it possible for a single firm to satisfy market demand at a lower cost per unit than could two or more firms, the single firm is considered a _____.

    d. A potential barrier to entry is a firm's control of a(n) _____ critical to production in the industry.

2. **BARRIERS TO ENTRY** Explain how economies of scale can be a barrier to entry.

3. **Case Study: Is a Diamond Forever?** How did the De Beers cartel try to maintain control of the price in the diamond market? How has this control been undermined?

4. **REVENUE FOR THE MONOPOLIST** How does the demand curve faced by a monopolist differ from the demand curve faced by a perfectly competitive firm?

5. **REVENUE FOR THE MONOPOLIST** Why is it impossible for a profit-maximizing monopolist to choose any price *and* any quantity it wishes?

6. **REVENUE SCHEDULES** Explain why the marginal revenue curve for a monopolist lies below its demand curve, rather than coinciding with the demand curve, as is the case for a perfectly competitive firm. Is it ever possible for a monopolist's marginal revenue curve to coincide with its demand curve?

7. **REVENUE CURVES** Why would a monopoly firm never knowingly produce on the inelastic portion of its demand curve?

8. **PROFIT MAXIMIZATION** Review the following graph showing the short-run situation of a monopolist. What output level does the firm choose in the short run? Why?

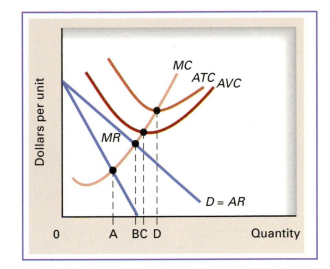

9. **ALLOCATIVE AND DISTRIBUTIVE EFFECTS** Why is society worse off under monopoly than under perfect competition, even if both market structures face the same constant long-run average cost curve?

10. **WELFARE COST OF MONOPOLY** Explain why the welfare loss of a monopoly may be smaller or larger than the loss shown in Exhibit 8 in this chapter.

11. **Case Study: The Mail Monopoly** Can the U.S. Postal Service be considered a monopoly in first-class mail? Why or why not? What has happened to the price elasticity of demand for first-class mail in recent years?

12. **CONDITIONS FOR PRICE DISCRIMINATION** List three conditions that must be met for a monopolist to price discriminate successfully?

13. **PRICE DISCRIMINATION** Explain how it may be profitable for South Korean manufacturers to sell new autos at a lower price in the United States than in South Korea, even with transportation costs included.

14. **PERFECT PRICE DISCRIMINATION** Why is the perfectly discriminating monopolist's marginal revenue curve identical to the demand curve it faces?

Problems and Exercises

15. **SHORT-RUN PROFIT MAXIMIZATION** Answer the following questions on the basis of the monopolist's situation illustrated in the following graph.

   a. At what output rate and price does the monopolist operate?
   b. In equilibrium, approximately what is the firm's total cost and total revenue?
   c. What is the firm's economic profit or loss in equilibrium?

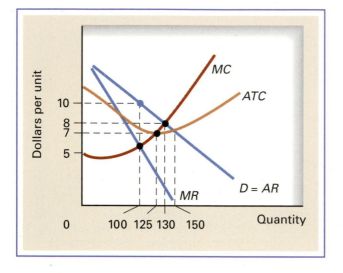

16. **MONOPOLY** Suppose that a certain manufacturer has a monopoly on the sorority and fraternity ring business (a constant-cost industry) because it has persuaded the "Greeks" to give it exclusive rights to their insignia.

   a. Using demand and cost curves, draw a diagram depicting the firm's profit-maximizing price and output level.
   b. Why is marginal revenue less than price for this firm?
   c. On your diagram, show the deadweight loss that occurs because the output level is determined by a monopoly rather than by a competitive market.
   d. What would happen if the Greeks decided to charge the manufacturer a royalty fee of $3 per ring?

Global Economic Watch Exercises

Login to www.cengagebrain.com and access the Global Economic Watch to do these exercises.

17. **GLOBAL ECONOMIC WATCH** Go to the Global Economic Crisis Resource Center. Select Global Issues in Context. In the Basic Search box at the top of the page, enter the phrase "Google monopoly." On the Results page, go to the Global Viewpoints section. Click on the link for the February 19, 2010, article "Is Google Gaining a Monopoly on the World's Information?"

Does Google enjoy a barrier to entry? What is the source of that barrier, if any?

18. **GLOBAL ECONOMIC WATCH** Go to the Global Economic Crisis Resource Center. Select Global Issues in Context. In the Basic Search box at the top of the page, enter the term "price discrimination." Write a paragraph about one example of an organization practicing price discrimination.

Monopolistic Competition and Oligopoly

10

- Why is Perrier water sold in green, tear-shaped bottles?
- Why are some shampoos sold only in salons?
- Why do some pizza makers deliver?
- Which market structure is like a golf tournament and which is like a tennis match?
- Why do airlines engage in airfare warfare?
- Why was the oil cartel, OPEC, created, and why has it met with only spotty success?
- Why is there a witness protection program?

To answer these and other questions, we turn in this chapter to the vast gray area that lies between perfect competition and monopoly.

Perfect competition and monopoly are extreme market structures. Under perfect competition, many suppliers offer an identical product and, in the long run, entry and exit erase economic profit. A monopolist supplies a product with no close substitutes in a market where natural and artificial barriers keep out would-be competitors, so a monopolist can earn economic profit in the long run. These polar market structures are logically appealing and offer a useful description of some industries observed in the economy.

But most firms fit into neither market structure. Some markets have many sellers producing goods that vary slightly, such as the many convenience stores that abound. Other markets consist of just a few sellers that in some industries produce essentially identical products, or commodities (such as oil), and in other industries produce differentiated goods (such as automobiles). This chapter examines the two remaining market structures that together include most firms in the economy.

Topics discussed include:

- Monopolistic competition
- Product differentiation
- Excess capacity
- Oligopoly
- Collusion
- Prisoner's dilemma

Monopolistic Competition

monopolistic competition

A market structure with many firms selling products that are substitutes but different enough that each firm's demand curve slopes downward; firm entry is relatively easy

As the expression *monopolistic competition* suggests, this market structure contains elements of both monopoly and competition. **Monopolistic competition** describes a market in which many producers offer products that are substitutes but are not viewed as identical by consumers. Because the products of different suppliers differ slightly—for example, some convenience stores are closer to you than others—the demand curve for each is not horizontal but slopes downward. Each supplier has some power over the price it can charge. Thus, the firms that populate this market are not *price takers,* as they would be under perfect competition, but are *price makers.* Because barriers to entry are low, firms in monopolistic competition can, in the long run, enter or leave the market with ease. Consequently, there are enough sellers that they behave competitively. There are also enough sellers that each tends to get lost in the crowd. For example, in a large metropolitan area, an individual restaurant, gas station, drugstore, dry cleaner, or convenience store tends to act *independently.* In other market structures, there may be only two or three sellers in each market, so they keep an eye on one another; they act *interdependently.* You will see the relevance of this distinction later in the chapter.

Product Differentiation

In perfect competition, the product is a commodity, meaning it's identical across producers, such as a bushel of wheat. In monopolistic competition, the product differs somewhat among sellers, as with the difference between one rock radio station and another, or one convenience store and another. Sellers differentiate their products in four basic ways.

Physical Differences

The most obvious way products differ is in their physical appearance and their qualities. Packaging is also designed to make a product stand out in a crowded field, such as a distinctive bottle of water (Perrier) and instant soup in a cup (Cup-a-Soup). Physical differences are seemingly endless: size, weight, color, taste, texture, and so on. Shampoos, for example, differ in color, scent, thickness, lathering ability, and bottle design. Particular brands aim at consumers with dandruff and those with normal, dry, or oily hair.

Location

The number and variety of locations where a product is available are other ways of differentiation—*spatial differentiation.* Some products seem to be available everywhere, including online; finding other products requires some search and travel. If you live in a metropolitan area, you are no doubt accustomed to the many convenience stores that populate the region. Each wants to be closest to you when you need milk, bread, or nachos—thus, the proliferation of stores. As the name says, these mini–grocery stores are selling *convenience*. Their prices are higher and selections more limited than at regular grocery stores, but they are usually closer to customers, don't have long lines, and some are open 24/7.

Services

Products also differ in terms of their accompanying services. For example, some products are delivered to your door, such as Domino's pizza and Amazon books; some products are delivered to your computer or wirelessly, like software and e-books; others products are cash and carry. Some products are demonstrated by a well-trained sales staff; others are mostly self-service. Some products include online support and toll-free help lines; others come with no help at all. Some sellers provide money-back guarantees; others say "no refunds." The quality and range of accompanying services often differentiate otherwise close substitutes.

Product Image

A final way products differ is in the image the producer tries to foster in the customer's mind. Producers try to create and maintain brand loyalty through product promotion and advertising. For example, suppliers of sportswear, clothing, watches, and cosmetics often pay for endorsements from athletes, fashion models, and other celebrities. Some producers emphasize the care and attention to detail in each item. For example, Hastens, a small, family-owned Swedish bedding company, underscores the months of labor required to craft each bed by hand—as a way to justify the $60,000 price tag. Some producers try to demonstrate high quality based on where products are sold, such as shampoo sold only in salons. Some products tout their all-natural ingredients, such as Ben & Jerry's ice cream, Tom's of Maine toothpaste, and Nantucket Nectars, or appeal to environmental concerns by focusing on recycled packaging, such as the Starbucks coffee cup insulating sleeve "made from 60% post-consumer recycled fiber." More generally, firms advertise to increase sales and profits. Research has found that each dollar of online advertising increased the firm's sales more than ten-fold.[1]

Short-Run Profit Maximization or Loss Minimization

Because each monopolistic competitor offers a product that differs somewhat from what others supply, each has some control over the price charged. This *market power* means that each firm's demand curve slopes downward. Because many firms offer close but not identical products, any firm that raises its price can expect to lose some customers to rivals. By way of comparison, a price hike by an individual firm would cost a monopolist fewer customers but would cost a perfect competitor *all* customers. Therefore, a monopolistic competitor faces a demand curve that tends to be more elastic than a monopolist's but less elastic than a perfect competitor's.

Recall that the availability of substitutes for a given product affects its price elasticity of demand. The price elasticity of the monopolistic competitor's demand depends on (1) the number of rival firms that produce similar products and (2) the firm's ability to differentiate its product from those of its rivals. *A firm's demand curve is more elastic the more substitutes there are and the less differentiated its product is.*

1. Randall Lewis and David Reiley, "Does Retail Advertising Work? Measuring the Effects of Advertising on Sales Via a Controlled Experiment on Yahoo!," Paper Presented at the American Economics Association Annual Meeting, 3 January 2010.

net 📖 bookmark

For products to be differentiated they have to be branded with a distinctive name. To protect the value of the name, the producer can apply for a trademark. Who has registered what names as trademarks? You can quickly find out for yourself using the U.S. Patent and Trademark Office's search engine at http://www.uspto. gov/. Try the names of some of your favorite products and brands. How many registered trademarks does Aerosmith have? What product is each one protecting?

EXHIBIT 1 Monopolistic Competitor in the Short Run

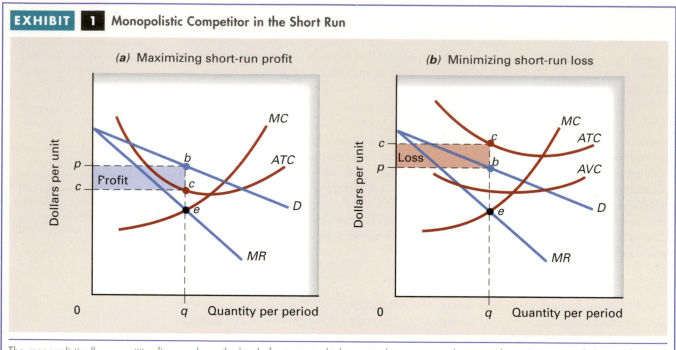

The monopolistically competitive firm produces the level of output at which marginal revenue equals marginal cost (point *e*) and charges the price indicated by point *b* on the downward-sloping demand curve. In panel (a), the firm produces *q* units, sells them at price *p*, and earns a short-run economic profit equal to ($p − c$) multiplied by *q*, shown by the blue rectangle. In panel (b), the average total cost exceeds the price at the output where marginal revenue equals marginal cost. Thus, the firm suffers a short-run loss equal to ($c − p$) multiplied by *q*, shown by the pink rectangle.

Marginal Revenue Equals Marginal Cost

From our study of monopoly, we know that a downward-sloping demand curve means the marginal revenue curve also slopes downward and lies beneath the demand curve. Exhibit 1 depicts demand and marginal revenue curves for a monopolistic competitor. The exhibit also presents average and marginal cost curves. Remember that the forces that determine the cost of production are largely independent of the forces that shape demand, so there is nothing special about a monopolistic competitor's cost curves. In the short run, a firm that can at least cover its variable cost increases output as long as marginal revenue exceeds marginal cost. A monopolistic competitor maximizes profit just as a monopolist does: *the profit-maximizing quantity occurs where marginal revenue equals marginal cost; the profit-maximizing price for that quantity is found up on the demand curve.* Exhibit 1 shows the price and quantity combinations that maximize short-run profit in panel (a), and minimize short-run loss in panel (b). In each panel, the marginal cost and marginal revenue curves intersect at point *e*, yielding equilibrium output *q*, equilibrium price *p*, and average total cost *c*.

Maximizing Profit or Minimizing Loss in the Short Run

Recall that the short run is a period too brief to allow firms to enter or leave the market. The demand and cost conditions shown in panel (a) of Exhibit 1 indicate that this firm earns economic profit in the short run. At the firm's profit-maximizing quantity, average total cost, *c*, is below the price, *p*. Price minus average total cost is the firm's profit per unit, which, when multiplied by the quantity, yields economic profit, shown by the blue rectangle. Again, the profit-maximizing quantity is found where marginal revenue equals marginal cost; price is found up on the demand curve at that quantity. Thus, a monopolistic competitor, like a monopolist, has no supply curve—that is, *there is no curve that uniquely relates prices and corresponding quantities supplied*.

The monopolistic competitor, like monopolists and perfect competitors, is not guaranteed an economic profit or even a normal profit. The firm's demand and cost curves could be as shown in panel (b), where the average total cost curve lies entirely above the demand curve, so no quantity allows the firm to escape a loss. In such a situation, the firm must decide whether to produce at a loss or to shut down in the short run. The rule here is the same as with perfect competition and monopoly: as long as price exceeds average variable cost, the firm in the short run loses less by producing than by shutting down. If no price covers average variable cost, the firm shuts down. Recall that the halt in production may be only temporary; shutting down is not the same as going out of business. Firms that expect economic losses to persist may, in the long run, leave the industry.

Short-run profit maximization in monopolistic competition is quite similar to that under monopoly. But the stories differ in the long run, as we'll see next.

Zero Economic Profit in the Long Run

Low barriers to entry in monopolistic competition mean that short-run economic profit attracts new entrants in the long run. Because new entrants offer similar products, they draw customers away from other firms in the market, thereby reducing the demand facing other firms. Entry continues in the long run until economic profit disappears. *Because market entry is easy, monopolistically competitive firms earn zero economic profit in the long run.*

On the other side of the ledger, economic losses drive some firms out of business in the long run. As firms leave the industry, their customers switch to the remaining firms, increasing the demand for those products. Firms continue to leave in the long run until the remaining firms have enough customers to earn normal profit, but not economic profit.

Exhibit 2 shows long-run equilibrium for a typical monopolistic competitor. In the long run, entry and exit shifts each firm's demand curve until economic profit disappears—that is, until price equals average total cost. In Exhibit 2, the marginal revenue curve intersects the marginal cost curve at point *a*. At the equilibrium quantity, *q*, the average total cost curve is tangent to the demand curve at point *b*. Because average total cost equals the price, the firm earns no economic profit but does earn a normal profit (how do we know this?). At all other quantities, the firm's average total cost curve lies above the demand curve, so the firm would lose money by reducing or expanding production.

Thus, because entry is easy in monopolistic competition, short-run economic profit attracts new entrants in the long run. The demand curve facing each monopolistic competitor shifts left until economic profit disappears. A short-run economic loss prompts some firms to leave the industry in the long run until remaining firms earn just a normal profit. In summary: *Monopolistic competition is like monopoly in the sense that firms in each industry face demand curves that slope downward. Monopolistic competition is like perfect competition in the sense that easy entry and exit eliminate economic profit or economic loss in the long run.*

One way to understand how firm entry erases short-run economic profit is to consider the evolution of an industry, as discussed in the following case study.

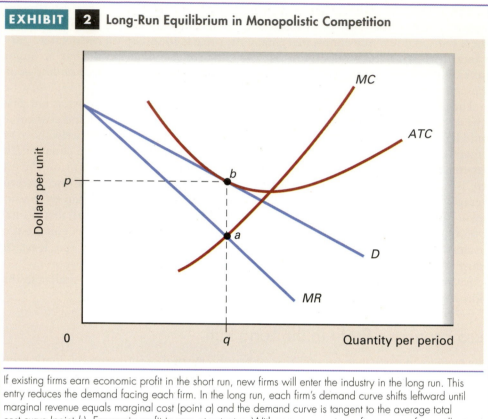

EXHIBIT   2   Long-Run Equilibrium in Monopolistic Competition

If existing firms earn economic profit in the short run, new firms will enter the industry in the long run. This entry reduces the demand facing each firm. In the long run, each firm's demand curve shifts leftward until marginal revenue equals marginal cost (point *a*) and the demand curve is tangent to the average total cost curve (point *b*). Economic profit is zero at output *q*. With zero economic profit, no more firms will enter, so the industry is in long-run equilibrium. The same long-run outcome occurs if firms suffer a short-run loss. Firms leave until remaining firms earn just a normal profit.

CASE STUDY

e activity

Check Blockbuster's website at http://www.blockbuster.com/. Is the company still operating? If yes, how is Blockbuster differentiating its product? If not, why do you think it shut down? Explain using economic concepts from this chapter.

WORLD OF BUSINESS

Fast Forward to Creative Destruction   The introduction in the 1970s of videocassette recorders, or VCRs, fueled demand for videotaped movies, which were originally so expensive ($75 to $100) that renting was the only way to go. The first wave of video rental stores required security deposits and imposed membership fees of up to $100. In those early days, most rental stores faced little competition so many outlets earned short-run economic profit. But because entry was relatively easy, this profit attracted competitors. Convenience stores, grocery stores, bookstores, even drugstores began renting videos as a sideline. Between 1982 and 1987, the number of rental outlets *quadrupled*, growing faster than VCR purchases.

Thus, the supply of video rentals increased faster than the demand. The 1990s brought more bad news for the industry, when hundreds of cable channels and pay-per-view options offered close substitutes for video rentals. The greater supply of rental outlets along with the increased availability of substitutes had the predictable effect on market prices. Rental rates crashed to as little as $0.99. Membership fees and tape deposits disappeared. So many outlets gave up on the business that a market developed to buy and resell their tape inventories.

The video rental business grew little during the 1990s. Even after the addition of DVDs and video games, the industry "shakeout" continued. One rental chain, Blockbuster, bought up weaker competitors and eventually accounted for more than a third of the U.S. market, with over 6,000 outlets. But Blockbuster faced its own growing pains, including an "excess inventory" of tapes and a failed effort to sell books, magazines, and snacks at its rental stores.

The latest threats to Blockbuster and other bricks-and-mortar rental stores are (1) on-demand movies delivered by broadband cable, (2) downloads from the Internet, (3) grab-and-go rental kiosks such as Redbox, and (4) online rental services that mail DVDs, such as QwikFliks and Netflix (Netflix offers 100,000 movie titles and mails out 2 million DVDs a day). In other developments, Wal-Mart bought Vudu in 2010 to stream movies over the Internet in high definition using Vudu's compression technology. And Best Buy teamed up with Cinema Now to stream movies online. Other download competition came from Amazon.com's Unbox, Microsoft's Xbox, Apple TV, and Netflix (half of Netflix's 12 million subscribers stream movies).

Technological change has created powerful rivals to the bricks-and-mortar movie rental business. Competition is fierce. Blockbuster announced in 2010 that it planned to close 1,560 of its remaining 3,750 outlets and warned that it may be forced into bankruptcy. As a measure of how far Blockbuster's fortunes have fallen, in 2002 the company stock sold for about $30 per share. By September 2010, the price was less than 10 cents a share. Such is the dynamic nature of a market economy—out with the old and in with the new, in a competitive process that has been aptly called *creative destruction*. This destruction is no fun for producers on the losing end, but consumers benefit from a wider choice and more competitive prices.

Sources: James Jarman, "Video Stores Crippled by Online, Kiosk, Mail Services," *Arizona Republic,* 27 February 2010. Mary Ellen Lloyd, "Blockbuster Considers Bankruptcy Filing," *Wall Street Journal,* 17 March 2010; and Stephen Grocer, "Wal-Mart Pays Up for Vudu. Should It Have Bought NetFlix?," *Wall Street Journal,* 22 February 2010.

Monopolistic Competition and Perfect Competition Compared

How does monopolistic competition compare with perfect competition in terms of efficiency? In the long run, neither earns economic profit, so what's the difference? The difference traces to the demand curves facing individual firms in each of the two market structures. Exhibit 3 presents the long-run equilibrium price and quantity for a typical firm in each market structure, assuming each firm has identical cost curves. In each case, the marginal cost curve intersects the marginal revenue curve at the quantity where the average total cost curve is tangent to the firm's demand curve.

A perfect competitor's demand curve is a horizontal line drawn at the market price, as shown in panel (a). This demand curve is tangent to the lowest point of the firm's long-run average total cost curve. Thus, a perfect competitor in the long run produces at the lowest possible average cost. In panel (b), a monopolistic competitor faces a downward-sloping demand curve because its product differs somewhat from those of other suppliers. In the long run, the monopolistic competitor produces less than re- quired to achieve the lowest possible average cost. Thus, the price and average cost in monopolistic competition, identified as p' in panel (b), exceed the price and average cost in perfect competition, identified as p in panel (a). *If firms have the same cost*

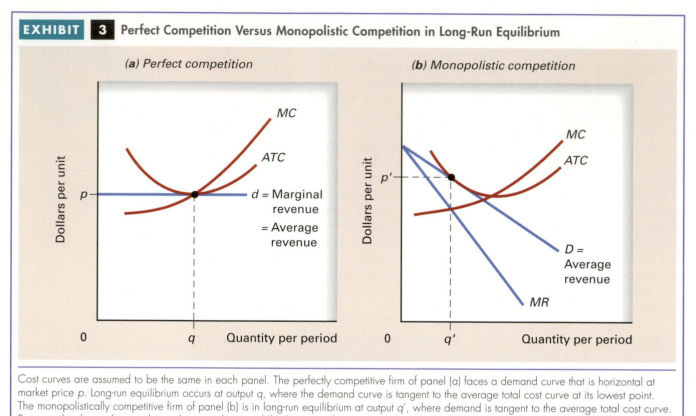

EXHIBIT **3** **Perfect Competition Versus Monopolistic Competition in Long-Run Equilibrium**

(a) Perfect competition

(b) Monopolistic competition

Cost curves are assumed to be the same in each panel. The perfectly competitive firm of panel (a) faces a demand curve that is horizontal at market price *p*. Long-run equilibrium occurs at output *q*, where the demand curve is tangent to the average total cost curve at its lowest point. The monopolistically competitive firm of panel (b) is in long-run equilibrium at output *q'*, where demand is tangent to the average total cost curve. Because the demand curve slopes downward in panel (b), however, the tangency does not occur at the minimum point of average total cost. Thus, the monopolistically competitive firm produces less output and charges a higher price than does a perfectly competitive firm with the same cost curves. Neither firm earns economic profit in the long run. The firm in monopolistic competition has excess capacity, meaning that it could reduce average cost by increasing its rate of output.

excess capacity

The difference between a firm's profit-maximizing quantity and the quantity that minimizes average cost; firms with excess capacity could reduce average cost by increasing quantity

curves, the monopolistic competitor produces less and charges more than the perfect competitor does in the long run, though neither earns economic profit.

Firms in monopolistic competition are not producing at minimum average cost. They are said to have **excess capacity**, because production falls short of the quantity that would achieve the lowest average cost. Excess capacity means that each producer could easily serve more customers and, in the process, lower average cost. *The marginal value of increased output would exceed its marginal cost, so greater output would increase social welfare.* Such excess capacity exists with gas stations, drugstores, convenience stores, restaurants, motels, bookstores, flower shops, and firms in other monopolistic competitive industries. A specific example is the funeral business. Industry analysts argue that the nation's 22,000 funeral directors could efficiently handle 4 million funerals a year, but only about 2.4 million people die. So the industry operates at only 60 percent of capacity, resulting in a higher average cost per funeral because valuable resources remain idle much of the time.

One other difference between perfect competition and monopolistic competition does not show up in Exhibit 3. Although the cost curves drawn in each panel of the exhibit are identical, firms in monopolistic competition spend more to differentiate their products than do firms in perfect competition, where products are identical. This higher cost of product differentiation shifts up the average cost curve.

Some economists have argued that monopolistic competition results in too many suppliers and in artificial product differentiation. The counterargument is that consumers are willing to pay a higher price for a wider selection. According to this latter view, consumers benefit from more choice among gas stations, restaurants, convenience stores, clothing stores, video stores, drugstores, textbooks, hiking boots, and many other goods and services. For example, what if half of the restaurants in your area were to close just so the remaining ones could reduce their excess capacity? Some consumers, including you, might be disappointed if a local favorite closed.

Perfect competitors and monopolistic competitors are so numerous in their respective markets that an action by any one of them has little or no effect on the behavior of others in the market. Another important market structure on the continuum between perfect competition and monopoly has just a few firms. We explore this market structure in the balance of the chapter.

An Introduction to Oligopoly

The final market structure we examine is *oligopoly,* a Greek word meaning "few sellers." When you think of "big business," you are thinking of **oligopoly,** an industry dominated by just a few firms. Perhaps three or four account for more than half the industry supply. Many industries, including steel, automobiles, oil, breakfast cereals, cigarettes, personal computers, and operating systems software, are *oligopolistic.* Because an oligopoly has only a few firms, each one must consider the effect of its own actions on competitors' behavior. Oligopolists are therefore said to be *interdependent.*

oligopoly
A market structure characterized by so few firms that each behaves interdependently

Varieties of Oligopoly

In some oligopolies, such as steel or oil, the product is identical, or undifferentiated, across producers. Thus, an **undifferentiated oligopoly** sells a commodity, such as an ingot of steel or a barrel of oil. But in other oligopolies, such as automobiles or breakfast cereals, the product is differentiated across producers. A **differentiated oligopoly** sells products that differ across producers, such as a Toyota Camry versus a Honda Accord.

The more similar the products, the greater the interdependence among firms in the industry. For example, because steel ingots are essentially identical, steel producers are quite sensitive to each other's pricing. A small rise in one producer's price sends customers to rivals. But with differentiated oligopoly, such as the auto industry, producers are not quite as sensitive about each other's prices. As with monopolistic competitors, oligopolists differentiate their products through (1) physical qualities, (2) sales locations, (3) services offered with the product, and (4) the image of the product established in the consumer's mind.

Because of interdependence, the behavior of any particular firm is difficult to predict. *Each firm knows that any changes in its product's quality, price, output, or advertising policy may prompt a reaction from its rivals. And each firm may react if another firm alters any of these features.* Monopolistic competition is like a professional golf tournament, where each player strives for a personal best. Oligopoly is more like a tennis match, where each player's actions depend on how and where the opponent hits the ball. Here's another analogy to help you understand the effects of interdependence: Did you ever find yourself in an awkward effort to get around someone coming toward you on a sidewalk? You each end up turning this way and that in a brief, clumsy encounter. You each are trying to figure out which way the other will turn. But since

undifferentiated oligopoly
An oligopoly that sells a commodity, or a product that does not differ across suppliers, such as an ingot of steel or a barrel of oil

differentiated oligopoly
An oligopoly that sells products that differ across suppliers, such as automobiles or breakfast cereal

neither can read the other's mind, neither can work out the problem independently. The solution is for one of you to put your head down and just walk. The other can then easily adjust.

Why have some industries evolved into oligopolies, dominated by only a few firms? Although the reasons are not always clear, *an oligopoly can often be traced to some form of barrier to entry, such as economies of scale, legal restrictions, brand names built up by years of advertising, or control over an essential resource.* In the previous chapter, we examined barriers to entry as they applied to monopoly. Those same principles apply to oligopoly.

Economies of Scale

Perhaps the most important barrier to entry is economies of scale. Recall that the minimum efficient scale is the lowest output at which the firm takes full advantage of economies of scale. If a firm's minimum efficient scale is relatively large compared to industry output, then only a few firms are needed to satisfy industry demand. For example, an automobile plant of minimum efficient scale could make enough cars to supply nearly 10 percent of the U.S. market. If there were 100 auto plants, each would supply such a tiny portion of the market that the average cost per car would be higher than if only 10 plants manufacture autos. In the automobile industry, economies of scale create a barrier to entry. To compete with existing producers, a new entrant must sell enough automobiles to reach a competitive scale of operation.

Exhibit 4 presents the long-run average cost curve for a typical firm in the industry. If a new entrant can sell only S cars, the average cost per unit, c_a, far exceeds the average cost, c_b, of a manufacturer that sells enough cars to reach the minimum efficient size, M. If autos sell for less than c_a, a potential entrant can expect to lose money, and this prospect discourages entry. For example, John Delorean tried to break into the auto industry in the early 1980s with a modern design featured in the *Back to the Future* movies. But his company managed to build and sell only 8,583 Deloreans before going bankrupt. If an auto plant costs $1 billion to build, just paying for the plant would have cost over $100,000 per Delorean.

The High Cost of Entry

Potential entrants into oligopolistic industries could face another problem. The total investment needed to reach the minimum efficient size is often gigantic. A new auto plant or new semiconductor plant can cost over $3 billion. The average cost of developing and testing a new drug exceeds $800 million (only 1 in 25 drug candidates identified by the industry ever makes it to market).[2] Advertising a new product enough to compete with established brands may also require enormous outlays.

High start-up costs and well-established brand names create huge barriers to entry, especially because the market for new products is so uncertain (four out of five new consumer products don't survive). An unsuccessful product could cripple an upstart firm. The prospect of such a loss discourages many potential entrants. That's why most new products come from established firms. For example, Colgate-Palmolive spent $100 million introducing Total toothpaste, as did McDonald's in its failed attempt to sell the Arch Deluxe. Unilever lost $160 million when its new detergent, Power, washed out.

Firms often spend millions and sometimes billions trying to differentiate their products. Some of these outlays offer consumers useful information and wider choice. But

---

2.   As reported in "Little Big Pharma," *Wall Street Journal*, 6 December 2006.

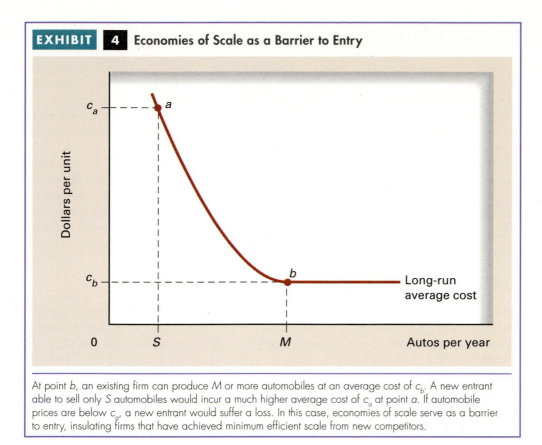

EXHIBIT   4   Economies of Scale as a Barrier to Entry

At point b, an existing firm can produce M or more automobiles at an average cost of c_b. A new entrant able to sell only S automobiles would incur a much higher average cost of c_a at point a. If automobile prices are below c_a, a new entrant would suffer a loss. In this case, economies of scale serve as a barrier to entry, insulating firms that have achieved minimum efficient scale from new competitors.

some spending seems to offer neither. For example, Pepsi and Coke spend billions on messages such as "It's the Cola" or "Open Happiness." Regardless, *product differentiation expenditures create a barrier to entry.*

Crowding Out the Competition

Oligopolies compete with existing rivals and try to block new entry by offering a variety of products. Entrenched producers may flood the market with new products in part to crowd out other new entries. For example, a few cereal makers offer more than a dozen products each. Many of these variations offer little that is new. One study of 25,500 new products introduced during one year found only 7 percent offered new or added benefits.[3] *Multiple products from the same brand dominate shelf space and attempt to crowd out new entrants.*

This does not mean that small producers can't survive. Brenda Jensen, for example, handcrafts two-pound wheels of cheese in her small business that produces only about 12,000 pounds a year. She survives because her cheese sells for $20 to $40 a pound at boutique retailers.[4]

3. The study was carried out by Market Intelligence Service and was reported in "Market Makers," *The Economist,* 14 March 1998.
4. Pervaiz Shallwani, "From Corporate to Camembert: Cheesemaking Lures Newcomers," *Wall Street Journal,* 7 November 2008.

Models of Oligopoly

Because oligopolists are interdependent, analyzing their behavior is complicated. No single model or single approach explains oligopoly behavior completely. At one extreme, oligopolists may try to coordinate their behavior so they act collectively as a single monopolist, forming a cartel, such as OPEC. At the other extreme, oligopolists may compete so fiercely that price wars erupt, such as those that break out among airlines, tobacco companies, computer chip makers, and wireless service providers.

Several theories have been developed to explain oligopoly behavior. We will study three of the better-known approaches: collusion, price leadership, and game theory. As you will see, each has some relevance in explaining observed behavior, although none is entirely satisfactory as a general theory of oligopoly. Thus, *there is no general theory of oligopoly but rather a set of theories, each based on the diversity of observed behavior in an interdependent market.*

Collusion and Cartels

collusion

An agreement among firms to increase economic profit by dividing the market and fixing the price

cartel

A group of firms that agree to coordinate their production and pricing decisions to reap monopoly profit

In an oligopolistic market, there are just a few firms so, to decrease competition and increase profit, these firms may try to *collude,* or conspire to rig the market. **Collusion** is an agreement among firms in the industry to divide the market and fix the price. A **cartel** is a group of firms that agree to collude so they can act as a monopoly to increase economic profit. Cartels are more likely among sellers of a commodity, like oil or steel. *Colluding firms, compared with competing firms, usually produce less, charge more, block new firms, and earn more profit. Consumers pay higher prices, and potential entrants are denied the opportunity to compete.*

Collusion and cartels are illegal in the United States. Still, monopoly profit can be so tempting that some U.S. firms break the law. For example, top executives at Archer Daniels Midland were convicted of conspiring with four Asian competitors to rig the $650 million world market for lysine, an amino acid used in animal feed. Some other countries are more tolerant of cartels and a few even promote cartels, as with the 12 member-nations of OPEC. If OPEC ever met in the United States, its representatives could be arrested for price fixing. Cartels can operate worldwide because there are no international laws against them.

Suppose all firms in an industry formed a cartel. The market demand curve, D, appears in Exhibit 5. What price maximizes the cartel's profit, and how is output allocated among participating firms? The first task of the cartel is to determine its marginal cost of production. Because a cartel acts like a monopoly that runs many plants, the marginal cost curve for the cartel in Exhibit 5 is the horizontal sum of each firm's marginal cost curve. The cartel's marginal cost curve intersects the market's marginal revenue curve to determine output that maximizes the cartel's profit. This intersection yields quantity Q. The cartel's price, p, is read off the demand curve at that quantity.

So far, so good. To maximize cartel profit, output Q must be allocated among cartel members so that each member's marginal cost equals c. Any other allocation would lower cartel profit. Thus, *for cartel profit to be maximized, output must be allocated so that the marginal cost for the final unit produced by each firm is identical.* Let's look at why this is easier said than done.

Differences in Average Cost

If all firms have identical average cost curves, output and profit would be easily allocated across firms (each firm would produce the same amount), but if costs differ, as they usually do, problems arise. The greater the difference in average costs across firms,

EXHIBIT **5** **Cartel as a Monopolist**

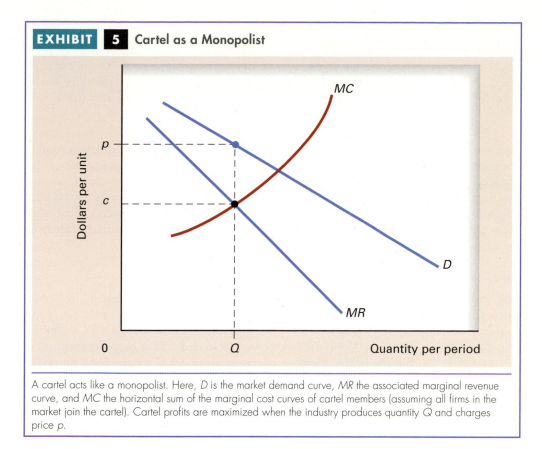

A cartel acts like a monopolist. Here, *D* is the market demand curve, *MR* the associated marginal revenue curve, and *MC* the horizontal sum of the marginal cost curves of cartel members (assuming all firms in the market join the cartel). Cartel profits are maximized when the industry produces quantity *Q* and charges price *p*.

the greater the differences in economic profit among them. If cartel members try to equalize each firm's total profit, a high-cost firm would need to sell more than would a low-cost firm. But this allocation scheme would violate the cartel's profit-maximizing condition. Thus, *if average costs differ across firms, the output allocation that maximizes cartel profit yields unequal profit across cartel members.* Firms earning less profit could drop out of the cartel, thereby undermining it. Usually, the allocation of output is the result of haggling among cartel members. Firms that are more influential or more adept at bargaining get a larger share of output and profit. Allocation schemes are sometimes based on geography or on the historical division of output among firms. OPEC, for example, allocates output in proportion to each member country's share of estimated oil reserves. Cartel members of Norway's cement market base output on each firm's share of industry capacity.[5]

Number of Firms in the Cartel

The more firms in an industry, the more difficult it is to negotiate an acceptable allocation of output among them. *Consensus becomes harder to achieve as the number of firms grows.* And the more firms in the industry, the more likely that some will become dissatisfied and bolt from the cartel.

5. Lars-Hendrik Roller and Frode Steen, "On the Workings of a Cartel: Evidence from the Norwegian Cement Industry," *American Economic Review* 96 (March 2006), p. 322.

New Entry Into the Industry

If a cartel can't prevent new entry into the market, new firms will eventually force prices down, squeeze economic profit, and disrupt the cartel. The profit of the cartel attracts entry, entry increases market supply, and increased supply forces the price down. A cartel's success therefore depends on barriers that block the entry of new firms.

Cheating

Perhaps the biggest problem in keeping the cartel together is the powerful temptation to cheat on the agreement. Because oligopolists usually operate with excess capacity, some cheat on the price. By offering a price slightly below the fixed price, any cartel member can usually increase sales and profit. Even if cartel members keep an eagle eye on each firm's price, one firm can increase sales by offering extra services, secret rebates, or other concessions. Research suggests that cheating increases as the number of firms in the cartel grows.[6] Cartels collapse once cheating becomes widespread.

OPEC's Spotty History

The problems of establishing and maintaining a cartel are reflected in the spotty history of OPEC. Many members are poor countries that rely on oil as their major source of revenue, so they argue over the price and their market share. OPEC members also cheat on the cartel. In 1980, the price of oil exceeded $85 a barrel (measured in 2010 dollars). During the 1990s, the price averaged around $32 a barrel and dipped as low as $10 a barrel. Prices topped $145 in 2008, but fell back to $45 by the end of that year. Like other cartels, OPEC has difficulty with new entry. The high prices resulting from OPEC's early success attracted new oil supplies from non-OPEC members operating in the North Sea, Mexico, and Siberia. The high price also made extraction from Canadian oil sands economical. As a result of new exploration and other oil sources, about 60 percent of the world's oil now comes from non-OPEC sources.

To Review: In those countries where cartels are legal, establishing and maintaining an effective cartel is more difficult if (1) the product is differentiated among firms, (2) average costs differ among firms, (3) there are many firms in the industry, (4) entry barriers are low, or (5) cheating on the cartel agreement becomes widespread. Efforts to cartelize the world supply of a number of products, including bauxite, copper, tin, and coffee, have failed so far. Russia is trying to form a natural gas cartel with other gas exporters, but obstacles abound.

Price Leadership

price leader

A firm whose price is matched by other firms in the market as a form of tacit collusion

An informal, or *tacit,* form of collusion occurs if there is a **price leader** who sets the price for the rest of the industry. Typically, a dominant firm sets the market price, and other firms follow that lead, thereby avoiding price competition. The price leader also initiates any price changes, and, again, others follow. The steel industry was an example of the price-leadership form of oligopoly. Typically, U.S. Steel, the largest firm in the industry, would set the price for various products. Public pressure on U.S. Steel not to raise prices eventually shifted the price-leadership role onto less prominent producers, resulting in a rotation of leadership among firms. Although the rotating price leadership reduced price conformity, price leadership kept prices high.

Like other forms of collusion, price leadership faces obstacles. Most importantly, the practice violates U.S. antitrust laws. Second, the greater the product differentiation

6.   John List, "The Economics of Open Air Markets," NBER Working Paper 15420 (October 2009).

among sellers, the less effective price leadership is as a means of collusion. Third, there is no guarantee that other firms will follow the leader. Firms that fail to follow a price increase take business away from firms that do. Fourth, unless there are barriers to entry, a profitable price attracts new entrants, which could destabilize the price-leadership agreement. And finally, as with formal cartels, some firms are tempted to cheat on the agreement to boost sales and profit.

Game Theory

How do firms act when they recognize their interdependence but either cannot or do not collude? Because oligopoly involves interdependence among a few firms, we can think of interacting firms as players in a game. **Game theory** examines oligopolistic behavior as a series of strategic moves and countermoves among rival firms. This approach analyzes the behavior of decision makers, or players, whose choices affect one another. Game theory is not really a separate model of oligopoly but a general approach, an approach that focuses on each player's incentives to cooperate—say, through cartels or price leaders—or to compete, in ways to be discussed now.

To get some feel for game theory, let's work through the **prisoner's dilemma,** the most widely examined game. The game originally considered a situation in which two thieves, let's call them Ben and Jerry, are caught near the crime scene and brought to police headquarters, where they are interrogated in separate rooms. The police know the two guys did it but can't prove it, so they need a confession. Each thief faces a choice of confessing, thereby "squealing" on the other, or "clamming up," thereby denying any knowledge of the crime. If one confesses, turning state's evidence, he is granted immunity from prosecution and goes free, while the other guy gets 10 years. If both clam up, each gets only a 1-year sentence on a technicality. If both confess, each gets 5 years.

What will Ben and Jerry do? The answer depends on the assumptions about their behavior—that is, what *strategy* each pursues. A **strategy** reflects a player's game plan. In this game, suppose each player tries to save his own skin—each tries to minimize his time in jail, regardless of what happens to the other (after all, there is no honor among thieves). Exhibit 6 shows the *payoff matrix* for the prisoner's dilemma. A **payoff matrix**

game theory
An approach that analyzes oligopolistic behavior as a series of strategic moves and countermoves by rival firms

prisoner's dilemma
A game that shows why players have difficulty cooperating even though they would benefit from cooperation

strategy
In game theory, the operational plan pursued by a player

payoff matrix
In game theory, a table listing the payoffs that each player can expect from each move based on the actions of the other player

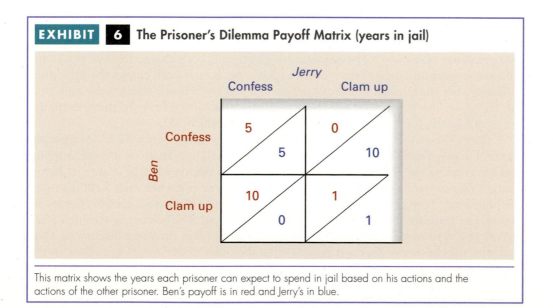

EXHIBIT 6   The Prisoner's Dilemma Payoff Matrix (years in jail)

This matrix shows the years each prisoner can expect to spend in jail based on his actions and the actions of the other prisoner. Ben's payoff is in red and Jerry's in blue.

is a table listing the rewards (or, in this case, the penalties) that Ben and Jerry can expect based on the strategy each pursues.

Ben's choices are shown down the left margin and Jerry's across the top. Each prisoner can either confess or clam up. The numbers in the matrix indicate the prison time in years each can expect based on the corresponding strategies. Ben's numbers are in red and Jerry's in blue. Take a moment now to see how the matrix works. Notice that the sentence each player receives depends on the strategy he chooses *and* on the strategy the other player chooses.

What strategies are rational assuming that each player tries to minimize jail time? For example, put yourself in Ben's shoes. You know that Jerry, who is being questioned in another room, will either confess or clam up. If Jerry confesses, the left column of Exhibit 6 shows the penalties. If you confess too, you both get 5 years in jail, but if you clam up, you get 10 years and Jerry "walks." So, if you think Jerry will confess, you should too.

What if you believe Jerry will clam up? The right-hand column shows the two possible outcomes. If you confess, you do no time, but if you clam up too, you each get 1 year in jail. Thus, if you think Jerry will clam up, you're better off confessing. In short, whatever Jerry does, Ben is better off confessing. The same holds for Jerry. He's better off confessing, regardless of what Ben does. So each has an incentive to confess and each gets 5 years in jail. This is called the **dominant-strategy equilibrium** of the game because each player's action does not depend on what he thinks the other player will do.

But notice that if each crook could just hang tough and clam up, both would be better off. After all, if both confess, each gets 5 years, but if both clam up, the police can't prove otherwise, so each gets only 1 year in jail. If each could trust the other to clam up, they both would be better off. But there is no way for the two to communicate or to coordinate their actions. That's why police investigators keep suspects apart, that's why organized crime threatens "squealers" with death, and that's why the witness protection program tries to shield "squealers."

Price-Setting Game

The prisoner's dilemma applies to a broad range of economic phenomena including pricing policy and advertising strategy. For example, consider the market for gasoline in a rural community with only two gas stations, Texaco and Exxon. Here the oligopoly consists of two sellers, or a **duopoly**. Suppose customers are indifferent between the brands and focus only on the price. Each station posts its daily price early in the morning before learning about the other station's price. To keep things simple, suppose only two prices are possible—a low price or a high price. If both charge the low price, they split the market and each earns a profit of $500 per day. If both charge the high price, they also split the market, but profit jumps to $700 each. If one charges the high price but the other the low one, the low-price station gets most of the business, earning a profit of $1,000, leaving the high-price station with only $200.

Exhibit 7 shows the payoff matrix, with Texaco's strategy down the left margin and Exxon's across the top. Texaco's profit appears in red, and Exxon's in blue. Suppose you are running the Texaco station and are trying to decide what to charge. If Exxon charges the low price, you earn $500 charging the low price but only $200 charging the high price. So you earn more charging the low price. If, instead, Exxon charges the high price, you earn $1,000 charging the low price and $700 charging the high price. Again, you earn more charging the low price. Exxon faces the same incentives. Thus, each charges the low price, regardless of what the other does.

The prisoner's dilemma outcome is an equilibrium because each player maximizes profit, given the price chosen by the other. Neither gas station can increase profit by changing its price, given the price chosen by the other firm. A situation in which a

dominant-strategy equilibrium

In game theory, the outcome achieved when each player's choice does not depend on what the other player does

duopoly

A market with only two producers; a special type of oligopoly market structure

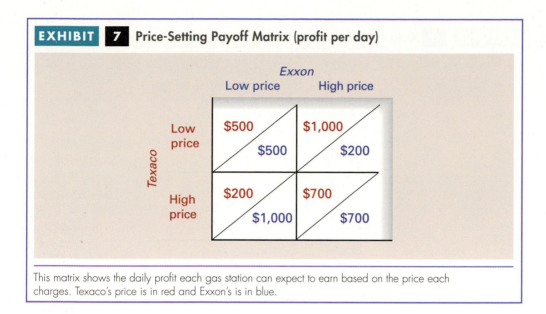

EXHIBIT 7 Price-Setting Payoff Matrix (profit per day)

Exxon

		Low price	High price
Texaco	**Low price**	$500 / $500	$1,000 / $200
	High price	$200 / $1,000	$700 / $700

This matrix shows the daily profit each gas station can expect to earn based on the price each charges. Texaco's price is in red and Exxon's is in blue.

player chooses its best strategy given the strategies chosen by other firms is called a **Nash equilibrium,** named after Nobel Prize winner and former Princeton professor John Nash. He inspired the award-winning movie *A Beautiful Mind* starring Russell Crowe as Nash.

In this prisoner's dilemma, each charges the low price, earning $500 a day, although each would earn $700 charging the high price. Think of yourself as a member of the oil cartel discussed earlier, where the cartel determines the price and sets production quotas for each member. If you think other firms in the cartel will stick with their quotas, you can increase your profit by cutting your price and thereby increasing quantity sold. If you think the other firms will cheat on the cartel by cutting the price, then you should too—otherwise, you will get your clock cleaned by those cheaters. Either way, your incentive as a cartel member is to cheat on the quota. All members have an incentive to cheat, although all would earn more by sticking with the agreement that maximizes joint profit. Cheating is a Nash equilibrium, unless the cartel has real teeth to keep members in line—that is, unless cartel members have the strategy imposed on them.

This incentive to cut prices suggests why price wars sometimes break out among oligopolists. Even in industries with just two or three firms, competition often locks these rivals in a steel-cage death match for survival. For example, in 2010, McDonald's and Burger King were each selling two beef patties with one slice of cheese on a bun for $1—a dollar-menu duel between the McDouble and the BK Dollar Double.[7] A bitter price war with Dell cut Hewlett-Packard's earnings on each $500 personal computer sold to a razor-thin $1.75.[8] Early profits in the animated movie business attracted entry, which over time cut profit and led to some bankruptcies. And just before a recent Thanksgiving weekend, a price war erupted in airfares. American Airlines first announced holiday discounts. Delta responded with cuts of up to 50 percent. Within hours, American, United, and other major carriers said they would match Delta's reductions. All these airlines were losing money at the time. So go the price wars.

Nash equilibrium
A situation in which a firm, or a player in game theory, chooses the best strategy given the strategies chosen by others; no participant can improve his or her outcome by changing strategies even after learning of the strategies selected by other participants

7. See Dollar Menu news at http://www.mcdonalds.com/content/usa/eat/features/mcdouble.html.
8. David Bank, "H-P Posts 10% Increase in Revenue," *Wall Street Journal,* 20 November 2003.

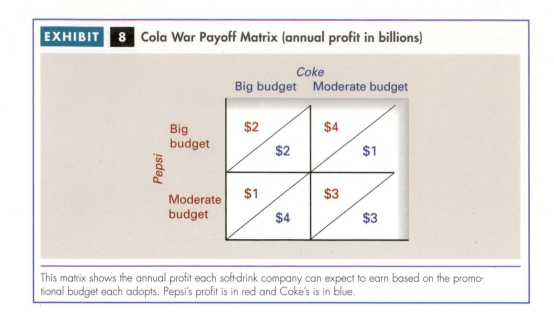

EXHIBIT 8 Cola War Payoff Matrix (annual profit in billions)

This matrix shows the annual profit each soft-drink company can expect to earn based on the promotional budget each adopts. Pepsi's profit is in red and Coke's is in blue.

Cola War Game

As a final example of a prisoner's dilemma, consider the marketing strategies of Coke and Pepsi. Suppose each is putting together a promotional budget for the coming year, not knowing the other's plans. The choice boils down to adopting either a moderate budget or a big budget—one that involves multiple Super Bowl ads, showy in-store displays, and other marketing efforts aimed mostly at attracting customers from each other. If each adopts a big budget, their costly efforts will, for the most part, cancel each other out and limit each company's profit to $2 billion a year. If each adopts a moderate promotional budget, the money saved boosts profit for each to $3 billion a year. And if one adopts a big budget but the other does not, the heavy promoter captures a bigger market share and earns $4 billion, while the other loses market share and earns only $1 billion. What to do, what to do?

Exhibit 8 shows the payoff matrix for the two strategies, with Pepsi's choices listed down the left margin and Coke's across the top. In each cell of the matrix, Pepsi's profit appears in red, and Coke's in blue. Let's look at Pepsi's decision. If Coke adopts a big promotional budget, Pepsi earns $2 billion by doing the same but only $1 billion by adopting a moderate budget. Thus, if Coke adopts a big budget, so should Pepsi. If Coke adopts a moderate budget, Pepsi earns $4 billion with a big budget and $3 billion with a moderate one. Again, Pepsi earns more with a big budget. Coke faces the same incentives, so both adopt big budgets, earning $2 billion each in profit, even though each would have earned $3 billion with a moderate budget.

One-Shot Versus Repeated Games

The outcome of a game often depends on whether it is a *one-shot game* or a *repeated game*. The classic prisoner's dilemma is a one-shot game. If the game is to be played just once, the strategy of confessing makes you better off regardless of what the other player does. Your choice won't influence the other player's behavior. But if the same players repeat the prisoner's dilemma, as would likely occur with the price-setting game, the cola war game, and the OPEC cartel, other possibilities unfold. In a repeated-game setting, each player has a chance to establish a reputation for cooperation and thereby may be able to encourage other players to do the same. After all, the cooperative solution—whether that involves clamming up, maintaining a high price, or adopting a moderate marketing budget—makes both players better off than if both fail to cooperate.

Experiments have shown that the strategy with the highest payoff in repeated games turns out to be the simplest—**tit-for-tat.** You begin by cooperating in the first round. On every round thereafter, you cooperate if the other player cooperated in the previous round, and you cheat if your opponent cheated in the previous round. In short, in any given round, you do whatever your opponent did in the previous round. The tit-for-tat strategy offers the other player immediate rewards for cooperation and immediate punishment for cheating. Some cartels seem to exhibit tit-for-tat strategies.

Coordination Game

In the **coordination game,** a Nash equilibrium occurs when each player chooses the same strategy. For example, you are driving on a country road and have to decide whether to drive on the right or the left side. Suppose you decide to drive on your left. If the driver coming from the opposite direction drives on his or her left, you pass each other without incident, so the cost to each of you is zero. But if the other player drives on the right-hand side, the probability of a crash increases. If, instead, you choose to drive on the right-hand side, you encounter no problems if the oncoming driver does the same, but face a greater likelihood of crashing if the other driver chooses the left-hand side. In this game, cost is minimized when both players choose the same strategy. And each strategy is a Nash equilibrium because no player can improve on that outcome, given the other player's choice. So if you choose the left-hand side and the other player chooses his or her left-hand side, then you can do no better and would do worse choosing the right-hand side.

To Review: Our discussion has given you some idea of game theory by focusing mostly on the prisoner's dilemma. Other games can be more complicated and involve more strategic interaction. Because firms are interdependent, oligopoly gives rise to all kinds of behavior and many approaches. Each approach helps explain certain behavior observed in oligopolistic markets. The *cartel*, or *collusion*, model shows why oligopolists might want to cooperate in fixing the market price; but that model also explains why a cartel is hard to establish and maintain. The *price-leadership* model explains why and how firms may charge the same price without explicitly establishing a formal cartel. Finally, *game theory*, expressed here mostly by the prisoner's dilemma, shows how difficult a cooperative solution might be even though cooperation benefits all players. Game theory is more of an approach to oligopoly rather than a distinct model.

Comparison of Oligopoly and Perfect Competition

As we have seen, each approach explains a piece of the oligopoly puzzle. But each has limitations, and none provides a complete picture of oligopoly behavior. Because there is no typical, or representative, model of oligopoly, "the" oligopoly model cannot be compared with the competitive model. We might, however, imagine an experiment in which we took the many firms that populate a competitive industry and, through a series of giant mergers, combined them to form, say, four firms. We would thereby transform the industry from perfect competition to oligopoly. How would firms in this industry behave before and after the massive merger?

Price Is Usually Higher Under Oligopoly

With fewer competitors after the merger, remaining firms would become more interdependent. Oligopoly models presented in this chapter suggest why firms may try to coordinate their pricing policies. *If oligopolists engaged in some sort of implicit or*

tit-for-tat
In game theory, a strategy in repeated games when a player in one round of the game mimics the other player's behavior in the previous round; an optimal strategy for getting the other player to cooperate

coordination game
A type of game in which a Nash equilibrium occurs when each player chooses the same strategy; neither player can do better than matching the other player's strategy

explicit collusion, industry output would be smaller and the price would be higher than under perfect competition. Even if oligopolists did not collude but simply operated with excess capacity, the price would be higher and the quantity lower with oligopoly than with perfect competition. The price could become lower under oligopoly compared with perfect competition if a price war broke out among oligopolists. Two rivals, Intel and Advanced Micro Devices, together account for the entire market for a specific type of computer chip, yet these two are always at each other's throat, thereby keeping prices and profits down. Behavior also depends on whether there are barriers to entry. The lower the barriers to entry into the oligopoly, the more oligopolists act like perfect competitors.

Higher Profits Under Oligopoly

In the long run, easy entry prevents perfect competitors from earning more than a normal profit. With oligopoly, however, there may be barriers to entry, such as economies of scale or a way to differentiate a product such as with brand names, which allow firms in the industry to earn long-run economic profit. *With barriers to entry, we should expect profit in the long run to be higher under oligopoly than under perfect competition.* Profit rates do in fact appear to be higher in industries where a few firms account for a high proportion of industry sales. Some economists view these higher profit rates as troubling evidence of market power. But not all economists share this view. Some note that the largest firms in oligopolistic industries tend to earn the highest rate of profit. Thus, the higher profit rates observed in oligopolistic industries do not necessarily stem from market power per se. Rather, these higher profit rates stem from the greater efficiency arising from economies of scale in these large firms. An individual firm can also achieve greater market power and higher profit by differentiating its product, as discussed in this closing case study.

e activity

Zara is owned by the Intidex Group, one of the world's largest fashion distributors, with over 3,300 stores in 68 countries—and Zara having over 1,000 of them. Visit the Intidex Web site at http://www.inditex.com/en to read about their philosophy and their dimensions of corporate responsibility—including their model of sustainability, and the social, environmental, and economic dimensions of the organization.

WORLD OF BUSINESS

Timely Fashions Boost Profit for Zara   One way a firm can increase market power is to offer a differentiated product. Zara, the largest fashion retailer in Europe, has been described as "possibly the most innovative and devastating retailer in the world." The company makes much of its clothing in its own workshops and factories, including designing, fabric dyeing, tailoring, and ironing. Zara also outsources some manufacturing to select suppliers that have developed the ability to make high-quality garments with the required flexibility and speed.

Zara's network of retail shops and clothing factories communicate through a sophisticated feedback mechanism for gathering market intelligence and putting it to work. Sales associates carry personal digital assistants to relay information on fashion trends and customer demand back to the company's team of 200 designers in Spain. Real-time sales data allow the factory to increase production of items that are selling and to bring out similar designs. Direct shipments from factory to shops also eliminate the need for costly warehouses.

Zara takes as little as two weeks to develop a new item and deliver it to one of its more than 1,000 retail stores. The industry average is six months. The company launches about 10,000 new designs a year, making new items in small batches at first so if something doesn't sell, there is not much left over. But if something catches on, stores can restock in a few days, so Zara doesn't miss out on a fashion wave. Thus, shops never have to wait long for fresh stock or to get an order filled. Whereas traditional stores such as the Gap may get new fashions twice a season, Zara distributes them twice a week. And in perhaps its most unusual of strategies, the company advertises little, relying instead on prime store location and word of mouth.

In short, Zara believes that making most of its own apparel and selectively outsourcing the rest, reduces delays, exploits customer feedback, maintains flexibility, and ensures quality. This steady supply of new clothing lines and continuous supply of popular items help Zara differentiate its products. Amancio Ortega, Zara's founder, opened his first store in 1975. With a personal fortune of $25 billion in 2010, he became the richest person in Spain and the ninth richest on the planet. The market rewards successful innovators.

Digital Vision/Jupiter Images

Sources: Nebahat Tokatli, "Insights from the Global Clothing Industry—The Case of Zara, A Fast Fashion Retailer," *Journal of Economic Geography*, 8 (January 2008): 21–38; Vanessa O'Connell, "How Fashion Makes Its Way from the Runway to the Rack," *Wall Street Journal*, 8 February 2007; "Supply-Chain Management," *The Economist*, 6 April 2009; and "The World's Billionaires," *Forbes*, 11 March 2010.

Conclusion

Firms in monopolistic competition and in oligopoly face a downward-sloping demand curve for their products. With monopolistic competition, there are so many firms in the market that each tends to get lost in the crowd. Each behaves independently. But with oligopoly, there are so few firms in the market that each must consider the impact that its pricing, output, and marketing decisions will have on other firms. Each oligopolist behaves interdependently, and this makes oligopoly difficult to analyze. As a result, there are different models and approaches to oligopoly, three of which were discussed in this chapter.

The analytical results derived in this chapter are not as clear-cut as for the polar cases of perfect competition and monopoly. Still, we can draw some general conclusions using perfect competition as a guide. In the long run, perfect competitors operate at minimum average cost, while other types of firms usually operate with excess capacity. Therefore, given identical cost curves, monopolists, monopolistic competitors, and oligopolists tend to charge higher prices than perfect competitors do, especially in the long run. In the long run, monopolistic competitors, like perfect competitors, earn only a normal profit because entry barriers are low. Monopolists and oligopolists can earn economic profit in the long run if new entry is restricted. In a later chapter, we examine government policies aimed at increasing competition. *Regardless of the market structure, however, profit maximization prompts firms to produce where marginal revenue equals marginal cost.*

This chapter has moved us from the extremes of perfect competition and monopoly to the gray area inhabited by most firms. Exhibit 9 compares features and examples of the four market structures. Please take a moment now to review these key distinctions. Some of these issues are revisited later when we explore the government's role in promoting market competition.

EXHIBIT | **9** | **Comparison of Market Structures**

	Perfect Competition	Monopoly	Monopolistic Competition	Oligopoly
Number of firms	Most	One	Many	Few
Control over price	None	Complete	Limited	Some
Product differences	None	Only one supplier	Some	None or some
Barriers to entry	None	Insurmountable	Low	Substantial
Examples	Wheat	Local electricity	Convenience stores	Automobiles

Summary

1. Whereas the output of a monopolist has no close substitutes, a monopolistic competitor must contend with many rivals. But because of differences among the products offered by different firms, each monopolistic competitor faces a downward-sloping demand curve.

2. Sellers in monopolistic competition and in oligopoly differentiate their products through (a) physical qualities, (b) sales locations, (c) services offered with the product, and (d) the product image.

3. In the short run, monopolistic competitors that can at least cover their average variable costs maximize profits or minimize losses by producing that quantity where marginal revenue equals marginal cost. In the long run, easy entry and exit of firms means that a monopolistic competitor earns only a normal profit, which occurs where its average total cost curve is tangent to the downward-sloping demand curve for its product.

4. An oligopoly is an industry dominated by a few sellers. In undifferentiated oligopolies, such as steel or oil, the product is a commodity—meaning that it does not differ across firms. In

differentiated oligopolies, such as automobiles or breakfast cereals, the product differs across firms.

5. Because an oligopoly consists of just a few firms, each may react to another firm's changes in quality, price, output, services, or advertising. Because of this interdependence, the behavior of oligopolists is difficult to analyze and predict. No single approach characterizes all oligopolistic markets.

6. In this chapter, we considered three approaches to oligopoly behavior: (a) collusion, in which firms form a cartel to act collectively like a monopolist; (b) price leadership, in which one firm, usually the biggest one, sets the price for the industry and other firms follow the leader; and (c) game theory, which analyzes oligopolistic behavior as a series of strategic moves by rival firms.

7. The prisoner's dilemma game shows why each player has difficulty cooperating even though all players would be better off if they did. In a variety of decisions such as what price to charge and how much to spend on marketing, rival firms could increase profit by cooperating. Yet each faces incentives that encourage noncooperation.

Key Concepts

Questions for Review

1. CHARACTERISTICS OF MONOPOLISTIC COMPETITION Why does the demand curve facing a monopolistically competitive firm slope downward in the long run, even after the entry of new firms?

2. PRODUCT DIFFERENTIATION What are four ways in which a firm can differentiate its product? What role can advertising play in product differentiation? How can advertising become a barrier to entry?

3. ZERO ECONOMIC PROFIT IN THE LONG RUN In the long run, a monopolistically competitive firm earns zero economic profit, which is exactly what would occur if the industry were perfectly competitive. Assuming that the cost curves for each firm are the same whether the industry is perfectly or monopolistically competitive, answer the following questions.

   a. Why don't perfectly and monopolistically competitive industries produce the same equilibrium quantity in the long run?
   b. Why is a monopolistically competitive industry said to be economically inefficient?
   c. What benefits might cause consumers to prefer the monopolistically competitive result to the perfectly competitive result?

4. VARIETIES OF OLIGOPOLY Do the firms in an oligopoly act independently or interdependently? Explain your answer.

5. COLLUSION AND CARTELS Why would each of the following induce some members of OPEC to cheat on their cartel agreement?

   a. Newly joined cartel members are less-developed countries.
   b. The number of cartel members doubles from 12 to 24.
   c. International debts of some members grow.
   d. Expectations grow that some members will cheat.

6. PRICE LEADERSHIP Why might a price-leadership model of oligopoly not be an effective means of collusion in an oligopoly?

7. MARKET STRUCTURES Determine whether each of the following is a characteristic of perfect competition, monopolistic competition, oligopoly, and/or monopoly:

   a. A large number of sellers
   b. Product is a commodity
   c. Advertising by firms
   d. Barriers to entry
   e. Firms are price makers

Problems and Exercises

8. SHORT-RUN PROFIT MAXIMIZATION A monopolistically competitive firm faces the following demand and cost structure in the short run:

Output	Price	FC	VC	TC	TR	Profit/Loss
0	$100	$100	$0	—	—	—
1	90	—	50	—	—	—
2	80	—	90	—	—	—
3	70	—	150	—	—	—
4	60	—	230	—	—	—
5	50	—	330	—	—	—
6	40	—	450	—	—	—
7	30	—	590	—	—	—

   a. Complete the table.
   b. What is the highest profit or lowest loss available to this firm?
   c. Should this firm operate or shut down in the short run? Why?
   d. What is the relationship between marginal revenue and marginal cost as the firm increases output?

9. Case Study: Fast Forward to Creative Destruction Use a cost-and-revenue graph to illustrate and explain the initial short-run profits in the video rental business in monopolistic competition. Then, use a second graph to illustrate the long-run situation. Explain fully.

10. MONOPOLISTIC COMPETITION AND PERFECT COMPETITION COMPARED Illustrated to the right are the marginal cost and average total cost curves for a small firm that is in long-run equilibrium.

   a. Locate the long-run equilibrium price and quantity if the firm is perfectly competitive.
   b. Label the price and quantity p_1 and q_1.
   c. Draw in a demand and marginal revenue curve to illustrate long-run equilibrium if the firm is monopolistically competitive. Label the price and quantity p_2 and q_2.
   d. How do the monopolistically competitive firm's price and output compare to those of the perfectly competitive firm?
   e. How do long-run profits compare for the two types of firms?

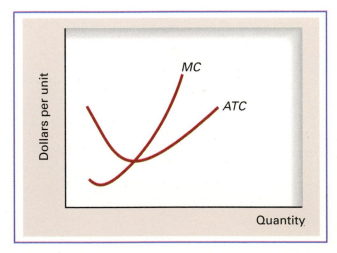

11. **COLLUSION AND CARTELS**   Use revenue and cost curves to illustrate and explain the sense in which a cartel behaves like a monopolist.

12. **GAME THEORY**   Suppose there are only two automobile companies, Ford and Chevrolet. Ford believes that Chevrolet will match any price it sets, but Chevrolet too is interested in maximizing profit. Use the following price and profit data to answer the following questions.

Ford's Selling Price in $	Chevrolet's Selling Price in $	Ford's Profits in $ (millions)	Chevrolet's Profits in $ (millions)
4,000	4,000	8	8
4,000	8,000	12	6
4,000	12,000	14	2
8,000	4,000	6	12
8,000	8,000	10	10
8,000	12,000	12	6
12,000	4,000	2	14
12,000	8,000	6	12
12,000	12,000	7	7

   a. What price will Ford charge?
   b. What price will Chevrolet charge once Ford has set its price?
   c. What is Ford's profit after Chevrolet's response?
   d. If the two firms collaborated to maximize joint profits, what prices would they set?
   e. Given your answer to part (d), how could undetected cheating on price cause the cheating firm's profit to rise?

13. **GAME THEORY**   While grading a final exam, an economics professor discovers that two students have virtually identical answers. She is convinced the two cheated but cannot prove it. The professor speaks with each student separately and offers the following deal: Sign a statement admitting to cheating. If both students sign the statement, each will receive an "F" for the course. If only one signs, he is allowed to withdraw from the course while the other student is expelled. If neither signs, both receive a "C" because the professor does not have sufficient evidence to prove cheating.

   a. Draw the payoff matrix.
   b. Which outcome do you expect? Why?

14. **Case Study: Timely Fashions Boost Profits for Zara**   Firms earn economic profit by offering a differentiated product. How does Zara differentiate its clothing?

Global Economic Watch Exercises

Login to www.cengagebrain.com and access the Global Economic Watch to do these exercises.

15. **GLOBAL ECONOMIC WATCH**   Go to the Global Economic Crisis Resource Center. Select Global Issues in Context. In the Basic Search box at the top of the page, enter the phrase "product and service differentiation." On the Results page, go to the News section. Click on the link for the April 1, 2010, article "Study Results from University of Adelaide Broaden Understanding of Research Policy." According to the article, are innovation-related activities enough to create product and service differentiation?

16. **GLOBAL ECONOMIC WATCH**   Go to the Global Economic Crisis Resource Center. Select Global Issues in Context. In the Basic Search box at the top of the page, enter the term "game theory." Write a paragraph about one example of game theory being used to analyze economic behavior.

Resource Markets

11

- ○ Why do surgeons earn twice as much as general practitioners?
- ○ Why do truck drivers in the United States earn at least 20 times more than bicycle-rickshaw drivers in India?
- ○ Why does prime Iowa corn acreage cost more than scrubland in the high plains of Montana?
- ○ Why are buildings taller in downtown Chicago than those in the suburbs?

To answer these and other questions, we turn to the demand and supply of resources.

You say you've been through this demand-and-supply drill already? True. But the earlier focus was on the product market—that is, on the market for final goods and services. Goods and services are produced by resources—labor, capital, natural resources, and entrepreneurial ability. Demand and supply in resource markets determine the price and quantity of resources. And the ownership of resources determines the distribution of earnings throughout the economy.

Because your earnings depend on the market value of your resources, you should find a study of resource markets particularly relevant to your future. Certainly one consideration in your career choice is the expected earnings associated with alternative careers. The next three chapters examine how demand and supply interact to establish market prices for various resources.

Topics discussed in this chapter include:

- Demand and supply of resources
- Opportunity cost and economic rent
- Marginal revenue product
- Marginal resource cost
- Changes in resource demand

The Once-Over

Just to prove you already know more about resource markets than you may think, try answering the questions that arise in the following examples of resource demand and supply.

Resource Demand

Let's begin with the demand for labor. The manager of Wal-Mart estimates that hiring another sales clerk would increase total revenue by $500 per week but increase total cost by $400 per week. Should Wal-Mart hire another sales clerk? Sure, because profit would increase by $100 per week. *As long as the additional revenue from employing another worker exceeds the additional cost, the firm should hire that worker.*

What about capital? Suppose that you run a lawn service during the summer, getting an average of $50 per lawn. You have all the business you can handle. You mow about 15 lawns a week, for total revenue of $750 a week. You are thinking of upgrading to a larger, faster mower called the Lawn Monster, but it would cost you an extra $500 per week. The bigger mower would cut your time per lawn in half, enabling you to mow 30 lawns per week, so your total revenue would double to $1,500. Should you make the switch? Because the additional revenue of $750 exceeds the additional cost of $500, you should move up to the Monster.

What about natural resources? A neighbor offers Farmer Jones the chance to lease 100 acres of farmland. Jones figures that farming the extra land would cost $70 per acre but would yield $60 per acre in additional revenue. Should Jones lease the extra land? What do you think? Because the additional cost of farming that land would exceed the additional revenue, the answer is no.

These examples show that a *producer demands another unit of a resource as long as its marginal revenue exceeds its marginal cost.*

Resource Supply

You likely also understand the logic behind resource supply. Suppose you are trying to decide between two jobs that are identical in all ways except that one pays more than the other. Is there any question which one you'll take? If the working conditions are equally attractive, you would choose the higher-paying job. Now let's say your choice is between two jobs that pay the same. One has normal 9 to 5 hours, but the other starts at 5 A.M., an hour when your body tends to reject conscious activity. Which would you choose? You would pick the one that suits your tastes.

People supply their resources to the highest-paying alternative, other things constant. Because other things are not always constant, people must be paid more for jobs less suited to their tastes. Your utility depends on both monetary and nonmonetary aspects of the job. Generally, people must be paid more for jobs that are dirty, dangerous, dull, exhausting, illegal, low status, have no future, have no benefits, and involve inconvenient hours than for jobs that are clean, safe, interesting, energizing, legal, high status, have bright prospects, have good benefits, and involve convenient hours.

net 📖 bookmark

What makes a good job good? Working for a good employer might be one factor. Each year, *Fortune* magazine lists the 100 best employers at http://money .cnn.com/magazines/fortune/ bestcompanies/. What factors other than compensation are cited in the report as creating a favorable work environment? What are the best and worst jobs? Go to http://money.cnn .com/magazines/moneymag/ bestjobs/.

The Demand and Supply of Resources

In the market for goods and services—that is, in the product market—households are the demanders and firms are suppliers. Households demand the goods and services that maximize utility, and firms supply the goods and services that maximize profit. In the

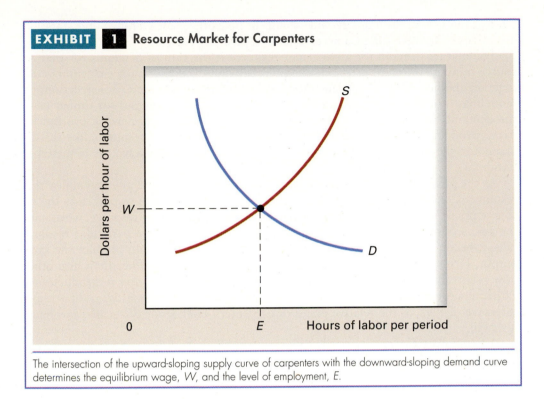

EXHIBIT   1   Resource Market for Carpenters

(y-axis: Dollars per hour of labor; x-axis: Hours of labor per period; curves S and D intersect at W, E)

The intersection of the upward-sloping supply curve of carpenters with the downward-sloping demand curve determines the equilibrium wage, *W*, and the level of employment, *E*.

resource market, roles are reversed: Firms are demanders and households are suppliers. Firms demand the resources that maximize profit, and households supply the resources that maximize utility. *Any differences between the profit-maximizing goals of firms and the utility-maximizing goals of households are sorted out through voluntary exchange in markets.*

Exhibit 1 presents the market for a particular resource—in this case, carpenters. As you can see, the demand curve slopes downward and the supply curve slopes upward. *Like the demand and supply for final goods and services, the demand and supply for resources depend on the willingness and ability of buyers and sellers to engage in market exchange.* This market converges to the equilibrium wage, or the market price, for this type of labor.

The Market Demand for Resources

Why do firms employ resources? Resources produce goods and services, which firms try to sell for a profit. A firm values not the resource itself but the resource's ability to produce goods and services. Because the value of any resource depends on the value of what it produces, the demand for a resource is said to be a **derived demand**—arising from the demand for the final product. For example, a carpenter's pay derives from the demand for the carpenter's output, such as a kitchen cabinet or a new deck. A professional baseball player's pay derives from the demand for ballgames. A truck driver's pay derives from the demand for transporting goods. The derived nature of resource demand helps explain why professional baseball players usually earn more than professional hockey players, why brain surgeons earn more than tree surgeons, and why drivers of big rigs earn more than drivers of delivery vans. Derived demand also explains

derived demand
Demand that arises from the demand for the product the resource produces

why, in the face of an industry-wide slump in box office sales, Hollywood stars like Tom Cruise, Brad Pitt, and Cameron Diaz accepted pay cuts.[1]

The market demand for a particular resource is the sum of demands for that resource in all its different uses. For example, the market demand for carpenters adds together the demands for carpenters in residential and commercial construction, remodeling, cabinetmaking, and so on. Similarly, the market demand for timber sums the demand for this resource as lumber, railway ties, furniture, pencils, toothpicks, paper products, firewood, and so on. The demand curve for a resource, like the demand for the goods produced by that resource, slopes downward, as depicted in Exhibit 1.

As the price of a resource falls, producers are more willing and able to employ that resource. Consider first the producer's greater *willingness* to hire resources as the resource price falls. In developing the demand curve for a particular resource, we assume the prices of other resources remain constant. So if the price of a particular resource falls, it becomes cheaper compared with other resources that could produce the same output. Firms therefore are more willing to hire this resource rather than hire other, now relatively more costly, resources. Thus, we observe *substitution in production*—carpenters for masons, coal for oil, security alarms for security guards, and backhoes for grave diggers, as the relative prices of carpenters, coal, security alarms, and backhoes fall.

A lower price for a resource also increases a producer's *ability* to hire that resource. For example, if the wage of carpenters falls, home builders can hire more carpenters for the same total cost. The lower resource price means the firm is *more able* to employ the resource. Another key resource in residential construction is lumber. The following case study discusses the derived demand for lumber.

CASE STUDY

e activity

The National Association of Home Builders (NAHB) publishes the framing lumber prices for 1,000 board feet from *Random Lengths* and the Chicago Mercantile Exchange (CME) Futures Price each week. For current and historic lumber prices, visit http://www.nahb.org and search for "framing lumber prices." Note how prices change from 2005 through 2009. Why do you think this is so? Examine the CME futures prices. Does the future look better or worse?

WORLD OF BUSINESS

Lumber Prices and Housing Markets   The demand for lumber, like that for carpenters, is a derived demand—derived from lumber demand in its many uses, particularly housing. When the demand for new housing increases, so does the demand for lumber. For example, as the U.S. economy recovered from the 2001 recession, the demand for housing increased. Housing prices rose. This fueled the demand for lumber, a key resource in residential construction. The demand curve for lumber shifted rightward. Increased demand for housing boosted lumber prices between late 2001 and mid-2004. For example, the price per thousand board feet of framing lumber jumped from $281 in October 2001 to $473 in August 2004, a rise of 68 percent.

But in 2005, the U.S. housing market began to slump, and the slide stretched into 2009. The decline in housing demand reduced the demand for building products, shifting the demand curve for lumber to the left. All this had the expected effect on lumber prices,

VisionsofAmerica/Joe Sohm/ © 2010 Jupiterimages Corporation

---

1.   John Hiscock, "Hollywood Stars Meet the Real World," *The Independent*, 16 July 2006.

which fell sharply—for some types of lumber, to levels not seen in a decade. For example, the price per thousand board feet of framing lumber bottomed at $140 in 2009, a 70 percent drop from the high of 2004. As the price of lumber declined, so did lumber's profitability. Lumber mills cut production by 45 percent between 2005 and 2009. Weyerhaeuser Corporation, for example, suspended production indefinitely at two of its mills. Louisiana-Pacific Corporation closed its major mills. But as housing recovered in 2010, so did lumber prices, increasing to about $300 per thousand board feet by March of that year.

The demand for lumber is a prime example of derived demand.

Sources: Liam Pleven and Lester Aldrich, "High Lumber Prices Threaten Housing Market," *Wall Street Journal*, 16 February 2010; Dawn Wotapka, "Builders Get Back in Game," *Wall Street Journal*, 3 March 2010; and "Framing Lumber Prices," National Association of Home Builders, at http://www.nahb.org/generic.aspx?genericContentID=527.

The Market Supply of Resources

The market supply curve for a resource sums all the individual supply curves for that resource. Resource suppliers are more *willing* and more *able* to increase quantity supplied as the resource price increases, so the market supply curve slopes upward, as in Exhibit 1. Resource suppliers are more *willing* because a higher resource price, other things constant, means more goods and services can be purchased with the earnings from each unit of the resource supplied. Resource prices are signals about the rewards for supplying resources. A high resource price tells the resource owner, "The market will reward you more for what you supply." Higher prices draw resources from lower-valued uses, including leisure. For example, as the wage for carpenters increases, the quantity of labor supplied increases. Some carpenters give up leisure to work more.

The second reason a resource supply curve slopes upward is that resource owners are more *able* to increase the quantity supplied as the resource price increases. For example, a higher carpenter's wage means more apprentices can afford to undergo the extensive training to become carpenters. A higher wage *enables* resource suppliers to increase their quantity supplied. Similarly, a higher timber price enables loggers to harvest trees in less accessible forests, a higher gold price enables miners to extract the metal from lower grade ore, and a higher oil price enables producers to drill deeper, to explore more remote parts of the world, and to squeeze oil from tar sands that contain less oil.

Temporary and Permanent Resource Price Differences

People have a strong interest in selling their resources to the highest bidder, other things constant. *Resources tend to flow to their highest-valued use.* If, for example, carpenters can earn more building homes than making furniture, and if the two activities are otherwise equally attractive, they shift into home building until wages in the two uses are equal. Because resource owners seek the highest pay, *other things constant*, earnings should tend toward equality for different uses of the same type of resource. For example, suppose carpenters who build homes earn $25 per hour, which is $5 more than carpenters who make furniture. This difference is shown in Exhibit 2 by an initial wage of $25 per hour in panel (a) and an initial wage of $20 per hour in panel (b). This gap encourages some carpenters to move from furniture making into home building, pulling up the wage in furniture making and driving down the wage in home building. Carpenters migrate into home building until wages equalize.

EXHIBIT 2 Market for Carpenters in Alternative Uses

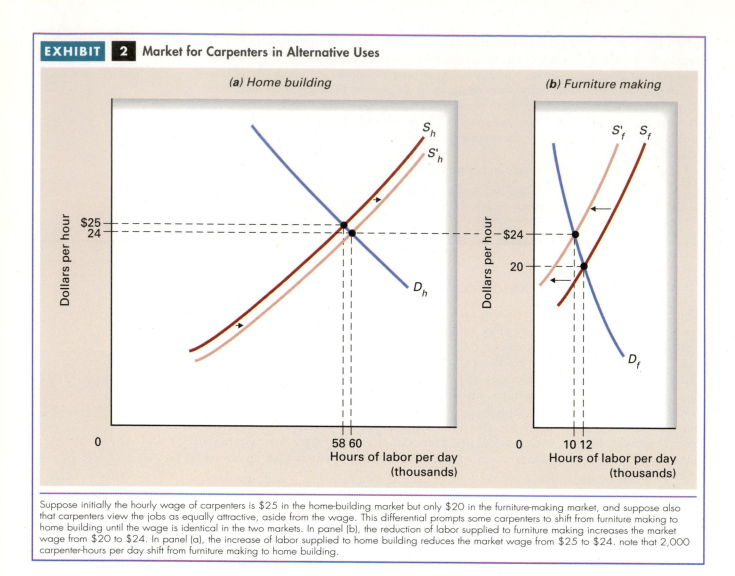

Suppose initially the hourly wage of carpenters is $25 in the home-building market but only $20 in the furniture-making market, and suppose also that carpenters view the jobs as equally attractive, aside from the wage. This differential prompts some carpenters to shift from furniture making to home building until the wage is identical in the two markets. In panel (b), the reduction of labor supplied to furniture making increases the market wage from $20 to $24. In panel (a), the increase of labor supplied to home building reduces the market wage from $25 to $24. note that 2,000 carpenter-hours per day shift from furniture making to home building.

In Exhibit 2, labor supply shifts leftward for furniture making and rightward for home building until the wage reaches $24 in both markets. Note that 2,000 hours of labor per day shift from furniture making to home building. *As long as the nonmonetary benefits of supplying resources to alternative uses are identical and as long as resources are freely mobile, resources adjust across uses until they earn the same in different uses.*

Sometimes earnings appear to differ for seemingly similar resources. For example, corporate economists on average earn more than academic economists, and land in the city goes for more than land in the country. As you will now see, these differences also reflect the workings of demand and supply.

Temporary Differences in Resource Prices

Resource prices might differ temporarily across markets because adjustment takes time. As you have seen, however, a difference between the prices of similar resources prompts resource owners and firms to make adjustments that drive resource prices toward equality, as with the carpenters in Exhibit 2. The process may take years, but when resource markets are free to adjust, price differences trigger the reallocation of resources, which equalizes earnings for similar resources.

Permanent Differences in Resource Prices

Not all resource price differences cause reallocation. For example, for the price of a square yard of land along New York's Fifth Avenue you could buy several acres of land in Upstate New York. Yet such a difference does not prompt upstaters to supply their land to New York City—obviously that's impossible. Likewise, the price of farmland varies widely, reflecting differences in the land's fertility and location. Such differences do not trigger shifts of resource supply. Similarly, certain wage differentials stem in part from the different costs of acquiring the education and training needed to perform particular tasks. This difference explains why brain surgeons earn more than tree surgeons, why ophthalmologists earn more than optometrists, and why airline pilots earn more than truck drivers.

Differences in the nonmonetary aspects of similar jobs also lead to pay differences. For example, other things constant, most people would require higher pay to work in a grimy factory than in a pleasant office. Similarly, academic economists earn less than corporate economists, in part because academic economists typically have more freedom in their daily schedules, their attire, their choices of research topics, and even in their public statements.

Some price differences are temporary because they spark shifts of resource supply away from lower-paid uses and toward higher-paid uses. Other price differences cause no such shifts and are permanent. Permanent price differences are explained by *a lack of resource mobility* (urban land vs. rural land), *differences in the inherent quality of the resource* (fertile land vs. scrubland), *differences in the time and money involved in developing the necessary skills* (certified public accountant vs. file clerk), or *differences in nonmonetary aspects of the job* (lifeguard at Malibu Beach vs. prison guard at San Quentin).

Opportunity Cost and Economic Rent

Shaquille O'Neal earned about $20 million during the season ending in 2010 playing basketball plus at least $10 million more from product endorsements, including his Nike sneakers. But he would probably have been willing to play basketball and endorse products for less. The question is, how much less? What was his best alternative? Suppose his best alternative was to become a full-time rap artist, something he did on the side (as of 2010, he had released six rap albums). Suppose, as a full-time rapper, he could earn $1 million a year, including endorsements. And suppose, aside from the pay gap, he was indifferent between basketball and rap, so the nonmonetary aspects of the two jobs even out. Thus, he had to be paid at least $1 million a year to remain in basketball, and this represents his opportunity cost. *Opportunity cost is what that resource could earn in its best alternative use.*

The amount O'Neal earned in excess of his opportunity cost is called *economic rent.* **Economic rent** is that portion of a resource's earnings that exceeds the amount necessary to keep the resource in its present use. Economic rent is, as the saying goes, "pure gravy." In O'Neal's case, economic rent was $29 million in 2010. Economic rent is producer surplus earned by resource suppliers. The *division* of earnings between opportunity cost and economic rent depends on the resource owner's elasticity of supply. *In general, the less elastic the resource supply, the greater the economic rent as a proportion of total earnings.* To develop a feel for the difference between opportunity cost and economic rent, let's consider three resource markets.

economic rent
Portion of a resource's total earnings that exceeds its opportunity cost; earnings greater than the amount required to keep the resource in its present use

Resource Market A: All Earnings Are Economic Rent

If the supply of a resource to a particular market is perfectly inelastic, that resource has no alternative use. Thus, there is no opportunity cost, and all earnings are economic rent. For example, scrubland in the high plains of Montana has no use other than for grazing cattle. The supply of this land is depicted by the red vertical line in panel (a) of Exhibit 3, which indicates that the 10 million acres have no alternative use. Because supply is fixed, the rent paid to graze cattle on this land has no effect on the quantity of land supplied for cattle grazing. *The land's opportunity cost is zero, so all earnings are economic rent, shown by the blue-shaded area.* Here, fixed supply determines the equilibrium quantity of the resource, but demand determines the equilibrium price.

Resource Market B: All Earnings Are Opportunity Cost

At the other extreme is the market in which a resource can earn as much in its best alternative use as in its present use. This situation is illustrated by the perfectly elastic supply curve in panel (b) of Exhibit 3, which shows the market for janitors in the local school system. Here, janitors earn $10 an hour and supply 1,000 hours of labor per day. If the school system paid less than $10 per hour, janitors could find jobs elsewhere, perhaps in nearby factories, where the wage is $10 per hour. *All earnings reflect opportunity cost.* There is no economic rent in the market for janitors. In this resource market, the horizontal supply curve determines the equilibrium wage, but demand determines the equilibrium quantity.

Resource Market C: Earnings Include Both Economic Rent and Opportunity Cost

If the supply curve slopes upward, most resource suppliers earn economic rent in addition to their opportunity cost. For example, if the market wage for semiskilled work in your college community increases from $10 to $20 per hour, the quantity of labor supplied would increase, as would the economic rent earned by these workers. This market occurs in panel (c) of Exhibit 3, where the pink shading identifies opportunity cost and the blue shading, economic rent. If the wage increases from $10 to $20 per hour, the quantity supplied increases by 5,000 hours per day. For those who had been willing to work for $10 per hour, the difference between $10 and $20 is economic rent. *When resource supply slopes upward, as it usually does, earnings consist of both opportunity cost and economic rent.* In the case of an upward-sloping supply curve and a downward-sloping demand curve, both demand and supply determine equilibrium price and quantity.

Note that specialized resources tend to earn a higher proportion of economic rent than do resources with alternative uses. Thus, Shaquille O'Neal earned a greater *proportion* of his income as economic rent than did the janitor who cleaned the team's locker room. O'Neal would have taken a huge pay cut if he didn't play professional basketball, but the janitor could probably have found another job that paid about the same.

To Review: Given a resource demand curve that slopes downward, when the resource supply curve is vertical (perfectly inelastic), all earnings are economic rent; when that supply curve is horizontal (perfectly elastic), all earnings are opportunity cost; and when that supply curve slopes upward (an elasticity greater than zero but less than infinity), earnings divide between economic rent and opportunity cost. Remember, *the opportunity cost of a resource is what that resource could earn in its best alternative use. Economic rent is earnings in excess of opportunity cost.* Economic rent to a resource holder is like economic profit to the firm.

EXHIBIT 3 Opportunity Cost and Economic Rent

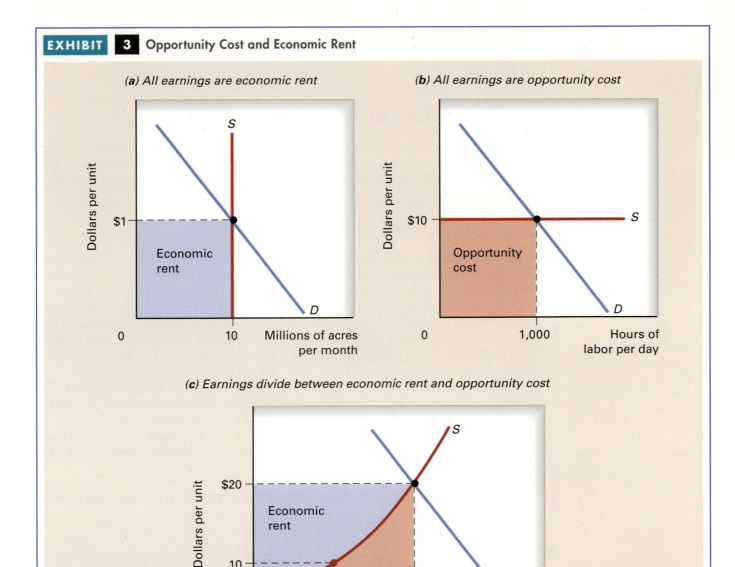

(a) All earnings are economic rent

(b) All earnings are opportunity cost

(c) Earnings divide between economic rent and opportunity cost

In panel (a), the resource supply curve is vertical, indicating that the resource has no alternative use. The price is demand-determined, and all earnings are economic rent. In panel (b), the resource supply curve is horizontal at $10 per hour, indicating that the resource can also earn that much in its best alternative use. Employment is demand-determined, and all earnings are opportunity cost. Panel (c) shows an upward-sloping resource supply curve. Earnings are partly opportunity cost and partly economic rent. Both demand and supply determine the equilibrium price and quantity.

This completes our introduction to resource demand and supply. In the balance of the chapter, we take a closer look at resource demand. The determinants of resource demand are largely the same whether we are talking about labor, capital, or natural resources. The supply of different resources, however, has certain peculiarities depending on the resource, so the supply of resources is taken up in the next chapter.

A Closer Look at Resource Demand

Although production usually involves many resources, we cut the analysis down to size by focusing on a single resource, assuming that employment of other resources remains constant. As usual, we assume that firms try to maximize profit and households try to maximize utility.

The Firm's Demand for a Resource

You may recall that when production costs were introduced in Chapter 7, we considered a moving company, where labor was the only variable resource in the short run. We examined the relationship between the quantity of labor employed and the amount of furniture moved per day. The same approach is used in Exhibit 4, where only one resource varies. Column (1) lists possible employment levels of the variable resource, here measured as workers per day. Column (2) lists the amount produced, or total product, and column (3) lists the marginal product. The *marginal product* of labor is the change in total product from employing one more unit of labor.

With only one worker, total product is 10 units as is the marginal product. The marginal product of a second worker is 9 units. Notice in this example that diminishing marginal returns set in immediately—that is, right after the first worker.

Although labor is the variable resource here, we could examine the marginal product of any resource. For example, we could consider the number of lawns cut per week

| EXHIBIT | 4 | Marginal Revenue Product When a Firm Sells in a Competitive Market |

(1) Workers per Day	(2) Total Product	(3) Marginal Product	(4) Product Price	(5) Total Revenue (5) = (2) × (4)	(6) Marginal Revenue Product (6) = (3) × (4)
0	0	—	$ 20	$ 0	—
1	10	10	20	200	$ 200
2	19	9	20	380	180
3	27	8	20	540	160
4	34	7	20	680	140
5	40	6	20	800	120
6	45	5	20	900	100
7	49	4	20	980	80
8	52	3	20	1040	60

Because of diminishing marginal returns, the marginal product of labor declines as more labor is employed, as shown in column (3). Because this firm sells in a competitive market, it can sell all it wants at the market price of $20 per unit of output, as shown in column (4). The marginal product of labor in column (3) times the product price of $20 in column (4) yields the marginal revenue product of labor in column (6). Labor's marginal revenue product is the change in total revenue as a result of hiring another unit of labor.

by varying the quantity of capital. We might start off with very little capital—imagine cutting grass with scissors—and then move up to a push mower, a power mower, and the Lawn Monster. By holding labor constant and varying the quantity of capital employed, we could compute the marginal product of capital. Likewise, we could compute the marginal product of natural resources by examining crop production for varying amounts of farmland, holding other inputs constant.

Marginal Revenue Product

The important question is: what happens to the firm's *revenue* when additional workers are hired? The first three columns of Exhibit 4 show how output changes with more workers. The *marginal revenue product* of labor indicates how much total revenue changes as more labor is employed, other things constant. The **marginal revenue product** of any resource is the change in the firm's total revenue resulting from employing an additional unit of the resource, other things constant. You could think of the marginal revenue product as the firm's "marginal benefit" from hiring one more unit of the resource. *Marginal revenue product depends on how much additional output the resource produces and at what price that output is sold.*

marginal revenue product
The change in total revenue when an additional unit of a resource is employed, other things constant

Selling Output in Competitive Markets

The calculation of marginal revenue product is simplest when the firm sells in a perfectly competitive market, which is the assumption underlying Exhibit 4. An individual firm in perfect competition can sell as much as it wants at the market price. The marginal revenue product, listed in column (6) of Exhibit 4, is the change in total revenue from hiring an additional unit of the resource. For the perfectly competitive firm, the marginal revenue product is simply the marginal product of the resource multiplied by the product price of $20. Notice that because of diminishing returns, the marginal revenue product falls steadily as the firm employs more of the resource.

Selling Output With Some Market Power

If the firm has some power in the product market—that is, some ability to set the price—the demand curve for that firm's output slopes downward. To sell more, the firm must lower its price. Exhibit 5 reproduces the first two columns of Exhibit 4. But column (3) now shows the price at which that output can be sold. Total output multiplied by the price yields the firm's total revenue, which appears in column (4).

The marginal revenue product of labor, which is the change in total revenue from adding another worker, appears in column (5). For example, the first worker produced 10 units per day, which sell for $40 each, yielding total revenue and marginal revenue of $400. Hiring the second worker adds 9 more units to total product, but to sell 9 more units, the firm must lower the price from $40 to $35. Total revenue increases to $665, which means the marginal revenue product from hiring a second worker is $265. For firms selling with some market power, the marginal revenue product curve slopes downward both because of diminishing marginal returns and because additional output can be sold only if the price falls. A profit-maximizing firm is willing and able to pay as much as the marginal revenue product for an additional unit of the resource. Thus, *the marginal revenue product curve can be thought of as the firm's demand curve for that resource.* You could think of the marginal revenue product curve as the marginal benefit to the firm of hiring each additional unit of the resource.

EXHIBIT 5 The Marginal Revenue Product When a Firm Sells with Market Power

(1) Workers per Day	(2) Total Product	(3) Product Price	(4) Total Revenue (4) = (2) × (3)	(5) Marginal Revenue Product
0	0	—	—	—
1	10	$ 40	$ 400	$ 400
2	19	35	665	265
3	27	31	837	172
4	34	28	952	115
5	40	25	1000	48
6	45	23	1035	35
7	49	21	1029	−6
8	52	19	988	−41

To sell more, this firm must lower the price, as indicated in column (3). Total revenue in column (4) equals total product in column (2) times the product price in column (3). Labor's marginal revenue product in column (5) equals the change in total revenue from hiring another worker. The marginal revenue product declines both because of diminishing marginal returns from labor and because the product price must fall to sell more.

To Review: Whether a firm sells its product in a competitive market or sells with some market power, the marginal revenue product of a resource is the change in total revenue resulting from a 1-unit change in that resource, other things constant. The marginal revenue product curve of a resource is also the demand curve for that resource—it shows the most a firm would be willing and able to pay for each additional unit of the resource. For firms selling in competitive markets, the marginal revenue product curve slopes downward only because of diminishing marginal returns to the resource. For firms selling with some market power, the marginal revenue product curve slopes downward both because of diminishing marginal returns and because additional output can be sold only if the price falls. *For all types of firms, the marginal revenue product is the change in total revenue resulting from hiring an additional unit of the resource.*

Marginal Resource Cost

marginal resource cost

The change in total cost when an additional unit of a resource is hired, other things constant

If we know a firm's marginal revenue product, can we determine how much labor that firm should employ to maximize profit? Not yet, because we also need to know how much labor costs the firm. Specifically, what is the **marginal resource cost**—what does another unit of labor cost the firm? The typical firm hires such a tiny fraction of the market supply that the firm's hiring decision has no effect on the market price of the resource. Thus, each firm usually faces a given market price for the resource and decides only on how much to hire at that price.

For example, panel (a) of Exhibit 6 shows the market for factory workers, measured as workers per day. The intersection of market demand and market supply determines the market wage of $100 per day. Panel (b) shows the situation for the firm. The market wage becomes the firm's marginal resource cost of labor. The *marginal resource cost* curve is the horizontal line drawn at the $100 level in panel (b); this is the labor supply curve to the firm. Panel (b) also shows the marginal revenue product curve, or resource demand curve, based on the schedule presented in Exhibit 4. The marginal revenue product curve indicates the additional revenue the firm gets from adding another worker.

Resource Employment to Maximize Profit or Minimize Loss

Given a marginal resource cost of $100 per worker per day, how much labor should the firm employ to maximize profit? *The firm hires more labor as long as doing so adds more to revenue than to cost—that is, as long as labor's marginal revenue product exceeds its marginal resource cost. The firm stops adding labor once the two are equal.* If marginal resource cost is a constant $100 per worker, the firm hires six workers per day because the marginal revenue product from hiring a sixth worker equals $100. Thus, the firm hires additional workers until

$$\text{Marginal revenue product} = \text{Marginal resource cost}$$

This equality holds for all types of resources employed, whether the firm sells in perfectly competitive markets or sells with some market power. Profit maximization occurs where labor's marginal revenue product equals the market wage. Based on data presented so far, we can't yet determine the firm's actual profit because we don't yet know about the firm's other costs. We do know, however, that in Exhibit 6, a seventh worker would add $100 to cost but would add less than that to revenue, so hiring a seventh worker would reduce the firm's profit (or increase its loss).

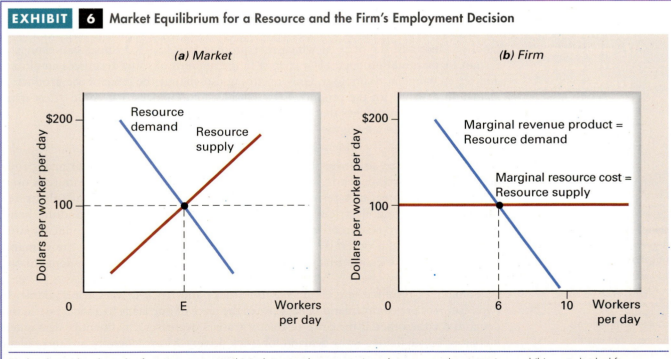

EXHIBIT 6 Market Equilibrium for a Resource and the Firm's Employment Decision

Market demand and supply of a resource, in panel (a), determine that resource's market wage and quantity. In panel (b), an individual firm can employ as much as it wants at the market wage, so that wage becomes the firm's marginal resource cost. The marginal resource cost curve also is the supply curve of that resource to the firm. In panel (b), a resource's marginal revenue product is the firm's demand curve for that resource. The firm maximizes profit (or minimizes its loss) by hiring a resource up to the point where the resource's marginal revenue product equals its marginal resource cost, which is six workers per day in this example.

Whether a firm sells in competitive markets or with some market power, the profit-maximizing level of employment occurs where the marginal revenue product of labor equals its marginal resource cost. Similarly, profit-maximizing employment of other resources, such as natural resources and capital, occurs where their respective marginal revenue products equal their marginal resource costs. Each unit of a resource must "pull its own weight"—that is, each unit must bring in additional revenue that at least covers the additional cost.

Optimal Input and Optimal Output Decisions Are Equivalent

In earlier chapters, you learned how to find the profit-maximizing level of output. Maximum profit (or minimum loss) occurs where the marginal revenue from *output* equals its marginal cost. Likewise, maximum profit (or minimum loss) occurs where the marginal revenue from an *input* equals its marginal resource cost. The two are equivalent ways of deriving the same principle of profit maximization. For example, in Exhibit 6, the firm maximizes profit by hiring six workers when the market wage is $100 per day. Exhibit 4 indicates that a sixth worker adds 5 units to output, which sell for $20 each, yielding labor's marginal revenue product of $100. The *marginal revenue* of that output is the change in total revenue from selling another unit of output, which is $20. The *marginal cost* of that output is the change in total cost, $100, divided by the change in output, 5 units; so the marginal cost of output is $100/5, or $20. Thus, *in equilibrium, the marginal revenue of output equals its marginal cost.* Now that you have some idea of how to derive the demand for a resource, let's discuss what could shift the resource demand curve.

Changes in Resource Demand

As we have seen, a resource's marginal revenue product depends on the resource's marginal product and the price at which that product is sold. Two things can change a resource's marginal product: (1) a change in the amount of other resources employed and (2) a change in technology. Only one thing can change the price of the product: a change in demand for the product. Let's consider first changes that could affect marginal product, then changes that could affect demand for the product.

Change in Other Resources Employed

Although our focus so far has been on a single input, in reality the marginal product of any resource depends on the quantity and quality of other resources used in production. Sometimes resources are *substitutes*. For example, coal substitutes for oil in generating electricity. And ATMs substitute for tellers in handling bank transactions. If two resources are **substitutes**, an increase in the price of one increases the demand for the other. An increase in the price of oil increases the demand for coal, and an increase in the market wage of tellers increases the demand for ATMs.

Sometimes resources are *complements*—trucks and truck drivers, for example. If two resources are **complements**, a decrease in the price of one leads to an increase in the demand for the other. If the price of tractor-trailers decreases, the quantity demanded increases, which increases the demand for truck drivers. More generally, any increase in the quantity and quality of a complementary resource, such as trucks, raises the marginal productivity of the resource in question, such as truck drivers, and so increases the demand for that resource. A bigger and better truck makes the driver more productive. One big reason a truck driver in the United States earns much more than a bicycle-rickshaw driver in India is the truck.

resource substitutes

Resources that substitute in production; an increase in the price of one resource increases the demand for the other

resource complements

Resources that enhance one another's productivity; a decrease in the price of one resource increases the demand for the other

Changes in Technology

Technological improvements can boost the productivity of some resources but make other resources obsolete. The introduction of computer-controlled machines increased the demand for computer-trained machinists but reduced the demand for machinists without computer skills. The development of synthetic fibers, such as rayon and Orlon, increased the demand for acrylics and polyesters but reduced the demand for natural fibers, such as cotton and wool. Breakthroughs in fiber-optic and satellite telecommunications increased the demand for fiberglass and satellites and reduced the demand for copper wire.

Computer programs are changing job prospects in fields such as law, medicine, accounting, and architecture. For example, Quicken's WillMaker software has written more wills than any lawyer alive. In medicine, software such as Skyscape's 5-Minute Clinical Consult is a handheld program that helps doctors diagnose more than a thousand medical and surgical conditions. In accounting, software such as TurboTax completes tax forms with ease. And in architecture, three-dimensional modeling programs such as 3D Home Architect help configure all aspects of a structure. As software and hardware get cheaper, better, and easier to use, the demand for some professional services declines.

Changes in the Demand for the Final Product

Because the demand for a resource is *derived* from the demand for the final output, any change in the demand for output affects resource demand. For example, an increase in the demand for video games increases their market price and thereby increases the marginal revenue product of game programmers.

To Review: The demand for a resource depends on its marginal revenue product, which is the change in total revenue resulting from employing one more unit of the resource. Any change that increases a resource's marginal revenue product increases resource demand.

The Optimal Use of More Than One Resource

As long as marginal revenue product exceeds marginal resource cost, a firm can increase profit or reduce a loss by employing more of that resource. Again, the firm hires more of a resource until the marginal revenue product just equals the marginal resource cost. This principle holds for each resource employed. The opening paragraph asked why buildings in downtown Chicago are taller than those in the suburbs. Land and capital, to a large extent, substitute in the production of building space. Because land is more expensive downtown than in the suburbs, builders downtown substitute capital for land, building up instead of out. Hence, buildings are taller closer to the center of the city and are tallest in cities where land is most expensive. Buildings in Chicago and New York City are taller than those in Salt Lake City and Tucson, for example.

The high price of land in metropolitan areas has other implications for the efficient use of resources. For example, in New York City, as in many large cities, food carts seem to be on every corner. New York City has more than 3,000 of them. Why are they so popular? Consider the resources needed to supply sidewalk food: land, labor, capital, food, and perhaps a tiny morsel of entrepreneurial ability. Which of these do you suppose is most expensive in New York City? Retail space along Madison Avenue's Golden Mile can rent for an average $800 a year per square foot (even after the drop that followed the financial crisis of 2008). Because operating a food cart requires about 6 square yards (or 54 square feet), renting that space could cost as much as $43,000 a year. Aside from the necessary public permits, however, space on the public sidewalk is free to vendors. Profit-maximizing street vendors substitute public sidewalks for costly commercial space. (Incidentally, does free public space mean sidewalk vendors earn long-run economic profit?)

Government policy can affect resource allocation in other ways, as discussed in this closing case study.

CASE STUDY

PUBLIC POLICY

The McMinimum Wage   In 2007, Congress and the president passed a law increasing the minimum wage from $5.15 to $7.25 an hour in three steps of 70 cents over two years. At the time, only about 4 percent of all workers earned less than $7.25 an hour. That group included mostly young workers, the majority part time, primarily in service and sales jobs. When the law was passed, 30 states plus the District of Columbia had their own minimum wages exceeding $5.15, with Washington State the highest at $7.93. In addition, more than 100 municipalities across the nation have introduced so-called *living-wage laws* that set minimum wages exceeding federal or state minimums. In Washington, D.C., for example, certain employers must pay at least $11.75 per hour.

Ever since a federal minimum wage of 25 cents was established in 1938, economists have been debating the benefits and costs of the law. The law initially covered only 43 percent of the workforce—primarily workers in large firms involved in interstate commerce. Over the years, the minimum wage has been raised and the coverage has been broadened. By 2010, coverage more than doubled to about 90 percent of the workforce (groups still not covered include those working in small retail establishments and in small restaurants).

Advocates of minimum-wage legislation argue that it can increase the income of the poorest workers. Critics claim that it can cause employers either to cut nonwage compensation or to eliminate jobs. Dozens of studies have examined the effects of the minimum wage on employment. A few found a small positive effect on employment, but most found either no effect or a negative effect, particularly for teenage workers. One reason a higher minimum wage may not reduce total employment is that employers often respond by substituting part-time jobs for full-time jobs, by substituting more-qualified minimum-wage workers (such as college students) for less-qualified workers (such as high school dropouts), and by adjusting nonwage components of the job to reduce costs or increase worker productivity.

Here are some nonwage adjustments an employer could impose on workers in response to a higher minimum wage: reduced work hours, less convenient work hours, greater expected work effort, less on-the-job training, less time for meals and breaks,

less extra pay for night shifts, fewer paid vacation days, fewer paid holidays, less sick leave, fewer health-care benefits, tighter limits on arriving late for work or leaving early, greater restrictions on personal phone calls or texting, and so on. For example, one researcher found that restaurants responded to a higher minimum wage by reducing vacation time and cutting night-shift premiums. Other researchers found that the imposition of a living-wage ordinance in Los Angeles caused employers to switch from untrained workers to those with formal training.

Of most concern to economists is a possible reduction in on-the-job training of young workers, especially those with little education. A higher minimum wage also raises the opportunity cost of staying in school. According to one study, a higher minimum wage encouraged some 16- to 19-year-olds to quit school and look for work, though many failed to find jobs. Thus, an increase in the minimum wage may have the unintended consequence of cutting school enrollment. And those who had already dropped out were more likely to become unemployed. By December 2009, more than half of African American males in their teens who wanted to work could not find jobs.

A survey of 193 labor economists found that 87 percent believed "a minimum wage increases unemployment among young and unskilled workers." Minimum-wage increases, however, have broad public support. In one poll, the highest support, 81 percent, came from those aged 18 to 29, the group most likely to be affected by a hike in the minimum wage.

Sources: David Fairris and Leon Bujanda, "The Dissipation of Minimum Wage Gains for Workers Through Labor-Labor Substitution: Evidence from the Los Angeles Living Wage Ordinance," *Southern Economic Journal*, 75 (October 2008): 473–96; Robert Whaples, "Is There Consensus Among American Labor Economists?" *Journal of Labor Research* 27 (Fall 1996): 725–734; William Alpert, *The Minimum Wage in the Restaurant Industry* (Praeger, 1986); "Lost Wages of Youth," *Wall Street Journal*, 5 March 2010; and Joseph Sabia, "Identifying Minimum Wage Effects," *Industrial Relations*, 48 (April 2009): 311–328.

Conclusion

A firm hires each resource until the marginal revenue product of that resource equals its marginal cost. The objective of profit maximization ensures that to produce any given level of output, firms employ the least-cost combination of resources and thereby use the economy's resources most efficiently. Although our focus has been on the marginal productivity of each resource, we should keep in mind that an orchestra of resources combines to produce output, so the marginal productivity of a particular resource depends in part on the amount and quality of other resources employed.

Summary

1. Firms demand resources to maximize profit. Households supply resources to maximize utility. The profit-maximizing goals of firms and the utility-maximizing goals of households are reconciled through voluntary exchange in resource markets.

2. Because the value of any resource depends on what it produces, the demand for a resource is a derived demand—arising from the demand for the final product. Resource demand curves slope downward because firms are more willing and able to increase quantity demanded as the price of a resource declines. Resource supply curves slope upward because resource owners are more willing and able to increase quantity supplied as their reward for doing so increases.

3. Some differences in the market prices of similar resources trigger the reallocation of resources to equalize those prices. Other price differences do not cause a shift of resources among uses because of a lack of resource mobility, differences in the inherent quality of the resources, differences in the time and money involved in developing necessary skills, and differences in nonmonetary aspects of jobs.

4. Resource earnings divide between (a) opportunity cost and (b) economic rent—that portion of earnings that exceeds opportunity cost. If a resource has no other use, earnings consist entirely of economic rent. If a resource has other uses that pay just as well, earnings consist entirely of opportunity cost. Most resources earn both economic rent and opportunity cost.

5. A firm's demand curve for a resource is the resource's marginal revenue product curve, which shows the change in total revenue from employing one more unit of the resource, other things constant. If a firm sells output in a competitive market, the marginal revenue product curve slopes downward because of diminishing marginal returns. If a firm has some power in the product market, the marginal revenue product curve slopes downward both because of diminishing marginal returns and because the price must fall to sell more.

6. The demand curve for a resource shifts to the right if (a) its marginal productivity increases, (b) the output price increases, (c) the price of a substitute resource increases, or (d) the price of a complement resource decreases.

7. Marginal resource cost is the change in total cost resulting from employing one more unit of the resource, other things constant. A firm maximizes profit by employing each resource up to the point where its marginal revenue product equals its marginal resource cost. This is the flip side of the profit-maximizing output decision that equates marginal revenue with marginal cost.

Key Concepts

Questions for Review

1. **RESOURCE DEMAND AND SUPPLY**   Answer each of the following questions about the labor market:

   a. Which economic decision makers determine the demand for labor? What is their goal, and what decision criteria do they use in trying to reach that goal?

   b. Which economic decision makers determine the supply of labor? What is their goal and what decision criteria do they use in trying to reach that goal?

   c. In what sense is the demand for labor a derived demand?

2. **Case Study: Housing Markets and Lumber Prices**   Between 2001 and 2009, how was the demand for lumber affected by the demand for housing? In what sense is the demand for lumber a derived demand?

3. **MARKET SUPPLY FOR RESOURCES**   Explain why the market supply curve of a resource slopes upward.

4. **RESOURCE PRICE DIFFERENCES**   Distinguish between how the market reacts to a temporary difference in prices for the same resource and how the market reacts to a permanent difference. Why do the reactions differ?

5. **OPPORTUNITY COST AND ECONOMIC RENT**   On-the-job experience typically enhances a person's productivity in that particular job. If the person's salary increases to reflect increased experience but the additional experience has no relevance for other jobs, does this higher salary reflect an increase in opportunity cost or in economic rent?

6. **FIRM'S DEMAND FOR A RESOURCE**   How does the law of diminishing marginal returns affect a firm's demand for labor?

7. **SHIFTS OF RESOURCE DEMAND**   Many countries are predominantly agricultural. How would changes in the supply of fertilizer affect the marginal product, and thus the income, of farmers in such countries?

8. **OPTIMAL USE OF MORE THAN ONE RESOURCE**   Explain the rule for determining optimal resource use when a firm employs more than one resource.

Problems and Exercises

9. **OPPORTUNITY COST AND ECONOMIC RENT**   Define economic rent. In the graph below, assume that the market demand curve for labor is initially D_1.

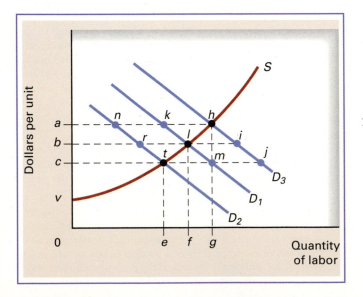

a. What are the equilibrium wage rate and employment level? What is the economic rent?

b. Next assume that the price of a substitute resource increases, other things constant. What happens to demand for labor? What are the new equilibrium wage rate and employment level? What happens to economic rent?

c. Suppose instead that demand for the final product drops, other things constant. Using labor demand curve D_1 as your starting point, what happens to the demand for labor? What are the new equilibrium wage rate and employment level? Does the amount of economic rent change?

10. **FIRM'S DEMAND FOR A RESOURCE**   Use the following data to answer the questions below. Assume a perfectly competitive product market.

Units of Labor	Units of Output
0	0
1	7
2	13
3	18
4	22
5	25

a. Calculate the marginal revenue product for each additional unit of labor if output sells for $3 per unit.
b. Draw the demand curve for labor based on the above data and the $3-per-unit product price.
c. If the wage rate is $15 per hour, how much labor will be hired?
d. Using your answer to part (c), compare the firm's total revenue to the total amount paid for labor. Who gets the difference?
e. What would happen to your answers to parts (b) and (c) if the price of output increased to $5 per unit, other things constant?

11. SELLING OUTPUT AS A PRICE TAKER   If a competitive firm hires another full-time worker, total output increases from 100 units to 110 units per week. Suppose the market price of output is $25 per unit. What is the maximum weekly wage at which the firm would hire that additional worker?

12. SHIFTS OF RESOURCE DEMAND   A local pizzeria hires college students to make pizza, wait on tables, take phone orders, and deliver pizzas. For each situation described, determine whether the demand for student employees by the restaurant would increase, decrease, or remain unchanged. Explain each answer.

a. The demand for pizza increases.
b. Another pizzeria opens up next door.
c. An increase in the minimum wage raises the cost of hiring student employees.
d. The restaurant buys a computer system for taking phone orders.

13. Case Study: The McMinimum Wage   Describe some ways that an employer might adjust to an increase in the minimum wage.

Global Economic Watch Exercises

Login to www.cengagebrain.com and access the Global Economic Watch to do these exercises.

14. GLOBAL ECONOMIC WATCH   Go to the Global Economic Crisis Resource Center. Select Global Issues in Context. In the Basic Search box at the top of the page, enter the phrase "minimum wage face-off." Click on the link for the May 11, 2010, editorial "The Minimum Wage Face-Off." According to the editorial, what is one advantage and one disadvantage of raising the Nigerian minimum wage?

15. GLOBAL ECONOMIC WATCH   Go to the Global Economic Crisis Resource Center. Select Global Issues in Context. In the Basic Search box at the top of the page, enter the term "housing market." Write a paragraph about the recent housing market in a foreign country. How are resource costs affecting housing prices? Alternatively, how is housing demand affecting resource prices?

Labor Markets and Labor Unions

12

AP Photo/Robert Coplin

○ How do you divide your time between work and leisure?

○ Why do some people work *less* if the wage increases enough?

○ For example, why do unknown rock bands play hours for peanuts, while famous bands play much less for much more?

○ Why are butchers more likely than surgeons to mow their own lawns?

○ What determines the wage structure in the economy?

○ What else besides the wage affects your labor supply?

○ In what sense have labor unions become the victims of their own success?

This chapter digs deeper into labor markets and wage determination.

You can be sure of one thing: demand and supply play a central role in all this. You have already considered the demand for resources. Demand depends on a resource's marginal revenue product. The first half of this chapter focuses on the supply of labor, then brings demand and supply together to arrive at the market wage. The second half considers the role of labor unions.

We examine the economic impact of unions and review recent trends in union membership.

Topics discussed include:

* Theory of time allocation
* Backward-bending labor supply curve
* Nonwage factors in labor supply
* Why wages differ
* Unions and collective bargaining
* Union wages and employment
* Trends in union membership

Labor Supply

As a resource supplier, you have a labor supply curve for each of the many possible uses of your labor. To some markets, your quantity supplied is zero over the realistic range of wages. The qualifier "over the realistic range" is added because, for a high enough wage (say, $1 million per hour), you might supply labor to just about *any* activity. In most labor markets, your quantity supplied may be zero either because you are *willing* but *unable* to perform the job (professional golfer, airline pilot, novelist) or because you are *able* but *unwilling* to do so (soldier of fortune, prison guard, P.E. instructor). You have as many individual supply curves as there are labor markets, just as you have as many individual demand curves as there are markets for goods and services. Your labor supply to each market depends, among other things, on your abilities, your taste for the job, and the opportunity cost of your time. Your supply to a particular labor market assumes that wages in other markets are constant, just as your demand for a particular product assumes that other prices are constant.

Labor Supply and Utility Maximization

Recall the definition of economics: *the study of how people use their scarce resources in an attempt to satisfy their unlimited wants*—that is, how people use their scarce resources to maximize their utility. Two sources of utility are of special interest in this chapter: the consumption of goods and services and the enjoyment of leisure. The utility derived from consumption serves as the foundation of demand. Another valuable source of utility is leisure—time spent relaxing with friends, sleeping, eating, watching TV, gaming, reading for pleasure, and in other recreation. Leisure is a normal good that, like other goods, is subject to the law of diminishing marginal utility. Thus, the more leisure time you have, the less you value an additional hour of it. Sometimes you may have so much leisure that you "have time on your hands" and are "just killing time." As that sage of the comic page Garfield the cat once lamented, "Spare time would be more fun if I had less to spare." Or as Shakespeare wrote, "If all the year were playing holidays, to sport would be as tedious as to work." Leisure's diminishing marginal utility explains why some of the "idle rich" may grow bored in their idleness.

Three Uses of Time

Some of you are at a point in your careers when you have few resources other than your time. Time is the raw material of life. You can use your time in three ways. First, you can undertake **market work**—selling your time in the labor market. In return for a wage, you surrender control of your time to the employer. Second, you can undertake **nonmarket work**—using time to produce your own goods and services. Nonmarket work includes the time you spend doing your laundry, making a sandwich, or cleaning up after yourself. Nonmarket work also includes the time spent acquiring skills and education that enhance your productivity. Although studying and attending class may provide little immediate utility, you expect that the knowledge and perspective so gained will enrich your future. Third, you can spend time in **leisure**—using your time in nonwork pursuits.

Work and Utility

Unless you are among the fortunate few, work is not a pure source of utility, as it's often boring, uncomfortable, and aggravating. In short, time spent working can be "a real pain," a source of *disutility*—the opposite of utility. And work is subject *to increasing marginal disutility*—the more you work, the greater the marginal disutility of working

market work
Time sold as labor

nonmarket work
Time spent getting an education or on do-it-yourself production for personal consumption

leisure
Time spent on nonwork activities

another hour. In the extreme, you get burned out from overwork. You may work none-theless, because your earnings buy goods and services. You expect the utility from these products to more than offset the disutility of work. Thus, the *net utility of work*—the utility of the additional consumption possibilities from earnings minus the disutility of the work itself—usually makes some amount of work an attractive use of your time. In the case of market work, your income buys goods and services. In the case of non-market work, either you produce goods and services directly, as in making yourself a sandwich, or you invest your time in education with an expectation of higher future earnings and higher future consumption possibilities.

Utility Maximization

Within the limits of a 24-hour day, seven days a week, you balance your time among market work, nonmarket work, and leisure to maximize utility. As a rational consumer, *you attempt to maximize utility by allocating your time so that the expected marginal utility of the last unit of time spent in each activity is identical.* Thus, in the course of a week or a month, the expected marginal utility of the last hour of leisure equals the ex-pected net marginal utility of the last hour of market work, which equals the expected net marginal utility of the last hour of nonmarket work. In the case of time devoted to acquiring more human capital, you must consider the marginal utility expected from the future increase in earnings that result from your enhanced productivity.

Maybe at this point you are saying, "Wait a minute. I don't know what you're talk-ing about. I don't allocate my time like that. I just sort of bump along, doing what feels good." Economists do not claim that you are even aware of making these marginal calculations. But as a rational decision maker, you allocate your scarce time trying to satisfy your unlimited wants, or trying to maximize utility. And utility maximization, or "doing what feels good," implies that you act *as if* you allocated your time to derive the same expected net marginal utility from the last unit of time spent in each alterna-tive use.

You probably have settled into a rough plan for meals, work, entertainment, study, sleep, and so on—a plan that fits your immediate objectives. This plan is probably in constant flux as you make expected and unexpected adjustments in your use of time. For example, last weekend you may have failed to crack a book, despite good inten-tions. This morning you may have overslept because you were up late. Over a week, a month, or a year, however, your use of time is roughly in line with an allocation that maximizes utility as you perceive it at the time. Put another way, if you could alter your use of time to increase your utility, you would do so. Nobody's stopping you! You may emphasize immediate gratification over long-term goals, but, hey, that's your choice and you bear the consequences. *This time-allocation process ensures that at the margin, the expected net utilities from the last unit of time spent in each activity are equal.*

Because information is costly and because the future is uncertain, you sometimes make mistakes. You don't always get what you expect. Some mistakes are minor, such as going to a movie that turns out to be a waste of time. But other mistakes can be costly. For example, some people are now studying for a field that will grow crowded by the time they graduate, or some people may be acquiring skills that new technology will soon make obsolete.

Implications

The theory of time allocation described thus far has several implications for individual choice. First, consider the choices among market work, nonmarket work, and leisure. The higher your market wage, other things constant, the higher your opportunity cost of leisure and nonmarket work. For example, those who earn a high wage spend less time in nonmarket work, other things constant. Surgeons are less likely to mow their lawns than are butchers. And among those earning the same wage, those more productive in nonmarket work—handy around the house, good cooks—do more for themselves. Conversely, those who are all thumbs around the house and have trouble boiling water hire more household services and eat out more.

By the same logic, the higher the expected earnings right out of high school, other things constant, the higher the opportunity cost of attending college. Most young, successful movie stars do not go to college, and many even drop out of high school, as noted earlier. Promising athletes often turn professional as soon as they can. But the vast majority of people, including female basketball stars, do not face such a high opportunity cost of higher education. As one poor soul lamented, "Since my wife left me, my kids joined a cult, my job is history, and my dog died, I think now might be a good time to go back for an MBA."

Wages and Individual Labor Supply

To breathe life into the time-allocation problem, consider your choices for the summer. If you can afford to, you can take the summer off, spending it entirely on leisure, perhaps as a fitting reward for a rough academic year. Or you can get a job. Or you can undertake nonmarket work, such as cleaning the garage, painting the house, or attending summer school. As a rational decision maker, you select the mix of leisure, market work, and nonmarket work that you expect will maximize your utility. And the optimal combination is likely to involve allocating time to each activity. For example, even if you work, you might still take one or two summer courses.

Suppose the only summer job available is some form of unskilled labor, such as working in a fast-food restaurant or for the municipal parks department. For simplicity, let's assume that you view all such jobs as equally attractive (or unattractive) in terms of their nonmonetary aspects, such as working conditions, working hours, and so on. (These nonmonetary aspects are discussed in the next section.) If there is no difference among these unskilled jobs, the most important question for you in deciding how much market labor to supply is: What's the market wage?

Suppose the wage is $7 per hour, not even the legal minimum. Rather than working for a wage that low, you might decide to work around the house, attend summer school, take a really long nap, travel across the country to find yourself, or perhaps pursue some combination of these. In any case, you supply no market labor at such a low wage. The market wage must rise to $8 before you supply any market labor. Suppose at a wage of $8, you supply 20 hours per week, perhaps taking fewer summer courses and shorter naps.

As the wage increases, your opportunity cost of time spent in other activities rises, so you substitute market work for other uses of your time. You decide to work 30 hours per week at a wage of $9 per hour, 40 hours at $10, 48 hours at $11, and 55 hours at $12. At a wage of $13 you go to 60 hours per week; you are starting to earn serious money—$780 a week. If the wage hits $14 per hour, you decide to cut back to 58 hours per week. Despite the cutback, your weekly pay rises to $812, which is more than when the wage was $13. Finally, if the wage hits $15, you cut back to 55 per week, earning $825. To explain why you may eventually reduce the quantity of labor supplied, let's consider the impact of wage increases on your time allocation.

Substitution and Income Effects

A higher wage has two effects on your use of time. First, because each hour of work now buys more goods and services, a higher wage increases the opportunity cost of leisure and nonmarket work. Thus, as the wage increases, you substitute market work for other activities. This is the **substitution effect of a wage increase.** Second, a higher wage means a higher income for a given number of hours. This higher income increases your demand for all normal goods. Because leisure is a normal good, a higher income increases your demand for leisure, thereby reducing your allocation of time to market work. The **income effect of a wage increase** tends to reduce the quantity of labor supplied to market work. As the Greek philosopher Aristotle observed, "The end of labor is to gain leisure."

As the wage increases, the substitution effect causes you to work more, but the income effect causes you to work less and demand more leisure. In our example, the substitution effect exceeds the income effect for wages up to $13 per hour, resulting in more labor supplied as the wage increases. When the wage reaches $14, however, the income effect exceeds the substitution effect, causing you to reduce the quantity of labor supplied.

Backward-Bending Labor Supply Curve

The labor supply curve just described appears in Exhibit 1. As you can see, this slopes upward until the wage reaches $13 per hour; then the curve bends backward. The **backward-bending supply curve** gets its shape because the income effect of a higher wage eventually dominates the substitution effect, reducing the quantity of labor supplied as the wage increases. We see evidence of a backward-bending supply curve particularly among high-wage individuals, who reduce their work and consume more leisure as their wage increases. For example, entertainers typically perform less as they become more successful. Unknown musicians play for hours for hardly any money; famous musicians play much less for much more. But the backward-bending supply curve may also apply to ordinary workers, such as you during the summer or to New York City taxi drivers, who reduced their hours after an increase in taxi fares.[1] The income effect of rising real wages helps explain the decline in the U.S. workweek from an average of 60 hours in 1900 to about 40 hours in 1960 to about 34 hours today.

Flexibility of Hours Worked

The model we have been discussing assumes that workers have some control over how much they work. Opportunities for part-time work and overtime allow workers to put together their preferred quantity of hours. Workers also have some control over the timing and length of their vacations. More generally, individuals usually have some control over how long to stay in school, when to enter or leave the workforce, and when to retire. Thus, most people actually have more control over the number of hours worked than you might think.

Nonwage Determinants of Labor Supply

The supply of labor to a particular market depends on a variety of factors other than the wage, just as the demand for a particular good depends on factors other than the price. As we have already seen, the supply of labor to a particular market depends on wages in other labor markets. What nonwage factors shape a college student's labor supply for the summer?

substitution effect of a wage increase
A higher wage encourages more work because other activities now have a higher opportunity cost

income effect of a wage increase
A higher wage raises a worker's income, increasing the demand for all normal goods, including leisure, so the quantity of labor supplied to market work decreases

backward-bending supply curve of labor
As the wage rises, the quantity of labor supplied may eventually decline; the income effect of a higher wage increases the demand for leisure, which reduces the quantity of labor supplied enough to more than offset the substitution effect of a higher wage

1. Orley Ashenfelter, Kirk Doran, and Bruce Schaller, "A Shred of Credible Evidence on the Long Run Elasticity of Labor Supply," NBER Working Paper 15746, (February 2010).

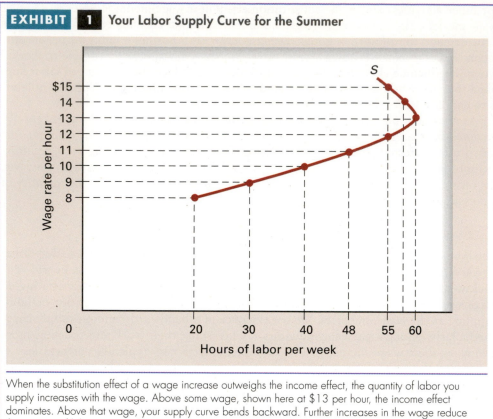

EXHIBIT | **1** | Your Labor Supply Curve for the Summer

When the substitution effect of a wage increase outweighs the income effect, the quantity of labor you supply increases with the wage. Above some wage, shown here at $13 per hour, the income effect dominates. Above that wage, your supply curve bends backward. Further increases in the wage reduce the quantity of labor you supply.

Other Sources of Income

Although some jobs are rewarding in a variety of nonmonetary ways, the main reason people work is to earn money. Thus, your willingness to supply labor depends on income from other sources, including from family, savings, student loans, and scholarships. A student who receives a generous scholarship, for example, faces less pressure to work in the summer or during the college term. More generally, wealthy people have less incentive to work. For example, multimillion-dollar lottery winners often quit their jobs. And those who inherit a large sum are more likely to retire early.[2]

Nonmonetary Factors

Labor is a special kind of resource. Unlike capital or natural resources, which can be supplied regardless of the whereabouts of the resource owner, the supplier of labor must be where the work is performed. Because individuals must usually be physically present to supply labor, such *nonmonetary factors* as the difficulty of the job, the quality of the work environment, and the status of the position become important to labor suppliers. For example, deckhands on crab boats in the icy waters off Alaska can earn over $10,000 for five days of work, but the job is dangerous, winter temperatures seldom exceed zero, and daily shifts allow only three hours of sleep.

2. As found in research by Jeffrey Brown, Courtney Coile, and Scott Weisbenner, "The Effect of Inheritance Receipt on Retirement," *Review of Economics and Statistics*, 92 (May 2010): 425–434.

Consider the different working conditions you might encounter. A campus job that lets you study on the job is more attractive than one with no study time. Some jobs offer flexible hours; other work schedules are rigid. Is the workplace air-conditioned, or do you have to sweat it out? The more attractive the working conditions, the more labor you supply to that market, other things constant. Finally, some jobs convey more status than others. For example, the president of the United States earns less than one-tenth that of corporate heads, but there is no shortage of applicants for the job. Similarly, U.S. Supreme Court justices typically took a huge pay cut to accept the job.

The Value of Job Experience

All else equal, you are more inclined to take a position that provides valuable job experience. Serving as the assistant treasurer for a local business during the summer provides better job experience and looks better on a résumé than serving mystery meat at the college cafeteria. Some people are willing to accept relatively low wages now for the promise of higher wages in the future. For example, new lawyers are eager to fill clerkships for judges, though the pay is low and the hours long, because these positions offer experience and contacts future employers value. Likewise, athletes who play in the minor leagues for little pay believe that experience will give them a shot at the major leagues. Thus, *the more a job enhances future earning possibilities, the greater the supply of labor, other things constant.* Consequently, the pay in such jobs is usually lower than for jobs that impart less valuable experience. Sometimes the pay is zero, as with some internships.

Taste for Work

Just as the taste for goods and services differs among consumers, the taste for work also differs among labor suppliers. Some people prefer physical labor and hate office work. Some become surgeons; others can't stand the sight of blood. Some become airline pilots; others are afraid to fly. Teenagers prefer jobs at Starbucks and Gap to those at McDonald's and Burger King. Many struggling writers, artists, actors, and dancers could earn more elsewhere, but prefer the creative process and the chance, albeit slim, of becoming rich and famous in the arts (for example, the 120,000 members of the Screen Actors Guild average less than $10,000 a year from acting). Some people have such strong preferences for certain jobs that they expect no pay, such as auxiliary police officers or volunteer firefighters.

As with the taste for goods and services, economists do not try to explain how work preferences develop. They simply argue that your preferences are relatively stable and you supply more labor to jobs you like. Based on taste, workers seek jobs in a way that tends to minimize the disutility of work. This is not to say that everyone ends up in his or her most preferred position. The transaction costs of job information and of changing jobs may prevent some matchups that might otherwise seem desirable. But in the long run, people tend to find jobs that suit them. We are not likely to find tour guides who hate to travel, zookeepers who are allergic to animals, or garage mechanics who hate getting their hands dirty.

Market Supply of Labor

In the previous section, we considered those factors, both monetary and nonmonetary, that influence individual labor supply. *The supply of labor to a particular market is the horizontal sum of all the individual supply curves.* The horizontal sum at each particular wage is found by adding the quantities supplied by each worker. If an individual supply curve of labor bends backward, does this mean that the market supply curve for

EXHIBIT 2 Deriving the Market Labor Supply Curve From Individual Labor Supply Curves

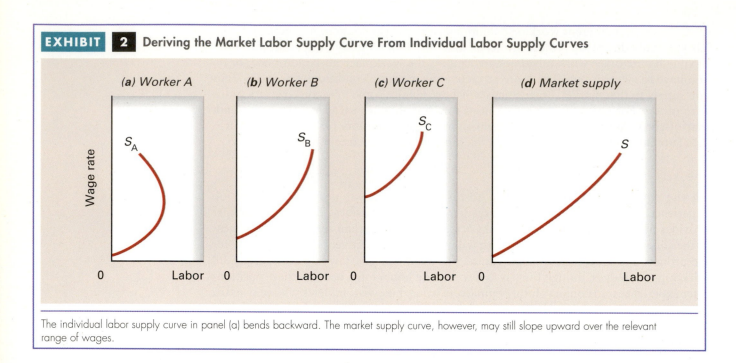

The individual labor supply curve in panel (a) bends backward. The market supply curve, however, may still slope upward over the relevant range of wages.

labor also bends backward? Not necessarily. Because different individuals have different opportunity costs and different tastes for work, the bend in the supply curve occurs at different wages for different individuals. And, for some individuals, the labor supply curve may not bend backward over the realistic range of wages. Exhibit 2 shows how just three individual labor supply curves sum to yield a market supply curve that slopes upward.

Why Wages Differ

Just as both blades of scissors contribute equally to cutting paper, both labor demand and labor supply determine the market wage. Exhibit 3 shows average hourly wages for more than 130 million U.S. workers. Workers are sorted into 22 occupations from the highest to the lowest wage as of May 2009. Management earns the highest wage, at $49.47 an hour. The lowest is the $10.04 an hour averaged by workers preparing and serving food. Wage differences across labor markets trace to differences in labor demand and in labor supply, as you will see. The previous chapter discussed the elements that influence the demand for resources and examined labor in particular. In brief, *a profit-maximizing firm hires labor up to the point where labor's marginal revenue product equals its marginal resource cost*—that is, where the last unit employed increases total revenue enough to cover the added cost. Because we have already discussed what affects the demand for labor—namely, labor's marginal revenue product—let's focus more on labor supply.

Differences in Training, Education, Age, and Experience

Some jobs pay more because they require a long and expensive training period, which reduces market supply because few are willing to incur the time and expense required. But such training increases labor productivity, thereby increasing demand for the skills. Reduced supply and increased demand both raise the market wage. For example,

EXHIBIT **3** **Average Hourly Wage by Occupation in the United States**

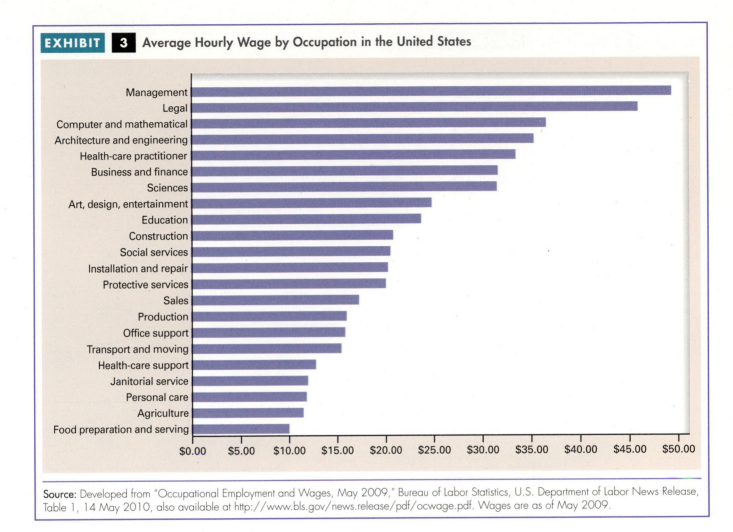

Source: Developed from "Occupational Employment and Wages, May 2009," Bureau of Labor Statistics, U.S. Department of Labor News Release, Table 1, 14 May 2010, also available at http://www.bls.gov/news.release/pdf/ocwage.pdf. Wages are as of May 2009.

certified public accountants (CPAs) earn more than file clerks because the extensive training of CPAs limits the supply to this field and because this training increases the productivity of CPAs compared to file clerks.

Exhibit 4 shows how education and experience affect earnings. Age groups are indicated on the horizontal axis and average annual earnings on the vertical axis. To standardize things, pay is for the highest level of education achieved. The relationship between income and education is clear. At every age, those with more education earn more. For example, among those ages 55–64, workers with professional degrees earned more than twice those with bachelor's degrees and more than five times those without high school diplomas.

Age itself also has an important effect on income. Earnings tend to increase as workers acquire job experience and get promoted. Among educated workers, experience pays more. For example, among those with professional degrees, workers in the 55–64 age group earned on average 70 percent more than those in the 25–34 age group. But among those without high school diplomas, workers in the 55–64 age group earned on average only 14 percent more than those in the 25–34 age group. Differences in earnings reflect the normal workings of resource markets, whereby workers are rewarded according to their marginal productivity.

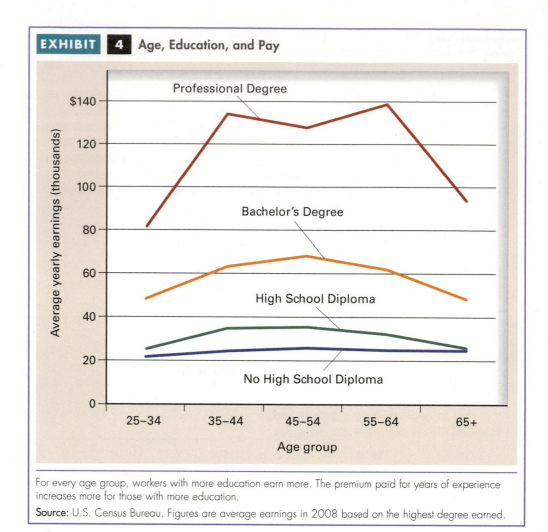

EXHIBIT 4   Age, Education, and Pay

For every age group, workers with more education earn more. The premium paid for years of experience increases more for those with more education.

Source: U.S. Census Bureau. Figures are average earnings in 2008 based on the highest degree earned.

Differences in Ability

Because they are more able and more talented, some people earn more than others with the same training and education. For example, two lawyers may have identical educations, but earnings differ because of differences in underlying ability. Most executives have extensive training and business experience, but only a few get to run large corporations. In professional basketball, some players earn up to 50 times more than others. From lawyers to executives to professional athletes, pay differences reflect differing abilities and different marginal productivities. The following case study examines why the premium awarded greater marginal productivity has grown in recent decades.

WORLD OF BUSINESS

Winner-Take-All Labor Markets   Each year *Forbes* magazine lists the multimillion-dollar earnings of top entertainers and professional athletes. Oprah Winfrey has made that list each year for more than two decades. Her annual income adds up. With wealth now in the billions, she ranks among the world's richest people. Entertainment and pro sports have come to be called **winner-take-all labor markets** because a few key people critical to the overall success of an enterprise are richly rewarded. For example, the credits at the end of a movie list a hundred or more people directly involved in the production. Hundreds, sometimes thousands, more work behind the scenes. Despite a huge cast and crew, the difference between a movie's financial success and failure usually depends on the performance of just a few critical people—the screenwriter, the director, and the lead actors. The same happens in sports. In professional golf tournaments, attendance and TV ratings are significantly higher with Tiger Woods in the mix. In professional basketball, LeBron James has been credited with filling once-empty seats and boosting the value of his team by $160 million. Thus, top performers generate a high marginal revenue product.

But high productivity alone is not enough to get paid a lot. To be paid anywhere near their marginal revenue product, there must be an open competition for top performers. This bids up pay, such as the $20 million per movie garnered by top stars—about 2,000 times the average annual acting earnings of Screen Actors Guild members. Simon Cowell reportedly earned $36 million judging *American Idol* in his final contract year; he was expected to leave that show to develop a new one that could earn him twice as much. In professional sports, before the free-agency rule was introduced (which allows players to seek the highest bidder), top players couldn't move on their own from team to team. They were stuck with the team that drafted them, earning only a fraction of their marginal revenue product.

Relatively high pay in entertainment and sports is not new. What is new is the spread of winner-take-all to other U.S. markets. The "star" treatment now extends to such fields as management, law, banking, finance, even academia. Consider, for example, corporate pay. In 1980, the chief executive officers (CEOs) of the 200 largest U.S. corporations earned about 42 times more than the average production worker. Now, this multiple tops 200. Comparable multiples are much lower in Germany and Japan. Why the big U.S. jump?

First, the U.S. economy has grown sharply in recent decades and is by far the largest in the world—with the value of total output equaling that of the next three economies combined. So U.S. businesses serve a wider market, making the CEO potentially more productive and more valuable. Second, breakthroughs in communications, production, and transportation mean that a well-run U.S. company can now usually sell a valued product around the world. Third, wider competition for the top people has increased their pay. For example, in the 1970s, U.S. businesses usually hired CEOs from company ranks, promoting mainly from within (a practice still common today in Germany and Japan). Because other firms were not trying to bid away the most talented executives, companies were able to retain them for just a fraction of the pay that now prevails in a more competitive market. Today top executives are often drawn from outside the firm—even outside the industry and the country. Fourth, although CEO pay has increased more than sixfold on average since 1980, so has the stock market value of the corporations they run. Fifth, a study of 732 firms in the United States, France, Germany, and the United Kingdom found that U.S. firms on average are more efficient than those in the other countries. One final reason why top CEO pay has increased in America is that high salaries are more socially acceptable here than they once were. High pay is still frowned on in some countries, such as Japan and Germany.

Some top executives are no doubt paid more than they are worth, but nobody claims the market for resources works perfectly. The claim is that an open competition for resources will

winner-take-all labor markets

Markets in which a few key employees critical to the overall success of an enterprise are richly rewarded

e activity

For current news stories about executive compensation, visit *Forbes* magazine's subsection about trends in this area at http://www.forbes.com/. Then search on "Special Report: CEO Compensation." What is the latest explanation for the pay differential? Who are the highest-paid CEOs? For a union's view on executive pay, go to http://www.aflcio.org/corporatewatch/paywatch/ and check the trends on executive pay. Do stock compensation for executives improve executives' performance?

© RD./Leon/Retna Digital—Image by © Leon/Retna Ltd./Corbis

tend to offer the most to those resources contributing the most. And in those cases where marginal productivity is huge, so is the pay.

Sources: Nicholas Bloom and John Van Reenan, "Measuring and Explaining Management Practices Across Firms and Countries," *Quarterly Journal of Economics*, 122 (November 2007): 1351–1408. Bill Livingston, "LeBron," *Cleveland Plain Dealer*, 6 May 2007; "Paula Abdul Stays Focussed on Her Craft," *The Los Angeles Times*, 5 May 2009. Urs Fischbacher and Christian Thoni, "Winner Take All Markets Are Inefficient," *Journal of Economic Behavior and Organization*," 67 (July 2008): 150–163; Xavier Gabaix and Augustin Landier, "Why Has CEO Pay Increased So Much," *Quarterly Journal of Economics*, 123 (February 2008): 49–100. *Economic Report of the President*, February 2010, at http://www.gpoaccess.gov/eop/.

Differences in Risk

Research indicates that jobs with a higher probability of injury or death, such as coal mining, usually pay more, other things constant. Russians working at the partially disabled nuclear power plant, Chernobyl, earned 10 times the national average, but workers there face continued health risk from radiation exposure. Sex workers in Mexico earn 23 percent more for unprotected sex.[3] Truck drivers for American contractors in Iraq earn over $100,000 a year, but the job is dangerous. Workers also earn more, other things constant, in seasonal jobs such as construction, where the risk of unemployment is greater.

Geographic Differences

People have a strong incentive to sell their resources in the market where they earn the most. For example, the National Basketball Association attracts talent from around the world. About 20 percent come from abroad. Likewise, thousands of foreign-trained physicians migrate to the United States each year for the high pay. The same goes for nurses (a nurse from the Philippines can earn six times more in the United States). The flow of labor is not all one way: Some Americans seek their fortune abroad, with American basketball players going to Europe and baseball players to Japan. Workers often face migration hurdles. Any reduction in these hurdles would reduce wage differentials across countries.

Discrimination

Sometimes wage differences stem from racial or gender discrimination in the job market. Although such discrimination is illegal, history shows that certain groups—including African Americans, Hispanics, and women—have systematically earned less than others of equal ability. This is discussed in a later chapter.

To Review: Wage differences trace to training, education, age, experience, ability, risk of injury, risk of job loss, geography, and racial and gender discrimination. Other things equal, members of organized labor earn more than nonmembers. The balance of this chapter discusses the effects of labor unions on labor markets.

Unions and Collective Bargaining

Few aspects of labor markets make news more than labor unions. Labor negotiations, strikes, picket lines, confrontations between workers and employers—all fit TV's "action news" format. Despite media attention, only about one in eight U.S. workers is a

3.   See Paul Gertler et al., "Risky Business: The Market for Unprotected Commercial Sex," *Journal of Political Economy*, 113 (June 2005): 518–550.

union member and nearly all union agreements are reached without a strike. But labor unions are more important than their current membership indicates. Let's examine the tools that unions use to seek higher pay and better benefits for their members.

Types of Unions

A **labor union** is a group of workers who join together to improve their terms of employment. Labor unions in the United States date back to the early days of national independence, when workers in a particular craft—such as carpenters, shoemakers, or printers—formed a local group to seek higher wages and better working conditions. A **craft union** is limited to workers with a particular skill, or craft. Each craft union kept its individual identity but combined forces with other craft unions to form a national organization in 1886, the *American Federation of Labor (AFL)*. The Clayton Act of 1914 exempted labor unions from antitrust laws, meaning that *unions at competing companies could legally join forces.* Unions were also tax exempt. Membership jumped during World War I but fell by half between 1920 and 1933, as the government retreated from its support of union efforts.

The *Congress of Industrial Organizations (CIO)* was formed in 1935 to serve as a national organization of unions in mass-production industries, such as autos or steel. Whereas the AFL organized workers in particular crafts, such as plumbers or carpenters, the CIO consisted of unions whose membership embraced all workers in a particular industry. These **industrial unions** included unskilled, semiskilled, and skilled workers in an industry, such as all autoworkers or all steelworkers.

Collective Bargaining, Mediation, and Arbitration

Collective bargaining is the process by which representatives of union and management negotiate a mutually agreeable contract specifying wages, employee benefits, and working conditions. A tentative agreement, once reached, goes to the membership for a vote. If accepted by the membership, the agreement holds for the years of the contract. If the agreement is rejected, the union can return to the bargaining table to continue negotiations. If negotiations reach an impasse and the public interest is involved, government officials may ask an independent mediator to step in. A **mediator** is an impartial observer who listens to each side separately and then suggests a resolution. If each side still remains open to a settlement, the mediator brings them together to work out a contract, but the mediator has no power to impose a settlement. In certain critical sectors, such as police and fire protection, where a strike could harm the public interest, differences are sometimes settled through **binding arbitration.** A neutral third party evaluates each position and issues a ruling that both sides must accept. Some disputes skip the mediation and arbitration steps and go directly from impasse to strike.

The Strike

A major source of union power is a **strike,** which is a union's attempt to withhold labor to stop production, thereby hoping to force the firm into accepting the union's position. But strikes are also risky for workers, who earn no pay or benefits during the strike and could lose their jobs. Union funds and, in some states, unemployment benefits, may aid strikers some, but incomes still fall substantially. *Although neither party usually wants a strike, both sides, rather than concede on key points, usually act as if they could endure one.* Unions usually picket to prevent or discourage so-called strikebreakers, or "scabs," from crossing the picket lines to work. But the targeted firm, by hiring temporary workers and nonstriking union workers, can sometimes continue production.

labor union
A group of workers who organize to improve their terms of employment

craft union
A union whose members have a particular skill or work at a particular craft, such as plumbers or carpenters

industrial union
A union consisting of both skilled and unskilled workers from a particular industry, such as all autoworkers or all steelworkers

collective bargaining
The process by which union and management negotiate a labor agreement

mediator
An impartial observer who helps resolve differences between union and management

binding arbitration
Negotiation in which union and management must accept an impartial observer's resolution of a dispute

strike
A union's attempt to withhold labor from a firm to halt production

Some industries are more vulnerable to strikes—industries that deal in perishable goods, such as strawberries, and industries where picket lines can turn away lots of customers, such as Broadway theaters. But in other industries, advances in technology have reduced the effectiveness of strikes, as petroleum and chemical workers learned when strikers found that skeleton crews of supervisors could run computer-controlled refineries for a long time.

Union Wages and Employment

Samuel Gompers, the AFL's founder and long-time head, was once asked what unions want. "More!" he roared. Union members, like everyone else, have unlimited wants. But because resources are scarce, choices must be made. A menu of union desires includes higher wages, more benefits, greater job security, better working conditions, and so on. To keep the analysis manageable, let's focus on a single objective, higher wages, and consider three ways unions might increase wages: (1) by forming an inclusive, or industrial, union; (2) by forming an exclusive, or craft, union; and (3) by increasing the demand for union labor.

Inclusive, or Industrial, Unions: Negotiating a Higher Industry Wage

The market demand and supply curves for a particular type of labor are labeled D and S in panel (a) of Exhibit 5. In the absence of a union, the market wage is W and industry employment is E. At the market wage, each firm faces a horizontal, or perfectly elastic,

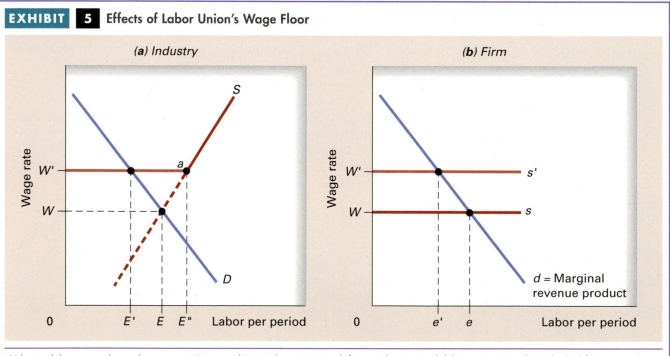

EXHIBIT   5   Effects of Labor Union's Wage Floor

(a) Industry

(b) Firm

Without a labor union, the market wage is W in panel (a). At that wage, each firm can hire as much labor as it wants. The individual firm in panel (b) hires more labor until the marginal revenue product equals the market wage, W. Each firm hires e units of labor, and industry employment is E. If a union negotiates a wage W', which is above the market wage W, the supply curve facing the firm shifts up from s to s'. Each firm hires less labor, e', so industry employment falls to E'. At the union wage there is now an excess quantity of labor supplied equal to $E''-E'$.

supply of labor, as depicted by *s* in panel (b) of Exhibit 5. Thus, each firm can hire as much labor as it wants at the market wage of *W*. The firm hires workers up to the point where labor's marginal revenue product equals its marginal resource cost, resulting in *e* units of labor in panel (b). As we saw earlier, in equilibrium, labor is paid a wage just equal to its marginal revenue product.

With the *inclusive, or industrial,* approach, the union tries to negotiate industry-wide wages for each class of labor. Suppose the union negotiates a wage above the market-clearing level. Specifically, suppose the negotiated wage is *W'* in panel (a), meaning that no labor is supplied at a lower wage. In effect, the market supply of labor is perfectly elastic at the union wage out to point *a*. To the right of point *a*, however, the wage floor no longer applies; *aS* becomes the relevant portion of the labor supply curve. For an industry facing a wage floor of *W'*, the entire labor supply curve becomes *W'aS*, which has a kink where the wage floor joins the upward-sloping portion of the original labor supply curve.

Once this wage floor is negotiated for the industry, each firm in the industry faces a horizontal supply curve of labor at the collectively bargained wage, *W'*. Because the union wage is higher than the market-clearing wage, each firm hires less labor. Consequently, the higher wage leads to a reduction in employment; the quantity of labor demanded by the industry drops from *E* to *E'* in panel (a). At wage *W'* workers in the industry would like to supply, *E"*, which exceeds the quantity of labor demanded, *E'*. Ordinarily this excess quantity supplied would force the wage down. But because union members agree *collectively* to the union wage, individual workers can't work for less, nor can employers hire them for less. *With the inclusive, or industrial, union, which negotiates with the entire industry, the wage is higher and employment lower than they would be in the absence of a union.*

The union must somehow ration the limited jobs available, such as by awarding them based on worker seniority, personal connections within the union, or lottery. Those who can't find union jobs must turn to the nonunion sector. *This increases the supply of labor in the nonunion sector, which drives down the nonunion wage.* So wages are relatively higher in the union sector first, because unions bargain for a wage that exceeds the market-clearing wage, and second, because those unable to find union jobs crowd into the nonunion sector. Studies show that union wages average about 15 percent above the wages of similarly qualified nonunion workers. Exhibit 6 compares median weekly earnings of union and nonunion workers. Note that unions are less successful at raising wages in more competitive sectors. For example, unions have less impact on manufacturing and retail trade, where product markets tend to be competitive. Unions have greater success in services, government, transportation, and construction—sectors that tend to be less competitive. When there is more competition in the product market, employers cannot easily pass along higher union wages as higher product prices. New, nonunion, firms can enter the industry, pay market wages, and sell the product for less.

Exclusive, or Craft, Unions: Reducing Labor Supply

One way to increase wages while avoiding an excess quantity of labor supplied is to somehow reduce the supply of labor, shown in Exhibit 7 as a leftward shift of the labor supply curve in panel (a). This supply reduction increases the wage and reduces employment. Successful supply restrictions of this type require that the union first limit its membership and second force all employers in the industry to hire only union members. The union can restrict membership with higher initiation fees, longer apprenticeship periods, tougher qualification exams, more restrictive licensing

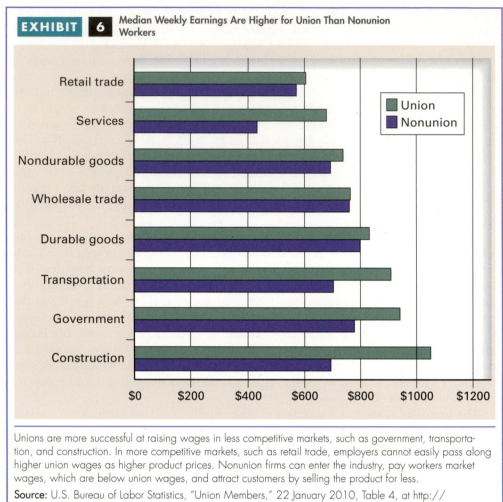

EXHIBIT **6** Median Weekly Earnings Are Higher for Union Than Nonunion Workers

Unions are more successful at raising wages in less competitive markets, such as government, transportation, and construction. In more competitive markets, such as retail trade, employers cannot easily pass along higher union wages as higher product prices. Nonunion firms can enter the industry, pay workers market wages, which are below union wages, and attract customers by selling the product for less.

Source: U.S. Bureau of Labor Statistics, "Union Members," 22 January 2010, Table 4, at http://www.bls.gov/news.release/union2.t04.htm. Figures are for full-time workers in 2009.

requirements, and so on. But even if unions restrict membership, they still have difficulty unionizing all firms in the industry.

Whereas wage setting is more typical of industrial unions, such as autos or steel, restricting supply is more typical of craft unions, such as unions of carpenters, plumbers, or bricklayers. Professional groups—doctors, lawyers, and accountants, for instance—also impose entry restrictions through education, examination, and licensing requirements. These restrictions, usually defended as protecting the public, are often little more than self-serving attempts to increase wages by restricting labor supply.

Increasing Demand for Union Labor

A third way to increase wages is to increase the demand for union labor by somehow shifting the labor demand curve outward as from D to D'' in panel (b) of Exhibit 7. This is an attractive alternative *because it increases both the wage and employment,* so there is no need to restrict labor supply or to ration jobs among union members. Here are some ways unions try to increase the demand for union labor.

EXHIBIT 7 Effect of Reducing Labor Supply or Increasing Labor Demand

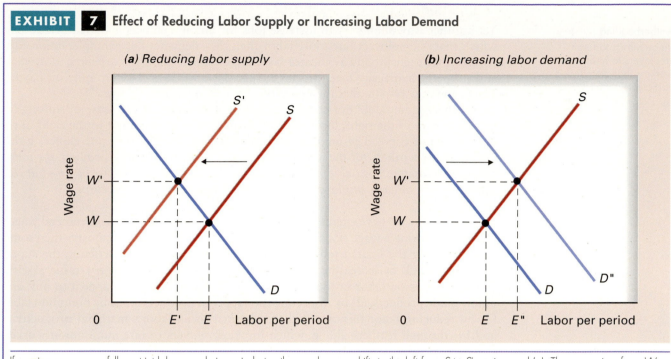

If a union can successfully restrict labor supply in an industry, the supply curve shifts to the left from S to S', as in panel (a). The wage rises from W to W', but at the cost of reducing employment from E to E'. If a union can increase the demand for union labor, as in panel (b), the demand curve shifts right from D to D", raising the wage and increasing employment.

Increase Demand for Union-Made Goods

The demand for union labor may be increased through a direct appeal to consumers to buy only union-made products. Because the demand for labor is a derived demand, increasing the demand for union-made products increases the demand for union labor.

Restrict Supply of Nonunion-Made Goods

Another way to increase the demand for union labor is to restrict the supply of products that compete with union-made products. This approach also relies on the derived nature of labor demand. The United Auto Workers, for example, has supported restrictions on imported cars. Fewer imported cars means greater demand for cars produced by U.S. workers, who are mostly union members. This strategy became less effective when foreign automakers, such as Toyota, established nonunion plants in the United States.

Increase Productivity of Union Labor

Some observers claim union representation improves labor-management relations. According to this theory, unions increase worker productivity by minimizing conflicts, resolving differences, and at times even straightening out workers who goof off. In the absence of a union, a dissatisfied worker may simply quit, increasing job turnover. Turnover is costly to the firm because the departing worker leaves with company-specific, on-the-job training that increases productivity. With a union, however, workers can resolve problems through union channels. Quit rates are in fact significantly lower among union workers (although this could also be due to the higher pay). If unions increase the productivity of workers, the demand for union labor increases.

Featherbedding

Yet another way unions try to increase jobs for union members is by **featherbedding**, which makes employers hire more labor than they demand. For example, union rules require that each Broadway theater have a permanent "house" carpenter, electrician, and property manager. Once the play opens, these workers show up only on payday. The union may require that the box office be staffed by three people.

Featherbedding does not create an increase in demand, in the sense of shifting the demand curve to the right. Instead, it forces an employer to a point to the right of the labor demand curve. The union tries to limit a firm to an all-or-none choice: Either hire so many workers for the job, or we'll strike. Thus, with featherbedding, *the union attempts to dictate not only the wage but also the quantity that must be hired at that wage, thereby moving employers to the right of their labor demand curve.*

To Review: We have examined three ways that unions try to raise members' wages: (1) by negotiating a wage floor above the equilibrium wage for the industry then somehow rationing the limited jobs among union members, (2) by restricting the supply of labor, and (3) by increasing the demand for union labor. Unions try to increase the demand for union labor in four ways: (1) through a direct public appeal to buy only union-made products, (2) by restricting the supply of products made by nonunion labor, (3) by reducing labor turnover and thereby increasing labor's marginal productivity, and (4) through featherbedding, which forces employers to hire more union workers than they want or need.

Trends in Union Membership

In 1955, about 35 percent of U.S. workers belonged to unions. Since then, union membership as a fraction of the workforce has declined steadily. By 2009, only 12 percent of U.S. workers belonged to unions, about the same rate as in 1900. Government workers are much more unionized than other workers—37 percent of government workers are unionized versus just 7 percent of private sector workers; most union members are now government workers. A typical union member is a schoolteacher. Compared with other industrialized countries, the United States ranks relatively low in the extent of unionization, though rates abroad have been declining as well.

The bar graph in Exhibit 8 indicates U.S. union membership rates by age and gender in 2009. The rates for men, shown by the green bars, are higher than the rates for women, in part because women work more in the service sector, where union membership is lower. The highest membership rates are for middle-aged males. Although the exhibit does not show it, black workers have a higher union membership rate than white workers (14 percent vs. 12 percent), in part because African Americans are employed more by government and by heavy industries such as autos and steel, where union representation is higher. Union membership is below average among Asians and those of Hispanic origin (10 percent each).

Union membership rates also vary across states. New York had the highest unionization rate at 25 percent and North Carolina, the lowest at 3 percent. Unionization rates in right-to-work states average only half the rates in other states. In **right-to-work states,** workers in unionized companies do not have to join the union or pay union dues. Over the years, the number of right-to-work states has increased and this has hurt the union movement.

The decline in union membership rates is also due to structural changes in the U.S. economy. Unions have long been more important in the industrial sector than in the service sector. But employment in the industrial sector, which includes manufacturing, mining, and construction, has declined in recent decades as a share of all jobs. What's

EXHIBIT **8** Unionization Rates by Age and Gender

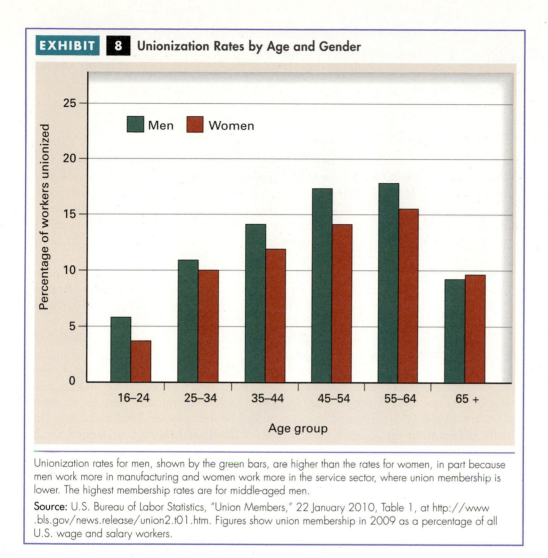

Unionization rates for men, shown by the green bars, are higher than the rates for women, in part because men work more in manufacturing and women work more in the service sector, where union membership is lower. The highest membership rates are for middle-aged men.

Source: U.S. Bureau of Labor Statistics, "Union Members," 22 January 2010, Table 1, at http://www .bls.gov/news.release/union2.t01.htm. Figures show union membership in 2009 as a percentage of all U.S. wage and salary workers.

more, union jobs are a dwindling share of jobs in the industrial sector. For example, in the last three decades, U.S. manufacturing jobs have declined from 20 million to 16 million. But the union share of those jobs dropped from 8 million to only 2 million. Nonunion jobs in manufacturing increased.

Another factor in the decline of the union movement is a growth in market competition, particularly from imports. Increased competition from nonunion employers, both foreign and domestic, has reduced the ability of unionized firms to pass on higher labor costs as higher prices. And fewer union members mean fewer voters who belong to unions, so unions have lost political clout.

Finally, the near disappearance of the strike has cut union power. During the 1970s, an average of about 300 strikes a year in the United States involved 1,000 or more workers. Since 2000, there were only about 20 such strikes a year on average. Worse still for organized labor, many recent strikes have ended badly for union workers; companies such as Caterpillar, Continental Airlines, Hormel Foods, International Paper, and Phelps Dodge Copper hired replacement workers. Union members are now less inclined to strike because of the increased willingness of employers to hire strikebreakers and the increased willingness of workers—both union and nonunion—to work during a strike. Strikes also cut company profits, which hurts workers whose pay is tied to profits, thus dampening the incentive to strike.

The final case study examines the impact of the United Auto Workers on American automakers.

CASE STUDY

e activity

Visit the United Auto Workers at http://www.uaw.org/ to view their history and newsfeed. If you select Where We Work, you will find a list of industries in which the UAW represents workers. Is the UAW a craft union, an industrial union, or some combination of the two?

PUBLIC POLICY

Federal Bailout of GM, Chrysler, and the UAW　In the 1970s, the United Auto Workers (UAW) negotiated what have been called "gold-plated benefits" for their workers and retirees. General Motors, Ford, and Chrysler, the so-called Big Three, believed that because they dominated the U.S. auto market and because they all faced the same labor costs, any higher costs could simply be passed along to car buyers. What could go wrong? Well, what went wrong was an onslaught of fierce competition from foreign automakers who would develop a reputation for high quality at competitive prices. These foreign automakers also began building plants in the United States operated by mostly nonunion workers. Pay and benefits for these nonunion workers, while still attractive, amounted to about three quarters of what UAW workers were getting (and UAW pay was double what average Americans earned).

Not only were UAW wages higher, but union work rules—some 5,000 pages detailing what each worker could and could not be asked to do—imposed expensive inefficiencies on production. If work rules were violated, a union representative could shut down the assembly line. General Motors, Ford, and Chrysler, were making costly vehicles that not enough people wanted to buy, and the companies were losing money by the truckload. GM, for example, lost over $60 billion between 2005 and 2008. Hard hit by fallout from the global financial crisis of 2008 and facing bankruptcy, the Big Three turned to the federal government for help. After some UAW pressure and political wrangling, federal officials agreed on a bailout of about $85 billion, with most of that going to GM (Ford ultimately decided not to accept federal aid).

The agreement called for GM and Chrysler to file for bankruptcy. By doing so, both companies were able to walk away from huge debt burdens built up from years of making costly products that didn't sell well enough. Those who had owned the companies, the stockholders, got wiped out in the bankruptcy—they got nothing. Bondholders and other creditors also took a beating—they would get back less than a third of what they had lent the automakers. Some suppliers were also left hanging and many dealerships were shut down. The group that benefited most from the bailout was UAW workers. They ended up owning 10 percent of the new GM and a majority of the new Chrysler. In years leading up to the bailout, many workers had taken buyouts, meaning that the

company paid them a chunk of money to leave their jobs. The union also made some concessions, but mostly on the pay and benefits of workers hired in the future. Existing workers gave up little in the bailout agreement—certainly little compared to the drubbing suffered by company stockholders, creditors, suppliers, and car dealers.

The new GM emerged from bankruptcy with the federal government owning 61 percent in return for its $43 billion "investment." Much of the federal bailout money would be used to buy out existing workers and shore up the health care fund for union retirees. The Big Three are hoping to hire new workers at lower wages, but recently-laid-off workers still have first claim on any job openings, and they must be rehired at their previous high wages, not the lower wages to be paid new workers.

The Congressional Budget Office estimated that the government bailout would ultimately cost taxpayers $34 billion. That translates into $300 per U.S. household to support the pay and benefits of those making twice what average American workers earn. We can't necessarily blame the UAW for the demise of the American auto industry. Demanding higher pay, better benefits, and more restrictive work rules sounds like the job description of union representatives. But we can blame the managements for going along with these demands. Top auto executives lost their jobs in the bankruptcy. UAW workers gave up little in the bankruptcy.

In today's competitive marketplace, only an efficient, flexible work force will thrive. Technology advances too rapidly to drag along wages that exceed the market rate and featherbedding work rules that slow down production.

Sources: David Leonhardt, "$73 an Hour: Adding It Up," *New York Times*, 10 December 2008; Jonathan Welsh, "General Motors Says It Repaid Bailout. Not True, Says Watchdog Group," *Wall Street Journal*, 4 May 2010; Nick Bunkley, "Progress for Automakers After Losses," *New York Times*, 21 April 2010; and Bill Koenig, "Unions Resist Yielding More as GM, Ford, Chrysler Seek Aid," *Bloomberg*, 12 November 2009.

Conclusion

The first half of this chapter focused on labor supply and explained why wages differ across occupations and among individuals within an occupation. The interaction of labor demand and supply determines wages and employment. The second half of the chapter explored the effect of unions on the labor market. At one time unions dominated some key industries. But as global competition intensifies, employers have a harder time passing higher union labor costs along to consumers. Both in the United States and in other industrial economies, union members represent a dwindling segment of the labor force. Now only 7 percent of private sector workers are union members.

Summary

1. The labor demand curve shows the relationship between the wage and the quantity of labor that producers are willing and able to hire, other things constant. The labor supply curve shows the relationship between the wage and the quantity of labor that workers are willing and able to supply, other things constant. The intersection of labor demand and labor supply determines the market wage and market employment.

2. People allocate their time to maximize utility. There are three uses of time: market work, nonmarket work, and leisure. A person attempts to maximize utility by allocating time so that the expected marginal utility of the last unit of time spent in each activity is identical.

3. The higher the wage, other things constant, the more goods and services can be purchased with that wage, so a higher wage encourages people to substitute market work for other uses of their time. But a higher wage also increases income for a given

amount of work, increasing the demand for all normal goods, including leisure. The net effect of a higher wage on the quantity of labor supplied depends on both the substitution effect and the income effect.

4. The supply of labor depends on factors other than the wage, including (a) other sources of income, (b) job amenities, (c) the value of job experience, and (d) worker tastes.

5. Market wages differ because of (a) differences in training and education; (b) differences in the skill and ability of workers; (c) risk differences, both in terms of the workers' safety and the chances of getting laid off; (d) geographic differences; (e) racial and gender discrimination; and (f) union membership.

6. Labor unions and employers try to negotiate a labor contract through collective bargaining. A major source of union power has been the threat of a strike, which is an attempt to withhold labor from the firm.

7. Inclusive, or industrial, unions attempt to establish a wage floor that exceeds the competitive, or market-clearing, wage. A union wage above the market-clearing level creates an excess quantity of labor supplied, so the union must somehow ration the limited jobs available among its members. Exclusive, or craft, unions try to raise union wages by restricting the supply of labor. Another way to raise union wages is to increase the demand for union labor.

8. Union membership as a percentage of the labor force has been falling for half a century. Reasons for the decline include right-to-work laws, growing global competition, a shift in employment from goods to services, a greater willingness to hire replacements for striking workers, a greater willingness of union members and others to work during strikes, and less political support for the labor movement.

Key Concepts

Questions for Review

1. **USES OF TIME**   Describe the three possible uses of an individual's time, and give an example of each.

2. **WORK AND UTILITY**   Explain the concept of the "net utility of work." How is it useful in developing the labor supply curve?

3. **UTILITY MAXIMIZATION**   How does a rational consumer allocate time among competing uses?

4. **SUBSTITUTION AND INCOME EFFECTS**   Suppose that the substitution effect of an increase in the wage rate exactly offsets the income effect as the hourly wage increases from $12 to $13. What would the supply of labor curve look like over this range of wages? Why?

5. **SUBSTITUTION AND INCOME EFFECTS**   Suppose that the cost of living increases, thereby reducing the purchasing power of your income. If your money wage doesn't increase, you may work *more* hours because of this cost-of-living increase. Is this response predominantly an income effect or a substitution effect? Explain.

6. **NONWAGE DETERMINANTS OF LABOR SUPPLY**   Suppose that two jobs are exactly the same except that one is performed in an air-conditioned workplace. How could you measure the value workers attach to such a job amenity?

7. **WHY WAGES DIFFER**   Why might permanent wage differences occur between different markets for labor or within the same labor market?

8. **Case Study: Winner-Take-All Labor Markets**   What characterizes a winner-take-all labor market? Offer some reasons why corporate heads now earn relatively more than they did in 1980.

9. **MEDIATION AND ARBITRATION**   Distinguish between mediation and binding arbitration. Under what circumstances do firms and unions use these tools? What is the role of a strike in the bargaining process?

10. **THE STRIKE**   Why might firms in industries with high fixed costs be inclined to prevent strikes or end strikes quickly?

11. **INDUSTRIAL UNIONS**   Why are unions more effective at raising wages in oligopolistic industries than in competitive industries?

12. **CRAFT UNIONS**   Both industrial unions and craft unions attempt to raise their members' wages, but each goes about it differently. Explain the difference in approaches and describe the impact these differences have on excess quantity of labor supplied.

13. **Case Study: Federal Bailout of GM, Chrysler, and the UAW**   How would the UAW benefit for increased demand for GM and Chrysler vehicles?

Problems and Exercises

14. **MARKET SUPPLY OF LABOR** The following table shows the hours per week supplied to a particular market by three individuals at various wage rates. Calculate the total hours per week (Q_T) supplied to the market.

Hourly Wage	Hours per Week			
	Q_1	Q_2	Q_3	Q_T
$15	20	0	0	___
16	25	0	0	___
17	35	10	0	___
18	45	25	10	___
19	42	40	30	___
20	38	37	45	___

Which individuals, if any, have backward-bending supply curves in the wage range shown? Does the market supply curve bend backward in the wage range shown in the table?

15. **INDUSTRIAL UNIONS** Review the logic underlying Exhibit 5. Then determine the effect, on the industry and a typical firm, of an increase in the demand for industry output. Show your conclusions on a graph. Does the magnitude of the increase in demand make a difference?

Global Economic Watch Exercises

Login to www.cengagebrain.com and access the Global Economic Watch to do these exercises.

16. **GLOBAL ECONOMIC WATCH** Go to the Global Economic Crisis Resource Center. Select Global Issues in Context. In the Basic Search box at the top of the page, enter the phrase "nonmarket work." On the Results page, go to the News Section. Click on the link for the January 7, 2008, article "Research on Marriage and Family Described by Scientists at University of California." According to the article, what are some differences between work by boys and girls in Indonesia?

17. **GLOBAL ECONOMIC WATCH** Go to the Global Economic Crisis Resource Center. Select Global Issues in Context. In the Basic Search box at the top of the page, enter the term "union strike." Find a website with a date within the two most recent years. Analyze the union situation described.

Capital, Interest, Entrepreneurship, and Corporate Finance

13

AP Photo/Paul Sakuma

○ Why is a movie rental or download only half the price of a movie ticket?

○ Why do you burn your mouth eating pizza?

○ What's seed money and why can't Farmer Jones grow a thing without it?

○ What's the harm in pirated software, music, and DVDs?

○ Why are state lottery jackpots worth much less than the advertised millions?

○ Who is and is not an entrepreneur?

These and other questions are answered in this chapter, which examines how businesses get started and how they are financed.

So far, our discussion of resources has focused primarily on labor markets. This emphasis is appropriate because labor generates most income—more than two-thirds of the total. The rewards to labor, however, depend in part on the amount and quality of the other resources employed, particularly capital. A farmer plowing a field with a tractor is more productive than one scraping the soil with a stick. This chapter first looks at the role of capital in production—its cost and its expected return. Secondly, we consider the role the entrepreneur plays in driving the economy forward. Finally, we explore the sources of corporate finance.

Topics include:

- Production, saving, and time
- Consumption, saving, and time
- Optimal investment
- Loanable funds market
- Present value and discounting
- Role of the entrepreneur
- Corporate finance
- Stocks, bonds, and retained earnings

The Role of Time in Production and Consumption

Time is important in both production and consumption. In this section, we first consider the role of time in the production decision, then show why firms borrow household savings. Next, we consider the role of time in the consumption decision and show why households are rewarded to save, or to defer consumption. By bringing together borrowers and savers, we find the market interest rate.

Production, Saving, and Time

Suppose Jones is a primitive farmer in a simple economy. Isolated from any neighbors or markets, he literally scratches out a living on a plot of land, using only some crude sticks. While his crop is growing, none of it is available for current consumption. Because production takes time, to survive, Jones must rely on food saved from prior harvests. The longer the growing season, the more he must save. Thus, even in this simple example, it is clear that *production cannot occur without savings.*

With his current resources, consisting of land, labor, seed corn, fertilizer, and some crude sticks, Jones grows about 100 bushels of corn a year. He soon realizes that if he had a plow—a type of investment good, or capital—his productivity would increase. Making a plow in such a primitive setting, however, is time consuming and would keep him away from his fields for a year. Thus, the plow has an opportunity cost of 100 bushels of corn. He could not survive this drop in production without enough saved from previous harvests.

The question is: Should he invest his time in the plow? The answer depends on the cost and benefit of the plow. We already know that the plow's opportunity cost is 100 bushels—the forgone output. The benefit depends on how much the plow increases crop production and how long it lasts. Jones figures that the plow would boost annual yield by 50 bushels and would last his lifetime. In making the investment decision, he compares the current cost to the future benefit. Suppose he decides that adding 50 bushels a year outweighs the one-time cost of 100 bushels to make the plow.

In making the plow, Jones engages in *roundabout production.* Rather than working the soil with his crude sticks, he produces capital to increase his productivity. More roundabout production in an economy means more capital, so more goods can be produced in the future. Advanced industrial economies are characterized by much roundabout production and thus abundant capital accumulation.

You can see why production cannot occur without savings. *Production requires savings because both direct and roundabout production take time—time during which goods and services are not available from current production.* Now let's modernize the example by introducing the ability to borrow. Many farmers visit the bank each spring to borrow enough "seed money" to get by until the harvest. Likewise, other businesses often borrow at least a portion of the start-up funds needed to get going. Thus, in a modern economy, producers need not rely just on their own savings. Banks and other financial institutions serve as *intermediaries* between savers and borrowers. Financial markets for stocks and bonds also help channel savings to producers.

Let's take a look at the incentive to save.

Consumption, Saving, and Time

Did you ever burn the roof of your mouth eating a slice of pizza? Have you done this more than once? Why do you persist in such self-mutilation? You persist because that bite of pizza is worth more to you now than the same bite a minute from now. In fact, you are willing to risk burning your mouth rather than wait until the pizza has lost its destructive properties. In a small way, this reflects the fact that you and other consumers value *present* consumption more than *future* consumption. Not pie in the sky; pie now. You and other consumers are said to have a **positive rate of time preference**.

Because you value present consumption more than future consumption, you are willing to pay more to consume now rather than wait. And prices often reflect this greater willingness to pay. Consider the movies. You pay about twice as much for a movie ticket than to rent the DVD or download it three months later. The same is true for books. By waiting for the paperback, you can save more than half the hardback price. Photo developers, dry cleaners, fast-food restaurants, furniture stores promising same-day delivery, cable news networks, and other suppliers tout the speed of their services, knowing that consumers prefer earlier availability. Thus, *impatience* is one explanation for a positive rate of time preference. Another is *uncertainty*. If you wait, something might prevent you from consuming the good. A T-shirt slogan captures this point best: "Life is uncertain. Eat dessert first."

Because people value present consumption more than future consumption, they must be rewarded to postpone consumption—to delay gratification. By saving a portion of their incomes in financial institutions such as banks, people forgo present consumption for a greater ability to consume in the future. Interest is the reward for postponing consumption. The **interest rate** is the annual reward for saving as a percentage of the amount saved. For example, if the interest rate is 5 percent, the reward, or interest, is $5 per year for each $100 saved. The higher the interest rate, other things constant, the more consumers are rewarded for saving, so the more they save. You will learn more about this later in the chapter.

positive rate of time preference

Consumers value present consumption more than future consumption

interest rate

Interest per year as a percentage of the amount saved or borrowed

Optimal Investment

In a market economy characterized by specialization and exchange, Farmer Jones no longer needs to produce his own capital, nor need he rely on his own savings. He can purchase capital with borrowed funds. More generally, firms invest now in the expectation of a future return. Because the return is in the future, a would-be investor must estimate how much a particular investment will yield this year, next year, the year after, and in all years during the productive life of the investment. *Firms buy new capital goods only if they expect this investment to yield a higher return than other possible uses of their funds.*

To understand the investment decision in a modern economy, let's switch from the farm to a golf course to consider another simple example. The operators of the Hacker Haven Golf Course are thinking about buying some solar-powered golf carts. The model under consideration, called the Weekend Warrior, sells for $5,000, requires no maintenance or operating expenses, and is expected to last indefinitely. *The expected rate of return of each cart equals the expected annual earnings divided by the cart's purchase price.* More generally, the **expected rate of return on capital** is the expected annual earnings divided by capital's purchase price. The first cart is expected to generate rental income of $1,000 per year. This income, divided by the cost of the cart, yields an expected rate of return on the investment of $1,000/$5,000, or 20 percent per year. Additional carts will be used less. A second is expected to generate $750 per year in rental income, yielding a rate of return of $750/$5,000, or 15 percent; a third cart, $500 per year, or 10 percent; and a fourth cart, $250 per year, or 5 percent. They don't expect a fifth cart to get rented at all, so it has a zero expected rate of return.

Should the operators of Hacker Haven invest in golf carts, and if so, how many? Suppose they plan to borrow the money to buy the carts. The number of carts they purchase depends on the interest rate they must pay for borrowing. If the market interest

expected rate of return on capital

The expected annual earnings divided by capital's purchase price rate exceeds 20 percent, the cost of borrowing would exceed the expected rate of return for even the first cart, so the club would buy no carts. What if the operators have enough cash on hand to buy the carts? Suppose the market interest rate also reflects what club owners could earn on savings. If the interest rate earned on savings exceeded 20 percent, course owners would earn more saving their money than buying golf carts. *The market interest rate is the opportunity cost of investing in capital.*

What if the market rate is 8 percent per year? At that rate, the first three carts, all with expected returns exceeding 8 percent, would each yield more than the market rate. A fourth cart would lose money, because its expected rate of return is only 5 percent. Exhibit 1 measures the interest rate along the vertical axis and the amount invested in golf carts along the horizontal axis. The step-like relationship shows the expected rate of return earned on additional dollars invested in golf carts. This relationship also indicates the amount invested in golf carts at each interest rate, so you can view this step-like relationship as Hacker Haven's demand curve for this type of investment. For example, the first cart costs $5,000 and earns a rate of return of 20 percent. A firm should reject any investment with an expected rate of return that falls below the market rate of interest.

The horizontal line at 8 percent indicates the market interest rate, which is Hacker Haven's opportunity cost of investing. The course operators' objective is to choose an investment strategy that maximizes profit. Profit is maximized when $15,000 is invested in the carts—that is, when three carts are purchased. The expected return from a fourth cart is 5 percent, which is below the opportunity cost of funds. Therefore, investing in four or more carts would reduce total profit.

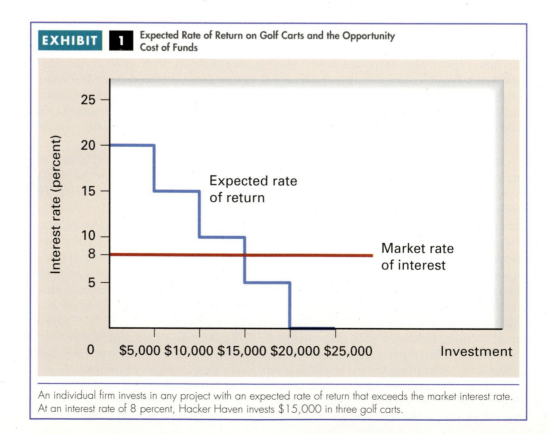

EXHIBIT 1   Expected Rate of Return on Golf Carts and the Opportunity Cost of Funds

An individual firm invests in any project with an expected rate of return that exceeds the market interest rate. At an interest rate of 8 percent, Hacker Haven invests $15,000 in three golf carts.

So far, we have looked at the investment decision for a single golf course, but there are over 16,000 golf courses in the United States. The industry demand for golf carts shows the relationship between the amount all courses invest and the expected rate of return. Like the step-like relationship in Exhibit 1, the investment demand curve for the golf industry slopes downward. The lower the market rate of interest, the more invested in golf carts.

Let's move beyond golf carts and consider the investment decisions of all industries: publishing, software, farming, fast food, sporting goods, and thousands more. Individual industries have downward-sloping demand curves for investment. More is invested when the opportunity cost of borrowing is lower, other things constant. A downward-sloping investment demand curve for the entire economy can be derived, with some qualifications, from a horizontal summation of all industries' downward-sloping investment demand curves.

We have now discussed investing in physical capital. Whether the firm borrows money or draws on savings, the market interest rate represents the opportunity cost of investment. Let's shift gears and turn to a less tangible form of capital in the following case study about intellectual capital.

THE INFORMATION ECONOMY

The Value of a Good Idea—Intellectual Property   One potentially valuable capital resource is information, or so-called **intellectual property**, which is any intangible asset created by human knowledge and ideas. Intellectual property is costly to produce, but, once produced, it can be supplied at low cost. For example, the first copy of a new Windows operating system may cost Microsoft over $1 billion to develop, but each additional copy can be streamed over the Internet for virtually nothing. As soon as Microsoft sells a copy, that first customer becomes a potential supplier of that product.

Because of this special supply characteristic, the original producer often has difficulty controlling the distribution and may have trouble getting paid. To help with these problems, the U.S. Constitution granted Congress the power "to promote the Progress of Science and useful Arts, by securing for limited Times to Authors and Inventors the exclusive Right to use their respective Writings and Discoveries." This was the only "Right" spelled out in the U.S. Constitution as initially ratified by the states (the Bill of Rights, the first ten amendments to the Constitution, was ratified later). Originators are thereby better able to benefit from their creations. A *patent* establishes property rights to an invention or other technical advances. A *copyright* confers property rights to an original expression of an author, artist, composer, or computer programmer. And a *trademark* establishes property rights in unique commercial marks and symbols, such as McDonald's golden arches, Nike's swoosh, or Apple's apple with a bite out of it.

Granting property rights is one thing; enforcing them is another. (Do you have any pirated software, music, or DVDs?) Much of the software, music CDs, and DVDs sold around the world, particularly in Indonesia, Zimbabwe, Vietnam, China, India, and Russia, are pirated editions of products developed in the United States. For example, Windows 7, which retails for about $320 in the United States, was available in China in pirated form for as little as $3 even before its U.S. release date. Worldwide more than 40 percent of all software in use is pirated. The ready availability of pirated software stunts development of a homegrown software industry in countries where piracy thrives. And some movies are available on the black market as DVDs even before they open in U.S. theaters.

CASE STUDY

e activity

Wired News covers events in business and technology with daily updates at http://www .wired.com/, including many stories about conflicts over copyright. What are some of the current issues in protecting intellectual property rights that appear in the headlines? Do a search for "intellectual property" on the *Wired* site.

intellectual property
An intangible asset created by human knowledge and ideas

AP Photo/EyePress

Enforcing property rights is costly, and this diminishes the incentive to create new products and new ideas. For example, in May 2010 makers of *The Hurt Locker*, the 2010 Oscar winner for best picture, filed copyright suits against 5,000 IP addresses that downloaded pirated copies of the movie. And the U.S. Copyright Group sued about 50,000 illegal downloaders of a dozen other movies. Pirated videos, music, computer games, and software bring no royalties to the artists, no wages to industry workers, no income to the producers or programmers, and no taxes to the government. Even within the United States, the music industry has been devastated by the ease with which music can be shared online. CD sales in 2010 were only half that of a decade earlier. Sharing music files is not a victimless crime: between 2000 and 2010, for example, more than one-fourth of music industry workers lost their jobs as sales declined. Most musicians now earn more from touring than from record sales.

Intellectual property is an intangible asset that fuels the digital economy. How society nurtures incentives to create new ideas, inventions, and artistic creations will affect economic development around the globe.

Sources: Jeff Leeds, "Plunge in CD Sales Shakes Up Big Labels," *New York Times*, 28 May 2007; Joel Mokyr, "Intellectual Property Rights, the Industrial Revolution, and the Beginning of Modern Economic Growth," *American Economic Review*, 99 (May 2009): 349–355. "Software Pirates in China Beat Microsoft to the Punch," Reuters, 18 October 2009; the World Intellectual Property Organization at http://www.wipo.int/; and Greg Sandoval, "*Hurt Locker* Downloaders, You've Been Sued," *CNET News*, 28 May 2010 at http://news.cnet.com/8301-31001_3-20006314-261.html.

The Market for Loanable Funds

You earlier learned why producers are willing to pay interest to borrow money: *Money provides a command over resources, making both direct production and roundabout production possible.* The simple principles developed for Farmer Jones and Hacker Haven can be generalized to other producers. The major demanders of loans are entrepreneurs who borrow to start firms and to invest in physical capital, such as machines, trucks, and buildings, and in intellectual capital, such as patents, copyrights, and trademarks. At any time, a firm has a variety of investment opportunities. The firm ranks these from highest to lowest, based on the expected rates of return. The firm increases investment until the expected rate of return just equals the market interest rate. With other inputs held constant, the demand curve for investment slopes downward.

But entrepreneurs are not the only demanders of loans. As we have seen, households value present consumption more than future consumption; they are willing to pay extra to consume now rather than later. One way to ensure that goods and services are available now is to borrow for present consumption, as reflected by home mortgages, car loans, and credit card purchases. Some people also borrow to invest in their human capital, as reflected by college loans. The household's demand curve for loans, like the firm's demand for loans, slopes downward, indicating that consumers are more willing and able to borrow at lower interest rates, other things constant. The government sector and the rest of the world are also demanders of loans.

Demand for Loanable Funds

demand for loanable funds

The negative relationship between the market interest rate and the quantity of loanable funds demanded, other things constant

The **demand for loanable funds** curve shows the negative relationship between the market interest rate and the quantity of loans demanded, other things constant. This curve is based on the expected rate of return these borrowed funds yield when invested in capital. Each firm has a downward-sloping demand curve for loanable funds, reflecting a declining rate of return on investment. With some qualifications, the demand for loanable funds of each firm can be summed horizontally to yield the market demand for loanable funds, shown as *D* in Exhibit 2. Factors assumed constant along this demand curve include the expected rate of inflation, the prices of other resources, the level of technology, the customs and conventions of the market, and the tax laws.

Supply of Loanable Funds

Banks are willing to pay interest on savings because they can, in turn, lend these savings to those who need credit, such as farmers, golf courses, construction companies, home buyers, college students, and entrepreneurs looking to start a new business or buy new capital. Banks and other financial institutions play the role of *financial intermediaries* in what is known as the market for loanable funds. The higher the interest rate, other things constant, the greater the reward for saving. As people save more, the quantity of loanable funds increases. The **supply of loanable funds** curve shows the positive relationship between the market interest rate and the quantity of savings supplied, other things constant, as reflected by the usual upward-sloping supply curve shown as *S* in Exhibit 2. In recent years, a lot of savings have come from abroad, especially China. Factors assumed constant along this supply curve include the expected rate of inflation and people's retirement plans.

supply of loanable funds
The positive relationship between the market interest rate and the quantity of loanable funds supplied, other things constant

Market Interest Rate

The **loanable funds market** brings together borrowers, or demanders of loanable funds, and savers, or suppliers of loanable funds, to determine the market interest rate. The demand and supply of loanable funds come together, as in Exhibit 2, to determine the

loanable funds market
The market in which savers (suppliers of loanable funds) and borrowers (demanders of loanable funds) come together to determine the market interest rate and the quantity of loanable funds exchanged

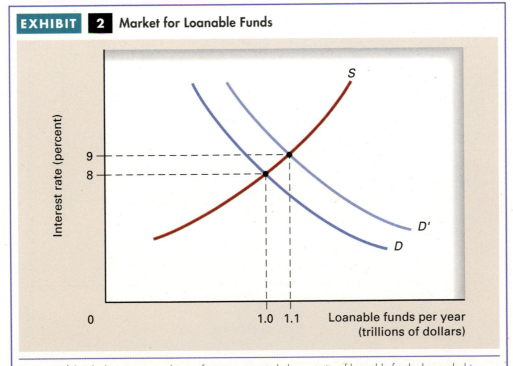

EXHIBIT 2 Market for Loanable Funds

Because of the declining expected rate of return on capital, the quantity of loanable funds demanded is inversely related to the interest rate. The market rate of interest, 8 percent, is found where the demand curve for loanable funds intersects the supply curve of loanable funds. An increase in the demand for loanable funds from D to D' raises the market interest rate from 8 percent to 9 percent and increases the equilibrium quantity of loanable funds from $1.0 trillion to $1.1 trillion.

market interest rate. In this case, the equilibrium interest rate of 8 percent is the only one that exactly matches the wishes of borrowers and savers. The equilibrium quantity of loanable funds is $1.0 trillion per year. Any change in the demand or supply of loanable funds changes the market interest rate. For example, a major technological breakthrough that increases the productivity of capital increases its expected rate of return, shifting the demand curve for loanable funds rightward, as shown in the movement from D to D'. Such an increase in the demand for loanable funds would raise the equilibrium interest rate to 9 percent and increase the market quantity of loanable funds to $1.1 trillion per year.

Why Interest Rates Differ

So far, we have been talking about *the* market interest rate, implying that only one rate prevails in the loanable funds market. At any particular time, however, a range of interest rates coexist in the economy. Exhibit 3 shows interest rates for loans in various markets. The interest rate for home mortgages is relatively low because this loan is backed up by the home itself. The so-called **prime rate** is the interest rate lenders

prime rate

The interest rate lenders charge their most trustworthy business borrowers

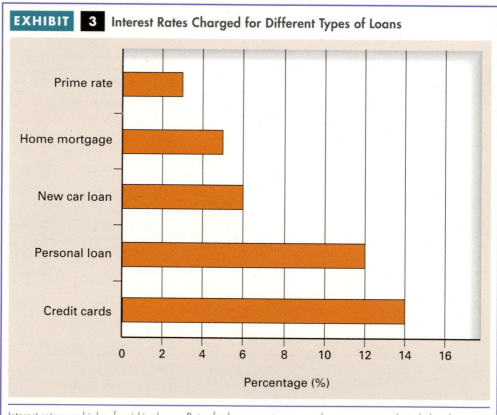

EXHIBIT   3   Interest Rates Charged for Different Types of Loans

Interest rates are higher for riskier loans. Rates for home mortgages and new cars are relatively low because these loans are backed up by the home or car as collateral. Personal loans and credit card balances face the highest rates, because these loans are riskier—that is, the likelihood borrowers fail to repay the loans is greater and the borrower offers no collateral.

Source: Federal Reserve Board; Bankrate.com; and Moneycentral.msn.com. Rates are as of April 2010.

charge their most trustworthy business borrowers. The highest is the rate charged on credit card balances, which is nearly triple the rate on mortgages. Let's see why interest rates differ.

Risk

Some borrowers are more likely than others to *default* on their loans—that is, not to pay them back. Before a bank lends money, it usually requires a borrower to put up **collateral,** which is an asset pledged by the borrower that can be sold to pay off the loan in the event of a default. With business loans, any valuable asset—land, buildings, machinery—the firm owns can serve as collateral. With a home mortgage, the home itself becomes collateral. And with a car loan, the car becomes collateral. The more valuable the collateral backing up the loan, other things constant, the lower the interest rate charged on that loan. For example, the interest rate charged on car loans is usually higher than on home loans. A car loses its value more quickly than a home does, and a car can be driven away by a defaulting borrower, whereas a home usually increases in value and stays put (home prices declined during the recent economic crisis, creating trouble for both borrowers and banks, but that was unusual). So a car typically offers worse collateral than a home—hence, the interest charged on a car loan is higher. Interest rates are higher still for personal loans and credit cards, because such borrowers usually provide no collateral.

collateral
An asset pledged by the borrower that can be sold to pay off the loan in the event the borrower defaults

Duration of the Loan

The future is uncertain, and the further into the future a loan is to be repaid, the more uncertain that repayment becomes. Bad things can happen over time. Thus, as the duration of a loan increases, lenders require a higher interest rate to compensate for the greater risk. The **term structure of interest rates** is the relationship between the duration of a loan and the interest rate charged. *The interest rate usually increases with the duration of the loan, other things constant.*

term structure of interest rates
The relationship between the duration of a loan and the interest rate charged; typically interest rates increase with the duration of the loan, because longer loans are considered more risky

Administration Costs

The costs of executing the loan agreement, monitoring the loan, and collecting payments are called the *administration costs* of the loan. These costs, as a proportion of the loan, decrease as the size of the loan increases. For example, the cost of administering a $100,000 loan is less than 10 times the cost of administering a $10,000 loan. Consequently, that portion of the interest charge reflecting administration costs becomes smaller as the size of the loan increases, other things constant, thus reducing the interest rate for larger loans.

Tax Treatment

Differences in the tax treatment of different types of loans also affects the interest rate charged. For example, the interest earned on loans to state and local governments is not subject to federal income taxes. Because lenders focus on their after-tax rate of interest, state and local governments pay a lower interest rate than otherwise similar borrowers pay.

    To Review: The demand and supply of loanable funds determine the market interest rate. At any given time, interest rates may differ because of differences in risk, maturity, administrative costs, and tax treatment. Now we move on to consider the value of some future benefit.

Present Value and Discounting

Because you value present consumption more than future consumption, present and future consumption cannot be compared directly. Someone who "eats like there's no tomorrow" apparently values present consumption much more than consumption tomorrow. A way of standardizing the discussion is to measure all consumption in terms of its present value. **Present value** is the current value of a payment or payments to be received in the future. For example, how much would you pay now to receive $100 one year from now? Put another way, what is the *present value* to you of receiving $100 one year from now?

present value

The value today of income to be received in the future

Present Value of Payment One Year Hence

Suppose the market interest rate is 8 percent and you can either lend or borrow at that rate. One way to determine how much you would pay for the opportunity to receive $100 one year from now is to ask how much you would have to save now, at the market interest rate, to end up with $100 one year from now. Here's the problem we are trying to solve: What amount of money, if saved at an interest rate of, say, 8 percent, would accumulate to $100 one year from now? We can calculate the answer with a simple formula:

$$\text{Present value} \times 1.08 = \$100$$

or:

$$\text{Present value} = \frac{100}{1.08} = \$92.59$$

Thus, if the interest rate is 8 percent, $92.59 is the present value of receiving $100 one year from now; it is the most you would pay today to receive $100 one year from now. Rather than pay more than $92.59, you could simply deposit your $92.59, earn the market interest rate of 8 percent, and end up with $100 a year from now (ignoring taxes). Dividing the future payment by 1 plus the prevailing interest rate to express it in today's dollars is called **discounting.**

The present value of $100 to be received one year from now depends on the interest rate. The more that present consumption is preferred to future consumption, the more must be offered savers to defer consumption. *The higher the interest rate, the more any future payment is discounted and the lower its present value.* Put another way, the higher the interest rate, the less you need to save now to yield a given amount in the future. For example, if the interest rate is 10 percent, the present value of receiving $100 one year from now is $100/1.10, which equals $90.91.

On the other hand, the less present consumption is preferred to future consumption, the less savers need to be paid to defer consumption, so the lower the interest rate. The lower the interest rate, the less the future income is discounted and the greater its present value. A lower interest rate means that you must save more now to yield a given amount in the future. As a general rule, the present value of receiving an amount one year from now is:

discounting

Converting future dollar amounts into present value

$$\text{Present value} = \frac{\text{Amount received one year from now}}{1 + \text{interest rate}}$$

For example, when the interest rate is 5 percent, the present value of receiving $100 one year from now is:

$$\text{Present value} = \frac{\$100}{1 + 0.05} = \frac{\$100}{1.05} = \$95.24$$

Present Value for Payments in Later Years

Now consider the present value of receiving $100 two years from now. What amount of money, if deposited at the market interest rate of 5 percent, would total $100 after two years? After one year, the value would be the present value times 1.05, which would then earn the market interest rate during the second year. After two years, the deposit would have accumulated to the present value times 1.05 times 1.05. Thus, we have the equation:

$$\text{Present value} \times 1.05 \times 1.05 = \text{Present value} \times (1.05)^2 = \$100$$

Solving for the present value yields:

$$\text{Present value} = \frac{\$100}{(1.05)^2} = \frac{\$100}{1.1025} = \$90.70$$

If the $100 were to be received three years from now, we would discount the payment over three years:

$$\text{Present value} = \frac{\$100}{(1.05)^3} = \$86.38$$

If the interest rate is i, the present value of M dollars received t years from now is:

$$\text{Present value} = \frac{M}{(1 + i)^t}$$

Because $(1 + i)$ is greater than 1, the more times it is multiplied by itself (as determined by t), the larger the denominator and the smaller the present value. Thus, *the present value of a given payment is smaller the further into the future that payment is to be received.*

Present Value of an Income Stream

So far, we have figured out the present value of a single sum to be received in the future. Most investments, however, yield a stream of income over time. In cases where the income is received for a period of years, the present value of each receipt can be computed individually and the results summed to yield the present value of the entire income stream. For example, the present value of receiving $100 next year and $150 the year after is simply the present value of the first year's receipt plus the present value of the second year's receipt. If the interest rate is 5 percent:

$$\text{Present value} = \frac{\$100}{1.05} + \frac{\$150}{(1.05)^2} = \$231.29$$

Present Value of an Annuity

annuity
A given sum of money received each year for a specified number of years

A given sum of money received each year for a specified number of years is called an **annuity.** Such an income stream is called a *perpetuity* if it continues indefinitely. The present value of receiving a certain amount forever seems like it should be a very large sum indeed. But because future income is valued less the more distant into the future it is to be received, the present value of receiving a particular amount forever is not much more than that of receiving it for, say, 20 years.

To determine the present value of receiving $100 a year forever, we need only ask how much money must be deposited in a savings account to yield $100 in interest each year. If the interest rate is 8 percent, a deposit of $1,250 will earn $100 per year. Thus, the present value of receiving $100 a year indefinitely when the interest rate is 8 percent is $1,250. More generally, the present value of receiving a sum each year forever equals the amount received each year divided by the interest rate.

$$\text{Present value of receiving } M \text{ dollars each year forever} = \frac{M}{i}$$

The concept of present value is useful for investment decisions. What about your decision to invest in human capital—to go to college? A chart in the previous chapter showed that those with at least a college degree earned nearly twice as much as those with just a high school diploma. We could compute the present value of an education by discounting earnings based on that level of education, then summing total earnings over your working life. Even without doing the calculations, we can say with reasonable certainty that the present value of at least a college education will be nearly twice that of just a high school education. To develop an appreciation for present value and discounting, let's put the payoff from state lotteries in perspective.

CASE STUDY

e activity

Virginia has two big cash prize lotteries: Mega Millions and Lotto South. Winners in either can get a lump sum or payments over time. Visit the Web site at http://www .valottery.com to find out how each works. Note that the prizes are not awarded similarly. How is the value of the jackpot determined in each case? What interest rate is used?

BRINGING THEORY TO LIFE

The Million-Dollar Lottery?   Since 1963, when New Hampshire introduced the first modern state-run lottery, 43 states and the District of Columbia have followed suit, generating profits of about $20 billion a year. Publicity photos usually show the winner receiving an oversized check in the millions. But winners get paid in annual installments, so the present value of the prize is much less than advertised. For example, a million-dollar prizewinner usually gets $33,333 a year for 30 years. To put this in perspective, keep in mind that at an interest rate of 8 percent, the $33,333 received in the 30th year has a present value of only $3,313. If today you deposited $3,313 in an account earning 8 percent interest, you would wind up with $33,333 in 30 years (if we ignore taxes).

If the interest rate is 8 percent, the present value of a $33,333 annuity for the next 30 years is $375,256. Thus, the present value is much less than half of the promised million, which is why lottery officials pay in installments. Incidentally, we might consider the present value of receiving $33,333 a year forever. Using the formula for an annuity discussed earlier, the present value with an interest rate of 8 percent is $33,333/0.08 = $416,662. Because the present value of receiving $33,333 for 30 years is $375,256, continuing the $33,333 annual payment *forever* adds only $41,406 to the present value.

In most states, lottery winners have a choice of getting annual installments or taking a lump sum right away. For example, a $258 million Powerball winner in 2010 had a choice of getting 30 annual installments of $8.6 million each or taking a lump-sum payout of $125 million. The lump sum was less than half the advertised jackpot, and the implied discount rate was about 6 percent. After state and federal income taxes, the lump sum reduced to about $67 million—no question, still an awesome amount but only 26 percent of the headline prize of $258 million.

Among all the types of legal gambling, state lotteries offer the smallest payout—only about $0.55 of each dollar wagered goes to winners. Still, some people apparently view lotteries as good bets, especially the 5 percent of the population that buys half of all lottery tickets sold. To strengthen the state's monopoly grip over lotteries, private and foreign lotteries are outlawed in the United States. The value of one state's lottery monopoly was underscored when the governor of Texas proposed selling that state's lottery to a private firm—for $14 billion.

Sources: "Missouri Store Clerk Wins $258 Million Powerball Jackpot," Associated Press, 22 April 2010; and an index of lottery sites found at http://www.state.wv.us/lottery/links.htm.

This discussion of present value and discounting concludes our treatment of capital and interest. We now turn to a special factor of production, entrepreneurial ability, or entrepreneurship.

Entrepreneurship

In a market economy, people are free to risk their time and savings to start a business. If the business succeeds, they are rewarded with profit. If it fails, they could lose their life's savings. Chances of success are not great—most new businesses don't last five years. But many survive, some thrive, and a few make their founders rich. Despite the high failure rate, the profit motive and the drive to create something of lasting value, to make a mark in the world, attract many would-be entrepreneurs.

Role of the Entrepreneur

An entrepreneur comes up with an idea, turns that idea into a marketable product, accepts the risk of success or failure, and claims any resulting profit or loss. That idea might be a new product, a better version of an existing product, or a more efficient way of making something already available. Because each of those activities often involves long and costly development, such ventures are risky. Entrepreneurs must have the confidence to accept that risk and must inspire confidence in others needed to succeed, such as resource suppliers, lenders, investors, and consumers.

Because there is no formal market for entrepreneurship, entrepreneurs become their own bosses—that is, they hire themselves. In addition to entrepreneurship, or entrepreneurial ability, some supply other resources to the firm. Imagine an entrepreneur who comes up with a good idea, borrows start-up money from a bank, and hires a manager to line up all the other resources required to bring that idea to life. The entrepreneur promises to pay resource suppliers at least their opportunity cost; otherwise, they would go elsewhere. This entrepreneur, by hiring a manager and by agreeing to pay all resources, supplies nothing other than entrepreneurship. Yet the entrepreneur has acquired the right to control these resources in return for the promise to pay at least the market rate. Despite what may seem like limited involvement, this entrepreneur owns the firm, and the firm consists of a bundle of contracts or agreements between the entrepreneur and resource suppliers. At the end of the week or month or year, the entrepreneur can claim as profit whatever is left after paying all other resources. The entrepreneur is the *residual claimant*, the one who gets to keep what's left over and who is responsible for covering any loss.

What distinguishes the role of the entrepreneur is not the management of resources in the firm, but the power to choose who manages those resources. An entrepreneur who decides to manage the firm, and many do, would still delegate some decisions to employees. Therefore, don't think that an entrepreneur must manage the firm. *An entrepreneur must simply have the authority to hire and fire the manager.*

In reality, an entrepreneur seldom has the limited role described above. An entrepreneur often manages the business, at least in the beginning, and usually supplies at least some of the financial capital required to get the business off the ground, because banks may be reluctant to lend to a risky startup.

Entrepreneurs Drive the Economy Forward

Entrepreneurs create new or better products, new production methods, or new ways of doing business. These are sources of technological progress and economic growth in the economy. Successful entrepreneurs initiate creative change, thereby earning a profit and driving the economy forward.

New Products

Some entrepreneurs come up with new products, opening up markets that had not before existed. For example, Levi Strauss and his partner Jacob Davis in 1873 won a patent for fastening blue denim with small metal studs to create the most popular clothing in the world, now called Levi's jeans. As another example, Dean Kamen developed the Segway® Human Transporter, a personal transport device, which went on the market in 2001 as an alternative to walking or riding a bicycle.

Improve Existing Products

Some entrepreneurs begin with an existing product and make it better. For example, Howard Schultz took the simple cup of coffee and turned it into a $20 billion corporation by offering higher quality and greater variety in a more inviting setting. Founded by Schultz in 1985, Starbucks now employs more than 140,000 people at about 9,000 locations around the world. Guy Laliberte founded Cirque du Soleil in 1984 as a modern update on the circus. By 2010 he had created 21 different shows, some staying put and some touring. For his creative efforts, he accumulated an estimated net worth of $2.5 billion as of 2010.[1]

New Production Methods

Some entrepreneurs combine resources more efficiently to reduce costs. They use less costly materials, employ newer technology, and generally make better use of resources. Henry Ford, for example, introduced the assembly line, where automobiles move along a conveyer and the workers stay put. Ford didn't invent the automobile, but his assembly line made owning one affordable for millions of Americans. Similarly, Ray Croc didn't invent the hamburger or the hamburger stand, but he applied the principles of mass production to make McDonald's hamburgers quickly and cheaply, first across the nation then around the world.

1. Joan Acocella, "Night at the Circus," *The New Yorker*, 7 June 2010, p. 82.

New Ways of Doing Business

Some entrepreneurs step outside existing business models to create new ways of doing business. For example, Michael Dell began in 1984 with $1,000 and an idea to sell personal computers directly to customers rather than through retailers. His made-to-order computers sold by phone and now over the Internet make Dell one of the world's largest computer sellers, with sales exceeding $150 million *a day*. Mary Kay Ash did the same for skin care products and cosmetics, selling more than $2 billion a year directly to consumers around the world through independent Mary Kay consultants.

Who Are Not Entrepreneurs?

Some people may carry out a particular function of an entrepreneur. For example, they may dream up a new product or process, they may manage resources, or they may assume the risk of success or failure. But carrying out just one of these roles does not usually make for an entrepreneur. One way of appreciating the role of an entrepreneur is to identify those who are not serving that role.

Corporate Inventors

Inventors are considered entrepreneurs if they bear the risk of success or failure. But most inventors are hired hands. Corporations such as Pfizer, Dupont, and Apple employ thousands of scientists and engineers to improve existing products, develop new ones, and devise more efficient ways to make things. These corporate inventors still get paid even in years when their creative juices slow to a trickle. Because these hired inventors take no more risk than most other employees, they are not considered entrepreneurs.

Exhibit 4 shows the sources of invention since 1990 as measured by the number of U.S. patents awarded. Patents increased 76 percent between 1990 and 2008. But the share of patents awarded to individual inventors fell from 19 percent in 1990 to

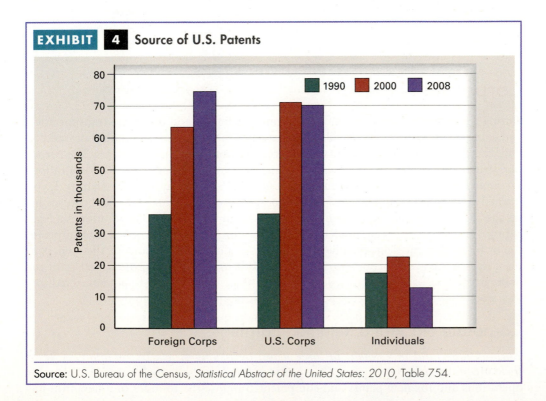

EXHIBIT 4 Source of U.S. Patents

Source: U.S. Bureau of the Census, *Statistical Abstract of the United States: 2010*, Table 754.

only 8 percent in 2008. Individual inventors usually are considered entrepreneurs, even those who sell their ideas for others to develop and market. These inventors take on risks in a way that inventors who work for corporations do not. So self-employed inventors usually are considered entrepreneurs.

Managers

Most entrepreneurs do more than simply sell their good ideas for others to run with. They try to bring their ideas to the market by going into business. But, as already noted, founding a business does not necessarily mean the entrepreneur must manage it. For example, Dean Kamen, inventor of the Segway, created a company to make and market his invention. He hired a manager to run the company because he was too busy inventing things (besides the Segway, Kamen holds patents for a water purifier, a mobile dialysis system, the first insulin pump, and an all-terrain electric wheelchair, among other things). Even though he doesn't manage the business himself, he is still an entrepreneur because he has the power to hire and fire the manager. The manager is a well-paid and important employee, but he is not an entrepreneur.

Stockholders

More than half of all households in the United States own corporate stock, either directly or indirectly, and thus take on the risk of a corporation's success or failure. Does this risk-bearing make the stockholder an entrepreneur? No. Entrepreneurs do more than assume the risk of success or failure. They begin with a bright idea and usually figure out how to profit from that idea. An individual stockholder, on the other hand, typically has little say in a firm's operation (and most like it that way).

To Review: The entrepreneur is a prime mover in a market economy—a visionary, someone who can see what others can't. By coming up with new products, making existing products better, finding better ways to make things, of finding new ways of doing business, the entrepreneur drives the economy forward. This concludes our discussion of entrepreneurs. You now have sufficient background to consider how firms, especially corporations, are financed.

Corporate Finance

During the Industrial Revolution, labor-saving machinery and improved transportation and communication networks made large-scale production more profitable, but building huge factories filled with heavy machinery required substantial investments. The corporate structure became the easiest way to finance such outlays, and by 1920, corporations accounted for most employment and output in the U.S. economy. Back in Chapter 3, you learned about the pros and cons of the corporate form of business. Thus far, however, little has been said about corporate finance. As noted in Chapter 3, a corporation is a legal entity, distinct from its shareholders. The corporation may own property, earn a profit, sue or be sued, incur debt, even be found guilty of a crime. Stockholders, the owners of the corporation, are liable only to the extent of their investment in the firm. Use of the abbreviation Inc. or Corp. in the company name serves as a warning to potential creditors that stockholders will not accept personal liability for debts of the company.

Corporate Stock and Retained Earnings

Corporations fund investment in three ways: by issuing stock, by retaining some of their profits, and by borrowing. Corporations issue and sell stock to raise money for operations and for new plants and equipment. Suppose the founder of a new firm has met with early success, but finds that to remain competitive, the firm needs to achieve economies of scale, which means the firm must grow fast. To fund that growth, the entrepreneur decides to incorporate. The newly incorporated company issues 1,000,000 shares of stock. The entrepreneur takes 100,000 shares as *owner's equity* in the corporation. The rest are sold to the public for $50 per share, which raises $45 million for the company. The entrepreneur, in effect, has already paid for his or her shares with the "sweat equity" required to come up with the idea, found the company, and get it rolling. The initial sale of stock to the public is called an **initial public offering,** or **IPO.** A *share* of **corporate stock** is a claim on the net income and assets of a corporation, as well as the right to vote on corporate directors and on other important matters. A person who buys 1 percent of the 1,000,000 shares issued thereby owns 1 percent of the corporation, is entitled to 1 percent of any profit, and gets to cast 1 percent of the votes on important corporate decisions.

Corporations must pay corporate income taxes on any profit. After-tax profit is either paid as **dividends** to shareholders or reinvested in the corporation. Reinvested profit, or **retained earnings,** helps the firm grow. Stockholders usually expect dividends, but the corporation is not required to pay dividends, and most new firms don't. Once shares are issued, their price tends to fluctuate directly with the firm's profit prospects. People buy stock because the firm is expected to eventually pay dividends and because they hope the share price will appreciate, or increase, over time.

Corporate Bonds

Again, a corporation can acquire funds by issuing stock, by retaining earnings, or by borrowing. To borrow money, the corporation can go to a bank for a loan or it can issue and sell bonds. A **bond** is the corporation's promise to pay back the holder a fixed sum of money on the designated *maturity date* plus make interest payments until that date. For example, a corporation might sell for $1,000 a bond that promises to make an annual interest payment of, say, $80 for 20 years and to repay the $1,000 at the end of 20 years.

The payment stream for bonds is more predictable than that for stocks. Unless this corporation goes bankrupt, it must pay bondholders as promised. In contrast, stockholders are last in line when resource suppliers get paid, so bondholders get paid before stockholders. Investors usually consider bonds less risky than stocks, although bonds involve risks as well. Risks include corporate bankruptcy and higher market interest rates. For example, suppose you buy a bond that pays 8 percent interest. Soon after that purchase, the market interest rate increases, so newly issued bonds pay 10 percent interest. Your 8 percent bond is less attractive than the new bonds, so the market value of your bond declines. The value of your bond declines until bond buyers are indifferent between buying your 8 percent bond and buying a 10 percent bond.

Securities Exchanges

Once stocks and bonds have been issued and sold, owners of these securities are free to resell them on *securities exchanges*. In the United States, the *Securities and Exchange Commission (SEC)* is the federal body that regulates securities markets. The largest securities market is the New York Stock Exchange (now NYSE Euronext), which trades the securities of about 2,800 major corporations, including about 500 non-U.S. companies. Altogether approximately 10,000 corporations trade on various U.S. exchanges. These are called publicly traded companies, to be distinguished from privately owned companies. Although privately owned companies, such as sole proprietors and

initial public offering (IPO)
The initial sale of corporate stock to the public

corporate stock
Certificate reflecting part ownership of a corporation

dividends
After-tax corporate profit paid to stockholders rather than retained by the firm and reinvested

retained earnings
After-tax corporate profit reinvested in the firm rather than paid to stockholders as dividends

bond
Certificate reflecting a firm's promise to pay the lender periodic interest and to repay the borrowed sum of money on the designated maturity date

partnerships, make up the overwhelming share of U.S. businesses in terms of numbers, corporations account for the overwhelming share of employment and sales.

Nearly all the securities traded each business day are *secondhand securities* in the sense that they have already been issued by the corporation. So the bulk of daily transactions do not finance firms in need of investment funds. Most money from daily trading goes from a securities buyer to a securities seller. *Institutional investors,* such as banks, insurance companies, and mutual funds, account for most of the trading volume on major exchanges. By providing a *secondary market* for securities, exchanges enhance the *liquidity* of securities—that is, the exchanges make the securities more readily sold for cash and thus more attractive to own. Of growing importance in securities exchanges are *hedge funds*, which often follow complex strategies to invest for institutions and wealthy clients.

The secondary markets for stocks also determine the current market value of the corporation. The market value of a firm at any given time can be found by multiplying the share price by the number of shares issued. Because the share price fluctuates throughout the trading day, so does the value of the corporation. In theory, the share price reflects the present value of the discounted stream of expected profit. Just to give you some idea, Exxon Mobil, the top-valued U.S. corporation, had a market value of $280 billion at the close of the trading day on June 4, 2010. The 2,300 U.S. corporations traded on the New York Stock Exchange had a combined market value of more than $10 trillion.

Securities prices give corporate management some indication of the wisdom of raising investment funds through retained earnings, new stock issues, or new bond issues. The greater a corporation's expected profit, other things constant, the higher the value of shares on the stock market and the lower the interest rate that would have to be paid on new bond issues. Securities markets usually promote the survival of the fittest by allocating investment funds to those firms able to make the most profitable use of them. *Thus, securities markets allocate funds more readily to successful firms than to firms in financial difficulty.* Some firms may be in such poor shape that they can't issue new securities.

One final point: When economists talk about investing, they have in mind purchases of new capital, such as new machines and new buildings. When the media talk about investing, they usually mean buying stocks and bonds. To an economist, Farmer Jones is investing only when he buys new farm machinery, not when he buys stocks. As noted already, the overwhelming share of stock transactions are in secondary markets, so the money goes from buyers to sellers, and does not go toward new capital purchases. Regardless, secondary markets make shares more readily convertible into cash and thus more attractive to own.

Conclusion

This chapter introduced you to capital, interest, entrepreneurship, and corporate finance. Capital is a more complicated resource than this chapter has conveyed. For example, the demand curve for investment is a moving target, not the stable relationship drawn in Exhibit 1. An accurate depiction of the investment demand curve calls for knowledge of the marginal product of capital and the price of output in the future. But capital's productivity changes with breakthroughs in technology and with changes in the employment of other resources. The future price of the product can also vary widely. Consider, for example, the dilemma of a firm contemplating an investment in oil-drilling rigs in recent years, when the price of crude oil fluctuated between $10 and $145 per barrel, as it has over the last two decades.

Summary

1. Production cannot occur without savings, because both direct production and roundabout production require time—time during which the resources required for production must be paid. Because people value present consumption more than future consumption, they must be rewarded to defer consumption. Interest is the reward to savers for forgoing present consumption and the cost to borrowers for being able to spend now.

2. Choosing the profit-maximizing level of capital is complicated because capital purchased today yields a stream of benefits for years into the future. The expected rate of return on capital equals the expected annual earnings of that capital divided by that capital's purchase price. The profit-maximizing firm invests up to the point where the expected rate of return on capital equals the market rate of interest. The market interest rate is the opportunity cost of investing.

3. The demand and supply of loanable funds determine the market interest rate. At any given time, interest rates may differ because of differences in risk, maturity, administrative costs, and tax treatment.

4. The current value of future payments is the present value. The process of translating future payments into present value is called discounting. The present value of a given payment is smaller the further into the future that payment is to be received. A given sum of money received each year for a specified number of years is called an annuity. The present value of receiving a sum each year forever is the amount received each year divided by the market interest rate.

5. An entrepreneur is a profit-seeker who comes up with an idea, tries to turn that idea into a marketable product, and accepts the risk of success or failure. The entrepreneur need not supply any resource other than entrepreneurial ability, though many manage the firm and provide some start-up funds. By developing new products, improving existing ones, employing better production methods, and finding new ways of doing business, successful entrepreneurs earn a profit and drive the economy forward.

6. Corporations fund new investment from three main sources: new stock issues, retained earnings, and borrowing (either directly from financial institutions or by issuing bonds). Once new stocks and bonds are issued, they can then be bought and sold on securities markets. The value of corporate stocks and bonds tends to vary directly with the firm's profit prospects. More profitable firms have better access to funds needed for expansion.

Key Concepts

Questions for Review

1. Role of Time   Complete the following sentences with a word or a phrase:
   a. If Bryan values present consumption more than future consumption, he has a _____.
   b. The reward to households for forgoing present consumption is _____.
   c. Producing capital goods rather than producing final goods is known as _____.

2. Consumption, Saving, and Time   Explain why the supply of loanable funds curve slopes upward to the right.

3. Case Study: The Value of a Good Idea—Intellectual Property   Many who use pirated software and illegal downloads of music and movies believe their actions are harmless. Identify some downsides for individuals and the economy of violating intellectual property rights.

4. Why Interest Rates Differ   At any given time, a range of interest rates prevails in the economy. What are some factors that contribute to differences among interest rates?

5. Present Value of an Annuity   Why is $10,000 a close approximation of the price of an annuity that pays $1,000 each year for 30 years at 10 percent annual interest?

6. Present Value of an Annuity   Suppose you are hired by your state government to determine the profitability of a lottery offering a grand prize of $10 million paid out in equal annual

installments over 20 years. Show *how* to calculate the cost to the state of paying out such a prize. Assume payments are made at the end of each year.

7. **Case Study: The Million-Dollar Lottery?**   In many states with lotteries, people can take their winnings in a single, discounted, lump-sum payment or in a series of annual payments for 20 or 30 years. What factors should a winner consider in determining how to take the money?

8. ENTREPRENEURSHIP   What entrepreneurial idea do you have? How would your idea contribute to the economy?

9. CORPORATE FINANCE   Describe the three ways in which corporations acquire funds for investment.

10. SECURITIES EXCHANGES   What role do securities exchanges play in financing corporations?

Problems and Exercises

11. OPTIMAL INVESTMENT   Review Exhibit 1 in this chapter. If the operators of the golf course revised their revenue estimates so that each cart is expected to earn $250 less, how many carts would they buy at an interest rate of 8 percent? How many would they buy if the interest rate is 3 percent?

12. MARKET FOR LOANABLE FUNDS   Using the demand-supply for loanable funds diagram, show the effect on the market interest rate of each of the following:
    a. An increase in the purchase price of capital
    b. An increase in the productivity of capital
    c. A shift in preferences toward present consumption and away from future consumption

13. PRESENT VALUE   Calculate the present value of each of the following future payments. (For some of these problems you may wish to use the online calculator available at http://www.moneychimp.com/articles/finworks/ fmpresval.htm.)
    a. A $10,000 lump sum received 1 year from now if the market interest rate is 8 percent
    b. A $10,000 lump sum received 2 years from now if the market interest rate is 10 percent

    c. A $1,000 lump sum received 3 years from now if the market interest rate is 5 percent
    d. A $25,000 lump sum received 1 year from now if the market interest rate is 12 percent
    e. A $25,000 lump sum received 1 year from now if the market interest rate is 10 percent
    f. A perpetuity of $500 per year if the market interest rate is 6 percent

14. PRESENT VALUE OF AN INCOME STREAM   Suppose the market interest rate is 10 percent. Would you be willing to lend $10,000 if you were guaranteed to receive $1,000 at the end of each of the next 12 years plus a $5,000 payment 15 years from now? Why or why not?

Global Economic Watch Exercises

Login to www.cengagebrain.com and access the Global Economic Watch to do these exercises.

15. GLOBAL ECONOMIC WATCH   Go to the Global Economic Crisis Resource Center. Select Global Issues in Context. In the Basic Search box at the top of the page, enter the phrase "Whose Concept Was It, Anyway." On the Results page, go to the Global Viewpoints Section. Click on the link for the July 11, 2010, column "Whose Concept Was It Anyway?." Which outcome would benefit the economy more, Jane Wyler having a patent on all reusable dry-cleaning bags or Rick Siegel developing a cheaper reusable bag?

16. GLOBAL ECONOMIC WATCH   Go to the Global Economic Crisis Resource Center. Select Global Issues in Context. In the Basic Search box at the top of the page, enter the term "initial public offering." Read about an IPO within the two most recent years. How much money was raised? For what will the money be used?

Transaction Costs, Imperfect Information, and Behavioral Economics

14

PhotoLink/Getty Images

- Why do some firms, such as Domino's Pizza, specialize in a single product, while other firms, such as General Electric, make hundreds of different products?

- Why stop at hundreds? Why not thousands? In fact, why doesn't a giant firm make everything?

- Why is proper spelling important on your résumé?

- Why is buying a used car such a gamble?

- Why do some winners of online auctions end up losers?

- What have economists learned from psychologists about the limits of rational self-interest?

Answers to these and other seemingly unrelated questions are addressed in this chapter, which digs deeper into assumptions about firms, the information required for competitive markets, and why some people make choices that seem inconsistent with their self-interest.

In the first third of this chapter, we step inside the firm to reconsider some simplifying assumptions about how firms work. We ask: Why do firms exist? How do they decide what to make themselves and what to buy from other firms? These steps toward realism move us beyond the simple depiction of the firm employed to this point. In the second third of this chapter, we challenge some simplifying assumptions about the information available to market participants. We ask: How does the lack of certain information affect behavior and shape market outcomes? And in the final third of the chapter, we consider why some economists are drawing on findings from psychology to enrich models of economic behavior. Specifically, we consider why many people eat too much, drink too much, smoke too much, and do other things that appear to be at odds with their rational self-interest.

Overall, this chapter should help you develop a more realistic view of how the economy works.

Topics discussed include:

- Transaction costs
- Vertical integration
- Bounded rationality
- Economies of scope
- Optimal search
- Winner's curse

- Asymmetric information
- Adverse selection
- Principal-agent problem
- Moral hazard
- Signaling and screening
- Behavioral economics

Rationale for the Firm and its Scope of Operation

The competitive model assumes that all participants in the market know everything they need to about the price and availability of all inputs, outputs, and production processes. The firm is assumed to be headed by a brilliant decision maker with a computer-like ability to calculate all the relevant marginal products. This individual knows everything necessary to solve complex production and pricing problems. The irony is that if the marginal products of all inputs could be measured easily and if prices for all inputs could be easily determined, there would be little reason for production to take place in firms. In a world characterized by perfect competition, perfect information, constant returns to scale, and costless exchange, the consumer could bypass the firm to deal directly with resource suppliers, purchasing inputs in the appropriate amounts. Someone who wanted a table could buy timber, have it milled, hire a carpenter, hire a painter, and end up with a finished product. The consumer could carry out transactions directly with each resource supplier.

The Firm Reduces Transaction Costs

So why is production carried out within firms? About 75 years ago, in a classic article, Nobel Prize winner Ronald Coase asked the question, "Why do firms exist?"[1] Why do people organize in the hierarchical structure of the firm and coordinate their decisions through a manager rather than simply rely on market exchange? His answer would not surprise today's students of economics: *Organizing activities through the hierarchy of the firm is usually more efficient than market exchange because production requires the coordination of many transactions among many resource suppliers.* In short, firms are superior to markets when production is complicated.

Consider again the example of purchasing a table by contracting directly with all the different resource suppliers—from the logger to the painter who applied the finishing varnish. Using resource markets directly involves (1) the cost of determining what

1. "The Nature of the Firm," *Economica*, 4 (November 1937): 386–405.

inputs are needed and how they should be combined and (2) the cost of reaching an agreement with each resource supplier *over and above* the direct costs of the timber, nails, machinery, paint, and labor required to make the table. Where inputs are easily identified, measured, priced, and hired, production can be carried out through a price-guided "do-it-yourself" approach using the market. For example, getting your house painted is a relatively simple task: You can buy the paint and brushes and hire painters by the hour. You become your own painting contractor, hiring inputs in the market and combining them to do the job. Likewise you could talk about different approaches to a European vacation. One traveler plans every aspect of a trip—booking flights, reserving hotel rooms, planning excursions, transportation, meals, and so on. A second traveler buys a packaged tour that includes everything. And a third traveler buys a land package covering hotels and excursions, but books all the flights.

Where the costs of identifying the appropriate inputs and negotiating for each specific contribution are high, the consumer minimizes transaction costs by purchasing the finished product from a firm. For example, although some people serve as their own contractor when painting a house, fewer do so when building a house; most buy a home already built or hire a building contractor. *The more complicated the task, the greater the ability to economize on transaction costs through specialization and centralized control.* For example, attempting to buy a new car by contracting with the thousands of suppliers required to assemble one would be time consuming, costly, and impossible for most anyone. What type of skilled labor should be hired and at what wages? How much steel, aluminum, plastic, glass, paint, and other materials should be purchased? How should resources be combined and in what proportions? Anyone without a detailed knowledge of auto production couldn't do it. (General Motors and Ford, for example, each deals with more than 20,000 suppliers.) That's why consumers buy assembled cars rather than contract separately with each resource supplier.

At the margin, some activities could go either way, with some consumers using firms and some hiring resources directly in markets. The choice depends on each consumer's skill and opportunity cost of time. For example, some people may not want to be troubled with hiring all the inputs to get their house painted. Instead, they simply hire a firm for an agreed-on price—they hire a painting contractor. As you will see later in the chapter, however, hiring a contractor may give rise to other problems of quality control.

The Boundaries of the Firm

So far, the chapter has explained why firms exist: *Firms minimize the transaction costs and the production costs of economic activity.* The next question is: What are the efficient boundaries of the firm? The theory of the firm described in earlier chapters is largely silent on the boundaries of the firm—that is, on the appropriate degree of vertical integration. **Vertical integration** is the expansion of a firm into stages of production earlier or later than those in which it specializes. For example, a steel company may decide (1) to integrate backward to mine iron ore and even mine the coal used to smelt iron ore or (2) to integrate forward to fashion raw steel into various components. A large manufacturer employs an amazing variety of production processes, but on average about half of the cost of production goes to purchase inputs from other firms. For example, General Motors and Ford each spends over $50 billion a year on parts, materials, and services. The total exceeds the annual output of some countries.

Outsourcing occurs when a firm buys products, such as auto parts, or services, such as data processing, from outside suppliers. How does the firm determine which activities to undertake and which to purchase from other firms? A firm relies on the division of labor and the law of comparative advantage to focus on what it does best, what it

vertical integration
The expansion of a firm into stages of production earlier or later than those in which it specializes, such as a steel maker that also mines iron ore

outsourcing
A firm buys inputs from outside suppliers

core competency
Area of specialty; the product or phase of production a firm supplies with greatest efficiency

net 📖 bookmark
To learn more about outsourcing, visit the Outsourcing FAQ at http://www.outsourcingfaq .com/. The Outsourcing Institute (http://www.outsourcing .com/) provides an Internet B2B ("B2B" is short for "business to business") meeting place for outsourcing managers, consultants, and others. Go to http://www.elance.com for an online talent marketplace.

bounded rationality
The notion that there is a limit to the information that a firm's manager can comprehend and act on

considers its **core competency**. Should Dell manufacture its own computer chips or buy them from another firm? The answer depends on the benefits and costs of internal production versus market purchases. The point bears repeating: *Internal production and market purchases are alternative ways of organizing transactions*. The choice depends on which is a more efficient way of carrying out the transaction in question. Keep in mind that market prices coordinate transactions *between* firms, whereas managers coordinate activities *within* firms. The market coordinates resources by meshing the independent plans of separate decision makers, but a firm coordinates resources through the conscious direction of the manager.

The usual assumption is that transactions are organized by market exchange unless markets pose problems. Market exchange allows each firm to benefit from specialization and comparative advantage. For example, Apple can specialize in making computers and buy chips from Intel, a specialist. At this point, it might be useful to discuss specific criteria firms consider when deciding whether to purchase a particular input from the market.

Bounded Rationality of the Manager

To direct and coordinate activity in a conscious way in the firm, a manager must understand how all the pieces of the puzzle fit together. As the firm takes on more and more activities, however, the manager may start losing track of details, so the quality of managerial decisions suffers. The more tasks the firm takes on, the longer the lines of communication between the manager and the production workers who must implement the decision. One constraint on vertical integration is the manager's **bounded rationality,** which limits the amount of information a manager can comprehend about the firm's operation. As the firm takes on more and more functions, coordination and communication become more difficult. The firm can experience diseconomies similar to those it experiences when it expands output beyond the efficient scale of production. The solution is for the firm to reduce its functions to those where it has a comparative advantage.

Incidentally, outsourcing is growing on college campuses. The number of college bookstores run by outside companies has more than doubled since 1992. Barnes & Noble, for example, runs over 600 college bookstores. But college outsourcing has moved beyond bookstores to dozens of activities including food service, custodial service, real estate management, laundry, parking, printing, and security. The growing consensus is that colleges should focus on their core competency, teaching and research, leaving other functions to specialists in each area.

Minimum Efficient Scale

As noted when firm costs were introduced, the *minimum efficient scale* is the minimum rate of output at which economies of scale are fully exploited. For example, suppose that minimum efficient scale in the production of personal computers is 1 million per month, as shown by the firm's long-run average cost curve in panel (a) of Exhibit 1. Suppose this also turns out to be the amount that maximizes profit. Because the computer chip is an important component in a personal computer, should the PC maker integrate backward into chip production? What if the minimum efficient scale in chip production is 5 million per month? As you can see in panel (b) of Exhibit 1, the average cost of producing 1 million chips is much higher than the average cost at the minimum efficient scale of chip production. The PC manufacturer therefore minimizes costs by buying chips from a chip maker of optimal size. More generally, *other things constant, a firm should buy an input if the market price is below what it would cost the firm to make.*

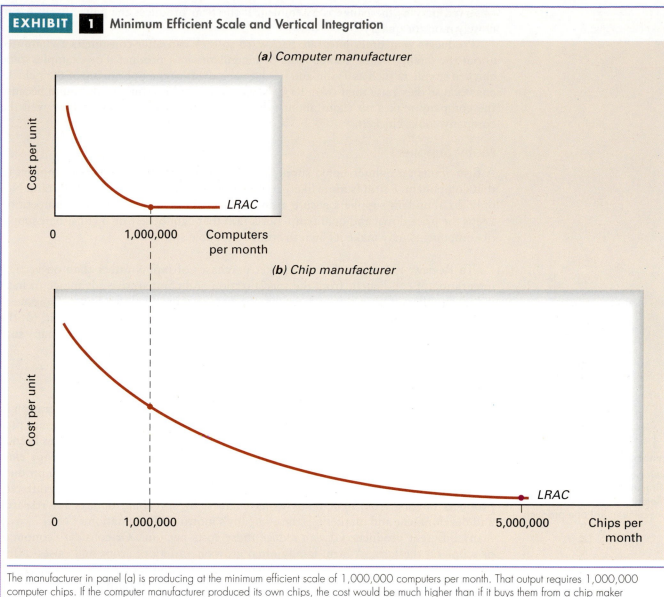

EXHIBIT 1 Minimum Efficient Scale and Vertical Integration

(a) Computer manufacturer

Cost per unit

LRAC

0   1,000,000   Computers
per month

(b) Chip manufacturer

Cost per unit

LRAC

0   1,000,000   5,000,000   Chips per
month

The manufacturer in panel (a) is producing at the minimum efficient scale of 1,000,000 computers per month. That output requires 1,000,000 computer chips. If the computer manufacturer produced its own chips, the cost would be much higher than if it buys them from a chip maker operating on a much larger scale. As panel (b) shows, economies of scale in chip production are far from exhausted when 1,000,000 chips a month are produced.

Easily Observable Quality

If an input is well defined and its quality is easily determined at the time of purchase, that input is more likely to be purchased in the market than produced internally, other things constant. For example, a flour mill typically buys wheat in the market rather than grow its own, as the quality of the wheat can be easily assessed upon inspection. In contrast, the quality of certain inputs can be determined only during production. Firms whose reputations depend on the operation of a key component are likely to produce the component, especially if the quality varies widely across producers over time and can't be easily observed by inspection. For example, suppose that the manufacturer of a sensitive measuring instrument requires a crucial gauge, the quality of which can be observed only as the gauge is assembled. If the firm produces the gauge itself, it can closely monitor quality.

Producers sometimes integrate backward so they can offer consumers a guarantee about the quality of the components or ingredients in a product. For example, some chicken suppliers such as Tyson and Perdue can advertise the upbringing of their chickens because they raise their own. KFC, however, omits this family background because the company makes no claim about raising them, focusing instead on how well the company cooks chicken.

Many Suppliers

A firm wants an uninterrupted supply of components. If there are many suppliers of that component, a firm is more likely to buy it than make it, other things constant. Not only do abundant suppliers ensure a dependable source of components, competition keeps the price down and quality up. But a firm that cannot rely on a consistent supply of components may make its own to ensure a reliable source.

To Review: If a firm relies on market purchases of inputs rather than on vertical integration, it can benefit from the specialization and comparative advantage of individual suppliers. Other things constant, the firm is more likely to buy a component rather than produce it if (1) buying the component is cheaper than making it, (2) the component is well defined and its quality easily observable, and (3) there are many suppliers of the component.

Economies of Scope

economies of scope
Average costs decline as a firm makes a range of different products rather than specialize in just one product

So far we have considered issues affecting the optimal degree of vertical integration in producing a particular product. Even with outsourcing, the focus is on how best to produce a particular product, such as an automobile or a computer. But some firms branch into product lines that do not have a vertical relationship. **Economies of scope** exist when it's cheaper to produce two or more different items in one firm than to produce them in separate firms. For example, General Electric produces hundreds of different products ranging from light bulbs to jet engines. By spreading outlays for research and development and marketing (the company's motto is "Imagination at work") over many different products, GE can reduce those costs per unit. Or consider economies of scope on the farm. A farm family often grows a variety of crops and raises different farm animals—animals that recycle damaged crops and food scraps into meat and fertilizer. With economies of *scale*, the average cost per unit of output falls as the *scale* of the firm increases; *with economies of scope, average costs per unit fall as the firm supplies more types of products—that is, as the scope of the firm increases.* The cost of some fixed resources, such as specialized knowledge, can be spread across product lines.

Our focus has been on why firms exist, why they often integrate vertically, why they outsource, and why they sometimes produce a range of products. These steps toward realism move us beyond the simple picture of the firm created earlier. The next section challenges some simplifying assumptions about the amount of information available to market participants.

Market Behavior With Imperfect Information

For the most part, our analysis of market behavior has assumed that market participants have full information about products and resources. For consumers, full information involves knowledge about a product's price, quality, and availability. For firms, full information includes knowledge about the marginal productivity of various resources, about the appropriate technology for combining them, and about the demand for the firm's product. In reality, *reliable information is often costly for both consumers and producers*. This section examines the impact of less-than-perfect information on market behavior.

Optimal Search With Imperfect Information

Suppose you want to buy a new computer. You need information about the quality and features of each model and the prices at various retail outlets and online sites. To learn more about your choices, you may talk with friends and experts, read promotional brochures and computer publications, and visit online sites. Once you narrow your choice to one or two models, you may visit the mall, or let your fingers do the walking through the *Yellow Pages,* computer catalogs, online search engines, newspaper ads, and the like. Searching for the lowest price for a particular model involves a cost, primarily the opportunity cost of your time. This cost obviously varies from individual to individual and from item to item. Some people actually enjoy shopping, as you will see later in the chapter, but this "shop 'til you drop" attitude does not necessarily carry over to all purchases. *For most of us, the process of gathering consumer information can be considered nonmarket work.*

Marginal Cost of Search

In your quest for product information, you gather the easy and obvious information first. You may check on the price and availability at the few electronics stores at the mall. But as your search widens, the *marginal cost* of information increases, both because you may have to travel greater distances to check prices and services and because the opportunity cost of your time increases as you spend more time acquiring information. Consequently, the marginal cost curve for information slopes upward, as is shown in Exhibit 2. Note that a certain amount of information, I_f, is common knowledge and is freely available, so its marginal cost is zero.

Marginal Benefit of Search

The *marginal benefit* of acquiring additional information is a better quality for a given price or a lower price for a given quality. The marginal benefit is relatively large at first, but as you gather more information and grow more acquainted with the market, additional information yields less and less marginal benefit. For example, the likelihood of uncovering valuable information, such as an added feature or a lower price, at the second store or Web site visited is greater than the likelihood of finding this information at the twentieth store or Web site visited. Thus, the marginal benefit curve for additional information slopes downward, as is shown in Exhibit 2.

Optimal Search

Market participants continue to gather information as long as the marginal benefit of additional information exceeds its marginal cost. *Optimal search occurs where the marginal benefit just equals the marginal cost,* which in Exhibit 2 is where the two marginal curves intersect. Notice that at search levels exceeding the equilibrium amount, the marginal benefit of additional information is still positive but below marginal cost. Notice also that at some point the value of additional information reaches zero, as identified by I_p on the horizontal axis. This level of information could be identified as *full information.* The high marginal cost of acquiring I_p, however, makes it impractical to become fully informed. Thus, firms and consumers, by gathering the optimal amount

net bookmark

For most Americans, a house is the single biggest investment they will ever make. The larger the investment, the more worthwhile it is to gather information. The search process is made easier with http://www.realtor.com, the official Web site of the National Association of Realtors®. What types of information are provided on the introductory Web page? From there you can search for homes for sale in any part of the country, filtering the selection according to various criteria. Try finding a home you might like. Read 20 steps on how to buy a house at http://www.ehow.com/how_110971_buy-house.html.

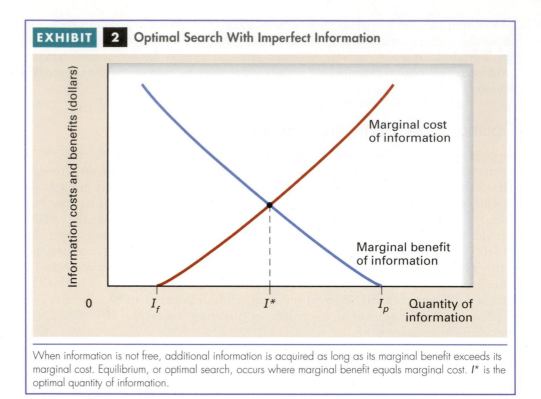

EXHIBIT 2 Optimal Search With Imperfect Information

When information is not free, additional information is acquired as long as its marginal benefit exceeds its marginal cost. Equilibrium, or optimal search, occurs where marginal benefit equals marginal cost. *I** is the optimal quantity of information.

of information, I^*, have less-than-full information about the price, availability, and quality of products and resources.

Implications

This search model was developed by Nobel laureate George Stigler, who showed that the price of a product can differ among sellers because some consumers are unaware of lower prices elsewhere.[2] Thus, *search costs result in price dispersion, or different prices for the same product.* Some sellers call attention to price dispersions by claiming to have the lowest prices around and by promising to match any competitor's price—for example, Wal-Mart makes such a promise. *Search costs also lead to quality differences across sellers, even for identically priced products, because consumers find the expected marginal cost of finding a higher quality product outweighs the expected marginal benefit.*

There are other implications of Stigler's search model. The more expensive the item, the greater the price dispersion in dollar terms, so the greater the expected marginal benefit from shopping around. You are more likely to shop around for a new car than for a new toothbrush. Also, as earnings increase, so does the opportunity cost of time, resulting in less searching and more price dispersion. On the other hand, any technological change that reduces the marginal cost of information lowers the marginal cost curve in Exhibit 2, increasing the optimal amount of information and reducing price dispersion. For example, some online sites, like mySimon.com, identify the lowest

2. George Stigler, "The Economics of Information," *Journal of Political Economy,* 69 (June 1961): 213–225.

prices for books, airfares, automobiles, computers, and dozens of other products. And some online sellers, like Buy.com, maintain the lowest prices on the Web as a way of attracting customers who undertake such searches. As a result of more readily available price information, consumers have become much more price-sensitive.[3] Thus, by reducing search costs, the Internet reduces price dispersion.

Here's another example of how information technology can improve market performance and enhance social welfare. Between 1997 and 2001, mobile phone service was introduced throughout a state in India with a large fishing industry. Researchers found that the adoption of mobile phones by fishermen and wholesalers sharply reduced price dispersions, in the process increasing both consumer and producer welfare.[4]

The Winner's Curse

In 1996, the federal government auctioned off leases to valuable space on the scarce radio spectrum. The space was to be used for cell phones, wireless networks, and portable fax machines. The bidding was carried out in the face of much uncertainty about what were then new markets. Bidders had little experience with the potential value of such leases. At the time, 89 companies made winning bids for 493 licenses totaling $10.2 billion. But by 1998, it became clear that many of the winning bidders couldn't pay, and many went bankrupt.[5] The auction eventually collected only half the amount of the winning bids. In auctions for products of uncertain value, such as wireless communications licenses, why do so many "winners" end up losers?

When bids were submitted, the true value of space on the radio spectrum could only be estimated. Suppose the average bid for a license was $10 million, with some higher and others lower. Suppose also that the winning bid was $20 million. The winning bid was not the average bid, which may have been the most reliable estimate of the true value, but the highest bid, which was the most optimistic estimate. Winners of such bids are said to experience the **winner's curse** because they often lose money after winning the bid, paying the price of being overly optimistic. (It will be interesting to see if similar problems result from the 2008 wireless spectrum auction, which raised $19.6 billion.)

The winner's curse applies to all cases of bidding in which the true value is unknown at the outset. For example, online auctions, such as eBay, often sell items of unknown value. Movie companies often bid up the price of screenplays to what some argue are unrealistic levels (only about 5 percent of screenplays studios purchase ever become movies). Likewise, publishers get into bidding wars over book manuscripts and even book proposals that are little more than titles. Team owners bid and often overpay for athletes who become free agents. And research shows that professional basketball players improve their performance in the year before signing a multiyear contract, but performance declines after that.[6] NBC lost money on the 2008 summer Olympics in Beijing and the 2010 winter Olympics in Vancouver; at the time of the bid for broadcast rights, the Olympic cities had not even been selected.

With perfect information about market value, potential buyers would never bid more than that market value. But *when competitive bidding is coupled with imperfect information, the winning bidder often ends up an overly optimistic loser.*

winner's curse

The plight of the winning bidder who overestimates an asset's true value

3.   Glenn Ellison and Sara Ellison, "Search, Obfuscation, and Price Elasticities on the Internet." *Econometrica*, 77 (March 2009): 427–452.
4.   Robert Jensen, "The Digital Provide: Information (Technology), Market Performance, and Welfare in the South Indian Fisheries Sector," *Quarterly Journal of Economics*, 122 (August 2007): 879–924.
5.   Scott Ritter, "FCC Says Several Bidders to Return Wireless Licenses," *Wall Street Journal*, 18 June 1998.
6.   Kevin Stiroh, "Playing for Keeps: Pay and Performance in the NBA," *Economic Inquiry*, 45 (January 2007): 145–161.

Asymmetric Information in Product Markets

We have considered the effects of costly information and limited information on market behavior. But the issue becomes more complicated when one side of the market knows more than the other side does, a problem of **asymmetric information**. There are two types of information that a market participant may want but lack: information about a product's *characteristics* and information about *actions* taken by the other party to the transaction. This section examines several examples of asymmetric information in the product market and the effects on market efficiency.

Hidden Characteristics: Adverse Selection

When one side of the market knows more than the other side about important product characteristics, the asymmetric information problem involves **hidden characteristics.** For example, the seller of a used car normally has abundant personal experience with important *characteristics* of that car, such as any accidents, breakdowns, gas mileage, maintenance record, performance in bad weather, and so on. A prospective buyer can only guess at these characteristics based on the car's appearance, ratings in *Consumer Reports*, and perhaps a test drive. The buyer cannot really know how well the car performs without driving it under varying traffic and weather conditions.

To simplify the problem, suppose there are only two types of used cars for sale: good ones and bad ones, or "lemons." A buyer who is certain about a car's type would be willing to pay $10,000 for a good used car but only $4,000 for a lemon. Again, only the seller knows which type is for sale. Prospective buyers believe that half the used cars on the market are good ones and half are lemons and are willing to pay, say, $7,000 for a car of unknown quality (the average expected value of cars on the market). Would $7,000 become the market price of used cars?

So far, the analysis has ignored the actions of potential sellers, who know which type of car they have. Because sellers of good cars can get only $7,000 for cars they know to be worth $10,000 on average, many will keep their cars or will sell them only to friends or relatives. But sellers of lemons will find $7,000 an attractive price for a car they know to be worth only $4,000. As a result, the proportion of good cars on the market will fall and the proportion of lemons will rise, reducing the average value of used cars on the market. As buyers come to realize that the mix has shifted toward lemons, they will reduce what they are willing to pay for cars of unknown quality. As the market price of used cars falls, potential sellers of good cars become even more reluctant to sell at such a low price, so the proportion of lemons increases, leading to still lower prices. The process could continue until few good cars are for sale on the open market. More generally, *when sellers have better information about a product's quality than buyers do, lower-quality products dominate the market.*

When those on the informed side of the market self-select in a way that harms the uninformed side of the market, the problem is one of **adverse selection.** In our example, car sellers, the informed side, self-select—that is, they decide whether or not to offer their cars for sale—in a way that increases the proportion of lemons for sale. Because of adverse selection, those still willing to buy on the open market often get stuck with lemons. There is empirical support for adverse selection in used car markets. For example, one researcher found that owners of lemons try to sell them to ill-informed buyers while owners of good cars hold onto theirs.[7]

asymmetric information
One side of the market has better information about the product than does the other side

hidden characteristics
One side of the market knows more than the other side about product characteristics that are important to the other side

adverse selection
Those on the informed side of the market self-select in a way that harms those on the uninformed side of the market

7.   George Seldon, "The Market for Used Cars: New Evidence of the Lemons Phenomenon," *Applied Economics*, 41 (Issue 22, 2009): 2867–2885.

Hidden Actions: The Principal-Agent Problem

A second type of problem occurs when one side of a transaction can pursue an unobservable *action* that affects the other side. Whenever one side of an economic relationship can take a relevant action that the other side cannot observe, the situation is described as one of **hidden actions.** In this age of specialization, there are many tasks we do not perform for ourselves because others do them better and because others have a lower opportunity cost of time. Suppose your car isn't working and you have no clue what's wrong. The mechanic you hire may have other objectives, such as minimizing on-the-job effort or maximizing the garage's profit. But the mechanic's actions are hidden from you. Although your car's problem may be only a loose connection wire, the mechanic could inflate the bill by charging you for work not needed or not performed. This asymmetric information problem occurs because one side of a transaction can pursue *hidden actions* that affect the other side. When buyers have difficulty monitoring and evaluating the quality of goods or services purchased, some suppliers may substitute poor-quality resources or exercise less diligence in providing the service.

The problem that arises from hidden actions is called the **principal-agent problem,** which describes a relationship in which one party, known as the **principal,** contracts with another party, known as the **agent,** in the expectation that the agent will act on behalf of the principal. *The problem arises when the goals of the agent are incompatible with those of the principal **and** when the agent can pursue hidden actions.* For example, you are the *principal* and the garage mechanic is your *agent.* You could also confront a principal-agent problem when you deal with a doctor, lawyer, stockbroker, plumber, building contractor, or real estate agent, to name a few. For example, real estate agents are usually better informed than their clients about the housing market. Research suggests that agents exploit this asymmetry by encouraging their clients to sell their homes too cheaply and too quickly.[8]

Any employer-employee relationship could become a principal-agent problem, with the employer as the principal and the employee as the agent. Again, the problem arises because the agent's objectives are not the same as the principal's *and* because the agent's actions are hidden. Not all principal-agent relationships pose a problem. For example, when you hire someone to cut your hair or your lawn, there are no hidden actions so you can judge the results for yourself.

Asymmetric Information in Insurance Markets

Asymmetric information also creates problems in insurance markets. For example, from an insurer's point of view, the ideal candidate for health insurance is someone who leads a long, healthy life, then dies peacefully while sleeping. But many people are poor risks for health insurers because of hidden characteristics (bad genes) or hidden actions (smoking and drinking excessively, getting exercise only on trips to the refrigerator, and thinking a balanced meal consists of some beef jerky and a six-pack of beer). In the insurance market, it is the buyers, not the sellers, who have more information about the characteristics and actions that predict their likely need for insurance in the future.

If the insurance company has no way of distinguishing among applicants, it must charge those who are good health risks the same price as those who are poor ones. This price is attractive to poor risks but not to good ones, some of whom will not buy insurance. The insured group becomes less healthy on average, so rates must rise, making

hidden actions
One side of an economic relationship can do something that the other side cannot observe

principal-agent problem
The agent's objectives differ from those of the principal's, and one side can pursue hidden actions

principal
A person or firm who hires an agent to act on behalf of that person or firm

agent
A person or firm who is supposed to act on behalf of the principal

---

8. Steven Levitt and Chad Syverson, "Market Distortions When Agents Are Better Informed: The Value of Information in Real Estate Transactions," *Review of Economics and Statistics,* 90 (November 2008): 599–611.

insurance even less attractive to healthy people. *Because of adverse selection, insurance buyers tend to be less healthy than the population as a whole.* Adverse selection was used as an argument for the health care reform introduced in 2010.

The insurance problem is compounded by the fact that once people buy insurance, their behavior may change in a way that increases the probability that a claim will be made. For example, those with health insurance may take less care of their health, and those with theft insurance may take less care of their valuables. This incentive problem is referred to as *moral hazard*. **Moral hazard** occurs when an individual's behavior changes in a way that increases the likelihood of an unfavorable outcome. More generally, *moral hazard is a principal-agent problem because it occurs when those on one side of a transaction have an incentive to shirk their responsibilities because the other side is unable to observe them.* The responsibility could be to repair a car, maintain one's health, or safeguard one's valuables. Both the mechanic and the insurance buyer may take advantage of the ignorant party. In the car-repair example, the mechanic is the agent; in the insurance example, the policy buyer is the principal. Thus, moral hazard arises when someone can undertake hidden action; this could be either the agent or the principal, depending on the situation.

Moral hazard was a frequent topic of debate each time the federal government decided to bail out or not bail out a company or industry during the 2008 global financial crisis. For example, if an investment bank was rescued after its past risky behavior, would such a bank be more inclined to take similar risks in the future? Some observers believe the answer is yes.

moral hazard

A situation in which one party, as a result of a contract, has an incentive to alter their behavior in a way that harms the other party to the contract

Coping With Asymmetric Information

There are ways of reducing the consequences of asymmetric information. An incentive structure or an information-revealing system can be developed to reduce the problems associated with the lopsided availability of information. For example, all states now have "lemon laws" that offer compensation to buyers of new or used cars that turn out to be lemons. Used-car dealers may also offer warranties to reduce the buyer's risk of getting stuck with a lemon. Most garages provide written estimates before a job is done, and many return the defective parts to the customer as evidence that the repair was necessary and was carried out. People often get multiple estimates for major repairs.

Insurance companies deal with adverse selection and moral hazard in a variety of ways. Prior to recent federal legislation, most required applicants to undergo a physical exam and to answer questions about their medical history and lifestyle (false information could block benefits). Preexisting medical conditions were not usually covered. To avoid adverse selection, an insurer often covers all those in a group, such as all company employees, not just those who would otherwise self-select. Insurers reduce moral hazard by making the policyholder pay, say, the first $250 of a claim as a "deductible" and by requiring the policyholder to copay a percentage of a claim. Also, as more claims are filed, insurance premiums go up and the policy could be canceled. Property insurers reduce premiums for those who install security systems, smoke alarms, sprinkler systems, and who take other safety precautions.

Asymmetric Information in Labor Markets

Our market analysis for particular kinds of labor typically assumes that workers are more or less interchangeable. In equilibrium, each worker in a particular labor market is assumed to be paid the same wage, a wage equal to the marginal revenue product of the last unit of labor hired. But what if ability differs across workers? Differences in ability present no particular problem as long as these differences can be readily observed by the employer. If the productivity of each worker is easily quantified through measures such as crates of oranges picked, quantity of garments sewn, or number of cars sold, these can and do serve as the basis for pay. And such incentives seem to affect output. For example, when the British National Health Service changed the pay basis of dentists from "contact hours" with patients to the number of cavities filled, dentists found more cavities and filled them in only a third of the time they took under the contact-hour pay scheme.[9]

Because production often requires a team effort, the employer may not be able to attribute specific outputs to particular workers. When information about each worker's marginal productivity is hard to come by, employers usually pay workers by the hour. Sometimes the pay combines an hourly rate and incentive pay linked to a measure of productivity. For example, a sales representative typically earns a base salary plus a commission tied to sales. At times, the task of evaluating performance is left to customers. Workers who provide personal services, such as waiters, barbers, beauticians, pizza deliverers, and bellhops, rely partly or mostly on tips. These services are "personal" and visible, so customers are usually in the best position to judge the quality and timeliness of service and to tip accordingly.

Adverse Selection in Labor Markets

A job applicant's true abilities—motivation, work habits, skills, ability to get along with others, and the like—are, to a large extent, *hidden characteristics*. In a labor market with hidden characteristics, employers might be better off offering a higher wage. The higher the wage, the more attractive the job is to more-qualified workers. Paying a higher wage also encourages those who are hired not to goof off or otherwise jeopardize an attractive job. Paying above-market wages to attract and retain more-productive workers is called paying **efficiency wages,** something that Henry Ford did.

> **efficiency wage theory**
> The idea that offering high wages attracts a more talented labor pool and encourages those hired to perform well to keep their jobs

Signaling and Screening

The person on the side of the market with hidden characteristics and hidden actions has an incentive to say the right thing. For example, a job applicant might say, "Hire me because I am hardworking, reliable, prompt, highly motivated, and just an all-around great employee." Or a manufacturer might say, "At Ford, quality is job one." But such claims appear self-serving and thus are not necessarily believable. To cut through this fog, both sides of the market try to develop credible ways of communicating reliable information about qualifications.

Signaling is the attempt by the informed side of the market to communicate information that the other side would find valuable. Consider signaling in the job market. Because some jobs require abilities that are unobservable on a résumé or in an interview, job applicants offer proxy measures, such as years of education, college grades, and letters of recommendation. A proxy measure is called a *signal*, which is an observable indicator of some hidden characteristic. A signal is sent by the informed side of the market to the uninformed side and is useful as long as less-qualified applicants face more difficulty sending the same signal.

> **signaling**
> Using a proxy measure to communicate information about unobservable characteristics; the signal is more effective if more-productive workers find it easier to send than do less-productive workers

To identify the best workers, employers try to *screen* applicants. **Screening** is the attempt by the uninformed side of the market to uncover the relevant but hidden characteristics of the informed party. An initial screen might check each résumé for spelling and typographical errors. Although not important in themselves, such errors

> **screening**
> The process used by employers to select the most qualified workers based on observable characteristics, such as a job applicant's level of education and course grades

---

9. John Pencavel, "Piecework and On-the-Job Screening," *Working Paper*, Stanford University, (June 1975).

suggest a lack of attention to detail—which could reduce labor productivity. The uninformed party must identify signals that less-productive individuals have more difficulty sending. A signal that can be sent with equal ease by all workers, regardless of their productivity, does not provide a useful way of screening applicants. But if, for example, more-productive workers find it easier to graduate from college than do less-productive workers, a college degree is a measure worth using to screen workers. In this case, education may be valuable, not so much because of its direct effect on a worker's productivity, but simply because it enables employers to distinguish between types of workers. In fact, the actual pay increase from a fourth year of college that results in graduation is several times the pay increase from just a third year of college. This finding is consistent with the screening theory of education.

To Review: Because the potential productivity of job applicants cannot be measured directly, an employer must rely on proxy measures to screen applicants. *The most valuable proxy is a signal that can be sent more easily by more-productive workers and also is a good predictor of future productivity.* The problems of adverse selection, signaling, and screening are discussed in the following case study of how McDonald's selects franchisees.

CASE STUDY

e activity

McDonald's maintains a Web site devoted to information about obtaining a U.S. franchise at http://www .aboutmcdonalds.com/mcd/ franchising/us_franchising .html. Look over the FAQ file. How much cash does a potential franchisee currently need to qualify? How many partners can be involved in a franchise? Who selects the sites and who constructs the building?

McDonalds/Feature Photo Service/Newscom

WORLD OF BUSINESS

Reputation of a Big Mac   McDonald's has 32,000 restaurants in more than 120 countries and employs more than a million people. The secret to their success is that customers around the world can count on product consistency whether in Phoenix, Anchorage, Moscow, or Hong Kong. *McDonald's has grown because it has attracted competent and reliable franchise owners and has provided them with appropriate incentives and constraints to offer a product of consistent quality.*

To avoid adverse selection, McDonald's seldom advertises for franchisees yet still has plenty of applicants. Even to be granted an interview, an applicant must show substantial financial resources and good business experience. An applicant who passes the initial screening must come up with a security deposit and complete the nine-month full-time training program. A franchise costs anywhere from $950,000 to $1,800,000, depending on the size and location, plus an opening fee of $45,000. Of that amount, the new franchisee must have "non-borrowed personal resources," of at least $500,000 in cash; this money can't come from friends or relatives. In effect, the applicant must have saved this amount or own assets such as property or stock that could be sold to raise the cash. Those with more savings have an edge in the selection process. McDonald's uses personal wealth as a signal of the individual's business sense and ability to manage money. The rest can be borrowed from a bank but must be paid back in no more than seven years. McDonald's is using the bank's loan officers to screen the applicant's creditworthiness. During the training period, the applicant is paid nothing, not even expenses. Some who complete training are rejected for a franchise. Once the restaurant opens, a franchisee must work full time. McDonald's does not offer franchises to partnerships or to groups of investors.

Thus, the franchisee has a deep financial stake in the success of the operation. As a further incentive, successful owners may get additional restaurants. If all goes well, the franchise is valid for 20 years and renewable after that, but it can be canceled at any time if the restaurant fails the company's standards of quality, pricing, cleanliness, hours of operation, and so on. The franchisee is bound to the company by highly specific investments of money and human capital, such as the time invested learning McDonald's operating system. The loss of a franchise would represent a huge financial blow. Through its franchise policies, McDonald's is trying to protect its most valuable asset—its reputation for "quality, service, cleanliness, and value." The golden arches are the second most recognized corporate symbol in the world (the stylized lettering of Coca-Cola ranks first). In selecting and monitoring franchisees, McDonald's has successfully addressed problems stemming from hidden characteristics and hidden actions.

Sources: Andrew Martin, "At McDonald's the Happiest Meal Is Hot Profits," *New York Times*, 10 January 2009; Esther Fung, "McDonald's to Double Restaurants in China," *Wall Street Journal*, 29 March 2010; D. L. Noren, "The Economics of the Golden Arches," *American Economist*, 34 (Fall 1990): 60–64; and "McDonald's Corporate Franchising" at http://www.aboutmcdonalds.com/mcd/franchising/us_franchising.html.

Behavioral Economics

Traditional economics assumes that people act rationally to maximize their overall well-being. People know what they want, they try to make the most of what they have, they make choices that are fairly consistent given the circumstances, and they follow through with those choices. In short, *the traditional economic approach assumes that people pursue their rational self-interest*. And according to Adam Smith, the pursuit of self-interest promotes the general good, so the market system works in a reinforcing and beneficial cycle. In the extreme, this standard approach views the economy as populated by calculating, unemotional maximizers who make choices consistent with rational self-interest and then follow through on those choices.

Viewing people as robot-like maximizers is a simplification that can be defended on the grounds that this approach is easy to spell out in a theoretical model and it yields clear, testable implications about how people behave. Much empirical work backs up this version of human nature. And even if people don't actually make such complex calculations, they act as if they do. For example, they act as if they can maximize utility by equating the relevant marginal utilities.

On the other hand, psychologists have come to believe that people are prone to mistakes, are fickle and inconsistent, and often do not get the best deal when making choices. Psychologists investigate the biases, faulty assumptions, and errors that affect how people make decisions in all aspects of life. In recent decades, some economists have begun to rely on findings from psychology to look at instances where people do not act according to traditional economic theory. The convergence of economics and psychology eventually created a new field of study referred to as behavioral economics, a field pursued by a small but growing band of economists. **Behavioral economics** borrows insights from psychology to help explain some economic decisions. This approach questions some assumptions of traditional economics, particularly the assumptions of (1) unbounded rationality and (2) unbounded willpower.

behavioral economics
An approach that borrows insights from psychology to help explain economic choices

Unbounded Rationality

Nobel Prize winner Herbert Simon was an early critic of the idea that people have unlimited information-processing capabilities. He introduced the term "bounded rationality" to describe a more realistic conception of human problem-solving ability, a term introduced earlier in this chapter to help explain optimal firm size. Because we have only so much brainpower and only so much time, we cannot be expected to solve complex production or consumption problems optimally. When faced with lots of information that we aren't sure how to process, most of us rely on simple rules of thumb for guidance. The simplest rule of thumb in the face of a difficult decision is to do nothing.

Psychologists find that people are prone to inertia, even when doing nothing may cost them money. In the face of uncertainty, doing nothing or doing little also means that people are inclined to accept default rules. For example, employees have a strong tendency to stick to whatever savings option an employer presented to them as the default option, even when they are free to choose better options. Many accept the default option even when that option is not to save at all, and thereby miss out on any free money available through a company-match. Inertia is also why, once a decision is made, or made for them, the chooser tends to stick with that option even when circumstances change. In short, we humans try to avoid making some decisions even when the consequences of no decision are costly. In that regard, we do not seem to be pursuing our self-interest.

Unbounded Willpower

A second assumption of traditional economics is that people, once they make a decision, have unbounded willpower—that is, they have complete self-control. But we humans, even when we know what's best for us, often lack the discipline to follow through. Most of us have, despite our best intentions, ended up eating, drinking, or spending too much, and exercising, saving, or studying too little. For example, nearly two-thirds of American adults are overweight. Let's close this chapter with a case study that looks at issues of self-control.

BEHAVIORAL ECONOMICS

Self-Control: Just Don't Do It!   In the late 1960s, Walter Mischel, a psychologist at Stanford University, conducted an experiment to measure the self-control of children at a campus nursery school. A child was ushered into a small room and invited to choose a treat from a tray of marshmallows, cookies, and pretzel sticks. The child was then seated at a small table with the treat on a plate and made an offer: The child could eat the selected treat anytime, but a child who could wait 15 minutes before eating it would be rewarded with another of that same treat. After explaining the deal, the researcher left the room. These experiments were conducted with hundreds of children over several years. Films of the experiment show how each child struggled to delay gratification. Most held out no more than three minutes before eating the treat, but about 30 percent got the second treat by holding out the 15 minutes.

About a dozen years later, Professor Mischel surveyed the parents, teachers, and academic advisors of students involved in the experiment. He found that the children who were able to wait longer at age 4 or 5 grew into adolescents who were described as more academically and socially competent, more attentive, better planners, and more able to deal with frustration and stress. He and his colleagues continued to track these subjects into their late thirties and found that those who couldn't wait as children had a significantly higher body-mass index as adults and were more likely to have encountered problems with drug addiction.

A different experiment looking at the relationship between self-control and academic performance among 164 eighth-graders found that the ability to delay gratification—students were given a choice between a dollar right away or $2 the following week—was much more powerful at predicting academic performance than was I.Q. For decades, researchers viewed intelligence as a key variable in predicting success in life. But many researchers now believe that intelligence is at the mercy of self-control. After all, to succeed, even the smartest students still need to do their assignments.

What has come to be called "the marshmallow test" is a microcosm of many will-power issues, from watching TV instead of studying for a final exam to spending impulsively now rather than saving for something that really matters. From morning weigh-ins to New Year's resolutions, we all use devices to help boost our willpower. More generally, market and nonmarket solutions have evolved to help people overcome self-control problems. People who want to study more, save more, exercise more, quit smoking, lose weight, quit drinking, shop less impulsively, get off drugs, or stop gambling are often willing to pay time and money for help, as with tutors and enforced study hours, payroll-savings plans and excessive tax withholding (to ensure a refund later), fitness trainers and club memberships, nicotine gum and patches, diet plans and weight-loss surgery, Alcoholics Anonymous, Shopaholics Anonymous, rehab treatment, and Gamblers Anonymous. Some casinos allow problem gamblers to ban themselves from the premises; they will be turned away if they show up and can be denied any winnings if they do manage to gamble and win.

To pursue long-term goals, people must be able to postpone at least some immediate gratification. More economists are now looking at willpower issues. For example, Dean Karlan, a Yale economist, has developed a Web site at www. stickk.com to help people stick to their goals.

Sources: Walter Mischel et al., "The Nature of Adolescent Competencies Predicted by Preschool Delay of Gratification," *Journal of Personal and Social Psychology*, 54 (Winter 1988): 687–696; Angela Duckworth and Martin Seligman, "Self-Discipline Outdoes I.Q. in Predicting Academic Performance in Adolescents," *Psychological Science*, 16 (December 2005): 939–944; Tabea Bucher-Koenen and Carsten Schmidt, "Instant Gratification and Self-Control in Experiments with Children and Teenagers," American Economic Association Meetings, 5 January 2010; and Lex Borghans, Angela Duckworth, and James Heckman, "The Economics and Psychology of Personality Traits," *Journal of Human Resources*, 43 (Fall 2008): 972–1059.

Conclusion

The firm has evolved through a natural selection process as the form of organization that minimizes both transaction and production costs. Ways of organizing production that are more efficient will be selected by the economic system for survival. Attributes that yield an economic profit will thrive, and those that do not will fall away. The form of organization selected may not be optimal in the sense that it cannot be improved, but it is the most efficient of those that have been tried. If there is a way to organize production that is more efficient, some entrepreneur will stumble on it one day and will be rewarded with greater profit. The improvement may not always be the result of conscious design. Once a more efficient way of organizing production is uncovered, others will imitate it.

In conventional demand-and-supply analysis, trades occur in impersonal markets, and the buyer has no special concern about who is on the sell side. But with asymmetric information, the mix and characteristics of the other side of the market become important. When the problem of adverse selection is severe enough, some markets may cease to function. Market participants try to overcome the limitations of asymmetric information by signaling, screening, and trying to be quite explicit and transparent about the terms of the transaction.

Behavioral economists have borrowed insights from psychology to help explain some economic choices that seem inconsistent with rational self-interest. Psychologists argue that because people have trouble with complex choices, they tend to do nothing or go with whatever default option is presented. And people often lack the self-control to put up with near-term costs for long-term benefits.

Summary

1. According to Ronald Coase, firms arise when production is more efficient using the hierarchy of the firm than using market transactions. Because production requires elaborate coordination of many resources, all this activity can usually be carried out more efficiently under the direction of a firm's manager than by having a consumer negotiate detailed performance contracts with many resource suppliers.

2. The extent to which a firm integrates vertically depends on the transaction costs and the production costs of economic activity. Other things constant, the firm is more likely to buy a component rather than produce it if (a) it's cheaper to buy it than make it, (b) the item is well defined and its quality easily determined, and (c) there are many suppliers of the component.

3. Economies of scope exist when it is cheaper to produce two or more different products in one firm than to produce them in separate firms.

4. A buyer searches for product information as long as the marginal benefit of search exceeds its marginal cost. Because information is costly, product prices may differ across suppliers of otherwise identical products. A new technology, such as the Internet, that reduces search costs will increase the amount of search and reduce price differences for a given product.

5. Asymmetric information occurs when one side of the market is better informed about a product than the other side is. The uninformed side may not know about hidden characteristics or about hidden actions. Because of adverse selection, those on the uninformed side of the market may find they are dealing with exactly the wrong people.

6. When the productivity of job applicants cannot be directly observed, an employer may try to screen them based on some signal, such as the level of education or college grades, that more-productive workers can send more easily than can less-productive workers.

7. Standard economics assumes that people are rational in pursuing their self-interest. They have computer-like abilities to make marginal calculations and have sufficient willpower to follow through on decisions that involve near-term costs for long-term gains. Psychologists question the ability of humans to make complex decisions and to follow through on choices that involve near-term costs. Behavioral economics borrows insights from psychology to help explain some economic decisions that otherwise seem inconsistent with rational self-interest.

Key Concepts

Vertical integration   315

Outsourcing   315

Core competency   316

Bounded rationality   316

Economies of scope   318

Winner's curse   321

Asymmetric information   322

Hidden characteristics   322

Adverse selection   322

Hidden actions   323

Principal-agent problem   323

Principal   323

Agent   323

Moral hazard   324

Efficiency wage theory   325

Signaling   325

Screening   325

Behavioral economics   327

Questions for Review

1. **RATIONALE FOR THE FIRM**   Explain Ronald Coase's theory of why firms exist. Why isn't all production consolidated in one large firm?

2. **BOUNDARIES OF THE FIRM**   Define vertical integration. What factors should a firm consider when determining what degree of vertical integration to undertake?

3. **BOUNDARIES OF THE FIRM**   Ashland Oil buys its crude oil in the market. Larger oil refiners, such as Texaco, drill for their own crude oil. Why do some oil companies drill for their own crude oil and others buy crude oil in the market?

4. **BOUNDARIES OF THE FIRM**   In the movement to downsize government, advocates often recommend turning over some government services to private firms hired by the government. What are the potential benefits and costs of such outsourcing? Prepare your answer by reviewing. The Outsourcing

Institute's "Top 10 Reasons Companies Outsource" at http://www.horizontech.net/toptenreasons.htm.

5. **ECONOMIES OF SCOPE**   Distinguish between economies of scale and economies of scope. Why do some firms produce multiple product lines, while others produce only one?

6. **SEARCH WITH IMPERFECT INFORMATION**   Fifty years ago, people shopped by mail using catalogs from large mail-order houses. In the last few years, catalog shopping has again become a widely used method of buying. Online shopping is also growing. What reasons can you suggest for the growth in these forms of shopping?

7. **ASYMMETRIC INFORMATION**   Define asymmetric information. Distinguish between hidden characteristics and hidden actions. Which type of asymmetric information contributes to the principal-agent problem?

8. THE PRINCIPAL-AGENT PROBLEM Discuss the nature of the principal-agent problem. Determine which is the principal and which is the agent in each of the following relationships:

    a. A firm that produces goods for export and the export management company that helps market its goods overseas
    b. The management of a firm and its stockholders
    c. A homeowner and the plumber hired to make repairs
    d. A dentist and a patient
    e. An employee-pension management firm and the company using its services

9. ADVERSE SELECTION AND MORAL HAZARD Describe the problems faced by health insurance companies as a result of adverse selection and moral hazard. How do insurance companies try to reduce these problems?

10. SIGNALING Give an example of signaling in each of the following situations:

    a. Choosing a doctor
    b. Applying to graduate school
    c. Filling out a form for a dating service

11. SIGNALING AND SCREENING What roles do signaling and screening play in a labor market with asymmetric information?

12. Case Study: The Reputation of a Big Mac Explain how the time and financial requirements involved in obtaining a McDonald's franchise relate to the hidden-characteristics problem. Why would existing franchise owners have an interest in the maintenance of high application standards for new franchise owners?

Problems and Exercises

13. BEHAVIORAL ECONOMICS A management consultant advised a small business owner to fully analyze all transaction costs, delineate the boundaries of the business, and develop an equation to calculate exactly economies of scope. The owner replied that there were not enough hours in the day to gather all this information and so the owner would just keep running the business in the same way as usual. What assumption from traditional economics is in dispute here?

14. SEARCH WITH IMPERFECT INFORMATION The following questions concern the accompanying graph.

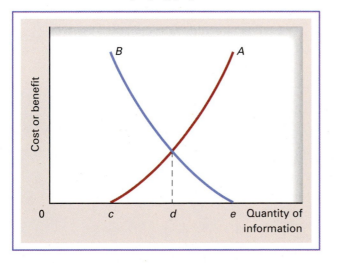

a. Identify the two curves shown on the graph, and explain their upward or downward slopes.
b. Why does curve A intersect the horizontal axis?
c. What is the significance of quantity d?
d. What does e represent?
e. How would the optimal quantity of information change if the marginal benefit of information increased—that is, if the marginal benefit curve shifted upward?

15. SEARCH WITH IMPERFECT INFORMATION Determine the effect of each of the following on the optimal level of search.

    a. The consumer's wage increases.
    b. One seller guarantees to offer the lowest price on the market.
    c. The technology of gathering and transmitting market information improves.

Global Economic Watch Exercises

Login to www.cengagebrain.com and access the Global Economic Watch to do these exercises.

16. GLOBAL ECONOMIC WATCH Go to the Global Economic Crisis Resource Center. Select Global Issues in Context. In the Basic Search box at the top of the page, enter the phrase "behavioral economics." On the Results page, go to the Global Viewpoints Section. Click on the link for the July 15, 2010, editorial "Economics Behaving Badly." The authors stated, "Behavioral economics should complement, not substitute for, more substantive economic interventions." Use one of the examples from the editorial to explain this statement.

17. GLOBAL ECONOMIC WATCH Go to the Global Economic Crisis Resource Center. Select Global Issues in Context. In the Basic Search box at the top of the page, enter the term "moral hazard." Choose an article published in the most recent two years. Explain how the article illustrates the concept of moral hazard.

Economic Regulation and Antitrust Policy

15

JIM BRYANT/UPI/Landov

- If the "invisible hand" of competition yields such desirable results for the economy, why does the government need to regulate business?
- Is monopoly ever better than competition?
- Who benefits most when government regulates monopoly?
- Why did the U.S. government haul Microsoft into court, and what about recent regulator interest in Apple and in Google?
- Is the U.S. economy becoming more competitive or less competitive?

Answers to these and other questions are addressed in this chapter, which discusses government regulation of business.

Businesspeople praise competition but they love monopoly. They praise competition because it harnesses the diverse and often conflicting objectives of various market participants and channels them into the efficient production of goods and services. Competition does this as if by "an invisible hand." Businesspeople love monopoly because it provides the surest path to economic profit in the long run—and, after all, profit is the name of the game for any business. The fruits of monopoly are so tempting that a firm might try to eliminate competitors or conspire with them to raise prices. As Adam Smith observed more than two centuries ago, "People of the same trade seldom meet together, even for merriment or diversion, but the conversation ends in a conspiracy against the public, or in some contrivance to raise prices."

The tendency of firms to seek monopolistic advantage is understandable, but monopoly usually harms consumers and other producers. Public policy can play a role by promoting competition in those markets where competition seems desirable and by reducing the harmful effects of monopoly in those markets where the output can be most efficiently supplied by one or just a few firms.

Topics discussed include:

- Regulating natural monopolies
- Theories of economic regulation
- Deregulation
- Antitrust policy
- Per se illegality
- Rule of reason
- Merger waves
- Competitive trends

Types of Government Regulation

You'll recall that a monopolist supplies a product with no close substitutes, so a monopolist can usually charge a higher price than would prevail with competition. When only a few firms serve a market, those firms are sometimes able to coordinate their actions, either explicitly or implicitly, to act like a monopolist. The ability of a firm to raise the price without losing all its sales to rivals is called **market power**. Any firm facing a downward-sloping demand curve has some control over the price and thus some market power. The presumption is that a monopoly, or a group of firms acting as a monopoly, restricts output to charge a higher price than competing firms would charge. With output restricted, the marginal benefit of the final unit sold exceeds its marginal cost, so expanding output would increase social welfare. *By failing to expand output to the point where marginal benefit equals marginal cost, firms with market power produce less of the good than would be socially optimal.*

Other distortions have also been associated with monopolies. For example, some critics argue that because a monopoly is insulated from competition, it is not as innovative as aggressive competitors would be. Worse still, because of their size and economic importance, monopolies may influence public choices to protect and enhance their monopoly power.

Three kinds of government policies are designed to alter or control firm behavior: social regulation, economic regulation, and antitrust policy. **Social regulation** tries to improve health and safety, such as control over unsafe working conditions and dangerous products. Health care reform is another example of social regulation; the 2010 health care act was the broadest social legislation since the Great Depression. Social regulation can have far-reaching economic consequences, but that's not the focus of this chapter. **Economic regulation** aims to control the price, output, the entry of new firms, and the quality of service *in industries in which monopoly appears inevitable or even desirable.* Government controls over *natural monopolies,* such as local electricity transmission, local phone service, and a subway system, are examples of economic regulation. Several other industries, such as land and air transportation, have also been regulated in the past. Federal, state, and local governments carry out economic regulation. **Antitrust policy** outlaws attempts to monopolize, or cartelize, markets in which competition is desirable. Antitrust policy is pursued in the courts by government attorneys and by individual firms that charge other firms

market power
The ability of a firm to raise its price without losing all its customers to rival firms

social regulation
Government regulations aimed at improving health and safety

economic regulation
Government regulation of natural monopoly, where, because of economies of scale, average production cost is lowest when a single firm supplies the market

antitrust policy
Government regulation aimed at preventing monopoly and fostering competition in markets where competition is desirable

with violating antitrust laws. Economic regulation and antitrust policy are examined in this chapter. Let's turn first to economic regulation—specifically, the regulation of natural monopolies.

Regulating a Natural Monopoly

Because of economies of scale, a natural monopoly has a long-run average cost curve that slopes downward over the range of market demand. This means that the lowest average cost is achieved when one firm serves the entire market. For example, a subway system is a natural monopoly. If two competing systems tunnel parallel routes throughout a city, the average cost per trip would be higher than if a single system provided this service.

Unregulated Profit Maximization

Exhibit 1 shows the demand and cost conditions for a natural monopoly, in this case a metropolitan subway system. A natural monopoly usually faces huge initial capital costs, such as those associated with digging a subway system, building a natural gas pipeline, launching a communications satellite, or wiring a city for electricity or cable TV. Once capital is in place, average cost falls as output increases, so the average cost curve slopes downward over a broad range of output. In this situation, average cost is lowest when a single firm supplies the market.

An unregulated monopolist, like any other firm, chooses the price-quantity combination that maximizes profit. In Exhibit 1, the monopolist—in this case, the operator of a subway system—maximizes profit by producing where marginal revenue equals marginal cost—that is, where 50 million riders per month pay $4 per trip. The monopolist reaps the profit identified by the blue-shaded rectangle. The *abc* triangle, which is the area below the demand curve and above the $4 price, measures the consumer surplus—consumers' net gain from riding the subway. The problem with letting the monopolist maximize profit is that the resulting price-output combination is inefficient in terms of social welfare. Consumers pay a price that far exceeds the marginal cost of providing the service. *The marginal value of additional output exceeds its marginal cost, so social welfare would increase if output expanded.*

Government can increase social welfare by forcing the monopolist to lower the price and expand output. To accomplish this, government can either operate the monopoly itself, as it does with most urban transit systems, or government can *regulate* a privately owned monopoly, as it does with some urban transit systems, local phone services, cable TV service, and electricity transmission. Government-owned or government-regulated monopolies are called **public utilities**. Here we focus on government regulation, though the issues discussed are similar if the government owns the monopoly.

public utilities
Government-owned or government-regulated monopolies

Setting Price Equal to Marginal Cost

Many facets of a natural monopoly have been regulated, but the price-output combination gets the most attention. Suppose government regulators require the monopolist to produce the level of output that is efficient—that is, where the price, which also measures the marginal benefit to consumers, equals the marginal cost of the good. This price-output combination is depicted in Exhibit 1 as point *e,* where the demand curve, or the marginal benefit curve, intersects the marginal cost curve, yielding a price of $0.50 per trip and quantity of 105 million trips per month. Consumers clearly prefer this price to the $4 charged by the unregulated monopolist. The consumer surplus from riding the subway jumps from triangle *abc* without regulation to triangle *aef* with regulation.

EXHIBIT **1** **Regulating a Natural Monopoly**

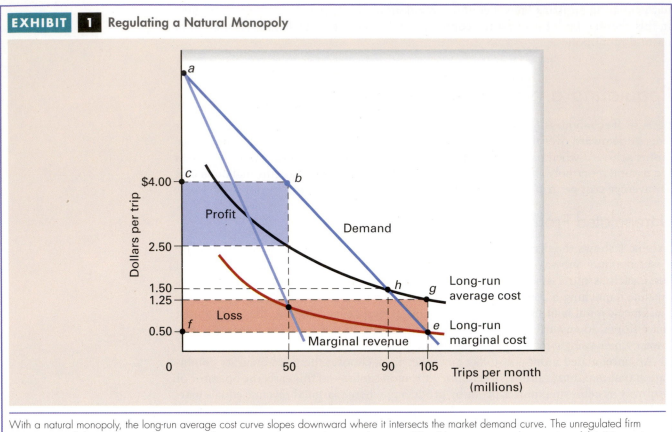

With a natural monopoly, the long-run average cost curve slopes downward where it intersects the market demand curve. The unregulated firm maximizes profit by producing where marginal revenue equals marginal cost, in this case, 50 million trips per month at a price of $4.00 per trip. This outcome is inefficient because price, or marginal benefit, exceeds marginal cost. To achieve the efficient output rate, regulators could set the price at $0.50 per trip. The subway would sell 105 million trips per month, which would be an efficient outcome. But at that price, the subway would lose money and would require a subsidy to keep going. As an alternative, regulators could set the price at $1.50 per trip. The subway would sell 90 million trips per month and would just break even (because price equals average cost). Social welfare could still be increased by expanding output as long as the price, or marginal benefit, exceeds marginal cost, but that would result in an economic loss.

Notice, however, that the monopolist now has a problem. The average cost of supplying each of the 105 million trips per month is $1.25, identified by point *g* on the average cost curve. This is more than double the regulated price of $0.50. Rather than earning a profit, the monopolist suffers a loss—in this case, $0.75 per trip, for a total loss of $79 million a month, identified by the pink-shaded rectangle. *Forcing a natural monopolist to produce where price, or marginal benefit, equals marginal cost results in an economic loss to this monopolist.* In the long run, the monopolist would go out of business rather than endure such a loss.

Subsidizing the Natural Monopolist

How can regulators encourage the monopolist to stay in business yet still produce where price equals marginal cost? The government can cover the loss—*subsidize* the firm so it earns a normal profit. Bus and subway fares are typically set below the average cost of providing the service, with the difference made up by a government subsidies. For example, government subsidies pay more than 40 percent of the Washington, DC, Metro subway system. Amtrak gets a federal subsidy covering about a third of its operating budget. One drawback with the subsidy solution is that, to provide the subsidy, the government must raise taxes or forgo public spending in some other area. Thus, the subsidy has an opportunity cost and could easily result in inefficiencies elsewhere in the economy.

Setting Price Equal to Average Cost

Although some public utilities are subsidized, most are not. Instead, regulators try to establish a price that provides the monopolist with a "fair return." Recall that the average cost curve includes a normal profit. Thus, *setting price equal to average cost* provides a normal, or "fair," profit for the monopolist. In Exhibit 1, the demand curve intersects the average cost curve at point *h*, yielding a price of $1.50 per trip and a quantity of 90 million trips a month. This price-output combination allows the monopolist to stay in business without a subsidy.

Setting price equal to average total cost enhances social welfare compared to the unregulated situation. The monopolist would prefer an economic profit but accepts a normal profit to stay in business. After all, a normal profit is the most this firm could expect if resources were redirected to their best alternative uses. But note that the marginal benefit of the 90 millionth trip exceeds its marginal cost. Therefore, expanding output beyond 90 million trips per month would increase social welfare.

The Regulatory Dilemma

Setting price equal to marginal cost yields the *socially optimal* allocation of resources because *the consumers' marginal benefit from the last unit sold equals the marginal cost of producing that last unit*. In our example, setting the price at $0.50 equates marginal benefit and marginal cost, but the monopolist faces losses unless government provides a subsidy. These losses disappear if price equals average cost, which in our example is $1.50. The higher price ensures a normal profit, but output falls 15 million trips short of the socially optimal level.

Thus, the dilemma facing the regulator is whether to set price equal to marginal cost, which is socially optimal but requires a government subsidy, or to set a break-even price even though output falls short of the socially optimal level. There is no right answer. Compared with the unregulated profit-maximizing price of $4, both reduce the price, increase output, erase economic profit, increase consumer surplus, and increase social welfare. Although Exhibit 1 lays out the options neatly, regulators usually face a cloudier picture. Demand and cost curves can only be estimated, and the regulated firm may withhold or distort information. For example, a natural monopoly may overstate costs so it can charge more.

Alternative Theories of Economic Regulation

Why do governments regulate certain industries? Why not let market forces allocate resources? There are two views of government regulation. The first has been implicit in the discussion so far—namely, economic regulation is in the *public interest*. Economic regulation promotes social welfare by keeping prices down when one or just a few firms serve a market. A second, darker, view is that economic regulation is not in the public interest but is in the *special interest* of producers. According to this view, *well-organized producer groups expect to profit from economic regulation and persuade public officials to impose restrictions that existing producers find attractive, such as limiting entry into the industry or preventing competition among existing firms*. Individual producers have more to gain or to lose from regulation than do individual consumers. Producers typically are also better organized and more focused than consumers and are therefore better able to bring about regulations that favor producers.

Producers' Special Interest in Economic Regulation

To understand how and why producer interests could influence public regulation, think back to the last time you got a haircut. Most states regulate the training and licensing of barbers and beauticians. If any new regulation affecting the profession is proposed, who do you suppose has more interest in that legislation, you or someone who cuts hair for a living? *Producers have an intense interest in matters that affect their livelihood, so they try to shape such legislation.* Those who cut hair for a living often try to restrict entry by requiring thousands of hours of instruction. At any public hearings on haircut regulations, industry officials provide self-serving testimony, while consumers largely ignore the whole thing.

As a consumer, you do not specialize in getting haircuts. You purchase haircuts, cold cuts, hardware, software, underwear, and thousands of other goods and services. You have no *special interest* in haircuts. Some economists argue that because consumers ignore such matters, regulators often favor producer interests. Well-organized producer groups, as squeaky wheels in the legislative machinery, get the most grease in the form of favorable regulations. Such regulations are usually introduced under the guise of advancing consumer interests or protecting the public. Producer groups may argue that unbridled competition in their industry would hurt consumers. For example, the alleged problem of "cutthroat" competition among taxi drivers led to regulations that eliminated price competition and restricted the number of taxis in most large metropolitan areas. New York City has 10,000 fewer taxis now than it did 70 years ago (Mexico City has many more taxis per resident). As a result, taxis in New York City are harder to find and fares are higher. To operate a cab in New York City, someone must purchase a "medallion." The purchase price reflects the market value to taxi owners of regulations that restrict entry and set fares above the competitive level. The average price of a taxi medallion increased from $27,000 in 1968 to more than $700,000 in 2010. Regulation gives medallion owners an abiding interest in blocking entry. If market entry and taxi fares were deregulated, cabs would become more plentiful, fares would fall to competitive levels, and medallions would become worthless.

Regulation may be introduced under the guise of quality control, such as keeping "quacks" out of certain professions. But entry restrictions usually reduce competition and increase prices. The special-interest theory may be valid even when the initial intent of the legislation was in the consumer interest. Over time, the regulatory machinery may shift toward the special interests of producers, who, in effect, "capture" the regulating agency. This **capture theory of regulation** was discussed by George Stigler, the Nobel laureate mentioned in the previous chapter. He argued that "as a general rule, regulation is acquired by the industry and is designed and operated for its benefit."[1]

Critics charge that the Securities and Exchange Commission failed to uncover the massive fraud by Bernie Madoff, despite numerous complaints to the agency, because it was captured by the industry it was supposed to regulate. For example, SEC lawyers didn't want to ruffle feathers because they hoped to land high-paying jobs in the securities industry after building contacts and experience in Washington.[2] Perhaps it would be useful at this point to discuss the regulation and, more recently, deregulation of another industry—airlines.

capture theory of regulation
Producers' political power and strong stake in the regulatory outcome lead them, in effect, to "capture" the regulating agency and prevail on it to serve producer interests

---

1. George Stigler, "The Theory of Economic Regulation," *Bell Journal of Economics and Management Science,* 3 (Spring 1971): 3.
2. See Erin Arvedlund, *Too Good to Be True: The Rise and Fall of Bernie Madoff,* (Penguin Group, 2009): 199.

PUBLIC POLICY

Airline Regulation and Deregulation   The Civil Aeronautics Board (CAB), established in 1938, once tightly regulated interstate airlines. Anyone trying to enter a particular airline market first had to persuade the CAB that the route needed another airline. During the 40 years prior to deregulation, potential entrants submitted more than 150 applications for long-distance routes, *but not a single new interstate airline was authorized.* The CAB also enforced strict compliance with regulated prices. In effect, the CAB created a cartel that fixed prices among the 10 major airlines and blocked new entry. Airlines reflected the capture theory of regulation.

Regulation insulated the industry from price competition, allowing labor unions to secure higher wages than they could in a more competitive setting. Working less than two weeks a month, airline pilots in 1978 earned more than $325,000 a year on average (in today's dollars). Some had so much free time they pursued second careers at the same time. The CAB had no regulatory power over airlines that flew only *intrastate* routes—flights between Los Angeles and San Francisco, for instance. Fares on intrastate airlines were only half those on identical routes flown by regulated airlines (Southwest Airlines sharpened its competitive skills as an intrastate operator in Texas).

Despite opposition from the existing airlines and labor unions, Congress deregulated airlines in 1978, thereby allowing price competition and new entry. Airfares in inflation-adjusted dollars are now more than one-quarter below regulated prices. Competition helps keep airfares lower. The airlines could also afford to lower fares because they became more efficient by filling a greater percentage of seats.

Deregulation in the United States spurred deregulation abroad. For example, after flights between Dublin and London were deregulated in 1986, that became the busiest international route in Europe, jumping from 2 million passengers a year before deregulation to 72 million passengers a year most recently.

Critics of deregulation worried that quality and safety would deteriorate. But the Federal Aviation Administration still regulates quality and safety. Since deregulation, accident rates have declined by anywhere from 10 to 45 percent, depending on the specific measure used (worldwide, donkeys and mules kill more people than plane crashes). Also, because of lower fares, more people fly rather than drive (air passenger miles have tripled), thereby saving thousands of lives that would have been lost driving (per passenger mile, flying is about 20 times safer than driving). Researchers found that during the three months following the 9/11 attacks, people drove more and flew less, resulting in about one thousand more driving deaths.

Some air passengers complain that service has declined in recent years, but that's because most people seem to prefer the lower fares of no-frills airlines. Most consumers view air travel as a commodity, and consider airlines as interchangeable. Thus, consumers seek the lowest fare. Low-cost, no-frills carriers such as Southwest Airlines and JetBlue are grabbing market share and forcing down fares wherever they fly. Competition is fierce. And even where they don't yet fly, just the threat of entry by the likes of Southwest Airlines reduces fares in that market. Many airlines have merged, disappeared, or gone bankrupt. Even with baggage fees and other new charges, major airlines still lost a total of $30 billion between 2005 and 2010. This has pushed down wages in the industry, making airline jobs across the board less attractive than during the regulated era. For example, pilot pay for major airlines now starts at about $40,000 per year, and the top pay in inflation-adjusted dollars is only half what it

e activity
The concerns of airline pilots about employment security and getting what they see as their fair share of industry revenues are presented through the Air Line Pilots' Association Web site at http://www.alpa.org/. What particular issues are of current concern to the pilots? A Report to Congressional Committees at the Government Accounting Office Web site—http://www.gao.gov/new.items/d06630.pdf—indicates that re-regulating the airline industry could reverse the consumer benefits of deregulation and would not necessarily save airline pensions. Read this report from the point of view of a pilot.

Photo by George Frey/Getty Images

was prior to deregulation. Pay at regional airlines is even lower. But, on the whole, deregulation has benefited consumers by lowering fares, increasing the number of flights, and saving lives.

Sources: Austan Goolsbee and Chad Syverson, "How Do Incumbents Respond to Threats of Entry? Evidence from Major Airlines," *Quarterly Journal of Economics*, 123 (November 2008): 1611–1633; Sean Barrett, "Exporting Deregulation: Alfred Kahn and the Celtic Tiger," *Review of Network Economics*, 7 (December 2008): 573–602; Mike Esterl and Susan Carey, "Pressure Will Rise for Other Mergers," *Wall Street Journal*, 3 May 2010; Garrick Blalock et al., "Driving Fatalities After 9/11: A Hidden Cost of Terrorism," *Applied Economics*, 42 (Issue 14, 2009): 1717–1729; and Scott McCartney, "Pilot Pay: Want to Know How Much Your Captain Earns?" *Wall Street Journal*, 16 June 2009.

Recall the alternative views of regulation: one holds that regulation is in the public, or consumer, interest; the other holds that regulation is in the special, or producer, interest. In the airline industry, regulation initially appeared more in accord with producer interests, and producer groups fought deregulation, which benefited consumers.

To Review: Economic regulation tries to reduce the harmful consequences of monopolistic behavior in those markets where the output can be most efficiently supplied by one or a few firms. We now turn to antitrust policy, which tries to promote competition in those markets where competition seems desirable.

Antitrust Law and Enforcement

Although competition typically ensures the most efficient use of the nation's resources, an individual competitor would rather be a monopolist. If left alone, a firm might try to create a monopoly by driving competitors out of business, by merging with competitors, or by colluding with competitors. *Antitrust policy* reflects the government's attempt to reduce anticompetitive behavior and promote a market structure that leads to greater competition. *Antitrust policy attempts to promote socially desirable market performance.*

Origins of Antitrust Policy

Economic developments in the last half of the 19th century created bigger firms serving wider markets. Perhaps the two most important developments were (1) technological breakthroughs that led to a larger optimal plant size in manufacturing and (2) the rise of the railroad from 9,000 miles of track in 1850 to 167,000 miles by 1890, which reduced transport costs. *Economies of scale and cheaper transport costs extended the geographical size of markets,* so firms grew larger to serve this bigger market.

Sharp declines in the national economy in 1873 and in 1883, however, panicked large manufacturers. Because their heavy fixed costs required large-scale production, they cut prices in an attempt to stimulate sales. Price wars erupted, creating economic turmoil. Firms desperately sought ways to stabilize their markets. One solution was for competing firms to form a **trust** by transferring their voting stock to a single board of trustees, which would vote in the interest of the industry. Early trusts were formed in the sugar, tobacco, and oil industries. Although the impact of these early trusts is still debated today, they allegedly pursued anticompetitive practices to develop and maintain a monopoly advantage. Gradually the word **trust** came to mean any firm or group of firms that tried to monopolize a market.

---

net 📖 bookmark

Read about the Federal Antitrust Acts at the Legal Information Institute (http://topics.law.cornell.edu/wex/Antitrust). There are many intersections between economics and law.

---

trust

Any firm or group of firms that tries to monopolize a market

Sherman Antitrust Act of 1890

In the presidential election of 1888, the major political parties put antitrust planks in their platforms. This consensus culminated in the **Sherman Antitrust Act of 1890,** the first national legislation in the world against monopoly. The law prohibited trusts, restraint of trade, and monopolization, but the law's vague language allowed room for much anticompetitive activity.

Clayton Act of 1914

The **Clayton Act of 1914** was passed to outlaw certain practices not prohibited by the Sherman Act and to help government stop a monopoly before it develops. For example, the Clayton Act outlaws price discrimination when this practice creates a monopoly. You'll recall that *price discrimination* charges different customers different prices for the same good. The act also prohibits *tying contracts* and *exclusive dealing* if they substantially lessen competition. **Tying contracts** require the buyer of one good to purchase another good as part of the deal. For example, a seller of a patented machine might require customers to buy other supplies. **Exclusive dealing** means a customer must agree not to buy any of the product from other suppliers. For example, a manufacturer might sell computer chips to a computer maker only if the computer maker agrees not to buy chips from other manufacturers. Another prohibition of the act is **interlocking directorates,** whereby the same individual serves on the boards of directors of competing firms. For example, in 2009 two individuals serving on the boards of both Apple and Google were forced to resign from one.[3] Finally, acquiring the corporate stock of a competing firm is outlawed if this would substantially lessen competition.

Federal Trade Commission Act of 1914

The **Federal Trade Commission (FTC) Act of 1914** established a federal body to help enforce antitrust laws. The president appoints the five commissioners, who are assisted by a staff of economists and lawyers. The Sherman, Clayton, and FTC acts provide the framework for U.S. antitrust laws. Subsequent amendments and court decisions have clarified and embellished these laws. A loophole in the Clayton Act was closed in 1950 with the passage of the *Celler-Kefauver Anti-Merger Act,* which prevents one firm from buying the *physical assets* of another firm if the effect is to reduce competition. This law can block both **horizontal mergers,** or the merging of firms that produce the same product, such as Coke and Pepsi, and **vertical mergers,** or the merging of firms where one supplies inputs to the other or demands output from the other, such as Microsoft software going into Dell hardware.

Antitrust Enforcement

Any law's effectiveness depends on the vigor and vigilance of enforcement. The pattern of antitrust enforcement goes something like this. Either the Antitrust Division of the U.S. Justice Department or the FTC charges a firm or group of firms with breaking the law. Federal agencies are usually acting on a complaint by a customer or a competitor. At that point, those charged with wrongdoing may be able, without admitting guilt, to sign a **consent decree,** whereby they agree not to do whatever they had been charged with. If the accused contests the charges, evidence from both sides is presented in a court trial, and a judge decides. Some decisions may be appealed all the way to the Supreme Court, and in such cases the courts may render new interpretations of existing laws.

3.   Miguel Helft, "Google and Apple Eliminate Another Tie," *New York Times*, 13 October 2009.

Sherman Antitrust Act of 1890

First national legislation in the world against monopoly; prohibited trusts, restraint of trade, and monopolization, but the law was vague and, by itself, ineffective

Clayton Act of 1914

Beefed up the Sherman Act; outlawed certain anticompetitive practices not prohibited by the Sherman Act, including price discrimination, tying contracts, exclusive dealing, interlocking directorates, and buying the corporate stock of a competitor

tying contract

A seller of one good requires a buyer to purchase other goods as part of the deal

exclusive dealing

A supplier prohibits its customers from buying from other suppliers of the product

interlocking directorate

A person serves on the boards of directors of two or more competing firms

Federal Trade Commission (FTC) Act of 1914

Established a federal body to help enforce antitrust laws; run by commissioners assisted by economists and lawyers

horizontal merger

A merger in which one firm combines with another that produces the same type of product

vertical merger

A merger in which one firm combines with another from which it had purchased inputs or to which it had sold output

consent decree

The accused party, without admitting guilt, agrees not to do whatever it was charged with if the government drops the charges

Per Se Illegality and the Rule of Reason

per se illegal

In antitrust law, business practices deemed illegal regardless of their economic rationale or their consequences

rule of reason

Before ruling on the legality of certain business practices, a court examines why they were undertaken and what effect they have on competition

predatory pricing

Pricing tactics employed by a dominant firm to drive competitors out of business, such as temporarily selling below marginal cost or dropping the price only in certain markets

The courts have interpreted antitrust laws in essentially two different ways. One set of practices has been declared **per se illegal**—that is, illegal regardless of the economic rationale or consequences. For example, under the Sherman Act, all agreements among competing firms to fix prices, restrict output, or otherwise restrain competition are viewed as per se illegal. To prove guilt under a per se rule, the government need only show that the offending practice took place. Thus, the government need only examine the firm's *behavior*.

Another set of practices falls under the **rule of reason**. Here the courts take into account the facts surrounding the particular offense—namely, the reasons why the offending practice was adopted and its effect on competition. The rule of reason was first set forth in 1911, when the Supreme Court held that Standard Oil had illegally monopolized the petroleum refining industry. Standard Oil allegedly had come to dominate 90 percent of the market by acquiring more than 120 competitors and by practicing **predatory pricing** to drive remaining rivals out of business—for example, by temporarily selling below marginal cost or dropping the price only in certain markets. In finding Standard Oil guilty, the Court focused on both the company's *behavior* and the *market structure* that resulted from that behavior. Based on this approach, the Court found that the company had behaved *unreasonably* and ruled that the monopoly should be broken up.

But in 1920, the rule of reason led the Supreme Court to find U.S. Steel not guilty of monopolization. In that case, the Court ruled that not every contract or combination in restraint of trade is illegal—only those that "unreasonably" restrained trade violated antitrust laws. The Court said that *mere size is not an offense*. Although U.S. Steel clearly possessed market power, the company, in the Court's view, had not violated antitrust laws because it had not unreasonably used that power. The Court switched positions in 1945, ruling that although Alcoa's conduct might be reasonable and legal, its mere possession of market power—Alcoa controlled 90 percent of the aluminum ingot market—violated antitrust laws per se. Here the Court was using *market structure* rather than firm *behavior* as the test of legality.

Mergers and Public Policy

Herfindahl-Hirschman Index, or HHI

A measure of market concentration that squares each firm's percentage share of the market then sums these squares

Some firms have pursued rapid growth by merging with other firms or by acquiring other firms. Much of what the Antitrust Division in the U.S. Justice Department and the FTC's Bureau of Competition do is approve or reject proposed mergers and acquisitions. As a guiding rule, regulators challenge any merger that would "create, enhance, or entrench market power." In determining possible harmful effects that a merger might have on competition, regulators sometimes consider its impact on the share of sales accounted for by the largest firms in the industry. If a few firms account for a relatively large share of sales, the industry is said to be *concentrated*. As a measure of sales concentration, the Justice Department and FTC often use the **Herfindahl-Hirschman Index, or HHI**, which is found by squaring the percentage of market share of each firm in the market and then summing these squares. For example, if the industry consists of 100 firms of equal size, the HHI is 100 [= $100 \times (1)^2$]. If the industry is a pure monopoly, its index is 10,000 [= $(100)^2$], the largest possible value. *The more firms in the industry and the more equal their size, the smaller the HHI.* This index gives greater weight to firms with larger market shares, as can be seen in Exhibit 2. Each industry has 44 firms, but, for ease of exposition, only the market share of the top 4 firms differs across industries. Note that the index for Industry III is nearly triple

EXHIBIT 2   Herfindahl-Hirschman Index (HHI) Based on Market Share in Three Industries

Firm	Industry I Market Share (percent)	Industry I Market Share Squared	Industry II Market Share (percent)	Industry II Market Share Squared	Industry III Market Share (percent)	Industry III Market Share Squared
A	23	529	15	225	57	3,249
B	18	324	15	225	1	1
C	13	169	15	225	1	1
D	6	36	15	225	1	1
Remaining 40 firms	1 each	40	1 each	40	1 each	40
HHI		1,098		940		3,292

Each of the three industries shown has 44 firms. The HHI is found by squaring each firm's market share then summing the squares. Under each industry, each firm's market share is shown in the left column and the square of the market share is shown in the right column. For ease of exposition, only the market share of the top four firms differs across industries. The remaining 40 firms have 1 percent market share each. The HHI for Industry III is nearly triple that for each of the other two industries.

that for each of the two other industries. Please take a minute now to work through the logic of the exhibit.

The Justice Department and FTC guidelines sort all mergers into one of two categories: *horizontal mergers*, which involve firms in the same market, and *nonhorizontal mergers*, which include all other types of mergers. Of greatest interest for antitrust purposes are horizontal mergers, such as a merger between competing oil companies like Shell and Chevron. The government challenges any merger in an industry that meets two conditions: (1) the HHI exceeds 2,500 and (2) the merger increases the index by more than 200 points. Mergers in an industry with an index of less than 1,500 are seldom challenged.[4] Other factors, such as the ease of entry into the market, the stability of market shares, and gains in efficiency, are considered for indexes between 1,500 and 2,500. For example, regulators are less likely to challenge a merger in an industry where market share fluctuates a lot.

Merger Waves

There have been four merger waves in this country over the last 125 years, as outlined in Exhibit 3. Between 1887 and 1904 some of the twentieth century's largest firms, including U.S. Steel and Standard Oil, were formed. Mergers during this first wave tended to be horizontal. For example, the firm that is today the United States Steel Corporation was created in 1901 through a billion-dollar merger that involved dozens of individual steel producers and two-thirds of the industry's production capacity. This merger wave was a reaction to technological progress in transportation, communication, and manufacturing. Simply put, it became easier and cheaper to run a corporation

4.   Merger guidelines were under revision in 2010. See the proposed guidelines at http://www.ftc.gov/os/2010/04/100420hmg.pdf.

EXHIBIT **3** U.S. Merger Waves in the Past Century

Wave	Years	Dominant Type of Merger	Examples	Stimulus
First	1887–1904	Horizontal	U.S. Steel, Standard Oil	Span national markets
Second	1916–1929	Vertical	Copper refiner with fabricator	Stock market boom
Third	1948–1969	Conglomerate	Litton Industries	Diversification
Fourth	1982–present	Horizontal and vertical	Banking, telecommunications, health services, insurance	Span national and global markets, stock market boom

that stretched across the nation, so firms merged to reach national markets. During this first wave, similar merger activity occurred in Canada, Great Britain, and elsewhere, creating dominant firms, some of which still exist. The U.S. merger wave cooled with the severe national recession of 1904 and with the first stirrings of antitrust laws with real bite.

Because antitrust laws began to restrain *horizontal* mergers, *vertical* mergers became more common during the second merger wave, between 1916 and 1929. A vertical merger is one between a firm that either supplies the other firm inputs or demands the other firm's outputs—the merger of firms at different stages of the production process. For example, a copper refiner merges with a fabricator of copper piping. The stock market boom of the 1920s fueled this second wave, and the stock market crash of 1929 stopped it cold.

The Great Depression and World War II cooled mergers for two decades, but the third merger wave got under way after the war. More than 200 of the 1,000 largest firms in 1950 disappeared by the early 1960s as a result of the third merger wave, which stretched between 1948 and 1969. In that span, many large firms were absorbed by other, usually larger, firms. The third merger wave peaked during 1964 to 1969, when **conglomerate mergers**, which join firms in different industries, accounted for four-fifths of all mergers. For example, Litton Industries combined firms that made calculators, appliances, electrical equipment, and machine tools. Merging firms were looking to diversify their product mix and perhaps achieve some *economies of scope*—meaning, to reduce average costs by producing a variety of goods.

The fourth merger wave began in 1982 and involved both horizontal and vertical mergers. Some large conglomerate mergers from the third wave were dissolved during the fourth wave, as the core firm sold off unrelated operations. About one-third of mergers in the 1980s resulted from *hostile takeovers,* where one firm would buy control of another against the wishes of the target firm's management. Hostile takeovers dwindled to less than one-tenth of mergers during the 1990s and later.

Merger activity gained momentum during the latter half of the 1990s, with the dollar value of each new merger topping the previous record. Most mergers during this period were financed by the exchange of corporate stock and were spurred on by a booming stock market (like the mergers of the 1920s). The dissolution of the Soviet Union ended the Cold War and boosted capitalism around the world. Companies merged to achieve a stronger competitive position in global markets. The largest mergers in history took

conglomerate merger

A merger of firms in different industries

place since the late 1990s, with the biggest action in banking, radio and television, insurance, telecommunications, and health services. The fourth merger wave continues, as the global economic slump of 2008 and 2009 forced firms in some industries, especially banking and finance, to merge in order to survive. But not all mergers work out. For example, Daimler-Benz bought Chrysler for $36 billion in 1998. After nearly a decade of disappointing results, the merged company had to pay $650 million in 2007 to unload 80 percent of its Chrysler division (Chrysler stayed in business in 2009 only after filing for bankruptcy then getting billions in aid from the federal government for the newly reorganized company).

In recent years, there have been fewer objections to mergers on antitrust grounds either from academics or regulatory officials. The government shifted from rules that restrict big mergers to a more flexible approach that allows big companies to merge. For example, after several months of review, the U.S. Justice Department concluded that Whirlpool's acquisition of Maytag would not reduce competition substantially and could achieve efficiencies and cost savings. What's more, growing competition from Asia would prevent the merged company from raising prices.

Antitrust officials ask "will the merger hurt competition?" Most, apparently, do not. Regulators ultimately have challenged only about 2 percent of all mergers proposed in recent years, though just the threat of a legal challenge has probably deterred many potentially anticompetitive mergers and acquisitions.

Competitive Trends in the U.S. Economy

For years, there has been concern about the sheer size of some firms because of the real or potential power they might exercise in the economy. One way to measure the power of the largest corporations is to calculate the share of the nation's corporate assets controlled by the 100 largest manufacturing firms. They now control about half of all manufacturing assets in the United States, up from 40 percent after World War II. We should recognize, however, that size alone is not the same as market power. A very big firm, such as a large chip maker, may face stiff competition from another large chip maker foreign or domestic. On the other hand, the only movie theater in an isolated community may be able to raise its price with less concern about competition.

Competition Over Time

More important than the size of the largest firms in the nation is the market structure of each industry. Various studies have examined the level of competition by industry and changes in competition over the years. All began with some measure of market share, such as the HHI. Among the most comprehensive is the research of William G. Shepherd, who relied on a variety of sources to determine the competitiveness of each industry in the U.S. economy.[5] He sorted industries into four groups: (1) pure monopoly, in which a single firm controlled the entire market and was able to block entry; (2) dominant firm, in which a single firm had more than half the market share and no close rival; (3) tight oligopoly, in which the top four firms supplied more than 60 percent of market output, with stable market shares and evidence of cooperation; and

---

5. William G. Shepherd, "Causes of Increased Competition in the U.S. Economy, 1939–1980," *Review of Economics and Statistics*, 64 (November 1982); and William G. Shepherd and Joanna M. Shepherd, *The Economics of Industrial Organization*, 5th ed. (Waveland, 2004).

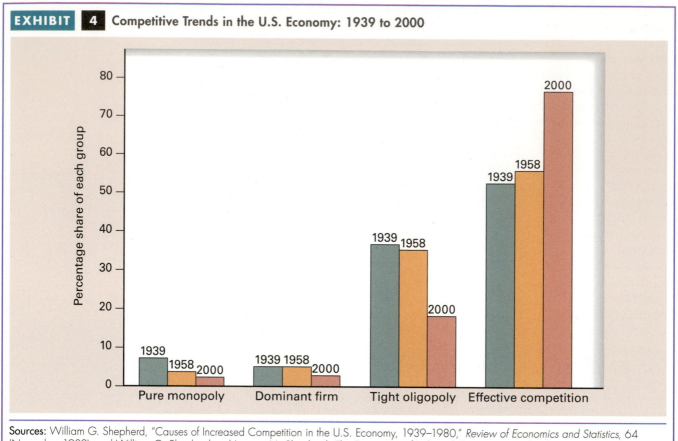

EXHIBIT 4   Competitive Trends in the U.S. Economy: 1939 to 2000

Sources: William G. Shepherd, "Causes of Increased Competition in the U.S. Economy, 1939–1980," *Review of Economics and Statistics,* 64 (November 1982); and William G. Shepherd and Joanna M. Shepherd, *The Economics of Industrial Organization,* 5th ed. (Long Grove, Illinois: Waveland Press, 2004), p. 15.

(4) effective competition, in which firms in the industry exhibited low concentration, low entry barriers, and little or no collusion.

Exhibit 4 presents Shepherd's breakdown of U.S. industries into the four categories for 1939, 1958, and 2000. Between 1939 and 1958, the table shows a modest growth in competition, with the share of those industries rated as "effectively competitive" increasing from 52 percent to 56 percent of all industries. Between 1958 and 2000, however, the share of effectively competitive industries jumped from 56 percent to 77 percent.

According to Shepherd, the growth in competition from 1958 to 2000 can be traced to three sources: (1) *competition from imports,* (2) *deregulation,* and (3) *antitrust policy*. Foreign imports between 1958 and 2000 increased competition in more than a dozen industries, including autos, tires, and steel. The growth in imports accounted for one-sixth of the overall increase in competition. Imports were attractive to consumers because of their higher quality and lower price. Finding themselves at a cost and technological disadvantage, U.S. producers initially sought protection from foreign competitors through trade barriers, such as quotas and tariffs.

Shepherd argues that deregulation accounted for one-fifth of the increase in competition. Trucking, airlines, securities trading, banking, and telecommunications were among the industries deregulated between 1958 and 2000. We have already discussed some of the effects of deregulation in airlines, particularly in reducing barriers to entry and in eliminating uniform pricing schedules.

Although it is difficult to attribute an increase in competition to specific antitrust cases, Shepherd credits antitrust policy with two-fifths of the growth in competition between 1958 and 2000. To summarize: According to Shepherd, the three primary reasons for increased competition were international trade, deregulation, and antitrust policy. One-sixth of the growth in competition between 1958 and 2000 came from imports, one-fifth from deregulation, and two-fifths, the largest share, from antitrust policy. In light of the important role that Shepherd accords antitrust policy, let's look at the most significant antitrust case of the last two decades.

PUBLIC POLICY

CASE STUDY

Microsoft on Trial   The U.S. Justice Department and 20 state attorneys general filed lawsuits in 1998 alleging that Microsoft tried to protect its operating-system monopoly and to extend that monopoly into Internet software. Windows software operated 90 percent of the nation's computers. The government charged that Microsoft's integration of its browser, Internet Explorer, into Windows 98 was not, as the company claimed, solely to make life easier for customers, but was aimed at boosting Explorer's market share. Government officials wanted Windows customers to have a choice of browsers. Microsoft disputed the charges and said the government was interfering with its right to create new products that benefit consumers.

The government argued during the trial that Microsoft engaged in predatory practices aimed at winning the browser war and harming competitors. The government, by focusing on why Microsoft did what it did and the impact on competition, was using a rule-of-reason approach. Microsoft, for its part, characterized itself as an aggressive but legal player in a fiercely competitive industry. Microsoft's lawyers said that the company would not hold such a huge market share if it failed to improve quality and value with each new version. They argued that the high market share "does not begin to reflect the intense competitive dynamic in the software industry." Even such a market share, they said, was "susceptible to rapid deterioration should the market leader fail to innovate at a rapid and competitive pace."

After 78 days of testimony and months of deliberation, the judge ruled that Microsoft maintained a monopoly in operating-system software by anticompetitive means and attempted to monopolize the browser market by unlawfully "tying" Internet Explorer with Windows. Microsoft appealed the ruling but eventually reached an out-of-court settlement with the Justice Department and with most of the state attorneys general. The settlement gave personal-computer makers greater freedom to install non-Microsoft software on new machines. It also banned retaliation against companies that take advantage of these freedoms, prohibited exclusive contracts, and required Microsoft to disclose design information to hardware and software makers so they can build competing products that run smoothly with Windows. The court approved this settlement. It was not until 2009, eleven years after the lawsuits began, that Microsoft had settled suits with all states and the District of Columbia.

Across the Atlantic, Microsoft had to defend itself against antitrust charges brought by the European Union. After years of litigation and fines topping a billion dollars, the company settled most charges there by 2010. Windows software still operates 90 percent of the world's computers, and Microsoft remains a powerful company, with a stock market value of about $225 billion in May 2010. But when the U.S. antitrust suits were filed in 1998, Microsoft had a market value six times that of Apple. In May 2010, however, Apple topped Microsoft to become the

e activity

The New York Times maintains an archive of its articles about the lawsuit at http://www .nytimes.com/library/tech/ reference/index-microsoft .html, and Microsoft maintains its own archive of articles at its Microsoft Legal News Center Web site at http://www .microsoft.com/presspass/ legal/default.mspx. After the domestic suit was resolved came the European Union's antitrust suit. ITPRO in the UK provides a timeline of Microsoft's EU antitrust activities at http://www.itpro.co.uk/ applications/news/125084/ microsofts-eu-antitrust-timeline.html. The EU came to its decision in September 2007, largely rejecting the company's appeal of the landmark March 2004 antitrust ruling (http:// blog.seattlepi.nwsource.com/ microsoft/archives/121932.asp).

© George Frey/epa/Corbis

most valuable technology company in the world. And Google, which in 1998 was still six years away from becoming a publicly traded company, was by May 2010 worth two-thirds as much as Microsoft. While Microsoft officials were tied down for more than a decade by antitrust suits here and abroad, the technology world changed around them. Antitrust scrutiny has now shifted to Apple and to Google, especially Apple's requirements for developing iPhone and iPad applications and Google's decisions about which search results to show first.

Sources: Thomas Catan and Yukari Kane, "Apple Draws Scrutiny from Regulators," *Wall Street Journal*, 4 May 2010; Miguel Helft, "Justice Dept. Criticizes Latest Google Book Deal," *New York Times*, 5 May 2010; R. Jai Krishna et al., "Ballmer Dismisses Microsoft Value Issue," *Wall Street Journal*, 27 May 2010; and Brad Stone, "Sure It's Big. But Is That Bad?," *New York Times*, 21 May 2010.

Recent Competitive Trends

Shepherd's analysis of competition extended to 2000. What has been the trend since then? Growing world trade has increased competition in the U.S. economy. For example, the share of the U.S. auto market controlled by General Motors, Ford, and Chrysler fell from 80 percent in 1970 to 45 percent by 2010. And federal action to deregulate international phone service forced down the average price of international phone calls from $0.88 a minute in 1997 to well under $0.10 a minute by 2010. In an effort to reduce international phone rates, federal officials even subpoenaed Filipino phone executives who were attending a conference in Hawaii, alleging they colluded on phone rates to the United States.

Technological change is boosting competition in many markets, especially the market for media. For example, the prime-time audience share of the three major television networks (NBC, CBS, and ABC) dropped from 90 percent in 1980 to under 30 percent today as FOX became a fourth major network, and as cable and satellite technology delivered hundreds of networks and channels. About 90 percent of U.S. households have either cable or satellite television. And the 14,000 radio stations now available is double the number in 1970 (satellite radio alone has about 20 million subscribers).

Despite Microsoft's dominance in operating systems, the software market barely existed in 1980 but now flourishes in a technology-rich environment populated by nearly 10,000 producers, with Microsoft scrambling to catch up with search technology and with social networking. And the Internet has opened far-ranging possibilities for greater competition in a number of industries, from online stock trading to all manner of electronic commerce and information distribution.

Let's not forget that competition benefits society by forcing producers to become more efficient. A recent study of 732 firms in the United States, France, Germany, and the United Kingdom found that firms in competitive industries are more efficient than other firms.[6]

Problems With Antitrust Policy

There is growing doubt about the economic value of the lengthy antitrust cases pursued in the past. A case against Exxon, for example, was in the courts for 17 years before the company was cleared of charges in 1992. Another case began in 1969 when

6.   Nicholas Bloom and John Van Reenan, "Measuring and Explaining Management Practices Across Firms and Countries," *Quarterly Journal of Economics*, 122 (November 2007): 1351–1408.

IBM, with nearly 70 percent of domestic sales of electronic data-processing equipment, was accused of monopolizing that market. In 1982, the government dropped the case, noting that the threat of monopoly had diminished enough that the case was "without merit." As noted already, the U.S. case against Microsoft took nearly six years to resolve; the case dragged on in state courts five more years.

Competition May Not Require That Many Firms

Joseph Schumpeter argued half a century ago that competition should be viewed as a dynamic process, one of "creative destruction." Firms are continually in flux—introducing new products, phasing out old ones, trying to compete for the consumer's dollar in a variety of ways. In light of this, antitrust policy should not necessarily aim at increasing the *number* of firms in each industry. In some cases, firms grow large because they are better than rivals at offering what consumers want. Accordingly, firm size should not be the primary concern. Moreover, as noted in the chapter on perfect competition, economists have shown through market experiments that most of the desirable properties of perfect competition can be achieved with relatively few firms.[7] For example, the two leading chip makers, Intel and Advanced Micro Devices, have been locked in a price war for years, as each fights for market share. Likewise, Boeing, the only U.S. maker of commercial jets, competes fiercely with Europe's Airbus for every new contract. And it was not that long ago that Google was the upstart among Internet search engines. Now it dominates 65 percent of that market, but may face a fierce competitor as Microsoft and Yahoo join forces. And all three are laggards to Facebook and Twitter in social networking.

Antitrust Abuses

Parties that can show injury from firms that violate antitrust laws can sue the offending company and recover three times the damages sustained. These so-called *treble damage* suits increased after World War II. More than 1,000 are filed each year. Courts have been relatively generous to those claiming to have been wronged. Even foreign firms have started suing in U.S. courts. And, in an unusual twist, foreign firms are now suing other foreign firms using U.S courts, laws, and lawyers. But studies show that such suits can be used to intimidate an aggressive competitor or to convert a contract dispute between, say, a firm and its supplier into treble damage payoffs. The result can have a chilling effect on competition. Many economists now believe that the anticompetitive costs from this abuse of treble damage suits may exceed any competitive benefits of these laws.

Growth of International Markets

Finally, a standard approach to measuring the market power of a firm is its share of the market. With greater international trade, however, the local or even national market share becomes less relevant. General Motors may still dominate U.S. auto manufacturing, accounting for 42 percent of national sales by U.S. firms in 2010. But when Japanese and European producers are included, GM's share of the U.S. auto market falls to only about 20 percent of all sales. GM's share of world production has declined steadily since the mid-1950s. After 77 years as the world's largest automaker, GM was surpassed by Toyota in 2008. GM and Chrysler's very survival came into question in

7. See, for example, Vernon Smith, "Markets as Economizers of Information: Experimental Examination of the 'Hayek Hypothesis,'" *Economic Inquiry*, 20 (April 1982): 165–179; and Douglas Davis and Charles Holt, *Experimental Economics* (Princeton, N.J.: Princeton University Press, 1993).

2009 as the two car makers sought and received federal aid. *Where markets are open to foreign competition, antitrust enforcement that focuses on domestic producers makes less economic sense.*

In response to the global nature of markets, antitrust policy is starting to take an international approach. The U.S. government has signed cooperative agreements with some other governments, including Japan and the European Union, to promote antitrust enforcement and reduce conflicting decisions. For example, investigators from the United States, the European Union, and Japan simultaneously raided car-parts manufacturers in a price fixing probe.[8] Through the International Competition Network, more than 100 nations discuss antitrust procedures and policies. Such discussions have thrown light on anticompetitive regulations in place around the world. Many countries for decades have sheltered firms in some politically powerful industries. For example, until recently, regulations in India restricted entry into the hotel business. As a result, there were fewer hotel rooms in all of India, a country with more than a billion people, than in New York City, with less than 1 percent that population.

Bailing Out Troubled Industries

Finally, the collapse of housing prices in 2007 and 2008 caused mortgage defaults and led to rising unemployment. The federal government responded by aiding affected industries, especially financial institutions and two of the big three automakers. The intent was to promote financial stability and keep the economy from sinking further. But the long-term effect of such market intervention on competition remains to be seen.

Conclusion

Competition has been growing in recent decades because of changing technology, greater international trade, industry deregulation, and antitrust policy. Consumers benefit as firms compete by offering lower prices, better products, and new services to keep existing customers and attract new ones. Competition also ensures that the economy's resources find their most efficient uses. Through the process of creative destruction, competition promotes the survival of the fittest. Market forces continuously pressure firms to innovate—that is, to develop new and better products, services, methods of doing business, and technologies.

Summary

1. In this chapter, we examined two forms of government regulation of business: (a) economic regulation, such as the regulation of natural monopolies, and (b) antitrust policy, which promotes competition and prohibits efforts to monopolize, or to cartelize, an industry.

2. Governments regulate natural monopolies so that output is greater and prices lower than if the monopolist was allowed

to maximize profits. One problem with regulation is that the price that maximizes social welfare results in an economic loss, whereas the price that allows the firm to earn a normal profit does not maximize social welfare.

3. There are two views of economic regulation. The first is that economic regulation is in the public, or consumer, interest because it controls natural monopolies where production by one

---

8. Jeff Bennett and Peppi Kiviniemi, "Car-Parts Makers Raided in Price-Fixing Probe," *Wall Street Journal*, 26 February 2010.

or just a few firms is most efficient. A second view is that regulation is more in the special interest of producers who use regulations to fix prices, block entry, and increase profits.

4. Regulations in effect for 40 years in the airline industry restricted entry and fixed prices. Deregulation in 1978 stimulated new entry, unleashed price competition, and reduced prices overall. Price wars in the industry are now common, and benefit consumers.

5. Antitrust laws are aimed at promoting competition and prohibiting efforts to cartelize, or monopolize, an industry. The Sherman, Clayton, and FTC acts provide the legal and institutional framework for antitrust enforcement, a framework that subsequent amendments and court cases have clarified and embellished.

6. Competition in U.S. industries has been increasing since World War II. Four sources of increased competition are greater international trade, deregulation, antitrust policy, and technological change.

Key Concepts

Market power   334

Social regulation   334

Economic regulation   334

Antitrust policy   334

Public utilities   335

Capture theory of regulation   338

Trust   340

Sherman Antitrust Act
   of 1890   341

Clayton Act of 1914   341

Tying contract   341

Exclusive dealing   341

Interlocking directorate   341

Federal Trade Commission (FTC)
   act of 1914   341

Horizontal merger   341

Vertical merger   341

Consent decree   341

Per se illegal   342

Rule of reason   342

Predatory pricing   342

Herfindahl-Hirschman Index,
   or HHI   342

Conglomerate merger   344

Questions for Review

1. BUSINESS BEHAVIOR AND PUBLIC POLICY   Define market power, and then discuss the rationale for government regulation of firms with market power.

2. GOVERNMENT REGULATION   What three types of government policies are used to alter or control firm behavior? Determine which type of regulation is used for each of the following:

   a. Preventing a merger that the government believes would lessen competition
   b. The activities of the Food and Drug Administration
   c. Regulation of fares charged by a municipal bus company
   d. Occupational safety and health regulations that affect working conditions

3. REGULATING NATURAL MONOPOLIES   What is the "regulatory dilemma?" That is, what trade-offs do regulators have to consider when deciding how to control a natural monopoly?

4. THEORIES OF REGULATION   Why do producers have more interest in government regulations than consumers do?

   a. Compare and contrast the public-interest and special-interest theories of economic regulation. What is the capture theory of regulation?
   b. Which of these theories best describes the case of airline deregulation? Which best explains the government's case against Microsoft?

5. Case Study: Airline Regulation and Deregulation   Consumers now treat air travel like a commodity and meals on some airlines are nonexistent. Does this mean that consumers have suffered because of airline deregulation?

6. ANTITRUST LAW AND ENFORCEMENT   Discuss the difference between per se illegality and the rule of reason.

7. ANTITRUST ACTIVITY   "The existence of only two or three big U.S. auto manufacturers is evidence that the market structure is anticompetitive and that antitrust laws are being broken." Evaluate this assertion.

8. MERGERS AND PUBLIC POLICY   Under what circumstances, and why, would the government be opposed to a merger of two firms? How does the Justice Department decide which mergers to challenge?

9. COMPETITIVE TRENDS IN THE U.S. ECONOMY   William Shepherd's study of U.S. industries showed a clear increase in competition in the U.S. economy between 1958 and 2000. How did Shepherd explain this trend?

Problems and Exercises

10. **REGULATING NATURAL MONOPOLIES** The following graph represents a natural monopoly.

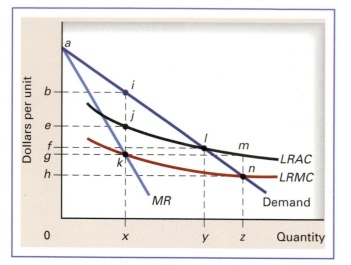

a. Why is this firm considered a natural monopoly?
b. If the firm is unregulated, what price and output would maximize its profit? What would be its profit or loss?
c. If a regulatory commission establishes a price with the goal of achieving allocative efficiency, what would be the price and output? What would be the firm's profit or loss?
d. If a regulatory commission establishes a price with the goal of allowing the firm a "fair return," what would be the price and output? What would be the firm's profit or loss?
e. Which one of the prices in parts b, c, and d maximizes consumer surplus? What problem, if any, occurs at this price?

11. **ORIGINS OF ANTITRUST POLICY** Identify the type of anticompetitive behavior illustrated by each of the following:

a. A university requires buyers of season tickets for its basketball games to buy season tickets for its football games as well.
b. Dairies that bid on contracts to supply milk to school districts collude to increase what they charge.
c. The same individual serves on the boards of directors of General Motors and Ford.
d. A large retailer sells merchandise below cost in certain regions to drive competitors out of business.
e. A producer of carbonated soft drinks sells to a retailer only if the retailer agrees not to buy from the producer's major competitor.

12. **MERGERS AND PUBLIC POLICY** Calculate the Herfindahl-Hirschman Index (HHI) for each of the following industries. Which industry is the most concentrated?

a. An industry with five firms that have the following market shares: 50 percent, 30 percent, 10 percent, 5 percent, and 5 percent
b. An industry with five firms that have the following market shares: 60 percent, 20 percent, 10 percent, 5 percent, and 5 percent
c. An industry with five firms, each of which has a 20 percent market share

13. **Case Study: Microsoft on Trial** What was the government's argument in the Microsoft trial and what was the company's defense? Which side prevailed?

Global Economic Watch Exercises

Login to www.cengagebrain.com and access the Global Economic Watch to do these exercises.

14. **GLOBAL ECONOMIC WATCH** Go to the Global Economic Crisis Resource Center. Select Global Issues in Context. In the Basic Search box at the top of the page, enter the phrase "law on antitrust." On the Results page, go to the News Section. Click on the link for the July 27, 2009, article "Obama Aide Is Aiming to Tighten Law on Antitrust." What does this article reveal about the role of politics in setting antitrust policy?

15. **GLOBAL ECONOMIC WATCH** Go to the Global Economic Crisis Resource Center. Select Global Issues in Context. In the Basic Search box at the top of the page, enter the term "regulation." Choose one article and analyze whether it is in favor of or opposed to government regulation. Summarize the article's arguments.

Public Goods and Public Choice 16

- ○ How do public goods differ from private goods?
- ○ Why do most people remain largely ignorant about what's happening in the public sector?
- ○ Why is it so difficult to interest the public in the public interest?
- ○ Why is voter turnout so low?
- ○ Why do some politicians express concern for average Americans, but vote for special interests?
- ○ Why are incumbents more likely than challengers to support campaign spending limits?

Answers to these and related questions are discussed in this chapter, which focuses on the public sector—both the rationale for public goods and public choices about those goods.

The effects of government are all around us. Stitched into the clothes you put on this morning are government-required labels providing washing instructions. Government subsidies affect the price of your Cheerios and the milk and sugar you put on them. Governments regulate the motor vehicle you get around in as well the speed and the sobriety of the driver. Taxpayers subsidize your education in a variety of ways. Yes, government plays a major role in the economy. The federal government alone spends about $3,700,000,000,000—about $3.7 *trillion*. Spending by governments at all levels tops $5.0 trillion.

The role of government has been discussed throughout this book. For the most part, we assumed that government makes optimal adjustments to the shortcomings of the private sector—that is, when confronted with market failure, government adopts and implements the appropriate program to address the problem. But, just as there are limits to the market's effectiveness, there are limits to government's effectiveness.

In this chapter, we look at the pros and cons of government activity. We begin with public goods, discuss the decision-making process, and then examine the limitations of that process.

Topics discussed include:

- Private versus public goods
- Representative democracy
- Rational ignorance
- Special-interest legislation
- Rent seeking
- The underground economy
- Bureaucratic behavior
- Private versus public production

Public Goods

Throughout most of this book, we have been talking about *private goods*, such as pizzas and haircuts ("goods" in this chapter usually mean goods and services). As noted in Chapter 3, private goods have two important features. First, they are *rival* in consumption, meaning that the amount consumed by one person is unavailable for others to consume. For example, when you and friends share a pizza, each slice others eat is one less available for you (which is why you tend to eat a little faster when sharing). A second key feature of private goods is that suppliers can easily *exclude* those who don't pay. Only paying customers get pizzas. Thus, private goods are said to be *rival* and *exclusive*.

Private Goods, Public Goods, and In Between

In contrast to private goods, *public goods*, such as national defense, the national weather service, the Centers for Disease Control, or a local mosquito-control program, are *nonrival* in consumption. One person's consumption does not diminish the amount available to others. Once produced, such goods are available to all in equal amount; the good can be supplied to an additional consumer for zero marginal cost. But once a public good is produced, suppliers cannot easily deny it to those who don't pay. There are no vending machines for public goods. For example, if a firm sprays a neighborhood for mosquitoes, all those in the neighborhood benefit. The firm can't easily exclude those who fail to pay. Thus, the mosquito spraying is *nonexclusive*—it benefits all those in the neighborhood. Some people figure, "Since I can enjoy the benefits without paying, why bother paying?" As a consequence, for-profit firms can't profitably sell public goods. In this case of market failure, the government comes to the rescue by providing public goods and paying for them through enforced taxation. Sometimes nonprofit agencies also provide public goods, funding them through contributions and other revenue sources.

But the economy consists of more than just the polar cases of private and public goods. Some goods are *nonrival* but *exclusive*. For example, additional households can watch a TV show without affecting the reception of other viewers. It's not as if there is only so much TV signal to go around. Television signals are nonrival in consumption. Yet the program's producers, should they choose to, could charge each household for reception, as with cable TV, so the TV signal is nonrival but exclusive. A good that is nonrival but exclusive is called a *natural monopoly*, a term already introduced. Along the same lines, short of the point of congestion, additional people can benefit from a subway system, golf course, swimming pool, rock concert, or highway without diminishing the benefit to other users. These goods, when not congested, are nonrival. Yet producers can, with relative ease, exclude anyone who doesn't pay the subway fare, greens fee, pool admission, ticket price, or road toll. These uncongested goods are both nonrival and exclusive and are therefore natural monopolies. Once congestion sets in, however, these goods become rival—space is scarce on a stuffed subway car, on a backed-up golf course, in a crowded swimming pool, at a jam-packed concert, or on a bumper-to-bumper highway. Once congestion sets in, these natural monopolies morph into private goods—both rival and exclusive.

Some other goods are *rival* but *nonexclusive*. The fish in the ocean are rival in the sense that every fish caught is no longer available for others to catch; the same goes for migratory game, like geese. But ocean fish and migratory game are nonexclusive in that it would be costly if not impossible for someone to block access to these goods. A good that is rival but nonexclusive is called an **open-access good**. Problems that arise with open-access goods will be examined in the next chapter.

Exhibit 1 sorts out the four categories of goods. Across the top, goods are classified as either *rival* or *nonrival,* and along the left margin, goods are classified as either *exclusive* or *nonexclusive*. Private goods are usually provided by the private sector. Natural monopolies are sometimes provided by the private sector, as with a private golf course, and sometimes provided by government, as with a municipal golf course. Open-access goods are usually regulated by government, as you will see in the next chapter. And public goods are usually provided by government.

open-access good
A good such as ocean fish that is rival in consumption but nonpayers cannot be excluded easily

Optimal Provision of Public Goods

Because private goods are rival in consumption, the market demand for a private good at a given price is the sum of the quantities demanded by each consumer. For example, the market quantity of pizza demanded when the price is $10 is the quantity demanded by Alan plus the quantity demanded by Maria plus the quantity demanded by all other

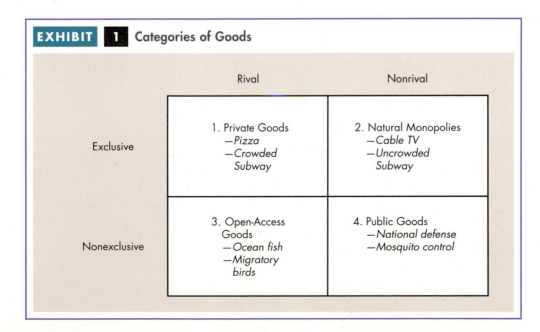

EXHIBIT 1 Categories of Goods

	Rival	Nonrival
Exclusive	1. Private Goods —Pizza —Crowded Subway	2. Natural Monopolies —Cable TV —Uncrowded Subway
Nonexclusive	3. Open-Access Goods —Ocean fish —Migratory birds	4. Public Goods —National defense —Mosquito control

consumers in the market. The market demand curve for a private good is the *horizontal* sum of individual demand curves, an idea developed in Exhibit 7 of Chapter 6. The efficient quantity of a private good occurs where the market demand curve intersects the market supply curve.

But a public good is nonrival in consumption, so that good, once produced, is available in that amount to all consumers. For example, the market demand for a given level of mosquito control reflects the marginal benefit that Alan gets from that amount plus the marginal benefit that Maria gets plus the marginal benefit that all others in the community get from that amount of the good. Therefore, the market demand curve for a public good is the *vertical* sum of each consumer's demand for the public good. To arrive at the efficient level of the public good, we find where the market demand curve intersects the marginal cost curve—that is, where the sum of the marginal valuations equals the marginal cost.

Suppose the public good in question is mosquito control in a neighborhood, which, for simplicity, has only two households, one headed by Alan and the other by Maria. Alan spends more time in the yard than does Maria and thus values a mosquito-free environment more than she does. Their individual demand curves are shown in Exhibit 2 as D_a and D_m, reflecting the marginal benefits that Alan and Maria enjoy at each rate of output. Quantity is measured here as hours of mosquito spraying per week. By vertically summing marginal valuations at each rate of output, we derive the neighborhood demand curve, D, for mosquito spraying. For example, when the town

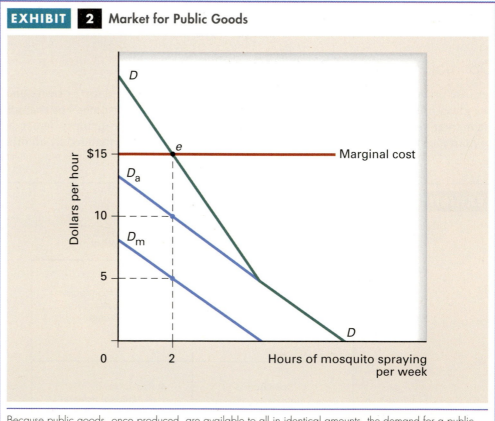

EXHIBIT   2   Market for Public Goods

Because public goods, once produced, are available to all in identical amounts, the demand for a public good is the vertical sum of each individual's demand. Thus, the market demand for mosquito spraying is the vertical sum of Maria's demand, D_m, and Alan's demand, D_a. The efficient level of provision is found where the marginal cost of mosquito spraying equals its marginal benefit. This occurs at point *e*, where the marginal cost curve intersects the market demand curve, D.

sprays two hours a week, Maria values the second hour at $5 and Alan values it at $10. To get the market demand for the second hour of spraying, we simply add each resident's marginal benefit to get $15, as identified by point *e*.

How much mosquito spraying should the government provide? Suppose the marginal cost of spraying is a constant $15 an hour, as shown in Exhibit 2. The efficient level of output is found where the marginal benefit to the neighborhood equals the marginal cost, which occurs where the neighborhood demand curve intersects the marginal cost curve. In our example, these curves intersect where quantity is two hours per week.

Paying for Public Goods

Suppose the government pays for the mosquito spray through taxes. The efficient approach would be to impose a tax on each resident equal to his or her marginal valuation. Simple enough, but there are at least two problems with this. First, once people realize their taxes are based on government estimates of how much they value the good, some people tend to understate their true valuation. Why admit you really value the good if, as a result, you get socked with a higher tax bill? After all, people in the neighborhood can enjoy mosquito abatement whether or not they pay for it. So taxpayers tend to understate their true valuation of public goods. This creates the **free-rider problem,** which occurs because some people try to benefit from the public good without paying for it.

But even if the government has accurate information about everyone's marginal valuations, some households have a greater ability to pay taxes than others. In our example, Alan values mosquito control more because he spends more time in the yard than does Maria. What if Alan is around more because he can't find a job? Should his taxes be double those of Maria, who has, say, a high-paying job? *Taxing people according to their marginal valuations of the public good may be efficient, but it may not be fair if the ability to pay differs.*

Once the public good is produced, only that quantity is available, such as two hours of mosquito spraying per week. With private goods, each consumer can buy any quantity he or she demands and each can purchase a different amount. Thus, *public goods are more complicated than private goods in terms of what goods should be provided, in what quantities, and who should pay.* These decisions are thrashed out through public choices, which we explore in the balance of this chapter.

free-rider problem
Because nobody can be easily excluded from consuming a public good, some people may try to reap the benefits of the good without paying for it

Public Choice in Representative Democracy

Government decisions about public goods and taxes are *public choices*. In a democracy, public choices usually require approval by a majority of voters. About 60 percent of the world's 200 independent nations are democracies. Thus, issues raised in this section about majority rule apply to most of the world, including all of Western Europe and nearly all of the Americas.

Median-Voter Model

As it turns out, we can usually explain the outcome of majority rule by focusing on the preferences of the median voter. The *median voter* is the one whose preferences lie in the middle of all voters' preferences. For example, if the issue is the size of the government budget, half the voters prefer a larger budget than the median voter and half prefer a smaller one. The **median-voter model** predicts that under certain conditions, the preference of the median, or middle, voter will dominate other choices. Here's an example. Suppose you and two roommates have just moved into an apartment, and the three of

median-voter model
Under certain conditions, the preferences of the median, or middle, voter will dominate the preferences of all other voters

you must decide on furnishings. You agree to share common expenses equally and to make choices by majority rule. The issue at hand is whether to buy a TV and, if so, of what size. You each have a different preference. Your studious roommate considers a TV an annoying distraction and would rather go without; otherwise, the smaller, the better. Your other roommate, an avid TV watcher, prefers a 48-inch screen but would settle for a smaller one rather than go without. A 27-inch screen is your first choice, but you would prefer the 48-inch screen rather than go without. What to do, what to do?

You all agree to make the decision by voting on two alternatives at a time, then pairing the winner against the remaining alternative until one choice dominates the others. When the 27-inch screen is paired with the no-TV option, the 27-inch screen gets both your vote and the TV fan's vote. When the 27-inch screen is then paired with the 48-inch screen, the 27-inch screen wins again, this time because your studious roommate sides with you.

Majority voting in effect delegates the public choice to the person whose preference is the median for the group. As the median voter in this example, you get your way. You have the votes for any choice between no TV and a 48 incher. Similarly, *the median voter in an electorate often determines public choices. Political candidates try to get elected by appealing to the median voter.* This is why candidates focus their rhetoric on "hard-working Americans," "middle-class America," or "American families." They are targeting median voters. This is one reason why candidates often seem so much alike. Note that under majority rule, only the median voter gets his or her way. Other voters must go along with the median choice. Thus, other voters usually end up paying for what they consider to be either too much or too little of the public good. On the contrary, in private markets each individual gets whatever amount he or she is willing and able to buy.

People vote directly on issues at New England town meetings and on the occasional referendum, but *direct democracy* is not the most common form of public choice. When you consider the thousands of choices made in the public sector—from the number of teachers to hire to what software to use for municipal records—it becomes clear that direct democracy for all public choices through referenda would be unwieldy and impractical. Rather than make decisions by direct referenda, voters elect *representatives*, who, at least in theory, make public choices that reflect their constituents' views. More than 500,000 elected officials serve in the United States. Under certain conditions, the resulting public choices reflect the preferences of the median voter. Some complications of representative democracy are explored next.

Special Interest and Rational Ignorance

We assume that consumers maximize utility and firms maximize profit, but what about governments? As noted in Chapter 3, there is no common agreement about what, if anything, governments try to maximize or, more precisely, what elected officials try to maximize. One theory that stems from the rational self-interest assumption of economic behavior is that elected officials try to *maximize their political support*.

To maximize political support, elected officials may cater to special interests rather than serve the interest of the public. The possibility arises because of the asymmetry between special interest and public interest, an idea introduced in the previous chapter. Consider only one of the thousands of decisions elected representatives make: funding an obscure federal program that subsidizes U.S. wool production. Under the wool-subsidy program, the federal government guarantees that a floor price is paid to sheep farmers for each pound of wool they produce, a subsidy that has cost taxpayers over $75 million since 2000. During deliberations to renew the program, the only person to testify before Congress was a representative of the National Wool Growers Association, who claimed that the subsidy was vital to the nation's economic welfare. Why didn't a single taxpayer challenge the subsidy?

Households consume so many different public and private goods and services that they have neither the time nor the incentive to understand the effects of public choices on every product. What's more, voters realize that each of them has but a tiny possibility of influencing public choices. And even if an individual voter is somehow able to affect the outcome, the impact on that voter is likely to be small. For example, if a taxpayer could have successfully staged a grassroots campaign in 2000 to eliminate the wool subsidy, the average taxpayer would have saved about 50 cents in federal income taxes since then. Therefore, unless voters have a *special* interest in the legislation, they adopt a stance of **rational ignorance,** which means that they remain largely oblivious to most public choices. The cost to the typical voter of acquiring information about each public choice and acting on it usually exceeds any expected benefit. It's not easy to interest the public in the public interest. Or as Joseph Pulitzer, who funded the Pulitzer Prize, said, "What is everybody's business is nobody's business—except the journalist's."

In contrast, consumers have much more incentive to gather and act on information about market decisions because they benefit directly and immediately from such information. *Because information and the time required to acquire and digest it are scarce, consumers concentrate on private choices rather than public choices. The payoff in making better private choices is usually more immediate, more direct, and more substantial.* For example, a consumer in the market for a new car has an incentive to examine the performance records of different models, test-drive a few, and check prices at dealerships and online. That same person has less incentive to examine the performance records of candidates for public office because that single voter has virtually no chance of deciding the election. What's more, because candidates aim to please the median voter anyway, they often take positions that are similar.

Distribution of Benefits and Costs

Let's turn now to a different topic—how the benefits and costs of public choices are spread across the population. Depending on the issue, particular legislation may benefit only a small group or much of the population. Likewise, the costs of that legislation may be imposed only on a small group or on much of the population. The combinations of benefits and costs yield four possible categories of distributions: (1) widespread benefits and widespread costs, (2) concentrated benefits and widespread costs, (3) widespread benefits and concentrated costs, and (4) concentrated costs and concentrated benefits.

Traditional public-goods legislation, such as for national defense, a justice system, or cancer research, involve widespread benefits and widespread costs—nearly everyone benefits and nearly everyone pays. Traditional public-goods legislation usually has a positive impact on the economy because total benefits exceed total costs.

With **special-interest legislation,** benefits are concentrated but costs widespread. For example, as you'll see shortly, price supports for dairy products have benefited a small group—dairy farmers. To benefit dairy farmers, a special interest, the program spread costs across nearly all taxpayers and consumers. Legislation that caters to special interests usually harms the economy, on net, because total costs often exceed total benefits. Special-interest legislation benefitting a narrow geographical interest is called **pork-barrel spending.** To boost their reelection prospects, members of Congress "bring home the bacon" by delivering pork-barrel programs for their constituents. For example, a recent federal budget appropriated $50,000 for a tattoo removal program in San Luis Obispo, California; $150,000 to restore the Augusta Historic Theater in Georgia; and $2 million for a statue of a Roman god in Birmingham, Alabama.[1]

rational ignorance
A stance adopted by voters when they realize that the cost of understanding and voting on a particular issue exceeds the benefit expected from doing so

traditional public-goods legislation
Legislation that involves widespread costs and widespread benefits—nearly everyone pays and nearly everyone benefits

special-interest legislation
Legislation with concentrated benefits but widespread costs

pork-barrel spending
Special-interest legislation with narrow geographical benefits but funded by all taxpayers

1. Robert Novak, "Senate Sneaks Preserve Pork," *New York Post,* 19 April 2007.

populist legislation
Legislation with widespread benefits but concentrated costs

Populist legislation involves widespread benefits but concentrated costs. Populist legislation usually has a tough time getting approved because the widespread group that benefits typically remains rationally ignorant about the proposed legislation, so these voters provide little political support. But the concentrated group who would get whacked by the taxes object strenuously. Most economists agree that tort-reform legislation, for example, would benefit the economy as a whole by limiting product liability lawsuits, reducing insurance costs, and bringing some goods to the market that, because of liability suits, have all but disappeared, such as personal aircraft. But trial lawyers, the group that would be most harmed by such limits, have successfully blocked reforms for years. Because the small group that bears the cost is savvy about the impact of such proposals but those who would reap the benefits remain rationally ignorant, populist legislation has little chance of approval. The only way such measures get approved is if some political entrepreneur raises enough visibility about the issue to gather public attention and votes. For example, a candidate for governor may run against high electric bills. The key is to somehow get the issue on voters' radar screens.

competing-interest legislation
Legislation that confers concentrated benefits on one group by imposing concentrated costs on another group

Finally, **competing-interest legislation** involves both concentrated benefits and concentrated costs, such as labor unions versus employers, or steel makers versus steel-using industries. These are fierce political battles because both sides have a heavy stake in the outcome.

Exhibit 3 arrays the four categories of distributions. Across the top, benefits of legislation are either *widespread* or *concentrated,* and along the left margin, costs are either *widespread* or *concentrated.* Box 1 shows *traditional public-goods legislation,* such as national defense, with both widespread benefits and widespread costs. Box 2 shows *special-interest legislation,* such as farm subsidies, with concentrated benefits but widespread costs. Box 3 shows *populist legislation,* such as tort reform, with widespread benefits but concentrated costs. And Box 4 shows *competing-interest legislation,* such as labor union issues, with both concentrated benefits and concentrated costs.

The following case study considers a special-interest program—farm price supports.

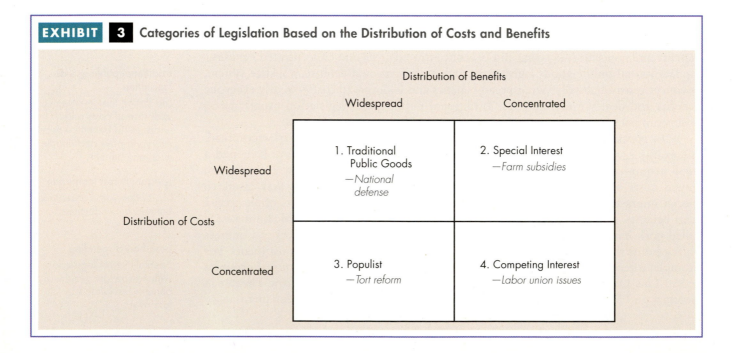

EXHIBIT 3   Categories of Legislation Based on the Distribution of Costs and Benefits

	Distribution of Benefits	
	Widespread	**Concentrated**
Widespread	1. Traditional Public Goods —*National defense*	2. Special Interest —*Farm subsidies*
Concentrated	3. Populist —*Tort reform*	4. Competing Interest —*Labor union issues*

Distribution of Costs

PUBLIC POLICY

Farm Subsidies   The Agricultural Marketing Agreement Act became law in 1937 to prevent what was viewed as "ruinous competition" among farmers. At the time, one in four Americans lived on a farm. In the years since, the government introduced a variety of policies that set floor prices for a wide range of farm products. Now, only one in fifty Americans lives on a farm, but this program is still with us. Subsidies in the 2008 Farm Act cost U.S. taxpayers $15.4 billion in 2009. Worse still, the U.S. government often sells surplus crops overseas for lower prices. That sounds altruistic, but U.S. exports put some poor farmers around the world out of business. U.S. farm subsidies continue to be a sticking point in negotiating freer international trade agreements.

Let's see how price supports have worked in the dairy industry, using a simplified example. Exhibit 4 presents the market for milk. Without government intervention, suppose the market price of milk would average $1.50 per gallon for a market quantity of 100 million gallons per month. In long-run equilibrium, dairy farmers would earn a normal profit in this competitive industry. Consumer surplus is shown by the blue-shaded area. Recall that consumer surplus is the difference between the most that consumers would be willing to pay for that quantity and the amount they actually pay.

Now suppose the dairy lobby persuades Congress that milk should not sell for less than $2.50 per gallon. The higher price encourages farmers to increase their quantity supplied to 150 million gallons. Consumers, however, reduce their quantity demanded to 75 million gallons. To make the floor price of $2.50 stick, the government every month must buy the 75 million gallons of surplus milk generated by the floor price or somehow get dairy farmers to cut output to only 75 million gallons per month. For example, to reduce supply, the government spent about $1 billion on milk products in 2009 under one federal program.

Consumers end up paying dearly to subsidize farmers. First, the price consumers pay increases, in this example by $1 per gallon. Second, as taxpayers, consumers must also pay for the surplus milk or otherwise pay farmers not to produce that milk. So consumers pay $2.50 for each gallon they buy on the market and pay another $2.50 in higher taxes for each surplus gallon the government must buy. Instead of paying a free-market price of just $1.50 for each gallon consumed, the typical consumer-taxpayer in effect pays $5.00 for each gallon actually consumed.

How do farmers make out? Each receives an extra $1 per gallon in revenue compared to the free-market price. As farmers increase their quantity supplied in response to the higher price, however, their marginal cost of production increases. At the margin, the higher price just offsets the higher marginal cost of production. The government subsidy also bids up the price of specialized resources, such as cows and especially pasture land. Anyone who owned these resources when the subsidy was introduced would benefit. Farmers who purchased them after that (and, hence, after resource prices increased) earn only a normal rate of return on their investment. Because farm subsidies were originally introduced more than half a century ago, most farmers today earn just a normal return on their investment, despite the billions spent annually on subsidies.

If the extra $1 per gallon that farmers receive for milk were pure profit, farm profit would increase by $150 million per

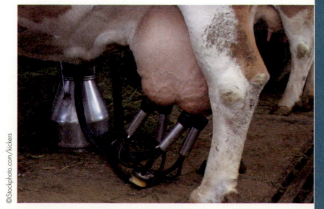

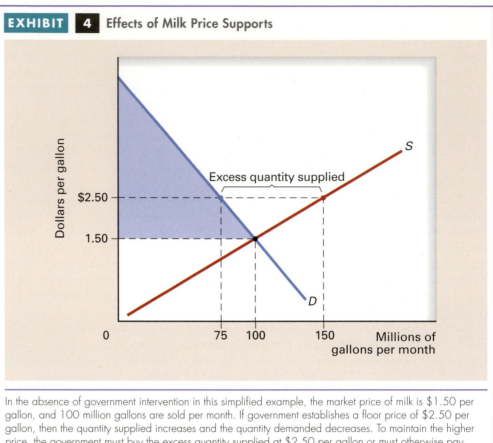

EXHIBIT **4** **Effects of Milk Price Supports**

In the absence of government intervention in this simplified example, the market price of milk is $1.50 per gallon, and 100 million gallons are sold per month. If government establishes a floor price of $2.50 per gallon, then the quantity supplied increases and the quantity demanded decreases. To maintain the higher price, the government must buy the excess quantity supplied at $2.50 per gallon or must otherwise pay farmers to limit their quantity supplied to only 75 million gallons a month.

month under the government program. But total outlays by consumer-taxpayers jumped from $150 million per month for 100 million gallons to $375 million per month for just 75 million gallons. Thus, cost to consumer-taxpayers increases by $225 million, though they drink 25 million fewer gallons. Like other special-interest legislation, farm subsidies have a negative impact on the economy, as the losses outweigh the gains. The real winners are those who owned specialized resources when the subsidy was first introduced. Young farmers must pay more to get into a position to reap the subsidies. Ironically, subsidies aimed at preserving the family farm raise the costs of farming.

Sources: Barratt Kirwan, "The Incidence of U.S. Agricultural Subsidies on Farmland Rental Rates," *Journal of Political Economies*, 117 (February 2009): 138–164; Ani Katchova, "A Comparison of Economic Well-Being of Farm and Nonfarm Households," *American Journal of Agricultural Economics*, 90 (August 2008): 733–747; Bill Egbert, "Councilman Eric Gioia Having a Cow Over Milk Prices: $6 A Gallon Is Too High, He Says," *New York Daily News*, 5 July 2009; Calitza Jimenez, "USDA Pulls Plug on Some Farm Subsidy Data," Center for Public Integrity, 21 May 2010, at http://www.publicintegrity.org/data_mine/entry/2100/; and Joseph Glauber, "Statement Before the Senate Judiciary Committee," 19 September 2009, at http://www.usda.gov/oce/newsroom/archives/testimony/2009/VermontDairy.pdf.

Rent Seeking

An important feature of representative democracy is the incentive and political power it offers interest groups to increase their wealth, either from direct government transfers or from favorable public expenditures and regulations. Special-interest groups, such as dairy farmers, trial lawyers, and other producers, seek from government some special advantage or some outright transfer or subsidy. Such benefits are often called *rents* because they exceed what the producer would require to supply the product. Thus, rents represents earnings that exceed opportunity cost. The activity that interest groups undertake to secure these special favors from government is called *rent seeking*, a term already introduced.

The government frequently bestows some special advantage on a producer or group of producers, and abundant resources are expended to acquire these advantages. For example, *political action committees,* known more popularly as *PACs,* contribute millions to congressional campaigns. Seven of the top ten spending PACs in 2009–2010 were labor unions.

To the extent that special-interest groups engage in rent seeking, they shift resources from productive endeavors that create output and income to activities that focus more on transferring income to their special interests. *Resources employed to persuade government to redistribute income and wealth to special interests are unproductive because they do nothing to increase total output and usually end up reducing it.* Often many firms compete for the same government advantage, thereby wasting still more resources. If the advantage conferred by government on some special-interest group requires higher income taxes, the earnings people expect from working and investing fall, so they may work less and invest less. If this happens, productive activity declines.

As a firm's profitability relies more and more on decisions made in Washington, resources are diverted from productive activity to rent seeking, or lobbying efforts. One firm may thrive because it secured some special government advantage at a critical time; another firm may fail because its managers were more concerned with productive efficiency than with rent seeking.

Special-interest groups have little incentive to make the economy more efficient. In fact, they usually support legislation that transfers wealth to them even if the economy's overall efficiency suffers. For example, suppose lawyers are able to change product liability laws in a way that boosts their annual incomes by a total of $1 billion, or about $1,800 for each of the 550,000 lawyers in private practice. Suppose, too, that this measure drives up the insurance premiums of producers, raising the total cost of production by, say, $2 billion per year. Lawyers themselves have to bear part of this higher cost, but because their personal consumption accounts for only about 1 percent of total spending in the economy, they bear only about 1 percent of the $2 billion in higher costs, or about $20 million. This amounts to $36 per lawyer per year. Thus, the legislation is a good deal for lawyers because their annual incomes grow about $1,800 each but their annual costs increase only about $36 each, resulting in the net average gain of $1,764 per lawyer in private practice. Much special-interest legislation leads to a net reduction in social welfare. For example, some of the nation's best minds are now occupied devising schemes to avoid taxes or divert income to favored groups at the expense of market efficiency.

There are hundreds of special-interest groups representing farmers, physicians, lawyers, teachers, manufacturers, barbers, and so on. One way special interests try to gain access to the political process is through campaign contributions. The tricky issue of campaign finance reform is discussed in the following case study.

PUBLIC POLICY

Campaign Finance Reform   Critics have long argued that American politics is awash in special-interest money. Most Americans seem to agree. Two-thirds of those surveyed support public financing of campaigns if it eliminates funding from large private donations and organized interest groups. Since the 1970s, presidential campaigns have been in part publicly funded, but not congressional races. Candidates who accept public funds must abide by campaign spending limits. But, by rejecting public funds, candidates can ignore spending limits.

Senators John McCain and Russ Feingold proposed a ban on so-called soft-money contributions to national parties. *Soft money* allows political parties to raise unlimited amounts from individuals, corporations, and labor unions and to spend it freely on party-building activities, such as get-out-the-vote efforts, but not on direct support for candidates. *Hard money* is the cash parties raise under rules that limit individual contributions and require public disclosure of donors. The McCain-Feingold measure was approved as the Bipartisan Campaign Reform Act of 2002. The act bans the solicitation of soft money by federal candidates and prohibits political advertising by special interest groups in the weeks just before an election. The contribution limit to a presidential candidate is $2,300 for the primary and $2,300 for the general election, or a combined $4,600 for both.

Limits on special-interest contributions may reduce their influence in the political process, but such caps also increase the advantage of incumbents. Although there was anti-incumbent sentiment in the 2010 congressional election, historically about 95 percent of congressional incumbents usually get reelected. Incumbents benefit from a taxpayer-funded staff and free mailing privileges; these mailings often amount to campaign literature masquerading as official communications. Limits on campaign spending

also magnify the advantages of incumbency by reducing a challenger's ability to appeal directly to voters. Some liberal *and* conservative thinkers agree that the supply of political money should be increased, not decreased. As Curtis Gans, director of the Committee for the Study of the American Electorate argued, "The overwhelming body of scholarly research . . . indicates that low spending limits will undermine political competition by enhancing the existing advantages of incumbency." *Money matters more to challengers* because the public knows less about them. Challengers must be able to spend enough to get their message out. One study found a positive relationship between spending by challengers and their election success but found no relationship between spending by incumbents and their reelection success. So campaign spending limits favor incumbents.

The U.S. Supreme Court in 2010 ruled that the federal government may not ban certain types of political spending by corporations and labor unions, ruling that: "When governments seek to use its full power, including the criminal law, to command where a person may get his or her information, . . . it uses censorship to control thought."

Barack Obama and John McCain together spent a little more than $1 billion in the 2008 presidential race (with most of that spent by Obama). More than a billion dollars sounds like a lot of money, but Coke spends at least twice that on advertising each year. The point is that even well-meaning legislation often has unintended consequences. Efforts to limit campaign spending may or may not reduce the influence of special-interest groups, but *by reducing a challenger's ability to reach the voters, spending limits increase the advantage of incumbency, thus reducing political competition.*

Sources: Michael Ensley, "Individual Campaign Contributions and Candidate Ideology," *Public Choice,* 138 (January 2009): 229–238; Jess Bravin, "Supreme Court Reverses Limits on Campaign Spending," *Wall Street Journal,* 21 January 2010; Jonathan Salant, "Spending Doubled as Obama Led Billion-Dollar Campaign," *Bloomberg News,* 27 December 2008, at http://www.bloomberg.com/apps/news?pid=20601087&sid=apxzrZEHqU1o&refer=home#; the Federal Election Commission at http://www.fec.gov/; and Common Cause at http://www.commoncause.org.

The Underground Economy

A government subsidy promotes production, as we saw in the case study on milk price supports. Conversely, a tax discourages production. Perhaps it would be more accurate to say that when government taxes productive activity, less production gets *reported*. If you ever worked as a waitress or waiter, did you faithfully report all your tip income to the Internal Revenue Service? If not, your unreported income became part of the underground economy. The **underground economy** describes all market activity that goes unreported either to evade taxes or because the activity itself is illegal. Income arising in the underground economy ranges from unreported tips to the earnings of drug dealers.

underground economy

An expression used to describe market activity that goes unreported either because it is illegal or because those involved want to evade taxes

Taxing productive activity has two effects. First, resource owners may supply less of the taxed resource because the after-tax earnings decline. Second, to evade taxes, some people shift from the formal, reported economy to an underground, "off the books" economy. Thus, when the government taxes market exchange and the income it generates, less market activity and less income get reported. The underground economy is known by a variety of other names in different countries, including the shady economy, informal economy, second economy, cash economy, hidden economy, unrecorded economy, parallel economy, off-the-books economy, and black economy.

We should take care to distinguish between tax *avoidance* and tax *evasion*. Tax avoidance is a *legal* attempt to arrange one's economic affairs to pay the least tax possible, such as buying municipal bonds because they yield interest free of federal income taxes. Tax evasion, on the other hand, is *illegal*; it takes the form of either failing to file a tax return or filing a fraudulent return by understating income or overstating deductions. Research around the world indicates that the underground economy grows more when (1) government regulations increase, (2) tax rates increase, and (3) government corruption is more widespread.[2]

The U.S. Commerce Department estimates that official figures capture only about 90 percent of U.S. income. And an Internal Revenue Service survey estimates that only about 90 percent of taxable income gets reported on tax returns. These studies suggest an underground economy of about $1.5 trillion in 2010.

Those who pursue rent-seeking activity and those involved in the underground economy view government from opposite sides. Rent seekers want government to become actively involved in transferring wealth to them, but those in the underground economy want to avoid government contact. *Subsidies and other advantages bestowed by government draw some people closer to government; taxes and regulations drive some others underground.*

Bureaucracy and Representative Democracy

Elected representatives approve legislation, but the task of implementing that legislation is typically left to **bureaus**, which are government agencies whose activities are financed by appropriations from legislative bodies.

bureaus

Government agencies charged with implementing legislation and financed by appropriations from legislative bodies

Ownership and Funding of Bureaus

We can get a better feel for government bureaus by comparing them to corporations. Stockholders own a corporation and share any profit or loss. Stockholders also get to vote on important corporate matters based on the number of shares owned. Corporate shares can be bought and sold in the stock market: ownership is *transferable* to whomever buys the shares. Taxpayers are in a sense the "owners" of government bureaus.

2. For a summary of these studies, see Simon Johnson et al., "Regulatory Discretion and the Unofficial Economy," *American Economic Review*, 88 (May 1998): 387–392.

If the bureau earns a "profit," taxes may decline; if the bureau operates at a "loss," as most do, this loss must be made up by taxes. Each taxpayer has just one vote, regardless of the taxes he or she pays. Ownership in the bureau is surrendered only if the taxpayer dies or moves out of the jurisdiction, but ownership is not transferable—it cannot be bought or sold directly.

Whereas corporations cover their costs if enough people buy their products, bureaus are usually financed by government appropriation, most of which comes from taxpayers. Bureaus do not have to meet a market test. Some bureaus get revenue through user charges, such as admission fees to state parks or tuition at state colleges, but even these bureaus typically rely on taxes for part of their revenue. Because of these differences in the forms of ownership and in the sources of funding, bureaus have different incentives than do for-profit firms, so they are likely to behave differently, as we'll see next.

Ownership and Organizational Behavior

A central assumption of economics is that people behave rationally and respond to economic incentives. The more tightly compensation is linked to individual incentives, the more people behave in accordance with those incentives. For example, if a letter carrier's pay is based on customer satisfaction, the carrier will make a greater effort to deliver mail promptly and intact.

A private firm receives a steady stream of consumer feedback. If the price is too high or too low to clear the market, surpluses or shortages become obvious. Not only is consumer feedback abundant, but the firm's owners have a profit incentive to act on that information to satisfy consumer wants. The promise of profits also creates incentives to produce output at the least cost. Thus, the firm's owners stand to gain from any improvement in customer satisfaction for a given cost or any reduction in cost for a given level of consumer satisfaction.

Because public goods and services are not sold in markets, government bureaus receive less consumer feedback and have less incentive to act on any feedback they do receive. There are usually no prices and no obvious shortages or surpluses. For example, how would you know whether there was a shortage or a surplus of police protection in your community? Not only do bureaus receive less consumer feedback than firms do, bureaus have less incentive to act on the information available. If a corporation is run poorly, someone could buy most of the shares, improve performance, then profit from a higher share price. But because the ownership of bureaus is not transferable, there is less incentive to eliminate waste and inefficiency.

Voters could pressure their elected representatives to make bureaus more responsive. But this discipline is rather crude. Most voters remain rationally ignorant about government performance in part because each voter has little impact on the outcome and each stands to gain so little from any increase in efficiency. For example, suppose that you are one of a million taxpayers in a city and you learn that by having FedEx Offices do all public copying, the city could save $1 million a year. If, through letters to the editor and calls to local officials, you somehow convince the city to adopt this cost-saving measure, you, as a typical taxpayer, would save yourself about a dollar a year in taxes.

Voters can leave a jurisdiction if they believe government is inefficient. This mechanism, whereby people "vote with their feet," does promote some efficiency and consumer satisfaction at the state and local levels, but it's also crude. What if you like some public programs but not others? Moreover, voters dissatisfied with the biggest spender and taxer, the federal government, cannot easily vote with their feet. If you were to move abroad, you, as a U.S. citizen, must still pay U.S. federal taxes on your worldwide income even if you did not earn a dime from U.S. sources (most other countries tax only the domestic income of those living abroad).

Because of differences between public and private organizations—in the owners' ability both to transfer ownership and to appropriate profits—we expect bureaus to be less concerned with satisfying consumer demand or with minimizing costs than private firms are. A variety of empirical studies compares costs for products that are provided by both public bureaus and private firms, such as garbage collection. Of those studies that show a difference, most find private firms are more efficient.

Bureaucratic Objectives

Assuming that bureaus are not simply at the beck and call of the legislature—that is, assuming that bureaucrats have some autonomy—what sort of objectives do *they* pursue? The traditional view is that bureaucrats are "public servants," who try to serve the public as best they can. No doubt some public employees do just that, but is this a realistic assumption for bureaucrats more generally? Why should we assume self-sacrificing behavior by public-sector employees when we make no such assumption about private-sector employees?

One widely discussed theory of bureaucratic behavior claims that bureaus try to *maximize their budget,* for along with a bigger budget come size, prestige, amenities, staff, and pay—all features that are valued by bureaucrats.[3] According to this view, bureaus are monopoly suppliers of their output to elected officials. Rather than charge a price per unit, bureaus offer the entire amount as a package deal in return for the requested appropriation. This theory assumes that the elected officials have only limited ability to dig into the budget and cut particular items. If elected officials do try to cut the bureau's budget, the bureau may threaten to make those cuts as painful to constituents as possible. For example, if city officials attempt to slow the growth of the school budget, school bureaucrats, rather than increase teaching loads or reducing pay raises, may threaten to eliminate kindergarten, abolish the high school football team, or disband the school band. If such threats force elected officials to back off, the government budget turns out to be larger than the public would prefer. *Budget maximization results in a larger budget than that desired by the median voter.* The key to this argument is that bureaus are monopoly suppliers of public goods and elected officials have only limited ability to cut that budget. If taxpayers have alternatives in the private sector or if elected officials can dig into the budget, the monopoly power of the bureau is diminished.

Private Versus Public Production

Simply because some goods and services are *financed* by the government does not mean that they must be *produced* by the government. Elected officials may contract directly with private firms to produce public output. For example, city officials may contract with a private firm to collect garbage for the city. In some jurisdictions, for-profit firms now provide everything from fire protection to prisons. Elected officials may also use a combination of bureaus and firms to produce the desired output. For example, the Pentagon, a giant bureau, hires and trains military personnel, yet contracts with private firms to develop and produce various weapon systems. State governments typically hire private contractors to build highways but employ state workers to maintain them. The mix of firms and bureaus varies over time and across jurisdictions, but the trend is toward increased *privatization,* or production by the private sector, of public goods and services.

When governments produce public goods and services, they are using *the internal organization of the government*—the bureaucracy—to supply the product. When governments contract with private firms to produce public goods and services, they are using *the market* to supply the product. While private firms have more incentives to be efficient than bureaus do, public officials sometimes prefer dealing with bureaus. Public

3.   William A. Niskanen Jr., in *Bureaucracy and Representative Government* (Aldine-Atherton, 1971).

officials may have more control over the bureau than over a private firm. Bureaus may also offer public officials more opportunities to appoint friends and political supporters to government jobs.

In situations where it would be difficult to specify a contract for the public good in question, a bureau may be more responsive to public concerns than a for-profit firm would be. Suppose the service provided by social workers is put out for bid. The firm that wins the bid may be tempted to skimp on quality, particularly if quality can be determined only by direct observation at the time the service is provided. The governments would have difficulty monitoring the quality provided by a private contractor. The services of social workers might be better provided by a government bureau. Because profit is not its goal, a bureau may be less inclined to minimize cost by reducing quality. For example, one study found that privately operated juvenile correction facilities in Florida had lower costs but experienced higher rates of recidivism than state-operated juvenile correction facilities. The lower costs of privately operated facilities were more than offset by the increased recidivism, making state operation the better choice.[4]

Conclusion

Governments attempt to address market failures in the private economy. But simply turning problems of perceived market failure over to government may not always be the best solution, because government has limitations and failings of its own. Participation in markets is based on voluntary exchange. Governments, however, have the legal power to enforce public choices. We should employ at least as high a standard in judging the performance of government, where allocations have the force of law, as we do in judging the private market, where allocations are decided by voluntary exchange between consenting parties. In other words, we should scrutinize a system that is compulsory at least as much as we scrutinize a system that is voluntary. After all, nobody is forcing you to buy tofu, but if you refuse to pay taxes to fund public programs you hate, you could go to prison.

Summary

1. Private goods are rival and exclusive, such as a pizza. Public goods are nonrival and nonexclusive, such as national defense. Goods that are in between public and private goods include natural monopolies, which are nonrival but exclusive, such as cable TV, and open-access goods, which are rival but nonexclusive, such as ocean fish. Because private-sector producers cannot easily exclude nonpayers from consuming a public good, public goods are typically provided by government, which has the power to enforce tax collections.

2. Public choice based on majority rule usually reflects the preferences of the median voter. Other voters often must "buy" either more or less of the public good than they would prefer.

3. Producers have an abiding interest in any legislation that affects their livelihood. Consumers, however, purchase thousands of different goods and services and thus have no special interest in legislation affecting any particular product. Most consumers adopt a stance of rational ignorance, because the expected costs of keeping up with special-interest issues usually outweigh the expected benefits.

4. The intense interest that producer groups have in relevant legislation, coupled with the rational ignorance of voters regarding most issues, leave government vulnerable to rent seeking by special interests. Elected officials trying to maximize their political support sometimes serve special interests at the expense of the public interest.

5. Bureaus differ from firms in the amount of consumer feedback they receive, in their incentives to minimize costs, and in the transferability of their ownership. Because of these differences, bureaus may not be as efficient or as sensitive to consumer preferences as for-profit firms are.

4. Patrick Bayer and David Pozen, "The Effectiveness of Juvenile Correction Facilities: Public Versus Private Management," *Journal of Law and Economics*, 48 (October 2005): 549–589.

Key Concepts

Questions for Review

1. **PRIVATE AND PUBLIC GOODS** Distinguish among private goods, natural monopolies, open-access goods, and public goods. Provide examples of each.

2. **FREE RIDER** Does the free-rider problem arise from the characteristics of consumption rivalry, excludability, or both?

3. **MEDIAN-VOTER MODEL** In a single-issue majority vote, such as the TV example in this chapter, does the median voter always get his or her most preferred outcome?

4. **REPRESENTATIVE DEMOCRACY** Major political parties typically offer "middle of the road" platforms rather than take extreme positions. Is this consistent with the concepts of the median voter and rational ignorance discussed in this chapter?

5. **DISTRIBUTION OF COSTS AND BENEFITS** Why are consumer interest groups usually less effective than producer lobbies in influencing legislation?

6. **DISTRIBUTION OF COSTS AND BENEFITS** Which groups typically bear the costs and which groups enjoy the benefits of (a) traditional public goods, (b) special-interest legislation, and (c) competing-interest legislation?

7. **Case Study: Farm Subsidies** "Subsidizing the price of milk or other agricultural products is not very expensive considering how many consumers there are in the United States. Therefore, there is little harmful effect from such subsidies." Evaluate this statement.

8. **Case Study: Farm Subsidies** Subsidy programs are likely to have a number of secondary effects in addition to the direct effect on dairy prices. What impact do you suppose farm subsidies are likely to have on the following?

   a. Housing prices
   b. Technological change in the dairy industry
   c. The price of dairy product substitutes

9. **RENT SEEKING** Explain how rent seeking can lead to a drop in production of goods and services. What role might the underground economy play in lessening the drop in productive activities?

10. **THE UNDERGROUND ECONOMY** What is the underground economy? What is the impact on the underground economy of instituting a tax on a certain productive activity?

11. **BUREAUCRACY AND REPRESENTATIVE DEMOCRACY** How do the incentives and feedback for government bureaus differ from those for profit-making firms?

12. **BUREAUCRACY AND REPRESENTATIVE DEMOCRACY** A firm is described as combining managerial coordination with market exchange in order to produce its good or service. Does similar behavior occur in government bureaus? Explain.

13. **Case Study: Campaign Finance Reform** The motivation behind campaign finance reform was to limit the influence of special interests. In what sense could that legislation have the opposite effect?

Problems and Exercises

14. **OPTIMAL PROVISION OF PUBLIC GOODS** Using at least two individual consumers, show how the market demand curve is derived from individual demand curves (a) for a private good and (b) for a public good. Once you have derived the market demand curve in each case, introduce a market supply curve and then show the optimal level of production.

15. **DISTRIBUTION OF COSTS AND BENEFITS** Suppose that the government decides to guarantee an above-market price for a good by buying up any surplus at that above-market price.

Using a conventional supply-demand diagram, illustrate the following gains and losses from such a price support:

a. The loss of consumer surplus
b. The gain of producer surplus in the short run
c. The cost of running the government program (assuming no storage costs)
d. What is the total cost of the program to consumers?
e. Are the costs and benefits of the support program widespread or concentrated?

Global Economic Watch Exercises

Login to www.cengagebrain.com and access the Global Economic Watch to do these exercises.

16. GLOBAL ECONOMIC WATCH   Go to the Global Economic Crisis Resource Center. Select Global Issues in Context. In the Basic Search box at the top of the page, enter the phrase "public goods." On the Results page, go to the Global Viewpoints Section. Click on the link for the July 2003 editorial "Global Public Goods and Health." What is a global public good?

17. GLOBAL ECONOMIC WATCH   Go to the Global Economic Crisis Resource Center. Select Global Issues in Context. In the Basic Search box at the top of the page, enter one of the following terms: "underground economy," "shadow economy," or "informal economy." Choose one article about a foreign country and write an analysis of the underground economy there.

Externalities and the Environment

17

REUTERS/Sean Gardner/Landov

- Why do people fish until the fish are gone?

- Why might environmentalists buy rights to pollute the air and water?

- How did barbed wire tame the Wild West?

- In what sense was the biggest environmental disaster in U.S. history not a negative externality?

- And how does someone else's antitheft device affect the chances that your car will get stolen?

These and other questions are answered in this chapter, which looks at externalities and the environment.

The rivers in Jakarta, Indonesia, are dead—killed by acid, alcohol, and oil. Coral reefs in the South Pacific are being ripped apart by dynamite fishing. BP's drilling accident could affect the Gulf of Mexico for years. The tropical rainforest is shrinking because of slash-and-burn claims on the land's resources. The build-up of greenhouse gases threatens to warm the oceans and near-surface air. Some streams in Colorado are still considered toxic from gold mining that ended more than a century ago. These environmental problems are all negative externalities, which result from the actions of producers or consumers that affect many others. Markets can allocate resources efficiently only as long as property rights are well defined and can be easily enforced. But property rights to clean water, air, and soil, to fish in the ocean, to peace and quiet, and to scenic vistas are hard to establish and enforce. This lack of property rights to some resources results in externalities.

Externalities may be either negative, such as air and water pollution, or positive, such as the general improvement in the civic climate that results from better education.

This chapter discusses externalities and explores how public policies can reduce negative externalities and increase positive externalities.

Topics discussed include:

- Exhaustible resources
- Renewable resources
- Common-pool problem
- Private property rights
- Optimal pollution

- Marginal social cost
- Marginal social benefit
- Coase theorem
- Markets for pollution rights
- Environmental protection

Externalities and the Common-Pool Problem

exhaustible resource
A resource in fixed supply, such as crude oil or coal

Let's begin by distinguishing between exhaustible resources and renewable resources. An **exhaustible resource** such as oil or coal does not renew itself and so is available in a finite amount. Technology may improve the ability to extract and utilize these resources, but each gallon of oil burned is gone forever. Sooner or later, all oil wells will run dry. The world's oil reserves are *exhaustible*.

Renewable Resources

renewable resource
A resource that regenerates itself and so can be used indefinitely if used conservatively, such as a properly managed forest

A resource is **renewable** if, when used conservatively, it can be drawn on indefinitely. Thus, timber is a **renewable resource** if trees are cut at sustainable rates and replaced with seedlings. The atmosphere and rivers are renewable resources to the extent that they can absorb and neutralize a certain level of pollutants. More generally, biological resources like fish, game, forests, rivers, grasslands, and agricultural soil are renewable if managed appropriately.

common-pool problem
Unrestricted access to a renewable resource results in overuse

Some renewable resources are also open-access resources, an idea introduced in the previous chapter. An open-access resource is rival in consumption, but exclusion is costly. Fish caught in the ocean, for example, are not available for others to catch, so fish are rival in consumption. Yet it would be difficult, if not impossible, for a person or a firm to "own" fish still swimming in open waters and to prevent others from catching them, so ocean fish are nonexclusive. An open-access good is often subject to the **common-pool problem,** which results because people harvest a resource as long as the marginal benefit exceeds marginal cost. For example, people will fish the oceans as long as the marginal benefit of catching more fish exceeds the marginal cost. Practically speaking, unless otherwise checked, people will fish until the oceans become "fished out." Open-access goods are overfished, overhunted, overharvested, and overused. Because the atmosphere is an open-access resource, it's used as a dump for unwanted gases. Air pollution is a negative externality imposed on society by polluters. The problem is that people exploit any resource as long as their personal marginal benefit exceeds their personal marginal cost. As we'll see, personal marginal cost ignores the costs imposed on others.

In a market system, specific individuals usually own the rights to resources and therefore have a strong interest in using those resources efficiently. *Private property rights*, a term introduced in Chapter 2, allow individuals to use resources or to charge others for their use. Private property rights are defined and enforced by government, by informal social actions, and by ethical norms. As Robert Frost wrote, "Good fences make good neighbors."[1] But because defining and enforcing property rights to open-access resources, such as the air, are quite costly or even impossible, these resources usually are not owned as private property.

Pollution and other negative externalities arise because there are no practical, enforceable, private property rights to open-access resources, such as the air. Market prices usually fail to include the costs that negative externalities impose on society. For example, the price you pay for a gallon of gasoline does not reflect the costs imposed by the greenhouse gases, sootier air, oil spills, and the greater traffic congestion your driving creates. Electric rates do not reflect the negative externalities, or external costs, caused by fossil-fueled power plants. Note that externalities are unintended side effects of actions that are themselves useful and purposeful. Electricity producers, for example, did not go into business to pollute.

Resolving the Common-Pool Problem

Users of the atmosphere, waterways, wildlife, or other open-access resources tend to ignore the impact of their use on the resource's renewal ability. As quality and quantity diminish from overuse, the resource grows scarcer and could disappear. For example, Georges Bank, located off the New England coast, long one of the world's most productive fishing grounds, became so depleted by overfishing that by the 1990s the catch was down 85 percent from peak years. Tuna, once abundant in the Mediterranean, now faces extinction there. The United Nations reports that 11 of the world's 15 primary fishing grounds are seriously depleted.

By imposing restrictions on resource use, government regulations may reduce the common-pool problem. Output restrictions or taxes could force people to use the resource at a rate that is socially optimal. For example, in the face of the tendency to overfish and to catch fish before they are sufficiently mature, the U.S. government has imposed a variety of restrictions on the fishing industry. The laws limit the total catch, the size of fish, the length of the fishing season, the equipment used, and other aspects of the business.

More generally, when imposing and enforcing private property rights would be too costly, government regulations may improve allocative efficiency. For example, stop signs and traffic lights allocate the scarce space at intersections, minimum size restrictions control lobster fishing, hunting seasons control the stock of game, and enforced study hours may calm the din in the college dormitory.

But not all regulations are equally efficient. For example, fishing authorities sometimes limit the total industry catch and allow all firms to fish until that limit is reached. Consequently, when the fishing season opens, there is a mad scramble to catch as much as possible before the industry limit is reached. Because time is of the essence, fishing boats make no effort to fish selectively. And the catch reaches processors all at once, creating congestion throughout the supply chain. Also, each firm has an incentive to expand its fishing fleet to catch more in those precious few weeks. Thus, large fleets of technologically efficient fishing vessels operate for a few weeks until the limit is reached and then sit in port for the rest of the year. Each operator is acting rationally, but the collective effect of the regulation is grossly inefficient in terms of social welfare. Consider the complicated and sometimes confounding fishing regulations in Iceland:

> *The Icelandic government realized that it would have to curb the capacity of its own fleet. But the fishermen compensated by buying more trawlers. Then the*

net 📖 bookmark

Read the history of the U.S. Environmental Protection Agency at http://www.epa.gov/ history/index.htm. Search on "market-based incentives" to find evidence of the role of incentives in environmental policy. The Acid Rain program is often cited by economists as an example of how such incentives can be implemented. This topic is well documented at http:// www.epa.gov/acidrain/. For introductory information about almost any environmental problem, go to the EPA's Student Center at http://www.epa .gov/students/.

---

1. From the poem "Mending Wall" in Robert Frost, *You Come Too* (Holt, Rinehart, and Winston, 1967): 64.

government restricted the size of the fleet and the number of days at sea; the fishermen responded by buying larger, more efficient gear. The cod stocks continued to decline. In 1984, the government introduced quotas on species per vessel per season. This was a controversial and often wasteful system. A groundfish hauled up from 50 fathoms [300 feet] is killed by the change in pressure. But if it is a cod and the cod quota has been used up, it is thrown overboard. Or if the price of cod is low that week and cod happens to come in the haddock net, the fishermen will throw them overboard because they do not want to use up their cod quota when they are not getting a good price.[2]

Ocean fish remain a common-pool resource because firms have not yet been able to establish and enforce rights to particular schools of fish. But advances in technology may some day allow the creation of private property rights to ocean fish, migrating birds, and other open-access resources. Establishing property rights to cattle on the Great Plains once seemed impossible, but the invention of barbed wire allowed ranchers to fence the range. Patented in 1867, barbed wire was advertized as "The finest fence in the world. Light as air. Stronger than whiskey. Cheaper than dirt." In a sense, barbed wire tamed the Wild West.

Optimal Level of Pollution

Though the science is not yet fully resolved, fossil fuel used to power the likes of automobiles and electricity generators produces carbon dioxide, which mixes with other greenhouse gases that may contribute to climate change. Electricity production from fossil fuels, therefore, involves the external cost of using the atmosphere as a gas dump. This section considers a way to analyze such externalities.

External Costs With Fixed Technology

Suppose *D* in Exhibit 1 depicts the demand for electricity. Recall that a demand curve reflects consumers' marginal benefit of each unit. The lower horizontal line reflects the marginal private cost of electricity using fossil fuels. If producers base their pricing and output decisions on their marginal private costs, the equilibrium quantity per month is 50 million kilowatt-hours and the equilibrium price is \$0.10 per kilowatt-hour. At that price and quantity, identified by point *a*, the marginal private cost of production just equals the marginal benefit enjoyed by consumers of electricity.

Electricity production involves not only the private cost of the resources employed but also the external cost of using the atmosphere as a dump for greenhouse gases. Suppose that the marginal external cost imposed on the environment by the generation of electricity is \$0.04 per kilowatt-hour. If the only way to cut emissions is to reduce electricity production, then the relationship between electricity production and pollution is fixed; the pollution in this case occurs with **fixed-production technology**.

The vertical distance between the marginal private cost curve and the marginal social cost curve in Exhibit 1 shows the marginal external cost of \$0.04 per kilowatt-hour. The **marginal social cost** includes both the marginal private cost and the marginal external cost that production imposes on society. Because the marginal external cost here is assumed to be a constant \$0.04 per kilowatt-hour, the two cost curves are parallel. Notice that at the private-sector equilibrium output level of 50 million kilowatt-hours, the marginal social cost, identified at point *b*, exceeds society's marginal benefit of

fixed-production technology
Occurs when the relationship between the output rate and the generation of an externality is fixed; the only way to reduce the externality is to reduce the output

marginal social cost
The sum of the marginal private cost and the marginal external cost of production or consumption

2.   Mark Kurlansky, *Cod: A Biography of the Fish That Changed the World* (New York: Walker., 1997), p. 172.

EXHIBIT **1** **Negative Externalities: The Market for Electricity in the Midwest**

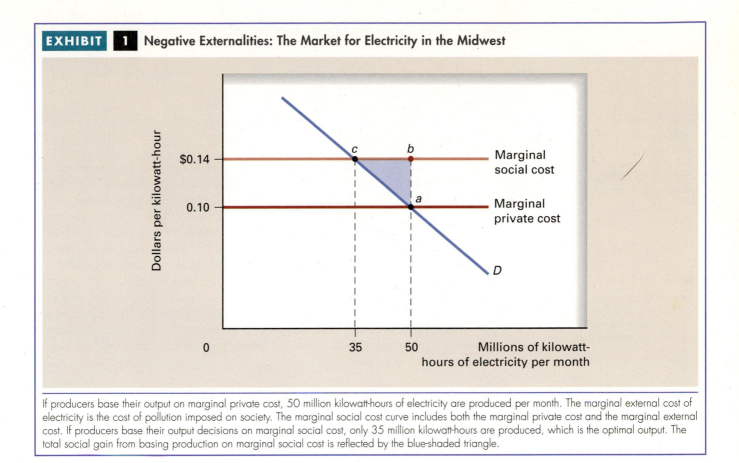

If producers base their output on marginal private cost, 50 million kilowatt-hours of electricity are produced per month. The marginal external cost of electricity is the cost of pollution imposed on society. The marginal social cost curve includes both the marginal private cost and the marginal external cost. If producers base their output decisions on marginal social cost, only 35 million kilowatt-hours are produced, which is the optimal output. The total social gain from basing production on marginal social cost is reflected by the blue-shaded triangle.

electricity, identified on the demand curve at point *a*. The 50-millionth kilowatt-hour of electricity costs society $0.14 but yields only $0.10 of marginal benefit. Because the marginal social cost exceeds the marginal benefit, too much electricity is produced.

The efficient quantity of 35 million kilowatt-hours is found where the demand, or marginal benefit, curve intersects the marginal social cost curve. This intersection is identified at point *c*. How could output be restricted to the socially efficient amount? If regulators knew the demand and marginal cost curves, they could simply limit production to 35 million kilowatt-hours, the efficient quantity. Or, on each kilowatt-hour produced, they could impose a tax equal to the marginal external cost of $0.04. Such a pollution tax would lift the marginal private cost curve up to the marginal social cost curve. Thus, the tax would bring private costs in line with social costs.

With a tax of $0.04 per kilowatt-hour, the equilibrium combination of price and output moves from point *a* to point *c*. The price rises from $0.10 to $0.14 per kilowatt-hour, and output falls to 35 million kilowatt-hours. Setting the tax equal to the marginal external cost results in the efficient level of output. At point *c*, the marginal social cost of production equals the marginal benefit. Notice that greenhouse gas emissions are not eliminated at point *c*, but the utilities no longer generate electricity for which marginal social cost exceeds marginal benefit. The social gain from reducing production to the socially optimal level is shown by the blue-shaded triangle in Exhibit 1. This triangle also measures the social cost of allowing firms to ignore the external cost of production. Although Exhibit 1 offers a tidy solution, the external costs of greenhouse gases often cannot be easily calculated or taxed. At times, government intervention may result in more or less production than the optimal solution requires.

External Costs With Variable Technology

The previous example assumes that the only way to reduce greenhouse gases is to reduce output. But power companies, particularly in the long run, can usually change their resource mix to reduce emissions for any given level of electricity. If pollution can be reduced by altering the production process rather than by simply adjusting the quantity, these externalities are said to be produced under conditions of **variable technology**. With variable technology, the idea is to find the optimal level of pollution for a given quantity of electricity.

Let's look at Exhibit 2. The horizontal axis measures greenhouse gas emissions for a given level of electricity production. Emissions can be reduced by adopting cleaner production technology. Yet the production of cleaner air, like the production of other goods, is subject to diminishing returns. Cutting emissions of the most offensive greenhouse gases may involve simply changing the fuel mix, but further reductions call for more sophisticated and more expensive processes. Thus, the marginal social cost of reducing greenhouse gases increases, as shown by the upward-sloping marginal social cost curve in Exhibit 2.

The **marginal social benefit** curve reflects the additional benefit society derives from greenhouse gas reductions. When emissions are high, an improvement can save lives and thus is valued by society more than when emissions are low. Cleaner air, like other goods, has a declining marginal benefit to society (though the total benefit still increases). The marginal social benefit curve from cleaner air therefore slopes downward, as shown in Exhibit 2.

variable technology

Occurs when the amount of externality generated at a given rate of output can be reduced by altering the production process

marginal social benefit

The sum of the marginal private benefit and the marginal external benefit of production or consumption

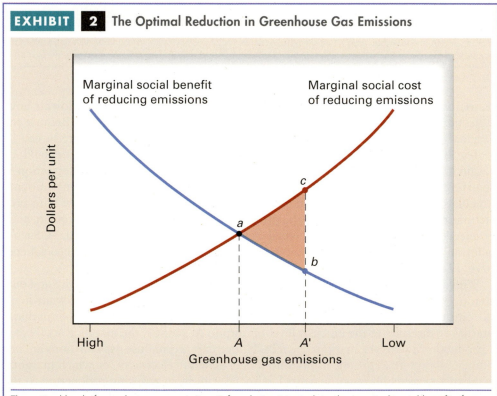

EXHIBIT 2   **The Optimal Reduction in Greenhouse Gas Emissions**

The optimal level of greenhouse gas emissions is found at point *a*, where the marginal social benefit of reducing such emissions equals the marginal social cost. If some lower level of emissions were dictated by the government, such as *A′*, the marginal social cost would exceed the marginal social benefit, and social waste would result. The total social waste resulting from a lower than optimal level of emissions is shown by the pink-shaded triangle.

The optimal level of air quality for a given quantity of electricity is found at point *a*, where the marginal social benefit of cleaner air equals the marginal social cost. In this example, the optimal level of greenhouse gas emissions is *A*. If firms made their production decisions based simply on their private cost—that is, if the emission cost is external to the firm—then firms would have little incentive to search for production methods that reduce greenhouse gas emission, so too much production would result.

What if government regulators decree that greenhouse gas emission levels should be no greater than *A'*? For example, suppose a law establishes *A'* as the maximum acceptable level of emissions. The marginal social cost, identified as *c*, of achieving that level of air quality exceeds the marginal social benefit, identified as *b*. The total social waste associated with imposing a greater-than-optimal level of air quality is shown by the pink-shaded triangle, *abc*. This area is the total amount by which the additional social costs of cleaner air (associated with a move from *A* to *A'*) exceed the additional social benefits. Improving air quality benefits society only as long as the marginal social benefit of cleaner air exceeds its marginal social cost.

What would happen to the optimal level of emissions if either the marginal cost curve or the marginal benefit curve shifted? For example, suppose some technological breakthrough reduces the marginal cost of cutting greenhouse gas emissions. As shown in panel (a) of Exhibit 3, the marginal social cost curve of reducing emissions would shift downward to *MSC'*, leading to cleaner air as reflected by the movement from *A* to *A'*. *The simple logic is that the lower the marginal cost of reducing greenhouse gases, other things constant, the cleaner the air.*

An increase in the marginal benefit of air quality would have a similar effect. For example, suppose research indicates that the effects of a one degree increase in the Earth's average surface temperature would be much more devastating than previously believed. This finding would increase the perceived benefits of reducing greenhouse gases. Thus, the marginal benefit of cleaner air would increase, as reflected in panel

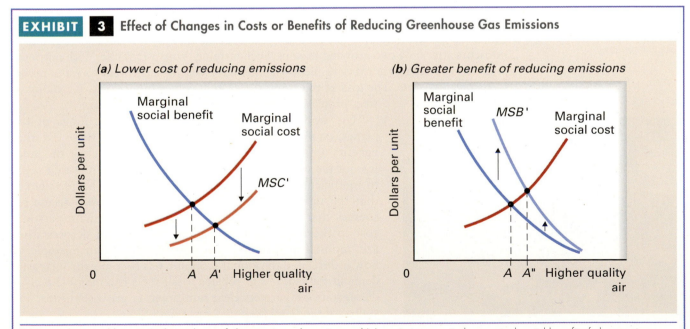

EXHIBIT 3   **Effect of Changes in Costs or Benefits of Reducing Greenhouse Gas Emissions**

Either a reduction in the marginal social cost of cleaner air, as shown in panel (a), or an increase in the marginal social benefit of cleaner air, as shown in panel (b), increases the optimal level of air quality.

(b) of Exhibit 3 by an upward shift of the marginal social benefit curve to *MSB'*. As a result, air quality would improve, moving from A to A" in panel (b) of Exhibit 3. *The greater the marginal benefit of reducing greenhouse gases, other things constant, the cleaner the air.* As another example, recent research indicates that deaths from heart and lung disease would decrease 0.7 percent in large U.S. cities if suspended particulates in the air decrease by just 1/100,000th of a gram per cubic meter of air.[3] This finding increases the perceived benefits of cleaner air, leading to an increase in the optimal quality of air.

The atmosphere has the ability to cleanse itself of some emissions, but the destruction of the tropical rainforest has reduced this ability, as discussed in the following case study.

CASE STUDY

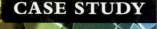

e activity

The Rainforest Alliance at http://www.rainforest-alliance.org/ is an international nonprofit organization dedicated to the conservation of tropical forests. Its goal is to promote economically viable alternatives to the destruction of this endangered natural resource. Look through this site to find examples of the role economics plays in the projects and research the group supports. The Rainforest Action Network is another group devoted to rainforest conservation but focuses more on citizen activism. Go to its site at http://www.ran.org/ and compare the approaches of these two groups.

PUBLIC POLICY

The Lungs of the Planet

The tropical rainforests have been called the lungs of the planet because they naturally recycle carbon dioxide into oxygen and wood, thus eliminating heat-trapping gases and helping to maintain the world's atmospheric balance. These rainforests cover just 6 to 7 percent of the Earth's land surface but contain over half of the world's plant and animal species. The Amazon rainforest, for example, contains the largest collection of plant and animal life on Earth, along with 20 percent of the world's supply of fresh water.

The world's rainforests are located in countries that are relatively poor, such as Bolivia, Brazil, Colombia, Indonesia, Venezuela, and the Philippines. Landless peasants and settlers burn down these forests to create farmland and pastures. Worse yet, to meet the growing demand for timber, loggers strip rainforests. Because most of the rainforest amounts to an open-access resource, where property rights are not easily established, poor settlers and timber companies usually pursue a slash-and-burn approach. The world's tropical forests have been cut in half in the last 50 years.

Burning the world's rainforests spells trouble for the environment. The fires add greenhouse gases to the atmosphere. Destruction of tropical forests around the world is estimated to be responsible for about 20 percent of global greenhouse gas emissions. The loss of trees reduces the atmosphere's ability to cleanse itself and increases flash flooding and mud slides. Stripped of trees, the land contains huge amounts of carbon subject to oxidization. Soil gets eroded by rains and baked by the sun and runs out of nutrients after only two growing seasons. Such farming is unsustainable. With nutrients lost, the ecosystem is not very resilient—*it takes a century for a clear-cut forest to return to its original state*. The loss of the tropical forests involves other costs. A canopy of trees protects a rich, genetically diverse, ecosystem.

The tropical rainforests, by serving as the lungs of the planet, confer benefits around the globe. But these external benefits are usually ignored in the decision to clear the land. It's not the greed of peasants and timber companies that leads to inefficient, or wasteful, uses of resources. The problem is that the rainforests and the atmosphere are open-access resources that can be degraded with little immediate personal cost to those who clear the land. The costs of deforestation are imposed on people around the globe. As an example of how interrelated the global economy has become, the increased demand for biofuels to replace fossil fuels is a major driver of deforestations. Farmers clear rainforests to grow soybeans, one source of biodiesel fuel.

3.   Jonathan M. Samet et al., "Fine Particulate Air Pollution and Mortality in 20 U.S. Cities, 1987–1994," 343 *New England Journal of Medicine*, (14 December 2000): 1742–1749.

Poverty in the rainforest countries combined with the lack of legal title to the land encourage people to exploit that timber and soil rather than maximize the long-term value of these resources. For example, a secure property right to the land would reduce the need to clear it in order to claim some value. A farmer with title to the land could even leave a forest bequest to heirs. Research shows that people granted rights to the Amazon rainforest manage their land more conservatively. Property rights promote efficient harvesting of hardwoods and reforestation, allowing the forest to serve as an air filter. For example, the frequency of reforestation among those settlers granted land title was about 15 times greater than among those without title. Without title, the only way to capture some of the land's value is through a slash-and-burn approach. Thus, granting peasants and settlers property rights could help conserve the rainforests.

Sources: Alexai Barrionuevo, "Giants in Cattle Industry Agree to Help Fight Deforestation," *New York Times,* 6 October 2009; R. Godoy et al., "The Role of Tenure Security and Private Time Preference in Neotropical Deforestation," *Land Economics,* 74 (May 1998): 162–170; Charles Wood and Robert Walker, "Saving the Trees by Helping the Poor," *Resources for the Future* (Summer 1999): 14–17; and *State of the World's Forests: 2009,* Food and Agricultural Organization of the United Nations, at http://www.fao.org/docrep/011/i0350e/i0350e00.htm.

The Coase Theorem

The traditional analysis of externalities assumes that market failures arise because people ignore the external effects of their actions. For example, suppose a manufacturer of heavy machinery is next door to a research laboratory that tests delicate equipment. The vibrations caused by the manufacturing process throw off the delicate equipment next door. Professor Ronald Coase, who won the Nobel Prize in 1991, would argue that the negative externality in this case is not necessarily imposed by the heavy machinery— rather, it arises from the incompatible activities of the two firms. The externality is the result of both vibrations created by the factory *and* the location of the testing lab next door. Solutions might include modifying the factory, moving the factory, making the test equipment more shock resistant, or moving the testing lab.

According to Coase, the efficient solution depends on which party can avoid the externality at the lower cost. Suppose it would cost $2 million for the factory to reduce vibrations enough for the lab to function normally. On the other hand, if the factory makes no changes, the lab can't insulate its testing equipment enough to operate accurately, so the lab would have to relocate at a cost of $1 million. Based on this information, the least-cost solution would be for the testing lab to relocate at a cost of $1 million. Coase argues that, as long as transaction costs are low, the parties will reach the efficient solution if one party is assigned the property right. And here's Coase's special insight: *This efficient solution will be achieved regardless of which party gets the property right.*

Suppose the testing lab is granted the right to operate free of vibrations from next door, so the testing lab can force the factory to reduce its vibration. Rather than cut vibrations at a cost of $2 million, the factory can pay the lab to relocate. Any payment greater than $1 million but less than $2 million makes both sides better off, because the lab would receive more than its moving cost and the factory would pay less than its cost of reducing vibrations. Thus, the lab will move, which is the efficient outcome.

Alternatively, suppose the factory is granted the right to generate vibrations in its production process, regardless of the impact on the testing lab. For the factory, this means business as usual. Because the minimum payment the factory would accept to reduce vibrations is $2 million, the lab would rather relocate at a cost of $1 million. Thus, whether property rights are granted to the lab or to the factory, the lab will move, which is the efficient, or least-cost, solution. The **Coase theorem** says that as long as bargaining costs are small, merely assigning the property right will generate an efficient solution to an externality

Coase theorem
As long as bargaining costs are low, an efficient solution to the problem of externalities is achieved by assigning property rights to one party or the other, it doesn't matter which

problem regardless of which party is assigned that right. A particular assignment determines which side bears the externality costs but does not affect the efficient outcome.

Inefficient outcomes do occur, however, when the transaction costs of arriving at a solution are high. For example, an airport located in a populated area would have difficulty negotiating noise levels with all the affected residents. Or peasants contemplating clearing a portion of the tropical rainforest would be unable to negotiate with the millions, and perhaps, billions, of people ultimately affected by that decision. *When the number of parties involved in the transaction is large, Coase's solution of assigning property rights may not be enough.*

Markets for Pollution Rights

According to the Coase theorem, the assignment of property rights is often sufficient to resolve the market failure typically associated with externalities. Additional government intervention is not necessary. If pollution can be easily monitored and polluters easily identified, the government may be able to achieve an efficient solution to the problem of pollution simply by assigning the right to pollute. To see how this could work, let's look at an example. Firms that dump into a river evidently value the ability to discharge waste in this way. For them, the river provides a zero cost outlet for by products that otherwise would have to be disposed of at greater cost. The river provides a disposal service, and the demand curve for that service slopes downward, just like the demand for other resources.

The demand for the river as a discharge system is presented as D in Exhibit 4. The horizontal axis measures the tons of discharge dumped into the river per day, and the

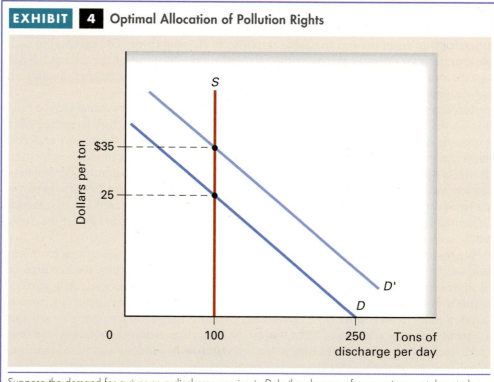

EXHIBIT   4   Optimal Allocation of Pollution Rights

Suppose the demand for a river as a discharge service is D. In the absence of any environmental controls, polluters dump 250 tons per day, where the marginal benefit of discharge is zero. If regulatory authorities establish 100 tons as the maximum daily level of discharge and then sell the rights, the market for these pollution rights clears at $25 per ton. If the demand for pollution rights increases to D', the market-clearing price of pollution rights rises to $35 per ton.

vertical axis measures firms' marginal benefit of disposing of each ton of waste in this way. The demand curve thus measures the marginal value to firms of using the river as a disposal service. With no restrictions on river pollution—that is, if all firms were free to dump waste into the river—dumping would continue as long as it provided firms some marginal benefit. This marginal benefit falls to zero in Exhibit 4 when 250 tons per day are discharged. At that point the marginal private cost of dumping, which is zero, equals the marginal private benefit.

The river, like the atmosphere, the soil, and the sea can absorb and neutralize a certain amount of discharge per day without deteriorating in quality. What if voters make the public choice that the river should remain clean enough for swimming and fishing? Suppose engineers determine this level of water quality can be maintained as long as no more than 100 tons are discharged per day. Thus, the "supply" of the discharge service provided by the river is fixed at 100 tons per day, shown by the vertical supply curve, S, in Exhibit 4.

If government regulators can easily identify polluters and monitor their behavior, authorities can allocate permits to discharge 100 tons per day. If polluters are simply given these permits (that is, if the price of permits is zero), there will be an excess demand for them, because the quantity supplied is 100 tons but the quantity demanded at a price of zero would be 250 tons. An alternative is to sell permits for 100 tons of pollution at the market-clearing price. The intersection of supply curve S and demand curve D yields a permit price of $25 per ton, which is the marginal value of discharging the 100th ton into the river each day. To most permit buyers, the marginal value of a permit exceeds $25 per ton.

The beauty of this system is that producers who value the discharge rights the most ultimately end up with them. Producers who attach a marginal value below $25 per ton apparently have cheaper ways of resolving their waste problems, including changing production techniques. And if conservation groups, such as the Sierra Club, want a cleaner river than the government's standard, such as water clean enough to drink, they can purchase pollution permits but not exercise them.

What if additional firms spring up along the river that are willing to pay more than $25 per ton for pollution rights? This greater demand is reflected in Exhibit 4 by D'. This increase of demand would bid up the market price of pollution permits to, say, $35 per ton. Some existing permit holders would sell their rights to those who value them more. Regardless of the comings and goings of would-be polluters, the total quantity of discharge rights is restricted to 100 tons per day, so the river's quality will be maintained. Thus, *the value of pollution permits, but not the total amount of pollution, may fluctuate over time.*

If the right to pollute could be granted, monitored, and enforced, then what had been a negative externality problem could be solved through market allocation. Historically, the U.S. government had relied on setting discharge standards and fining offenders. But in 1989, a pollution rights market for fluorocarbon emissions was established and was followed in 1990 by a market for sulfur dioxide. During the 1990s, sulfur dioxide emissions in the nation fell by more than half, exceeding the goals of the authorizing legislation. The "cap-and-trade" proposal by President Obama aims to create a market for greenhouse gas emissions. So the market for pollution rights is alive and growing.[4] Even China is now experimenting with this approach. Some companies and even celebrities have used a variant of pollution rights to become "carbon neutral"—that is, by estimating their carbon emissions then offsetting this impact by paying for projects

4. For a discussion of the market for sulfur dioxide emissions, see Paul Joskow, Richard Schmalensee, and Elizabeth Bailey, "The Market for Sulfur-Dioxide Emissions," *American Economic Review*, 88 (September 1998): 669–685.

to neutralize, or "sop up," equivalent emissions.[5] For example, Delta Air Lines until recently allowed online ticket buyers to pay an extra $5.50 for domestic flights or $11 for international flights for tree plantings to help offset flight emissions. And the band Coldplay funded the planting of 10,000 mango trees in India to help sop up emissions related to the release of a new CD.[6]

Pollution Rights and Public Choice

Unfortunately, legislation dealing with pollution is affected by the same problems of representative democracy that trouble other public policy questions. Big polluters have a special interest in government proposals relating to pollution, and they fight measures to reduce pollution. But members of the public remain rationally ignorant about pollution legislation. So pollution regulations may be less in accord with the public interest than with the special interests of polluters. To win their cooperation, a portion of pollution permits are often *given* to existing firms or offered at below-market prices. For example, under the sulfur dioxide program, the nation's 101 dirtiest power plants were granted credits equal to between 30 and 50 percent of the pollution they emitted before the program began. Because they received something of value, polluters were less inclined to oppose the legislation. Once permits were granted, some recipients found it profitable to sell their permits to other firms that valued them more. Thus, a market emerged that led to an efficient allocation of pollution permits. According to some analysts, the sulfur dioxide program saves up to $3 billion annually compared with the old system. More generally, a system of marketable pollution rights can reduce the cost of pollution abatement by as much as 75 percent.

Before 1990, **command-and-control environmental regulations** were the norm—an approach that required polluters, such as electric utilities, to introduce particular technologies to reduce emissions by specific amounts. These regulations were based on engineering standards and did not recognize unique circumstances across generating plants, such as plant design, ability to introduce scrubbers, and the ease of switching to low-sulfur fuels. But the market for pollution rights reflects an **economic efficiency approach** that offers each electric utility the flexibility to reduce emissions in the most cost-effective manner, given its unique operation. Firms with the lowest costs of emission control have an incentive to implement the largest reduction in emissions and then sell unused pollution permits to those with greater control costs.

Now that you know something about the theory of externalities, let's turn to an important application of the theory—environmental protection.

command-and-control environmental regulations

An approach that required polluters to adopt particular technologies to reduce emissions by specific amounts; inflexible regulations based on engineering standards that ignore each firm's unique ways of reducing pollution

economic efficiency approach

An approach that offers each polluter the flexibility to reduce emissions as cost-effectively as possible, given its unique cost conditions; the market for pollution rights is an example

Environmental Protection

Federal efforts to address the common-pool problems of air, water, and soil pollution are coordinated by the Environmental Protection Agency (EPA). Four federal laws and subsequent amendments underpin U.S. efforts to protect the environment: (1) the Clean Air Act of 1970, (2) the Clean Water Act of 1972, (3) the Resource Conservation and Recovery Act of 1976 (which governs solid waste disposal), and (4) the Superfund law of 1980 (legislation focusing on toxic waste dumps). When the EPA was created in 1970, it began with about 4,000 employees and a budget of $1.2 billion (in 2011 dollars). By 2011, it had about 18,000 employees and a $10.0 billion budget.

---

5.   See Andrew Revkin, "Carbon-Neutral Is Hip, But Is It Green," *New York Times*, 29 April 2007.
6.   Michael Hill, "Can Planting a Tree Absolve Your Eco-Sins?" *Arizona Republic*, 28 May 2007.

According to EPA estimates, compliance with pollution-control regulations cost U.S. producers and consumers about $300 billion in 2011, an amount equivalent to 2 percent of gross domestic product, the market value of all final goods and services produced in the economy. We can divide pollution control spending into three categories: spending for air pollution abatement, spending for water pollution abatement, and spending for solid waste disposal. About 40 percent of the pollution control expenditures in the United States goes toward cleaner air, another 40 percent goes toward cleaner water, and 20 percent goes toward disposing of solid waste. (These figures are from a typical year, and do not include cleanup costs after the drilling accident in the Gulf of Mexico.) In this section, we consider, in turn, air pollution, water pollution, Superfund activities, and disposing of solid waste.

Air Pollution

In the Clean Air Act of 1970 and in subsequent amendments, Congress set national standards for the amount of pollution that could be released into the atmosphere. Congress thereby recognized the atmosphere as an economic resource, which, like other resources, has alternative uses. The air can be used as a source of life-giving oxygen, as a prism for viewing breathtaking vistas, or as a dump for carrying away unwanted soot and gases. The 1970 act gave Americans the right to breathe air of a certain quality and at the same time gave producers the right to emit particular amounts of specified pollutants. Research shows that people value clean air and are willing to pay more to live in communities with less pollution.[7]

Smog is the most visible form of air pollution. Automobile emissions account for 40 percent of smog. Another 40 percent comes from consumer-oriented products, such as paint thinner, fluorocarbon sprays, dry-cleaning solvents, and baker's yeast by products. Surprisingly, only 15 percent of smog comes from manufacturing. The 1970 Clean Air Act mandated a reduction of 90 percent in auto emissions, leaving it to the auto industry to achieve this target. At the time, automakers said the target was impossible. Between 1970 and 1990, however, average emissions of lead fell 97 percent, carbon monoxide emissions fell 41 percent, and sulfur dioxide emissions fell 25 percent. In fact, an EPA study concluded that because auto emissions and industrial smoke have been reduced so much, *air pollution on average is now greater indoors than outdoors*. For example, in the Los Angeles area, a smog alert, meaning the air reached dangerous levels, occurred on a weekly basis during the 1980s, but the city did not experience a smog alert between 2003 and the heavy forest-fire season of 2008. U.S. air quality is now considered good compared to the air quality in much of the world. For example, no U.S. city ranks among the world's worst in sulfur dioxide. Despite recent improvements in air quality, the United States is still a major source of fossil-fuel carbon dioxide emissions, a major greenhouse gas. As you can see from Exhibit 5, which shows the world's 25 worst nations in annual fossil-fuel carbon dioxide emissions per capita, the United States ranks fourth worst with 5.2 tons per capita.

There have been efforts to address greenhouse gases on an international scale. A report by the Intergovernmental Panel on Climate Change, a group sponsored by the United Nations, was approved in May 2007 by more than 120 nations.[8] The study says, to fight climate change, the world must cut emissions of carbon dioxide and other greenhouse gases by (1) sharply improving energy efficiency in buildings, vehicles, and machines; (2) shifting from fossil fuels to nuclear, wind, solar, and other renewable

---

7. Kenneth Chay and Michael Greenstone, "Does Air Quality Matter? Evidence from the Housing Market," *Journal of Political Economy*, 113 (April 2005): 376–424.
8. For panel reports, go to http://www.ipcc.ch/.

EXHIBIT 5 Fossil-Fuel Carbon Dioxide Emissions per Capita: The 25 Worst Nations

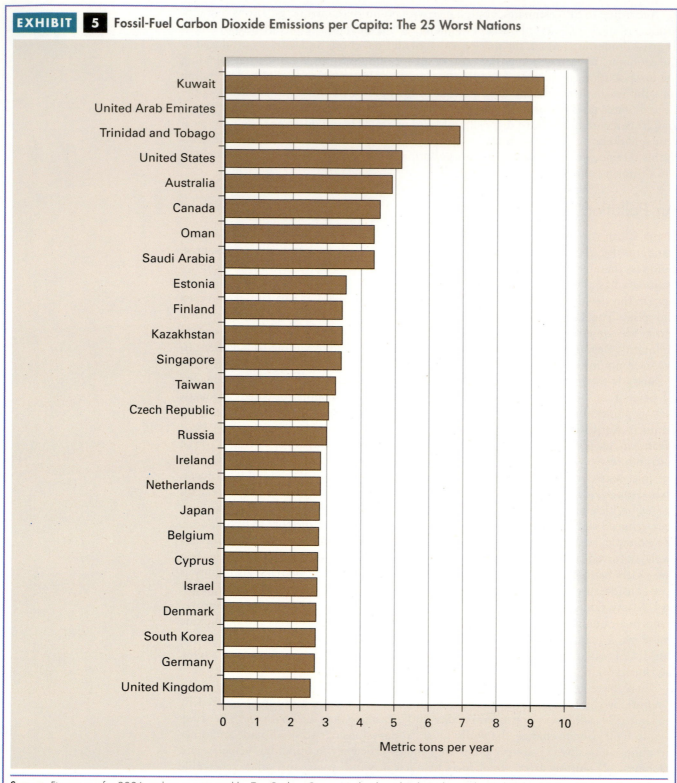

Sources: Figures are for 2006 and were estimated by Tom Boden, Gregg Marland, and Bob Andres at the Oak Ridge National Laboratory and can be found at http://cdiac.ornl.gov/trends/emis/top2006.cap. Excluded are nations with fewer than one million people.

energy sources; (3) preserving forests as absorbers of carbon dioxide, or as "carbon sinks"; and (4) capping agricultural emissions. The United States and China, which account for more than 40 percent of the world's emissions, approved the report but offered no indication that they would reverse their opposition to mandatory emission reductions. The report said that such reforms would require lifestyle changes, increased prices for some basics including gasoline and electricity, and greater investment in research and development.

Water Pollution

Three major sources of water pollution are sewage, chemicals, and oil. For decades, U.S. cities had an economic incentive to dump their sewage directly into waterways rather than clean it up first. Water current or tides would carry off the waste to become someone else's problem. Although each community found it rational, based on a narrow view of the situation, to dump into waterways, the combined effect of these local choices was water pollution, a negative externality imposed by one community on other communities. Federal money over the years has funded thousands of sewage treatment plants, which cut water pollution substantially. Nearly all U.S. cities now have modern sewage treatment systems. Hundreds of once-polluted waterways have been cleaned up enough for swimming and fishing.

Chemicals are a second source of water pollution. Chemical pollution may conjure up an image of a pipe spewing chemicals into a river, but only about 10 percent of chemical pollution in the water comes from point pollution—pollution from factories and other industrial sites. About two-thirds come from nonpoint pollution—mostly runoff from agricultural pesticides and fertilizer. Congress has been reluctant to limit the use of pesticides, although pesticides pollute water and contaminate food. Industrial America seems an easier target than Old MacDonald's farm. In 1970, Congress shifted control of pesticides from the U.S. Department of Agriculture to the newly created Environmental Protection Agency (EPA). But the EPA already had its hands full administering the Clean Water Act, so it turned pesticide regulation over to the states. Most states gave the job to their departments of agriculture, which usually promote the interests of farmers, not restrict what farmers can do. The EPA now reports that in most states pesticides have fouled some groundwater.[9]

A third source of water pollution is oil. The cleanup of oil spills on land are overseen by the EPA. About 600,000 underground storage tanks for oil and chemicals pose a potential threat of contamination for groundwater, the source of drinking water for half of Americans. The cleanup of offshore oil spills is overseen by the U.S. Coast Guard. The most notable offshore spill in U.S. history is discussed in the following case study.

PUBLIC POLICY

CASE STUDY

BP's Oil Spill in the Gulf On April 20, 2010, the Deepwater Horizon oil rig exploded in the Gulf of Mexico in a drilling accident that killed 11 workers and hospitalized many. Both BP and the government initially underestimated the size of the spill, and neither had a response plan in place. Though the oil industry had experienced blowouts at shallower depths, an accident a mile down was new and devastating. Federal regulators seemed lax prior to the accident, perhaps captives of the industry. The size of the Gulf spill combined with live video of the gushing well and photos of oil-soaked birds marked this tragedy in the public's mind. President Obama called it the worst environmental disaster in U.S. history.

9. John Cushman, "E.P.A. and States Found to Be Lax on Pollution Law," *New York Times*, 7 June 1998.

The explosion and resulting oil spill, accidental byproducts of BP's efforts to supply oil, threatened the livelihood of tens of thousands around the Gulf and could impose lasting damage on the habitat. BP spent billions on cleanup in the first three months, but that was peanuts compared to the costs company owners have and will face. More than 150 class-action lawsuits named BP as a defendant. Hoping to attract more clients, law firms purchased domain names such as offshoreinjuries.com and bigoilspills.com and advertised with billboards along the Gulf Coast. Environmental groups filed suits of their own. President Obama warned BP against "nickel and diming" the economic victims of the accident. And the Justice Department opened a criminal probe against BP for possible violations of the Clean Water Act and other environmental laws.

Here's a question: Was this oil spill a negative externality? Was this an unpriced by-product that affected neither buyer nor seller but third parties? The buyers in this case were customers for BP gasoline and the seller was BP. Market competition may make it difficult for BP to pass along its spill-related costs, so BP consumers may not be much affected. How about BP?

A.J. SISCO/UPI/Landov

If this were truly an externality, then the accident would have had little impact on the supplier, BP, or the company BP hired to drill the well, Transocean. But both have been profoundly affected. Because BP has been reviled by everyone from President Obama on down, the company's brand name will be tarnished for a generation, becoming the poster child of polluters in the public's mind, in the media, even in textbooks. Lawsuits will likely cost the company billions and may take years to settle (some Exxon-Valdez suits from the 1989 Alaska spill took more than two decades to resolve). For its part, Transocean, the owners of the rig, saw 11 workers die in the explosion and many more hospitalized. The drilling rig itself, which cost Transocean $375 million, sank two days after the explosion.

Although lawsuits may be in the courts for years, share owners of BP and Transocean didn't have to wait long to see their losses reflected in stock prices. Within six weeks of the accident, the share price of each company sank 50 percent. In BP's case, that meant a loss in the market value of the company of about $90 billion. Because Transocean was a smaller company, its market value fell about $15 billion. Although the exact amount of the spill may never be known, let's say the total turns out to be about 200 million gallons, a figure higher than any reported estimate. This would imply that BP and Transocean stockholders together lost more than $500 in market value for each of the 200 million gallons of crude oil spilled into the Gulf. There remained some question whether the companies will survive. For example, BP established a $20 billion fund to compensate those affected by the spill. The company was forced to sell rights to some oil fields to pay for the cleanup and was expected to issue bonds to raise more money. No question, many in the Gulf region have been harmed by the spill, and some of the damage could last for years. But many people will be compensated for their losses. The legal system, the government, the media, and the stock market have placed much of the cost of this accident squarely on BP and Transocean, and to that extent, most of what otherwise would have been external costs became internalized.

Sources: Michael Shear and Steven Mufson, "Obama to BP: Take Care of Gulf Victims," *Washington Post*, 5 June 2010; Justin Gillis and Leslie Kaufman, "After Oil Spill, Hidden Damage Can Last for Years," *New York Times*, 17 July 2010; Dionne Searcey, "Attorneys Scramble to Gather the Most Plaintiffs for the Broadest Action Possible," *Wall Street Journal*, 2 June 2010; and Brian Baskins, "BP: 'No Evidence' of Problems with New Caps," *Wall Street Journal*, 17 July 2010.

Hazardous Waste and the Superfund

The U.S. synthetic chemical industry has flourished in the last 50 years, and over 50,000 chemicals are now in common use. But some have harmful effects on humans and other living creatures. These chemicals can pose risks at every stage of their production, use, and disposal. New Jersey manufactures more toxic chemicals than any other state and, not surprisingly, has the worst toxic waste burden. Prior to 1980, the disposal of toxic waste created get-rich-quick opportunities for anyone who could rent or buy a few acres of land to open a toxic waste dump. As an extreme example, one site in New Jersey took in 71 million gallons of hazardous chemicals during a three-year period.[10]

Before 1980, once a company paid someone to haul away its hazardous waste, that company was no longer responsible. The Comprehensive Environmental Response, Compensation, and Liability Act of 1980, known more popularly as the Superfund law, requires any company that generates, stores, or transports hazardous wastes to pay to clean up any wastes that are improperly disposed of. A producer or hauler who is the source of even one barrel of pollution dumped at a site can be held liable for cleaning up the entire site.

The Superfund law gave the federal government authority over sites contaminated with toxins. But to get an offending company to comply, the EPA frequently must sue. The process is slow, and nearly half the budget goes to lawyers, consultants, and administrators rather than to site cleanups. The law did not require that benefits of a cleanup exceed costs or even that such comparisons be attempted. Although billions have been spent so far, a recent EPA study concluded that the health hazards of Superfund sites have been vastly exaggerated. Chemicals in the ground usually move slowly, sometimes taking years to travel a few feet, so any possible health threat is confined to the site itself. People know when they live near toxic waste sites, and they can exert political pressure to get something done, whereas people exposed to polluted air, water, and pesticide residue may develop health problems but never make the connection to their environment. Thus, people see less reason to press public officials for cleaner air and water (though the threat of climate change has focused more attention on greenhouse gas emissions). Toxic waste sites, because of their greater political urgency and media appeal (witness the movies on the subject), tend to receive more attention than air or water pollution. And with the federal government picking up the tab, localities demand all the cleanup they can get. But research indicates that Superfund cleanups have little or no impact on residential property values, property rental rates, the housing supply, total population, or the types of individuals living near the sites.[11] In short, Superfund cleanups seem to be much to do about not much.

Solid Waste: "Paper or Plastic?"

Throughout most of human history, households tossed their trash outside as fodder for pigs and goats. New York City, like other cities, had no trash collections, so domestic waste was thrown into the street, where it mixed with mud and manure (until recently, many residents of Beijing and other parts of China did the same thing).[12] Decades of such accumulation explain why the oldest Manhattan streets are anywhere from 3 to 15 feet above their original levels. Until the last century, people buried their trash near their homes or took it to a local dump. Most localities now forbid trash burning.

U.S. households generate about 4 pounds of garbage per resident per day—more than twice the 1960 level and the most in the world. Much of the solid waste consists

10. Jason Zweig, "Real-Life Horror Story," *Forbes*, 12 December 1988.
11. Michael Greenstone and Justin Gallagher, "Does Hazardous Waste Matter? Evidence from the Housing Market and Superfund Programs," *Quarterly Journal of Economics*, 123 (August 2008): 951–1003.
12. Laurence Brahm, "Hygiene? It's a Load of Rubbish," *South China Morning Post*, 1 November 2005.

of packaging. The question is, how do we dispose of the more than 200 million tons of household garbage generated in this country each year? Advanced economies produce and buy more than less developed economies, so there is more to throw away. And because of higher incomes in advanced economies, the opportunity cost of time is higher, so Americans tend to discard items rather than repair or recycle them. For example, it's cheaper to buy a new toaster for $20 than to pay $40 an hour to fix a broken one, assuming you can even find a repair service. (Look up "Appliance Repair, Small" in the *Yellow Pages* and see if you can find even one such service in your area.)

About 70 percent of the nation's garbage is bulldozed and covered with soil in landfills. Although a well-managed landfill poses few environmental concerns, at one time, communities dumped all kinds of toxins in them—stuff that could leach into the soil, contaminating wells and aquifers. So landfills got a bad reputation. Now, the prevailing attitude with landfills is Nimby! (Not in my backyard!). We all want our garbage picked up but nobody wants it put down anywhere nearby.

As the cost of solid waste disposal increases, some state and local governments are economizing, charging households by the pound for trash pickups, and requiring more recycling and returnable bottles. **Recycling** is the process of converting waste products into reusable materials. Nearly half of U.S. households participate in curbside recycling programs. Still, according to the EPA, only about 15 percent of U.S. garbage gets recycled; about 15 percent is incinerated and, as noted already, the remaining 70 percent goes into landfills. Of the recycled material, three-quarters consists of corrugated boxes, newspapers, office paper, and other paper products. Some paper is shipped to Korea, Taiwan, and China, where it becomes packaging material for U.S. imports such as Blu-ray players and computer components. Exhibit 6 ranks the world's top 25 recyclers of paper and cardboard among major economies. Ireland heads the list, recycling 78 percent. The United States is in a five-way tie for 18th, recycling 50 percent (but more than double that of 1985). Poorer countries recycle much less—Mexico, for example, only 7 percent.

Most of the 15 percent of garbage that is incinerated gets burned in trash-to-energy plants, which generate electricity using the heat from incineration. Until recently, such plants looked like the wave of the future, but less favorable tax treatment and environmental concerns over incinerator locations (Nimby strikes again!) have taken the steam out of the trash-to-energy movement.

To repeat, only 30 percent of U.S. garbage is recycled or incinerated, and about 70 percent goes to landfills. In contrast, the Japanese recycle or incinerate 73 percent, sending only 27 percent to landfills. Japanese households sort their trash into as many as 21 categories. Because land is scarcer in Japan—we know this because it costs relatively more—it is not surprising that the Japanese deposit a smaller share of their garbage in landfills.

Some recycling is clearly economical—such as aluminum cans, which are a relatively cheap source of aluminum compared to producing raw aluminum. About two out of three aluminum cans now get recycled, though only 11 states require returnable deposits on such cans. Still, returnable deposit laws increase recycling. Incentives matter. Even if you decide to discard your empties, chances are that someone down the line with a lower opportunity cost than you will find them and claim the deposits. For example, researchers found an average of 47 bottles and cans along a one-block path of city park each day prior to the enactment of deposit law, but one year after the law was introduced, they found an average of only two bottles and cans each day along the same path.[13]

Recycling paper and cardboard is also economical and occurred long before the environmental movement. Such old standbys as paper drives, drop-off bins, and redemption centers collect more tonnage than curbside programs. Most recycling results from salvaging scrap material from business and industry, a practice that dates back decades.

13. J. Trinkaus, "A Bottle Law: An Informal Look," *Perceptual and Motor Skills*, 59 (December 1984): 806.

recycling
The process of converting waste products into reusable material

EXHIBIT 6 Paper and Cardboard Recycling: Top 25 Among Advanced Economies

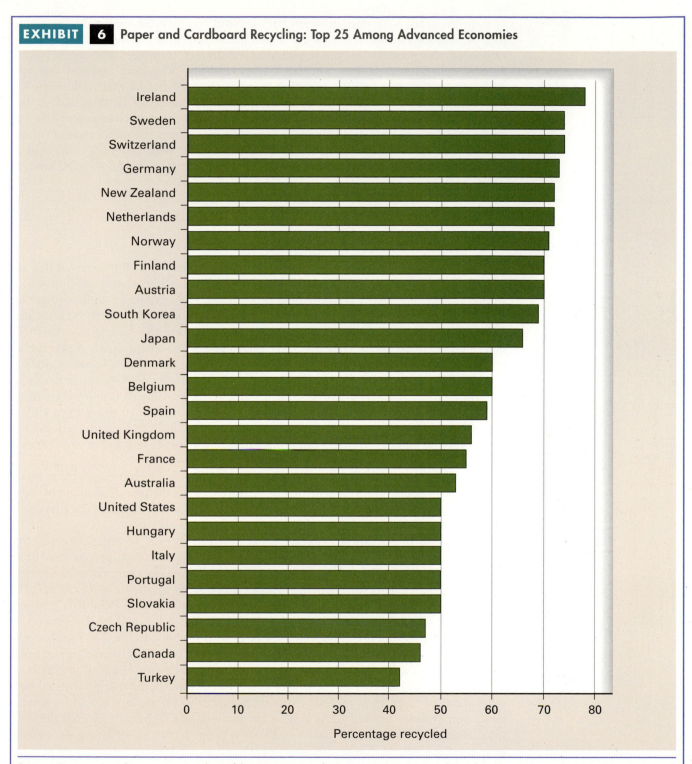

Percentage recycled

Sources: Figures are rankings among members of the Organization of Economic Cooperation and Development as reported in *OECD Environmental Data 2006/2007*, Table 4A, p. 25. This can be found at http://www.oecd.org/dataoecd/60/59/38106368.pdf. Figures are for 2005, except for South Korea, Germany, Sweden, and the U.K., which are for 2004, and for Japan and Turkey, which are for 2003.

Governments have tried to stimulate demand for recycled material—for example, by requiring newspapers to use a minimum percentage of recycled newsprint. Other recycled products are not in such demand. In fact, some recycled products have become worthless and must be hauled to landfills. Recycling imposes its own environmental cost. Curbside recycling requires fleets of trucks that pollute the air. Newsprint must first be de-inked, creating a sludge that must be disposed of. But greater environmental awareness has made consumers more receptive to more efficient packaging. For example, liquid laundry detergent now comes in a concentrated "ultra" form, which cuts volume in half, and Unilever's brand All Small & Mighty cuts volume by two-thirds. Labels for all kinds of products proudly identify the recycled content of the packaging.

Positive Externalities

To this point, we have considered only negative externalities. But externalities are sometimes positive, or beneficial. Positive externalities occur when consumption or production benefits other consumers or other firms. For example, people who get inoculated against a disease reduce their own likelihood of contracting the disease (the personal benefit), but they reduce the risk of transmitting the disease to others (the external benefit). Parents who don't get their children vaccinated risk triggering an epidemic, so the vaccination decision is not simply a private matter. Likewise, society as a whole receives external benefits from education because those with more education become better citizens, can read road signs, are better able to support themselves and their families, and are less likely to require public assistance or to resort to violent crime for income. Researchers found that more schooling significantly reduces the probability of incarceration.[14] Thus, your education benefits you but it also benefits others.

The effect of external benefits is illustrated in Exhibit 7, which presents the demand and supply of education. The demand curve, *D*, represents the private demand for education, which reflects the marginal private benefit for those who acquire the education. More education is demanded at a lower price than at a higher price.

The benefit of education, however, spills over to others in society. If we add this positive externality, or marginal external benefit, to the marginal private benefit of education, we get the marginal social benefit of education. *The marginal social benefit includes all the benefits society derives from education, both private and external.* The marginal social benefit curve is above the private demand curve in Exhibit 7. If education were a strictly private decision, the amount purchased would be determined by the intersection of the private demand curve *D* with supply curve *S*. The supply curve reflects the marginal cost of producing each unit of the good. This intersection at point *e* yields education level *E*, where the marginal private benefit of education equals its marginal cost, as reflected by the supply curve. But at level *E*, the marginal social benefit, identified as point *b*, exceeds the marginal cost. Social welfare would increase if education expands beyond *E*. As long as the marginal social benefit exceeds the marginal cost, social welfare increases as education expands. Social welfare is maximized at point *e'* in Exhibit 7, where *E'* units of education are provided—that is, where the marginal social benefit equals the marginal cost. The blue-shaded triangle identifies the increase in social welfare that results from increasing education from *E*, the private optimum, to *E'*, the social optimum.

14. Lance Lochner and Enrico Moretti, "The Effects of Education on Crime: Evidence from Prison Inmates," *American Economic Review*, 94 (March 2004): 155–189.

EXHIBIT **7** **Education and Positive Externalities**

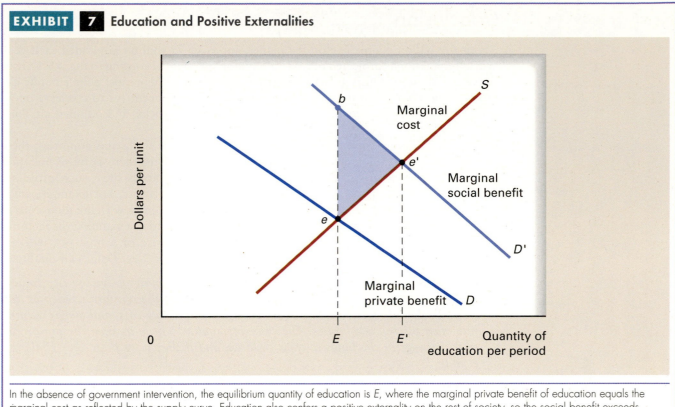

In the absence of government intervention, the equilibrium quantity of education is *E*, where the marginal private benefit of education equals the marginal cost as reflected by the supply curve. Education also confers a positive externality on the rest of society, so the social benefit exceeds the private benefit. At quantity *E*, the marginal social benefit, point *b*, exceeds the marginal cost, point *e*, so more education increases social welfare. In this situation, government tries to increase education to *E'*, where the marginal social benefit equals the marginal cost.

Thus, society is better off if the level of education exceeds the private equilibrium. With positive externalities, decisions based on private marginal benefits result in less than the socially optimal quantity of the good. Thus, like negative externalities, positive externalities typically point to market failure, which is why government often gets into the act. When there are external benefits, public policy aims to increase quantity beyond the private optimum. For example, governments try to increase education by providing free primary and secondary education, by requiring students to stay in school until they reach 16 years of age, by subsidizing public higher education, and by offering tax breaks for some education costs.

Another source of externalities stems from precautions people take to avoid becoming crime victims, such as LoJack, a device used to track and recover a stolen vehicle. Because the device is completely undetectable by a potential thief, the more LoJacks installed, the more nervous thieves get and the fewer vehicles stolen in general. Thus, car owners without LoJack get a positive externality when others install the device. Researchers estimated that a 1 percent increase in LoJack installations cuts car thefts in general by at least 20 percent.[15] On the other hand, the use of The Club, a very visible lock for the steering wheel, generates a negative externality, because it increases the likelihood that vehicles without The Club will get stolen. In terms of social welfare, there are not enough LoJacks installed and too many Clubs.

15. Ian Ayres and Steven Levitt, "Measuring Positive Externalities for Unobservable Victim Precautions: An Empirical Analysis of Lojack," *Quarterly Journal of Economics*," 113 (February 1998): 43–77.

Conclusion

About 6.9 billion people live on the planet, and over 72 million are added each year. World population is projected to reach 9.3 billion by 2050, according to the U.S. Census Bureau, with most of this growth occurring in countries where most people barely eke out a living. Population pressure coupled with a lack of incentives to conserve open-access resources results in deforestation, dwindling fish stocks, and polluted air, land, and water.

Ironically, because of the tighter pollution controls in industrial countries, these countries are less polluted than developing countries, where there is more pollution from what little industry there is. Most developing countries have such profound economic problems that environmental quality is not a priority. For example, when India's Supreme Court tried to close some polluting factories in New Delhi, thousands of workers torched buses, threw stones, and blocked major roads, demanding the factories stay open. Although New Delhi's pollution masks any trace of a blue sky, workers believe their jobs are more important. Here's one account of New Delhi's air quality:

> In the heat of the afternoons, a yellow-white mixture hung above the city, raining acidic soot into the dust and exhaust fumes. At night the mixture condenses into a dry, choking fog that envelops the headlights of passing cars, and creeps its stink into even the tightest houses. The residents could do little to keep the poison out of their lungs or the lungs of their children, and if they were poor, they could not even try.[16]

Market prices can direct the allocation of resources only as long as property rights are well defined. Pollution arises not so much from the greed of producers and consumers as from the fact that open-access resources are subject to the common-pool problem.

Summary

1. An exhaustible resource is available in fixed supply, such as crude oil or coal. A renewable resource can regenerate itself if used conservatively, such as a properly managed forest. Some renewable resources suffer from a common-pool problem because unrestricted access leads to overuse.

2. Production that generates negative externalities results in too much output. Production that generates positive externalities results in too little output. Public policy should tax or otherwise limit production that generates negative externalities and should subsidize or otherwise promote production that generates positive externalities.

3. The optimal amount of environmental quality occurs where the marginal social benefit of an improvement equals its marginal social cost. An upward shift of the marginal benefit curve of environmental quality or a downward shift of its marginal cost curve increases the optimal level of environmental quality.

4. The world's tropical rainforests recycle greenhouse gases into oxygen and wood. Because rainforests are open-access resources, settlers and loggers cut them down to make a living. This destruction reduces the environment's ability to cleanse itself of greenhouse gases, which may contribute to climate change.

5. The Coase theorem argues that as long as bargaining costs are low, assigning property rights to one party leads to an efficient solution to the externality problem. The market for pollution permits reflects the Coase theorem in action.

6. Aside from greenhouse gases, America's air and waterways are getting cleaner. The air is cleaner because of stricter emissions standards for motor vehicles, and waterways are cleaner because of billions spent on sewage treatment plants. Toxic waste sites do not pose as great a health threat as other forms of pollution such as smog and pesticide residue, but toxic waste sites often get more media and political attention.

16. William Langewiesche, "The Shipbreakers," *Atlantic Monthly* (August 2000): 42.

Key Concepts

Questions for Review

1. **EXTERNALITIES**   Complete each of the following sentences:
   a. Resources that are available only in a fixed amount are _____ resources.
   b. The possibility that a open-access resource is used until the marginal value of additional use equals zero is known as the _____.
   c. Resources for which periodic use can be continued indefinitely are known as _____ resources.

2. **RESOLVING THE COMMON-POOL PROBLEM**   Why have authorities found it so difficult to regulate the fishing catch in the open ocean to allow for a sustainable yield?

3. **OPTIMAL LEVEL OF POLLUTION**   Explain the difference between fixed-production technology and variable technology. Should the government set a goal of reducing the marginal social cost of pollution to zero in industries with fixed-production technology? Should they do so in industries with variable technology?

4. **Case Study: Destruction of the Tropical Rainforests**   Why does a solution to the overharvesting of timber in the tropical rainforests require some form of international cooperation? Would this be a sufficient solution to the deforestation problem?

5. **THE COASE THEOREM**   Suppose a firm pollutes a stream that has a recreational value only when pollution is below a certain level. If transaction costs are low, why does the assignment of property rights to the stream lead to the same (efficient) level of pollution whether the firm or recreational users own the stream?

6. **THE COASE THEOREM**   Ronald Coase points out that a market failure does not arise simply because people ignore the external cost of their actions. What other condition is necessary? What did Coase consider to be an efficient solution to a negative externality?

7. Four federal laws and subsequent amendments underpin U.S. environmental protection. Identify these laws.

8. **Case Study: BP's Oil Spill in the Gulf**   Should the government require deepwater oil companies to spend whatever it takes to reduce the chance of future spills to zero?

9. **POSITIVE EXTERNALITIES**   The value of a home depends in part on how attractive other homes and yards in the neighborhood are. How do local zoning ordinances try to promote land uses that generate external benefits for neighbors?

Problems and Exercises

10. **EXTERNAL COSTS WITH FIXED-PRODUCTION TECHNOLOGY**   Review the situation illustrated in Exhibit 1 in this chapter. If the government sets the price of electricity at the socially optimal level, why is the net gain equal to triangle *abc*, even though consumers now pay a higher price for electricity? What would the net gain be if the government set the price above the optimal level?

11. **NEGATIVE EXTERNALITIES**   Suppose you wish to reduce a negative externality by imposing a tax on the activity that creates that externality. When the amount of the externality produced per unit of output increases as output increases, the correct tax can be determined by using a demand-supply diagram; show this. Assume that the marginal private cost curve slopes upward.

12. **EXTERNAL COSTS**   Use the data in the table from the next page to answer the following questions.
    a. What is the external cost per unit of production?
    b. What level is produced if there is no regulation of the externality?
    c. What level should be produced to achieve economic efficiency?
    d. Calculate the dollar value of the net gain to society from correcting the externality.

Quantity	Marginal Private Benefit (demand) ($)	Marginal Private Cost (supply) ($)	Marginal Social Cost ($)
0	—	0	0
1	10	2	4
2	9	3	5
3	8	4	6
4	7	5	7
5	6	6	8
6	5	7	9
7	4	8	10
8	3	9	11
9	2	10	12
10	1	11	13

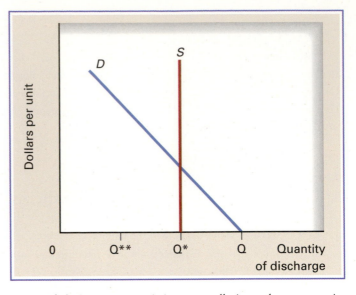

13. EXTERNAL COSTS WITH VARIABLE TECHNOLOGY Think of an industry that pollutes the water and has access to variable technology for reducing that pollution. Graphically illustrate and explain the impact of each of the following, other things constant, on the optimal level of water quality:

   a. New evidence is discovered about a greater risk of cancer from water pollution.
   b. The cost of pollution-control equipment increases.
   c. A technological improvement reduces the cost of pollution control.

14. MARKET FOR POLLUTION RIGHTS The following graph shows the market for pollution rights.

   a. If there are no restrictions on pollution, what amount is discharged?
   b. What is the quantity supplied and the quantity demanded if the government restricts the amount of discharge to Q* but gives the permits away?
   c. Where is market equilibrium if the government sells the permits? Illustrate this on the graph.
   d. What happens to market equilibrium if the government reduces the amount of discharge permitted to Q**? Illustrate this on the graph.

Global Economic Watch Exercises

Login to www.cengagebrain.com and access the Global Economic Watch to do these exercises.

15. GLOBAL ECONOMIC WATCH and Case Study: Destruction of the Tropical Rainforests Go to the Global Economic Crisis Resource Center. Select Global Issues in Context. In the Basic Search box at the top of the page, enter the phrase "carbon ranching." On the Results page, go to the Global Viewpoints Section. Click on the link for the June 16, 2007, editorial "Home on the Rainforest." Is the program described an example of command-and-control environmental regulation or of the economic efficiency approach?

16. GLOBAL ECONOMIC WATCH Go to the Global Economic Crisis Resource Center. Select Global Issues in Context. Go to the menu at the top of the page and click on the tab for Browse Issues and Topics. Choose Environment and Climate Change. Choose one of the topics listed and read the overview for that topic. Analyze the marginal social benefit and marginal social cost involved in your chosen topic.

Income Distribution and Poverty

18

- Why are some people poor even in the most productive economy on Earth?

- Who are the poor, how did they get that way, and how long do they stay poor?

- What's been the trend in U.S. poverty?

- What's been the impact of the changing family structure on poverty?

- What public programs aim to reduce poverty, and how well have they worked?

- Why was someone fined more than $200,000 for speeding 25 miles over the limit?

- And which group will likely get little sympathy for being hit hard by the recent recession?

Answers to these and related questions are addressed in this chapter, which discusses income distribution and poverty in America.

To establish a reference point, we first consider the distribution of income in the United States, paying special attention to trends in recent decades. We then examine the "social safety net"—government programs aimed at helping poor people. We also consider the impact of the changing family structure on poverty, focusing in particular on the increase in households headed by women.

We close by examining recent welfare reforms.

Topics discussed include:

- Distribution of income
- Official poverty level
- Public policy and poverty
- The feminization of poverty
- Poverty and discrimination
- Welfare reforms

The Distribution of Household Income

In a market economy, income depends primarily on earnings, which depend on the productivity of one's resources. The problem with allocating income according to productivity is that some people have few resources to sell. People with mental or physical disabilities, a poor education, those facing discrimination, bad luck, or the demands of caring for small children, and the elderly may be less productive and unable to earn a living.

Income Distribution by Quintiles

As a starting point, let's consider the distribution of income in the economy and see how it has changed over time, focusing on the household as the economic unit. After sorting U.S. households based on income into five groups of equal size, or *quintiles*, we can examine the percentage of total income received by each quintile. Such a division is presented in Exhibit 1 since 1980. Take a moment to look over this exhibit. Notice that households in the lowest, or poorest, fifth of the population received only 4.3 percent of the income in 1980, whereas households in the highest, or richest, fifth received 43.7 percent of the income. The U.S. Census Bureau measures income after cash transfer payments are received but before taxes are paid or in-kind transfers are received (from food vouchers, Medicare, Medicaid, public housing, and employer-provided benefits).

EXHIBIT 1 Share of Aggregate Household Income by Quintile

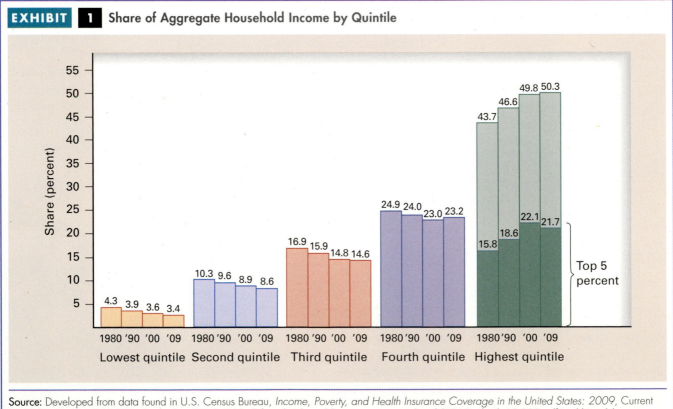

Source: Developed from data found in U.S. Census Bureau, *Income, Poverty, and Health Insurance Coverage in the United States: 2009*, Current Population Reports P-60-238, September 2010, Table 3 found at http://www.census.gov/prod/2010pubs/p60-238.pdf and http://www.census.gov/hhes/www/income/histinc/h02ar.html.

In recent decades, the share of income going to the top fifth has increased, and the share going to the bottom fifth has declined. The richest fifth's share of income increased from 43.7 percent in 1980 to 50.3 percent in 2009. A primary contributor to the larger share of income going to the highest group has been the growth of two-earner households in that top group. Three out of four households in the top quintile have two or more people working. A primary contributor to the smaller share going to the lowest group has been the growth of single-parent households in the bottom group. Only about one in three households in the bottom quintile has anybody working, and only about one in seven has anybody working full time.

Also shown in Exhibit 1 is the share of income going to the top 5 percent of households; that share has grown since 1980, accounting for nearly all the growth of the top 20 percent of households. Because of substantial reductions in the top marginal tax rates in 1981 and 1986, high-income people had less incentive to engage in tax avoidance, so their reported income increased, boosting the share of reported income going to the richest 5 percent of households.

The Lorenz Curve

We have just examined the distribution of income using a bar chart. Another way to picture that distribution is with a Lorenz curve. A **Lorenz curve** shows the percentage of total income received by any given percentage of households when incomes are arrayed from smallest to largest. As shown in Exhibit 2, the cumulative percentage of households is measured along the horizontal axis, and the cumulative percentage of income is measured along the vertical axis. Any given distribution of income can be compared to an equal distribution of income among households. If income were evenly distributed, each 20 percent of households would also receive 20 percent of the total income, and the Lorenz curve would be a straight line with a slope equal to 1.0, as shown by the "equal distribution" line in Exhibit 2.

As the distribution becomes more uneven, the Lorenz curve pulls down to the right, away from the line of equal distribution. The Lorenz curves in Exhibit 2 were calculated for 1980 and 2009 based on the data in Exhibit 1. As a reference, point *a* on the 1980 Lorenz curve indicates that in that year, the bottom 80 percent of families received 56.3 percent of the income, and the top 20 percent received 43.7 percent of the income. The Lorenz curve for 2009 is farther from the line of equal distribution than is the Lorenz curve for 1980, showing that income among households has become more unevenly distributed. Point *b* on the 2009 curve shows that the bottom 80 percent received 49.7 percent of the income and the top 20 percent received 50.3 percent of the income.

Why Incomes Differ

Income differences across households stem in part from differences in the *number* of workers in each household. Thus, *one reason household incomes differ is that the number of household members who are working differs.* For example, among households in the bottom 20 percent based on income, only one in seven includes a full-time, year-round worker. Consider the link between median income and the number of workers. The **median income** of all households is the middle income when incomes are ranked from lowest to highest. In any given year, half the households are above the median income and half are below it. The median income for households with two earners is 91 percent higher than for households with only one earner and is more than four times higher than for households with no earners.

lorenz curve

A curve showing the percentage of total income received by a given percentage of recipients whose incomes are arrayed from smallest to largest

median income

The middle income when all incomes are ranked from smallest to largest

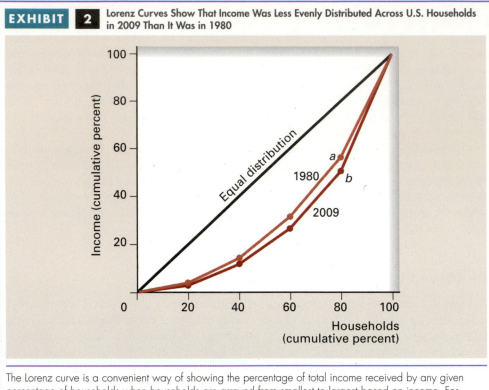

EXHIBIT 2 Lorenz Curves Show That Income Was Less Evenly Distributed Across U.S. Households in 2009 Than It Was in 1980

The Lorenz curve is a convenient way of showing the percentage of total income received by any given percentage of households when households are arrayed from smallest to largest based on income. For example, point a shows that in 1980, the bottom 80 percent of households received 56.3 percent of all income. Point b shows that in 2009, the share of all income going to the bottom 80 percent of households was lower than in 1980. If income were evenly distributed across households, the Lorenz curve would be a straight line.

Incomes also differ for all the reasons labor earnings differ, such as differences in education, ability, job experience, and so on. At every age, those with more education earn more, on average. As noted a few chapters back, those with a professional degree earn at least five times more than those without a high school diploma. Age itself also has an important effect on income. As workers mature, they acquire valuable job experience, get promoted, and earn more.

Differences in earnings based on age and education reflect a normal *life cycle* pattern of income. In fact, most income differences across households reflect the normal workings of resource markets, whereby workers are rewarded according to their productivity. Because of these lifetime patterns, it is not necessarily the same households that remain rich or poor over time. Indeed, one study of income mobility found that more than three-quarters of people in the bottom 20 percent in one particular year had moved into the top 40 percent for at least one year during the following 16 years.[1]

Despite this income mobility over time, we can still characterize rich and poor households at a point in time. *A high-income household usually consists of a well-educated couple with both spouses employed. A low-income household is usually one person living alone or is a family headed by a single parent who is young, female, poorly educated, and not working.* Low incomes are a matter of public concern, especially when children are involved, as we see in the next section.

1. W. Michael Cox and Richard Arm, "By Our Own Bootstraps," *Federal Reserve Bank of Dallas: 1995 Annual Report.*

A College Education Pays More

Also contributing to the dominance of the top group is an increased pay advantage for those with college educations. In the last two decades, the median wage (adjusted for inflation) for people with only high school diplomas declined 6 percent, while the median wage for college graduates rose 12 percent. The **median wage** is the middle wage when wages are ranked from lowest to highest. Why have more-educated workers done better? First, trends such as industry deregulation, declining unionization, and freer international trade and migration have reduced the pay for workers with less education. Labor unions, for example, raised the wages of many workers who would have otherwise ended up in the bottom half of the income distribution. But the share of the workforce that is unionized declined from 26 percent in 1973 to only 12 percent in 2009. More generally, an increasing fraction of jobs in the U.S. labor market explicitly pay workers for their productivity using bonus pay, commissions, or piece-rate contracts. Research suggests that productivity pay has increased earnings inequality.[2]

Second, new computer-based information technologies have reduced the demand for low-skilled clerical workers, because their jobs became computerized. Computers also offered more timely and accurate information to management, allowing for organizational innovations that made managers and other professionals more productive.[3] So computers reduced the demand for workers with low skills, such as clerical staff and bank tellers, and increased the demand for those who use computers to boost labor productivity, such as managers and accountants.

Third, the supply of less-educated workers increased more than the supply of more-educated workers, thus increasing the rewards of education. For example, compared to average residents, recent U.S. immigrants tend to be less educated, including an estimated 12 million illegal immigrants, more than half from Mexico. The Hispanic population more than doubled between the 1980 census and 2000 census, and the percentage of foreign-born Hispanics increased. Among males age 25 and older, only 57 percent of Hispanics had at least a high school education in 2000, compared with 85 percent of whites and 79 percent of blacks. More generally, the foreign-born share of the U.S. population more than doubled from 5 percent in 1970 to over 12 percent today, the largest share since the 1930s. Thus, immigration has increased the supply of relatively poorly educated workers, which has depressed wages of the less educated generally.

Finally, marriage trends have reinforced the income gap, as discussed in the following case study.

median wage
The middle wage when wages of all workers are ranked from lowest to highest

.net bookmark

Data and analytical reports about income distribution can be found at the U.S. Census Bureau's Web site at http://www.census.gov/hhes/www/income.html. This Income page includes a link to a page devoted to income inequality. There you can find data on the distribution of income by quintile and the report, "The Changing Shape of the Nation's Income Distribution, 1947–98." What is used in this report to measure income distribution? In what year was income least unequal? What is the most recent trend?

PUBLIC POLICY

Marital Sorting and Income Inequality In the not too distant past, lawyers married secretaries and doctors married nurses. Now, Americans with increasing frequency are pairing off by education levels—lawyers marry lawyers, and doctors marry doctors. Why the change? Women have made huge inroads into the professions. In 1970, only about 10 percent of law or medical school enrollees were women. Now it's about 50 percent. More generally, women make up 54 percent of those ages 18 to 24 enrolled in college, graduate school, or professional school. Thus, men and women are now more likely to meet their future spouses in college, law school, medical school, graduate school, or some other advanced educational setting.

CASE STUDY

e activity
According to the U.S. Census Bureau, Connecticut, the District of Columbia, New Jersey, and Massachusetts had median earnings for men that were above $55,000 in 2008. Connecticut, New Jersey, and Maryland were the only states where median earnings for women were above $44,000, as was the

2. Thomas Lamieux et al., "Performance Pay and Wage Inequality," *Quarterly Journal of Economics,* 124 (February 2009): 1–49.
3. Lex Borghans and Bas ter Weel, "The Diffusion of Computers and the Distribution of Wages," *European Economic Review,* 51 (April 2007): 715–748.

...continued

e activity continued

District of Columbia. In each of the 50 states and the District of Columbia, median earnings were less for women than they were for men in 2008—in the District of Columbia, women earned about 88 cents for every dollar that men earned, higher than in any of the states. Go to the Census Bureau's site at http://pubdb3.census. gov/macro/032007/perinc/ new10_000.htm and compare the wages by gender and race.

As a result of their educational strides, particularly in the professions, a growing number of women, for the first time in history, now have high-paying jobs and professional careers. The extent to which couples are educational equals has reached its highest point in decades. Choosing a marriage partner based on income is also on the rise. Studies find a growing similarity between women's wages before marriage and the future earnings of the men they marry.

So this power couple marries and has children, and these offspring benefit from the high income and any other advantages passed along from their well-educated parents, including better health. With this head start in life, many from that next generation, in turn, go to the best colleges, where they are likely to meet their future spouses. A study of the nation's top 147 colleges found that only 9 percent of admissions come from families in the bottom half of the income distribution. The whole cycle thereby gets reinforced and perpetuated.

The flip side of this is that someone with only a high school education is now less likely to marry a college graduate than was once the case. What's more, among women born after 1960, someone with only a high school education is less likely

to ever marry than is someone with a college education. Only about 11 percent of all births in 1970 were to unmarried mothers; that share climbed to 41 percent by 2008. As you will see, children born to single mothers typically face special challenges, not the least of which is a higher rate of poverty. *A growth in power couples and in unmarried mothers anchors the top and bottom ends of the income distribution, contributing to the widening income gap observed in the U.S. economy.*

Sources: Raquel Fernández and Richard Rogerson, "Sorting and Long-Term Inequality," *Quarterly Journal of Economics*, 116 (4, 2001): 1305–1341; Ashlesha Datar et al., "Endowments and Parental Investment in Infancy and Early Childhood," *Demography*, 47 (February 2010): 145–162; and Chinhui Juhn and Kristin McCue, "Trends in Earnings Instability of Couples: How Important Is Marital Sorting?" NBER Working Paper, (September 2009).

So economic forces, immigration, and marriage trends have hurt those at the low end of the income distribution and have benefited those at the high end, and this helps explain the growing disparity in household income.

Income in the United States is less evenly distributed than in other developed countries throughout the world, such as Canada, France, Great Britain, Italy, and Australia, but is more evenly distributed than in most developing countries, such as Brazil, Chile, Mexico, Nigeria, and the Philippines.

Problems With Distribution Benchmarks

One problem with assessing income distributions is that there is no objective standard for evaluating them. The usual assumption is that a more equal distribution of income is more desirable, but is equal distribution most preferred? If not, then how uneven should it be? For example, among major league baseball players, well over half the pay goes to 20 percent of the players. Professional basketball pay skews even more, with top NBA players earning up to 50 times more than the bottom players. Does this mean the economy, as a whole, is in some sense "fairer" than these professional sports?

A second problem is that because Exhibits 1 and 2 measure money income after cash transfers but before taxes, they neglect the effects of taxes and in-kind transfers, such as food vouchers and free medical care for poor families. The tax system as a whole is progressive, meaning that families with higher incomes pay a larger fraction of their incomes in taxes. In-kind transfers benefit the lowest income groups the most. Consequently, if Exhibit 1 incorporated the effects of taxes and in-kind transfers, the share of income going to the lower groups would increase, the share going to the higher groups would decrease, and income would become more evenly distributed.

Third, focusing on the share of income going to each income quintile overlooks the fact that household size differs across quintiles. Most households in the bottom quintile consist of one person living alone. Only one in 16 households in the top quintile consists of one person living alone. Fourth, Exhibits 1 and 2 include only *reported* income. If people receive payment "under the table" to evade taxes, or if they earn money through illegal activities, their actual income will exceed their reported income. The omission of unreported income distorts the data if unreported income as a percentage of total family income differs across income levels.

Finally, Exhibits 1 and 2 focus on the distribution of *income*, but a better measure of household welfare would be the distribution of *spending*. Available evidence indicates that *spending by quintiles is much more evenly distributed than income by quintiles*.

Redistribution Programs

Because poverty is such a relative concept, how do we measure it objectively, and how do we ensure that the measure can be applied with equal relevance over time? The federal government has developed a method for calculating an official poverty level, which serves as a benchmark for poverty analysis in the United States.

Official Poverty Level

To derive the **U.S. official poverty level**, the U.S. Department of Agriculture in 1959 first estimated the cost of a nutritionally adequate diet. Then, based on the assumption that the poor spend about one-third of their income on food, the official poverty level was calculated by multiplying this food cost by three. The U.S. Census Bureau tracks the official poverty level, making adjustments for family size and for inflation. For example, the official poverty level of money income for a family of four was $22,050 in 2009; a family of four below that income threshold was regarded as living in poverty. Poverty levels in 2009 ranged from $10,830 for a person living alone to $40,750 for a family of nine. The poverty definition is based on pretax money income, including cash transfers, but it excludes the value of noncash transfers such as food vouchers, Medicaid, subsidized housing, or employer-provided health insurance.

Each year since 1959, the Census Bureau has conducted a survey comparing each family's cash income to the annual poverty level applicable to that family. Results of this survey are presented in Exhibit 3, which indicates both the millions of people living below the official poverty level and the percentage of the U.S. population below that level. Periods of U.S. recession are also shown (a recession is usually defined as two or more successive quarters of declining output in the economy). Note that poverty increased during recessions.

The biggest decline in poverty occurred before 1970; *the poverty rate dropped from 22.4 percent in 1959 to 12.1 percent in 1969*. During that period, the number of poor people decreased from about 40 million to 24 million. The poverty rate has not shown huge fluctuations since that initial drop. After declining from 1994 to 2000, the poverty rate and the number of poor people drifted higher over the next five years because of the national recession in 2001. The recession of 2007–2009 increased the number of people in poverty to 43.6 million in 2009 and the poverty rate to 14.3 percent, or one in seven U.S. residents.

U.S. official poverty level
Benchmark level of income computed by the federal government to track poverty over time; initially based on three times the cost of a nutritionally adequate diet

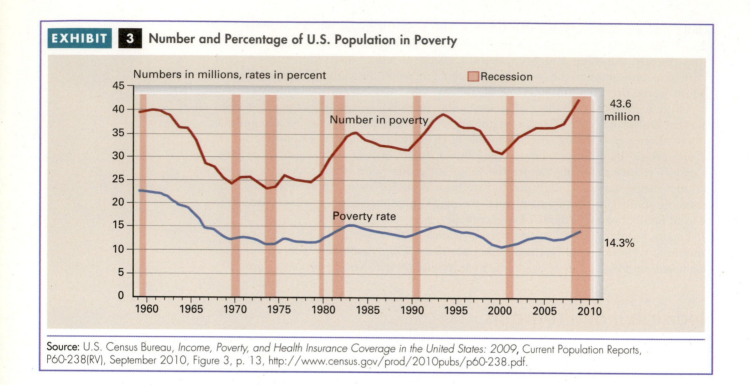

EXHIBIT   3   Number and Percentage of U.S. Population in Poverty

Source: U.S. Census Bureau, *Income, Poverty, and Health Insurance Coverage in the United States: 2009,* Current Population Reports, P60-238(RV), September 2010, Figure 3, p. 13, http://www.census.gov/prod/2010pubs/p60-238.pdf.

Poverty is a relative term. If we examined the distribution of income across countries, we would find huge gaps between rich and poor nations. The U.S. official poverty level of income is much greater than the average income for three-fourths of the world's population. The U.S. poverty level for a family of four in 2009 works out to be a $15.10 per person per day. Most nations employ a much lower poverty threshold. About 40 percent of the world's population lives on $2 a day or less.[4]

Programs to Help the Poor

What should society's response to poverty be? The best predictor of poverty is whether someone has a job. Adults with full-time jobs in 2009 had a poverty rate of 2.7 percent; adults who did not work during the year had a rate of 22.7 percent. One way government can try to reduce poverty, therefore, is to promote a healthy economy. The stronger the economy, the greater the job opportunities, and the more likely people find work. Perhaps the best indicator of whether or not jobs are readily available is the *unemployment rate*, which shows the percentage of the labor force out of work. The *lower* the unemployment rate, the *higher* the likelihood that someone who wants a job can find one. Thus, the lower the unemployment rate, the lower the poverty rate. Exhibit 4 shows poverty rates and unemployment rates in the United States each year since 1969. As you can see, the poverty rate, shown by the top line, tends to rise when the unemployment rate increases and to fall when the unemployment rate declines.

Thus, the government's first line of defense in fighting poverty is promoting a healthy economy. Yet even when the unemployment rate is low, some people are still poor. Although some antipoverty programs involve direct market intervention, such as minimum-wage laws, the most visible antipoverty programs redistribute income after the market has made an initial distribution. Since the mid-1960s, social welfare

---

4.   As reported in Daryl Collins et al., *Portfolios of the Poor: How the World's Poor Live on $2 a Day,* (Princeton University Press, 2009).

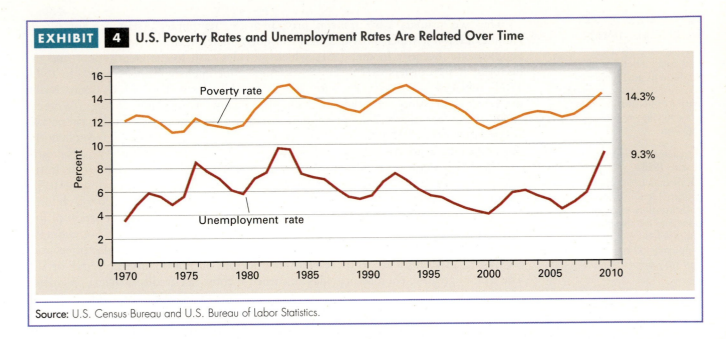

EXHIBIT **4** **U.S. Poverty Rates and Unemployment Rates Are Related Over Time**

Source: U.S. Census Bureau and U.S. Bureau of Labor Statistics.

expenditures at all levels of government have increased significantly. We can divide these programs into two broad categories: social insurance and income assistance.

Social Insurance

Social insurance programs are designed to help make up for the lost income of people who worked but are now retired, temporarily unemployed, or unable to work because of disability or work-related injury. The major social insurance program is **Social Security,** established during the Great Depression to supplement retirement income of those with a work history and a record of contributing to the program. **Medicare,** another social insurance program, provides health insurance for short-term medical care, mostly to those ages 65 and older, regardless of income. There are over 47 million Social Security and Medicare beneficiaries. Other social insurance programs include *unemployment insurance,* which supports those who have lost jobs, and *workers' compensation,* which supports workers injured on the job; both programs require that beneficiaries have a history of employment.

The social insurance system deducts "insurance premiums" from workers' pay to provide benefits to other retired, disabled, and unemployed individuals. These programs protect some families from poverty, particularly the elderly, but they are aimed more at those with a work history. Still, the social insurance system tends to redistribute income from rich to poor and from young to old. Most current Social Security beneficiaries will receive far more in benefits than they ever paid into the program, especially those with a brief work history or a record of low wages.

Income Assistance

Income assistance programs—what we usually call welfare programs—provide cash and in-kind assistance to the poor. Unlike social insurance, income assistance programs do not require recipients to have a work history or to have paid into the program. Income assistance programs are means tested. Those with sufficient means are not eligible. In a **means-tested program,** a household's income and assets must be below a certain level to qualify for benefits. The federal government funds about two-thirds of welfare spending, and state and local governments fund about one-third.

social insurance
Government programs designed to help make up for lost income of people who worked but are now retired, unemployed, or unable to work because of disability or work-related injury

Social Security
Supplements retirement income to those with a record of contributing to the program during their working years; by far the largest government redistribution program

Medicare
Social insurance program providing health insurance for short-term medical care to older Americans, regardless of income

income assistance programs
Welfare programs that provide money and in-kind assistance to the poor; benefits do not depend on prior contributions

means-tested program
A program in which, to be eligible, an individual's income and assets must not exceed specified levels

Temporary Assistance for Needy Families (TANF)

An income assistance program funded largely by the federal government but run by the states to provide cash transfer payments to poor families with dependent children

Supplemental Security Income (SSI)

An income assistance program that provides cash transfers to the elderly poor and the disabled; a uniform federal payment is supplemented by transfers that vary across states

earned-income tax credit

A federal program that supplements the wages of the working poor

Medicaid

An in-kind transfer program that provides medical care for poor people; by far the most costly welfare program

SNAP

An in-kind transfer program that offers low-income households vouchers redeemable for food; benefit levels vary inversely with household income

The two primary *cash transfer* programs are **Temporary Assistance for Needy Families (TANF)**, which provides cash to poor families with dependent children, and **Supplemental Security Income (SSI)**, which provides cash to the elderly poor and the disabled. Cash transfers vary inversely with family income from other sources. In 1997, TANF replaced Aid for Families with Dependent Children (AFDC), which began during the Great Depression and originally supported widows with young children. Whereas AFDC was a federal *entitlement* program, meaning that anyone who met the criteria was *entitled* to benefits, TANF is under the control of each state and carries no federal entitlement. The federal government gives each state a fixed grant to help fund TANF programs.

The SSI program provides support for the elderly and disabled poor. It is the fastest-growing cash transfer program with outlays exceeding $100 billion in 2010. SSI coverage has been broadened to include people addicted to drugs and alcohol, children with learning disabilities, and, in some cases, the homeless. The federal portion of this program is uniform across states, but states can supplement federal aid. For example, benefit levels in California average twice those in Alabama. Most states also offer modest *General Assistance* aid to those who are poor but do not qualify for TANF or SSI. The federal government also provides an **earned-income tax credit,** which supplements wages of the working poor. For example, a low-income family with three children would not only pay no federal income tax but would receive a cash transfer of up to $5,700 in 2010. More than 20 million tax filers received such transfers in 2010, when outlays of more than $40 billion for the program were double federal spending for TANF. The earned income tax credit lifts millions of families out of poverty. Twenty-three states and the District of Columbia also offer earned-income tax credits on top of the federal plan.

In addition to cash transfers, a variety of *in-kind transfer* programs provide health care, food vouchers, and housing assistance to the poor. **Medicaid** pays for medical care for those with low incomes who are aged, blind, disabled, or are in families with dependent children. *Medicaid is by far the largest welfare program, costing more than all cash and other in-kind transfer programs combined*. It has grown more than any other poverty program, quadrupling in the last decade and accounting for nearly a quarter of the typical state's budget (though states receive federal grants covering half or more of their Medicaid budget). The qualifying level of income is set by each state, and some states are stricter than others. Therefore, the proportion of poor people covered by Medicaid varies across states. More than 57 million, or more than one in six U.S. residents, received Medicaid benefits at a total cost of over $400 billion in 2010 (about 10 million Medicaid beneficiaries also receive Medicare). For many elderly, Medicaid covers long-term nursing care, which can cost taxpayers up to $100,000 a year per recipient.

The Supplemental Nutrition Assistance Program, or **SNAP**, provides vouchers that the poor can redeem for food. Forty million people received vouchers in an average month of 2010, and the monthly benefit averaged $290 per household. SNAP outlays exceeded $60 billion in 2010. Still, many of those eligible for food vouchers do not apply for them. *Housing assistance* programs include direct assistance for rental payments and subsidized low-income housing for over 10 million people. Federal spending alone came to about $58 billion in 2010. Other in-kind transfer programs for the poor include support for day care, school lunches, extra food for pregnant women, energy assistance, and education and training, such as Head Start. *In all, the federal government funds more than 80 means-tested programs*.

Here's an overview: Federal redistribution programs totaled about $1.8 trillion in 2010, more than twice the amount spent on national defense. Adding in state and local outlays pushes the total to $2.4 trillion. Exhibit 5 shows the growth in federal redistribution programs since 1962. To eliminate the effects of inflation, figures are expressed in dollars of constant purchasing power. Overall, redistribution outlays have grown at an annual average of 6 percent since 1962, even after netting out the

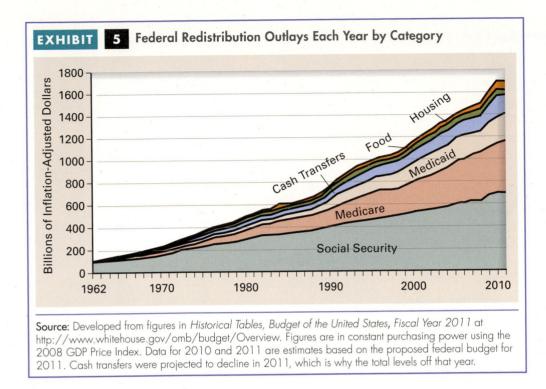

EXHIBIT **5** **Federal Redistribution Outlays Each Year by Category**

Source: Developed from figures in *Historical Tables, Budget of the United States, Fiscal Year 2011* at http://www.whitehouse.gov/omb/budget/Overview. Figures are in constant purchasing power using the 2008 GDP Price Index. Data for 2010 and 2011 are estimates based on the proposed federal budget for 2011. Cash transfers were projected to decline in 2011, which is why the total levels off that year.

effects of inflation. Social Security and Medicare, programs that mostly benefit the elderly, make up the greatest share throughout the period. Next is Medicaid, which, as noted earlier, exceeds outlays for cash transfers and other in-kind transfers combined. Although more than half the federal welfare budget goes for health care, about 50 million U.S. residents still lacked health insurance in 2009, or about one in six. Health care coverage is expected to increase after the adoption of federal health care reform in 2010.

Some countries also have far more extensive redistribution programs than does the United States, basing a variety of public policies on income. The heir to a sausage fortune who was caught speeding 50 miles per hour in a 25 mile-an-hour zone paid a $204,000 fine.[5]

Who Are the Poor?

Who are the poor, and how has their composition changed over time? We will slice poverty statistics in several ways to examine the makeup of the group. Keep in mind that we are relying on official poverty estimates, which ignore the value of in-kind transfers, so, to that extent, official estimates overstate poverty.

Poverty and Age

Earlier we looked at poverty among the U.S. population. Here we focus on poverty and age. Exhibit 6 presents the poverty rates for three age groups since 1959: people less than 18 years old, those between 18 and 64, and those 65 and older. As you can see, poverty rates for each group declined between 1959 and 1968. The rate among

5.   Lisa Moore, "Sticking It to the Scofflaw," *U.S. News & World Report,* March 18, 2007.

EXHIBIT **6** U.S. Poverty Rates by Age

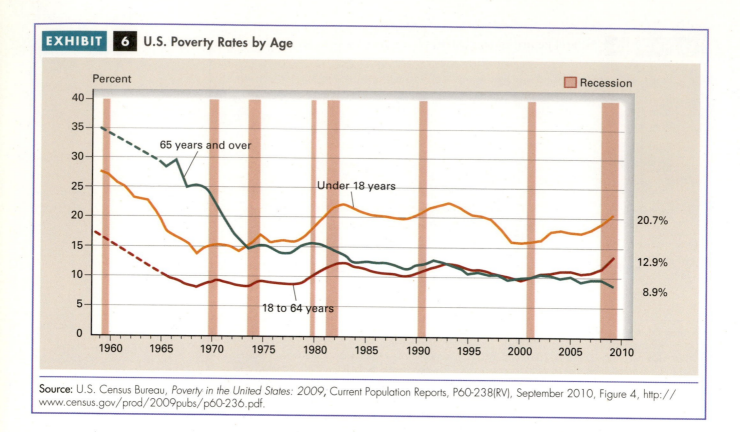

Source: U.S. Census Bureau, *Poverty in the United States: 2009*, Current Population Reports, P60-238(RV), September 2010, Figure 4, http://www.census.gov/prod/2009pubs/p60-236.pdf.

those under 18 trended upward between the mid-1970s and the early 1980s. The rate then remained around 20 percent for a dozen years, declined during the 1990s, before rising to 20.7 percent by 2009.

In 1959, the elderly were the poorest group, with a poverty rate of 35 percent. Poverty among the elderly declined to 8.9 percent by 2009, the lowest rate on record and below the rate of 12.9 percent for people 18 to 64 years of age. The decline in poverty among the elderly stems from the tremendous growth in spending for Social Security and Medicare. In real terms—that is, after adjusting for the effects of inflation—those two programs have grown more than twelvefold since 1959 (Medicare didn't even exist until 1965). *Although not welfare programs in a strict sense, Social Security and Medicare have been hugely successful in reducing poverty among the elderly.*

Poverty and Public Choice

In a democracy, public policies depend very much on the political influence of the interest groups involved. In recent years, the elderly have become a powerful political force. The voter participation rate of those 65 and over is higher than that of any other age group. For example, people 65 years of age and older vote at triple the rate of those between 18 and 24 and four times that of welfare recipients. The political muscle of the elderly has been flexed whenever a question of Social Security or Medicare benefits is considered.

Unlike most interest groups, the elderly make up a group we all expect to join one day. The elderly are supported by at least five constituencies: (1) the elderly themselves; (2) people under 65 who are concerned about the current benefits of their parents or other elderly relatives; (3) people under 65 who are concerned about their own benefits in the future; (4) people who earn their living by caring for the elderly, such as doctors, nurses, and nursing-home operators; and (5) candidates for office who want to harvest the votes that seniors deliver. So the elderly have a broad constituency, and this pays off in terms of redistribution of wealth to the elderly and in the reduction of poverty among this group. The poverty rate among those 65 and over in 2009 was less than half that among those under 18.

The Feminization of Poverty

Another way to look at poverty is based on the status of the household head. Exhibit 7 compares poverty rates among families headed by females with no husband present with poverty rates for other families. Two trends are unmistakable. First, poverty rates among families headed by females are much higher than rates among other families— about four times higher. Second, poverty rates among female-headed families have trended down since the early 1990s, falling from 39.7 percent in 1991 to 32.5 percent in 2009.

The exhibit compares poverty among female householders to other families. What it doesn't show is the growth in the number of people in female-headed households. The number of people in families headed by women increased 177 percent between 1965 and 2009, while the number in all other families grew just 25 percent. The percentage of births to unmarried mothers is five times greater today than in the 1960s. In 1960, only 1 in 200 children lived with a single parent who had never married. Today, 1 in 10 children lives with a single parent who has never married.

The United States has the highest teenage pregnancy rate in the developed world— twice the rate of Great Britain and 15 times that of Japan. Most recently, more than 85 percent of teen mothers were unmarried when they gave birth. Because fathers in such cases typically provide little support, children born outside marriage are likely to be poorer than other children. *The growth in the number of poor families since 1965 results overwhelmingly from a growth in the number of female householders.*

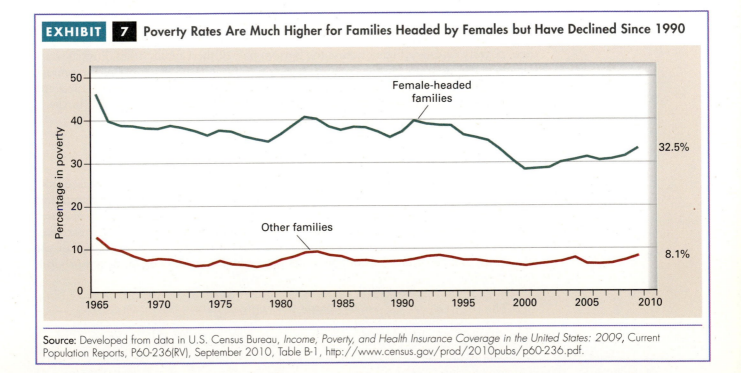

EXHIBIT   7   Poverty Rates Are Much Higher for Families Headed by Females but Have Declined Since 1990

Source: Developed from data in U.S. Census Bureau, *Income, Poverty, and Health Insurance Coverage in the United States: 2009,* Current Population Reports, P60-236(RV), September 2010, Table B-1, http://www.census.gov/prod/2010pubs/p60-236.pdf.

The number of jobs in the U.S. economy more than doubled in the last four decades. Families with a female householder were in the worst position to take advantage of this job growth. *Children of female householders are five times more likely to live in poverty than are other children. Young, single motherhood is a recipe for poverty.* Often the young mother drops out of school, which reduces her future earning possibilities when and if she seeks work outside the home. Even a strong economy is little help to households with nobody in the labor force. Worse yet, young, single mothers-to-be are less likely to seek adequate medical care; the result is a higher proportion of premature, underweight babies. This is one reason why the U.S. infant mortality rate exceeds that of some other industrialized countries. Compared to two-parent families, children in one-parent families are twice as likely to drop out of school, and girls from one-parent families are twice as likely to become single mothers themselves.

Because of a lack of education and limited job skills, most single mothers go on welfare. Before recently imposed lifetime limits on welfare, the average never-married mother had been on welfare for a decade, twice as long as divorced mothers on welfare. Of all teenagers who gave birth, the proportion unmarried was 13 percent in 1950, 30 percent in 1970, 67 percent in 1990, and 87 percent in 2008.[6]

Poverty has therefore become increasingly feminized, mostly because female householders have become more common. Children from mothers who finished high school, married before having a child, and gave birth after age 20 are 10 times less likely to be poor than children from mothers who fail to do these things.[7] Because the number of female householders has grown more rapidly among African Americans, the feminization of poverty has been more dramatic in those households. Seventy-two percent of all births to non-Hispanic black mothers in 2008 were to unmarried women, compared with 52 percent among women of Hispanic origin, 29 percent among non-Hispanic whites, and 17 percent among Asians and Pacific Islanders.[8] But we should be careful in drawing conclusions about the role of race or ethnicity per se, because black and Hispanic households are poorer on average than other households. Low income alone could account for much of the difference in birth rates. In other words, a better comparison would adjust for income differences across groups, but such data are not available.

Exhibit 8 shows poverty rates for each of the 50 states. States with a deeper shade of red have higher poverty rates. States with no shading have lower rates. As you can see, poverty rates are higher across the bottom half of the United States. Poverty rates tend to be higher in states where births to single mothers make up a larger percentage of all births. For example, Louisiana and Mississippi have the highest poverty rates and among the highest rates of births to unmarried mothers. Nearly half of all births in these states are to unmarried mothers.

Poverty and Discrimination

To what extent has racial discrimination limited job opportunities and increased poverty among minorities? Discrimination can occur in many ways: in school funding, in housing, in employment, in career advancement. Also, discrimination in one area can affect opportunities in another. For example, housing discrimination can reduce job opportunities if a black family cannot move within commuting distance of the best jobs, or cannot take advantage of the job networking available in neighborhoods

6. "Births: Preliminary Data for 2008," *National Vital Statistics Report* 58, No. 16 (April 2010), Table 7 at http://www.cdc.gov/nchs/data/nvsr/nvsr58/nvsr58_16.pdf.
7. James Q. Wilson, "Human Remedies for Social Disorder," *Public Interest* (Spring 1998): 27.
8. "Births: Preliminary Data for 2008," *National Vital Statistics Report* 58, No. 16 (April 2010), Table 1, found at http://www.cdc.gov/nchs/data/nvsr/nvsr58/nvsr58_16.pdf.

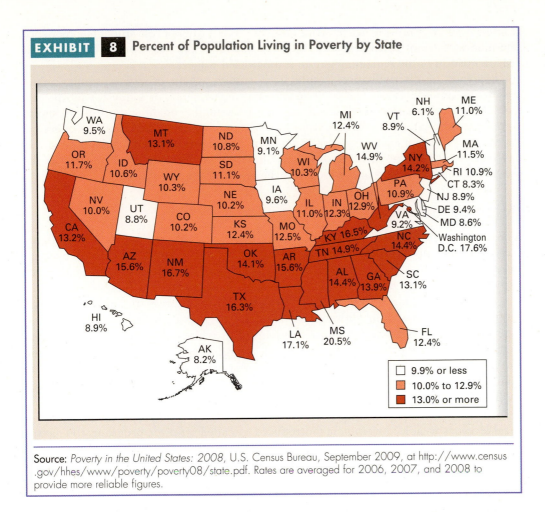

EXHIBIT 8   Percent of Population Living in Poverty by State

Source: *Poverty in the United States: 2008*, U.S. Census Bureau, September 2009, at http://www.census.gov/hhes/www/poverty/poverty08/state.pdf. Rates are averaged for 2006, 2007, and 2008 to provide more reliable figures.

where more people are working.[9] Job-market discrimination can take many forms. An employer may fail to hire a black job applicant because the applicant lacks training. But this lack of training can arise from discrimination in the schools, in union apprenticeship programs, or in training programs run by other employers. For example, evidence suggests that black workers receive less on-the-job training than otherwise similar white workers.

After adjusting for a variety of factors that could affect the wage, such as education and work experience, research shows that white workers earn more than black workers. The gap between the two narrowed between 1940 and 1976 to the point where black workers earned only 7 percent less than white workers; then it widened somewhat.[10] Since 1993, the gap has again narrowed. Could explanations besides job discrimination account for the wage gap? Though the data adjust for *years* of schooling, some research suggests that black workers received a lower *quality* of schooling than white workers. For example, black students were less likely to use computers in school. Inner-city schools often have more problems with classroom discipline, which takes time and

9. Researchers have found that individuals living in the same city block are more likely to work together than those living in nearby blocks. See Patrick Bayer, Stephen L. Ross, and Giorgio Topa, "Place of Work and Place of Residence: Informal Hiring Networks and Labor Market Outcomes," *Journal of Political Economy*, 116 (December 2008): 1150–1197.

10. M. Boozer, A. Krueger, and S. Wolken, "Race and School Quality Since *Brown v. Board of Education*," *Brookings Papers on Economic Activity: Microeconomics* (1992): 269–326.

attention away from instruction. And schools serving the poorest students experience the highest rates of teacher absences.[11] Such quality differences could account for at least a portion of the remaining gap in standardized wages.

Evidence of discrimination comes from studies where otherwise similar white and black candidates are sent to seek jobs, rent apartments, or apply for mortgages. For example, white and black job applicants with similar qualifications and résumés applied for the same job. These studies find that employers are less likely to interview or offer a job to minority applicants. Minority applicants also tend to be treated less favorably by real estate agents and lenders. One study concluded that one quarter of the wage gap between blacks and whites was the result of discrimination.[12]

Affirmative Action

The Equal Employment Opportunity Commission, established by the Civil Rights Act of 1964, monitors cases involving unequal pay for equal work and unequal access to promotion. All companies doing business with the federal government had to set numerical hiring, promotion, and training goals to ensure that these firms did not discriminate in hiring on the basis of race, sex, religion, or national origin. Black employment increased in those firms required to file affirmative action plans.[13] The fraction of the black labor force employed in white-collar jobs increased from 16.5 percent in 1960 to 40.5 percent in 1981—an increase that greatly exceeded the growth of white-collar jobs in the labor force as a whole. Research also suggests that civil rights legislation played a role in narrowing the black-white earnings gap between 1960 and the mid-1970s.[14]

Attention focused on hiring practices and equality of opportunity at the state and local levels as well, as governments introduced so-called *set-aside* programs to guarantee minorities a share of contracts. But a 1995 U.S. Supreme Court decision challenged affirmative action programs, ruling that Congress must meet a rigorous legal standard to justify any contracting or hiring practice based on race, especially programs that reserve jobs for minorities and women. Programs must be shown to be in response to injustices created by past discrimination, said the Court.

In summary, evidence suggests that black workers earn less than white workers after adjustment for other factors that could affect wages, such as education and job experience. Part of this wage gap may also reflect differences in the quality of education, differences that could themselves be the result of discrimination.[15] Keep in mind that unemployment rates are higher among blacks than among whites and are higher still among black teenagers, the group most in need of job skills and job experience. *But we should also note that black families are not a homogeneous group. In fact, the distribution of income is more uneven among black families than among the population as a whole.*

On the upside, there is a growing middle class among black households. Since 1970, the number of black doctors, nurses, college professors, and newspaper reporters has

---

11. Charles Clotfelter et al., "Are Teacher Absences Worth Worrying About in the United States?" *Education Finance and Policy*, 4 (Spring 2009): 115–149.

12. Kerwin Kofi Charles and Jonathan Guryan, "Prejudice and Wages: An Empirical Assessment of Becker's *The Economics of Discrimination*," *Journal of Political Economy*, 116 (October 2008): 773–809.

13. James Smith and Finis Welch, "Black Economic Progress After Myrdal," *Journal of Economic Literature*, 27 (June 1989): 519–563.

14. David Card and Alan Krueger, "Trends in Relative Black-White Earnings Revisited," *American Economic Review*, 83 (May 1993): 85–91.

15. Huoying Wu, "Can the Human Capital Approach Explain Life-Cycle Wage Differentials Between Races and Sexes," *Economic Inquiry*, 45 (January 2007): 24–39.

more than tripled; the number of black engineers, computer programmers, accountants, managers, and administrators has quadrupled; the number of black elected officials has increased fivefold; and the number of black lawyers has increased more than sixfold. In Georgia, for example, the number of black lawyers increased from just 54 in 1970 to more than 2,000 today. Two of the most admired Americans are African American— President Barack Obama and talk show host Oprah Winfrey.

Unintended Consequences of Income Assistance

On the plus side, antipoverty programs increase the consumption possibilities of poor families, and that's a good thing, especially because children are the largest poverty group. But programs to assist the poor have secondary effects that limit their ability to reduce poverty over time. Here we consider some unintended consequences.

Society, through government, tries to provide families with an adequate standard of living, but society also wants to ensure that only the needy receive benefits. As we have seen, income assistance consists of a combination of cash and in-kind transfer programs. Because these programs are designed to help the poor and only the poor, benefits decrease as income from other sources increases. With transfers declining sharply as earned income increases, welfare recipients face a high marginal tax rate on earned income. An increase in earnings may reduce benefits from TANF, Medicaid, SNAP (food vouchers), housing assistance, energy assistance, and others among the 80 means-tested programs. With a loss in support from each program as earned income increases, working may lead to little or no increase in total income. Over certain income ranges, a welfare recipient may lose more than $1 in welfare benefits for each additional $1 in earnings. Thus, the *marginal tax rate* on earned income could exceed 100 percent!

Holding even a part-time job involves some costs—for clothing, transportation, and child care, for instance—not to mention the loss of free time. Such a system of perverse incentives can frustrate people trying to work their way off welfare. *The high marginal tax rate discourages employment and self-sufficiency.* In many cases, welfare benefits exceed the income resulting from full-time employment.

The longer people stay out of the labor force, the more their job skills deteriorate, so when they do look for work, their productivity is lower than when they were last employed. This reduces their expected wage, making work even less attractive. Some economists argue that in this way, welfare benefits can lead to long-term dependency. While welfare seems to be a rational choice in the short run, it has unfavorable long-term consequences for the family, for society, and for the economy.

Welfare programs can cause other disincentives. For example, children may be eligible for Supplemental Security Income if they have a learning disability. According to one firsthand account, some low-income parents encouraged poor performance in school so their children could qualify for this program.[16]

A serious concern is whether children on welfare are more likely to end up on welfare as adults. Is there a cycle of dependency? Why might we expect one? Children in welfare households may learn the ropes about the welfare system and may come to view welfare as a normal way of life rather than as a temporary bridge over a rough patch. Research indicates that daughters from welfare families are more likely than daughters from other families to participate in the welfare system themselves and are more likely to have premarital births.[17] It is difficult to say whether welfare "causes"

---

16. Jacqueline Goldwyn Kingon, "Education Life: A View from the Trenches," *New York Times*, 8 April 2001.
17. Robert Moffitt, "Welfare Reform: The U.S. Experience," *From Welfare to Work*, Paper Presented at the Economic Council of Sweden Conference, 7 May 2007.

the link between mother and daughter, because the same factors that contribute to a mother's welfare status can also contribute to her daughter's welfare status. Evidence of a link is weaker when it comes to sons from welfare families.

Welfare Reform

There has been much dissatisfaction with the welfare system among both those who pay for the programs and direct beneficiaries. Welfare reforms introduced more than a decade ago have been aimed at reducing long-term dependency.

Recent Reforms

Some analysts believe that one way to reduce poverty is to provide welfare recipients with job skills and make them find jobs. Even before the 1996 federal reform of welfare, to be discussed shortly, some sort of "workfare" component for welfare recipients operated in most states. In these states, as a condition of receiving welfare, the head of the household had to participate in education and training programs, search for work, or take some paid or unpaid position. The idea was to expose people on welfare to the job market. Evidence from various states indicates that programs involving mandatory job searches, short-term unpaid work, and training could operate at low cost and could increase employment. The government saved money because those in welfare-to-work programs left welfare rolls sooner.

Reforms at the state level set the stage for federal reforms. By far the biggest reform in the welfare system in the last 70 years came with the 1996 legislation that replaced Aid to Families with Dependent Children (AFDC) with Temporary Assistance for Needy Families (TANF). Whereas the AFDC program set eligibility rules and left federal costs open-ended through matching grants to the states, TANF offers a fixed grant to the states to run their welfare programs. States ended AFDC and began TANF by July 1, 1997. Under the new system, states have much more control over their own welfare programs. But concerns about welfare dependency fostered some special provisions. The act imposes a five-year lifetime limit on cash transfers and requires states to move a certain percentage of people from welfare to work.

Aside from the time limits and work participation rates imposed by the federal government, states are free to set benefit levels and experiment however they choose. For example, about half the states impose time limits shorter than five years. Some observers fear that states now have an incentive to keep welfare costs down by cutting benefits. To avoid becoming destinations for poor people—that is, to avoid becoming "welfare magnets"—states may be tempted to offer relatively low benefits. The fear is that states will undercut benefits in what has been called a "race to the bottom."

Welfare Rolls Have Declined

Work requirements and time limits have resulted in substantial declines in the welfare caseload. The number of welfare recipients peaked in January 1994 at 14.2 million, mostly single women with children. By September 2009, the rolls had fallen to 4.1 million—71 percent below the peak. Exhibit 9 shows since 1960 the percentage of the U.S. population on welfare. Note the sharp decline in recent years. As a share of the U.S. population, welfare recipients fell from 5.5 percent in 1994 to 1.3 percent in 2009, only a tiny bit above the 1.2 rate for 2008, which was the lowest rate in the last half century.

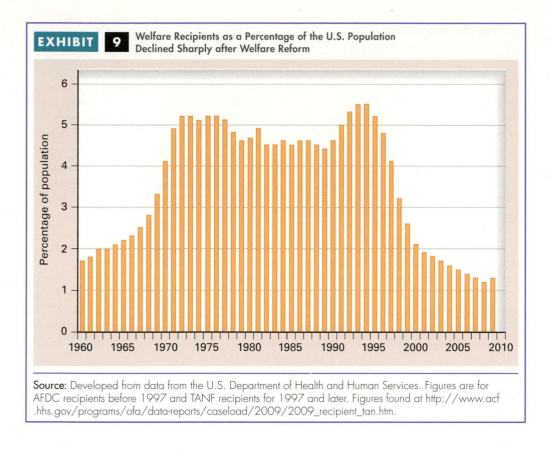

EXHIBIT 9 Welfare Recipients as a Percentage of the U.S. Population Declined Sharply after Welfare Reform

Source: Developed from data from the U.S. Department of Health and Human Services. Figures are for AFDC recipients before 1997 and TANF recipients for 1997 and later. Figures found at http://www.acf.hhs.gov/programs/ofa/data-reports/caseload/2009/2009_recipient_tan.htm.

A major result of welfare reform has been a substantial increase in employment among mothers who head families, especially those who have never married. About two-thirds found work during the period immediately after reform, and many more got jobs in the next year or two. This is a remarkable improvement from historical employment rates of women on welfare of about 10 percent. Their incomes went up on average, and they tended to hang onto their jobs. New York City officials reported that 85 percent of those getting off welfare did so because they had found work.

Because the welfare rolls have declined but federal grants have not, welfare spending per recipient increased significantly. Most states combined tough new eligibility rules with an expanded menu of welfare services. States have made large investments in work-related services such as job placement, transportation, and especially child care. Most of those going to work can continue to receive food vouchers, child care, and Medicaid. The earned-income tax credit also helps low-income workers—boosting pay up to $5,700 in 2009. Twenty-three states have added their own earned-income tax credits.

Despite the good news, some poor people are still having a hard time, particularly because of the recent downturn in the economy. Because many on welfare are poorly educated and have few job skills, wages for some remain low, and part-time work is common. Still, welfare reform has been quite successful in getting people off welfare and into jobs.

We close this chapter with a case study that looks at how another income class has been affected by the recent recession, a group that won't get much sympathy.

CASE STUDY

e activity

To track dividends'
contribution to personal
income, go to http://www.
bea.gov/national/nipaweb/
index.asp. Click on "list of
Selected NIPA Tables." In the
new window, scroll down to
Section 2 and click on Table
2.1. Personal Income and Its
Disposition. Choose the years
that you want to examine
and look for Line 15: Personal
dividend income.

PUBLIC POLICY

The Rich Got Poorer During the Recession   The sharp and painful national recession of
2007–2009 was hard on many Americans. The unemployment rate doubled between
2007 and 2009. To help people through this rough patch, the social safety net was
broadened. Extra months were added to unemployment benefits; in many states
benefits were extended to nearly two years, or four times the usual duration. Spending
targeted for the poor (see the programs identified in Exhibit 5) grew by 13 percent
between 2007 and 2009, even after adjusting for inflation. The progressive income
tax rate declined for all but those in the highest-income brackets, as falling incomes
meant lower tax brackets. Indeed, an estimated 47 percent of households paid no
federal personal income taxes in 2009. No question, some people were still having a
rough time, but public programs softened the blow, particularly at the low end of the
income distribution.

It may seem odd, but one of the hardest hit groups, at least on a relative basis, was
high-income households, many of whom lost a ton with the double whammy of a stock
market crash and a real-estate crash. High-income households also depend more on
corporate dividends, which experienced their sharpest drop since the government began
keeping records a half century ago.

Jonathan Parker and Annette Vissing-Jorgensen, economists at Northwestern
University, found that incomes of the affluent tend to fall more, in both absolute dollars
and in percentage terms, during a recession than do the incomes of the typical household. The exposure to economic fluctuations of households in the top 10 percent based
on income is about five times greater than the exposure of the typical household. And
the incomes of the super rich, defined as the top one-hundredth of 1 percent, fall the
most in percentage terms. Along with the decline in income of the rich comes a decline
in consumption. The two researchers expected that the recession of 2007–2009 would
cause a sharp reduction in consumption inequality across income classes. In short, the
rich were hit harder in relative terms by the recession than were other income groups,
so they cut their consumption more.

How has the declining fortunes of the rich affected the economy more broadly?
A drop in their income and wealth reduced contributions to universities, charities,
museums, and other institutions that rely on their generosity. Federal and state tax
revenues were also down sharply because these sources rely so much on the taxes paid
by the affluent. For example, most recently the top 1 percent of tax filers based on
income paid over 40 percent of all federal income taxes collected.

High-income households aren't just cash cows for tax collec-
tors. The rich often get that way by starting successful businesses
that create jobs. Consumption by the rich, including spending on
luxuries, also helps create jobs in the economy. But a recession is
a bad time for costly luxuries. In 2009, for example, 1,312 homes
with mortgage balances in excess of $5 million were foreclosed on
and went to public auction in the United States. That foreclosure
rate more than doubled in early 2010, and included the 11,817
square-foot Tudor mansion of actor Nicolas Cage. Other luxuries
also took a hit during the recession. Diamond sales worldwide fell
16 percent in 2009; thousands of U.S. jewelry stores closed their
doors. The best seats at the new Yankee Stadium failed to sell until
prices were cut in half. And hundreds of luxury boats, too costly
to maintain, were abandoned or purposely run aground. Florida
recently had to remove more than a hundred derelict boats from
public waterways, up from only a handful the year before.

Photo by James Aylot/Online USA

Troubles of the rich will never elicit much public sympathy, but high-income households represent a critical source of tax revenue, charitable giving, and job creation in the economy.

Sources: Jonathan Parker and Annette Vissing-Jorgensen, "Who Bears Aggregate Fluctuations and How," *American Economic Review*, 99 (May 2009): 399–405; David Leonhart and Geraldine Fabrikant, "Rise of Superrich Hits a Sobering Wall," *New York Times*, 21 August 2009; Craig Karmin and James Hagerty, "Foreclosures Hit Rich and Famous," *Wall Street Journal*, 9 April 2010; and David Streitfeld, "Boats Too Costly to Keep Are Littering Coastlines," *New York Times*, 1 April 2009.

Conclusion

Government redistribution programs have been most successful at reducing poverty among the elderly. But poverty rates among children increased because of the growth in the number of female householders. We might ask why transfer programs have reduced poverty rates more among the elderly than among female householders. Transfer programs do not encourage people to get old; that process occurs naturally and is independent of the level of transfers. But the level and availability of transfer programs at the margin could influence some young unmarried women as they are deciding whether or not to have a child and may, at the margin, influence a married mother's decision to get divorced.

Most transfers in the economy are not from the government but are in-kind transfers within the family, from parents to children. Thus, any change in a family's capacity to earn income has serious consequences for dependent children. *Family structure is a primary determinant of family income.* About one in five children in the United States lives in poverty. Children are the innocent victims of the changing family structure. Recent welfare reforms have succeeded in reducing welfare roles and increasing employment among single mothers.

Summary

1. Money income in the United States has become less evenly distributed since 1980. The poverty rate has dropped most among the elderly, thanks to Social Security and Medicare.

2. Young, single motherhood is a recipe for poverty. Often the young mother drops out of school, which reduces her future earning possibilities when and if she seeks work outside the home. Growth in the number of female householders in the last four decades increased poverty among children, though the overall poverty rate among households headed by females has declined since peaking in 1993. More unmarried mothers are working than ever.

3. The wage gap between black and white workers narrowed between 1940 and 1976, widened until the early 1990s, and has been narrowing again since 1993. Affirmative action programs and gains in education seem to have increased employment opportunities among black workers.

4. One undesirable effect of income assistance is a high marginal tax rate on earned income, which discourages employment and encourages welfare dependency. Worse still, welfare dependency could be passed on to the next generation. Research suggests that daughters from welfare families are more likely than daughters from other families to participate in the welfare system themselves and are more likely to have premarital births.

5. Welfare reforms introduced by the states set the stage for federal welfare reforms aimed at breaking the cycle of poverty and promoting the transition from welfare to work. The states began experimenting with different systems to encourage more personal responsibility. As a result of state reforms and federal welfare reform, welfare rolls dropped by more than two-thirds since 1994.

Key Concepts

Questions for Review

1. **DISTRIBUTION OF HOUSEHOLD INCOME**   Look back at Exhibit 1 in this chapter. How would you explain the shift of the U.S. income distribution in the last two decades?

2. **LORENZ CURVE**   What is a Lorenz curve? What does the Lorenz curve in Exhibit 2 illustrate?

3. **Case Study: Marital Sorting and Income Inequality**   How have marriage trends widened the gap between low-income and high-income households?

4. **OFFICIAL POVERTY LEVEL**   Although the poverty rate among single mothers has decreased since 1960, the number of poor children from such families has more than doubled. Explain.

5. **INCOME DIFFERENCES**   List some reasons why household incomes differ. Which factors are the most important?

6. **OFFICIAL POVERTY LEVEL**   How does the U.S. Department of Agriculture calculate the official poverty level? What government assistance programs does the Census Bureau consider when calculating household income? What programs are ignored?

7. **PROGRAMS TO HELP THE POOR**   Distinguish between social insurance programs and income assistance programs. Identify key examples of each.

8. **POVERTY AND AGE**   Poverty among the elderly fell dramatically between 1959 and 1974 and has continued to decline. However, poverty among that portion of the U.S. population that is less than 18 years old is no lower today than in the 1970s. Why have the experiences of these two age groups differed?

9. **POVERTY AND PUBLIC CHOICE**   Why is it difficult to pass legislation to reduce the growth in Social Security or Medicare benefits?

10. **POVERTY AND DISCRIMINATION**   Which types of discrimination may cause an earnings gap between white and black workers? Consider discrimination in schooling, for example. How would researchers detect such discrimination?

11. **DISINCENTIVES**   How does the implicit tax on earned income (in the form of lost benefits from government assistance programs as earned income increases) affect work incentives? How do some people avoid the implicit tax?

12. **WELFARE REFORM**   What has happened to the number of people on welfare since 1994? What explains the change over time?

13. **Case Study: The Rich Got Poorer During the Recession**   List the ill effects that the 2007–2009 recession had on high-income households and therefore on the economy.

Global Economic Watch Exercises

Login to www.cengagebrain.com and access the Global Economic Watch to do these exercises.

14. **GLOBAL ECONOMIC WATCH**   Go to the Global Economic Crisis Resource Center. Select Global Issues in Context. In the Basic Search box at the top of the page, enter the word "poverty." On the Results page, click on the link to View Full Overview. What is the difference between absolute and relative poverty?

15. **GLOBAL ECONOMIC WATCH**   Go to the Global Economic Crisis Resource Center. Select Global Issues in Context. In the Basic Search box at the top of the page, enter the words "poverty discrimination." Find an article about the effects of poverty and discrimination in a foreign country. Has discrimination increased poverty in that country?

International Trade

19

AP Photo/Reed Saxon

❍ This morning you pulled on your Levi's jeans from Mexico, pulled over your Benetton sweater from Italy, and laced up your Timberland boots from Thailand. After a breakfast that included bananas from Honduras and coffee from Brazil, you climbed into your Volvo from Sweden fueled by Venezuelan oil and headed for a lecture by a visiting professor from Hungary. If the United States is such a rich and productive country, why do we import so many goods and services?

❍ Why don't we produce everything ourselves?

❍ How can the U.S. economy grow if we import more goods and services?

❍ And why do some producers try to block imports?

Answers to these and other questions are addressed in this chapter.

The world is a giant shopping mall, and Americans are big spenders. For example, the U.S. population is less than 5 percent of the world's population, but Americans buy more than half the Rolls Royces and diamonds sold around the world. Americans also buy Japanese cars, French wine, European vacations, Chinese products galore, and thousands of other goods and services from around the globe. Foreigners buy U.S. products too—grain, aircraft, movies, software, trips to New York City, and thousands of other goods and services.

In this chapter, we examine the gains from international trade and the effects of trade restrictions on the allocation of resources. The analysis is based on the familiar tools of demand and supply.

Topics discussed include:

- Gains from trade
- Absolute and comparative advantage revisited
- Tariffs and quotas
- Cost of trade restrictions
- Arguments for trade restrictions
- Free trade agreements

The Gains From Trade

A family from Virginia that sits down for a meal of Kansas prime rib, Idaho potatoes, and California string beans, with Georgia peach cobbler for dessert, is benefiting from interstate trade. You already understand why the residents of one state trade with those of another. Back in Chapter 2, you learned about the gains arising from specialization and exchange. You may recall how you and your roommate could maximize output when you each specialized. The law of comparative advantage says that the individual with the lowest opportunity cost of producing a particular good should specialize in that good. Just as individuals benefit from specialization and exchange, so do states and, indeed, nations. To reap the gains that arise from specialization, countries engage in international trade. *Each country specializes in making goods with the lowest opportunity cost.*

A Profile of Exports and Imports

Just as some states are more involved in interstate trade than others, some nations are more involved in international trade than others. For example, exports account for about one-quarter of the gross domestic product (GDP) in Canada and the United Kingdom; about one-third of GDP in Germany, Sweden, and Switzerland; and about half of GDP in the Netherlands. Despite the perception that Japan has a huge export sector, exports make up only about one-sixth of its GDP.

U.S. Exports

U.S. exports of goods and services amounted to $1.6 trillion, or 11 percent of GDP in 2009. The left panel of Exhibit 1 shows the composition by major category. The largest category is services, which accounted for 32 percent of U.S. exports in 2009. U.S. service exports include transportation, insurance, banking, education, consulting, and tourism. Capital goods ranked second at 27 percent of exports, with aircraft the largest export industry (Boeing is the top U.S. exporter in any industry). Third most important are industrial supplies, at 19 percent of the total, with chemicals and plastics most important here. Capital goods and industrial supplies help foreign producers make stuff and together accounted for nearly half of U.S. exports. Consumer goods (except food, which appears separately) accounted for only 10 percent of exports (pharmaceuticals tops this group). Consumer goods include entertainment products, such as movies and recorded music.

U.S. Imports

U.S. imports of goods and services in 2009 totaled $1.9 trillion, or about 14 percent relative to GDP. The right panel of Exhibit 1 shows the composition of U.S. imports. The biggest category, at 25 percent, is industrial supplies, with oil-related products accounting for most of this. Whereas consumer goods accounted for only 10 percent of U.S. exports, they were 23 percent of U.S. imports, with pharmaceuticals the largest item. Ranked third in importance is capital goods, at 20 percent, with computers the largest item. Note that services, which accounted for 32 percent of U.S. exports, were only 19 percent of imports.

Trading Partners

To give you some feel for America's trading partners, here were the top 10 destinations for merchandise exports for 2009 in order of importance: Canada, Mexico, China, Japan, United Kingdom, Germany, Netherlands, South Korea, France, and Brazil. The

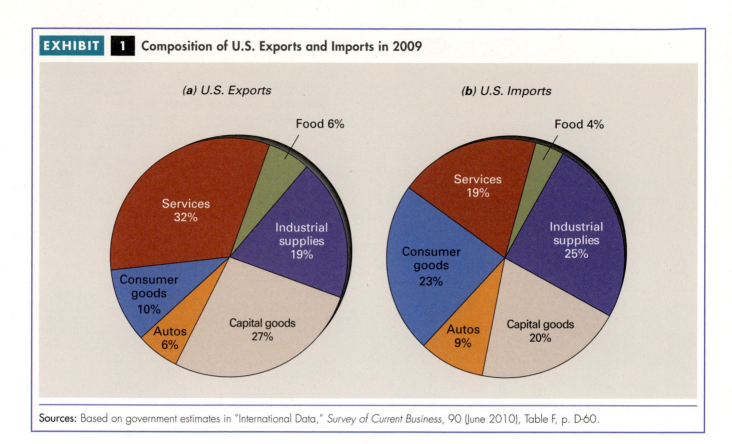

EXHIBIT   1   Composition of U.S. Exports and Imports in 2009

(a) U.S. Exports

Food 6%

Services 32%

Industrial supplies 19%

Consumer goods 10%

Autos 6%

Capital goods 27%

(b) U.S. Imports

Food 4%

Services 19%

Consumer goods 23%

Industrial supplies 25%

Autos 9%

Capital goods 20%

Sources: Based on government estimates in "International Data," *Survey of Current Business*, 90 (June 2010), Table F, p. D-60.

top 10 sources of merchandise imports in order of importance were China, Canada, Mexico, Japan, Germany, United Kingdom, South Korea, France, Taiwan, and Ireland.

Production Possibilities without Trade

The rationale behind most international trade is obvious. The United States grows little coffee because our climate is not suited to coffee. More revealing, however, are the gains from trade where the comparative advantage is not so obvious. Suppose that just two goods—food and clothing—are produced and consumed and that there are only two countries in the world—the United States, with a labor force of 100 million workers, and the mythical country of Izodia, with 200 million workers. The conclusions derived from this simple model have general relevance for international trade.

Exhibit 2 presents production possibilities tables for each country, based on the size of the labor force and the productivity of workers in each country. The exhibit assumes that each country has a given technology and that labor is efficiently employed. If no trade occurs between countries, Exhibit 2 also represents each country's *consumption possibilities* table. The production numbers imply that each worker in the United States can produce either 6 units of food or 3 units of clothing per day. If all 100 million U.S. workers produce food, they make 600 million units per day, as shown in column U_1 in panel (a). If all U.S. workers make clothing, they produce 300 million units per day, as shown in column U_6. The columns in between show some workers making food and some making clothing. Because a U.S. worker can produce either 6 units of food or 3 units of clothing, *the opportunity cost of 1 more unit of clothing is 2 units of food.*

| EXHIBIT 2 | Production Possibilities Schedules for the United States and Izodia |

(a) United States						
Production Possibilities with 100 Million Workers (millions of units per day)						
	U_1	U_2	U_3	U_4	U_5	U_6
Food	600	480	360	240	120	0
Clothing	0	60	120	180	240	300

(b) Izodia						
Production Possibilities with 200 Million Workers (millions of units per day)						
	I_1	I_2	I_3	I_4	I_5	I_6
Food	200	160	120	80	40	0
Clothing	0	80	160	240	320	400

Suppose Izodian workers are less educated, work with less capital, and farm less fertile soil than U.S. workers, so each Izodian worker can produce only 1 unit of food or 2 units of clothing per day. If all 200 million Izodian workers specialize in food, they can make 200 million units per day, as shown in column I_1 in panel (b) of Exhibit 2. If they all make clothing, total output is 400 million units per day, as shown in column I_6. Some intermediate production possibilities are also listed in the exhibit. Because an Izodian worker can produce either 1 unit of food or 2 units of clothing, *the opportunity cost of 1 more unit of clothing is 1/2 unit of food.*

We can convert the data in Exhibit 2 to a production possibilities frontier for each country, as shown in Exhibit 3. In each diagram, the amount of food produced is measured on the vertical axis and the amount of clothing on the horizontal axis. U.S. combinations are shown in the left panel by U_1, U_2, and so on. Izodian combinations are shown in the right panel by I_1, I_2, and so on. Because we assume for simplicity that resources are perfectly adaptable to the production of each commodity, each production possibilities curve is a straight line. The slope of this line differs between countries because the opportunity cost of production differs between countries. The slope equals the opportunity cost of clothing—the amount of food a country must give up to produce another unit of clothing. The U.S. slope is -2, and the Izodian slope is $-1/2$. The U.S. slope is steeper because its opportunity cost of producing clothing is greater.

Exhibit 3 illustrates possible combinations of food and clothing that residents of each country can produce and consume if all resources are efficiently employed and there is no trade between the two countries. **Autarky** is the situation of national self-sufficiency, in which there is no economic interaction with foreign producers or consumers. Suppose that U.S. producers maximize profit and U.S. consumers maximize utility with the combination of 240 million units of food and 180 million units of clothing—combination U_4. This is called the *autarky equilibrium.* Suppose also that Izodians are in autarky equilibrium, identified as combination I_3, of 120 million units of food and 160 million units of clothing.

autarky

National self-sufficiency; no economic interaction with foreigners

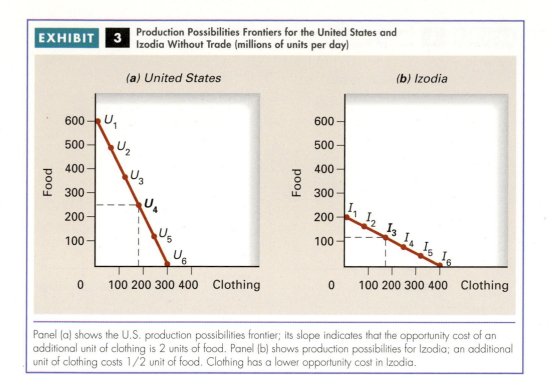

EXHIBIT **3** Production Possibilities Frontiers for the United States and Izodia Without Trade (millions of units per day)

Panel (a) shows the U.S. production possibilities frontier; its slope indicates that the opportunity cost of an additional unit of clothing is 2 units of food. Panel (b) shows production possibilities for Izodia; an additional unit of clothing costs 1/2 unit of food. Clothing has a lower opportunity cost in Izodia.

Consumption Possibilities Based on Comparative Advantage

In our example, each U.S. worker can produce more clothing and more food per day than can each Izodian worker, so Americans have an *absolute advantage* in the production of both goods. Recall from Chapter 2 that having an absolute advantage means being able to produce something using fewer resources than other producers require. Should the U.S. economy remain in autarky—that is, self-sufficient in both food and clothing productions—or could there be gains from specialization and trade?

As long as the opportunity cost of production differs between the two countries, there are gains from specialization and trade. *According to the law of comparative advantage, each country should specialize in producing the good with the lower opportunity cost.* The opportunity cost of producing 1 more unit of clothing is 2 units of food in the United States compared with 1/2 unit of food in Izodia. Because the opportunity cost of producing clothing is lower in Izodia than in the United States, both countries gain if Izodia specializes in clothing and exports some to the United States, and the United States specializes in food and exports some to Izodia.

Before countries can trade, however, they must agree on how much of one good exchanges for another—that is, they must agree on the **terms of trade**. As long as Americans can get more than ½ a unit of clothing for each unit of food produced, and as long as Izodians can get more than ½ a unit of food for each unit of clothing produced, both countries will be better off specializing. Suppose that market forces shape the terms of trade so that 1 unit of clothing exchanges for 1 unit of food. Americans thus trade 1 unit of food to Izodians for 1 unit of clothing. To produce 1 unit of clothing themselves, Americans would have to sacrifice 2 units of food. Likewise, Izodians trade 1 unit of clothing to Americans for 1 unit of food, which is only half what Izodians would sacrifice to produce 1 unit of food themselves.

Exhibit 4 shows that with 1 unit of food trading for 1 unit of clothing, Americans and Izodians can consume anywhere along their blue consumption possibilities frontiers.

terms of trade

How much of one good exchanges for a unit of another good

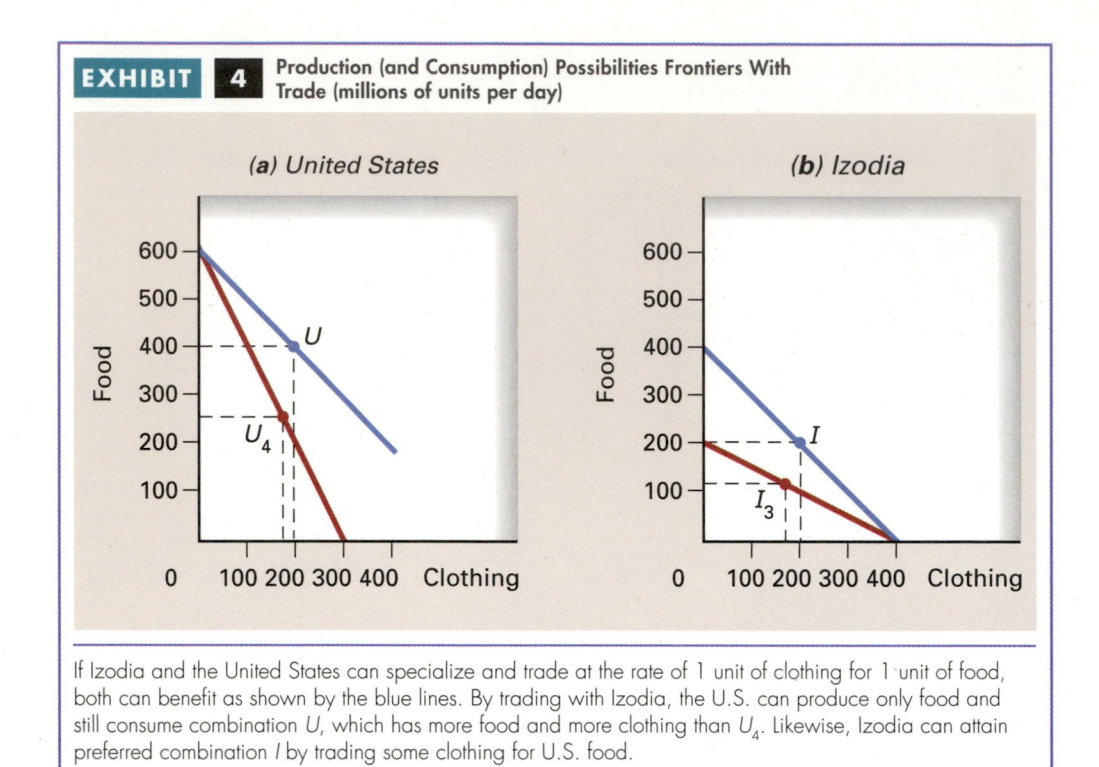

EXHIBIT 4 Production (and Consumption) Possibilities Frontiers With Trade (millions of units per day)

If Izodia and the United States can specialize and trade at the rate of 1 unit of clothing for 1 unit of food, both can benefit as shown by the blue lines. By trading with Izodia, the U.S. can produce only food and still consume combination U, which has more food and more clothing than U_4. Likewise, Izodia can attain preferred combination I by trading some clothing for U.S. food.

The consumption possibilities frontier shows a nation's possible combinations of goods available as a result of specialization and exchange. (Note that the U.S. consumption possibilities curve does not extend to the right of 400 million units of clothing, because Izodia could produce no more than that.) The amount each country actually consumes depends on the relative preferences for food and clothing. Suppose Americans select combination U in panel (a) and Izodians select point I in panel (b).

Without trade, the United States produces and consumes 240 million units of food and 180 million units of clothing. With trade, Americans specialize to produce 600 million units of food; they eat 400 million units and exchange the rest for 200 million units of Izodian clothing. This consumption combination is reflected by point U. Through exchange, Americans increase their consumption of both food and clothing.

Without trade, Izodians produce and consume 120 million units of food and 160 million units of clothing. With trade, Izodians specialize to produce 400 million units of clothing; they wear 200 million and exchange the rest for 200 million units of U.S. food. This consumption combination is shown by point I. Through trade, Izodians, like Americans, are able to increase their consumption of both goods. How is this possible?

Because Americans are more efficient in the production of food and Izodians more efficient in the production of clothing, total output increases when each specializes. Without specialization, world production was 360 million units of food and 340 million units of clothing. With specialization, food increases to 600 million units and clothing to 400 million units. Thus, both countries increase consumption with trade. *Although the United States has an absolute advantage in both goods, differences in the opportunity cost of production between the two nations ensure that specialization and exchange result in mutual gains.* Remember that comparative advantage, not absolute advantage, creates gains from specialization and trade. The only constraint on trade is that, for each good, *world production must equal world consumption.*

We simplified trade relations in our example to highlight the gains from specialization and exchange. We assumed that each country would completely specialize in producing a particular good, that resources were equally adaptable to the production of either good, that the costs of transporting goods from one country to another were inconsequential, and that there were no problems in arriving at the terms of trade. The world is not that simple. For example, we don't expect a country to produce just one good. Regardless, specialization based on the law of comparative advantage still leads to gains from trade.

Reasons for International Specialization

Countries trade with one another—or, more precisely, people and firms in one country trade with those in another—because each side expects to gain from exchange. How do we know what each country should produce and what each should trade?

Differences in Resource Endowments

Differences in resource endowments often create differences in the opportunity cost of production across countries. Some countries are blessed with an abundance of fertile land and favorable growing seasons. The United States, for example, has been called the "breadbasket of the world" because of its rich farmland ideal for growing wheat. Coffee grows best in the climate and elevation of Colombia, Brazil, and Jamaica. Honduras has the ideal climate for bananas. Thus, the United States exports wheat and imports coffee and bananas. Seasonal differences across countries also encourage trade. For example, in the winter, Americans import fruit from Chile, and Canadians travel to Florida for sun and fun. In the summer, Americans export fruit to Chile, and Americans travel to Canada for camping and hiking.

Resources are often concentrated in particular countries: crude oil in Saudi Arabia, fertile soil in the United States, copper ore in Chile, rough diamonds in South Africa. The United States grows abundant supplies of oil seeds such as soybeans and sunflowers, but does not have enough crude oil to satisfy domestic demand. Thus, the United States exports oil seeds and imports crude oil. More generally, *countries export products they can produce more cheaply in return for products that are unavailable domestically or are cheaper elsewhere.*

Exhibit 5 shows, for 12 key resources, U.S. production as a percentage of U.S. consumption. If production falls short of consumption, this means the United States imports the difference. For example, because America grows coffee only in Hawaii, U.S. production is only 1 percent of U.S. consumption, so nearly all coffee is imported. The exhibit also shows that U.S. production falls short of consumption for oil and for metals such as gold, zinc, copper, and aluminum. If production exceeds consumption, the United States exports the difference. For example, U.S.-grown cotton amounts to 417 percent of U.S. cotton consumption, so most U.S. grown cotton is exported. U.S. production also exceeds consumption for other crops, including wheat, oil seeds, and coarse grains (corn, barley, oats). In short, when it comes to basic resources, the United States is a net importer of oil and metals and a net exporter of crops.

Economies of Scale

If production is subject to *economies of scale*—that is, if the long-run average cost of production falls as a firm expands its scale of operation—countries can gain from trade if each nation specializes. Such specialization allows firms in each nation to produce

EXHIBIT 5 U.S. Production as a Percentage of U.S. Consumption for Various Resources

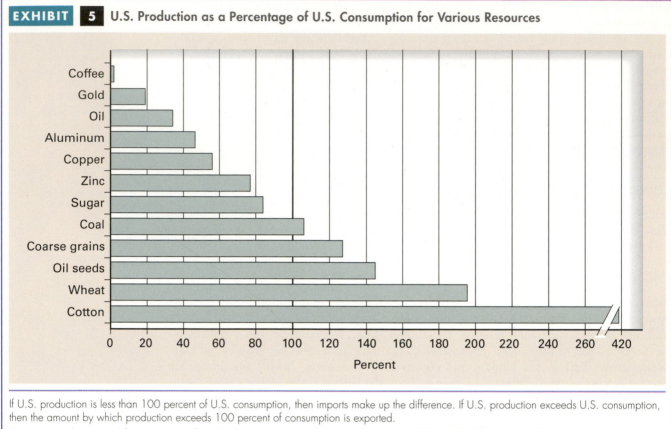

If U.S. production is less than 100 percent of U.S. consumption, then imports make up the difference. If U.S. production exceeds U.S. consumption, then the amount by which production exceeds 100 percent of consumption is exported.

Source: Based on annual figures selected from *The Economist Pocket World in Figures: 2010 Edition* (Profile Books, 2010).

more, which reduces average costs. The primary reason for establishing the single integrated market of the European Union was to offer producers there a large, open market of now more than 500 million consumers. Producers could thereby achieve economies of scale. Firms and countries producing at the lowest opportunity costs are most competitive in international markets. For example, 60 percent of the world's buttons come from a single Chinese city.

Differences in Tastes

Even if all countries had identical resource endowments and combined those resources with equal efficiency, each country would still gain from trade as long as tastes differed across countries. Consumption patterns differ across countries and some of this results from differences in tastes. For example, the Czechs and Irish drink three times as much beer per capita as do the Swiss and Swedes. The French drink three times as much wine as do Australians. The Danes eat twice as much pork as do Americans. Americans eat twice as much chicken as do Hungarians. Americans like chicken, but not all of it. The United States is the world's leading exporter of chicken feet, and China is the world's leading importer (Tyson Foods alone sends more than 2.8 billion chicken feet to China each year). Soft drinks are four times more popular in the United States than in Europe. The English like tea; Americans, coffee. Algeria has an ideal climate for growing grapes (vineyards there date back to Roman times). But Algeria's population is 99 percent Muslim, a religion that forbids alcohol consumption. Thus, Algeria exports wine.

Trade Restrictions and Welfare Loss

Despite the benefits of exchange, nearly all countries at one time or another erect trade barriers, which benefit some domestic producers but harm other domestic producers and all domestic consumers. In this section, we consider the effects of trade barriers and the reasons they are imposed.

Consumer Surplus and Producer Surplus From Market Exchange

Before we explore the net effects of world trade on social welfare, let's develop a framework showing the benefits that consumers and producers get from market exchange. Consider a hypothetical market for apples shown in Exhibit 6. The height of the demand curve shows what consumers are willing and able to pay for each additional pound of apples. In effect, the height of the demand curve shows the *marginal benefit* consumers expect from each pound of apples. For example, the demand curve indicates that some consumers in this market are willing to pay $3.00 or more per pound for the first few pounds of apples. But every consumer gets to buy apples at the market-clearing price,

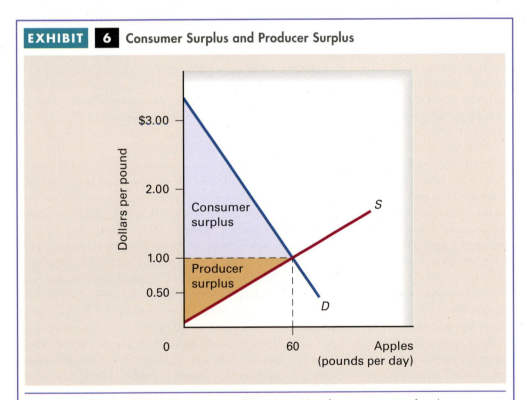

EXHIBIT 6 **Consumer Surplus and Producer Surplus**

Consumer surplus, shown by the blue triangle, indicates the net benefits consumers reap from buying 60 pounds of apples at $1.00 per pound. Some consumers would have been willing to pay $3.00 or more per pound for the first few pounds. Consumer surplus measures the difference between the maximum sum of money consumers would pay for 60 pounds of apples and the actual sum they pay. Producer surplus, shown by the gold triangle, indicates the net benefits producers reap from selling 60 pounds at $1.00 per pound. Some producers would have supplied apples for $0.50 per pound or less. Producer surplus measures the difference between the actual sum of money producers receive for 60 pounds of apples and the minimum amount they would accept for this amount.

which here is $1.00 per pound. Most consumers thus get a bonus, or a surplus, from market exchange.

The blue-shaded triangle below the demand curve and above the market price reflects the *consumer surplus* in this market, which is the difference between the most that consumers would pay for 60 pounds of apples per day and the actual amount they do pay. We all enjoy a consumer surplus from most products we buy.

Producers usually derive a similar surplus. The height of the supply curve shows what producers are willing and able to accept for each additional pound of apples. That is, the height of the supply curve shows the expected *marginal cost* from producing each additional pound. For example, the supply curve indicates that some producers face a marginal cost of $0.50 or less per pound for supplying the first few pounds. But every producer gets to sell apples for the market-clearing price of $1.00 per pound. The gold-shaded triangle above the supply curve and below the market price reflects the *producer surplus*, which is the difference between the actual amount that producers receive for 60 pounds and what they would accept to supply that amount.

The point is that market exchange usually generates a surplus, or a bonus, for both consumers and producers. In the balance of this chapter, we look at the gains from international trade and how trade restrictions affect consumer and producer surplus.

Tariffs

A *tariff,* a term first introduced in Chapter 3, is a tax on imports. (Tariffs can apply to exports, too, but we will focus on import tariffs.) A tariff can be either *specific,* such as a tariff of $5 per barrel of oil, or *ad valorem,* such as 10 percent on the import price of jeans. Consider the effects of a specific tariff on a particular good. In Exhibit 7, *D* is the U.S. demand for sugar and *S* is the supply of sugar from U.S. growers (there were about 10,000 U.S. sugarcane growers in 2010). Suppose that the world price of sugar is $0.10 per pound. The **world price** is determined by the world supply and demand for a product. It is the price at which any supplier can sell output on the world market and at which any demander can purchase output on the world market.

world price

The price at which a good is traded on the world market; determined by the world demand and world supply for the good

With free trade, any U.S. consumers could buy any amount desired at the world price of $0.10 per pound, so the quantity demanded is 70 million pounds per month, of which U.S. producers supply 20 million pounds and importers supply 50 million pounds. Because U.S. buyers can purchase sugar at the world price, U.S. producers can't charge more than that. Now suppose that a specific tariff of $0.05 is imposed on each pound of imported sugar, raising the U.S. price from $0.10 to $0.15 per pound. U.S. producers can therefore raise their own price to $0.15 per pound without losing business to imports. At the higher price, the quantity supplied by U.S. producers increases to 30 million pounds, but the quantity demanded by U.S. consumers declines to 60 million pounds. Because quantity demanded has declined and quantity supplied by U.S. producers has increased, U.S. imports fall from 50 million to 30 million pounds per month.

Because the U.S. price is higher after the tariff, U.S. consumers are worse off. Their loss in consumer surplus is identified in Exhibit 7 by the combination of the blue- and pink-shaded areas. Because both the U.S. price and the quantity supplied by U.S. producers have increased, their total revenue increases by the areas *a* plus *b* plus *f*. But only area *a* represents an increase in producer surplus. Revenue represented by the areas *b* plus *f* merely offsets the higher marginal cost U.S. producers face in expanding sugar output from 20 million to 30 million pounds per month. Area *b* represents part of the net welfare loss to the domestic economy because those 10 million pounds could have been imported for $0.10 per pound rather than produced domestically at a higher marginal cost.

Government revenue from the tariff is identified by area *c,* which equals the tariff of $0.05 per pound multiplied by the 30 million pounds imported, for tariff revenue

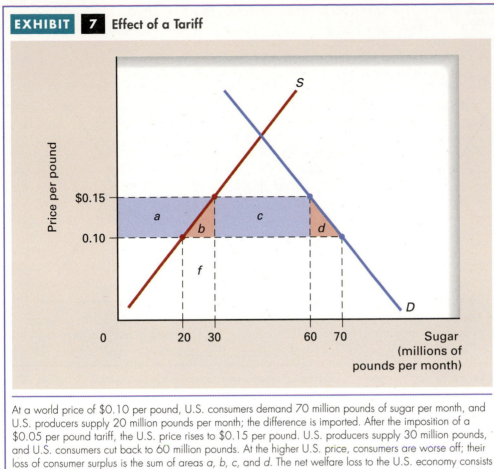

EXHIBIT **7** **Effect of a Tariff**

At a world price of $0.10 per pound, U.S. consumers demand 70 million pounds of sugar per month, and U.S. producers supply 20 million pounds per month; the difference is imported. After the imposition of a $0.05 per pound tariff, the U.S. price rises to $0.15 per pound. U.S. producers supply 30 million pounds, and U.S. consumers cut back to 60 million pounds. At the higher U.S. price, consumers are worse off; their loss of consumer surplus is the sum of areas *a, b, c,* and *d.* The net welfare loss to the U.S. economy consists of areas *b* and *d.*

of $1.5 million per month. Tariff revenue is a loss to consumers, but because the tariff goes to the government, it can be used to lower taxes or to increase public services, so it's not a loss to the U.S. economy. Area *d* shows a loss in consumer surplus because less sugar is consumed at the higher price. This loss is not redistributed to anyone else, so area *d* reflects part of the net welfare loss of the tariff. Therefore, areas *b* and *d* show the domestic economy's net welfare loss of the tariff; *the two triangles measure a loss in consumer surplus that is not offset by a gain to anyone in the domestic economy.*

In summary: Of the total loss in U.S. consumer surplus (areas *a, b, c,* and *d*) resulting from the tariff, area *a* goes to U.S producers, area *c* becomes government revenue, but areas *b* and *d* are net losses in domestic social welfare.

Import Quotas

An *import quota* is a legal limit on the amount of a commodity that can be imported. Quotas usually target imports from certain countries. For example, a quota may limit furniture from China or shoes from Brazil. To have an impact on the domestic market, a quota must be less than what would be imported with free trade. Consider a quota on the U.S. market for sugar. In panel (a) of Exhibit 8, *D* is the U.S. demand curve and *S* is the supply curve of U.S. sugar producers. Suppose again that the world price of sugar

EXHIBIT 8   Effect of a Quota

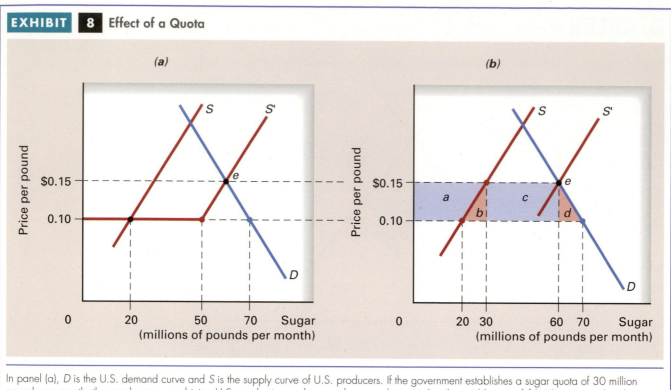

In panel (a), D is the U.S. demand curve and S is the supply curve of U.S. producers. If the government establishes a sugar quota of 30 million pounds per month, the supply curve combining U.S. production and imports becomes horizontal at the world price of $0.10 per pound and remains horizontal until the quantity supplied reaches 50 million pounds. For higher prices, the new supply curve equals the horizontal sum of the U.S. supply curve, S, plus the quota of 30 million pounds. The new U.S. price, $0.15 per pound, is determined by the intersection of the new supply curve, S', with the U.S. demand curve, D. Panel (b) shows the welfare effect of the quota. As a result of the higher U.S. price, consumer surplus is cut by the shaded area. The blue-shaded areas illustrate the loss in consumer surplus that is captured by domestic producers and those who are permitted to fulfill the quota, and the pink-shaded triangles illustrate the net welfare cost of the quota on the U.S. economy.

is $0.10 per pound. With free trade, that price would prevail in the U.S. market as well, and a total of 70 million pounds would be demanded per month. U.S. producers would supply 20 million pounds and importers, 50 million pounds. With a quota of 50 million pounds or more per month, the U.S. price would remain the same as the world price of $0.10 per pound, and the U.S. quantity would be 70 million pounds per month. In short, a quota of at least 50 million pounds would not raise the U.S. price above the world price because 50 million pounds were imported without a quota. A more stringent quota, however, would cut imports, which, as we'll see, would raise the U.S. price.

Suppose U.S. trade officials impose an import quota of 30 million pounds per month. As long as the U.S. price is at or above the world price of $0.10 per pound, foreign producers will supply 30 million pounds. So at prices at or above $0.10 per pound, the total supply of sugar to the U.S. market is found by adding 30 million pounds of imported sugar to the amount supplied by U.S. producers. U.S. and foreign producers would never sell in the U.S. market for less than $0.10 per pound because they can always get that price on the world market. Thus, the supply curve that sums domestic production and imports is horizontal at the world price of $0.10 per pound and remains so until the quantity supplied reaches 50 million pounds.

Again, for prices above $0.10 per pound, the new supply curve, S', adds horizontally the 30-million-pound quota to S, the supply curve of U.S. producers. The U.S. price is found where this new supply curve, S', intersects the domestic demand curve, which in

Exhibit 8 occurs at point *e*. *By limiting imports, the quota raises the domestic price of sugar above the world price and reduces quantity below the free trade level.* (Note that to compare more easily the effects of tariffs and quotas, this quota is designed to yield the same equilibrium price and quantity as the tariff examined earlier.)

Panel (b) of Exhibit 8 shows the distribution and efficiency effects of the quota. As a result of the quota, U.S. consumer surplus declines by the combined blue and pink areas. Area *a* becomes U.S. producer surplus and thus involves no loss of U.S. welfare. Area *c* shows the increased economic profit to those permitted by the quota to sell Americans 30 million pounds for $0.15 per pound, or $0.05 above the world price. If foreign exporters rather than U.S. importers reap this profit, area *c* reflects a net loss in U.S. welfare.

Area *b* shows a welfare loss to the U.S. economy, because sugar could have been purchased abroad for $0.10 per pound, and the U.S. resources employed to increase sugar production could instead have been used more efficiently producing other goods. Area *d* is also a welfare loss because it reflects a reduction in consumer surplus with no offsetting gain to anyone. Thus, areas *b* and *d* in panel (b) of Exhibit 8 measure the minimum U.S. welfare loss from the quota. If the profit from quota rights (area *c*) accrues to foreign producers, this increases the U.S. welfare loss.

Quotas in Practice

The United States has granted quotas to specific countries. These countries, in turn, distribute these quota rights to their exporters through a variety of means. *By rewarding domestic and foreign producers with higher prices, the quota system creates two groups intent on securing and perpetuating these quotas.* Lobbyists for foreign producers work the halls of Congress, seeking the right to export to the United States. This strong support from producers, coupled with a lack of opposition from consumers (who remain rationally ignorant for the most part), has resulted in quotas that have lasted decades. For example, sugar quotas have been around more than 50 years. For the past three decades, U.S. sugar prices have been double the world price, on average, costing U.S. consumers billions. Sugar growers, who account for only 1 percent of U.S. farm sales, have accounted for 17 percent of political contributions from agriculture since 1990.[1]

Some economists have argued that if quotas are to be used, the United States should auction them off to foreign producers, thereby capturing at least some of the difference between the world price and the U.S. price. Auctioning off quotas would not only increase federal revenue at a time when it's desperately needed, but an auction would reduce the profitability of quotas, which would reduce pressure on Washington to perpetuate them. American consumers are not the only victims of sugar quotas. Thousands of poor farmers around the world miss out on an opportunity to earn a living by growing sugar cane for export to America.

Tariffs and Quotas Compared

Consider the similarities and differences between a tariff and a quota. Because both have identical effects on the price in our example, they both lead to the same change in quantity demanded. In both cases, U.S. consumers suffer the same loss of consumer surplus, and U.S. producers reap the same gain of producer surplus. The primary difference is that the revenue from the tariff goes to the U.S. government, whereas the revenue from the quota goes to whoever secures the right to sell foreign goods in the U.S. market. *If quota rights accrue to foreigners, then the domestic economy is worse*

---

1. Michael Schroeder, "Sugar Growers Hold Up Push for Free Trade," *Wall Street Journal*, 3 February 2004.

off with a quota than with a tariff. But even if quota rights go to domestic importers, quotas, like tariffs, still increase the domestic price, restrict quantity, and thereby reduce consumer surplus and economic welfare. Quotas and tariffs can also raise production costs. For example, U.S. candy manufacturers face higher production costs because of sugar quotas, making them less competitive on world markets. Finally, and most importantly, *quotas and tariffs encourage foreign governments to retaliate with quotas and tariffs of their own, thus shrinking U.S. export markets, so the welfare loss is greater than shown in Exhibits 7 and 8.*

Other Trade Restrictions

Besides tariffs and quotas, a variety of other measures limit free trade. A country may provide *export subsidies* to encourage exports and *low-interest loans* to foreign buyers. Some countries impose *domestic content requirements* specifying that a certain portion of a final good must be produced domestically. Other requirements masquerading as health, safety, or technical standards often discriminate against foreign goods. For example, European countries once prohibited beef from hormone-fed cattle, a measure aimed at U.S. beef. Purity laws in Germany bar many non-German beers. Until the European Community adopted uniform standards, differing technical requirements forced manufacturers to offer as many as seven different versions of the same TV for that market. Sometimes exporters will voluntarily limit exports, as when Japanese automakers agreed to cut exports to the United States. The point is that *tariffs and quotas are only two of many devices used to restrict foreign trade.*

Recent research on the cost of protectionism indicates that international trade barriers slow the introduction of new goods and better technologies. So, rather than simply raising domestic prices, trade restrictions slow economic progress.

Freer Trade by Multilateral Agreement

Mindful of how high tariffs cut world trade during the Great Depression, the United States, after World War II, invited its trading partners to negotiate lower tariffs and other trade barriers. The result was the **General Agreement on Tariffs and Trade** (**GATT**), an international trade treaty adopted in 1947 by 23 countries, including the United States. Each GATT member agreed to (1) reduce tariffs through multinational negotiations, (2) reduce import quotas, and (3) treat all members equally with respect to trade.

Trade barriers have been reduced through trade negotiations among many countries, or "trade rounds," under the auspices of GATT. Trade rounds offer a package approach rather than an issue-by-issue approach to trade negotiations. Concessions that are necessary but otherwise difficult to defend in domestic political terms can be made more acceptable in the context of a larger package that also contains politically and economically attractive benefits. Most early GATT trade rounds were aimed at reducing tariffs. The Kennedy Round in the mid-1960s included new provisions against **dumping**, which is selling a commodity abroad for less than is charged in the home market or less than the cost of production. The Tokyo Round of the 1970s was a more sweeping attempt to extend and improve the system.

The most recently completed round was launched in Uruguay in September 1986 and ratified by 123 participating countries in 1994. The number of signing countries now exceeds 150. This so-called **Uruguay Round**, the most comprehensive of the eight postwar multilateral trade negotiations, included 550 pages of tariff reductions on 85 percent of world trade. The Uruguay Round also created the World Trade Organization (WTO) to succeed GATT.

General Agreement on Tariffs and Trade (GATT)
An international tariff-reduction treaty adopted in 1947 that resulted in a series of negotiated "rounds" aimed at freer trade; the Uruguay Round created GATT's successor, the World Trade Organization (WTO)

dumping
Selling a product abroad for less than charged in the home market or for less than the cost of production

Uruguay Round
The final multilateral trade negotiation under GATT; this 1994 agreement cut tariffs, formed the World Trade Organization (WTO), and will eventually eliminate quotas

The World Trade Organization

The **World Trade Organization (WTO)** now provides the legal and institutional foundation for world trade. Whereas GATT was a multilateral agreement with no institutional foundation, the WTO is a permanent institution in Geneva, Switzerland. A staff of about 500 economists and lawyers helps shape policy and resolves trade disputes between member countries. Whereas GATT involved only merchandise trade, the WTO also covers services and trade-related aspects of intellectual property, such as books, movies, and computer programs. The WTO will eventually phase out quotas, but tariffs will remain legal. As a result of the Uruguay Round, average tariffs fell from 6 percent to 4 percent of the value of imports (when GATT began in 1947, tariffs averaged 40 percent).

Whereas GATT relied on voluntary cooperation, the WTO settles disputes in a way that is faster, more automatic, and less susceptible to blockage than the GATT system was. The WTO resolved more trade disputes in its first decade than GATT did in nearly 50 years. Since 2000, developing countries have filed 60 percent of the disputes. But the WTO has also become a lightning rod for globalization tensions, as discussed in the following case study.

World Trade Organization (WTO)

The legal and institutional foundation of the multilateral trading system that succeeded GATT in 1995

BRINGING THEORY TO LIFE

CASE STUDY

Doha Round and Round   The trade-barrier reductions from the Uruguay Round were projected to boost world income by more than $500 billion when fully implemented, or about $72 per person. In poor countries around the world, any additional income from reduced trade barriers could be a lifesaver.

But when WTO members met in Seattle in November 1999 to set an agenda and timetable for the next round of trade talks (later to become known as the Doha Round), all hell broke loose, as 50,000 protesters disrupted the city. Most were peaceful, but police made more than 500 arrests over three days, and property damage reached $3 million. T-shirts sold the week before the meeting dubbed the event the "Battle in Seattle," and so it was.

Organizers used their objections to free trade as a recruiting and fund-raising tool for a variety of interest groups, including labor unions, environmentalists, and farmers. Union members feared losing jobs overseas, environmentalists feared that producers would seek out countries with lax regulations, farmers in Japan, South Korea, Europe, and the United States feared foreign competition, and other groups feared technological developments such as hormone-fed beef and genetically modified food. The Seattle protest was by far the largest demonstration against free trade in the United States.

Protestors would probably be surprised to learn that WTO members are not of one mind about trade issues. For example, the United States and Europe usually push to protect worker rights around the world, but developing countries, including Mexico, Egypt, India, and Pakistan, object strenuously to focusing on worker rights. These poorer nations are concerned that the clothing, shoes, and textiles they make have not gained access to rich nations quickly enough. Many developing countries view attempts to impose labor and environmental standards as just the latest effort to block goods coming from poor countries. For example, workers in China rioted when U.S. companies operating there proposed shortening the work week. Chinese workers wanted a longer work week, believing they could earn more.

Without international groups such as the WTO to provide a forum for discussing labor and environmental issues around the world, conditions in poor countries would likely be worse. Working conditions in many poor countries have been slowly improving, thanks in part to trade opportunities along with pressure for labor rights from

e activity

The World Trade Organization's Web site describes its role and functions and explains the value of reducing trade barriers. The basics on what the WTO is and how it operates can be found at http://www.wto.org/english/thewto_e/whatis_e/whatis_e.htm. What policies support the goal of nondiscriminatory trade? For an example of how one industry has been affected, read the WTO disputes involving textiles at http://www.wto.org/english/tratop_e/texti_e/texti_e.htm. For more on how Nike is responding to criticisms of its labor practices visit its Web site on the subject at http://www.nikebiz.com/responsibility/ (click on Workers/Factories, then on Audit Tools).

Imaginechina via AP Images

WTO and other international groups. For example, Cambodia is one of the poorest countries in the world, but the highest wages in the country are earned by those working in the export sector. Take, for example, Deth, a young mother who sewed T-shirts and shorts at the June Textile factory in Cambodia, mostly for Nike. She worked from 6:15 A.M. to 2:15 P.M. with a half hour for lunch, extra pay for overtime, and double pay for working holidays. Though her pay was low by U.S. standards, it supported her family and was more than twice what judges and doctors average in Cambodia. Factories tend to hire young women, a group otherwise offered few job opportunities. Factory jobs have provided women with status and social equality they never had. Still, protest groups in rich countries called the June Textile factory a "sweatshop" and wanted it shut down. In part because of media pressure, Nike ended its contract with the factory. Researchers have also found that freer trade with Mexico has increased job opportunities there for women.

After failing to get off the ground in Seattle, the round of talks was launched two years later in Doha, Qatar. In setting the agenda for the **Doha Round**, members agreed to improve market access around the world, phase out export subsidies, and substantially reduce distorting government subsidies in agriculture. Reaching agreement proved easier said than done. Headed by Brazil and India, a group of developing countries demanded stronger commitments to reduce agricultural subsidies in the United States, Europe, and Japan. But farmers in these industrial economies wanted to keep their subsidies and protection from imports. For example, the average farm in Japan is about four acres, so farming there is inefficient and costly (rice in Japan is triple the world price). Talks in Cancun in 2003, Hong Kong in 2005, and Geneva in 2006 and 2008 ended bitterly as the Doha Round went round and round. By late 2010 the Doha Round was still spinning its wheels.

Even in the absence of a Doha agreement, some countries continue to reduce trade barriers through *bilateral* agreements, or agreements between two countries. For example, the United States abolished tariffs on Korean flat TV screens and cars.

Sources: David Wessel, "Free-Trade Winds May Be Blowing Again," *Wall Street Journal*, 1 July 2010; Sewell Chan and Jackie Calmes, "White House to Push Free Trade Deal with South Korea," *New York Times*, 27 June 2010; Ernesto Aguayo-Tellez et al., "Did Trade Liberalization Help Women? The Case of Mexico in the 1990s," NBER Working Paper 16195, (July 2010); Gina Chon, "Dropped Stitches," *Asiaweek*, 22 December 2000; and the Web site for the World Trade Organization at http://www.wto.org.

Doha Round

The multilateral trade negotiation round launched in 2001, but still unsettled as of 2010; aims at lowering tariffs on a wide range of industrial and agricultural products; the first trade round under WTO

Common Markets

Some countries looked to the success of the U.S. economy, which is essentially a free trade zone across 50 states, and have tried to develop free trade zones of their own. The largest and best known is the European Union, which began in 1958 with a half dozen countries and expanded by 2010 to 27 countries and over 500 million people. The idea was to create a barrier-free European market like the United States in which goods, services, people, and capital are free to flow to their highest-valued use. Sixteen members of the European Union have also adopted a common currency, the *euro*, which replaced national currencies in 2002.

The United States, Canada, and Mexico have developed a free trade pact called the North American Free Trade Agreement (NAFTA). Through NAFTA, Mexico hopes to attract more U.S. investment by guaranteeing companies that locate there duty-free access to U.S. markets, which is where over two-thirds of Mexico's exports go. Mexico's 115 million people represent an attractive export market for U.S. producers, and Mexico's oil reserves could ease U.S. energy problems. The United States would also like to support Mexico's efforts to become more market oriented, as is reflected, for example, by Mexico's privatization of its phone system and banks. Creating job opportunities in Mexico also reduces pressure for Mexicans to cross the U.S. border illegally to find work. After more than a decade of NAFTA, agricultural exports to Mexico have doubled, as has overall trade among the three nations, but Americans still buy much more from Mexicans and Canadians than the other way around.

Free trade areas are springing up around the world. The United States signed a free trade agreement with the Dominican Republic and five Central American countries, called DR-CAFTA. Ten Latin American countries form Mercosur. The association of Southeast Asian nations make up ASEAN. And South Africa and its four neighboring countries form the Southern African Customs Union. Regional trade agreements require an exception to WTO rules because bloc members can make special deals among themselves and thus discriminate against outsiders. Under WTO's requirements, any trade concession granted to one country must usually be granted to *all other* WTO members.

Arguments for Trade Restrictions

Trade restrictions are often little more than handouts for the domestic industries they protect. Given the loss in social welfare that results from these restrictions, it would be more efficient simply to transfer money from domestic consumers to domestic producers. But such a bald payoff would be politically unpopular. Arguments for trade restrictions avoid mention of transfers to domestic producers and instead cite loftier goals. As we shall now see, none of these goals makes a strong case for restrictions, but some make a little more sense than others.

National Defense Argument

Some industries claim they need protection from import competition because their output is vital for national defense. Products such as strategic metals and military hardware are often insulated from foreign competition by trade restrictions. Thus, national defense considerations outweigh concerns about efficiency and equity. How valid is this argument? Trade restrictions may shelter the defense industry, but other means, such as government subsidies, might be more efficient. Or the government could stockpile basic military hardware so that maintaining an ongoing productive capacity would become less critical. Still, technological change could make certain weapons obsolete. Because most industries can play some role in national defense, instituting trade restrictions on this basis can get out of hand. For example, many decades ago U.S. wool producers secured trade protection at a time when some military uniforms were still made of wool.

The national defense argument has also been used to discourage foreign ownership of U.S. companies in some industries. For example, in 2005 a Chinese state-owned company was prevented from buying Unocal Oil. And in 2010, the Congressional Steel Caucus tried to block a Chinese plan to buy a Mississippi steel plant, saying that such a deal "threatens American jobs and our national security."[2]

2.   Yjun Zhang, "China Steel Group Accuses U.S. Lawmakers of Protectionism," *Wall Street Journal*, 5 July 2010.

Infant Industry Argument

The infant industry argument was formulated as a rationale for protecting emerging domestic industries from foreign competition. In industries where a firm's average cost of production falls as output expands, new firms may need protection from imports until these firms grow enough to become competitive. Trade restrictions let new firms achieve the economies of scale necessary to compete with mature foreign producers.

But how do we identify industries that merit protection, and when do they become old enough to look after themselves? Protection often fosters inefficiencies. The immediate cost of such restrictions is the net welfare loss from higher domestic prices. These costs may become permanent if the industry never realizes the expected economies of scale and thus never becomes competitive. As with the national defense argument, policy makers should be careful in adopting trade restrictions based on the infant industry argument. Here again, temporary production subsidies may be more efficient than import restrictions.

Antidumping Argument

As we have noted already, *dumping* is selling a product abroad for less than in the home market or less than the cost of production. Exporters may be able to sell the good for less overseas because of export subsidies, or firms may simply find it profitable to sell for less in foreign markets where consumers are more sensitive to prices. But why shouldn't U.S. consumers pay as little as possible? If dumping is *persistent,* the increase in consumer surplus would more than offset losses to domestic producers. *There is no good reason why consumers should not be allowed to buy imports for a persistently lower price.*

An alternative form of dumping, termed *predatory dumping,* is the *temporary* sale abroad at prices below cost to eliminate competitors in that foreign market. Once the competition is gone, so the story goes, the exporting firm can raise the price in the foreign market. The trouble with this argument is that if dumpers try to take advantage of their monopoly position by sharply increasing the price, then other firms, either domestic or foreign, could enter the market and sell for less. There are few documented cases of predatory dumping.

Sometimes dumping may be *sporadic,* as firms occasionally try to unload excess inventories. Retailers hold periodic "sales" for the same reason. Sporadic dumping can be unsettling for domestic producers, but the economic impact is not a matter of great public concern. Regardless, all dumping is prohibited in the United States by the Trade Agreements Act of 1979, which calls for the imposition of tariffs when a good is sold for less in the United States than in its home market or less than the cost of production. In addition, WTO rules allow for offsetting tariffs when products are sold for "less than fair value" and when there is "material injury" to domestic producers. For example, U.S. producers of lumber and beer frequently accuse their Canadian counterparts of dumping.

Jobs and Income Argument

One rationale for trade restrictions that is commonly heard in the United States, and is voiced by WTO protestors, is that they protect U.S. jobs and wage levels. Using trade restrictions to protect domestic jobs is a strategy that dates back centuries. One problem with such a policy is that other countries usually retaliate by restricting *their* imports to save *their* jobs, so international trade is reduced, jobs are lost in export industries, and potential gains from trade fail to materialize. That happened big time during the Great Depression, as high tariffs choked trade and jobs.

Wages in other countries, especially developing countries, are often a fraction of wages in the United States. Looking simply at differences in wages, however, narrows the focus too much. Wages represent just one component of the total production cost and may not necessarily be the most important. Employers are interested in the labor cost per unit of output, which depends on both the wage and labor productivity. Wages are high in the United States partly because U.S. labor productivity remains the highest in the world. High productivity can be traced to better education and training and to the abundant computers, machines, and other physical capital that make workers more productive. U.S. workers also benefit greatly from a relatively stable business climate.

But what about the lower wages in many developing countries? Low wages are often linked to workers' lack of education and training, to the meager physical capital available to each worker, and to a business climate that is less stable and hence less attractive for producers. But once multinational firms build plants and provide technological know-how in developing countries, U.S. workers lose some of their competitive edge, and their relatively high wages could price some U.S. products out of the world market. This has already happened in the consumer electronics and toy industries. China makes 80 percent of the toys sold in the United States. Some U.S. toy sellers, such as the makers of Etch A Sketch, would no longer survive had they not outsourced manufacturing to China.

Domestic producers do not like to compete with foreign producers whose costs are lower, so they often push for trade restrictions. But if restrictions negate any cost advantage a foreign producer might have, the law of comparative advantage becomes inoperative and domestic consumers are denied access to the lower-priced goods.

Over time, as labor productivity in developing countries increases, wage differentials among countries will narrow, much as they narrowed between the northern and southern United States during the last century. As technology and capital spread, U.S. workers, particularly unskilled workers, cannot expect to maintain wage levels that are far above comparable workers in other countries. So far, research and development has kept U.S. producers on the cutting edge of technological developments, but staying ahead in the technological race is a constant battle.

Declining Industries Argument

Where an established domestic industry is in jeopardy of closing because of lower-priced imports, could there be a rationale for *temporary* import restrictions? After all, domestic producers employ many industry-specific resources—both specialized labor and specialized machines. This human and physical capital is worth less in its best alternative use. If the extinction of the domestic industry is forestalled through trade restrictions, specialized workers can retire voluntarily or can gradually pursue more promising careers. Specialized machines can be allowed to wear out naturally.

Thus, in the case of declining domestic industries, trade protection can help lessen shocks to the economy and can allow for an orderly transition to a new industrial mix. But the protection offered should not be so generous as to encourage continued investment in the industry. Protection should be of specific duration and should be phased out over that period.

The clothing industry is an example of a declining U.S. industry. The 22,000 U.S. jobs saved as a result of one trade restriction paid an average of less than $30,000 per year. But a Congressional Budget Office study estimated that the higher domestic clothing prices resulting from trade restrictions meant that U.S. consumers paid two to three times more than apparel workers earned. Trade restrictions in the U.S. clothing and textile industry started phasing out in 2005 under the Uruguay Round of trade agreements.

Free trade may displace some U.S. jobs through imports, but it also creates U.S. jobs through exports. When Americans celebrate a ribbon-cutting ceremony for a new software company, nobody credits free trade for those jobs, but when a steel plant closes here, everyone talks about how those jobs went overseas. What's more, many foreign companies have built plants in the United States and employ U.S. workers. For example, a dozen foreign television manufacturers and all major Japanese automakers now operate plants in the United States.

The number employed in the United States has nearly doubled in the last four decades. To recognize this job growth is not to deny the problems facing workers displaced by imports. Some displaced workers, particularly those in steel and other unionized, blue-collar industries, are not likely to find jobs that pay nearly as well as the ones they lost. As with infant industries, however, the problems posed by declining industries need not require trade restrictions. To support the affected industry, the government could offer wage subsidies or special tax breaks that decline over time. The government has also funded programs to retrain affected workers for jobs that are in greater demand.

Problems With Trade Protection

Trade restrictions raise a number of problems in addition to those already mentioned. First, protecting one stage of production usually requires protecting downstream stages of production as well. Protecting the U.S. textile industry from foreign competition, for example, raised the cost of cloth to U.S. apparel makers, reducing *their* competitiveness. Thus, when the government protected domestic textile manufacturers, the domestic garment industry also needed protection. Second, the cost of protection includes not only the welfare loss from the higher domestic price but also the cost of the resources used by domestic producer groups to secure the favored protection. The cost of *rent seeking*—lobbying fees, propaganda, and legal actions—can sometimes equal or exceed the direct welfare loss from restrictions. A third problem with trade restrictions is the transaction costs of enforcing the myriad quotas, tariffs, and other trade restrictions. These often lead to smuggling and black markets. A fourth problem is that economies insulated from foreign competition become less innovative and less efficient. The final and biggest problem with imposing trade restrictions is that other countries usually retaliate, thus shrinking the gains from trade. Retaliation can set off still greater trade restrictions, leading to an outright trade war.

Consider steel tariffs discussed in the following case study.

CASE STUDY

e activity

Read news feeds about the steel industry at http://www. steelonthenet.com/feeds/. You can follow the steel industry in different regions of the world.

PUBLIC POLICY

Steel Tariffs   The U.S. steel industry has been slow to adopt the latest technology and consequently has suffered a long, painful decline for decades—a death from a thousand cuts. Between 1997 and 2001, about 30 percent of U.S. steel producers filed for bankruptcy, including Bethlehem Steel and National Steel. During that stretch, 45,000 U.S. steel jobs disappeared, leaving about 180,000 jobs remaining. Imports accounted for 30 percent of the U.S. market, with most of that steel coming from Europe.

Steel leaders turned to the White House for help, arguing that the industry needed a technological tune-up to become more competitive but needed trade protection during the process. This is a variant of the infant-industry argument. Many of the jobs lost were in "rust-belt" states, such as Ohio, West Virginia, and Pennsylvania, states also critical in presidential elections. We can only speculate what role politics played in the decision, but in March 2002, President George W. Bush imposed tariffs on steel, claiming that imports caused "material injury" to the U.S. steel industry. The tariffs, which ranged from 8 percent to 30 percent on 10 steel categories, were scheduled to last three years.

As expected, the tariffs cut imports and boosted the U.S. price of steel. By 2003, steel imports slumped to their lowest level in a decade. The higher domestic price of steel helped U.S. steel makers but made steel-using industries here less competitive on world markets. For example, the tariffs added about $300 to the average cost of a U.S. automobile. According to one estimate, the tariffs cost 15,000 to 20,000 jobs in steel-user industries.

The European Union and other steel-exporting nations filed a complaint, and in November 2003, the WTO ruled that the tariffs violated trade agreements. The European Union, with about 300,000 of its own steel jobs at stake, announced that if the tariffs were not repealed, EU countries would retaliate with tariffs on U.S. exports. Japan and South Korea also threatened retaliatory tariffs.

After the negative WTO ruling and facing threats of retaliation, the White House repealed the steel tariffs in December 2003, claiming that they had served their purpose. Approximately $650 million in higher tariffs was collected during the 21 months they were imposed. The steelworkers union called the repeal "an affront to all workers." But union members should not have been surprised in light of the WTO ruling, threatened retaliation from abroad, and the fact that several months earlier, the steelworkers union endorsed a Democrat for president.

A big threat to the steel industry has come not from foreign competition but from the financial crisis. In August 2008, U.S. steel makers were operating at 90 percent of capacity. The global financial panic of 2008 temporarily cut U.S. steel production to only 40 percent of capacity by December 2008.

The only tariff threats in recent years have been against Chinese exporters. In 2009, the Obama White House imposed a 35 percent tariff on Chinese tires. Despite minor trade skirmishes, and despite clamors in Washington to insulate U.S. jobs from Chinese goods, and despite the rocky going for the Doha Round, the trend among industrial economies is toward lower tariffs, especially on raw materials. The United States, the European Union, and Japan have eliminated nearly all tariffs on raw materials.

Sources: Steven Greenhouse, "With a Receptive White House, Labor Begins to Line-Up Battles," *New York Times*, 22 September 2009; James Areddy, "U.S. Businesses Back More Trade Action Vs. China," *Wall Street Journal*, 24 May 2010; Robert Guy Matthews, "Industry Cuts Back as Steel Prices Fall," *Wall Street Journal*, 6 July 2010; and "Steel Industry Executive Summary: May 2010," International Trade Administration, U.S. Dept. of Commerce at http://hq-web03.ita.doc .gov/License/Surge.nsf/webfiles/SteelMillDevelopments/$file/exec%20summ.pdf?openelement.

Conclusion

International trade arises from voluntary exchange among buyers and sellers pursuing their self-interest. Since 1950 world output has risen eightfold, while world trade has increased nearly twentyfold. World trade offers many advantages to the trading countries: access to markets around the world, lower costs through economies of scale, the opportunity to utilize abundant resources, better access to information about markets and technology, improved quality honed by competitive pressure, and, most importantly, lower prices for consumers. Comparative advantage, specialization, and trade allow people to use their scarce resources efficiently to satisfy their unlimited wants.

Despite the clear gains from free trade, restrictions on international trade date back centuries, and pressure on public officials to impose trade restrictions continues today. Domestic producers (and their resource suppliers) benefit from trade restrictions in their markets because they can charge domestic consumers more. Trade restrictions insulate domestic producers from the rigors of global competition, in the process stifling innovation and leaving the industry vulnerable to technological change from abroad. With trade quotas, the winners also include those who have secured the right to import goods at the world prices and sell them at the domestic prices. Consumers, who must pay higher prices for protected goods, suffer from trade restrictions, as do the domestic producers who import resources. Other losers include U.S. exporters, who face higher trade barriers as foreigners retaliate with their own trade restrictions.

Producers have a laser-like focus on trade legislation, but consumers remain largely oblivious. Consumers purchase thousands of different goods and thus have no special interest in the effects of trade policy on any particular good. Congress tends to support the group that makes the most noise, so trade restrictions often persist, despite the clear and widespread gains from freer trade.

Summary

1. Even if a country has an absolute advantage in all goods, that country should specialize in producing the goods in which it has a comparative advantage. If each country specializes and trades according to the law of comparative advantage, all countries will benefit from greater consumption possibilities.

2. Quotas benefit those with the right to buy goods at the world price and sell them at the higher domestic price. Both tariffs and quotas harm domestic consumers more than they help domestic producers, although tariffs at least yield government revenue, which can be used to fund public programs or to cut taxes.

3. Despite the gains from free trade, restrictions have been imposed for centuries. The General Agreement on Tariffs and Trade (GATT) was an international treaty ratified in 1947 to reduce trade barriers. Subsequent negotiations lowered tariffs and reduced trade restrictions. The Uruguay Round, ratified in 1994, lowered tariffs, phases out quotas, and created the World Trade Organization (WTO) as

the successor to GATT. The Doha Round was launched in 2001, but failed to reach an agreement as of 2010.

4. Arguments used by producer groups to support trade restrictions include promoting national defense, nurturing infant industries, preventing foreign producers from dumping goods in domestic markets, protecting domestic jobs, and allowing declining industries time to wind down and exit the market.

5. Trade restrictions impose a variety of strains on the economy besides the higher costs to consumers. These include (1) the need to protect downstream stages of production as well, (2) expenditures made by favored domestic industries to seek trade protection, (3) costs incurred by the government to enforce trade restrictions, (4) the inefficiency and lack of innovation that result when an industry is insulated from foreign competition, and (5), most important, the trade restrictions imposed by other countries in retaliation.

Key Concepts

Autarky   420
Terms of trade   421
World price   426

General Agreement on Tariffs
and Trade (GATT)   430
Dumping   430

Uruguay Round   430
World Trade Organization (WTO)   431
Doha Round   432

Questions for Review

1. PROFILE OF IMPORTS AND EXPORTS   What are the major U.S. exports and imports? How does international trade affect consumption possibilities?

2. REASONS FOR TRADE   What are the primary reasons for international trade?

3. GAINS FROM TRADE   Complete each of the following sentences:

   a. When a nation has no economic interaction with foreigners and produces everything it consumes, the nation is in a state of _____.

   b. According to the law of comparative advantage, each nation should specialize in producing the goods in which it has the lowest _____.

   c. The amount of one good that a nation can exchange for one unit of another good is known as the _____.

   d. Specializing according to comparative advantage and trading with other nations results in _____.

4. REASONS FOR INTERNATIONAL SPECIALIZATION   What determines which goods a country should produce and export?

5. TARIFFS   High tariffs usually lead to black markets and smuggling. How is government revenue reduced by such activity? Relate your answer to the graph in Exhibit 7 in this chapter. Does smuggling have any social benefits?

6. TRADE RESTRICTIONS   Exhibits 7 and 8 show net losses to the economy of a country that imposes tariffs or quotas on imported sugar. What kinds of gains and losses would occur in the economies of countries that export sugar?

7. THE WORLD TRADE ORGANIZATION   What is the World Trade Organization (WTO) and how does it help foster multilateral trade? (Check the WTO Web site at http://www.wto.org/.)

8. Case Study: The Doha Round and Round   What was the major sticking point holding up progress in the Doha Round?

9. ARGUMENTS FOR TRADE RESTRICTIONS   Explain the national defense, declining industries, and infant industry arguments for protecting a domestic industry from international competition.

10. ARGUMENTS FOR TRADE RESTRICTIONS   Firms hurt by cheap imports typically argue that restricting trade will save U.S. jobs. What's wrong with this argument? Are there ever any reasons to support such trade restrictions?

11. Case Study: Steel Tariffs   How did the steel tariff affect the domestic steel industry, the workers in the steel industry, workers in steel-use industries, and consumers?

Problems and Exercises

12. COMPARATIVE ADVANTAGE   Suppose that each U.S. worker can produce 8 units of food or 2 units of clothing daily. In Fredonia, which has the same number of workers, each worker can produce 7 units of food or 1 unit of clothing daily. Why does the United States have an absolute advantage in both goods? Which country enjoys a comparative advantage in food? Why?

13. COMPARATIVE ADVANTAGE   The consumption possibilities frontiers shown in Exhibit 4 assume terms of trade of 1 unit of clothing for 1 unit of food. What would the consumption possibilities frontiers look like if the terms of trade were 1 unit of clothing for 2 units of food?

14. IMPORT QUOTAS   How low must a quota be in effect to have an impact? Using a demand-and-supply diagram, illustrate and explain the net welfare loss from imposing such a quota. Under what circumstances would the net welfare loss from an import quota exceed the net welfare loss from an equivalent tariff (one that results in the same price and import level as the quota)?

15. TRADE RESTRICTIONS   Suppose that the world price for steel is below the U.S. domestic price, but the government requires that all steel used in the United States be domestically produced.
    a. Use a diagram like the one in Exhibit 7 to show the gains and losses from such a policy.
    b. How could you estimate the net welfare loss (deadweight loss) from such a diagram?
    c. What response to such a policy would you expect from industries (like automobile producers) that use U.S. steel?
    d. What government revenues are generated by this policy?

Global Economic Watch Exercises

Login to www.cengagebrain.com and access the Global Economic Watch to do these exercises.

18. GLOBAL ECONOMIC WATCH   Go to the Global Economic Crisis Resource Center. Select Global Issues in Context. In the Basic Search box at the top of the page, enter the phrase "Doha Round." On the Results page, go to the News Section. Click on the link for the October 1, 2010, article "America Embraces Trade Discrimination." In what ways does the author criticize U.S. trade policy?

19. GLOBAL ECONOMIC WATCH   Go to the Global Economic Crisis Resource Center. Select Global Issues in Context. Go to the menu at the top of the page and click on the tab for Browse Issues and Topics. Choose Business and Economy. Click on the link for Globalization. Find one article in favor of globalization and international trade and one article against. Compare and contrast the arguments in the articles.

International Finance

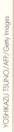
YOSHIKAZU TSUNO/AFP/Getty Images

- How can the United States export more than nearly any other country yet still have the world's highest trade deficit?
- Are high trade deficits a worry?
- What's the official "fudge factor" used to compute the balance of payments?
- What's meant by a "strong dollar"?
- Why does a nation try to influence the value of its currency?
- And what's up with China?

  Answers to these and other questions are explored in this chapter, which focuses on international finance.

If Starbucks wants to buy 1,000 espresso machines from the German manufacturer, Krups, it will be quoted a price in euros. Suppose the machines cost a total of €1 million (euros). How much is that in dollars? The dollar cost will depend on the exchange rate. When trade takes place across international borders, two currencies are usually involved. Supporting the flows of goods and services are flows of currencies that fund international transactions. The exchange rate between currencies—the price of one in terms of the other—is how the price of a product in one country translates into the price facing a buyer in another country. Cross-border trade therefore depends on the exchange rate.

In this chapter we examine the market forces that affect the relative value of one currency in terms of another.

Topics discussed include:

- Balance of payments
- Trade deficits and surpluses
- Foreign exchange markets
- Purchasing power parity
- Flexible exchange rates
- Fixed exchange rates
- International monetary system
- Bretton Woods agreement
- Managed float

Balance of Payments

A country's gross domestic product, or GDP, measures the economy's income and output during a given period. To account for dealings abroad, countries must also keep track of international transactions. A country's *balance of payments,* as introduced in Chapter 3, summarizes all economic transactions during a given period between residents of that country and residents of other countries. *Residents* include people, firms, organizations, and governments.

International Economic Transactions

The balance of payments measures economic transactions between a country and the rest of the world, whether these transactions involve goods and services, real and financial assets, or transfer payments. The balance of payments measures a *flow* of transactions during a particular period, usually a year. Some transactions do not involve actual payments. For example, if *Time* magazine ships a new printing press to its Australian subsidiary, no payment is made, yet an economic transaction involving another country has occurred. Similarly, if CARE sends food to Africa or the Pentagon provides military assistance to the Middle East, these transactions must be captured in the balance of payments. So remember, although we speak of the *balance of payments,* a more descriptive phrase would be the *balance-of-economic transactions.*

Balance-of-payments accounts are maintained according to the principles of *double-entry bookkeeping.* Some entries are called *credits,* and others are called *debits.* As you will see, the balance of payments consists of several individual accounts. An individual account may not balance, but a deficit in one or more accounts must be offset by a surplus in the other accounts. Because total credits must equal total debits, there is a *balance* of payments—hence, the name. During a given period, such as a year, the inflow of receipts from the rest of the world, which are entered as credits, must equal the outflow of payments to the rest of the world, which are entered as debits.

The first of two major categories in the balance of payments is the current account. The current account records *current* flows of funds into and out of the country, including imports and exports of goods and services, net income earned by U.S. residents from foreign assets, and net transfer payments from abroad. These are discussed in turn.

The Merchandise Trade Balance

The *merchandise trade balance,* a term introduced in Chapter 3, equals the value of merchandise exports minus the value of merchandise imports. The merchandise account reflects trade in goods, or tangible products (stuff you can put in a box), like French wine or U.S. computers, and is often referred to simply as the *trade balance.* The value of U.S. merchandise exports is a credit in the U.S. balance-of-payments account because U.S. residents get *paid* for the exported goods. The value of U.S. merchandise imports is a debit in the balance-of-payments account because U.S. residents *pay* foreigners for imported goods.

If merchandise exports exceed merchandise imports, the trade balance is in *surplus.* If merchandise imports exceed merchandise exports, the trade balance is in *deficit.* The merchandise trade balance, which is reported monthly, influences foreign exchange markets, the stock market, and other financial markets. The trade balance depends on a variety of factors, including the relative strength and competitiveness of the domestic

EXHIBIT **1** U.S. Imports Have Topped Exports Since 1976, and the Trade Deficit Has Widened

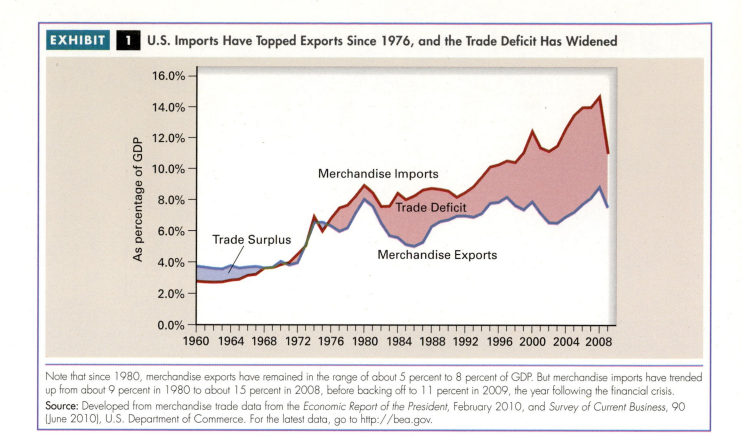

Note that since 1980, merchandise exports have remained in the range of about 5 percent to 8 percent of GDP. But merchandise imports have trended up from about 9 percent in 1980 to about 15 percent in 2008, before backing off to 11 percent in 2009, the year following the financial crisis.

Source: Developed from merchandise trade data from the *Economic Report of the President*, February 2010, and *Survey of Current Business*, 90 (June 2010), U.S. Department of Commerce. For the latest data, go to http://bea.gov.

economy compared with other economies and the relative value of the domestic currency compared with other currencies. Strong economies with growing incomes tend to buy more of everything, including imports.

U.S. merchandise trade since 1960 is depicted in Exhibit 1, where exports, the blue line, and imports, the red line, are expressed as a percentage of GDP. During the 1960s, exports exceeded imports, and the resulting trade surpluses are shaded blue. Since 1976, imports have exceeded exports, and the resulting trade deficits are shaded pink. Trade deficits as a percentage of GDP increased from 1.3 percent in 1991 to a peak of 6.3 percent in 2006. The recession of 2007–2009 slowed U.S. imports more than U.S. exports, so by 2009 the trade deficit relative to GDP fell to 3.5 percent, the lowest in more than a decade.

Because per capita income in the United States ranks among the highest in the world, the United States imports more goods from each of the world's major economies than it exports to them. Exhibit 2 shows the U.S. merchandise trade deficit with major economies or regions of the world in 2009. The $227 billion trade deficit with China was by far the largest, nearly four times that with Latin America, the European Union, or the OPEC nations. The Chinese bought $69 billion in U.S. goods in 2009, but Americans bought $296 billion in Chinese goods, or about $2,575 per U.S. household. So China sold America four times more than it bought from America. Chances are, most of the utensils in your kitchen were made in China; most toys are also Chinese made. The United States is the world's biggest importer and has a trade surplus with only a few major economies, including Australia, Brazil, and the Netherlands.

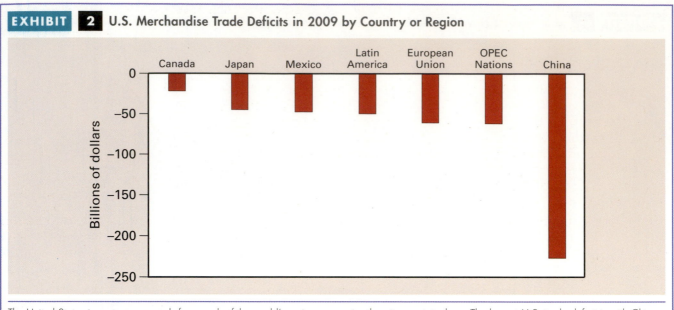

The United States imports more goods from each of the world's major economies than it exports to them. The largest U.S. trade deficit is with China, which exported four times more to the United States in 2009 than it imported from the United States.

Source: Developed from data in "Exports, Imports, and Trade Balance by Country and Area: 2009 Annual Totals," Exhibit 13, U.S. Bureau of Economic Analysis, 10 June 2010.

Balance on Goods and Services

The merchandise trade balance focuses on the flow of goods, but services are also traded internationally. *Services* are intangibles, such as transportation, insurance, banking, education, consulting, and tourism. Services are often called "invisibles" because they are not tangible. The value of U.S. service exports, as when an Irish tourist visits New York City, is listed as a credit in the U.S. balance-of-payments account because U.S. residents get paid for these services. The value of U.S. service imports, like computer programming outsourced to India, is listed as a debit in the balance-of-payments account because U.S. residents must pay for the imported services.

Because the United States exports more services than it imports, services have been in surplus for the last three decades. The **balance on goods and services** is the export value of goods and services minus the import value of goods and services, or *net exports*, a component of GDP.

Net Investment Income

U.S. residents earn investment income, such as interest and dividends, from assets owned abroad. This investment income flows to the United States and is a credit in the balance-of-payments account. On the other side, foreigners earn investment income on assets owned in the United States, and this payment flows out of the country. This outflow is a debit in the balance-of-payments account. **Net investment income from abroad** is U.S. investment earnings from foreign assets minus foreigners' earnings from their U.S. assets. From year to year, this figure bounces around

balance on goods and services

The portion of a country's balance-of-payments account that measures the value of a country's exports of goods and services minus the value of its imports of goods and services

net investment income from abroad

Investment earnings by U.S. residents from their foreign assets minus investment earnings by foreigners from their assets in the United States

between a positive and a negative number. In 2009, net investment income from foreign holdings was $89 billion.

Unilateral Transfers and the Current Account Balance

Unilateral transfers consist of government transfers to foreign residents, foreign aid, money workers send to families abroad, personal gifts to friends and relatives abroad, charitable donations, and the like. Money sent out of the country is a debit in the balance-of-payments account. For example, immigrants in the United States often send money to families back home. **Net unilateral transfers abroad** equal the unilateral transfers received from abroad by U.S. residents minus unilateral transfers sent to foreign residents by U.S. residents. U.S. net unilateral transfers have been negative since World War II, except for 1991, when the U.S. government received sizable transfers from foreign governments to help pay their share of the Persian Gulf War. In 2009, net unilateral transfers were a negative $130.2 billion, with private transfers accounting for most of that (government grants and transfers made up the rest). Net unilateral transfers abroad averaged about $430 per U.S. resident in 2009.

The United States places few restrictions on money sent out of the country. Other countries, particularly developing countries, strictly limit the amount that may be sent abroad. More generally, many developing countries, such as China, restrict the convertibility of their currency into other currencies.

When we add net unilateral transfers to net exports of goods and services and net income from assets owned abroad, we get the **balance on current account**, which is reported quarterly. Thus, *the current account includes all international transactions in currently produced goods and services, net income from foreign assets, and net unilateral transfers*. It can be negative, reflecting a current account deficit; positive, reflecting a current account surplus; or zero.

The Financial Account

The current account records international transactions in goods, services, asset income, and unilateral transfers. The **financial account** records international purchases of assets, including financial assets, such as stocks, bonds, and bank balances, and real assets such as land, housing, factories, and other physical assets. For example, U.S. residents purchase foreign securities to earn a higher return and to diversify their portfolios. Money flows out when Americans buy foreign assets or build factories overseas. Money flows in when foreigners buy U.S. assets or build factories here. The international purchase or sale of assets is recorded in the financial account.

Between 1917 and 1982, the United States ran a financial account deficit, meaning that U.S. residents purchased more foreign assets than foreigners purchased assets from the United States. The net income from these foreign assets improved our current account balance. But in 1983, for the first time in 65 years, foreigners bought more assets in the United States than U.S. residents purchased abroad. Since 1983, foreigners have continued to buy more U.S. assets most years than the other way around, meaning there has usually been a surplus in the financial account.

By the end of 2009, foreigners owned $21.1 trillion in U.S. assets and U.S. residents owned $18.4 trillion in foreign assets. Thus, foreigners owned $2.7 trillion more assets in the United States than U.S. residents owned abroad. This is not as bad as it sounds, because foreign purchases of assets in the United States add to America's productive capacity and promote employment and labor productivity here. But the income from these assets flows to their foreign owners, not to Americans. Remember, the investment income from these assets shows up in the current account.

net unilateral transfers abroad
The unilateral transfers (gifts and grants) received from abroad by U.S. residents minus the unilateral transfers U.S. residents send abroad

balance on current account
The portion of the balance-of-payments account that measures that country's balance on goods and services, net investment income from abroad, plus net unilateral transfers abroad

financial account
The record of a country's international transactions involving purchases or sales of financial and real assets

Deficits and Surpluses

Nations, like households, operate under a budget constraint. Spending cannot exceed income plus cash on hand and borrowed funds. We have distinguished between *current* transactions, which include exports, imports, asset income, and unilateral transfers, and *financial* transactions, which reflect purchases of foreign real and financial assets. Any surplus or deficit in one account must be offset by deficits or surpluses in other balance-of-payments accounts.

Exhibit 3 presents the U.S. balance-of-payments statement for 2009. All transactions requiring payments from foreigners to U.S. residents are entered as credits, indicated by a plus sign (+), because they result in an inflow of funds from foreign residents to U.S. residents. All transactions requiring payments to foreigners from U.S. residents are entered as debits, indicated by a minus sign (−), because they result in an outflow of funds from U.S. residents to foreign residents. As you can see, a surplus in the financial account of $197.7 billion was more than offset by a current account deficit of $419.8 billion. A *statistical discrepancy* is required to balance the payments, and that amounts to $222.1 billion. Think of the statistical discrepancy as the official "fudge factor" that (1) measures the error in the balance-of-payments and (2) satisfies the double-entry bookkeeping requirement that total debits must equal total credits. The statistical discrepancy was especially large in 2009, because the global financial crisis created unusual gyrations in international accounts.

Foreign exchange is the currency of another country needed to carry out international transactions. A country runs a deficit in its current account when the amount of foreign exchange received from exports, from foreign assets, and from unilateral transfers falls short of the amount needed to pay for imports, pay foreign holders of U.S. assets, and make unilateral transfers. If the current account is in deficit, the necessary foreign exchange must come from a net inflow in the financial account. Such an inflow

---

EXHIBIT 3   U.S. Balance of Payments for 2009 (billions of dollars)

Current Account

1. Merchandise exports	+1,045.5
2. Merchandise imports	−1,562.5
3. Merchandise trade balance (1 + 2)	−517.0
4. Service exports	+509.2
5. Service imports	−370.8
6. Goods and services balance (3 + 4 + 5)	−378.6
7. Net investment income from abroad	+89.0
8. Net unilateral transfers	−130.2
9. Current account balance (6 + 7 + 8)	−419.8

Financial Account

10. Change in U.S. owned assets abroad	−237.5
11. Change in foreign-owned assets in United States	+435.2
12. Financial account balance (10 + 11)	+197.7
13. Statistical discrepancy	+222.1
TOTAL (9 + 12 + 13)	0.0

Source: Computed from estimates in "U.S. International Transactions," *Survey of Current Business,* 90 (June 2010), Table F.2., p. D-61.

in the financial account could stem from borrowing from foreigners, selling domestic stocks and bonds to foreigners, selling a steel plant in Pittsburgh or a ski lodge in Aspen to foreigners, and so forth.

If a country runs a current account surplus, the foreign exchange received from exports, from foreign assets, and from unilateral transfers from abroad exceeds the amount needed to pay for imports, to pay foreign holders of U.S. assets, and to make unilateral transfers abroad. If the current account is in surplus, this excess foreign exchange results in a net outflow in the financial account through lending abroad, buying foreign stocks and bonds, buying a shoe plant in Italy or a villa on the French Riviera, and so forth.

When all transactions are considered, accounts must balance, though specific accounts usually don't. The statistical discrepancy ensures that, in the aggregate, accounts sum to zero. A deficit in a particular account should not necessarily be viewed as a source of concern, nor should a surplus be a source of satisfaction. The deficit in the U.S. current account in recent years has usually been offset by a financial account surplus. As a result, foreigners have been acquiring more claims on U.S. assets.

Foreign Exchange Rates and Markets

Now that you have some idea about international flows, we can take a closer look at the forces that determine the underlying value of the currencies involved. Let's begin by looking at exchange rates and the market for foreign exchange.

Foreign Exchange

Foreign exchange, recall, is foreign money needed to carry out international transactions. The **exchange rate** is the price measured in one country's currency of buying one unit of another country's currency. Exchange rates are determined by the interaction of the households, firms, private financial institutions, governments, and central banks that buy and sell foreign exchange. The exchange rate fluctuates to equate the quantity of foreign exchange demanded with the quantity supplied. Typically, foreign exchange is made up of bank deposits denominated in the foreign currency. When foreign travel is involved, foreign exchange often consists of foreign paper money.

The foreign exchange market incorporates all the arrangements used to buy and sell foreign exchange. This market is not so much a physical place as a network of telephones and computers connecting financial centers all over the world. Perhaps you have seen pictures of foreign exchange traders in New York, Frankfurt, London, or Tokyo in front of computer screens amid a tangle of phone lines. The foreign exchange market is like an all-night diner—it never closes. A trading center is always open somewhere in the world.

We will consider the market for the euro in terms of the dollar. But first, a little more about the euro. For decades the nations of Western Europe tried to increase their economic cooperation and trade. These countries believed they would be more productive and more competitive with the United States if they acted less like many separate economies and more like the 50 United States, with a single set of trade regulations and a single currency. Imagine the hassle involved if each of the 50 states had its own currency.

In 2002, euro notes and coins entered circulation in the 12 European countries adopting the common currency. The big advantage of a common currency is that Europeans no longer have to change money every time they cross a border or trade with another country in the group. Again, the inspiration for this is the United States, arguably the most successful economy in world history.

exchange rate
The price measured in one country's currency of purchasing one unit of another country's currency

So the euro is the common currency of the *euro zone,* as the now 16-country region is usually called. The price, or exchange rate, of the euro in terms of the dollar is the number of dollars required to purchase one euro. An increase in the number of dollars needed to purchase a euro indicates weakening, or **depreciation**, of the dollar. A decrease in the number of dollars needed to purchase a euro indicates strengthening, or **appreciation**, of the dollar. Put another way, a decrease in the number of euros needed to purchase a dollar is a depreciation of the dollar, and an increase in the number of euros needed to purchase a dollar is an appreciation of the dollar.

Because the exchange rate is usually a market price, it is determined by demand and supply: The equilibrium price is the one that equates quantity demanded with quantity supplied. To simplify the analysis, suppose that the United States and the euro zone make up the entire world, so the demand and supply for euros in international finance is the demand and supply for foreign exchange from the U.S. perspective.

The Demand for Foreign Exchange

Whenever U.S. residents need euros, they must buy them in the foreign exchange market, which could include your local bank, paying for them with dollars. Exhibit 4 depicts a market for foreign exchange—in this case, euros. The horizontal axis shows the quantity of foreign exchange, measured here in billions of euros per day. The vertical axis shows the price per unit of foreign exchange, measured here in dollars per euro. The demand curve D for foreign exchange shows the inverse relationship between the dollar price of the euro and the quantity of euros demanded, other things assumed constant. Assumed constant along the demand curve are the incomes and preferences of U.S. consumers, expected inflation in the United States and in the euro zone, the

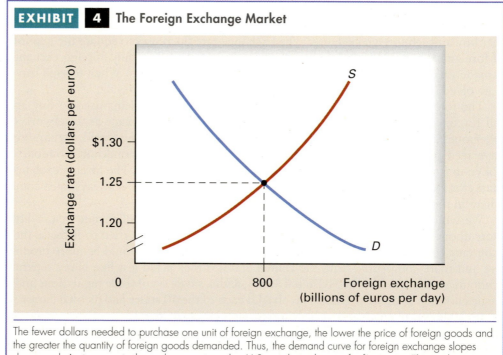

EXHIBIT   4   The Foreign Exchange Market

The fewer dollars needed to purchase one unit of foreign exchange, the lower the price of foreign goods and the greater the quantity of foreign goods demanded. Thus, the demand curve for foreign exchange slopes downward. An increase in the exchange rate makes U.S. products cheaper for foreigners. This implies an increase in the quantity of foreign exchange supplied. The supply curve of foreign exchange slopes upward.

euro price of goods in the euro zone, and interest rates in the United States and in the euro zone. U.S. residents have many reasons for demanding foreign exchange, but in the aggregate, the lower the dollar price of foreign exchange, other things constant, the greater the quantity of foreign exchange demanded.

A drop in the dollar price of foreign exchange, in this case the euro, means that fewer dollars are needed to purchase each euro, so the dollar prices of euro zone products (like German cars, Italian shoes, tickets to the Louvre, and euro zone securities), which list prices in euros, become cheaper. The cheaper it is to buy euros, the lower the dollar price of euro zone products to U.S. residents, so the greater the quantity of euros demanded by U.S. residents, other things constant. For example, a cheap enough euro might persuade you to tour Rome, climb the Austrian Alps, wander the museums of Paris, or crawl the pubs of Dublin.

The Supply of Foreign Exchange

The supply of foreign exchange is generated by the desire of foreign residents to acquire dollars—that is, to exchange euros for dollars. Euro zone residents want dollars to buy U.S. goods and services, acquire U.S. assets, make loans in dollars, or send dollars to their U.S. friends and relatives. Euros are supplied in the foreign exchange market to acquire the dollars people want. An increase in the dollar-per-euro exchange rate, other things constant, makes U.S. products cheaper for foreigners because foreign residents need fewer euros to get the same number of dollars. For example, suppose a Dell computer sells for $600. If the exchange rate is $1.20 per euro, that computer costs 500 euros; if the exchange rate is $1.25 per euro, it costs only 480 euros. The number of Dell computers demanded in the euro zone increases as the dollar-per-euro exchange rate increases, other things constant, so more euros will be supplied on the foreign exchange market to buy dollars.

The positive relationship between the dollar-per-euro exchange rate and the quantity of euros supplied on the foreign exchange market is expressed in Exhibit 4 by the upward-sloping supply curve for foreign exchange (again, euros in our example). The supply curve assumes that other things remain constant, including euro zone incomes and tastes, expectations about inflation in the euro zone and in the United States, and interest rates in the euro zone and in the United States.

Determining the Exchange Rate

Exhibit 4 brings together the demand and supply for foreign exchange to determine the exchange rate. At a rate of $1.25 per euro, the quantity of euros demanded equals the quantity supplied—in our example, 800 billion euros per day. Once achieved, this equilibrium rate will remain constant until a change occurs in one of the factors that affect supply or demand. If the exchange rate is allowed to adjust freely, or to *float,* in response to market forces, the market will clear continually, as the quantities of foreign exchange demanded and supplied are equated.

What if the initial equilibrium is upset by a change in one of the underlying forces that affect demand or supply? For example, suppose higher U.S. incomes increase American demand for all normal goods, including those from the euro zone. This shifts the U.S. demand curve for foreign exchange to the right, as Americans buy more Italian marble, Dutch chocolate, German machines, Parisian vacations, and euro zone securities.

This increased demand for euros is shown in Exhibit 5 by a rightward shift of the demand curve for foreign exchange. The demand increase from D to D' leads to an increase in the exchange rate per euro from $1.25 to $1.27. Thus, the euro increases in

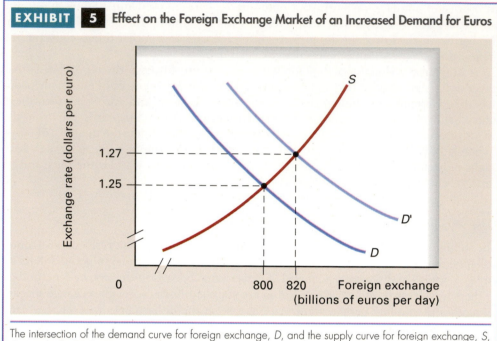

EXHIBIT 5 Effect on the Foreign Exchange Market of an Increased Demand for Euros

The intersection of the demand curve for foreign exchange, *D*, and the supply curve for foreign exchange, *S*, determines the exchange rate. At an exchange rate of $1.25 per euro, the quantity of euros demanded equals the quantity supplied. An increase in the demand for euros from *D* to *D'* increases the exchange rate from $1.25 to $1.27 per euro.

value, or appreciates, while the dollar falls in value, or depreciates. An increase in U.S. income should not affect the euro supply curve, though it does increase the *quantity of euros supplied*. The higher exchange value of the euro prompts those in the euro zone to buy more American products and assets, which are now cheaper in terms of the euro.

To Review: Any increase in the demand for foreign exchange or any decrease in its supply, other things constant, increases the number of dollars required to purchase one unit of foreign exchange, which is a depreciation of the dollar. On the other hand, any decrease in the demand for foreign exchange or any increase in its supply, other things constant, reduces the number of dollars required to purchase one unit of foreign exchange, which is an appreciation of the dollar.

Arbitrageurs and Speculators

Exchange rates between two currencies are nearly identical at any given time in markets around the world. For example, the dollar price of a euro is the same in New York, Frankfurt, Tokyo, London, Zurich, Hong Kong, Istanbul, and other financial centers. **Arbitrageurs**—dealers who take advantage of any difference in exchange rates between markets by buying low and selling high—ensure this equality. Their actions help to equalize exchange rates across markets. For example, if one euro costs $1.24 in New York but $1.25 in Frankfurt, an arbitrageur could buy, say, $1,000,000 worth of euros in New York and at the same time sell them in Frankfurt for $1,008,065, thereby earning $8,065 minus the transaction costs of the trades.

Because an arbitrageur buys and sells simultaneously, little risk is involved. In our example, the arbitrageur increased the demand for euros in New York and increased

arbitrageur
Someone who takes advantage of temporary geographic differences in the exchange rate by simultaneously purchasing a currency in one market and selling it in another market

the supply of euros in Frankfurt. These actions increased the dollar price of euros in New York and decreased it in Frankfurt, thereby squeezing down the difference in exchange rates. Exchange rates may still change because of market forces, but they tend to change in all markets simultaneously.

The demand and supply of foreign exchange arises from many sources—from importers and exporters, investors in foreign assets, central banks, tourists, arbitrageurs, and speculators. **Speculators** buy or sell foreign exchange in hopes of profiting by trading the currency at a more favorable exchange rate later. By taking risks, speculators aim to profit from market fluctuations—they try to buy low and sell high. In contrast, arbitrageurs take less risk, because they *simultaneously* buy currency in one market and sell it in another.

Finally, people in countries suffering from economic and political turmoil, such as occurred in Russia, Indonesia, the Philippines, and Zimbabwe, may buy *hard* currency as a hedge against the depreciation and instability of their own currencies. The dollar has long been accepted as an international medium of exchange. It is also the currency of choice in the world markets for oil and illegal drugs. But the euro eventually may challenge that dominance, in part because the largest euro denomination, the 500 euro note, is worth about six times the largest U.S. denomination, the $100 note. So it would be six times easier to smuggle euro notes than U.S. notes of equal value.

speculator
Someone who buys or sells foreign exchange in hopes of profiting from fluctuations in the exchange rate over time

Purchasing Power Parity

As long as trade across borders is unrestricted and as long as exchange rates are allowed to adjust freely, the **purchasing power parity (PPP) theory** predicts that the exchange rate between two currencies will adjust in the long run to reflect price differences between the two currency regions. *A given basket of internationally traded goods should therefore sell for about the same around the world (except for differences reflecting transportation costs and the like).* Suppose a basket of internationally traded goods that sells for $10,000 in the United States sells for €8,000 in the euro zone. According to the purchasing power parity theory, the equilibrium exchange rate should be $1.25 per euro. If this were not the case—if the exchange rate were, say, $1.20 per euro—then you could exchange $9,600 for €8,000, with which you buy the basket of commodities in the euro zone. You could then sell that basket of goods in the States for $10,000, yielding you a profit of $400 minus any transaction costs. Selling dollars and buying euros will also drive up the dollar price of euros.

purchasing power parity (PPP) theory
The idea that the exchange rate between two countries will adjust in the long run to equalize the cost between the countries of a basket of internationally traded goods

The purchasing power parity theory is more of a long-run predictor than a day-to-day indicator of the relationship between changes in the price level and the exchange rate. For example, a country's currency generally appreciates when inflation is low compared with other countries and depreciates when inflation is high. Likewise, a country's currency generally appreciates when its real interest rates are higher than those in the rest of the world, because foreigners are more willing to buy and hold investments denominated in that high-interest currency. As a case in point, the dollar appreciated during the first half of the 1980s, when real U.S. interest rates were relatively high, and depreciated during 2002 to 2004, when real U.S. interest rates were relatively low.

Because of trade barriers, central bank intervention in exchange markets, and the fact that many products are not traded or are not comparable across countries, the purchasing power parity theory usually does not explain exchange rates at a particular point in time that well. For example, if you went shopping in Switzerland tomorrow, you would soon notice a dollar does not buy as much there as it does in the United States. The following case study considers the purchasing power parity theory based on the price of Big Macs around the globe.

BRINGING THEORY TO LIFE

The Big Mac Index   As you have already learned, the PPP theory predicts that in the long run the exchange rate between two currencies should move toward equalizing the cost in each country of an identical basket of internationally traded goods. A lighthearted test of the theory has been developed by *The Economist* magazine, which compares prices around the world for a "market basket" consisting simply of one McDonald's Big Mac—a product that, though not internationally traded, is essentially the same in more than 100 countries. *The Economist* begins with the price of a Big Mac in the local currency and then converts that price into dollars based on the exchange rate prevailing at the time. A comparison of the dollar price of Big Macs across countries offers a crude test of the PPP theory, which predicts that prices should be roughly equal in the long run.

Exhibit 6 lists the dollar price of a Big Mac in March 2010, in 22 surveyed countries plus the euro zone average. By comparing the price of a Big Mac in the United States (shown as the green bar) with prices in other countries, we can derive a crude measure of whether particular currencies, relative to the dollar, are overvalued (red bars) or undervalued (blue bars). For example, because the price of a Big Mac in Norway, at $6.87, was 92 percent higher than the U.S. price of $3.58, the Norwegian krone was the most overvalued relative to the dollar of the countries listed. But Big Macs were cheaper in most of the countries surveyed. The cheapest was in China, where $1.83 was 49 percent below the U.S. price. Hence, the Chinese yuan was the most undervalued relative to the dollar.

Thus, Big Mac prices in March 2010 ranged from 92 percent above to 49 percent below the U.S. price. The euro was 29 percent overvalued. The price range lends little

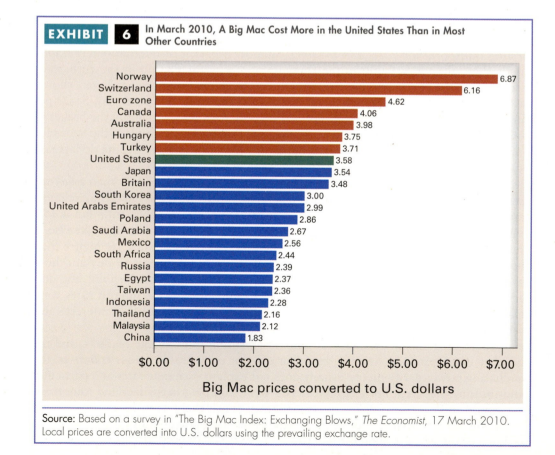

EXHIBIT 6   In March 2010, A Big Mac Cost More in the United States Than in Most Other Countries

Big Mac prices converted to U.S. dollars

Norway	6.87
Switzerland	6.16
Euro zone	4.62
Canada	4.06
Australia	3.98
Hungary	3.75
Turkey	3.71
United States	3.58
Japan	3.54
Britain	3.48
South Korea	3.00
United Arabs Emirates	2.99
Poland	2.86
Saudi Arabia	2.67
Mexico	2.56
South Africa	2.44
Russia	2.39
Egypt	2.37
Taiwan	2.36
Indonesia	2.28
Thailand	2.16
Malaysia	2.12
China	1.83

Source: Based on a survey in "The Big Mac Index: Exchanging Blows," *The Economist*, 17 March 2010. Local prices are converted into U.S. dollars using the prevailing exchange rate.

support to the PPP theory, but that theory relates only to traded goods. The Big Mac is not traded internationally. Part of the price of a Big Mac must cover rent, which can vary substantially across countries. Taxes and trade barriers, such as tariffs and quotas on beef, may also distort local prices. And wages differ across countries, with a McDonald's worker averaging about $8 an hour in the United States versus more like $1 an hour in China. So there are understandable reasons why Big Mac prices differ across countries.

Sources: "The Big Mac Index: Exchanging Blows," *The Economist*, 17 March 2010; David Parsley and Shang-Jin Wei, "In Search of a Euro Effect: Big Lessons from a Big Mac Meal?" *Journal of International Money and Finance*, 27 (March 2008): 260—276; Ali Kutan et al., "Toward Solving the PPP Puzzle: Evidence from 113 Countries," *Applied Economics*, 41 (Issue 24, 2009): 3057—3066; and the McDonald's Corporation international Web site at http://www.mcdonalds.com.

Flexible Exchange Rates

For the most part, we have been discussing a system of **flexible exchange rates**, which are determined by demand and supply. Flexible, or *floating*, exchange rates adjust continually to the myriad forces that buffet foreign exchange markets. Consider how the exchange rate is linked to the balance-of-payments accounts. Debit entries in the current or financial accounts increase the demand for foreign exchange, resulting in a depreciation of the dollar. Credit entries in these accounts increase the supply of foreign exchange, resulting in an appreciation of the dollar.

flexible exchange rate
Rate determined in foreign exchange markets by the forces of demand and supply without government intervention

Fixed Exchange Rates

When exchange rates are flexible, governments usually have little direct role in foreign exchange markets. But if governments try to set exchange rates, active and ongoing central bank intervention is often necessary to establish and maintain these **fixed exchange rates**. Suppose the European Central Bank selects what it thinks is an appropriate rate of exchange between the dollar and the euro. It attempts to *fix*, or to *peg*, the exchange rate within a narrow band around the particular value selected. If the euro threatens to climb above the maximum acceptable exchange rate, monetary authorities must sell euros and buy dollars, thereby keeping the dollar price of the euro down. Conversely, if the euro threatens to drop below the minimum acceptable exchange rate, monetary authorities must sell dollars and buy euros. This increased demand for the euro will keep its value up relative to the dollar. Through such intervention in the foreign exchange market, monetary authorities try to stabilize the exchange rate, keeping it within the specified band.

fixed exchange rate
Rate of exchange between currencies pegged within a narrow range and maintained by the central bank's ongoing purchases and sales of currencies

If monetary officials must keep selling foreign exchange to keep the value of their domestic currency from falling, they risk running out of foreign exchange reserves. Faced with this threat, the government has several options for eliminating the exchange rate disequilibrium. First, the pegged exchange rate can be increased, meaning that foreign currency costs more in terms of the domestic currency. This is a **devaluation** of the domestic currency. (A decrease in the pegged exchange rate is called a **revaluation**.) Second, the government can reduce the domestic demand for foreign exchange directly by imposing restrictions on imports or on financial outflows. Many developing countries do this. Third, the government can adopt policies to slow the domestic economy, increase interest rates,

currency devaluation
An increase in the official pegged price of foreign exchange in terms of the domestic currency

currency revaluation
A reduction in the official pegged price of foreign exchange in terms of the domestic currency

or reduce inflation relative to that of the country's trading partners, thereby indirectly decreasing the demand for foreign exchange and increasing the supply of foreign exchange. Several Asian economies, such as South Korea and Indonesia, pursued such policies to stabilize their currencies. Finally, the government can allow the disequilibrium to persist and ration the available foreign reserves through some form of foreign exchange control.

This concludes our introduction to the theories of international finance. Let's examine international finance in practice.

Development of the International Monetary System

gold standard
An arrangement whereby the currencies of most countries are convertible into gold at a fixed rate

From 1879 to 1914, the international financial system operated under a **gold standard**, whereby the major currencies were convertible into gold at a fixed rate. For example, the U.S. dollar could be redeemed at the U.S. Treasury for one-twentieth of an ounce of gold. The British pound could be redeemed at the British Exchequer, or treasury, for one-fourth of an ounce of gold. Because each British pound could buy five times as much gold as each dollar, one British pound exchanged for $5.

The gold standard provided a predictable exchange rate, one that did not vary as long as currencies could be redeemed for gold at the announced rate. But the money supply in each country was determined in part by the flow of gold between countries, so each country's monetary policy was influenced by the supply of gold. A balance-of-payments deficit resulted in a loss of gold, which theoretically caused a country's money supply to shrink. A balance-of-payments surplus resulted in an influx of gold, which theoretically caused a country's money supply to expand. The supply of money throughout the world also depended on the vagaries of gold discoveries. When gold production did not keep pace with the growth in economic activity, the price level dropped. When gold production exceeded the growth in economic activity, the price level rose. For example, gold discoveries in Alaska and South Africa in the late 1890s expanded the U.S. money supply, leading to inflation.

The Bretton Woods Agreement

During World War I, many countries could no longer convert their currencies into gold, and the gold standard eventually collapsed, disrupting international trade during the 1920s and 1930s. Once an Allied victory in World War II appeared certain, the Allies met in Bretton Woods, New Hampshire, in July 1944 to formulate a new international monetary system. Because the United States had a strong economy and was not ravaged by the war, the dollar was selected as the key reserve currency in the new international monetary system. All exchange rates were fixed in terms of the dollar, and the United States, which held most of the world's gold reserves, stood ready to convert foreign holdings of dollars into gold at a rate of $35 per ounce. Even though the rate that dollars could be exchanged for gold was fixed by the Bretton Woods agreement, *other* countries could adjust *their* exchange rates relative to the U.S. dollar if they found a chronic disequilibrium in their balance of payments—that is, if a country faced a large and persistent deficit or surplus.

International Monetary Fund (IMF)
An international organization that establishes rules for maintaining the international monetary system and makes loans to countries with temporary balance-of-payments problems

The Bretton Woods agreement also created the **International Monetary Fund (IMF)** to set rules for maintaining the international monetary system, to standardize financial reporting for international trade, and to make loans to countries with temporary balance-of-payments problems. The IMF lends a revolving fund of about $250 billion to economies in need of reserves; there are plans to double that. Headquartered in

Washington, D.C., the IMF has 186 member countries and a staff of 2,400 drawn from around the world (half the staff members are economists).

The Demise of the Bretton Woods System

During the latter part of the 1960s, inflation increased in the United States more than in other countries. Because of U.S. inflation, the dollar had become *overvalued* at the official exchange rate, meaning that the gold value of the dollar exceeded the exchange value of the dollar. In 1971, U.S. merchandise imports exceeded merchandise exports for the first time since World War II. Foreigners exchanged dollars for gold. To stem this gold outflow, the United States stopped exchanging gold for dollars, but this just made the dollar less attractive. In December 1971, the world's 10 richest countries met in Washington and devalued the dollar by 8 percent. They hoped this devaluation would put the dollar on firmer footing and would save the "dollar standard." With prices rising at different rates around the world, however, an international monetary system based on fixed exchange rates was doomed.

When the U.S. trade deficit tripled in 1972, it became clear that the dollar was still overvalued. In early 1973, the dollar was devalued another 10 percent, but this did not quiet foreign exchange markets. The dollar, for three decades the anchor of the international monetary system, suddenly looked vulnerable, and speculators began betting that the dollar would fall even more, so they sold dollars. Dollars were exchanged for German marks because the mark appeared to be the most stable currency. Bundesbank, Germany's central bank, tried to defend the dollar's official exchange rate by selling marks and buying dollars. Why didn't Germany want the mark to appreciate? Appreciation would make German goods more expensive abroad and foreign goods cheaper in Germany, thereby reducing German exports and increasing German imports. So the mark's appreciation would reduce German output and employment. But after selling $10 billion worth of marks, the Bundesbank gave up defending the dollar. As soon as the value of the dollar was allowed to float against the mark, the Bretton Woods system, already on shaky ground, collapsed.

The Current System: Managed Float

The Bretton Woods system has been replaced by a **managed float system**, which combines features of a freely floating exchange rate with sporadic intervention by central banks as a way of moderating exchange rate fluctuations among the world's major currencies. Most small countries, particularly developing countries, still peg their currencies to one of the major currencies (such as the U.S. dollar) or to a "basket" of major currencies. What's more, in developing countries, private international borrowing and lending are severely restricted; some governments allow residents to purchase foreign exchange only for certain purposes. In some countries, different exchange rates apply to different categories of transactions.

Critics of flexible exchange rates argue that they are inflationary, because they free monetary authorities to pursue expansionary policies; and flexible exchange rates have often been volatile. This volatility creates uncertainty and risk for importers and exporters, increasing the transaction costs of international trade. Furthermore, exchange rate volatility can lead to wrenching changes in the competitiveness of a country's export sector. These changes cause swings in employment, resulting in louder calls for import restrictions. For example, the exchange rate between the Japanese yen and the U.S. dollar has been relatively unstable, particularly because of international speculation.

Policy makers are always on the lookout for a system that will perform better than the current managed float system, with its fluctuating currency values. *Their ideal is a*

managed float system
An exchange rate system that combines features of freely floating rates with sporadic intervention by central banks

system that will foster international trade, lower inflation, and promote a more stable world economy. International finance ministers have acknowledged that the world must find an international standard and establish greater exchange rate stability.

The current system also allows some countries to manipulate their currencies to stimulate exports and discourage imports, as discussed in the following case study about China.

CASE STUDY

e activity

The New York Times reviews the basics of the U.S.-China exchange rate at http://www.nytimes.com/2010/09/19/weekinreview/19chan.html. The Bank of China publishes up-to-date exchange rates at http://www.boc.cn/sourcedb/whpj/enindex.html.

WORLD OF BUSINESS

What about China? The U.S. trade deficit with China of $227 billion in 2009 exceeded America's combined deficits with the European Union, OPEC countries, and Latin America. The deficit with China grew about 15 percent annually between 2000 and 2009. Americans spend four times more on Chinese products than the Chinese spend on American products. Between 2007 and 2010, China's holdings of U.S. Treasury securities more than doubled from $400 billion to $900 billion.

Many economists, politicians, and union officials argue that China manipulates its currency, the yuan, to keep Chinese products cheaper abroad and foreign products more expensive at home. This stimulates Chinese exports and discourages imports, thereby boosting Chinese production and jobs. At the same time, the average Chinese consumer is poorer because the yuan buys fewer foreign products.

As we have seen, any country that establishes a fixed exchange rate that undervalues or overvalues the currency must intervene continuously to maintain that rate. Thus, if the official exchange rate has chronically undervalued the Chinese yuan relative to the dollar, as appears to be the case, then Chinese authorities must continuously exchange yuan for dollars in foreign exchange markets. The increased supply of yuan keeps the yuan down, and the increased demand for dollars keeps the dollar up.

But the charge that China manipulates its currency goes beyond simply depressing the yuan and boosting the dollar. China's trading partners increasingly feel they are being squeezed out by Chinese producers without gaining access to Chinese markets. China seeks every trade advantage, especially for the 125 state-owned enterprises run directly by the central government. For example, China offers some domestic producers tax rebates and subsidies to promote exports, while imposing quotas and tariffs to discourage imports, such as a 25 percent tariff on auto-parts imports.

China has tried to soothe concerns about the trade deficit. Most importantly, Chinese authorities in 2005 began allowing the yuan to rise modestly against the dollar. As a result, the yuan rose a total of 20 percent against the dollar between July 2005 and July 2010. China also announced plans to cut tax rebates paid to its exporters and to lower some import duties. But these measures seem to have had little effect on America's monster deficit with China.

Prior to an international finance meeting in June 2010, a key European Central Bank official said "the rigidity of the Chinese monetary regime had slowed down the recovery in the developed world." Facing political pressure to do something, China announced that it would allow the exchange rate to become more flexible. We'll see.

Sources: Lee Branstetter and Nicholas Lardy, "China's Embrace of Globalization," NBER Working Paper 12373 (July 2006); Jason Dean and Shen Hong, "China Central Bank Tames Yuan Appreciation Hopes," *Wall Street Journal*, 22 June 2010; Yujan Zhang, "China Steel Group Accuses U.S. Lawmakers of Protectionism," *Wall Street Journal*, 5 July 2010; and Michael Casey, "Showdown Looms Over China's Currency at G-20," *Wall Street Journal*, 11 June 2010.

Conclusion

The United States is very much a part of the world economy, not only as the largest exporter nation but also as the largest importer nation. Although the dollar remains the unit of transaction in many international settlements—OPEC, for example, still states oil prices in dollars—gyrations of exchange rates have made those involved in international finance wary of putting all their eggs in one basket. The international monetary system is now going through a difficult period as it gropes for a new source of stability four decades after the collapse of the Bretton Woods agreement.

Summary

1. The balance of payments reflects all economic transactions between one country and the rest of the world. The current account measures flows from (a) goods; (b) services, including consulting and tourism; (c) income from foreign assets; and (d) unilateral transfers, or public and private transfer payments to and from foreign residents. The financial account measures international transactions in real and financial assets.

2. Foreign exchange pays for transactions across international borders. In the absence of government intervention, the demand and supply of foreign exchange determines the market exchange rate. According to the theory of purchasing power parity (PPP), the exchange rate between two countries will adjust in the long run to equalize the cost between the countries of a basket of internationally traded goods.

3. Under a system of flexible, or floating, exchange rates, the value of the dollar relative to foreign exchange varies with market forces. An increase in the demand for foreign exchange or a decrease in its supply, other things constant, increases the value

of foreign exchange relative to the dollar, which is a depreciation of the dollar. Conversely, a decrease in the demand for foreign exchange or an increase in its supply, other things constant, decreases the value of foreign exchange relative to the dollar, which is an appreciation of the dollar.

4. Under a system of fixed exchange rates, monetary authorities try to stabilize the exchange rate, keeping it between a specified ceiling and floor value. A country may try to hold down the value of its currency, so that exports will be cheaper to foreigners and imports will cost more to domestic consumers. One objective here is to increase domestic production and employment.

5. For much of the twentieth century, the international monetary system was based on fixed exchange rates. A managed float system has been in effect for the major currencies since the demise of the Bretton Woods system in the early 1970s. Although central banks often try to stabilize exchange rates, fluctuations in rates persist. These fluctuations usually reflect market forces but they still raise the transaction costs of international trade and finance.

Key Concepts

Balance on goods and services   444

Net investment income from abroad   444

Net unilateral transfers abroad   445

Balance on current account   445

Financial account   445

Exchange rate   447

Currency depreciation   448

Currency appreciation   448

Arbitrageur   450

Speculator   451

Purchasing power parity (PPP) theory   451

Flexible exchange rate   453

Fixed exchange rate   453

Currency devaluation   453

Currency revaluation   453

Gold standard   454

International Monetary Fund (IMF)   454

Managed float system   455

Questions for Review

1. BALANCE OF PAYMENTS Suppose the United States ran a surplus in its balance on goods and services by exporting goods and services while importing nothing.

    a. How would such a surplus be offset elsewhere in the balance-of-payments accounts?

    b. If the level of U.S. production does not depend on the balance on goods and services, how would running this surplus affect our *current* standard of living?

    c. What is the relationship between total debits and total credits in the balance on goods and services?

d. When all international economic transactions are considered, what must be true about the sum of debits and credits?

e. What is the role of the statistical discrepancy?

2. FOREIGN EXCHANGE   What is the difference between a depreciation of the dollar and a devaluation of the dollar?

3. ARBITRAGEURS   How do arbitrageurs help ensure that exchange rates are the same in markets around the world?

4. PURCHASING POWER PARITY   According to the theory of purchasing power parity, what will happen to the value of the dollar (against foreign currencies) if the U.S. price level doubles and price levels in other countries remain constant? Why is the theory more suitable for analyzing events in the long run?

5. Case Study: The Big Mac Index   The Big Mac Index computed by the *Economist* magazine has consistently found the U.S. dollar to be undervalued against some currencies and overvalued against others. This finding seems to call for a rejection of the purchasing power parity theory. Explain why this index may not be a valid test of the theory.

6. THE CURRENT SYSTEM: MANAGED FLOAT   What is a managed float? What are the disadvantages of freely floating exchange rates that led countries to the managed float system?

7. MERCHANDISE TRADE BALANCE   Explain why a U.S. recession that occurs as the rest of the world is expanding will tend to reduce the U.S. trade deficit.

8. Case Study: What about China?   Why would China want its own currency to be undervalued relative to the U.S. dollar? How does China maintain an undervalued currency?

Problems and Exercises

9. BALANCE OF PAYMENTS   The following are hypothetical data for the U.S. balance of payments. Use the data to calculate each of the following:

a. Merchandise trade balance
b. Balance on goods and services
c. Balance on current account
d. Financial account balance
e. Statistical discrepancy

	Billions of Dollars
Merchandise exports	350.0
Merchandise imports	2,425.0
Service exports	2,145.0
Service imports	170.0
Net income and net transfers	221.5
Outflow of U.S. capital	245.0
Inflow of foreign capital	100.0

10. BALANCE OF PAYMENTS   Explain where in the U.S. balance of payments an entry would be recorded for each of the following:

a. A Hong Kong financier buys some U.S. corporate stock.
b. A U.S. tourist in Paris buys some perfume to take home.
c. A Japanese company sells machinery to a pineapple company in Hawaii.

d. U.S. farmers make a gift of food to starving children in Ethiopia.
e. The U.S. Treasury sells a bond to a Saudi Arabian prince.
f. A U.S. tourist flies to France on Air France.
g. A U.S. company sells insurance to a foreign firm.

11. DETERMINING THE EXCHANGE RATE   Use these data to answer the following questions about the market for British pounds:

Pound Price (in $)	Quantity Demanded (of pounds)	Quantity Supplied (of pounds)
$4.00	50	100
3.00	75	75
2.00	100	50

a. Draw the demand and supply curves for pounds, and determine the equilibrium exchange rate (dollars per pound).
b. Suppose that the supply of pounds doubles. Draw the new supply curve.
c. What is the new equilibrium exchange rate?
d. Has the dollar appreciated or depreciated?
e. What happens to U.S. imports of British goods?

Global Economic Watch Exercises

Login to www.cengagebrain.com and access the Global Economic Watch to do these exercises.

12. GLOBAL ECONOMIC WATCH   Go to the Global Economic Crisis Resource Center. Select Global Issues in Context. In the Basic Search box at the top of the page, enter the phrase "China's exchange rate reform." On the Results page, go to the News Section. Click on the link for the July 30, 2010, article "China's Exchange Rate Reform on Right Track." What is China's exchange rate policy?

13. GLOBAL ECONOMIC WATCH   Go to the Global Economic Crisis Resource Center. Select Global Issues in Context. In the Basic Search box at the top of the page, enter the phrase "foreign exchange." From the past two years, choose one article about a foreign country. What did you learn about international finance in that country?

Economic Development

21

AP Photo/Kamran Jebreili

- Why are some countries so poor while others are so rich?

- What determines the wealth of nations?

- Why do families in low-income countries have more children than those in higher-income countries?

- Why have abundant natural resources such as oil or diamonds turned out to be a curse for some countries?

- And how might programs that send subsidized food and used clothing to poor countries have the unintended consequence of retarding economic development there?

People around the world face the day under quite different circumstances. Even during a national recession, most Americans rise from a comfortable bed in a nice home, select the day's clothing from a wardrobe, choose from a variety of breakfast foods, and drive to school or to work in one of the family's personal automobiles. But some of the world's 6.9 billion people have little housing, clothing, or food. They have no automobile and no formal job. Their health is poor, as is their education. Many cannot read or write. A billion people need eyeglasses but can't afford them.

In this chapter, we sort out rich nations from poor ones and try to explain the difference. We discuss sources of economic development, and weigh the pros and cons of foreign aid.

Topics discussed in this chapter include:

- Developing countries
- The key to development
- Privatization

- The poorest billion
- Foreign trade and development
- Foreign aid and development

Worlds Apart

Differences in economic vitality among countries are huge. Countries are classified in a variety of ways based on their economic development. The yardstick most often used to compare living standards across nations is the amount an economy produces per capita, or *output per capita*. The World Bank, an economic development institution affiliated with the United Nations (UN), estimates income per capita to classify economies. The measure begins with *gross national income (GNI)*, which is the market value of all goods and services produced by resources supplied by the countries' residents and firms, regardless of the location of the resource. For example, U.S. GNI includes profit earned by an American factory in Great Britain but excludes profits earned by a Japanese factory in Kentucky.

GNI measures both the value of output produced and the income that output generates. The World Bank computes the GNI per capita, then adjusts figures across countries based on the purchasing power of that income in each country. Using this measure, the World Bank sorts countries around the world into three major groups: *high-income economies*, *middle-income economies*, and *low-income economies*.

Data on world population and world output are summarized in Exhibit 1. High-income economies in 2009 made up only 16 percent of the 6.9 billion people on Earth, but accounted for 73 percent of world output. So high-income economies, *with only about one-sixth of the world's population, produced nearly three-quarters of the world's output*. Middle-income economies made up 69 percent of the world's population, but accounted for 26 percent of the world output. And low-income countries made up 15 percent of the world's population, but account for only 1 percent of world output.

Developing and Industrial Economies

The low- and middle-income economies are usually referred to as **developing countries**. Most high-income economies are also referred to as **industrial market countries**. So low- and middle-income economies, what are called developing countries, made up

---

developing countries

Nations typified by high rates of illiteracy, high unemployment, high fertility rates, and exports of primary products; also known as low-income and middle-income economies

industrial market countries

Economically advanced capitalist countries of Western Europe, North America, Australia, New Zealand, and Japan; also known as developed countries and high-income economies

---

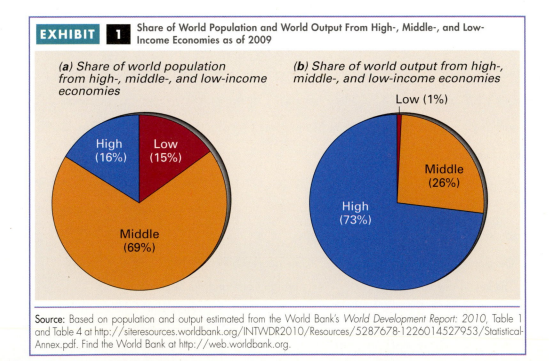

EXHIBIT 1 Share of World Population and World Output From High-, Middle-, and Low-Income Economies as of 2009

(a) Share of world population from high-, middle-, and low-income economies

High (16%)
Low (15%)
Middle (69%)

(b) Share of world output from high-, middle-, and low-income economies

Low (1%)
Middle (26%)
High (73%)

Source: Based on population and output estimated from the World Bank's *World Development Report: 2010*, Table 1 and Table 4 at http://siteresources.worldbank.org/INTWDR2010/Resources/5287678-1226014527953/Statistical-Annex.pdf. Find the World Bank at http://web.worldbank.org.

84 percent of the world's population in 2009 but produce only 27 percent of the output. Compared to industrial market countries, developing countries usually have higher rates of illiteracy, higher unemployment, faster population growth, and exports consisting mostly of agricultural products and raw materials.

On average, about half of the labor force in developing countries works in agriculture versus only about 3 percent in industrial market countries. Because farming methods are relatively primitive in developing countries, farm productivity is low and some households barely subsist. Industrial market countries or *developed countries* are primarily the economically advanced capitalist countries of Western Europe, North America, Australia, New Zealand, and Japan. They were the first to experience long-term economic growth during the 19th century.

Exhibit 2 presents income per capita in 2009 for a sample of high-, middle-, and low-income economies. Because most countries in the sample have large populations, together they account for 56 percent of the world population. Countries are listed from top to bottom in descending order based on income per capita. Again, figures have been adjusted to reflect the actual purchasing power of the local currency in its respective economy. The bars in the chart are color-coded, with high-income economies in blue, middle-income economies in orange, and low-income economies in red. Per capita income in the United States, the exhibit's top-ranked country, was seven times that of China, a middle-income economy. But per capita in China, in turn, was

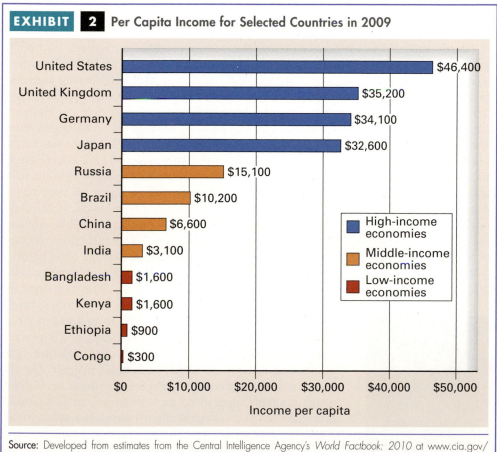

EXHIBIT 2 Per Capita Income for Selected Countries in 2009

Source: Developed from estimates from the Central Intelligence Agency's *World Factbook: 2010* at www.cia.gov/library/publications/the-world-factbook/index.html. Figures are based on the purchasing power of each country's currency.

about seven times that of Ethiopia and 22 times that of the Democratic Republic of the Congo, both, poor African nations. Residents of China likely feel poor relative to America, but they appear well off compared to the poorest nations. U.S per capita income was 51 times that of Ethiopia, and 155 times that of the Congo, one of the poorest nations on Earth. Thus, there is a tremendous range of per capita income around the world.

Exhibit 2 looks at income per capita, but neither income nor population is always measured accurately, especially in the poorest countries. Some economists have looked for simpler ways of measuring an economy, as discussed in the following case study.

CASE STUDY

e activity

To see city lights displayed across the earth, go to DaylightMap at http://www .daylightmap.com/?night=1.

THE INFORMATION ECONOMY

Night Lights and Income   GDP and economic growth are measured poorly for many developing economies. J. Vernon Henderson and two colleagues from Brown University have proposed a different measure of economic activity that does not rely on any of the usual statistics, such as employment, income, or output. Their approach uses photos taken at night from outer space to measure the density of light on the ground. Consumption of most goods and services in the evening requires light. As personal income rises, so does consumption and night lights. Using U.S. Air Force weather satellite photos, the researchers observe changes in a region's light density over a 10-year period. They use this change in light to supplement existing income growth measures.

For example, the trio examine the differential effects of the economic transition on income and light in former Soviet republics versus neighboring Eastern Europe. In particular, they compare the former Soviet republics of Moldova and Ukraine, where per capita income fell in the wake of the USSR's breakup, with neighboring Hungary, Poland, and Romania, countries that experienced a much smoother and more successful transition from central planning. The two photos below show night lights in Hungary, Poland, and Romania in the left portion of each photo and Moldova and Ukraine in the right portion of each photo. The photo on the left was taken in 1992 and the one on the right in 2002. The photos show that the more brightly lit areas in 2002 are in the Eastern European countries (the left half portion of the right-hand photo), where light intensity increases from 1992 to 2002. Also noticeable is the dimming of lights for their neighbors on the right of the photo, who were formerly part of the Soviet Union. In Moldova and in Ukraine, income per capita fell by an average of 33 percent, and light intensity dropped by an average of 57 percent. In Hungary, Poland, and Romania, where income per capita rose by an average of 40 percent, light intensity rose an average of 64 percent.

When the researchers use their approach on countries with especially low-quality national income data, the night-light measure sometimes differs from the standard measure of income. For example, in the Congo, night lights suggest a 27 percent rise in GDP from 1992 to 2002, but official estimates of income indicate a 23 percent drop over the same time period. Thus, the Congo seems to be growing faster than official estimates suggest. On the other hand, although official data for Myanmar are limited, what's available suggests an income growth of 128 percent during the ten years, but the night-light data imply growth of only 40 percent.

The night-light approach is most valuable where the quality of other data are poor, such as in many African

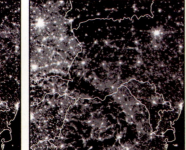

NOAA and USAF Weather Agency

economies, or when data are simply not available, such as for Somalia, Liberia, and North Korea. The three economists don't expect their night-light measure to replace official estimates of income and growth, but, rather, to complement these data, especially where statistics are of poor quality or nonexistent.

Sources: J. Vernon Henderson, Adam Storeygard, and David Weil, "Measuring Economic Growth from Outer Space," NBER Working Paper, (July 2009).

NOAA, National Geophysical Data Center, Data 1992 F-10 and 2002 F-15, http://www.ngdc.noaa.gov/dmsp/downloadV4composites.html#AXP

Health and Nutrition

Differences in stages of development among countries are reflected in a number of ways besides per capita income. For example, many people in developing countries suffer from poor health as a result of malnutrition and disease. AIDS is devastating some developing countries, particularly those in sub-Saharan Africa. In 2007, about 150 of every 1,000 people ages 15 to 49 in South Africa, Zambia, and Zimbabwe had HIV, compared to only 3 of every 1,000 among those in high-income economies. In sub-Saharan Africa, life expectancy at birth averaged 52 years versus 80 years in high-income economies, 69 years in middle-income economies, and 59 years in all low-income economies.

Malnutrition

Those in the poorest countries consume only half the calories of those in high-income countries. Even if an infant survives the first year, malnutrition can turn normal childhood diseases, such as measles, into life-threatening events. The World Health Organization cites malnutrition as the biggest single threat to the world's public health. Malnutrition is a primary or contributing factor in more than half of the deaths of children under the age of 5 in low-income countries. Diseases that are well controlled in the industrial countries—malaria, whooping cough, polio, dysentery, typhoid, and cholera—can become epidemics in poor countries. Many of these diseases are water borne, as safe drinking water is often hard to find. In low-income countries, about 28 percent of children under the age of 5 suffered from malnutrition in 2007. Among middle-income countries the figure was 23 percent. Among high-income countries, it was 3 percent.

Infant Mortality

Health differences among countries are reflected in child mortality. Child mortality rates are much greater in low-income countries than in high-income countries. As of 2007, the mortality rate for children up to 5 years of age was 7 per 1,000 live births in high-income economies, 58 in middle-income economies, and 120 in low-income economies. Rates for our representative sample of high-, medium-, and low-income economies appear in Exhibit 3. Again, high-income economies appear as blue bars, middle-income as orange bars, and low-income as red bars. Among the dozen countries shown, child mortality was highest in the sub-Saharan African nations of Congo, Ethiopia, and Kenya. Child mortality among all 48 sub-Saharan African countries averaged 21 times that in high-income countries.

High Birth Rates

Developing countries are identified not only by their low-incomes and high mortality rates but also by their high birth rates. This year, more than 80 million of the 90 million people added to the world's population will be born in developing countries. In fact,

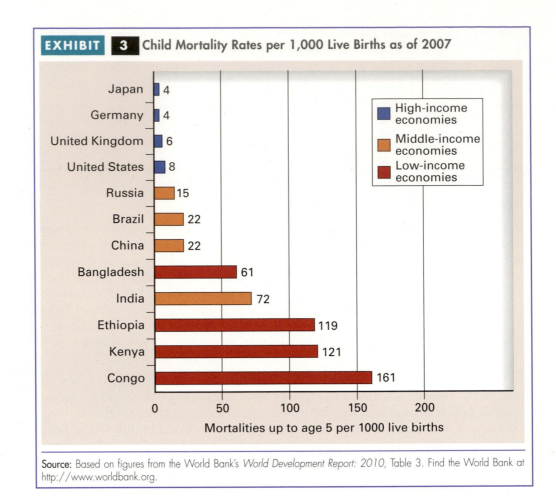

EXHIBIT **3** Child Mortality Rates per 1,000 Live Births as of 2007

Legend:
- High-income economies
- Middle-income economies
- Low-income economies

Japan	4
Germany	4
United Kingdom	6
United States	8
Russia	15
Brazil	22
China	22
Bangladesh	61
India	72
Ethiopia	119
Kenya	121
Congo	161

Mortalities up to age 5 per 1000 live births

Source: Based on figures from the World Bank's *World Development Report: 2010*, Table 3. Find the World Bank at http://www.worldbank.org.

the birth rate is one of the clearest ways of distinguishing between industrial and developing countries. Very few low-income economies have a fertility rate below 2.2 births per woman, but none of the industrial market economies has a fertility rate above that level.

Exhibit 4 presents total fertility rates per woman for selected countries as of 2010. Ethiopia and the Congo, the two poorest nations on the list, each has among the world's highest fertility rates at 6.1. This means each woman on average gives birth to 6.1 children during her lifetime. Note that the four low-income economies, shown as red bars, have the highest fertility rates. Historically, families tend to be larger in poor countries because children are viewed as a source of farm labor and as economic and social security as the parents age. Most developing countries have no pension or social security system for the aged. The higher child mortality rates in poorer countries also engender higher birth rates, as parents strive to ensure a sufficiently large family.

Sub-Saharan African nations are the poorest in the world and have the fastest-growing populations. Because of high fertility rates in the poorest countries, children under 15 years old make up 43 percent of the population there. In high-income countries, children make up only 18 percent of the population. Italy, a high-income economy, became the first country in history with more people over the age of 65 than under the age of 15. Germany, Greece, Spain, Portugal, Japan, Hungary, Switzerland, and

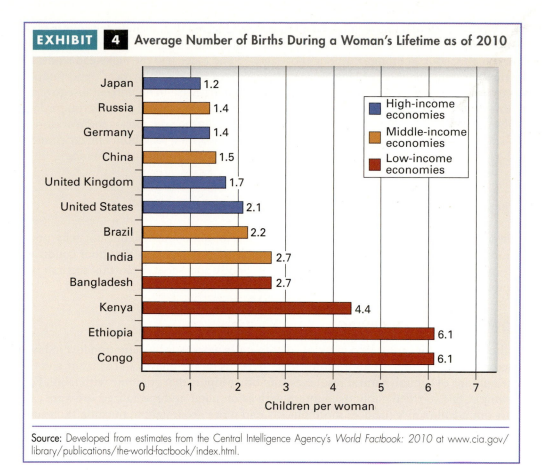

EXHIBIT 4 Average Number of Births During a Woman's Lifetime as of 2010

Japan — 1.2
Russia — 1.4
Germany — 1.4
China — 1.5
United Kingdom — 1.7
United States — 2.1
Brazil — 2.2
India — 2.7
Bangladesh — 2.7
Kenya — 4.4
Ethiopia — 6.1
Congo — 6.1

Legend:
- High-income economies
- Middle-income economies
- Low-income economies

X-axis: Children per woman (0 to 7)

Source: Developed from estimates from the Central Intelligence Agency's *World Factbook: 2010* at www.cia.gov/library/publications/the-world-factbook/index.html.

the United Kingdom have since followed. An aging population poses fiscal problems, because these same countries typically offer generous health and pension benefits to the elderly.

In some developing countries, the population growth rate has exceeded the growth rate in total production, so the standard of living as measured by per capita output has declined. Still, even in the poorest of countries, attitudes about family size are changing. According to the United Nations, the birth rate during a typical woman's lifetime in a developing country has fallen from six children in 1965 to under three children today. Evidence from developing countries more generally indicates that when women have employment opportunities outside the home, fertility rates decline. And as women become better educated, they earn more and tend to have fewer children.

Women in Developing Countries

Throughout the world, the poverty rate is higher for women than men, particularly women who head households. The percentage of households headed by women varies from country to country, but nears 50 percent in some areas of Africa and the Caribbean. Because women often must work in the home as well as in the labor market, poverty can impose a special hardship on them. In many cultures, women's responsibilities include gathering firewood and carrying water, tasks that are especially burdensome if firewood is scarce and water is far from home.

Women in developing countries tend to be less educated than men. In the countries of sub-Saharan Africa and South Asia, for example, only half as many women as men complete high school. In Ethiopia, among those ages 15 and older, half the males can read and write, but only one third of females can. Women have fewer employment opportunities and earn lower wages than men do. For example, Sudan's Muslim fundamentalist government bans women from working in public places after 5:00 P.M. In Algeria, Egypt, Jordan, Libya, and Saudi Arabia, women account for only about one-quarter of the workforce. Women are often on the fringes of the labor market, working long hours in agriculture. They also have less access to other resources, such as land, capital, and technology.

Productivity: Key to Development

We have examined some signs of poverty in developing countries, but not why poor countries are poor. At the risk of appearing simplistic, we might say that poor countries are poor because they do not produce many goods and services. In this section, we examine why some developing countries experience such low productivity.

Low Labor Productivity

Labor productivity, measured in terms of output per worker, is by definition low in low-income countries. Why? Labor productivity depends on the quality of the labor and on the amount of capital, natural resources, and other inputs that combine with labor. For example, one certified public accountant with a computer and specialized software can sort out a company's finances more quickly and more accurately than can a thousand high school–educated file clerks with pencils and paper.

One way a nation raises its productivity is by investing more in human and physical capital. This investment must be financed by either domestic savings or foreign funds. Income per capita in the poorest countries is often too low to support much investment. In poor countries with unstable governments, the wealthy minority frequently invests in more stable foreign economies. This leaves less to invest domestically in either human or physical capital; without sufficient capital, workers remain less productive.

Technology and Education

What exactly is the contribution of education to the process of economic development? Education helps people make better use of resources. If knowledge is lacking, other resources may not be used efficiently. For example, a country may be endowed with fertile land, but farmers may lack knowledge of irrigation and fertilization techniques. Or farmers may not know how to rotate crops to avoid soil depletion. In low-income countries, 36 percent of those 15 and older were illiterate in 2007, compared to 17 percent in middle-income countries, and only 1 percent in high-income countries. Many in developing countries drop out of school because the family can't afford it or would rather put the child to work. Child labor in developing countries obviously limits educational opportunities.

Education also makes people more receptive to new ideas and methods. Countries with the most advanced educational systems were also the first to develop. In the 20th century, the leader in schooling and economic development was the United States. In Latin America, Argentina was the most educationally advanced nation 100 years ago, and it is one of the most developed Latin American nations today. The growth of education in Japan during the 19th century contributed to a ready acceptance of technology and thus to Japan's remarkable economic growth in the 20th century.

Inefficient Use of Labor

Another feature of developing countries is that they use labor less efficiently than do industrial nations. Unemployment and underemployment reflect inefficient uses of labor. *Underemployment* occurs when skilled workers are employed in low-skill jobs or when people are working less than they would like—a worker seeking full-time employment may find only a part-time job. *Unemployment* occurs when those willing and able to work can't find jobs.

Unemployment is measured primarily in urban areas, because in rural areas farm work is usually an outlet for labor even if many workers are underemployed there. The unemployment rate in developing nations on average is about 10 percent to 15 percent of the urban labor force. Unemployment among young workers—those aged 15 to 24—is typically twice that of older workers. In developing nations, about 30 percent of the combined urban and rural workforce is either unemployed or underemployed. In Zimbabwe, the unemployment rate was 95 percent in 2010; it's no surprise why Zimbabwe is the poorest nation in the world—even poorer than the Congo.

In some developing countries, the average farm is as small as two acres. Productivity is also low because few other inputs, such as capital and fertilizer, are used. *Although more than half the labor force in developing countries works in agriculture, only about one-third of output in these countries stems from agriculture.* In the United States, where farmers account for only 2 percent of the labor force, a farmer with modern equipment can farm hundreds or even thousands of acres (the average U.S. farm is about 500 acres). In developing countries, a farmer with a hand plow or an ox-drawn plow can farm maybe 10 to 20 acres. U.S. farmers, though only one-fiftieth of the labor force, grow enough to feed a nation and to lead the world in farm exports. The average value added per U.S. farm worker is about 75 times that of farm workers in low- and middle-income countries.

Low productivity obviously results in low income, but low income can, in turn, affect worker productivity. Low income means less saving and less saving means less investment in human and physical capital. Low income can also mean poor nutrition during the formative years, which can retard mental and physical development. These difficult beginnings may be aggravated by poor diet and insufficient health care in later life, making workers poorly suited for regular employment. Poverty can result in less saving, less education, less capital formation, a poor diet, and little health care—all of which can reduce a worker's productivity. Thus, *low income and low productivity may reinforce each other in a cycle of poverty.*

Natural Resources

Some countries are rich in natural resources. The difference is most striking when we compare countries with oil reserves and those without. The Middle East countries of Bahrain, Kuwait, Qatar, Saudi Arabia, and the United Arab Emirates are classified as high-income economies because they were lucky enough to be sitting atop huge oil reserves. But oil-rich countries are the exception. Many developing countries, such as Chad and Ethiopia, have little in the way of natural resources. Most developing countries without oil reserves are in trouble whenever oil prices rise. Since oil must be imported, higher oil prices drain oil-poor countries of precious foreign exchange.

Oil-rich countries also show us that an abundant supply of a natural resource is not in itself enough to create a modern industrial economy. On the other hand, Japan has one of the most developed economies in the world, yet has few natural resources. Connecticut is consistently the most productive of the United States measured in per capita income, but the state has little in the way of natural resources (its main natural resource is gravel). In fact, many researchers believe that reliance on resource wealth can be something of a curse for a nation, as you will see in an upcoming case study.

Financial Institutions

Another requirement for development is an adequate and trusted system of financial institutions. An important source of funds for investment is the savings of house-holds and firms. People in some developing countries have little confidence in their currency because some governments finance a large fraction of public outlays by printing money. This practice results in high inflation and sometimes very high infla-tion, or hyperinflation, as has occurred recently in Zimbabwe, where annual inflation was just about incalculable. High and unpredictable inflation discourages saving and hurts development.

Developing countries have special problems because banks are often viewed with suspicion. At the first sign of economic problems, many depositors withdraw their funds. Because banks cannot rely on a continuous supply of deposits, they cannot make loans for extended periods. If financial institutions fail to serve as intermediar-ies between savers and borrowers, the lack of funds for investment becomes an ob-stacle to growth. During the global financial crisis of 2008, banks in industrial market countries also suffered from depositors' sagging confidence. One measure of banking presence is the credit provided by banks as a percent of that nation's total output. This percentage is more than five times greater in high-income countries than in low-income countries.

Capital Infrastructure

Production and exchange depend on a reliable infrastructure of transportation, com-munication, sanitation, and electricity. Roads, bridges, airports, harbors, and other transportation facilities are vital to commercial activity. Reliable mail service, tele-phone communications, Internet connections, clean water, and electricity are also essential for advanced production techniques. Imagine how difficult it would be to run even a personal computer if the supply of electricity and access to the Internet were unavailable or continually interrupted, as is often the case in many developing countries.

Some developing countries have serious deficiencies in their physical infrastructures. As just one measure, Exhibit 5 shows the number of fixed and mobile telephone lines per 1,000 people in 2009 for the 12 countries examined earlier. The high-income economies have about 7 times more phones per 1,000 people than the bottom four countries, which are low-income economies. Germany, the top rated in this category, had 1,929 phone lines per 1,000 people. Bottom-ranked Ethiopia had just 46 phone lines per 1,000 people. Still, more than half the world's population had cell phones in 2009.[1]

Phone lines help knit together an economy's communications network. Countries without reliable phone service have difficulty not only communicating but reaping the benefits of other technology advances, such as the Internet. Exhibit 6 shows Internet users as a percent of the population in 2008 for our sample countries. There is an unmistakable digital divide between high-income and low-income economies. In the four high-income economies, an average 75 percent of the population used the Internet. In low-income economies, just 2 percent used the Internet on average. Even in India, which has a reputa-tion as computer savvy, what with all the online support centers and software companies we read about, only 7 percent of the population were Internet users.

1.   "Father of the Cell Phone," *The Economist*, 6 June 2009.

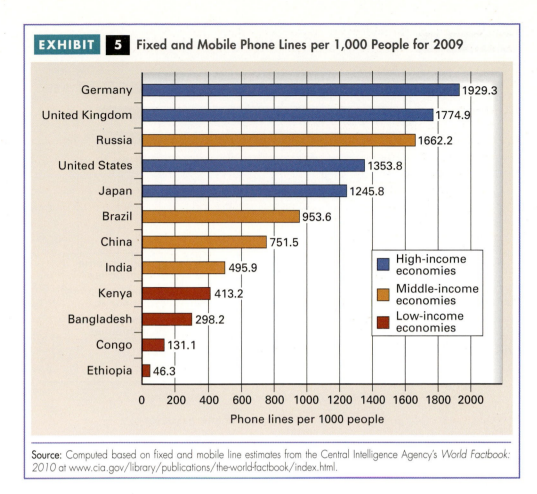

EXHIBIT 5 Fixed and Mobile Phone Lines per 1,000 People for 2009

Country	Phone lines per 1000 people
Germany	1929.3
United Kingdom	1774.9
Russia	1662.2
United States	1353.8
Japan	1245.8
Brazil	953.6
China	751.5
India	495.9
Kenya	413.2
Bangladesh	298.2
Congo	131.1
Ethiopia	46.3

- High-income economies
- Middle-income economies
- Low-income economies

Source: Computed based on fixed and mobile line estimates from the Central Intelligence Agency's *World Factbook: 2010* at www.cia.gov/library/publications/the-world-factbook/index.html.

Entrepreneurship

An economy can have abundant supplies of labor, capital, and natural resources, but without entrepreneurship, the other resources will not be combined efficiently to produce goods and services. Unless a country has entrepreneurs who are able to bring together resources and take the risk of profit or loss, development may never get off the ground. Many developing countries were once under colonial rule, a system of government that offered the local population fewer opportunities to develop entrepreneurial skills.

One source of entrepreneurial experience for developing countries comes from McDonald's and other international franchises. For example, by providing management training, McDonald's stimulates entrepreneurship directly through its franchises and indirectly by showing competitors how a business is run. Such franchises also demonstrate to customers what they should come to expect in the way of service, cleanliness, quality, and the like.[2]

Government officials sometimes decide that entrepreneurs are unable to generate the kind of economic growth the country needs. State enterprises are therefore created

---

2. Adrian Tschoegli, "McDonald's—Much Maligned, But an Engine of Economic Development," *Global Economy Journal, 7*(Issue 4 2007) at http://www.bepress.com/gej/vol7/iss4/5/.

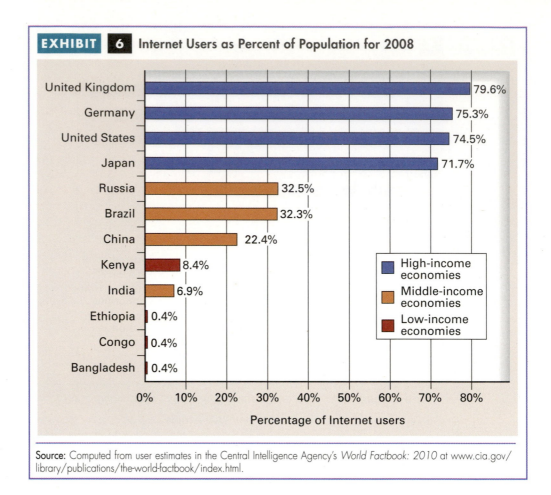

EXHIBIT 6 Internet Users as Percent of Population for 2008

- United Kingdom 79.6%
- Germany 75.3%
- United States 74.5%
- Japan 71.7%
- Russia 32.5%
- Brazil 32.3%
- China 22.4%
- Kenya 8.4%
- India 6.9%
- Ethiopia 0.4%
- Congo 0.4%
- Bangladesh 0.4%

Legend:
- High-income economies
- Middle-income economies
- Low-income economies

x-axis: 0% 10% 20% 30% 40% 50% 60% 70% 80%
Percentage of Internet users

Source: Computed from user estimates in the Central Intelligence Agency's *World Factbook: 2010* at www.cia.gov/library/publications/the-world-factbook/index.html.

to do what government believes the free market cannot do. But state-owned enterprises may have objectives other than producing goods efficiently—objectives that could include providing jobs for friends and relatives of government officials.

Rules of the Game

Finally, in addition to human capital, natural resources, financial institutions, capital infrastructure, and entrepreneurship, a successful economy needs reliable *rules of the game*. Perhaps the most elusive ingredients for development are the formal and informal institutions that promote production and exchange: the laws, customs, conventions, and other institutional elements that sustain an economy. A stable political environment with well-defined property rights is important. Little private-sector investment will occur if potential investors believe their capital might be appropriated by government, destroyed by civil unrest, blown up by terrorists, or stolen by thieves.

Under capitalism, the rules of the game include private ownership of most resources and the coordination of economic activity by the price signals generated by market forces. Market coordination answers the questions of what to produce, how to produce it, and for whom to produce it. Under socialism, the rules of the game include government ownership of most resources and the allocation of resources through central plans. For example, countries such as Cuba and North Korea carefully limit the private ownership of resources like land and capital. More generally, personal freedom is limited in centrally planned economies (for example, in North Korea, people need a government permit just to travel outside their own town).[3]

Although there is no universally accepted theory of economic development, around the world markets have been replacing central plans in many once-socialist countries. **Privatization** is the process of turning government enterprises into private enterprises in these transitional economies. Privatization is the opposite of *nationalization* (what Hugo Chávez has been doing in Venezuela). For example, Russian privatization began in 1992 with the sale of municipally owned shops. Exhibit 7 presents, for 10 transitional economies, the gross domestic product (GDP) per capita in 2009 based on the purchasing power of the domestic currency. Notice the dramatic differences across these economies, with GDP per capita in the Czech Republic nearly nine times greater than that in Vietnam. Russia's GDP per capita was midway between those two. The Czech Republic and Hungary, identified with blue bars, have joined the ranks of high-income economies. Seven of the 10 countries are middle-income economies, and are identified with orange bars. Vietnam, the red bar, is a low-income economy that still reflects vestiges of central planning. For example, banks there are more likely to lend to businesses that are politically connected than to those that are the most profitable. Thus, the most profitable Vietnamese firms tend to avoid banks and rely instead on reinvested earnings and informal loans.[4]

privatization
The process of turning government enterprises into private enterprises

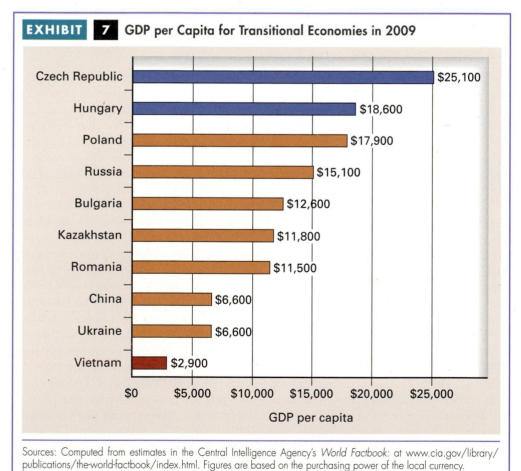

EXHIBIT 7 GDP per Capita for Transitional Economies in 2009

Sources: Computed from estimates in the Central Intelligence Agency's *World Factbook:* at www.cia.gov/library/publications/the-world-factbook/index.html. Figures are based on the purchasing power of the local currency.

3. Peter Wonacott, "The Mystery of North Korean Fans," *Wall Street Journal,* 26 June 2010.
4. Edmund J. Malesky and Markus Taussig, "Where Is Credit Due? Legal Institutions, Connections, and the Efficiency of Bank Lending in Vietnam," *Journal of Law, Economics, and Organization,* 25 (October 2009): 525–578.

High-income economies have developed a reliable and respected system of property rights and customs and conventions that nurture productive activity. These successful economies have also cultivated the social capital that helps the economy run more smoothly. **Social capital** consists of the shared values and trust that promotes cooperation in the economy. At the national level, social capital could be reflected in a sense of common purpose. For example, despite the troubling recession, polls show that Americans remain among the most patriotic people in the world. In a 2010 survey, 83 percent said they were "extremely" or "very" proud to be Americans.[5] At the local level, social capital could be expressed by a neighborhood crime watch, and there is evidence that such efforts help reduce property crime.[6] Low-income economies typically have poorly defined property rights, less social capital, and in the extreme, customs and conventions where bribery is commonplace and government corruption is an everyday practice. Worse still, civil wars have ravaged some of the poorest countries on Earth. Such violence and uncertainty make people less willing to invest in their own future or in the future of their country.

Although it is common to sort countries into advanced industrial economies and developing economies, there are broad differences among developing economies, as discussed in the following case study, which looks at the billion people living in the poorest economies.

CASE STUDY

BRINGING THEORY TO LIFE

The Poorest Billion   Not long ago, the world was one-sixth rich and five-sixths poor. Now, thanks to impressive growth in places like China, the world is more like one-sixth rich, two-thirds not rich but improving, and one-sixth poor and going nowhere. Most developing economies are experiencing a rising standard of living. But that still leaves about a billion people trapped in economies that are not only extremely poor, but stagnant or getting worse. All told, about 45 countries fit into this poorest-billion category, including 30 countries in sub-Saharan Africa plus the likes of Cambodia, Haiti, Laos, Myanmar, North Korea, and Yemen.

Economist Paul Collier, of Oxford University in England, has examined what went wrong with these "trapped countries." Based on decades of research, he identifies some poverty traps. About 750 million people of the bottom billion have recently lived through, or are still in the midst of, a civil war. Such wars can drag on for years with economically disastrous consequences. For example, the ethnic conflict in Burundi between the Hutus and the Tutsis has lasted three decades, which helps explain why that country is among the poorest in the world. And war in the Congo over the last dozen years has killed more than five million people. Unfortunately, the poorer a country becomes, the more likely it is to succumb to civil war. And once a country goes through one civil war, more are likely. Ethnic conflict, or *civil war*, is Collier's first poverty trap.

But why, aside from poverty itself, are so many sub-Saharan countries mired in civil war? He finds that three factors heighten the risk of such conflicts: (1) a relatively high proportion of young, uneducated men with few job prospects (who, thus, have a low opportunity cost); (2) an imbalance between ethnic groups, with one tending to outnumber the rest; and (3) a supply of natural resources like diamonds or oil, which both creates an incentive to rebel and helps finance that rebellion. The presence of

---

5.   Lexington, "Where Has All the Greatness Gone," *The Economist,* 17 July 2010.
6.   Paolo Buonanno, "Does Social Capital Reduce Crime," *Journal of Law and Economics,* 52 (February 2009): 145–170.

mineral wealth in an otherwise poor country can also undermine democracy itself. Government revenue from mineral sales reduces taxes, which dampens public debate about how taxes should be spent. For example, because of oil revenue, the Nigerian government relies less on taxes, so there is less pressure for government accountability, and hence fewer checks and balances on a corrupt government. Thus, *misuse of natural resource wealth* is Collier's second poverty trap. About 300 million of the poorest billion live in countries that have fallen into this trap.

This leads us to the third poverty trap: *a dysfunctional or corrupt government.* Government officials who pursue self-glorification and self-enrichment do serious harm to the economy. Much of the public budget disappears through wasteful programs rife with graft and payoffs. For example, a recent survey that tracked government funds for rural health clinics in Chad found that less than 1 percent of the money reached the clinics. About 750 million of the poorest billion live in countries that pursue disastrous economic policies or where government corruption harms the economy.

Can these poorest billion be helped? It will take more than band concerts. Collier doubts that unconditional foreign aid makes much of a difference. He points to the ill effects of oil as an unconditional source of government revenue. International trade may help, but because these countries have difficulty competing with the likes of China or Vietnam, they may need special trade advantages. Another way the rest of the world could help is by requiring Western banks to report deposits by corrupt officials. The rest of the world could also assist these poor countries develop laws and regulations to ensure the transparent management of natural resources, to help detect fiscal fraud, and to promote a free press. But even with all that, what these countries need most, Collier argues, is about 10 years of domestic peace—backed by an outside force if necessary, such as the UN. All that is a tall order, but the stakes are high for the billion people trapped and going nowhere in these poor nations.

Sources: Paul Collier, *The Bottom Billion: Why the Poorest Countries Are Failing and What Can Be Done About It,* (Oxford University Press, 2007); and Paul Collier, *The Plundered Planet,* (Oxford University Press, 2010).

Income Distribution Within Countries

Thus far the focus has been on income differences across countries, and these differences can be vast. But what about income differences within a country? Are poor countries uniformly poor or are there sizable income differences among that nation's population? One way to measure inequality across households is to look at the share of national income going to the poorest fifth of the population. As a point of reference, in the unlikely event that income in an economy were evenly distributed across all households, then the poorest fifth would also receive exactly one fifth, or 20 percent, of national income. More realistically, the poorest fifth receives less than 20 percent of the income, but how much less? Is the percentage of income going to the poorest fifth higher for low-income countries than for high-income countries? In other words, is income more evenly distributed among poor countries than among rich countries? Not necessarily. Among our 12 nations, the poorest fifth of the population got an average of 7.7 percent of the income in the high-income countries, 5.8 percent in middle-income countries, and 7.2 percent in low-income countries. So, at least in this sample, income was less evenly distributed among middle-income countries than in high- or low-income countries.

International Trade and Development

Developing countries need to trade with developed countries to acquire the capital and technology that will increase labor productivity on the farm, in the factory, in the office, and in the home. To import capital and technology, developing countries must first acquire the funds, or foreign exchange, needed to pay for imports. Exports usually generate more than half of the annual flow of foreign exchange in developing countries. Foreign aid and private investment make up the rest.

Trade Problems for Developing Countries

Primary products, such as agricultural goods and other raw materials, make up the bulk of exports from developing countries, just as manufactured goods make up the bulk of exports from industrial countries. About half the merchandise exports from low-income countries consist of raw materials, compared to only 20 percent among high-income countries. A problem for developing countries is that the prices of primary products, such as coffee, cocoa, sugar, and rubber, fluctuate more widely than do the prices of finished goods, because crop supplies fluctuate with the weather.

When developing countries experience trade deficits, they often try to restrict imports. Because imported food is critical to survival, developing countries are more likely to cut imports of capital goods—the very items needed to promote long-term growth and productivity. Thus, many developing countries cannot afford the modern machinery that will help them become more productive. Developing countries must also confront industrial countries' trade restrictions, such as tariffs and quotas, which often discriminate against primary products. For example, the United States strictly limits sugar imports and has done so for more than half a century. Such restrictions are one reason the Doha Round of trade agreements has not gone smoothly.

Migration and the Brain Drain

Migration plays an important role in the economies of developing countries. A major source of foreign exchange in some countries is the money sent home by migrants who find jobs in industrial countries. According to the World Bank, migrants sent home about $450 billion in 2008. Thus migration provides a valuable safety valve for poor countries. But there is a downside. Often the best and the brightest professionals, such as doctors, nurses, and engineers, migrate to developed countries. For example, every year thousands of nurses migrate from countries such as Kenya and the Philippines to the United States, where half the world's nurses are employed. The financial attraction is powerful: A nurse in the Philippines would start there at less than $6,000 a year, compared with at least $36,000 in the United States.

The Philippines economy benefits from the billions sent home by overseas workers. So the upside of the brain drain for the poor country is the money sent home by overseas workers. Still, a nation is hurt when its best and brightest leave for opportunities elsewhere. Some African countries are demanding compensation for educating the doctors and nurses who move to high-income economies.

Import Substitution Versus Export Promotion

An economy's progress usually involves moving up the production chain from agriculture and raw material to manufacturing then to services. If a country is fortunate, this transformation occurs gradually through natural market forces. For example, in 1850 most U.S. jobs were in agriculture. Now most jobs are in the service sector.

Sometimes governments try to speed up the evolution. Many developing countries, including Argentina and India, pursued a strategy called **import substitution**, whereby domestic manufacturers would make products that until then had been imported. To insulate domestic manufacturers from foreign competition, the government imposed stiff tariffs and quotas. This development strategy became popular for several reasons. First, demand already existed for these products, so the "what to produce" question was easily answered. Second, import substitution provided infant industries a protected market. Finally, import substitution was popular with those who supplied resources to the favored domestic industries.

Like all trade protection, however, import substitution erased the gains from specialization and comparative advantage among countries. Often the developing country replaced low-cost foreign goods with high-cost domestic versions of those same goods. And domestic producers, shielded from foreign competition, usually failed to become efficient. Worse still, other countries often retaliated with their own trade restrictions.

Critics of import substitution claim that export promotion is a surer path to economic development. **Export promotion** concentrates on producing for the export market. This development strategy begins with relatively simple products, such as textiles. As a developing country builds its technological and educational base—that is, as the developing economy learns by doing—producers can then make more complex products for export. Economists favor export promotion over import substitution because the emphasis is on comparative advantage and trade expansion rather than on trade restriction. Export promotion also forces producers to grow more efficient in order to compete on world markets. Research shows that facing global competition boosts domestic efficiency.[7] What's more, export promotion requires less government intervention in the market than does import substitution.

Of the two approaches, export promotion has been more successful around the world. For example, the newly industrialized countries of East Asia have successfully pursued export promotion, while Argentina, India, and Peru have failed with their import-substitution approach. In 1965, the newly industrialized economies of Hong Kong, South Korea, Singapore, and Taiwan had an average income only 20 percent that of high-income countries. Now these four are themselves high-income countries. Most Latin American nations, which for decades had favored import substitution, are now pursuing free trade agreements with each other and with the United States. Even India is dismantling trade barriers, with an emphasis on importing high-technology capital goods. One slogan of Indian trade officials is "Microchips, yes! Potato chips, no!"

Trade Liberalization and Special Interests

Although most people would benefit from freer international trade, some would be worse off. Consequently, governments in developing countries often have difficulty pursuing policies conducive to development. Often the gains from economic development are widespread, but the beneficiaries, such as consumers, do not recognize their potential gains. On the other hand, the losers tend to be concentrated, such as producers in an industry that had been sheltered from foreign competition, and they know quite well the source of their losses. So the government often lacks the political will and support to remove impediments to development, because the potential losers fight reforms that might harm their livelihood while the potential winners remain largely unaware of

import substitution
A development strategy that emphasizes domestic manufacturing of products that were imported

export promotion
A development strategy that concentrates on producing for the export market

---

7. See Martin Baily and Hans Gersbach, "Efficiency in Manufacturing and the Need for Global Competition," in *Brookings Papers on Economic Activity: Microeconomics*, M. Baily, P. Reiss, and C. Winston, eds. (Washington, D.C.: Brookings Institution, 1995): 307–347.

what's at stake. What's more, consumers have difficulty organizing even if they become aware of what's going on. A recent study by the World Bank suggests a strong link in Africa between governments that cater to special-interest groups and low rates of economic growth.

Nonetheless, many developing countries have been opening their borders to freer trade. People around the world have been exposed to information about the opportunities and products available on world markets. So consumers want the goods and firms want the technology and capital that are available abroad. Both groups want government to ease trade restrictions. Studies by the World Bank and others have underscored the successes of countries that have adopted trade liberalization policies.

Foreign Aid and Economic Development

We have already seen that because poor countries do not generate enough savings to fund an adequate level of investment, these countries often rely on foreign financing. Private international borrowing and lending are heavily restricted by the governments of developing countries. Governments may allow residents to purchase foreign exchange only for certain purposes. In some developing countries, different exchange rates apply to different categories of transactions. Thus, the local currency is not easily convertible into other currencies. Some developing countries also require foreign investors to find a local partner who must be granted controlling interest. All these restrictions discourage foreign investment. In this section, we will look primarily at foreign aid and its link to economic development.

Foreign Aid

foreign aid

An international transfer made on especially favorable terms for the purpose of promoting economic development

Foreign aid is any international transfer made on *concessional* (that is, especially favorable) terms for the purposes of promoting economic development. Foreign aid includes grants, which need not be repaid, and loans extended on more favorable repayment terms than the recipient could normally secure. Concessional loans have lower interest rates, longer repayment periods, or grace periods during which repayments are reduced or even waived (similar to some student loans). Foreign aid can take the form of money, capital goods, technical assistance, food, and so forth.

Some foreign aid is granted by a specific country, such as the United States, to another specific country, such as the Philippines. Country-to-country aid is called *bilateral* assistance. Other foreign aid goes through international bodies such as the World Bank. Assistance provided by organizations that use funds from a number of countries is called *multilateral*. For example, the World Bank provides loans and grants to support activities that are viewed as prerequisites for development, such as health and education programs or basic development projects like dams, roads, and communications networks. And the International Monetary Fund extends loans to countries that have trouble with their balance of payments.

During the last four decades, the United States has provided the developing world with over $400 billion in aid. Since 1961, most U.S. aid has been coordinated by the U.S. Agency for International Development (USAID), which is part of the U.S. Department of State. This agency concentrates primarily on health, education, and agriculture, providing both technical assistance and loans. USAID emphasizes long-range plans to meet the basic needs of the poor and to promote self-sufficiency. Foreign aid is a controversial, though relatively small, part of the federal budget. Since 1993, official U.S. aid has been less than 0.2 percent of U.S. GDP, compared to an average of 0.3 percent from 21 other industrialized nations.

Does Foreign Aid Promote Economic Development?

In general, foreign aid provides additional purchasing power and thus the possibility of increased investment, capital imports, and consumption. But it remains unclear whether foreign aid *supplements* domestic saving, thus increasing investment, or simply *substitutes* for domestic saving, thereby increasing consumption rather than investment. What is clear is that foreign aid often becomes a source of discretionary funds that benefit not the poor but their leaders. Historically, more than 90 percent of the funds distributed by USAID have gone to governments, whose leaders assume responsibility for distributing these funds.

Much bilateral funding is tied to purchases of goods and services from the donor nation, and such programs can sometimes be counterproductive—they have unintended consequences. For example, in the 1950s, the United States began the Food for Peace program, which helped sell U.S. farm products abroad, but some recipient governments turned around and sold that food to finance poorly conceived projects. Worse yet, the availability of low-priced food from abroad drove down farm prices in the developing countries, hurting poor farmers there. The same holds for clothing. Used clothing donated to thrift shops and charitable organizations in industrialized countries typically winds up for sale in Africa, where the low price discourages local production of clothing.[8] Before used clothing swamped the continent, Africa had a textile industry, but no more. Textiles are often the first rung on the ladder to developing a broader manufacturing base.

Foreign aid may have raised the standard of living in some developing countries, but it has not necessarily increased their ability to become self-supporting at that higher standard of living. Many countries that receive aid are doing less of what they had done well. Their agricultural sectors have suffered. For example, though we should be careful when drawing conclusions about causality, per capita food production in Africa has fallen since 1960. Outside aid has often insulated government officials from their own incompetence and from the fundamental troubles of their own economies. No country receiving U.S. aid in the past 25 years has moved up in status from developing to industrial. And most countries today that have achieved industrial status did so without foreign aid. Development success typically takes time and involves gradual movements toward freer markets.

Because of disappointment with the results of government aid, the trend is toward channeling funds through private nonprofit agencies such as CARE. More than half of foreign aid now flows through private channels. The privatization of foreign aid follows a larger trend toward privatization in transitional economies around the world.

Conclusion

Because no single theory of economic development has become widely accepted, this chapter has been more descriptive than theoretical. We can readily identify the features that distinguish developing from industrial economies. Education is key to development, both because of its direct effect on productivity and because those who are more educated tend to be more receptive to new ideas. A physical infrastructure of transportation and communication systems and utilities is needed to link economic participants. And trusted financial institutions help link savers and borrowers. A country needs entrepreneurs with the vision to move the economy forward. Finally, the most elusive

8. Garth Frazer, "Used-Clothing Donations and Apparel Production in Africa," *Economic Journal*, 118 (October 2008): 1764-1784.

ingredients are the laws, manners, customs and ways of doing business that nurture economic development. Economic history is largely a story of economies that have failed to produce a set of economic rules of the game that lead to sustained economic growth. Some transitional economies and some newly emerging industrial countries in Asia show that economic development continues to be achievable.

Summary

1. Developing countries are distinguished by low output per capita, poor health and nutrition, high fertility rates, poor education, and saving rates that are usually too low to finance sufficient investment in human and physical capital.

2. Worker productivity is low in developing countries because the stocks of human and physical capital are low, technological advances are not widely diffused throughout the economy, entrepreneurship is scarce, financial markets are not well developed, some talented professionals migrate to high-income countries, formal and informal institutions do not provide sufficient incentives for market activity, and governments may serve the interests of the group in power rather than the public interest.

3. The key to a rising standard of living is increased productivity. To foster productivity, developing nations must stimulate investment, support education and training programs, provide sufficient infrastructure, and foster supportive rules of the game.

4. Increases in productivity do not occur without prior saving, but low incomes in developing countries offer less opportunity to save. Even if some higher-income people in poor countries have the money to save, financial institutions are not well developed, and savings are often sent abroad, where there is a more stable investment climate.

5. Import substitution is a development strategy that emphasizes domestic production of goods that were imported. Export promotion concentrates on producing for the export market. Over the years, export promotion has been more successful than import substitution because it relies on specialization and comparative advantage.

6. Foreign aid has been a mixed blessing for most developing countries. In some cases, that aid has helped countries build the roads, bridges, schools, and other capital infrastructure necessary for development. In other cases, foreign aid has simply increased consumption and insulated government from painful but necessary reforms. Worse still, subsidized food and used clothing from abroad has undercut domestic production and economic development, particularly in Africa.

Key Concepts

Developing countries   460
Industrial market countries   460
Privatization   471

Social capital   472
Import substitution   475

Export promotion   475
Foreign aid   476

Questions for Review

1. Developing Countries   Why is agricultural productivity in developing countries usually so low?

2. Worlds Apart   Compare developing and industrial market economies on the basis of each of the following general economic characteristics, and relate the differences to the process of development:

   a. Diversity of the industrial base
   b. Child mortality rates
   c. Educational level of the labor force

3. Case Study: Night Lights and Income   Is the relationship between night lights and income an example of the association-is-causation fallacy? Why or why not?

4. Productivity and Development   Among the problems that hinder growth in developing economies are poor infrastructure, lack of financial institutions and a sound money supply, a low saving rate, poor capital base, and lack of foreign exchange. Explain how these problems are interconnected.

5. How does privatization contribute to productivity?

6. Classification of Economies   What are the arguments for using real per capita GNI to compare living standards between countries? What weakness does this measure have?

7. Case Study: The Poorest Billion   What three poverty traps help explain the plight of nations comprising the poorest billion people?

8. FOREIGN AID AND ECONOMIC DEVELOPMENT   Foreign aid, if it is to be successful in enhancing economic development, must lead to a more productive economy. Describe some of the problems in achieving such an objective through foreign aid.

9. INTERNATIONAL TRADE AND DEVELOPMENT   From the perspective of citizens in a developing country, what are some of the benefits and drawbacks of international trade?

10. FOREIGN AID AND ECONOMIC DEVELOPMENT   It is widely recognized that foreign aid that promotes productivity in developing economies is superior to merely shipping products like food to these countries. Yet the latter is the approach frequently taken. Why do you think this is the case?

Problems and Exercises

11. WORLDS APART   GNI per capita income most recently was about 155 times greater in the United States than in the Congo. Suppose GNI per capita grows an average of 3 percent per year in the richer country and 6 percent per year in the poorer country. Assuming such growth rates continue indefinitely into the future, how many years would it take before per capita income in the Congo exceeds that of the United States? (To simplify the math, suppose at the outset per capita income is $155,000 in the richer country and $1,000 in the poorer country.)

12. IMPORT SUBSTITUTION VERSUS EXPORT PROMOTION   Explain why domestic producers who supply a good that competes with imports would prefer an import-substitution approach to trade policy rather than an export-promotion approach. Which policy would domestic consumers prefer and why?

Global Economic Watch Exercises

Login to www.cengagebrain.com and access the Global Economic Watch to do these exercises.

13. GLOBAL ECONOMIC WATCH   Go to the Global Economic Crisis Resource Center. Select Global Issues in Context. In the Basic Search box at the top of the page, enter the phrase "import substitution." On the Results page, go to the News Section. Click on the link for the September 17, 2010, article "Uzbekistan Aims at Import Substitution." What is limiting the success of Uzbekistan's import substitution strategy?

14. GLOBAL ECONOMIC WATCH   Go to the Global Economic Crisis Resource Center. Select Global Issues in Context. Go to the menu at the top of the page and click on the tab for Browse Issues and Topics. Choose Business and Economy. Click on the link for the World Bank. Find one article supporting the work of the World Bank and one article against. Compare and contrast the arguments in the articles.

Glossary

ability-to-pay tax principle Those with a greater ability to pay, such as those earning higher incomes or those owning more property, should pay more taxes

absolute advantage The ability to make something using fewer resources than other producers use

accounting profit A firm's total revenue minus its explicit costs

adverse selection Those on the informed side of the market self-select in a way that harms those on the uninformed side of the market

agent A person or firm who is supposed to act on behalf of the principal

allocative efficiency The condition that exists when firms produce the output most preferred by consumers; marginal benefit equals marginal cost

annuity A given sum of money received each year for a specified number of years

antitrust policy Government regulation aimed at preventing monopoly and fostering competition in markets where competition is desirable

arbitrageur Someone who takes advantage of temporary geographic differences in the exchange rate by simultaneously purchasing a currency in one market and selling it in another market

association-is-causation fallacy The incorrect idea that if two variables are associated in time, one must necessarily cause the other

asymmetric information One side of the market has better information about the product than does the other side

autarky National self-sufficiency; no economic interaction with foreigners

average revenue Total revenue divided by quantity, or AR = TR/q; in all market structures, average revenue equals the market price

average total cost Total cost divided by output, or ATC = TC/q; the sum of average fixed cost and average variable cost, or ATC = AFC + AVC

average variable cost Variable cost divided by output, or AVC = VC/q

backward-bending supply curve of labor As the wage rises, the quantity of labor supplied may eventually decline; the income effect of a higher wage increases the demand for leisure, which reduces the quantity of labor supplied enough to more than offset the substitution effect of a higher wage

balance of payments A record of all economic transactions during a given period between residents of one country and residents of the rest of the world

balance on current account The portion of the balance-of-payments account that measures that country's balance on goods and services, net investment income from abroad, plus net unilateral transfers abroad

balance on goods and services The portion of a country's balance-of-payments account that measures the value of a country's exports of goods and services minus the value of its imports of goods and services

barrier to entry Any impediment that prevents new firms from entering an industry and competing on an equal basis with existing firms

barter The direct exchange of one product for another without using money

behavioral assumption An assumption that describes the expected behavior of economic decision makers, what motivates them

behavioral economics An approach that borrows insights from psychology to help explain economic choices

benefits-received tax principle Those who get more benefits from the government program should pay more taxes

binding arbitration Negotiation in which union and management must accept an impartial observer's resolution of a dispute

bond Certificate reflecting a firm's promise to pay the lender periodic interest and to repay the borrowed sum of money on the designated maturity date

bounded rationality The notion that there is a limit to the information that a firm's manager can comprehend and act on

bureaus Government agencies charged with implementing legislation and financed by appropriations from legislative bodies

capital The buildings, equipment, and human skills used to produce goods and services

capture theory of regulation Producers' political power and strong stake in the regulatory outcome lead them, in effect, to "capture" the regulating agency and prevail on it to serve producer interests

cartel A group of firms that agree to coordinate their production and pricing decisions to reap monopoly profit

circular-flow model A diagram that traces the flow of resources, products, income, and revenue among economic decision makers

Clayton Act of 1914 Beefed up the Sherman Act; outlawed certain anticompetitive practices not prohibited by the Sherman Act, including price discrimination, tying contracts, exclusive dealing, interlocking directorates, and buying the corporate stock of a competitor

Coase theorem As long as bargaining costs are low, an efficient solution to the problem of externalities is achieved by assigning property rights to one party or the other, it doesn't matter which

collateral An asset pledged by the borrower that can be sold to pay off the loan in the event the borrower defaults

collective bargaining The process by which union and management negotiate a labor agreement

collusion An agreement among firms to increase economic profit by dividing the market and fixing the price

command-and-control environmental regulations An approach that required polluters to adopt particular technologies to reduce emissions by specific amounts; inflexible regulations based on engineering standards that ignore each firm's unique ways of reducing pollution

commodity A standardized product, a product that does not differ across producers, such as bushels of wheat or an ounce of gold

common-pool problem Unrestricted access to a renewable resource results in overuse

comparative advantage The ability to make something at a lower opportunity cost than other producers face

competing-interest legislation Legislation that confers concentrated benefits on one group by imposing concentrated costs on another group

complements Goods, such as milk and cookies, that relate in such a way that an increase in the price of one shifts the demand for the other leftward

conglomerate merger A merger of firms in different industries

consent decree The accused party, without admitting guilt, agrees not to do whatever it was charged with if the government drops the charges

constant long-run average cost A cost that occurs when, over some range of output, long-run average cost neither increases nor decreases with changes in firm size

constant-cost industry An industry that can expand or contract without affecting the long-run per-unit cost of production; the long-run industry supply curve is horizontal

constant-elasticity demand curve The type of demand that exists when price elasticity is the same everywhere along the curve; the elasticity value is unchanged

consumer equilibrium The condition in which an individual consumer's budget is exhausted and the last dollar spent on each good yields the same marginal utility; therefore, utility is maximized

consumer surplus The difference between the most a consumer would pay for a given quantity of a good and what the consumer actually pays

cooperative An organization consisting of people who pool their resources to buy and sell more efficiently than they could individually

coordination game A type of game in which a Nash equilibrium occurs when each player chooses the same strategy; neither player can do better than matching the other player's strategy

core competency Area of specialty; the product or phase of production a firm supplies with greatest efficiency

corporate stock Certificate reflecting part ownership of a corporation

corporation A legal entity owned by stockholders whose liability is limited to the value of their stock ownership

craft union A union whose members have a particular skill or work at a particular craft, such as plumbers or carpenters

cross-price elasticity of demand The percentage change in the demand of one good divided by the percentage change in the price of another good; it's positive for substitutes, negative for complements, and zero for unrelated goods

currency appreciation With respect to the dollar, a decrease in the number of dollars needed to purchase one unit of foreign exchange in a flexible rate system

currency depreciation With respect to the dollar, an increase in the number of dollars needed to purchase one unit of foreign exchange in a flexible rate system

currency devaluation An increase in the official pegged price of foreign exchange in terms of the domestic currency

currency revaluation A reduction in the official pegged price of foreign exchange in terms of the domestic currency

deadweight loss of monopoly Net loss to society when a firm with market power restricts output and increases the price

demand A relation between the price of a good and the quantity that consumers are willing and able to buy per period, other things constant

demand curve A curve showing the relation between the price of a good and the quantity consumers are willing and able to buy per period, other things constant

derived demand Demand that arises from the demand for the product the resource produces

demand for loanable funds The negative relationship between the market interest rate and the quantity of loanable funds demanded, other things constant

developing countries Nations typified by high rates of illiteracy, high unemployment, high fertility rates, and exports of primary products; also known as low-income and middle-income economies

differentiated oligopoly An oligopoly that sells products that differ across suppliers, such as automobiles or breakfast cereal

discounting Converting future dollar amounts into present value

diseconomies of scale Forces that may eventually increase a firm's average cost as the scale of operation increases in the long run

disequilibrium The condition that exists in a market when the plans of buyers do not match those of sellers; a temporary mismatch between quantity supplied and quantity demanded as the market seeks equilibrium

dividends After-tax corporate profit paid to stockholders rather than retained by the firm and reinvested

division of labor Breaking down the production of a good into separate tasks

Doha Round The multilateral trade negotiation round launched in 2001, but still unsettled as of 2010; aims at lowering tariffs on a wide range of industrial and agricultural products; the first trade round under WTO

dominant-strategy equilibrium In game theory, the outcome achieved when each player's choice does not depend on what the other player does

dumping Selling a product abroad for less than charged in the home market or for less than the cost of production

duopoly A market with only two producers; a special type of oligopoly market structure

earned-income tax credit A federal program that supplements the wages of the working poor

economic efficiency approach An approach that offers each polluter the flexibility to reduce emissions as cost-effectively as possible, given its unique cost conditions; the market for pollution rights is an example

economic fluctuations The rise and fall of economic activity relative to the long-term growth trend of the economy; also called business cycles

economic growth An increase in the economy's ability to produce goods and services; reflected by an outward shift of the economy's production possibilities frontier

economic profit A firm's total revenue minus its explicit and implicit costs

economic regulation Government regulation of natural monopoly, where, because of economies of scale, average production cost is lowest when a single firm supplies the market

economic rent Portion of a resource's total earnings that exceeds its opportunity cost; earnings greater than the amount required to keep the resource in its present use

economic system The set of mechanisms and institutions that resolve the what, how, and for whom questions

economic theory, or economic model A simplification of reality used to make predictions about cause and effect in the real world

economics The study of how people use their scarce resources to satisfy their unlimited wants

economies of scale Forces that reduce a firm's average cost as the scale of operation increases in the long run

economies of scope Average costs decline as a firm makes a range of different products rather than specialize in just one product

efficiency wage theory The idea that offering high wages attracts a more talented labor pool and encourages those hired to perform well to keep their jobs

efficiency The condition that exists when there is no way resources can be reallocated to increase the production of one good without decreasing the production of another; getting the most from available resources

elastic demand A change in price has a relatively large effect on quantity demanded; the percentage change in quantity demanded exceeds the percentage change in price; the resulting price elasticity has an absolute value exceeding 1.0

elastic supply A change in price has a relatively large effect on quantity supplied; the percentage change in quantity supplied exceeds the percentage change in price; the price elasticity of supply exceeds 1.0

entrepreneur A profit-seeking decision maker who starts with an idea, organizes an enterprise to bring that idea to life, and assumes the risk of the operation

entrepreneurial ability The imagination required to develop a new product or process, the skill needed to organize production, and the willingness to take the risk of profit or loss

equilibrium The condition that exists in a market when the plans of buyers match those of sellers, so quantity demanded equals quantity supplied and the market clears

excess capacity The difference between a firm's profit-maximizing quantity and the quantity that minimizes average cost; firms with excess capacity could reduce average cost by increasing quantity

exchange rate The price measured in one country's currency of purchasing one unit of another country's currency

exclusive dealing A supplier prohibits its customers from buying from other suppliers of the product

exhaustible resource A resource in fixed supply, such as crude oil or coal

expected rate of return on capital The expected annual earnings divided by capital's purchase price

explicit cost Opportunity cost of resources employed by a firm that takes the form of cash payments

export promotion A development strategy that concentrates on producing for the export market

externality A cost or a benefit that affects neither the buyer nor seller, but instead affects people not involved in the market transaction

fallacy of composition The incorrect belief that what is true for the individual, or part, must necessarily be true for the group, or the whole

featherbedding Union efforts to force employers to hire more workers than demanded at a particular wage

Federal Trade Commission (FTC) Act of 1914 Established a federal body to help enforce antitrust laws; run by commissioners assisted by economists and lawyers

financial account The record of a country's international transactions involving purchases or sales of financial and real assets

firms Economic units formed by profit-seeking entrepreneurs who employ resources to produce goods and services for sale

fiscal policy The use of government purchases, transfer payments, taxes, and borrowing to influence economy-wide variables such as inflation, employment, and economic growth

fixed cost Any production cost that is independent of the firm's rate of output

fixed exchange rate Rate of exchange between currencies pegged within a narrow range and maintained by the central bank's ongoing purchases and sales of currencies

fixed resource Any resource that cannot be varied in the short run

fixed-production technology Occurs when the relationship between the output rate and the generation of an externality is fixed; the only way to reduce the externality is to reduce the output

flexible exchange rate Rate determined in foreign exchange markets by the forces of demand and supply without government intervention

foreign aid An international transfer made on especially favorable terms for the purpose of promoting economic development

foreign exchange Foreign money needed to carry out international transactions

free-rider problem Because nobody can be easily excluded from consuming a public good, some people may try to reap the benefits of the good without paying for it

game theory An approach that analyzes oligopolistic behavior as a series of strategic moves and countermoves by rival firms

General Agreement on Tariffs and Trade (GATT) An international tariff-reduction treaty adopted in 1947 that resulted in a series of negotiated "rounds" aimed at freer trade; the Uruguay Round created GATT's successor, the World Trade Organization (WTO)

gold standard An arrangement whereby the currencies of most countries are convertible into gold at a fixed rate

golden rule of profit maximization To maximize profit or minimize loss, a firm should produce the quantity at which marginal revenue equals marginal cost; this rule holds for all market structures

good A tangible product used to satisfy human wants

Herfindahl-Hirschman Index, or HHI A measure of market concentration that squares each firm's percentage share of the market then sums these squares

hidden actions One side of an economic relationship can do something that the other side cannot observe

hidden characteristics One side of the market knows more than the other side about product characteristics that are important to the other side

horizontal merger A merger in which one firm combines with another that produces the same type of product

hypothesis A theory about how key variables relate

implicit cost A firm's opportunity cost of using its own resources or those provided by its owners without a corresponding cash payment

import substitution A development strategy that emphasizes domestic manufacturing of products that were imported

income assistance programs Welfare programs that provide money and in-kind assistance to the poor; benefits do not depend on prior contributions

income effect of a price change A fall in the price of a good increases consumers' real income, making consumers more able to purchase goods; for a normal good, the quantity demanded increases

income effect of a wage increase A higher wage raises a worker's income, increasing the demand for all normal goods, including leisure, so the quantity of labor supplied to market work decreases

income elasticity of demand The percentage change in demand divided by the percentage change in consumer income; the value is positive for normal goods and negative for inferior goods

increasing marginal returns The marginal product of a variable resource increases as each additional unit of that resource is employed

increasing-cost industry An industry that faces higher per-unit production costs as industry output expands in the long run; the long-run industry supply curve slopes upward

individual demand The relation between the price of a good and the quantity purchased by an individual consumer per period, other things constant

individual supply The relation between the price of a good and the quantity an individual producer is willing and able to sell per period, other things constant

industrial market countries Economically advanced capitalist countries of Western Europe, North America, Australia, New Zealand, and Japan; also known as developed countries and high-income economies

Industrial Revolution Development of large-scale factory production that began in Great Britain around 1750 and spread to the rest of Europe, North America, and Australia

industrial union A union consisting of both skilled and unskilled workers from a particular industry, such as all autoworkers or all steelworkers

inelastic demand A change in price has relatively little effect on quantity demanded; the percentage change in quantity demanded is less than the percentage change in price; the resulting price elasticity has an absolute value less than 1.0

inelastic supply A change in price has relatively little effect on quantity supplied; the percentage change in quantity supplied is less than the percentage change in price; the price elasticity of supply is less than 1.0

inferior good A good, such as used clothes, for which demand decreases, or shifts leftward, as consumer income rises

Information Revolution Technological change spawned by the microchip and the Internet that enhanced the acquisition, analysis, and transmission of information

initial public offering (IPO) The initial sale of corporate stock to the public

innovation The process of turning an invention into a marketable product

intellectual property An intangible asset created by human knowledge and ideas

interest Payment to resource owners for the use of their capital

interest rate Interest per year as a percentage of the amount saved or borrowed

interlocking directorate A person serves on the boards of directors of two or more competing firms

International Monetary Fund (IMF) An international organization that establishes rules for maintaining the international monetary system and makes loans to countries with temporary balance-of-payments problems

labor The physical and mental effort used to produce goods and services

labor union A group of workers who organize to improve their terms of employment

law of comparative advantage The individual, firm, region, or country with the lowest opportunity cost of producing a particular good should specialize in that good

law of demand The quantity of a good that consumers are willing and able to buy per period relates inversely, or negatively, to the price, other things constant

law of diminishing marginal returns As more of a variable resource is added to a given amount of another resource, marginal product eventually declines and could become negative

law of diminishing marginal utility The more of a good a person consumes per period, the smaller the increase in total utility from consuming one more unit, other things constant

law of increasing opportunity cost To produce more of one good, a successively larger amount of the other good must be sacrificed

law of supply The amount of a good that producers are willing and able to sell per period is usually directly related to its price, other things constant

leisure Time spent on nonwork activities

linear demand curve A straight-line demand curve; such a demand curve has a constant slope but usually has a varying price elasticity

loanable funds market The market in which savers (suppliers of loanable funds) and borrowers (demanders of loanable funds) come together to determine the market interest rate and the quantity of loanable funds exchanged

long run A period during which all resources under the firm's control are variable

long-run average cost curve A curve that indicates the lowest average cost of production at each rate of output when the size, or scale, of the firm varies; also called the planning curve

long-run industry supply curve A curve that shows the relationship between price and quantity supplied by the industry once firms adjust in the long run to any change in market demand

lorenz curve A curve showing the percentage of total income received by a given percentage of recipients whose incomes are arrayed from smallest to largest

macroeconomics The study of the economic behavior of entire economies, as measured, for example, by total production and employment

managed float system An exchange rate system that combines features of freely floating rates with sporadic intervention by central banks

marginal cost The change in total cost resulting from a one-unit change in output; the change in total cost divided by the change in output, or $MC = \Delta TC / \Delta q$

marginal product The change in total product that occurs when the use of a particular resource increases by one unit, all other resources constant

marginal resource cost The change in total cost when an additional unit of a resource is hired, other things constant

marginal revenue (MR) The firm's change in total revenue from selling an additional unit; a perfectly competitive firm's marginal revenue is also the market price

marginal revenue product The change in total revenue when an additional unit of a resource is employed, other things constant

marginal social benefit The sum of the marginal private benefit and the marginal external benefit of production or consumption

marginal social cost The sum of the marginal private cost and the marginal external cost of production or consumption

marginal tax rate The percentage of each additional dollar of income that goes to the tax

marginal utility The change in your total utility from a one-unit change in your consumption of a good

Marginal valuation The dollar value of the marginal utility derived from consuming each additional unit of a good

marginal Incremental, additional, or extra; used to describe a change in an economic variable

market demand The relation between the price of a good and the quantity purchased by all consumers in the market during a given period, other things constant; sum of the individual demands in the market

market failure A condition that arises when the unregulated operation of markets yields socially undesirable results

market power The ability of a firm to raise its price without losing all its customers to rival firms

market structure Important features of a market, such as the number of firms, product uniformity across firms, firm's ease of entry and exit, and forms of competition

market supply The relation between the price of a good and the quantity all producers are willing and able to sell per period, other things constant

market work Time sold as labor

market A set of arrangements by which buyers and sellers carry out exchange at mutually agreeable terms

means-tested program A program in which, to be eligible, an individual's income and assets must not exceed specified levels

median income The middle income when all incomes are ranked from smallest to largest

median wage The middle wage when wages of all workers are ranked from lowest to highest

median-voter model Under certain conditions, the preferences of the median, or middle, voter will dominate the preferences of all other voters

mediator An impartial observer who helps resolve differences between union and management

Medicaid An in-kind transfer program that provides medical care for poor people; by far the most costly welfare program

Medicare Social insurance program providing health insurance for short-term medical care to older Americans, regardless of income

merchandise trade balance The value during a given period of a country's exported goods minus the value of its imported goods

microeconomics The study of the economic behavior in particular markets, such as that for computers or unskilled labor

minimum efficient scale The lowest rate of output at which a firm takes full advantage of economies of scale

mixed system An economic system characterized by the private ownership of some resources and the public ownership of other resources; some markets are regulated by government

monetary policy Regulation of the money supply to influence economy-wide variables such as inflation, employment, and economic growth

money income The number of dollars a person receives per period, such as $400 per week

monopolistic competition A market structure with many firms selling products that are substitutes but different enough that each firm's demand curve slopes downward; firm entry is relatively easy

monopoly A sole supplier of a product with no close substitutes

moral hazard A situation in which one party, as a result of a contract, has an incentive to alter their behavior in a way that harms the other party to the contract

movement along a demand curve Change in quantity demanded resulting from a change in the price of the good, other things constant

movement along a supply curve Change in quantity supplied resulting from a change in the price of the good, other things constant

Nash equilibrium A situation in which a firm, or a player in game theory, chooses the best strategy given the strategies chosen by others; no participant can improve his or her outcome by changing strategies even after learning of the strategies selected by other participants

natural monopoly One firm that can supply the entire market at a lower per-unit cost than could two or more firms

natural resources All gifts of nature used to produce goods and services; includes renewable and exhaustible resources

net investment income from abroad Investment earnings by U.S. residents from their foreign assets minus investment earnings by foreigners from their assets in the United States

net unilateral transfers abroad The unilateral transfers (gifts and grants) received from abroad by U.S. residents minus the unilateral transfers U.S. residents send abroad

nonmarket work Time spent getting an education or on do-it-yourself production for personal consumption

normal good A good, such as new clothes, for which demand increases, or shifts rightward, as consumer income rises

normal profit The accounting profit earned when all resources earn their opportunity cost

normative economic statement A statement that reflects an opinion, which cannot be proved or disproved by reference to the facts

not-for-profit organizations Groups that do not pursue profit as a goal; they engage in charitable, educational, humanitarian, cultural, professional, or other activities, often with a social purpose

oligopoly A market structure characterized by so few firms that each behaves interdependently

open-access good A good such as ocean fish that is rival in consumption but nonpayers cannot be excluded easily

opportunity cost The value of the best alternative forgone when an item or activity is chosen

other-things-constant assumption The assumption, when focusing on the relation among key economic variables, that other variables remain unchanged; in Latin, ceteris paribus

outsourcing A firm buys inputs from outside suppliers

partnership A firm with multiple owners who share the profits and bear unlimited liability for the firm's losses and debts

patent A legal barrier to entry that grants the holder the exclusive right to sell a product for 20 years from the date the patent application is filed

payoff matrix In game theory, a table listing the payoffs that each player can expect from each move based on the actions of the other player

per se illegal In antitrust law, business practices deemed illegal regardless of their economic rationale or their consequences

perfect competition A market structure with many fully informed buyers and sellers of a standardized product and no obstacles to entry or exit of firms in the long run

perfectly discriminating monopolist A monopolist who charges a different price for each unit sold; also called the monopolist's dream

perfectly elastic demand curve A horizontal line reflecting a situation in which any price increase would reduce quantity demanded to zero; the elasticity has an absolute value of infinity

perfectly elastic supply curve A horizontal line reflecting a situation in which any price decrease drops the quantity supplied to zero; the elasticity value is infinity

perfectly inelastic demand curve A vertical line reflecting a situation in which any price change has no effect on the quantity demanded; the elasticity value is zero

Perfectly inelastic supply curve A vertical line reflecting a situation in which a price change has no effect on the quantity supplied; the elasticity value is zero

populist legislation Legislation with widespread benefits but concentrated costs

pork-barrel spending Special-interest legislation with narrow geographical benefits but funded by all taxpayers

positive economic statement A statement that can be proved or disproved by reference to facts

positive rate of time preference Consumers value present consumption more than future consumption

predatory pricing Pricing tactics employed by a dominant firm to drive competitors out of business, such as temporarily selling below marginal cost or dropping the price only in certain markets

present value The value today of income to be received in the future

price ceiling A maximum legal price above which a product cannot be sold; to have an impact, a price ceiling must be set below the equilibrium price

price discrimination Increasing profit by charging different groups of consumers different prices for the same product

price elasticity formula Percentage change in quantity demanded divided by the percentage change in price; the average quantity and the average price are used as bases for computing percentage changes in quantity and in price

price elasticity of demand Measures how responsive quantity demanded is to a price change; the percentage change in quantity demanded divided by the percentage change in price

price elasticity of supply A measure of the responsiveness of quantity supplied to a price change; the percentage change in quantity supplied divided by the percentage change in price

price floor A minimum legal price below which a product cannot be sold; to have an impact, a price floor must be set above the equilibrium price

price leader A firm whose price is matched by other firms in the market as a form of tacit collusion

price maker A firm with some power to set the price because the demand curve for its output slopes downward; a firm with market power

price taker A firm that faces a given market price and whose quantity supplied has no effect on that price; a perfectly competitive firm that decides to produce must accept, or "take," the market price

prime rate The interest rate lenders charge their most trustworthy business borrowers

principal A person or firm who hires an agent to act on behalf of that person or firm

principal-agent problem The agent's objectives differ from those of the principal's, and one side can pursue hidden actions

prisoner's dilemma A game that shows why players have difficulty cooperating even though they would benefit from cooperation

private good A good, such as pizza, that is both rival in consumption and exclusive

private property rights An owner's right to use, rent, or sell resources or property

privatization The process of turning government enterprises into private enterprises

producer surplus A bonus for producers in the short run; the amount by which total revenue from production exceeds variable cost

product market A market in which a good or service is bought and sold

production function The relationship between the amount of resources employed and a firm's total product

Production possibilities frontier (PPF) A curve showing alternative combinations of goods that can be produced when available resources are used efficiently; a boundary line between inefficient and unattainable combinations

productive efficiency The condition that exists when production uses the least-cost combination of inputs; minimum average cost in the long run

profit Reward for entrepreneurial ability; sales revenue minus resource cost

progressive taxation The tax as a percentage of income increases as income increases

proportional taxation The tax as a percentage of income remains constant as income increases; also called a flat tax

public good A good that, once produced, is available for all to consume, regardless of who pays and who doesn't; such a good is nonrival and nonexclusive, such as a safer community

public utilities Government-owned or government-regulated monopolies

purchasing power parity (PPP) theory The idea that the exchange rate between two countries will adjust in the long run to equalize the cost between the countries of a basket of internationally traded goods

pure capitalism An economic system characterized by the private ownership of resources and the use of prices to coordinate economic activity in unregulated markets

pure command system An economic system characterized by the public ownership of resources and centralized planning

quantity demanded The amount of a good consumers are willing and able to buy per period at a particular price, as reflected by a point on a demand curve

quantity supplied The amount offered for sale per period at a particular price, as reflected by a point on a given supply curve

quota A legal limit on the quantity of a particular product that can be imported or exported

rational ignorance A stance adopted by voters when they realize that the cost of understanding and voting on a particular issue exceeds the benefit expected from doing so

rational self-interest Each individual tries to maximize the expected benefit achieved with a given cost or to minimize the expected cost of achieving a given benefit

real income Income measured in terms of the goods and services it can buy; real income changes when the price changes

recycling The process of converting waste products into reusable material

regressive taxation The tax as a percentage of income decreases as income increases

renewable resource A resource that regenerates itself and so can be used indefinitely if used conservatively, such as a properly managed forest

rent seeking Activities undertaken by individuals or firms to influence public policy in a way that increases their incomes

rent Payment to resource owners for the use of their natural resources

resource complements Resources that enhance one another's productivity; a decrease in the price of one resource increases the demand for the other

resource market A market in which a resource is bought and sold

resource substitutes Resources that substitute in production; an increase in the price of one resource increases the demand for the other

resources The inputs, or factors of production, used to produce the goods and services that people want; resources consist of labor, capital, natural resources, and entrepreneurial ability

retained earnings After-tax corporate profit reinvested in the firm rather than paid to stockholders as dividends

right-to-work states States where workers in unionized companies do not have to join the union or pay union dues

rule of reason Before ruling on the legality of certain business practices, a court examines why they were undertaken and what effect they have on competition

scarcity Occurs when the amount people desire exceeds the amount available at a zero price

screening The process used by employers to select the most qualified workers based on observable characteristics, such as a job applicant's level of education and course grades

secondary effects Unintended consequences of economic actions that may develop slowly over time as people react to events

service An activity, or intangible product, used to satisfy human wants

Sherman Antitrust Act of 1890 First national legislation in the world against monopoly; prohibited trusts, restraint of trade, and monopolization, but the law was vague and, by itself, ineffective

shift of a demand curve Movement of a demand curve right or left resulting from a change in one of the determinants of demand other than the price of the good

shift of a supply curve Movement of a supply curve left or right resulting from a change in one of the determinants of supply other than the price of the good

short run A period during which at least one of a firm's resources is fixed

shortage At a given price, the amount by which quantity demanded exceeds quantity supplied; a shortage usually forces the price up

short-run firm supply curve A curve that shows how much a firm supplies at each price in the short run; in perfect competition, that portion of a firm's marginal cost curve that intersects and rises above the low point on its average variable cost curve

short-run industry supply curve A curve that indicates the quantity supplied by the industry at each price in the short run; in perfect competition, the horizontal sum of each firm's short-run supply curve

signaling Using a proxy measure to communicate information about unobservable characteristics; the signal is more effective if more-productive workers find it easier to send than do less-productive workers

SNAP An in-kind transfer program that offers low-income households vouchers redeemable for food; benefit levels vary inversely with household income

social capital The shared values and trust that promote cooperation in the economy

social insurance Government programs designed to help make up for lost income of people who worked but are now retired, unemployed, or unable to work because of disability or work-related injury

social regulation Government regulations aimed at improving health and safety

Social Security Supplements retirement income to those with a record of contributing to the program during their working years; by far the largest government redistribution program

social welfare The overall well-being of people in the economy; maximized when the marginal cost of production equals the marginal benefit to consumers

sole proprietorship A firm with a single owner who has the right to all profits but who also bears unlimited liability for the firm's losses and debts

special-interest legislation Legislation with concentrated benefits but widespread costs

specialization of labor Focusing work effort on a particular product or a single task

speculator Someone who buys or sells foreign exchange in hopes of profiting from fluctuations in the exchange rate over time

strategy In game theory, the operational plan pursued by a player

strike A union's attempt to withhold labor from a firm to halt production

substitutes Goods, such as Coke and Pepsi, that relate in such a way that an increase in the price of one shifts the demand for the other rightward

substitution effect of a price change When the price of a good falls, that good becomes cheaper compared to other goods so consumers tend to substitute that good for other goods

substitution effect of a wage increase A higher wage encourages more work because other activities now have a higher opportunity cost

sunk cost A cost that has already been incurred, cannot be recovered, and thus is irrelevant for present and future economic decisions

Supplemental Security Income (SSI) An income assistance program that provides cash transfers to the elderly poor and the disabled; a uniform federal payment is supplemented by transfers that vary across states

supply curve A curve showing the relation between price of a good and the quantity producers are willing and able to sell per period other things constant

supply of loanable funds The positive relationship between the market interest rate and the quantity of loanable funds supplied, other things constant

supply A relation between the price of a good and the quantity that producers are willing and able to sell per period, other things constant

surplus At a given price, the amount by which quantity supplied exceeds quantity demanded; a surplus usually forces the price down

tariff A tax on imports

tastes Consumer preferences; likes and dislikes in consumption; assumed to remain constant along a given demand curve

tax incidence The distribution of tax burden among taxpayers; who ultimately pays the tax

Temporary Assistance for Needy Families (TANF) An income assistance program funded largely by the federal government but run by the states to provide cash transfer payments to poor families with dependent children

term structure of interest rates The relationship between the duration of a loan and the interest rate charged; typically interest rates increase with the duration of the loan, because longer loans are considered more risky

terms of trade How much of one good exchanges for a unit of another good

tit-for-tat In game theory, a strategy in repeated games when a player in one round of the game mimics the other player's behavior in the previous round; an optimal strategy for getting the other player to cooperate

total cost The sum of fixed cost and variable cost, or $TC = FC + VC$

total product A firm's total output

total revenue Price multiplied by the quantity demanded at that price

total utility The total satisfaction you derive from consumption; this could refer to either your total utility of consuming a particular good or your total utility from all consumption

traditional public-goods legislation Legislation that involves widespread costs and widespread benefits—nearly everyone pays and nearly everyone benefits

transaction costs The costs of time and information required to carry out market exchange

transfer payments Cash or in-kind benefits given to individuals as outright grants from the government

trust Any firm or group of firms that tries to monopolize a market

tying contract A seller of one good requires a buyer to purchase other goods as part of the deal

U.S. official poverty level Benchmark level of income computed by the federal government to track poverty over time; initially based on three times the cost of a nutritionally adequate diet

underground economy An expression used to describe market activity that goes unreported either because it is illegal or because those involved want to evade taxes

undifferentiated oligopoly An oligopoly that sells a commodity, or a product that does not differ across suppliers, such as an ingot of steel or a barrel of oil

unit-elastic demand curve Everywhere along the demand curve, the percentage change in price causes an equal but offsetting percentage change in quantity demanded, so total revenue remains the same; the elasticity has an absolute value of 1.0

unit-elastic demand The percentage change in quantity demanded equals the percentage change in price; the resulting price elasticity has an absolute value of 1.0

unit-elastic supply curve A percentage change in price causes an identical percentage change in quantity supplied; depicted by a supply curve that is a straight line from the origin; the elasticity value equals 1.0

unit-elastic supply The percentage change in quantity supplied equals the percentage change in price; the price elasticity of supply equals 1.0

Uruguay Round The final multilateral trade negotiation under GATT; this 1994 agreement cut tariffs, formed the World Trade Organization (WTO), and will eventually eliminate quotas

utility The satisfaction received from consumption; sense of well-being

variable cost Any production cost that changes as the rate of output changes

variable resource Any resource that can be varied in the short run to increase or decrease production

variable technology Occurs when the amount of externality generated at a given rate of output can be reduced by altering the production process

variable A measure, such as price or quantity, that can take on different values at different times

vertical integration The expansion of a firm into stages of production earlier or later than those in which it specializes, such as a steel maker that also mines iron ore

vertical merger A merger in which one firm combines with another from which it had purchased inputs or to which it had sold output

wages Payment to resource owners for their labor

winner's curse The plight of the winning bidder who overestimates an asset's true value

winner-take-all labor markets Markets in which a few key employees critical to the overall success of an enterprise are richly rewarded

world price The price at which a good is traded on the world market; determined by the world demand and world supply for the good

World Trade Organization (WTO) The legal and institutional foundation of the multilateral trading system that succeeded GATT in 1995

Index